# The Anticompetitive Impact of Regulation

The Fondazione Eni Enrico Mattei (FEEM) was established in 1989 as a non-profit, non-partisan research institute. The main objectives of the Fondazione are twofold: furthering research on the relationships between energy, environment and economic development and promoting interaction between academic, industrial and public policy spheres to find solutions to environmental problems.

The European University Institute was founded in 1976 by the European Community Member States with the objective of providing advanced academic training to PhD students and promoting research at the highest level. In 1992, a further element was added with the creation of the Robert Schuman Centre and the European Forum, two interdisciplinary centres. Over the past six years, these two centres have progressively merged and transformed themselves into a single Centre for Advanced Studies whose specific purpose is to focus on European problems (and in particular European integration); to develop and deepen its interdisciplinary character based upon the co-operation of four disciplines (Law, Economics, History and Civilisation, and Social and Political Sciences); and to enhance the training of promising young scholars.

# The Anticompetitive Impact of Regulation

*Edited by*

Giuliano Amato

*Former Prime Minister of Italy*
*External Professor, European University Institute, Florence, Italy*

and

Laraine L. Laudati

*Senior Research Fellow, European University Institute,*
*Legal Counsel to the European Commission, Florence, Italy*

**Edward Elgar**

Cheltenham, UK • Northampton, MA, USA

Published by
Edward Elgar Publishing Limited
Glensanda House
Montpellier Parade
Cheltenham
Glos GL50 1UA
UK

Edward Elgar Publishing, Inc.
136 West Street
Suite 202
Northampton
Massachusetts 01060
USA

A catalogue record for this book is available from the British Library

**Library of Congress Cataloguing in Publication Data**
The anticompetitive impact of regulation / edited by Giuliano Amato, Laraine Laudati.
   p. cm.
  Includes index.
  ISBN 1–84064–677–2
  1. Trade regulation. 2. Competition. I. Amato, Giuliano. II. Laudati, Laraine L.

  HD3612 .A56 2001
  338.6'048—dc21

                                                                2001023352

ISBN 1 84064 677 2
Printed and bound in Great Britain by MPG Books Ltd, Bodmin, Cornwall

# Contents

# Figures

# Tables

# Contributors

**Giuliano Amato** is a former Prime Minister of Italy. From 1996 to 1999, he was Professor of Law at the European University Institute in Florence. In 1999, he was Italian Minister of the Treasury; from 1998 to 1999, he was Italian Minister of Institutional Reform; from 1993 to 1997, he was Chairman of the Italian Antitrust Authority; from 1992 to 1993, he was Prime Minister of Italy; from 1987 to 1988, he was Deputy Prime Minister; from 1987 to 1989, he was Minister of the Treasury, and from 1983 to 1987, he was Undersecretary to the Prime Minister's Office. He became a Full Professor of Comparative Constitutional Law at the University of Rome, School of Political Science in 1975. Professor Amato has been full-time professor at the universities of Modena, Perugia and Florence. He has written books and articles on economy and political institutions, personal liberties, federalism and comparative government. His current area of research is competition law in Europe on a comparative basis.

**Mark Armstrong** is a Fellow in Economics at Nuffield College, Oxford University. He has previously held positions at Cambridge and Southampton. Much of his current research interests concern regulatory and competition policy, with a special emphasis on telecommunications issues; this includes, with Simon Cowan and John Vickers, *Regulatory Reform: Economic Analysis and British Experience* (1994). He is currently managing editor of the journal *Review of Economic Studies*. He has acted as economic advisor to Oftel and to the Monopolies and Mergers Commission.

**Manuel Ballbe** is Professor of Administrative Law at the Autonomous University of Barcelona. He has written a number of articles in various areas of Spanish law and European law, including European competition law.

**Darryl Biggar** is an economist at the Organization for Economic Cooperation and Development, where he is involved in researching competition and regulation issues in different sectors. Prior to working at the OECD, Dr Biggar worked on regulatory issues for the New Zealand Government, in the Ministry of Commerce and the New Zealand Treasury. He has also worked for the University of London, teaching law and economics.

**Bernardo Bortolotti** is Assistant Professor at the University of Turin and co-ordinator of the Privatization, Regulation and Antitrust unit at Fondazione Eni Enrico Mattei, Milan. His research interests are in privatization, regulation, corporate governance and auction theory. He has recently co-edited a book entitled *Organized Interests and Self-regulation: An Economic Approach*, and has a forthcoming book entitled *Privatisation and Institutions.*

**Ginevra Bruzzone** is Director for Regulation and Competition Policy at the Associazione fra le Società Italiane per Azioni (Assonime) in Rome, Italy. She was formerly Senior Economist at the Research Department of the Italian Competition Authority. Before joining the Authority, she worked for the Center for Financial and Monetary Studies of Bocconi University and the Institute for International Political Studies (ISPI) in Milan. She has published several articles on competition policy, corporate governance and banking.

**Blair Comley** is General Manager, Macroeconomic Policy Division of the Australian Treasury. During 1997, he was Director, Market Structure Section, Competition Policy Branch of the Australian Treasury. From late 1997 to 2000, he worked on tax reform as Manager (Specialist) and then General Manager of the Indirect Tax Division of the Australian Treasury.

**Mark Dutz** is a senior economist at the World Bank and the European Bank for Reconstruction and Development. At the World Bank, he is responsible for developing and implementing research initiatives and providing policy advice on issues related to competition policy, regulation and private involvement in infrastructure, with a focus on mechanisms to enhance the performance of enter-prises and the functioning of markets. He is also Course Director for a new World Bank course on competition policy for client country practitioners. Dr Dutz has taught at Princeton University, and has published related articles in journals and monographs.

**Marcella Fantini** is senior researcher at the Fondazione Eni Enrico Mattei and Lecturer in Economics at the University of Bergamo. Her interests are in applied econometrics and statistical analysis, privatization and financial market devel-opment. She has recently published a co-authored book on privatization and an article on environmental information and company behaviour.

**Allan Fels** has been Chairman of the Australian Competition and Consumer Commission since November 1995. He has a five-year appointment. Professor Fels was Chairman of the former Trade Practices Commission from 1991 to 1995. He was also Chairman of the Prices Surveillance Authority from 1989 to 1992. He was Director of the Graduate School of Management, Monash

University, from 1985 to 1990, and is now Honorary Professor in the Faculty of Business and Economics at Monash University. Professor Fels is the Co-Chairman of the Joint Group on Trade and Competition at the OECD.

**Chiara Fumagalli** is a post-doctoral researcher at Bocconi University in Milan. Her research activity is focused on industrial organization (in particular competition policy), corporate finance and international trade.

**Aydin Hayri** is a consulting economist at Deloitte & Touche specializing in benchmarking, pricing and valuation issues. Before joining Deloitte & Touche, he was an assistant professor of economics at Charles University, Prague; University of Warwick, England; and a research fellow at Princeton University. His primary specialization was industrial organization, with emphasis on the dynamics of competition in service-orientated industries and the design of competition and regulatory policy. On this subject, Dr Hayri taught courses, published articles, and provided consulting services for the European Commission and the World Bank.

**Alberto Heimler** is Director of the Research Department of the Italian Antitrust Authority. He is Adjunct Professor of the History of Economic Regulations at Luiss University in Rome and Chairman of Working Party 2, 'Competition and Regulation', of the Committee on Competition Law and Policy at the OECD. Before joining the Authority in 1991, he was a senior economist with the Confederation of Italian Industries. He has published extensively on applied economics and industrial economics.

**John C. Hilke** is an economist in the Bureau of Economics at the Federal Trade Commission and serves as the Bureau's Electricity Project Coordinator. In the latter role, he is the primary developer of FTC staff comments filed before the Federal Energy Regulatory Commission (FERC) and state regulators concerning electric industry restructuring. Dr Hilke joined the staff of the FTC in 1978 and has served as Assistant to the Director of the Bureau of Economics and as an expert economic witness in a number of antitrust merger cases. His research interests include antitrust, state securities regulation, international trade, privatization and regulatory reform. He is the author or co-author of two books and several journal articles on these subjects. He taught economics at Cornell University before joining the staff of the FTC.

**Frederic Jenny** is Vice-Chairman of the Conseil de la concurrence. Since 1997, he has chaired the World Trade Organization Working Group on the Interaction between Trade and Competition Policy. In 1996, he was appointed Special Advisor to the French Minister of International Trade and Competition on international trade and competition issues. In 1994, he was elected Chairman of the OECD Competition Law and Policy Committee. He was General Counsel (Rapporteur General) of the Conseil de la concurrence from 1985 to 1992. Professor Jenny served as special assistant to the French Minister for Consumer Affairs in 1977, where he was in charge of the revision of the French antitrust law. He has been Professor of Economics at ESSEC (Ecole Supérieure des Sciences Economiques et Commerciales) since 1972, and has published extensively in the areas of industrial organization and competition law. He has taught as visiting professor at Northwestern University (USA), Keio University (Japan), and the University of Capetown (South Africa).

**Michael Kohl** has studied law in Frankfurt and Madrid, and is currently completing a PhD thesis at the European University Institute in Florence. He specializes in intellectual property law and its interconnection with antitrust law and contract law, in a US/European comparative perspective.

**Laraine L. Laudati** is Senior Research Fellow at the European University Institute in Florence, Italy. She has worked with Giuliano Amato on various research projects involving competition law. She is also a legal counsel to the European Commission, and has worked extensively in that capacity with the Directorate General for Competition. She has practised law in the District of Columbia, USA. Dr Laudati has published numerous studies and articles concentrating on European Community competition law, and was co-editor with former DG Competition Director General Claus Dieter Ehlermann of the 1996 and 1997 editions of the Robert Schuman Centre Annual on European Competition Law.

**Kirti Mehta** is Director of Directorate A (Competition Policy, Coordination, International Affairs and Relations with the Other Institutions) of the Directorate General for Competition (DG IV) at the European Commission in Brussels. Dr Mehta joined the Commission in 1982, and worked with the Directorate General for Industrial Policy for several years before joining DG Competition in 1996. Prior to joining the Commission, he worked with the UK Department of Trade and Industry, the World Bank, and the Gill and Duffus Group (economists) in the UK.

**Massimo Motta** is Professor of Economics at the European University Institute in Florence, Italy and the Pompeu Fabra University in Barcelona. He is a Research Fellow at the Centre for Economic Policy Research in London, and associate editor of the *European Economic Review*, *Economica*, *Giornale degli Economisti* and *Mercato Concorrenza Regole*. His main research interests are in industrial organization and competition policy; he has also worked extensively in the areas of international trade and multinational firms.

**Giuseppe Nicoletti** is a senior economist at the OECD Economics Department in Paris, where he coordinates a project on regulation and performance in OECD countries. Before taking up his current position, Dr Nicoletti worked in the research department of the Italian Competition Authority and contributed to several other structural policy projects within the OECD.

**Carlos Padros** is Professor of Economic and European Law at the Autonomous University of Barcelona. He has written various articles in the area of European law, including competition and banking law.

**David Parker** is a Principal Administrator in the Competition Law and Policy Division of the OECD Secretariat. From 1998 to 2000 he was Minister-Counsellor (Economic Affairs) in the Australian Delegation to the OECD. From 1995 to 1997, he was Assistant Secretary for Competition Policy in the Australian Treasury. In this post, his responsibilities included implementation of the Australian National Competition Policy reforms.

**Carlo Scarpa** is Professor of Economics and Industrial Economics at the Faculty of Statistics, University of Bologna. Dr Scarpa's research focuses mainly on industry regulation, particularly in energy sectors, and privatization; he has also written papers on minimum quality standards and self-regulation in financial markets.

**Marius Schwartz** is the Economics Director of Enforcement at the Antitrust Division of the US Department of Justice; from January to June 1999 he also was the Acting Deputy Assistant Attorney General for Economics. From April 1995 to June 1996 he served as the Senior Economist at the President's Council of Economic Advisors responsible for industrial organization matters. He has also been a consultant to the Department of Justice on various competition matters, as well as to international agencies and private clients. He is on leave from Georgetown University, Washington, DC, where he is a Professor of Economics. His teaching and research fields are industrial organization, competition and regulation.

**Domenico Siniscalco** is Professor of Economics at the University of Turin, Managing Director of Fondazione Eni Enrico Mattei in Milan, and a member of the Italian Prime Minister's Council of Economic Advisors in Rome. He is also front-page columnist of *Il Sole 24 Ore*. He is currently involved in several European Commission research projects, and is associate editor of three international journals in economics. During the 1990s, he served as economic advisor to the Minister of Treasury, Finance, and as a member of several government committees. Professor Siniscalco has also held teaching and/or research positions at Luiss (Rome), Cambridge, Luovain La Neuve, and Johns Hopkins University. He has published extensively on game theory, coalition formation, industrial organization, privatization processes and environmental economics. He is past-president of the European Association of Environmental Economists (1995–87); associate of the Royal Institute of International Affairs; and member of the board of the Beijer Institute of the Swedish Royal Academy of Science.

**Michael O. Wise** works on regulatory reform issues with the OECD's Competition Law and Policy division. From 1991 to 1997, he managed the competition and consumer advocacy programme at the United States Federal Trade Commission (where he was also the manager of the Commission's programme of technical assistance to competition and consumer protection authorities in other countries). Before joining the FTC staff as a trial attorney in 1978, he practised law in Washington. He has published articles on legal history and antitrust policy and theory.

# Introduction

## Giuliano Amato and Laraine L. Laudati

A vast array of laws and regulations currently in force in the European Union, both at national level and Community level, are designed in such a way that they have an anticompetitive effect on the market in which they apply. This effect is similar to the negative economic effects of monopoly, leading to reduced economic growth and development with no corresponding social benefit.

Anticompetitive regulations are in effect with respect to both structurally competitive industries, such as manufacturing, transport and professional services, and structurally non-competitive industries, such as telecommunications, electricity and gas. For instance, as to the former, a typical regulatory scheme for a professional service would define conditions for entry into the profession through licensing requirements, establish the scope of permissible activities of a member of the profession, and set limits on the terms under which a member can provide professional services. Such regulatory schemes place severe restrictions on competition in the profession, ostensibly to protect the consumer who suffers from a lack of sufficient information to judge the competence of the professional. In fact, many of these restrictions are designed and administered by groups of incumbent professionals, who aim to restrict competition and preserve their own privileged position and high income level. As to the latter, structural regulations remain in force where supply and demand should operate freely to find the appropriate market equilibrium. Society bears a considerable cost as the result of such anticompetitive regulation.

Protection of competition was a fundamental principle underlying formation of the European Community, as is reflected by inclusion of provisions in the Treaty of Rome to this end. In the decades since the Community was formed, protection of competition has become a paramount concern.

Why, then, does anticompetitive regulation continue to exist in the European Union (EU), given our awareness of its harmful effects? Several reasons can be identified. First, strong political interests might oppose less-anticompetitive regulation. For instance, incumbent public service providers, such as the former monopolists in the telecommunications industry, seek to hold on to their privileges. These interests generally face little political resistance, as consumers have little understanding of the harmful effects that they suffer from such regulation, and are not organized to place countervailing political pressures on policy makers.

Second, national courts in Europe have narrowly defined their own scope of judicial review, and they have been reluctant to recognize economic unsoundness as a violation of the constitutionally-based proportionality principle. Moreover, European institutions have defined the boundaries of their jurisdiction in relation to anticompetitive state measures very narrowly. They have ruled that they have jurisdiction under Article 81 only when a state measure delegates power to a private undertaking that should be independently exercised by a public authority, or under Article 90 for state measures providing for state aid only when the limited exemption of Article 90(2) does not apply. A very close connection is needed, or the state measure is beyond the Court's and the Commission's jurisdiction.

Third, the historical roots of anticompetitive regulation in continental Europe date back to medieval times. The system of administrative law initially developed at that time as a tool that could be applied extensively to execute kingly prerogatives, such as building a national army and bureaucracy, and was deemed broadly applicable to the regulation of economic activities. A main feature of the continental administrative law system was its disrespect for other applicable rules whenever an activity was affected with a broadly defined 'public interest'.

Fourth, there is frequently no reason other than the culture of regulators, who tend to apply the typical normative scheme: if they must regulate, they must prohibit something. Regulation thus tends to be prescriptive.

In order to address the problem of anticompetitive regulation in the European Union, many puzzling questions must be answered: What methodologies should be used to analyse and measure the anticompetitive impact of regulation? Would it be feasible to review all EU laws and regulations to determine whether they have an anticompetitive effect and if so, to determine how to eliminate them? If it were feasible, how should it be designed and executed? What legal tools exist in the EU that might constitute the basis for taking action against anticompetitive regulation, at both national and European levels? What role should competition authorities play to combat anticompetitive regulation? How can public awareness of the problem, and public support for efforts to reform anticompetitive regulation, be increased?

In an effort to call upon economic reasoning to tackle some of these issues, and to help devise a blueprint for eliminating anticompetitive regulation in the EU, the editors of the current volume organized a Round Table on the Anticompetitive Impact of Regulation. The mission of the Round Table was to provide the economic foundation that would allow the editors to draft guidelines on the elimination of anticompetitive regulation in the EU and its member states.

The guidelines would also set forth suggestions for how they could be implemented, both from an institutional and a legal perspective.

This volume is composed of the collected written works and edited transcripts of dialogue that occurred during the Round Table. The first three parts (Parts I, II and III) include the papers presented and oral interventions made during the three panels of the Round Table. In particular, Part I covers regulations applicable to structurally competitive industries (the professions and private businesses); Part II covers regulations applicable to structurally noncompetitive industries (public services); and Part III deals with reform, regulatory institutions and the role of competition authorities. The recommendations made orally by the participants at the Round Table as to what should be included in the guidelines are then presented (Part IV). Finally, the recommended guidelines drafted by the editors, based on their own research and on all of the input from the Round Table participants, are set forth (Part V).

It is not our intention to summarize in a few pages the many insights that the reader will gather from study of this volume. It is, none the less, useful to present the main findings from the papers and discussions, as presented in the chapters that follow, to assist the reader in understanding the relevance of each paper to the overall theme, as well as how the guidelines were derived from the papers and panel discussions.

## REGULATIONS AFFECTING STRUCTURALLY COMPETITIVE INDUSTRIES: THE PROFESSIONS AND PRIVATE BUSINESSES

Structurally competitive industries include activities as varied as manufacturing goods of all types, and providing a broad array of services including the liberal professions, retailing, banking, travel agencies, driving schools and beauticians. Regulation of structurally competitive industries should correct market failures such as information asymmetries, negative or positive externalities, and it should ensure a minimum level of quality.

Participants focused mainly on regulation of the liberal professions. They identified information asymmetries as the main market failure, because consumers of professional services will often have difficulties in assessing the quality of services offered, either *ex ante* or *ex post*. Moreover, they may not even know where their demand curve lies – that is, they may not know what professional services they need.

Poorly designed regulations that are not well targeted to achieve their legitimate objectives can lead to regulatory failure, and to anticompetitive effects, such as price increases, impediments to efficient entry and stickiness in supply. These may, in turn, lead to adverse effects on growth, efficiency and distribution.

Participants agreed that certain types of regulations are very likely to bring about such regulatory failures, and therefore are not generally viewed to be effective regulatory instruments to attain public objectives. In service industries, they identified three main categories of regulations that can lead to anticompetitive effects for the markets involved: entry restrictions (such as licensing, certification and accreditation requirements); restrictions affecting business conduct (including price restrictions, restrictions on the scope of permissible activities and advertising restrictions); and restrictions affecting organizational and ownership form. For instance, rather than correcting the market failure of asymmetric information, restrictions on truthful advertising in markets for professional services further limit the information available to consumers. Removal of advertising restrictions is likely to increase entry, decrease concentration and prices but not quality, and therefore to lead to an overall increase in consumer welfare.

Reform of anticompetitive regulation in structurally competitive industries should begin with the establishment of some general principles and criteria. These should focus on what are the appropriate objectives of regulation, and how regulation should be designed in order best to achieve those objectives without leading to unintended consequences. Reformers should seek to identify the least-restrictive alternative form of regulation to achieve the legitimate objective.

Certain categories of restrictions were identified as likely to be the least-restrictive alternatives for correcting market failures. These include qualitative entry restrictions combined with minimum quality standards. However, even minimum quality standards can have negative effects on quality and structure, because they can restrict the pace at which a firm can react, and therefore limit its options. Self-regulation was viewed as a possible alternative in some cases. Self-regulation has the advantages of passing the role of regulator to those with greater information, and of being more flexible than regulation by public institutions. However, it can also be viewed as a form of collusion, as the self-regulatory organization will never go against the interests of its members. Thus, the issue is how to harness the best elements of self-regulation, but protect the public interest against abuse. One participant suggested that self-regulation seems to have the greatest potential when the number of agents is limited, the mobility of customers is high, and the regulator's uncertainty of firms' costs is substantial.

Participants emphasized the importance of approaching reform in such a way that it will raise the least opposition from affected groups. They agreed that reform should not be targeted to a single service, but should take a broad-based approach, which may have greater political appeal. The problems of regulatory capture must be addressed.

In addition, publicity is needed to raise the public's awareness of the need for reform, and to develop a political constituency that supports reform measures. Reformers should also consider how to provide consumers with the information they need in order to do comparison-shopping. One possibility would be to introduce independent auditing of professional services by either private or government agencies. Such auditing may impede professionals from strategic use of their dual role as the one who prescribes and provides services. Another possibility, applicable to sale of goods, would be to require the publication of information about the quality of the good being sold.

Finally, one participant suggested that it would be important to impose sanctions on the responsible government units to ensure that reform measures are properly implemented.

## REGULATIONS AFFECTING STRUCTURALLY NON-COMPETITIVE INDUSTRIES: THE PROVISION OF PUBLIC SERVICES

Structurally non-competitive industries include network industries (for example, gas, electricity, water, telecommunications, cable TV, postal services), public goods (for example, fire and police protection, sewer system, street lighting and cleaning, traffic control), and non-public goods (for example, local transport, health services, waste disposal, recreational services). Some of these services may be supplied by the market, although not at the desired level of price and quality, which is one reason why government intervention may be needed. Other reasons are to protect the health, safety and welfare of citizens, to address distributional considerations (especially those concerned with universal service obligations with respect to public utilities) and to conserve energy.

Participants identified a number of restrictions on competition that might result from government intervention in these markets. These fell into three main categories: (i) government restrictions aimed at protecting incumbents (for example, granting a monopoly franchise to an incumbent or otherwise restricting entry on behalf of the incumbent; asymmetric regulation of incumbents and entrants; lack of regulation of the incumbent's access charges for network industries); (ii) government restrictions aimed at protecting entrants (for example, limits on further entry; asymmetric tax treatment of entrants and incumbents; market share targets; premature deregulation of a market when substantial market power is still present; and regulation of the relationship between the incumbent's retail tariff and network access charges); and (iii) government restrictions aimed at protecting consumers (for example, price cap regulation, prohibiting incumbents from price discriminating, and requiring cross-subsidies in regulated tariffs). Moreover, participants discussed the problems that arise when strong interests that benefit from such anticompetitive regulations oppose reform efforts that threaten to deprive them of those benefits. Normally, there is no constituency that favours reform, because even though in the aggregate, consumers will realize substantial benefits from reform, the benefits felt by individual consumers will be negligible.

Many ideas for reform of anticompetitive regulation in structurally non-competitive industries were discussed. One participant argued that vertical separation of the structurally competitive component from the non-competitive component is a reform that would lead to a number of benefits. For instance, that the incumbent would no longer fight the regulator to restrict competition in downstream markets; the incumbent would be prevented from cost shifting; and innovation would be stimulated. In the electricity industry, potential buyers of generation facilities will demand vertical separation prior to purchase in order to be assured of future access to transmission facilities. With respect to government monopolies, another participant suggested that the market should be liberalized first, then privatized, in order to increase the success of the privatization effort. A reform method that has been used to liberalize the US telecommunications industry was also advocated, which is to allow the incumbent to enter new (long-distance) markets only if it achieves specified goals in opening the market which it dominates (local telephone services) to competition. Several participants noted the importance of addressing infrastructure problems in order fully to realize the benefits of liberalization.

Participants recognized that reforms in this area would lead to improved conditions, such as lower prices and improved quality of services, both in the market where the incumbent operates and in downstream markets.

Competition authorities have an important role to play in bringing about such reforms: to offset the coalition of interests that will be opposed to reform. One participant suggested that they could play this role more successfully if economists would devise more effective means for measuring economies of scope, which are key to the analysis of whether vertical separation is desirable.

## REFORM, REGULATORY INSTITUTIONS AND THE ROLE OF COMPETITION AUTHORITIES

Several institutional issues must be considered in conjunction with an effort to reform anticompetitive regulation. First, what is the appropriate institution to be responsible for review and reform? In Australia, where the most comprehensive reform effort to date is currently under way, a new agency, the National Competition Council (NCC), was created to administer the reform. To this end, it was empowered to conduct an initial review, through which it identified more than 2000 laws at every level of government that should be analysed, to determine whether the state and territory governments (which retained power to review their own laws and regulations) had conducted the reviews properly, and to reward them with the payment of substantial funds if they had. In the European Union, several participants suggested that the Commission should be empowered to play a role similar to that of the NCC, indicating that leaving the review entirely in the hands of the member states raises the danger that national governments would control the review process. Moreover, the Commission is the competition authority in Europe with the best reputation, has the know-how, and is situated far from national governments and lobbies, allowing it to take a broader view, which will be widely accepted. One participant suggested, however, that the process should be initiated by having an independent inquiry done by an independent body rather than the Commission. The importance of getting ongoing support for the review from the highest political levels was also noted.

Second, what should be the responsibilities of the competition authority as competition advocate, and how should the authority be structured to carry out this role effectively? The question of independence of the competition authority from the government was considered. On the one hand, participants recognized strong benefits of having the competition authority also act as competition advocate. One participant suggested that to be taken seriously, a competition advocate must have 'fist', and the competition authority's 'fist' is its responsibility for enforcement.

Some suggested that the head of the competition authority should be a cabinet minister, able to advocate competition in all government decision making. (This is the case in the European Union, where the competition commissioner is one of 20 commissioners, and is therefore in a key position to influence the initiation, implementation and monitoring of Community-wide regulatory actions in every sector. To date, however, the competition commissioner has not played a very major role as competition advocate.) In transition economies, the tradeoff of some independence for a higher level of influence in the political process is well worthwhile. In developed economies, this may not be the case. For instance, there would be the danger that a competition minister would have a junior position, and it may be preferable to have competition in the hands of the main economics minister, notwithstanding conflicts that he or she might have on some matters. Moreover, competition authorities have the know-how to be effective competition advocates, as there is no significant difference between assessing the anticompetitive impact of private conduct versus that of a regulation.

On the other hand, participants agreed that problems can arise when the competition authority acts also as competition advocate. People often resent the same institution doing too many things. An opinion from the competition authority on a legislative matter can be viewed as interference from other parts of the government. It enters the political arena and becomes part of the game. Accordingly, this may tarnish the reputation of independence of the competition authority.

Moreover, problems may result if the competition authority is not structurally independent from the government. Governments are generally interested in fostering national champions, an interest often at odds with competition considerations. Thus, there are strong benefits to structuring the competition authority in a manner that ensures its independence from government control. A strong and independent competition authority should have adequate technical and financial means, and sufficient powers of investigation.

In any event, in performing its role as advocate, the competition authority should have (or develop) a deep understanding of the industry concerned, be selective about which issues it will address, network with decision makers, and follow the issues closely. In the end, competition advocacy will be effective only to the extent that it is backed by political support, and perhaps by some legal powers.

Third, what should be the role of the courts in the reform of anticompetitive regulation? The proportionality principle could be used in European constitutional courts as the basis for judicial review of legislation with anticompetitive effects, with the possibility that the court would annul the legislative act. This would require these courts to apply economic analysis in order to determine whether a regulatory goal could be achieved in a less anti-competitive fashion. However, these courts do not do this, in part due to the European legal tradition, and in part due to concerns about the separation of powers and to the inadequate training of judges in economic matters. In addition, competition matters normally arrive in ordinary courts (as opposed to constitutional courts), on appeal of a decision that has been rendered by a competition authority. Although these courts have the power to make a factual appreciation of the case, they tend to assess only whether manifest error has occurred. Thus, courts tend to rely on the competition authority's decision, and not themselves to assess the facts by using economic analysis (although this may be changing). This supports the argument that judicial review would play a more significant role if competition authorities were empowered only to investigate and litigate, but not to decide cases. (However, one participant suggested that it is efficient for the competition authority not only to investigate and litigate, but also to decide cases, and it would be inefficient to separate the decision-making function.) Finally, ordinary courts in some member states, such as Germany and Italy, are empowered to refer matters to their respective constitutional courts. Thus, they could refer cases involving anticompetitive regulation to constitutional courts for a determination of whether a violation of the proportionality principle has occurred.

* * *

On the basis of the analysis in the chapters and panel discussions, as summarized above, the final part of this volume sets forth the Recommendations of the Round Table on Anticompetitive Regulation. The main recommendations of the participants are the following. All laws and regulations in the European Union, at both Community and national levels, should be reviewed pursuant to a regulatory review action plan. The results of such a review should be followed up by a benchmarking exercise, from which a 'procompetitive regulation' score would be attributed to each law and regulation. A Procompetitive Regulation Scoreboard would then report the results to the public, comparing the scores achieved by the Community and by each member state. The result would be to increase the degree of transparency as to the existence and effects of anticompetitive regulation throughout the Union, which would hopefully lead to reform. With respect to new legislation, a competitive impact statement should be prepared for each new legislative proposal, which would be provided to legislators and published.

Florence, Italy
Summer 2000

PART I


Regulations Affecting Structurally
Competitive Industries: The Professions
and Private Businesses

# Introduction

## Frederic Jenny

This part will address anticompetitive regulations affecting the professions and private business. It will focus on market failure and regulatory failure, and economists' failure to solve both market failure and regulatory failure. The chapters indicate that we are long on diagnosis but short on solutions or remedies. There seems to be agreement among several contributors that the market failure that characterizes the professions is due to an information asymmetry between the providers and the consumers of professional services. As a result of this information asymmetry, consumers have difficulties assessing the price/quality ratio of services provided by competing professionals. These professionals may thus engage in strategic behaviour and competition among them may not lead to efficiency.

One possible solution to this problem is self-regulation by professionals. However, Carlo Scarpa's chapter, using the example of minimum quality standards, shows that self-regulation may not be as innocuous as it is often considered to be and may create as many problems as it solves.

Several chapters (for example, those of Ginevra Bruzzone and Allan Fels) attempt to analyse the general conditions under which governmental regulations could correct this situation. A variety of regulatory devices, such as entry restrictions, advertising restrictions, restrictions on the scope of activity or the number of hours of operation, minimum quality standards and so on, are examined throughout the chapters. It is clear from these contributions that most or all of these devices restrict competition among professionals and therefore are of doubtful value. For example, Massimo Motta and Chiara Fumagalli, focusing on advertising restrictions that are widespread in the professions in Europe, show that those restrictions actually reduce welfare. Thus, they call for a removal of such restrictions. This call seems consistent with the approach taken by the US Supreme Court, under the commercial speech doctrine of the First Amendment of the US Constitution, which is analysed by Laraine Laudati. The US Supreme Court is reluctant to allow advertising bans in the professions and applies a very strict test when it examines such restrictions.

If self-regulation and regulations create risks of limiting competition and reducing welfare, should we conclude that liberalizing the professions and

*3*

ensuring that professionals compete with one another is the best course of action? Competition authorities tend to agree with this view and to advocate the elimination of regulatory constraints. However, eliminating regulations or self-regulations which may have adverse effects on competition and welfare does little to correct the market failure which lies at the heart of the problem. Thus, additional steps are necessary, which I discuss in Chapter 6.

# 1. Deregulation of structurally competitive services: economic analysis and competition advocacy

## Ginevra Bruzzone

*This chapter focuses on regulation of structurally competitive services, which include services as varied as retailing, banking, the liberal professions and the services of travel agencies, driving schools and beauticians. It discusses three sets of regulatory constraints that may be considered anticompetitive: entry restrictions, restrictions affecting business conduct (mainly, restrictions on price, on the scope of permissible activities and on advertising) and restrictions affecting organizational form and ownership relations. The analysis is divided into two parts: first, the substantive criteria to be used in an economic assessment of the competitive effects of the regulation of such services are considered; second, political elements of the regulatory decision-making process which may enhance or reduce the likelihood of procompetitive regulatory reform are taken into account.*

*The methodology for the competitive assessment of regulation of private services suggested by economic analysis is composed of three steps: analysis of market failures (including correction of information problems, negative or positive externalities, and ensuring a minimum level of service) and of the objectives of regulation; analysis of its economic impact (direct impact on price, impediment to entry by more efficient competitors, stickiness in supply, redistributive effects among consumers, consequences on the allocation of resources of associated rent-seeking activities), including its possible contribution to the correction of market failures; and identification of the least restrictive instruments needed to attain the relevant objectives (quantitative entry restrictions, restrictions on minimum prices, and restrictions on truthful advertising are normally not effective regulatory instruments to attain public objectives; qualitative entry restrictions combined with minimum quality standards may be appropriate for credence goods, while a case-by-case analysis is needed for experience goods).*

*Regarding the political aspects, liberalization is less likely when incumbents do not face any form of competition from other markets or foreign competi-*

*tion, when the business interests are homogeneous and when the perceived benefits of the regulation are small. Competition advocacy, even when it is not accompanied by any decision-making power, may foster liberalization by increasing the transparency of the economic impact of the regulation, which may change the perception of its costs and benefits.*

*The chapter ends by positing two questions. First, is it true that the closer the regulatory authority is to the regulated (European vis-à-vis national government; national vis-à-vis regional or local government), the less likely is liberalization? If so, a possible solution would be to centralize liberalization tasks. The alternative solution of structurally increasing the incentives of local regulators to take competition arguments into account should be considered. Second, is it true that the political appeal of liberalization initiatives directed at a single service is usually very small? If so, the solution would be to shift from a single-service approach to a liberalization-package approach, which may have greater political appeal. For instance, a review of all regulation of private services where a quantitative restriction on entry or a restriction on minimum prices still exists might be considered.*

## INTRODUCTION

Economic analysis offers important insights for the design of procompetitive reform of regulation applicable to private services. First, it helps identify the possible market failures for each business activity, and whether objectives of general interest exist that may justify a regulatory intervention, recognizing the proper distinctions among different services. Second, it highlights the costs and benefits of regulatory intervention. Third, it helps identify the most-efficient and least-anticompetitive instruments needed to correct the relevant market failures. This kind of analysis, however, is not sufficient to explain the varied evolution of regulation and the liberalization perspectives in each sector. For instance, it does not provide reasons why removal of merely protectionist regulatory barriers, not justified by general interest, is difficult to achieve and slow for some services.

This chapter will consider the example provided by the varying progress made in Italy towards procompetitive reform of regulation for a set of structurally competitive services (that is, services which are not provided under natural monopoly conditions), namely banking, retail distribution, the liberal professions and other professional business services. It will show that the elimination of clearly protectionist regulation in the banking sector has been more rapid than it has for other businesses, such as travel agencies or beauticians, although from an economic viewpoint, these latter services would seem to entail smaller problems of information asymmetries and externalities. By the mid-

1990s, most direct regulatory barriers to competition had been eliminated in the banking sector. With respect to retailing, an important step towards the removal of unjustified regulatory restrictions was taken with the adoption of Legislative Decree 31 March 1998, No. 114;[1] the scope of liberalization, however, has been significantly limited by the implementing regulations subsequently adopted by local governments. For the liberal professions, the debate on procompetitive regulatory reform has just begun; for several other business services, no progress towards liberalization has yet been achieved, notwithstanding the repeated competition advocacy efforts of the Italian Competition Authority.

To study liberalization as an endogenous variable, the standard economic analysis must be extended to consider the distribution of costs and benefits of regulation and deregulation in each sector and, more generally, the politics of the relevant regulatory decision making. This approach may also be useful for normative purposes, since it helps to identify the most serious obstacles to deregulation and how to overcome them.

The chapter is organized as follows. Section A will review the elements of economic analysis concerning regulation in structurally competitive sectors and identify the most obvious examples of merely protectionist regulation. Section B will consider current regulation of banking, retailing, the liberal professions and other professional services in Italy. An attempt is made to illustrate the major steps of the deregulation process in cases where a significant reduction of anticompetitive regulatory barriers has occurred. Section C will discuss the driving forces behind success in liberalization, and the most serious obstacles to the further elimination of restrictions, taking into account the characteristics of the regulatory decision-making process. The role played by the Italian Competition Authority in fostering liberalization in the Italian economy through its competition advocacy efforts is also discussed. The final section contains some concluding remarks.

## A.   THE ECONOMIC ANALYSIS OF REGULATION OF STRUCTURALLY COMPETITIVE SERVICES

### 1. Scope of Analysis

This section will set forth some results of economic analysis relevant to the assessment of regulation of structurally competitive services. It focuses on three sets of regulatory constraints which may be considered 'anticompetitive': those affecting entry into a market (especially quantitative restrictions such as ceilings on the number of competitors or minimum distances between retail outlets);

those affecting conduct (principally restrictions on price, scope of permissible activities and advertising); and those affecting ownership relations and the organizational arrangements for the provision of services.[2] It will consider market failures, the economic impact of regulatory constraints (including their contribution to the correction of market failures), and the suggestions derived from economic analysis for identifying the least-restrictive instruments to attain the relevant objectives.

## 2. Market Failures

Economic analysis helps identify cases in which the market may fail to ensure the provision or an adequate quality of service because of *information problems*. This is typically the case for credence goods, such as medical services, where the customer does not have adequate information before buying the service, and has difficulty in assessing the quality of the service even after the purchase. Adverse selection may discourage the provision of high-quality service and may result in the disappearance of the market. Moreover, suppliers may take advantage of the customer's lack of information and consciously overproduce the service, or may adopt other forms of opportunistic behaviour. Regarding experience goods, for which inadequate information exists only before the purchase, but *ex post* analysis of the quality of the service is possible, experience and reputation are usually sufficient to solve any problem. A failure may continue, however, when the potential damage (such as damage to personal safety) from an inadequate provision of the service is sufficiently serious, and obtaining *ex ante* information (such as information on the quality of a newcomer) is costly. Asymmetric information problems and their potential relevance are heterogeneous across the sectors considered in this chapter, with medical care and some legal and banking services at one extreme and non-food retailing at the other.

A second general interest requirement may be the correction of significant negative or positive *externalities* of private decisions which do not take their impact on other people into consideration. The relevance of externalities varies with services. For instance, in retail distribution, the impact of outlets on urban aesthetics, traffic and environmental protection may be relevant.[3]

A related concern, which may also be considered a general interest requirement, is *ensuring a minimum level of service*, in terms of availability in different geographical areas, compulsory opening hours or compulsory provision of a plurality of products, in cases where the market equilibrium is perceived to be different from that which would be socially desirable. Some examples are the regulation of taxis, pharmacies and newspaper kiosks. From an economic viewpoint, the concerns are similar to those with respect to the provision of public services.

Economists generally agree that regulatory intervention is not required to *reach an optimal market structure* in an oligopoly where the equilibrium number of firms may be different from the number that would maximize total surplus in a static framework.[4] As Gilbert observes in his classic survey of the economic analysis of entry conditions:

> Although many of the market equilibrium outcomes described in this chapter could in principle benefit from the invisible hand of an omniscient intervenor, they may be as good as may be expected given imperfect competition, imperfect information and the limited policy instruments available for the regulation of market performance.[5]

The changing nature of demand and supply in each market should also be considered. Even if it were possible to establish the optimal supply structure in a given instant, regulatory intervention may still distort dynamic market development, therefore producing more costs than benefits.

## 3. Economic Impact of Regulation

This section will consider the economic impact of regulatory restrictions on entry and restrictions concerning business conduct (regulation of price, restrictions on the scope of activities, restrictions on opening hours, minimum standard requirements, restrictions on organizational form and ownership links, and service requirements).

### a. Restrictions on entry

Freedom of entry of new competitors into a market has both a disciplinary effect on incumbents' behaviour and an impact on market equilibrium related to the possible increase in the number of firms. It also has a positive effect that is independent of the number of firms in the market, and depends on the variability of undertakings in terms of efficiency, innovation, quality of products and so on. The effect of actual or potential entry on welfare can be viewed not only in static terms, but also in a dynamic perspective. Geroski, Gilbert and Jacquemin correctly observe: '[It] can upset traditional patterns of market conduct, dethrone dominant firms, introduce new technology and fresh approaches to product design and marketing and lead to more competitive prices'.[6]

Regulatory restrictions on entry may *reduce the number of effective competitors* either directly, through quantitative restrictions, or indirectly, by increasing costs and therefore modifying the equilibrium conditions for the marginal entrant. Regulatory interventions resulting in a cost increase may take various forms, such as requirements to follow a specified training programme, to comply with given production standards, or to pay a licence fee.

Usually, the existence of entry restrictions leads to *higher prices*. The quantitative significance of the price increase will depend on the relevance of artificial entry costs with respect to the reference market and on the resulting artificial restriction in the number of competitors. The regulatory intervention may produce a negligible impact, or even have no impact, on price in a very fragmented market. However, it may also result in a shift from a competitive to a monopoly situation. Empirical research focusing on the impact of entry restrictions on price shows that the effect on individual consumers is often not large. For instance, in the US, one study showed that a 10 per cent reduction in the length of the required training programme for gaining access to the barber profession would produce a savings of $0.28 per haircut for consumers.[7]

However, even when the anticompetitive impact in terms of price is negligible, regulatory entry restrictions may produce a significant distortion on the competitive process by limiting entry of more efficient competitors and by introducing stickiness in the evolution of supply. When incumbents cannot sell their licences on the market, as in the case of Italian notaries, quantitative restrictions on the number of competitors prevent even a very efficient newcomer from entering the market. Moreover, when quantitative restrictions make entry possible only by acquiring an undertaking (including the licence) from an incumbent, a newcomer may meet significant constraints and therefore be less innovative than one who enters the market *ex novo*.

Even when an entry regulation that increases producers' costs succeeds in bringing about a higher quality of service, the impact on consumer surplus is not necessarily positive. Those who place high value on the increase in quality may be better off, but those who would have preferred the option to choose a lower quality at a lower price will be worse off. *Redistributive effects between consumer groups* therefore are significant.

Entry restrictions also have an impact with respect to artificially created *monopoly rents*. As shown above, entry restrictions usually result in a decrease in the number of effective competitors and in a corresponding increase in price (or more generally an increase in the incumbent market power). This does not mean, however, that the market incumbents are necessarily enjoying artificially created extra profits or monopoly rents. Demsetz demonstrated that if a licence has been purchased by the current incumbent either from the government or from a previous incumbent at a price corresponding to the discounted value of future expected related monopoly profits, he or she will not enjoy a monopoly rent.[8] For instance, this might be the case for taxi drivers who have bought their licence on the market. This is not, however, the case for competitors who have not fully paid the value of their licence in terms of related monopoly power, as in the case of Italian notaries. When the monopoly rent deriving from artificially created monopoly power is not entirely enjoyed by the current incumbent, it may be acquired by the government, the professional body which requires a payment to enrol in the register, the promoters of educational and training initiatives, legal assistants, or even corrupt public officials. The corresponding *rent-seeking activity generally produces a suboptimal allocation of resources.*[9]

To analyse the possible *contribution of entry restrictions to the solution of market failures*, a distinction must be made between qualitative and quantitative restrictions. Qualitative entry requirements may be justified to address information problems related to credence or experience goods. However, a regulatory intervention will be justified only when the risk to consumers with inadequate skills is significant. For instance, a taxi driver's driving licence may be sufficient to assure the safety of passengers. Moreover, the risk must be evaluated in conjunction with the potential relevance of the damage that would result from inadequate skills. The expected effectiveness of regulatory intervention and its overall costs, including the possible negative impact on price and market dynamics described above, must also be analysed. The market may provide spontaneous forms of skilfulness certification for some services where information problems exist. In some cases, regulation may simply establish a low minimum quality requirement for entering the market. This approach may allow diversity in the price and quality of available services, and avoid the costs resulting from excessive uniform regulatory requirements. The freedom to advertise may be essential to foster development of spontaneous forms of skilfulness certification.

On the other hand, quantitative restrictions to entry, such as ceilings on the number of licences, are generally ineffective in addressing any of the above described market failures. Public administrators are not able to establish the optimal market structure. Even assuming a benevolent regulator, not merely acting to protect incumbents but attempting to maximize total surplus, a structural market regulation may seriously distort the competitive process. Likewise, with respect to information problems, quantitative restrictions on the number of competitors and the possible resulting extra profits do not offer an *ex ante* guarantee with respect to quality. Nor do they solve *ex post* information problems for credence goods, since they do not impede the provision of low-quality services or the adoption of opportunistic behaviour. More direct instruments for correcting externalities and satisfying possible service requirements appear strongly preferable to quantitative restrictions on market structure. For instance, with respect to retailing, if the aim is to correct urban externalities, urban planning is much preferable to quantitative ceilings on the number of large outlets. With respect to pharmacies, if the aim is to ensure a given level of service throughout the country, including small centres and rural areas, guaranteeing the operation of a minimum number of outlets in all areas is preferable to quantitative ceilings on the number of outlets.

## b. Restrictions on business conduct

*Minimum prices*   Minimum prices have an obvious direct negative impact on customers, which is that they prevent customers from being able to obtain lower prices. In some cases, restrictions on price competition simply lead to stronger non-price competition, producing a 'competitive' equilibrium different, and usually inferior, to the one that would have prevailed as a free market outcome. The impact on artificially created monopoly profits will depend on how non-price competition occurs.

General interest justifications of regulatory minimum price fixing are unconvincing. For credence goods, minimum prices may prevent the disappearance of the market, but they are less effective in doing so than qualitative entry requirements. In fact, minimum prices do not guarantee either the quality of entrants or the absence of opportunistic behaviour. In short, contrary to what professionals often argue, minimum prices are not a proper instrument to correct market failures in the case of asymmetric information.

Nor are minimum prices justified to prevent externalities. For instance, with respect to banks, if the aim is to protect the stability of the system, regulatory restrictions on price competition are neither necessary nor efficient.

Finally, establishing minimum prices for a service in order to cross-subsidize the supply of other services with the objective of financing unprofitable service requirements is normally an inferior alternative to more direct and transparent subsidies.

*Restrictions on the scope of activities*   In principle, restrictions on the scope of activities would seem justifiable if the social cost of multiproduction (for instance, in terms of hygienic conditions or of possible conflicts of interest) exceeded the private cost for the seller (who, in the absence of information problems, would have to sustain a loss of reputation). The cost of such restrictions is the elimination of possible economies of scope and the introduction of some stickiness in the evolution of supply. Therefore, they may give rise to higher production costs and prices, and may hamper innovation. The relevance of such effects will vary, depending on the market involved. In general, however, policy makers should carefully consider whether other direct interventions aimed at correcting the externality, such as constraints on conduct, might be a satisfactory alternative to restrictions on productive specialization.

*Restrictions on hours of operation*   Regulatory restrictions on opening hours, often applied to retail establishments, constitute a restriction of non-price competition, since they limit the possibility of differentiating the service either horizontally (personalizing opening hours) or vertically (widening the opening hours interval). Regulatory restrictions that impose uniformity of the opening interval, for a given number of hours (restrictions in horizontal differentiation), worsen consumers' conditions and do not appear justifiable to protect the general interest. On the other hand, regulatory restrictions of the length of the opening interval reduce production costs and may therefore enhance efficiency and profits, although this is not necessarily the case. For some retailers, such as booksellers, the level of consumption depends on the width of the opening interval. However, total freedom to set opening hours, if not accompanied by flexibility in the possible use of part-time work, may unduly favour larger outlets with respect to small ones.[10]

*Maximum prices, advertising, organizational form and ownership links*
Maximum price fixing is often advocated on grounds of equity ('the service should be accessible to anybody') or of protection of customers who are in a particularly weak bargaining position. The main challenge for economic analysis is to find alternative instruments (for example, special insurance for less-wealthy people) to solve the problem without interfering with price competition.

Regulatory restrictions on the possibility of advertising truthfully raise barriers to entry, may limit innovation and price competition and are not justified in terms of the general interest.

Restrictions on organizational form and on proprietary links with other undertakings may reduce efficiency and the possibility of collecting equity capital, therefore limiting growth. The challenge for competition advocates is to find alternative ways of preventing significant conflicts of interests (arising, for instance, in the case of ownership of banks by non-financial companies) and, for professional services, to ensure adequate liability guarantees.

*Minimum quality standards* Minimum quality standards for the provision of services typically increase costs and prices. They may be justified, together with qualitative entry requirements, with respect to goods that give rise to significant information problems, since they can protect consumers and avoid opportunistic behaviour when this is not attained by private initiatives of spontaneous certification. If standards are not appropriately defined, or compliance with them is not effectively monitored, however, they may not be effective in increasing the quality of service.

The effect of quality standards on consumer surplus depends on how consumer groups value the increase in quality. Thus, an efficient solution may be to establish a low-quality standard and leave undertakings or professionals free to adopt higher standards, and to certify and publicize their acceptance of higher standards.

*Service requirements*   The most difficult issue with respect to service requirements is determining the cases in which the private provision of services would be less than the socially desirable level, so as to justify a regulatory intervention. In some cases, an activity that is not privately profitable when taken in isolation, may become profitable if undertaken together with other activities. This approach was followed in the 1998 Italian reform of retailing, which encouraged the combination of retail services and other services in the same outlet in order to maintain the presence of retail outlets in small rural centres. The need for regulatory intervention increases if constraints are imposed on pricing decisions. Moreover, the perception of what is socially desirable for pursuing different final objectives (for example, quality of life in urban centres and villages, pluralism of information) may change over time.

With respect to the choice of instruments, the main question concerns who should sustain the cost of the privately unprofitable service requirement. Either local or national taxpayers could finance direct subsidies. Other solutions may place the burden on all producers or a subset of them. The latter may unfairly burden the affected undertakings, if they must compete on the market with firms that do not sustain the same regulatory burden.

## 4. Suggestions for the Choice of the Most Effective Regulatory Instruments

The above review of economic insights on regulation of potentially competitive services shows that quantitative restrictions on entry, regulation of minimum prices and restrictions on fair advertising generally cannot be considered effective instruments for the correction of market failures. For credence goods, qualitative entry restrictions and minimum quality standards in principle represent the most-direct and least-anticompetitive instruments to protect consumers whenever a significant risk of inadequate skills, negligence or opportunism exists. For experience goods, a case-by-case analysis is needed to assess whether qualitative entry requirements should be imposed, taking the costs and expected benefits of regulation into consideration.

With respect to both externalities and service requirements, apart from the need for a careful case-by-case analysis of whether a regulatory intervention is necessary, the most-direct regulatory instruments are usually the most effective, and result in the smallest distortions of the competitive process.

Given these results, from a normative standpoint it is difficult to see why quantitative restrictions on entry, minimum price regulation and restrictions on advertising should not be rapidly eliminated. The Italian experience with deregulation in private services, however, shows that in some instances protectionist regulations are extremely persistent.

## B.   THE EVOLUTION OF REGULATION: CASES FROM THE ITALIAN EXPERIENCE

### 1. Banking

Under the 1936–38 Italian Banking Law, credit authorities enjoyed large dis-cretionary powers when deciding whether to accept or reject a demand for authorization to engage in banking or to open a new branch. For a long time, the establishment of a new branch would only be authorized in cases where this was perceived necessary to provide banking services in areas where such services were not previously available. Credit authorities could deny autho-rization for branching on the basis of an evaluation of the 'economic need' for a new branch in the area concerned. Although in the 'branching plans' of 1978, 1982 and 1985 the need to promote efficiency, together with stability, was increasingly taken into account by credit authorities, the logic behind public control of branching was direct regulation of market structure.

Enactment of the 1977 and 1989 European Community (EC) banking directives[11] led to the gradual reform of entry regulation, substantially elimi-nating the power of credit authorities to establish the 'optimal' market structure, both in terms of the number of competitors and of the number of branches.[12] In 1999, the European Commission intervened against the Portuguese government's veto of the acquisition by the Spanish *Banco Santander Central Hispano* of an important participation in the Portuguese financial group *Banca Champalimaud/Mundial Confianca*. This intervention demonstrated the Commission's current interest in ensuring that decisions by national govern-ments made on alleged prudential grounds do not violate the EC Treaty's competition rules and its rules on the freedom of establishment and of capital movements. It places a further limit on the discretionary powers of bank super-visory authorities to affect the market structure at national level.

Regarding pricing restrictions, the 1936–38 law allowed credit authorities to fix loan and deposit rates, although this provision was never used. Until 1974, however, the authorities supported bank agreements on interest rates. The 1993 Banking Law contains no provision allowing the authorities to restrict banks' freedom to fix interest rates (as well as the other prices); it simply requires banks to follow disclosure rules on terms and conditions of contract.[13]

Regarding line-of-business restrictions and ownership regulation, recent regulatory reforms have eliminated the previous distinction between banks that can raise short-term funds and those that cannot. All banks are presently allowed to issue instruments of deposit, as well as bonds, subject to supervisory rules for the control of maturity transformation. In addition to the activities of fund raising and granting credit, banks may engage in any other financial business (including all activities subject to mutual recognition on the basis of the Second EC Banking Directive), in accordance with the provisions applicable to each activity, and in related and instrumental activities. Restrictions on banks' shareholdings in financial companies and, in particular, in non-financial companies, established for prudential reasons, are more severe than the minimum required by EC Directive No. 89/646. If seen from a domestic standpoint, however, they are more flexible than those prevailing in the past. Stricter rules than those existing in other European Union (EU) member states limit the possibility of a non-financial undertaking to hold capital in banks.

In summary, if compared with the situation prevailing in the 1970s, current bank regulation does not allow authorities to limit entry and branching in order to establish the 'optimal' market structure, recognizes (with the partial exception of the 1996 usury law) that prices should be the result of the free market process and has removed previous restrictions on the scope of financial activities that banks can undertake. Prudential reasons have been invoked to justify Italy's restrictions on bank shareholdings and on the ownership of banks, which are stricter than restrictions prevailing in other EU member states.

## 2. Retail Distribution

Italy's 1926 retailing regulation was quite similar to the regulation of bank branches: local authorities granted licences only when the existing supply was considered insufficient to satisfy consumers' needs. This approach was maintained in Law 11 June 1971, No. 426, which constituted the regulatory framework until the recent reform undertaken with Legislative Decree No. 114/98.[14] Under the 1971 system, in order to operate in retailing, individuals were required to satisfy moral and professional requirements, and to be enrolled in a special Register (*Registro degli esercenti il commercio*). For each retail outlet, a municipal authorization was required, which was granted on the basis of predetermined 'municipal retail plans'. The authorization was needed not only to open the outlet, but also to enlarge it or change its location. Authorizations were granted with reference to a limited scope of activities (for example, sales of furniture, sales of clothes and shoes, sales of textile products), as defined in the 'Tables of categories of products' (*Tabelle merceologiche*). Therefore, once authorized to sell a given set of goods, retailers were not free to change their scope of activities. According to the law, the aim of retail planning was twofold: to enhance efficiency and to establish the proper equilibrium between supply and demand. To this end, ceilings were established limiting total surface area available for retailing of food, of clothes and shoes and for outlets with a surface above 400 m², respectively, in each municipality and in some cases also in smaller areas within municipalities. Once the ceiling was reached, no further authorizations were given. With respect to retail outlets with a surface above 400 m$^2$, the regional government was involved in the decision-making process, holding a veto power with respect to the authorization. The law also regulated opening hours, requiring outlets to be closed on the same days and during the same intervals within each day.

During the 1980s, some steps towards liberalization were taken. These reforms usually involved the automation of the authorization process, with special reference to the enlargement of existing outlets. This partial liberalization favoured incumbents *vis-à-vis* new entrants.

In 1993, the Italian Competition Authority presented a report to the government suggesting how to reform retail legislation in order to make it more consistent with market principles. A complete revision and reform of retail regulation was undertaken in 1998, with the enactment of Legislative Decree No. 114. The 1998 legislative decree abrogated the previous rules and abolished the special Register for retailers. The previous highly fragmented tables of categories of products were simplified considerably, such that only the two categories of food and non-food products are maintained. Professional requirements have been maintained only for selling food. Moreover, the opening of small outlets (with a surface of less than 250 m$^2$, or 150 m$^2$, depending on the area of location) has been liberalized, such that authorization is no longer required. Instead, a notification to the municipal government is all that is needed, as well as compliance with hygienic, safety and town-planning rules. Retailers also have greater flexibility in the choice of opening hours, both within each day and with respect to opening days. For medium-sized outlets (with a surface up to 1500 m$^2$ or 2500 m$^2$), an authorization by the municipal government is still required; for large outlets, an authorization by representatives of the municipal, provincial and regional governments is needed. Finally, the law requires regional governments to adopt general guidelines for programming the establishment of retail outlets as well as general criteria for urban development of the sector.

The 1971 law's objective of establishing the optimal market structure by finding the proper equilibrium between demand and supply is no longer mentioned in the 1998 decree. Instead, the latter refers to the more general concepts of competition, consumer protection, the promotion of small and medium enterprises and the balanced development of the sector. Until now, however, most regional governments have maintained a conservative attitude with respect to the liberalization challenge, repeated appeals by the Competition Authority notwithstanding. In particular, several regional governments have used all possible means provided by the law in order to limit the scope of liberalization. For instance, they have defined 'small outlets' (for which authorization is no longer needed) in a very restrictive way. Moreover, they have generally introduced total surface ceilings for the opening of large outlets, often blocking further entrance in the sector.

The European Commission has, until now, not intervened to compel member states to remove anticompetitive barriers. In its 1991 Notice entitled 'Towards a Single Market in Distribution', the Commission stated its intention to rely on the initiative of each member state to remove possible obstacles to market integration resulting from national legislation.[15] The January 1999 White Paper on Commerce, which delineates some priorities for Community action in terms of sectoral industrial policy, does not substantially change the Commission approach of no direct intervention against regulatory barriers to entry in the sector.[16] The only significant change is the express inclusion of commerce in the so-called BEST (Business Environment Simplification Taskforce) project, which provides that the Commission shall publish guidelines for the simplification of rules and administrative procedures in the sector. Moreover, the Commission promised to identify and publish 'best practices' with respect to public policy aimed at promoting the development of rural and less-favoured urban areas. In principle, the publication of regulatory best practices might be an indirect instrument by which the Commission promotes competition in sectors where it does not intervene directly in fostering liberalization.

## 3. Liberal Professions

In the liberal professions, including law, accounting, health and engineering/architecture, the current regulation stems from the statutory recognition of self-regulatory initiatives, which therefore now enjoy the force of law.[17] Among publicly regulated professions, licensed professionals enjoy an exclusive preserve. In order to attain a licence, in most professions a period of apprenticeship with an incumbent professional is required before taking the state examination. For notaries and pharmacies, a ceiling is placed on the number of new entrants and restrictions are placed on the geographic scope of activities. Representatives of publicly recognized professional bodies (*Ordini*) ensure compliance with professional codes of conduct. Moreover, they are deeply involved in the decision-making process concerning the entry of new competitors, taking part in examination commissions for the state qualifying examinations, which have considerable discretionary power, and in the determination of quantitative restrictions.

Minimum or fixed tariffs and charges are often established by law, and are based on the proposals made by professional bodies and subsequently approved by ministerial decree. Advertising is subject to strict limitations. Choice of organizational form was partially liberalized by Law 7 August 1997, No. 266, which removed the prohibition on provision of professional services in professional joint partnerships.[18] The limited liability company form is still not allowed, although it may, in principle, be accompanied by appropriate guarantees to safeguard the specific features of each profession.[19]

At European level, liberalization of professional services is advanced by the articles of the Treaty concerning freedom of establishment and freedom to provide services within the single market,[20] as well as from directives that define the mutual recognition system for professional requirements.[21] Moreover, in several decisions taken since 1993, the Commission has found some collective price-fixing practices and restrictions on advertising in the sector of professional services to violate Article 81, in cases where a significant impact on trade between member states was deemed to exist. The national legislation that expressly authorized these restrictions was considered irrelevant for the application of the prohibition. In one case, the national law itself was considered to violate Articles 10 and 81 of the Treaty.[22]

In 1997, the Italian Competition Authority published a general fact-finding inquiry on the liberal professions, which strongly spurred the domestic debate on regulatory reform. Following this intervention, no new licensed professions have been added to the existing ones, although a number of draft measures to this end were presented to Parliament. In its Economic and Financial Programme for the years 2000–2003, the Italian government expressly endorsed the objective of eliminating the administrative constraints limiting competition and ensuring monopoly rents to several liberal professions. The government stated that the creation of exclusive preserves should be limited to those sectors where true reasons of consumer protection exist, and that unjustified restrictions to the number of professionals should not be included when establishing appropriate rules of conduct. The representatives of licensed professions are extremely active in advancing their views on possible reforms. The *Ordine dei Commercialisti* (publicly recognized professional body of accountants) has, to some extent, anticipated the general reform by modifying its code of conduct, and eliminating its prohibition on advertising and its sanctions for non-compliance with minimum professional fees. Similarly, lawyers have removed some of the restrictions on advertising from their code of conduct.

Accordingly, some procompetitive reforms, such as elimination of compulsory minimum fees, elimination of restrictions on advertising, and transparency in the entry decision-making process, now appear to be widely accepted. However, strong opposition by incumbents still exists with respect to revision and reduction of exclusivity preserves. With respect to the possibility for non-professionals to hold shares in the capital of companies for the provision of professional services, incumbents are split, with most technical professions in favour of reform.

## 4. Other Private Services

In Italy, strict legal restrictions control entry conditions and, in some cases, the permissible scope of activities and pricing decisions in many private services (for example, bakeries, taxis, hairdressers and beauticians, driving schools, tour guides, alpine guides and ski teachers). For most of these services, regulatory restrictions are imposed not only at the national level, but also by regional, provincial or municipal governments. In several cases, subnational governments have substantial discretion to decide how restrictive regulation should be. Entry restrictions are often considerable, such as high formal professional requirements necessary to obtain a licence, requirements to enrol in special registers in order to operate, and frequent involvement of incumbents' representatives in the commissions for qualifying examinations. Quantitative limits on the permissible number of authorizations are imposed, at the local level, for activities such as driving schools, companies providing assistance for administrative matters relating to transport, taxis, cinemas, newspaper kiosks, bakeries, bars and restaurants, security guards and, in some regions, travel agencies, hairdressers and beauticians. Minimum prices are established by law for driving schools, companies providing assistance for administrative matters relating to transport, taxis, alpine guides and, in some regions, ski teachers. Limitations on the scope of activities exist for tour guides, interpreters and so on; restrictions on the permissible geographical area of operation limit freedom of action of tour guides, ski teachers, alpine guides and, in some regions, travel agencies.

Community-level liberalization initiatives affecting these sectors are those related to the freedom of establishment and to provide services by citizens of other member states. Thus, they centre on initiatives to ensure mutual recognition of professional requirements.

In most of these sectors, the Italian Competition Authority has sent competition advocacy reports and opinions to the relevant regulatory bodies at the national or local level. In some sectors (for example, cinemas, newspaper kiosks), partial attempts to introduce more flexibility in the existing regulation have been undertaken by the competent bodies. However, these suggestions have not in any case, to date, been completely accepted. The competition advocacy opinions have, however, succeeded in preventing the introduction of new regulatory restrictions, in particular new exclusive preserves or minimum prices, for a number of professions, including managers of apartment buildings, providers of auxiliary medical services and customs forwarding agents.

## C.    COMPETITION ADVOCACY AND PERSPECTIVES FOR REFORM: THE POLITICS OF DEREGULATION

### 1. Regulation and the Political Process

As shown above, the deregulation movement for structurally competitive services in Italy has, until now, been selective.[23] The 'public interest theory' or 'normative analysis as positive theory' approach used by economists until the 1960s, under which regulation was studied only with reference to the correction of market failures, is not sufficient to explain the differences in the evolution of regulation in the different services.

Public choice theorists have offered important insights that help explain why the removal of protectionist regulatory barriers to competition may not be an easy task. The 'economic theory' of regulation attempts to analyse the regulatory process by integrating the analysis of political behaviour with traditional economic analysis, and assuming that politicians and public officials are self-interest maximizers.[24] Complementary contributions to the understanding of regulation (and deregulation) as endogenous variables come from the more descriptive studies of political economists and of political scientists who, particularly since the 1980s, focused on analysis of the 'politics of regulation'.[25] These studies show that the perception of the costs and benefits of a policy matters in terms of the involvement of different interest groups in the political process and of the likely final regulatory result. When protectionist barriers to entry give rise to significant concentrated benefits for incumbents and to only small costs for a large number of dispersed consumers, incumbents will make strong efforts to oppose deregulation, while the damaged subjects may not be active in trying to foster liberalization. For instance, regarding the regulation of barbershops in the US, the estimated consumer loss is $0.28 for each haircut, but the estimated artificial yearly extra profit for an incumbent amounts to $6450.[26]

An additional and serious obstacle to liberalization exists in markets where the monopoly rent has been fully paid by the current incumbents (who, for instance, have bought a licence from previous incumbents on the belief that protectionist barriers would not be removed). This situation, described by Tullock as the 'transitional gain trap', leads to strong opposition to liberalization.[27] Incumbents will correctly argue that they are not enjoying artificial monopoly rents. Therefore, for them, removal of regulatory barriers would not cause a reduction of artificially increased extra profits, but a loss affecting the 'normal' profits resulting from the activity. An economist would object that the return on a licence, like the return on shares or other assets, is not riskless and that the expectation mechanism, when establishing the price of the licence, should take account of the possibility that regulatory barriers may be reformed at some point. But when the licence represents the main source of income for the incumbents, it may be politically very difficult to liberalize. On the other hand, protectionist barriers entail costs for consumers. Thus, it is essential that the expectation mechanism takes account of the possibility of future liberalization as credible, so as to adjust the market value of the licence gradually.[28]

Even in the simpler case where incumbents enjoy artificially created extra profits, liberalization is not straightforward. In order to promote the removal of anticompetitive regulation and to assess the perspectives of reform, the driving forces that have permitted deregulation in some sectors should be considered. The sections that follow will do so.

## 2. Political Demand

Factors that reduce the benefit of regulation or make regulation costly for incumbents may enhance the likelihood of regulatory reform. For instance, in the 1950s, the association of Italian manufacturers, *Confindustria*, initially opposed the removal of trade barriers within the Common Market. It subsequently changed this position when members understood that the cost of a protectionist position (a lower level of exports) would have been much larger, for most of them, than the benefit of limiting imports. However, in some instances, in the incumbents' perception the short-term benefits of protection outweigh the benefits of liberalization. For instance, in the case of multioutlet retail companies in Italy, the strict regulatory barriers that limited the number of large retail outlets may have given incumbents short-term monopoly profits. In the long run, however, these restrictions limited the growth and undermined the competitiveness and ability to expand abroad of large domestic retail companies. Some acquisitions by foreign companies have already occurred. The Italian association of large retailers is now pressuring regional governments not to introduce overly strict regulatory restrictions on the establishment of new outlets within the context of the 1998 reform (discussed above).

In the services sector, a political demand for removal of regulatory restrictions on conduct typically emerges when such restrictions limit the reaction of domestic incumbents to foreign competition. Where foreign competition will play a significant role, facilitated by EU measures based on mutual recognition and aimed at guaranteeing freedom of establishment and of provision of services, domestic incumbents are likely to demand the removal of restrictions which limit their flexibility. For instance, when the EC Banking Directives of 1977 and 1989 came into force, pressure from domestic banks was a powerful force towards the removal of restrictions on branching and on the scope of permissible activities in Italy. In some liberal professions (such as legal services), foreign competition is already being invoked as a justification for revision of existing regulation.

Another important factor affecting political demand is the degree of homogeneity of business interests *vis-à-vis* the measures to be liberalized. For instance, in the US, the uniformity of interests among the members of the American Trucking Association is deemed to have facilitated the lobbying action by the association against liberalization. In contrast, in air transport, divergence of interests among a small number of large and medium-sized incumbents impeded the adoption of a uniform position with respect to deregulation.[29] In Italy, the abolition of the monopoly of stock exchange trading by exchange brokers was facilitated by support from the banking sector. In retailing, the association of large retailers has traditionally supported the introduction of more flexibility in the choice of opening hours, while small retailers have opposed it. Currently, large and small retailers also disagree on the reform of restrictions on opening large outlets.

Heterogeneous interests are also emerging in the area of the professions. The Organization of Recognized Professional Bodies (*Comitato Unitario degli Ordini Professionali*) opposes an overly broad reform of the existing regulation. Concrete reform proposals that are more market-orientated, however, are being presented by several professional bodies belonging to the organization (for example, *Ordine dei periti industriali* (publicly recognized professional body of engineer surveyors)) and by the representatives of non-recognized professional associations. The association of 7000 registered pharmacists, limited in the operations by quantitative ceilings on the number of outlets, are demanding liberalization. The association of practitioners is demanding a simplification of rules governing access to the law profession.

Accordingly, politically organized business interests supporting deregulation may strongly facilitate progress towards the removal of protectionist barriers. The liberalization impact may be limited, however, when the choice of policy may be split in order to meet the specific demands. For instance, technical professions favour the allowance of limited companies for the provision of professional services, in which non-professionals would also be allowed to hold shares, subject to appropriate guarantees for consumer protection. Other professions oppose such a reform. The impact of this divergence on the overall reform process will depend on whether different rules for technical and non-technical professions will be adopted, or whether a single rule will be applied to all regulated professions.

## 3. Role of Competition Advocates

Political scientists have also suggested that 'opinion élites' play an important role in fostering procompetitive liberalization. For instance, economists can identify market failures, the costs and benefits of different regulatory instruments, and suggest the most effective regulatory instruments. Making public the economic analysis of the costs of an unjustified anticompetitive regulation may strongly affect liberalization. Moreover, by increasing the transparency of the impact of regulatory decisions, economic analysis can help the interest groups who suffer most from regulation to organize their political demand. It may also facilitate the introduction of the reform issue on the political agenda. For instance, at least since the 1970s, numerous economists and lawyers in Italy, both academics and public officials, have been studying how to promote a more market-orientated bank regulation. The active debate kept the relevant issues on the political agenda, and was particularly favourable to regulatory reform.

Under Law No. 287/90, the Italian Competition Authority has been attributed a consultative role with no decision-making power in the area of competition advocacy. The Authority's role as competition advocate has none the less had a practical importance. For instance, the Authority's success in preventing the introduction of new protectionist regulations in private services may be attributed to the transparency it has brought to the costs of such regulation. With respect to existing restrictions, the cases of the 1993 report on retail regulation and of the 1997 fact-finding enquiry on liberal professions are illustrative. Both reports attempted to identify the general interest requirements and the market failures in the relevant sector, the costs of the existing regulation, and both made suggestions as to how to reform regulation to make it more consistent with the operation of a competitive market. Both reports became landmarks in the domestic debate on sectoral regulation and strongly contributed to the inclusion of regulatory reform on the political agenda.

The peer reviews of member states' regulations promoted both by the Organization for Economic Cooperation and Development (OECD) and, after the 1998 Cardiff European Council, by the EU, have provided an additional vehicle to make public the regulatory costs and suggest how to proceed towards a more market-orientated regulation. Like the Italian Competition Authority, the relevant bodies have no decision-making power, and play only a consultative role. Such initiatives may, however, strongly facilitate liberalization at the domestic level.

## 4. Political Supply

In contrast to the most simplistic versions of the 'regulatory capture theory', studies in the politics of regulation stress that self-interest maximization by politicians does not always lead to the protection of concentrated interests, and that officials in regulatory administrative bodies do not always favour the maintenance of the most widespread regulation.[30] Some politicians, especially those with highly visible positions (such as the President, leaders of congressional committees and subcommittees, and heads of regulatory bodies in the US context) may have a structural incentive to protect widespread interests more than concentrated ones, especially when a consensus exists on the benefits of liberalization among opinion élites.

The convenience of following a market-orientated political strategy may depend on the level of decision making (for example, European, national, regional, local) and the institution involved (for example, European Commission versus European Parliament). In the Italian experience with structurally competitive services, deregulation has been mainly supported either by European decision makers (through their initiatives aimed at promoting market integration) or by the national government (which played a central role in starting the reform process for retailing and the liberal professions). The closer decision makers are to the involved interests (regional or local government), the more difficult it appears for them to promote the removal of protectionist barriers. The conservative attitude taken by regional governments with respect to the reform of retailing provides an important example.

A second group of problems concerns the appeal of liberalization initiatives from the point of view of politicians. As shown above, for some anticompetitive restrictions the cost to individual consumers may be very small. Is a politician likely to perceive it to be worthwhile to promote a reduction in entry barriers for barbers, if the benefit for consumers is only $0.28 per haircut? Thiel indicated that the answer is in the negative: 'Surveys show no overall dissatisfaction with the industry ... It is by no means clear that fighting off the encroachment of rent-seeking regulation would be perceived as worth the trouble'.[31] Perhaps for this reason, the liberalization suggestions of the Italian Competition Authority with respect to services such as ski teachers or travel agencies have not had any significant success to date.

Absence of interest in 'minor' liberalization is problematic because, even though individual costs may be small, the overall costs to society, including those resulting from obstacles to a dynamic market development, may be high. This problem is quite serious in a country like Italy where, as shown in Section C, unjustified anticompetitive regulation still exists in several sectors. One possible solution might be to shift from the single-sector approach in competition advocacy to a 'liberalization package' approach – that is, an overall revision of the relevant legislation. The political appeal of an initiative aimed at reforming the regulation of all private services for which quantitative restrictions to entry and regulatory limits on minimum prices still exist might be sufficient to include it on the political agenda.

## CONCLUSION

The economic analysis of market failures for the various services and of the costs and benefits of regulation helps to identify cases where existing regulation is unjustified or inefficient. Minimum rate regulation or quantitative restrictions on entry are normally not effective regulatory tools for pursuing objectives of general interest. The same holds for restrictions to truthful advertising. The results are less clear with respect to qualitative entry requirements and other restrictions on conduct. In these areas, economic theory is useful to define the subset of services for which this type of regulatory intervention might be justified.

The 'normative analysis as positive theory' of regulation does not fully explain the varied speed of procompetitive deregulation in the service sectors. In Italy, for instance, anticompetitive restrictions on entry and business conduct have already been eliminated in banking, but have been only partially reduced or are still in force with respect to other structurally competitive service sectors (retailing, liberal professions, other professional services). In order to understand deregulation in these sectors as an endogenous variable, consideration of the factors affecting the political supply and demand of regulation is a helpful complement to the standard economic analysis.

The Italian experience is useful for identifying factors affecting the likelihood of successful liberalization. Deregulation may be especially difficult when companies or professionals do not face a significant competition from outside, when business interests are homogeneous, when the perceived benefit of deregulation is relatively small, and when regulatory decision makers are close to the protected parties. Competition advocacy based on economic analysis may foster liberalization by helping change the perception of the costs and benefits of regulation.

How the level of regulatory decision making affects the convenience of promoting liberalization in private services is a delicate, but especially important issue, given the current trend to increase the regulatory powers of regional and local governments for several services (for example, retailing, tourism and so on). If liberalization is easier when decision makers are sufficiently far from the regulated undertakings and professionals ('proximity of the regulator trap'), one possible solution would be centralization of liberalization tasks. Future research should consider alternative solutions aimed at structurally increasing the incentives of members of regional and local governments to take competition advocacy arguments into account.

## NOTES

1. *Gazzetta Ufficiale* (*GU*) No. 80/L, ordinary supplement to *GU* No. 95 of 24 April 1998.
2. This chapter does not address other regulatory constraints, such as health and safety regulations, prudential requirements in the banking sector or urban planning provisions for retailing, whose effectiveness in attaining the general interest objectives and whose impact on competition might also be questioned.
3. Some authors stress that the externality and spillover notions are intellectually useful only when monetary estimation of the spillover effect, even if only rough, is possible. In other cases, such as elimination of the 'external costs' of chaos and disruption, or provision of goods such as justice and security, it is preferable to speak directly of non-economic reasons for or against a given action. This does not, however, impede economic evaluation of the regulatory instruments used to pursue such objectives. See, for example, Steven Breyer, *Regulation and its Reform* (Cambridge, MA: Harvard University Press, 1982).
4. For instance, in a symmetric Cournot game with fixed entry costs and homogeneous products, the equilibrium market outcome has a larger number of producers than the outcome that

maximizes total surplus. Too many or too few competitors, with respect to the 'optimal number', may emerge with differentiated goods, depending also on how consumers evaluate product diversity. See, for example, Christopher von Weiszacker, 'A Welfare Analysis of Barriers to Entry', 11 *Bell Journal of Economics* 399 (1980); W. Kip Viscusi, J. Vernon and J.E. Harrington, *Economics of Regulation and Antitrust* (Cambridge, MA: MIT Press, 1995).

5. Richard J. Gilbert, 'Mobility Barriers and the Value of Incumbency', in *Handbook of Industrial Organization* 531 (Richard Schmalensee and Robert Willig, eds, Amsterdam: North-Holland, 1989).

6. Paul Geroski, Richard Gilbert and Alexis Jacquemin, *Barriers to Entry and Strategic Competition* 1 (New York: Harwood Academic, 1990).

7. Stuart E. Thiel, 'The Cost of Hair Styling Regulation: Evidence' (1997) (unpublished mimeo).

8. Harold Demsetz, 'Barriers to Entry', 72 American Economic Review 47 (1982).

9. Richard Posner, 'The Social Cost of Monopoly and Regulation', 83 *Journal of Political Economy* 807 (1975).

10. Autorità Garante della Concorrenza e del Mercato, *Regolamentazione della distribuzione commerciale e concorrenza* (Regulation of commercial distribution and competition) (Rome, 1993).

11. Council Directive of 12 December 1977, No. 77/780, 1977 *Official Journal* (L 322); Council Directive of 15 December 1989, No. 89/646, 1989 *Official Journal* (L 386).

12. To establish a new bank in Italy, an authorization by the Bank of Italy is still required, based on a set of conditions listed in the 1993 Banking Law (Legislative Decree 1 September 1993, No. 385, in *GU* No. 230 of 30 September 1993) (minimum paid-up capital; legal status of limited company and so on). However, discretionary powers are limited to assessment of whether the submitted programme of operations, members' integrity records and the experience and integrity records of persons performing administrative, managerial or control functions show that a sound and prudent management is not ensured. For branching, the establishment of a new outlet by an Italian bank should be notified to the Bank of Italy, which may prohibit it only for reasons pertaining to the adequacy of the bank's organizational structure or to its financial situation. EC banks are free to establish branches and to provide services in Italy subject to the principles of minimum harmonization and mutual recognition contained in the EC banking directives.

13. An exception to the trend towards the elimination of direct regulatory restrictions on business choices is given by the enactment, in 1996, of a special law which, with the aim of preventing usury practices, establishes ceilings on lending interest rates (Law 7 March 1996, No. 108, in *GU* No. 58 of 9 March 1996). For homogeneous groups of operations, lending rates may not exceed 150 per cent of the average annual percentage rate (APR) of charge applied by registered intermediaries during the previous three months.

14. *GU* 6 July 1971, No. 168.

15. COM (91) 41.

16. COM (99) 0006.

17. Autorità Garante della Concorrenza e del Mercato, Indagine conoscitiva nel settore dei servizi professionali (Investigation in the professional services sector) (Rome, 1997); OECD Committee on Competition Law and Policy, Working Party No. 2 on Competition and Regulation, *Roundtable on Competition in Professional Services* (Paris: OECD: 1999) (provide a review of the existing regulation).

18. *GU* 11 August 1997, No. 186.

19. Some progress in this direction has already been achieved in the area of engineering services with Law 18 November 1998, No. 415 (*GU* No. 199/l, Ordinary Supplement to *GU* No. 284 of 4 December 1998) , which states that these services may be provided not only by partnerships but also by limited companies.

20. Articles 43–55 of the EC Treaty.

21. The proper enactment of such directives in the national legislation is extremely important for the effectiveness of the liberalization process. In July 1999 the Commission referred Italy to the European Court of Justice for the inadequate transposition of the EC directives aimed at ensuring access to the Italian market to lawyers and architects coming from other member states. One should also note that, in a context wider than the EU, the World Trade Organi-

zation (WTO) also tried to promote agreements between member states aimed at guaranteeing, in a transparent way, mutual recognition of professional requirements, although so far initiatives have substantially concerned only the provision of accounting services.

22. Consiglio Nazionale degli Spedizionieri Doganali (CNSD) (National Council of customs forwarding agents), 1993 *Official Journal* (L 203); Colegio Oficial de Agentes de la Propriedad Industrial (COAPI) (Official College of Industrial Property), 1995 *Official Journal* (L 122); EPI Code of Conduct, 1999 *Official Journal* (L 106). See also *Commission v. Republic of Italy*, 1998 Report of Cases before the Court of Justice of the European Communities, I-3851; Maria José Bicho, 'Professions Liberals: Aspects Essentiels de l'Action de la Commission en Matière d'Application des Règles de Concurrence' (Liberal professions: essential aspects of commission action in applying competition rules), 2 *Competition Policy Newsletter* 24 (reviews application by the European Commission of Article 81 of the Treaty to the sector of professional services).

23. See Sam Peltzman, 'The Economic Theory of Regulation After a Decade of Deregulation' (Washington, DC: Brookings Papers on Microeconomics 1989) (making similar remarks regarding the United States).

24. See, for example, Dennis Mueller, *Public Choice* (Cambridge: Cambridge University Press, 1975); Viscusi et al., *supra* note 4; George Stigler, 'The Theory of Economic Regulation', 2 *Bell Journal of Economics and Management Science* 3 (1971); Peltzman, *supra* note 23.

25. See, for example, Martha Derthick and Paul Quirk, *The Politics of Deregulation* (Washington, DC: Brookings Institution, 1985); Barry M. Mitnick, *The Political Economy of Regulation* (New York: Columbia University Press, 1980); James Q. Wilson, *The Politics of Regulation* (New York: Basic Books, 1980); Robert W. Hahn, 'State and Federal Regulatory Reform: a Comparative Perspective' (AEI-Brookings Working Paper 98–3, 1998); Randall S. Krozner and Philip Strahan, 'What Drives Deregulation? The Economics and Politics of the Relaxation of Bank Branching Restrictions' (unpublished mimeo, 1998); Michael Moran, 'Deregulating Britain, Deregulating America: the Case of the Securities Industry' (unpublished mimeo, European Consortium for Political Research (ECPR) Workshop on Deregulation in Western Europe, 1987).

26. Thiel, *supra* note 7.

27. Gordon Tullock, *Rent Seeking* (Locke Institute: Shaftesbury Papers No. 2, 1993).

28. Compensating the incumbent loss with a subsidy would not solve the problem. If a subsidy covered the entire loss, the cost to consumers of protectionist regulation would simply be transferred to taxpayers.

29. Derthick and Quirk, *supra* note 25.

30. See, for example, William Niskanen, *Bureaucracy and Representative Government* (Chicago: Aldine-Atherton, 1971).

31. Thiel, *supra* note 7, at 13.

# 2. The anticompetitive effects of minimum quality standards: the role of self-regulation

**Carlo Scarpa**

*In an unregulated equilibrium, firms usually tend to underprovide quality. The introduction of minimum quality standards is usually viewed as innocuous, but this chapter argues that it is not, based on recent theoretical and empirical literature. Minimum quality standards can have negative effects on quality and structure, reducing competition, forcing firms to exit the market, pre-empting entry by other firms, and reducing welfare. Self-regulation may be a solution in certain situations, but it raises many new problems.*

*The older theoretical literature, which relied on the duopoly model, argued that a severe enough minimum quality standard could force all firms in the market to improve their quality, having a welfare-increasing effect. However, new theoretical literature shows that the results are different when the duopoly model is not relied upon. Entry barriers, predatory behaviour, and welfare-reducing effects can result from minimum quality standards, because they restrict the pace at which a firm can move, and thus restrict its options. Rivals have an easier time ousting the firm from the market, because it cannot sufficiently differentiate its product from those of the rivals.*

*The current literature on minimum quality standards with complete information can be useful in providing a benchmark in asymmetric information models. It is more difficult to model oligopolistic behaviour with respect to such models, but current models help, in that at least they make it possible to have an idea of what certain regulations can do. More generally, when asymmetric information is present, many alternative solutions are possible.*

*Other models of quality regulation focus on long-run equilibria where quality levels are eventually revealed, and on the role of different types of intervention on such equilibria. Output quality regulation is an extreme case. Products are allowed in the market only if they pass a certain test that proves that they are reliable. It is an ex ante control that is present in certain markets but absent from other markets, especially when discussing professional services. Direct output control is, however, difficult; minimum quality standards on inputs, such as licensing requirements, are what normally apply with respect to professional services. Typically, they require that the member have a certain type of degree or training in order to enter the profession. The impact on quality is indirect; it is the input, not the output, that is regulated. The final impact on what consumers actually buy is relatively limited, but this regulation can have a similar entry pre-empting effect. Regulations requiring the provision of information, such as certification of professionals, are probably the lightest in the distortion they impose on market competition. Such regulations enable the state to provide information regarding an individual's previous experience, education and so on. The impact on final quality is not much less than it would be with input regulation, but entry cannot be pre-empted.*

*Self-regulation of quality is another very popular alternative because it passes the role of regulator to firms that have more information about their own market than the regulator has and are able to internalize the cost of regulation. Self-regulation also has greater flexibility than public procedures. However, a self-regulatory organization will never go against the interest of its members, which will be a form of collusion. Moreover, the monitoring of other firms' behaviour is a form of public good, which typically gives rise to inefficiencies. Self-regulation is thus likely to be a desirable alternative to minimum quality standards when the number of agents is limited, the mobility of customers is high and the regulator's uncertainty of the firm's costs is substantial.*

*The chapter concludes that minimum quality standards are not as innocuous as they are often considered to be, and that self-regulation is not necessarily a good alternative. Probably some sort of light public intervention is still desirable.*

## INTRODUCTION

The literature on quality choices by firms indicates – albeit with some ambiguities – that firms tend to underprovide quality. Thus, the traditional market failures that non-competitive markets generate in the quantity–price space appear in the quality space as well. A market failure provides a potential opening for state intervention. However, such intervention is subject to government failures, as stressed in the political economy literature.

Public intervention is often unable to provide an improvement relative to the free market equilibrium, even when it genuinely aims at maximizing social welfare. This chapter will show that the introduction of a minimum quality standard (MQS), which is the most obvious and seemingly neutral way of intervening, will often induce negative effects, including the decrease in average quality and the exit of firms from the market, which decrease market competition. Similar negative conclusions arise from asymmetric information models, which show that licensing (that is, allowing into the market only firms that satisfy certain requirements) has a strong anticompetitive effect without guaranteeing any quality improvements.

Self-regulation may be a solution in some cases, but it often creates at least as many problems as it solves. The use of self-regulation as a substitute (or a complement) of public intervention should be carefully considered, but also carefully monitored. The effectiveness of self-regulation as a device to limit entry has yet to be proved. Its difficulty in controlling behaviour is known in practice and emerges in theoretical models as well. The hope that self-regulation can actually improve market equilibrium has no strong foundation, and the scope of public intervention should, in most cases, be limited to the enforcement of liability rules and information diffusion.

The remainder of this chapter is organized as follows. Section A addresses the issue of quality determination and regulation with complete information. Section B does the same in the case of asymmetric information. Section C considers the alternative of self-regulation. Several concluding remarks are set forth in the final section.

## A.   ANTICOMPETITIVE EFFECTS OF MINIMUM QUALITY STANDARDS

Unfortunately, even in the simplest context, little can be said about the comparison between equilibrium quality levels and socially optimal quality levels. Spence[1] has shown that with full information, the quality level[2] a profit-maximizing monopolist[3] chooses might be either higher or lower than the socially optimal level. This depends on whether the consumer's *marginal* valuation of quality – the relevant parameter for profit maximization – is higher or lower than the *average* valuation of quality – crucial for welfare maximization.

Oligopolists, in contrast, typically differentiate their products in order to relax price competition. Oligopoly models tend to be complex because they introduce heavy assumptions to study market equilibrium, which lead to model-specific results. This makes it difficult to draw general conclusions about equilibrium and optimum. At least two factors should be considered: the number of firms observed and the quality levels produced. Regarding the number of firms, two opposite effects are present. On the one hand, as entry requires a fixed cost, the free entry equilibrium tends to have too many firms that duplicate fixed costs. In contrast, the tendency in vertically differentiated oligopolies is to have a limited number of firms, because competition in quality levels increases their fixed costs and sets an upper limit on the number of firms that can survive in equilibrium.[4] The monopolist's indeterminacy regarding the choice of quality levels carries over to the oligopoly equilibrium, although the models that are usually analysed show that equilibrium quality levels are lower than desirable.

An obvious and apparently innocuous way of intervening in such a situation is to introduce MQSs, such that only products above a certain level are allowed in the market. Several studies of the effects of MQSs in a duopoly with full information show that when only two firms are active in the market, a sufficiently low quality standard can improve overall welfare, as it induces *both* firms to improve their products.[5] The low-quality firm improves its product in order to comply with the rule, and the high-quality firm does the same to maintain a certain differentiation and avoid excessive price competition.

The limited empirical evidence on the effects of MQSs appears to be at odds with most of the above optimistic results, which point to the desirability of MQSs and to their quality-improving effect. For instance, a study analysing the regulation of electricians found that licensing restrictions reduce supply and decrease average quality (increase accident rates).[6] Studies in the health sector indicate that entry in these markets tends to be severely restricted by MQSs.[7] More recent work on this topic shows that MQSs increase the probability that a firm leaves the market, and that thereafter, the maximum quality supplied may decline.[8]

The idea that emerges from these papers is that the introduction of an MQS affects market structure, inducing some firms to exit, and that this decrease in competition can be associated with quality reductions. The theory has recently clarified some substantial negative effects of MQSs. In particular, an MQS can:

- *Decrease average quality, as long as there are more than two firms*[9]
  MQSs generally reduce the product space and thus reduce the possibility for firms to react to their rivals' moves. As simple non-cooperative forms of behaviour are less profitable, firms tend to avoid competition and to adopt a more aggressive line of conduct. The first result is a consequence of the second, in that with more than two firms in the market, the Ronnen effect (that the high-quality firm improves its product to maintain sufficient differentiation from the low-quality firm) cannot operate. The reaction of any firm of intermediate quality to an MQS is no longer obvious. Whichever way it changes its product, a firm in this position will see a reduction in the distance between itself and at least one of its competitors, with a consequent increase in price competition and loss of any incentive to produce high-quality goods. The fierce competition from below might cause the best firm to worsen its good, and the average quality of goods sold to decrease. The result is similar if one

considers the possibility of collusive behaviour. Collusion may be facilitated because the MQS restricts a firm's strategy space, and therefore deviating from a collusive arrangement is less profitable. Again, as a firm's individual profit opportunities are reduced, so is its incentive to deviate from a collusive strategy. Given that competition is less profitable, firms simply try to avoid it. While this result takes the number of firms as given, the two following points indicate the potential *structural* effects of the introduction of quality standards.

* *Make entry barriers possible* Setting a lower boundary to admissible quality implies setting a lower limit to a firm's costs. By following an appropriate pricing policy and adopting an adequate position in the market, the incumbent firm can prevent an entrant from achieving the market share necessary to cover such costs.

* *Help predatory behaviour*[10] In this context, predation means that following the introduction of the MQS, the high-quality firm, rather than adopting the duopoly equilibrium strategy, might attempt to drive the rival out of the market. This possibility clearly exists, as the MQS limits the ability of the low-quality firm to differentiate its output from the rival's. The duopoly will survive only for very low levels of MQS. For higher levels, predatory behaviour is indeed possible. Within a certain interval, two equilibria exist: a duopoly equilibrium and a predatory one, where the high-quality firm reduces its quality level and the rival leaves the market. When both equilibria exist, the criterion of risk dominance allows selection of the most likely equilibrium, and the duopoly equilibrium is ruled out for the entire admissible range of parameters, while predation emerges as the only equilibrium.[11]

Thus, this literature appears to contradict the initial optimistic results, stressing the negative consequences of MQSs. Not only do MQSs reduce the ability of firms to set quality levels and thus to pursue profit maximization, but they also induce firms to view the market differently. External constraints can be used either by all firms as commitment devices that help sustain collusion, or by stronger firms as weapons against their rivals.

The previous literature is typically based on an unnecessarily restrictive and quite implausible assumption, that is, that adapting to the new MQS (and to other firms' new quality choices) entails no adjustment costs. This leads to another important asymmetry, as the multistage structure of the game logically requires the quality choice to be a long-run choice, constraining the firm for a significant period of time. Therefore, models without adjustment costs can hardly provide a coherent representation of how incumbent firms react to the new standard.[12]

Indeed, in the international trade debate, the key problem is that the standard has an asymmetric impact on firms, as firms that already operate above the lower limit can afford to do business as usual, while lower-quality firms must pay additional costs to comply with new restrictions.[13]

Although the consequences of adjustment costs have not, to date, been fully analysed, the initial results seem to confirm the intuition that adjustment costs amplify the potential negative structural effects of the MQS.[14] This is hardly surprising, since the effects of the MQS are not simply to restrict competition, but also to introduce asymmetries between firms, an element traditionally recognized as capable of reducing the effectiveness of competition.

## B.  QUALITY AND INFORMATION

A different body of literature addresses quality regulation within the framework of asymmetric information. This chapter will focus on two situations involving asymmetric information: those where there is an unknown characteristic and where quality is produced before the product is purchased; and those where there is an unknown characteristic and where quality is produced after the product is purchased (particularly common in services).

The classic paper by George Akerlof was the first one to consider the situation where the predetermined characteristic of the good is unknown to the buyer.[15] He observed that in a market where quality levels are given but cannot be observed by customers before purchasing the goods, no customer will be willing to pay a price higher than others, so that all goods will be sold at the same price. Since high-quality firms receive an insufficient reward, they are not willing to sell what they would otherwise sell. Akerlof concludes that asymmetric information reduces the volume of transactions and the average quality of goods exchanged. The very existence of the market for high-quality goods is jeopardized. High-quality goods are penalized in this situation by 'adverse selection', one of the main potential market failures that can result from quality choices. The pervasiveness of informational problems in financial markets necessitates focusing on these issues in particular detail.

### Can the Market Overcome Information Problems?

To what extent is the market by itself able to overcome the main consequences of information problems? The answer depends on the features of the good sold. In all cases, at least some inefficiency will emerge in the short run. However, the main issue is whether the market is able to give producers the correct incentives to provide quality, inducing potential customers to buy.

Three types of goods can be traditionally distinguished:[16]

- *search goods*, for which asymmetric information on a good's features can be eliminated before consumption occurs through payment of a search cost;
- *experience goods*, for which the consumer can only become aware of the good's features by consuming the good;[17] and
- *credence goods*, for which the quality of the good does not become fully known to the consumer either before or after consumption.[18]

With search goods, the existence of asymmetric information creates an additional cost for consumers. The search process thus typically stops before full information is achieved, giving firms a lower incentive to produce quality, proportional to the difficulty of search. This is an obvious and banal distortion. From a policy perspective, however, when a good's quality can be detected before consumption, consumer protection can be achieved at a well-defined cost. The only issue remaining is the definition of benefits and their comparison with this cost. This scheme is most relevant when it concerns information on aspects of a product that can be objectively and precisely defined. Accordingly, this scheme is applied mainly to situations where a given good can be offered at different prices that a consumer can discover by shopping.

These models often indicate that informative advertising can increase welfare by increasing consumers' information. Moreover, as advertising reduces product differentiation, it also reduces firms' market power and profits. Thus, the prohibition of advertising in certain professional services can be a device to aid collusion, rather than one to protect consumers.

The most interesting features of a product are difficult to define without direct experience. Several experience models indicate that a plethora of equilibria exist.[19] One of these is a full-revelation equilibrium, where consumers become familiar with the product's qualities and producers earn a quality premium (pricing above marginal cost) in the long run.[20] A similar result emerges in signalling models, when the producer can provide warranties.[21]

The reason why firms have an incentive to produce goods of a consistent quality is that whenever they cheat, consumers will punish them by refusing to repeat the purchase. Accordingly, for this mechanism to work, repeat purchasing must be possible. Two elements are crucial in this respect:

- *Frequency of consumption* The consumer can punish the bad behaviour of the seller with respect to goods that he/she purchases frequently. However, certain intertemporal effects can prevent a consumer from doing so. In the extreme, a patient killed by his/her physician or an investor made bankrupt by a bad financial advisor is unlikely to be able to punish the seller. With respect to goods purchased infrequently, the consumer must rely on indirect reputation, through word of mouth. However, this channel is imperfect, as other consumers' information can be insufficient when tastes matter or when other customers' competence matters in evaluating the service received.

*   *Timing of quality determination*   Quality may be definitively determined, or it may change in every period. The former case is easier, the latter more difficult because firms can adopt an infinite number of strategies, and the multiplicity problem becomes unmanageable.

Even if the efficient equilibrium were eventually reached, this might occur only in the 'long run'. The vagueness of this expression requires that it be used carefully, especially for policy purposes.

Population changes also interfere with the learning process. This is a problem for both buyers and sellers, but especially for sellers. For instance, it is not useful to know that in ten years a seller will learn everything about the consumers currently in the market, if they will eventually disappear. Moreover, mobility among markets is considerable, and reputation does not always follow a seller from one market to another. An agent could be tempted to cheat the market as long as possible, and then to abandon it, moving to a different activity, or reappearing in the same market under a different commercial label. Even if firms' names are usually well known, their administrators' are often not. Moreover, if the convergence process takes excessively long, people might be tempted to drop from the market because they have lost confidence.

Accordingly, the short-run problem is crucial, supporting the conclusion that the market failure *potentially* justifies some form of public intervention.

## Public Intervention with Asymmetric Information

Other models of quality regulation typically focus on long-run equilibria where quality levels are eventually revealed, and on the role of different types of intervention on such equilibria. The equilibria that emerge in the different cases are not comparable. The situations are always second best, and in most cases, identification of the relevant tradeoffs is the best result that can be achieved. These models include:[22]

*   *Output regulation* in the form of an MQS, where the sale of goods below the MQS is assumed not to occur, as if the fine in case of the sale of these goods were infinite. Leland[23] introduces MQSs as remedies within an Akerlof-type model, showing that the MQS increases quality but decreases competition and thus increases prices. This implies a potential distributional problem, in that low-income consumers (more precisely, consumers with a low willingness to pay) will probably be excluded from the market.

The introduction of quality standards in cases where quality is difficult to assess is, however, highly disputable.[24] It makes little sense to provide a public guarantee when even the public authority is unlikely to be able to monitor the quality of the service. This is why the literature analyses alternatives that primarily focus on inputs (for example, the training level of a professional). However, the impact that any of these restrictions can have on the quality of the final good is necessarily indirect.

- *Input regulation* in the form of licensing, defined as a form of MQS on inputs, whereby only producers that satisfy certain requirements are allowed in the market. Shapiro[25] compares licensing and certification. While licensing sets a minimum level of quality-related investment that all producers must make, certification reduces the information asymmetry on the input used in the production process. Information remains asymmetric as long as quality levels are not fully revealed, thereby reducing the incentive to make only a small investment, and inducing more producers to provide high-quality goods. Both policies increase the average quality level,[26] but the cost of doing so may be so high as to reduce total surplus. Moreover, consumers with a low willingness to pay are typically worse off. Thus, the comparison yields no definite result.

- *Liability rules*, which impose no restrictions *ex ante*, but impose penalties if product quality is insufficient. This rule is similar to setting an MQS with no *ex ante* controls; quality can be not only observed, but verified in court. Polinsky and Rogerson[27] analyse the relationship between liability rules and market power. The latter is important because an industry in which firms have market power will react to the imposition of liability rules by excessively restricting output. Liability rules have such a distortionary effect only in industries where market power is present. Thus, in a competitive environment, strict liability is optimal; with less-competitive markets, liability rules should be made less stringent in order not to trigger a welfare-reducing reaction of firms.[28]

- *Diligence rules*, which impose no restrictions *ex ante*, but impose penalties if product quality is insufficient *and* it can be proved that the seller did not exert sufficient diligence. This is a weaker form of liability rule, since it requires a joint demonstration that the consumer obtained a poor result *and* that the firm has not made a sufficient effort. Shavell[29] observes that liability and diligence rules may be sufficient. Regulation is thus an imperfect tool, as the regulator cannot observe the magnitude of the harm each customer suffers in case the product fails. The joint use of both means of controlling quality is generally advantageous, a conclusion widely in accordance with observations.

- *Information provision* in the form of certification, which requires the public authority to provide consumers the relevant information on the amount invested (for example, the length of the training period).

The types of public intervention these papers consider are different, but their welfare consequences are similarly ambiguous. They all point to the redistributional problem that emerges when an increase in the minimum quality provided forces an increase in price. The effect of licensing on quality is very indirect, but its effect on entry requirements, and thus entry restrictions, is direct. The balance between the two seems typically negative from the social perspective.

In summary, none of the regulatory options considered seems to guarantee the effectiveness and desirability of public interventions. There is little guarantee that quality regulation increases social welfare or the average quality of products. Moreover, a quality-increasing regulation may create distributional problems, in that consumers with a lower willingness to pay are often penalized. When informational asymmetries impede the regulator's ability to observe quality levels or to enforce rules, the power of regulation is reduced even further.[30]

Licences should be restricted only when providing a service at a quality level below a certain limit threatens a major aspect of people's lives, such as health (the medical profession) or civil rights (the legal profession). Outside these areas, certification, which places a heavier reliance on the consumers' ability to choose for themselves, is preferable.

## C.   THE ROLE OF SELF-REGULATION

The aforementioned limitations of the process of public regulation of quality lead to consideration of an alternative that has become increasingly popular: self-regulation (SR).[31] SR is defined here to mean that important aspects of the management of regulation are left to bodies controlled by operating firms. In practice, the label SR might refer to a plethora of different arrangements, whereby a self-regulatory organization (SRO) may be:

- solely responsible for regulation, with autonomous rules and procedures;
- solely responsible for regulation, under the control of the law and with the support of the law (the SRO therefore has a semi-public role);
- responsible for regulation, but in competition with other SROs;
- part of a regulatory structure, where other private or public bodies are present at the same level;
- part of a regulatory structure, where a public body is present in a hierarchically superior position;

- part of a 'mixed' regulatory body, together with representatives either of consumers or of the community; or
- any combination of the above.

It is beyond the scope of this chapter to analyse the different alternatives in detail. However, the main reasons for SR and its potential consequences are set forth.[32] In particular, the term SR might mean either self-determination of rules, or self-management of the application of exogenous rules. This distinction might be important in reaching certain conclusions, although it is unlikely that any rule is so complete as to eliminate all margins of discretion in its application.

The limitations of external regulation is the primary reason for SR, including the asymmetric information between the regulator and the firm(s) and the rigidity of public procedures.[33] As to the former, SR has an advantage in that firms are likely to know market conditions better than the regulator. As to the latter, the advantage of SR is significantly less obvious. Many variables, although observable, are not easily verifiable by a third party, so that a court may not be able to punish improper behaviour due to a lack of sufficient evidence. Moreover, the formal process of regulation may not be sufficiently flexible to keep up with the pace of change in particularly dynamic markets. A system based on SR may be better able to cope.

While the latter part of the argument is the strongest, other aspects raise doubts. Public procedures typically are more rigid than procedures that a private body, such as an SRO, must follow. Accordingly, while a court needs hard evidence before punishing a firm, an SRO might be allowed to act on the basis of evidence that would not meet a court's high standard.

There is, however, a clear tradeoff between the formal power that an organization is given, and the degree of 'informality' that is acceptable. If an SRO is given considerable formal authority (for example, to fine its members, or to expel a firm from the market), it is unlikely to be allowed to operate without the safeguards that protect firms in their relationship with a public authority. Especially in a legal system of French tradition, the formality of legal procedures is difficult to escape, unless the SRO is viewed as having only an informal role. This would, however, call its relevance into question.

Furthermore, leaving regulation to a body in which only the regulated firms are represented has the obvious disadvantage that self-regulation will never go against the interest of the regulator, that is, the firms involved. Indeed, SR is often seen as the intervention of producers either as a cartel whose function is joint profit maximization, or as a cooperative whose function is maximizing profits per firm. The latter is probably a more reasonable alternative if the number of firms is predetermined when SR is introduced. Thus, benefits and costs must be carefully weighed, which requires a more precise analysis.

## Self-regulation and Access to the Profession

In practice, SR entails three steps: (i) a 'constitutional' phase, that is, identification on behalf of the public authority of the agents entitled to operate in a certain market, and to be responsible for SR; (ii) determination by these agents of certain rules within the domain established by the public authority; and (iii) enforcement of these rules, sometimes solely by the SRO, other times with the help of a public body.

When entry conditions are included in the set of rules delegated to the profession, SR implies that the agents belonging to the initial set will determine the number and characteristics of their competitors. This implies further that the initial set is determined through a public procedure (an examination, the establishment of certain training requirements and so on), whose administration is then delegated to the agents. As delegating power inevitably entails transferring some discretion, the risk is present that active firms will use SR unduly to restrict competition.

The approach of the theoretical literature is more direct. It assumes that identification of the members of the SRO is the same as establishment of the MQS. Thus, the SRO is viewed as a privately formed 'club', not the result of a public initiative, which determines the MQS. SR is considered in the context of exogenous quality levels, with respect to which there is asymmetric information between consumers and producers. The issue arises of the relationship between the MQS established by an SRO and the socially optimal MQS.

The first model that explicitly addresses this issue is that of Leland, who employs a typical Akerlof-type model.[34] As individual quality levels are not observable, consumers' willingness to pay depends on *average* quality. The two main results Leland obtains are the following. First, the establishment of an MQS ($L$) increases welfare if (i) price is low for low quality levels, (ii) price is sensitive to quality changes, (iii) demand is rigid, and (iv) cost does not increase rapidly with quality. Second, under certain conditions, the self-regulated MQS is too high. These results are somewhat obscure which, given the intrinsic complexity of the problem, is hardly surprising.

An extension of the Leland model is provided by Shaked and Sutton,[35] who develop a miniature general equilibrium model with two sectors, and in this way make endogenous the opportunity cost of supplying a good of given quality. In particular, they assume the existence of $N$ workers whose labour supply is inelastic and who must be allocated between the two sectors. Their skills (quality) are uniformly distributed in the interval $[0, N]$, so that all workers are different and can be ranked according to quality. The difference in skills translates into difference in output quality, depending on the sector where labour is employed. People working in sector A (called 'lawyers') differ in the quality of their output, while all those working in sector B (called 'workmen') produce a homogeneous output which does not depend on their skill.[36] Self-regulation of 'lawyers' consists of the determination of the MQS for lawyers, that is, of a skill level $L$, such that only the best $N - L$ people can practise the profession. The others must work with the generic labour force. This structure contains an important assumption on the effects of SR: with given quality levels, setting an MQS is equivalent to deciding the number of competitors in the sector. This means that any increase in the MQS entails an output reduction, and consequently, a price increase.[37] The demand for professional services depends on the quality of the service provided. While other lawyers can observe whether a person's quality is higher or lower than $L$, consumers cannot. Accordingly, demand for professional services depends on the *expected* quality of the profession $\bar{q}(L, N)$, which is assumed to increase in both arguments (a slightly more general formulation than Leland's). The higher the MQS, the higher the quality level consumers expect.[38] The MQS is decided by the SRO in order to maximize per seller earnings of its members. Thus, it is not surprising that the main result obtained by Shaked and Sutton confirms Leland's finding that the MQS set by the SRO is too high from a social viewpoint.[39]

These models assume that individual quality levels are given and costless. If quality is costly to produce in each period, however, there is a likely effect in the opposite direction: the distortion in entry due to the presence of an SRO is probably limited. However, when quality simply entails an initial set-up cost (for example, initial training), the suspicion that an SRO would unduly restrain entry seems well founded.

## Self-regulation and the Control of Individuals' Behaviour

As argued above, the issue of controlling *behaviour* and not just innate *characteristics* is more challenging. The main issue is no longer the study of the consequences of SR, but the analysis of the conditions under which an SRO is able (that is, has the incentive) to enforce a control on its members.

Shapiro[40] illuminates the role of self-regulation with moral hazard when experience matters. Under such conditions, regulation may serve two purposes only: to facilitate the detection of quality and to increase the minimum quality level. Both reduce the quality premium, that is, the price–cost margin that firms obtain in equilibrium as an incentive to produce goods of a quality higher than zero. If quality is detected immediately, there is no need to provide incentives against cheating, and competition should drive prices down to marginal costs. Moreover, the higher the minimum quality that can legally be produced, the lower the risk run by consumers, and the lower the compensation that firms obtain in equilibrium. Therefore, the SRO would not help detection of high-quality products and would set too low a standard.

Focusing on financial intermediaries with a clearer microeconomic foundation, Fletcher found that external regulation may be inferior to SR for an additional reason: it requires third-party verifiability of cheating, while under SR, generic observability can be sufficient, given the more informal nature of the procedures adopted.[41] In particular, quality levels $\theta_i$ are assumed to be observable by market operators but not verifiable by an external regulator, and the SRO, unlike the regulator, is assumed to be able to impose different fines on firms of different innate quality levels. Regulation thereby entails welfare maximization under the constraint that quality levels are non-verifiable, while SR involves profit maximization under appropriate incentives that the regulator can give to the SRO.

This chapter introduces an explicit distinction between 'cheating on quality' (that is, providing a service of zero quality when innate quality is higher) and fraud (that is, an additional damage consumers may suffer, for instance, because the firm runs away with their money). These types of consumer exploitation are substantially different, in that cheating on quality gives a reward equal to the price paid by consumers,[42] while fraud entails a reward independent of price. Different cases can thus be distinguished. When cheating on quality is the main problem, the highest level of regulation would be required by high-quality firms, in that the price they can get (that is, the reward they would get from cheating) is higher, and so is their incentive to cheat. In contrast, when fraud is the main problem, low-quality firms require the toughest regulation. Thus, the SRO is better equipped to design an optimal fine structure, given its ability to observe quality.

Since optimal fines can be made conditional on quality, SR may achieve a better result in terms of the range of quality levels admitted in the market. Quality is observed, which implies that low-quality firms can be given better incentives. With external regulation, punishing those who cheat on quality is more difficult, and it may be optimal to restrict product variety. In contrast, given the greater ability of the SRO to observe behaviour, it may be able to admit a wider range of firms. This is socially beneficial, given the heterogeneity of consumers' willingness to pay.

Finally, SR is more likely to be welfare improving relative to external regulation as:

- *Fraud is more important*   Low-quality firms should be monitored more closely, and the ability of the SRO to condition its decisions on $\theta$ is socially advantageous.
- *Sellers are more homogeneous*   When the members' interests tend to coincide, the SRO's job is easier.

- *The observation lag is longer*    When consumers are less able to punish cheaters by refusing to repeat the purchase, the role of SR and its ability to intervene taking $\theta$ into consideration become more important.
- *Demand is more elastic*    The SRO pursues profit maximization, and output reduction is smaller when demand is more elastic.

Gehrig and Jost[43] introduce another model that addresses similar issues, where $N$ producers operate in $N$ separate markets, each market having an identical number of potential consumers. If $t$ indicates time, when $t = 0$, firms decide their quality levels ($q$), which are known to all firms, but unknown to consumers; their choice cannot be reversed. When $t = 1$, consumers decide whether to buy one unit of the good or not to enter the market. Only after consumption do consumers become aware of the quality of the product they have consumed. Direct experience is the only means of learning. When $t = 2$, consumers know the quality of the goods they have consumed. The market game is repeated, but with an important change: a proportion $\lambda$ of consumers of each market migrates to other markets (mobility from one firm to another). Therefore, in each market, some consumers know the quality of the product, and others have no experience with the product offered in their new market.[44]

This highly stylized structure leads to several interesting observations: first, the mobility of consumers;[45] second, the relevance of reputation; third, the assumption that the learning process is imperfect, such that each firm faces at least some consumers who do not know its quality. Therefore, individual reputation is not all that matters; collective reputation also becomes important.

Regulation is managed by an SRO, which accepts as members all producers who supply a good the quality of which is at least equal to some minimum standard $q_{SR}$ and perfectly monitors its members. In the first period, consumers observe whether a firm is a member of an SRO. If so, they expect $q = q_{SR}$; otherwise, they expect $q = q^*$, the individual profit-maximizing level. Their demand, and hence the price they pay, depend on expected quality. In $t = 2$, consumers who confirm their initial choice already know the quality provided by their supplier, and do not need any further information. On the other hand, mobile consumers' expectations are partly determined by the reputation of the SRO. The crucial issues are whether, in the first period, their expectations of an SRO member proved to be correct, and, when an SRO member provided $q^* < q_{SR}$, what was the reaction of the SRO.

If no cheating occurred in the first period, consumers will maintain their trust in the SRO. If some consumers have been cheated, but the SRO has not expelled the firm, they will lose their faith in the SRO and will believe that the new firm will supply only quality $q^*$. This behaviour of the consumers gives complying firms an incentive to expel deviant firms. This is purely a reputational effect, as the structure of the model assumes away any direct competition.

Thus, SR functions if, for each producer, the incentive to expel deviant firms is large enough relative to the reward from cheating. SR is therefore feasible when the mobility of consumers is large enough, so that the SRO's reputation is important to each obedient firm, and when the number of firms is not too large. If, however, $N$ is very large, the number of dissatisfied consumers will be excessively diluted[46] in the sense that in the second period, each firm will face a very small number of consumers coming from each other market. Collective reputation thus matters less, and the punishment of a specific deviant firm becomes less crucial. This reasoning closely resembles the classic argument against competition in the production of public goods.[47] Moreover, SR is likely to be preferable to regulation if the regulator's uncertainty about firms' costs is substantial enough. In such a case, SR has the advantage of a greater ability to observe firms' characteristics.

However, the incentives cited for the SRO to punish cheaters are still not satisfactory. It has, until now, been assumed that an SRO will punish deviants out of a fear of losing its reputation *vis-à-vis* consumers. This is a correct, but partial, explanation. When the SRO punishes a member's behaviour, it publicizes that a member has pursued a line of conduct that the members of the SRO refuse to tolerate. In so doing, the SRO gives a signal to the market as to what is acceptable. However, it cannot tell the market how far that member's behaviour was from the acceptable level. Investors observe that the firm's behaviour might cause a downward revision of the expectation of other firms' behaviour, that is, of the 'general practice' of the profession.[48]

A satisfactory representation of an SRO's incentives to intervene should include both effects. It should demonstrate the SRO's decisions as emerging from the attempt to strike a balance between the risk that the information spreads in any event, which would damage the reputation of the SRO, and the risk that all SRO members suffer from a reputational externality when the fraudulent behaviour of one member is made public.[49]

Finally, if rules fixed in a purely ethical code do not correspond to punishments in case of violations, then the enforcement of such rules becomes problematic, and might work in particular circumstances but not in general.[50] If such rules are backed by punishments, then they refer not only to moral suasion, but also represent proper norms, to which the previous analysis applies. It is difficult to see a third alternative.

## CONCLUSION

Models where quality is exogenous differ from models where quality is a choice variable. With regard to the former, the result that the self-imposed MQS is set too high from a social viewpoint disappears. This is no surprise, given that if quality is costly, it is a force operating against a high MQS.[51] Whenever quality is a choice variable in each period, and firms may save on costs by reducing quality, the problem appears to be the opposite: that an SRO may have serious problems in enforcing quality standards.

With the extreme caution made necessary by the current gap between theory and policy, the models lead to two conclusions. First, at least some aspects of competition policy and SR are complementary. A greater mobility of consumers makes collective reputation more important. Lack of brand loyalty acts as a disciplinary device on the SRO, thereby forcing it to monitor its members. Removing all barriers to mobility of customers (for example, exit costs from a contract) aids regulation of a profession. However, this may be true only in certain sectors, where the notion of mobility makes sense.[52]

In contrast, SR and liberalization of access to a market are substitutes. Liberalizing market access renders the control of individual behaviour more difficult. This is because the existence of a large number of firms dilutes the effect of cheating by any one firm, and therefore punishing deviations from an agreed line of conduct becomes less important for the SRO. Moreover, liberalization makes the set of agents subject to regulation (and possibly even the set of agents entitled to execute regulation) quite unstable, which in turn, renders it difficult for reputational mechanisms properly to operate. However, greater liberalization makes regulation less effective, but also less relevant. Indeed, a greater number of competitors typically increases the choice set of consumers and reduces the need for regulation. Which of these effects is dominant can be answered only on a case-by-case basis.

# NOTES

1. Michael Spence, 'Monopoly, Quality and Regulation', 6 *Bell Journal of Economics* 417 (1975).
2. The definition of quality is not a banal issue. In economics, quality is an attribute of a good of which all consumers prefer more rather than less. A feature such as a product's safety thus can be considered 'quality' if consumers perceive it as desirable (independently of their willingness to pay for it). Notice that when a person's decision affects not just his/her health, but the health of others, then the case for restricting individual choices becomes much stronger.
3. This chapter will consider only the case of profit-maximizing firms. The evidence on the provision of quality by non-profit organizations appears mixed. See, for example, Naci H. Mocan, 'Quality Adjusted Cost Functions for Child Care Centers', 82 *American Economic Review* 409 (1995); Burton Weisbrod, *The Nonprofit Economy* (Cambridge, MA: Harvard University Press, 1998); Mark Schlesinger, 'Mismeasuring the Consequences of Ownership: External Influences and the Comparative Performance of Public, For Profit and Private Non-Profit Organizations', in *Private Action and the Public Good* (Walter Powell and Elisabeth Clemens, eds, New Haven, CT: Yale University Press, 1998).
4. Avner Shaked and John Sutton, 'The Self Regulating Profession', 48 *Review of Economic Studies* 217 (1981).

5.  Claude Crampes and Abraham Hollander, 'Duopoly and Quality Standards', 39 *European Economic Review* 71 (1995); Uri Ronnen, 'Minimum Quality Standards, Fixed Costs, and Competition', 22 *Rand Journal of Economics* 490 (1991).
6.  Sidney Carroll and Robert Gaston, 'Occupational Restrictions and the Quality of Service Received: Some Evidence', 47 *Southern Economic Journal* 959 (1991); see William Gormley, 'State Regulations and the Availability of Child Care Services', 10 *Journal of Policy Analysis and Management* 78 (1991) (confirming the supply-reducing effect).
7.  Shawn E. Kantor and Patrick Legros, 'The Economic Consequences of Legislative Oversight: Theory and Evidence from the Medical Profession' (National Bureau of Economic Research (NBER) Working Paper No. W4281, 1993).
8.  Tasneem Chipty and Ann Dryden Witte, 'An Empirical Investigation of Firms' Responses to Minimum Quality Standards Regulations' (NBER Working Paper 6104, 1997).
9.  Carlo Scarpa, 'Minimum Quality Standards with More Than Two Firms', 16 *International Journal of Industrial Organization* 665 (1998).
10. Luca Lambertini and Carlo Scarpa, 'Minimum Quality Standards and Predatory Behaviour', FEEM Note di Lavoro 86/99, Fondazione ENI Enrico Mattei, Milan (1999).
11. The same result is obtained under the more plausible assumption that shifting quality levels entails some adjustment cost. In this case, the duopoly equilibrium proves even more fragile.
12. This does not imply that previous models are incorrect, but only that they compare different and alternative scenarios (with and without MQS, or with MQS of different sizes) but not the *change* in behaviour of a firm and of an industry after the introduction of the MQS.
13. Nor are high-quality firms unaffected by the MQS. If low-quality firms change their products, the optimal response of other firms will in general *not* be to maintain previous quality levels.
14. Lambertini and Scarpa, *supra* note 10.
15. George Akerlof, 'The Market for Lemons', 84 *Quarterly Journal of Economics* 488.
16. The distinction between these categories is not as clear-cut as the definition might suggest. Search might be possible, but in practice too costly. Personal experience does not help unless purchase is sufficiently frequent. The view of other consumers is irrelevant when tastes differ. Some degree of uncertainty over a good's objective quality is likely always to be present, even after consumption. Thus, the distinction between experience and credence goods is a matter of how much uncertainty can be eliminated by consumption. Accordingly, application of this taxonomy requires considerable care.
17. This awareness can be achieved either through personal experience or, in certain cases, through word of mouth. In the case of services, the quality of the good purchased is often not observable before the customers decide to buy it. Indeed, production of services typically occurs after the service is acquired, which is the most extreme case of (*ex ante*) unobservability.
18. For instance, the full recovery after an illness may be due to the doctor's skill, but also to his/her luck. Several authors agree in classifying financial services as credence goods (for example, Thomas Gehrig and Peter Jost, 'Quacks, Lemons, and Self-regulation: A Welfare Analysis', 7 *Journal of Regional Economics* 309 (1995); Colin Mayer and Damien Neven, 'European Financial Regulation: A Framework for Policy Analysis', in *European Financial Integration* (Alberto Giovannini and Colin Mayer, eds, Cambridge: Cambridge University Press, 1991).
19. In the presence of multiple equilibria, a selection device is required, possibly based on an explicit learning mechanism. However, given the interaction between the learning processes on both sides of the market, it is difficult to see how this could eliminate the multiplicity problem. Using concepts from evolutionary game theory would probably represent a preferable alternative, in that it often allows the set of 'reasonable' outcomes to be narrowed down considerably, allowing one to link the final equilibrium to well-defined initial conditions. This latter aspect is the potentially main weakness and – at the same time – strength of this approach; only if one is able to 'tell a story' on where market dynamics starts from, do evolutionary arguments really help understand the future evolution of the market itself.
20. Benjamin Klein and Keith Leffler, 'The Role of Market Forces in Assuring Contractual Performance', 89 *Journal of Political Economy* 615 (1981); Carl Shapiro, 'Premiums for High Quality Products as Rents to Reputation', 98 *Quarterly Journal of Economics* 659 (1983).

21. Although it is correct to consider informational problems as a useful starting-point, the cost of doing so is to skip the issues emerging from imperfect competition, and thereby not really to model oligopolistic interaction. Given that oligopoly models with asymmetric information between consumers and firms are quite underdeveloped, the literature on this topic cannot be considered conclusive.

22. Many other contributions are not reviewed here, essentially because the qualitative conclusions one can reach (in the direction we are interested in) would not be affected by stretching the list of references even further.

23. Wayne Leland, 'Quacks, Lemons and Licensing: A Theory of Minimum Quality Standards', 87 *Journal of Political Economy* 1328 (1979).

24. The issue is further complicated when consumers are unable to judge their own needs, as occurs in the case of illness, when doctors may induce demand.

25. Carl Shapiro, 'Investment, Moral Hazard and Occupational Licensing', 53 *Review of Economic Studies* 843 (1986).

26. Producers simply choose whether to produce high- or low-quality goods, but these quality levels are exogenous. The only endogenous factor is the number of producers who decide to provide each quality level. Thus, these interventions affect the product mix supplied, but do not affect individual quality levels. With no competition in quality levels (that are not choice variables), none of the previously mentioned effects can be observed.

27. Mitchell Polinsky and William Rogerson, 'Products Liability, Consumer Misperception and Market Power', 14 *Rand Journal of Economics* 581 (1983) (distinguishing between strict liability, which fully insures consumers, and a no-negligence rule, which requires a firm to compensate consumers only if it can be shown that firms did not exert 'sufficient' care in providing their service).

28. The conclusion that seems to emerge is thus, that the law should be strong against the weak, and weak against the strong. Although formally correct, one wonders to what extent such a principle can really be implemented.

29. Steven Shavell, 'A Model of the Optimal Use of Liability and Safety Regulation', 15 *Rand Journal of Economics* 271 (1984).

30. The previous results are based on the assumption that regulation is carried out by benevolent policy makers, whose objective function is increasing social welfare. The literature on regulation, however, indicates that the regulator might be captured by producers, or at least that he/she might have private objectives, and that the interventions of the political authority might be at least partially determined by the influence of pressure groups. George Stigler, 'The Theory of Economic Regulation', 2 *Bell Journal of Economics* 3 (1971). In such cases, public regulation will achieve even less impressive results, which should be recalled when drawing policy conclusions.

31. This phenomenon is somehow parallel to the flourishing of independent administrative bodies (the 'Authorities'), to which the political power delegates substantial responsibilities.

32. *See* Carlo Scarpa, 'The Theory of Quality Regulation and Self-regulation: Towards an Application to Financial Markets', in *Organized Interests and Self-Regulation* (Bernardo Bortolotti and Gianluca Fiorentini, eds, Oxford: Oxford University Press, 1999).

33. Finally, SR has the advantage of internalizing the cost of regulation, and probably the ability to minimize it. Unfortunately, this aspect is, to date, absent from the theoretical literature.

34. Leland, *supra* note 23.

35. Shaked and Sutton, *supra* note 4.

36. Thus, in contrast to the argument of Leland, *supra* note 23, the opportunity cost of producing in sector A is independent of quality. This entails a *loss* of generality.

37. Scarpa, *supra* note 9, shows how this assumption may not hold when quality levels are not given, but instead chosen by the producers.

38. When quality levels are endogenous and information is symmetric, the average quality of the product does not necessarily increase with the MQS. Scarpa, *supra* note 9.

39. A recent analysis done by the Italian Competition Authority on self-regulation in professional groups reaches a similar conclusion (Autorità garante della concorrenza e del mercato, 'Indagine conoscitiva nel settore degli ordini e collegi professionali', (Investigation in the professional associations sector), Rome, 1997).

40. Shapiro, *supra* note 20.
41. Amelia Fletcher, 'Theories of Self-regulation' (unpublished D. Phil. Thesis, Nuffield College, Oxford University, 1993). An action may be observable by some people but not verifiable when a third party, such as a court, cannot find sufficient evidence on what has been done. Usually, formal legal procedures require the latter, more stringent feature.
42. The reason is that the price paid is in line with the intrinsic quality of the seller, and consumers would have been willing to pay zero for a zero-quality product.
43. Gehrig and Jost, *supra* note 18.
44. The distribution of migrants to other markets is such that the number of potential consumers in each market remains constant. A number $\lambda/(N-1)$ of consumers goes from market 1 to each other market, and so on.
45. Unfortunately, the proportion of mobile consumers is totally exogenous, and does not depend on how happy consumers are with their initial choice, that is, on the behaviour of producers. This is probably the least-acceptable assumption of the model.
46. In the second period, each firm (particularly the members of the SRO) receives $\lambda/(N-1)$ consumers coming from each other market.
47. William Oakland, 'Theory of Public Goods', in *Handbook of Public Economics* (Alan Auerbach and Martin Feldstein, eds, Amsterdam: North-Holland, 1987).
48. Similarly, by informing all customers that a firm acts in a certain way, the SRO indicates what a member could hope to do without being detected or punished: '[E]xposure might be a negative signal about the average quality of remaining members' and 'a sign that the fraudulent member thought that vigilance was low enough for there to be a reasonable chance of getting away with it'. John Vickers, 'Discussion of Mayer and Neven', in Alberto Giovannini and Colin Mayer (eds), *European Financial Integration* (Cambridge: Cambridge University Press, 1991). Thus, an SRO might have an incentive to cover up deviations of its members in the fear that public knowledge of such deviations might harm even its honest members.
49. Furthermore, although several authors agree that some services present cases of credence goods, the models on SR introduce some assumptions on observability of quality that clash with this view. This attitude could be justifiable on the ground of the difficulty in dealing with credence goods, but seriously undermines some of the policy implications.
50. In particular, it might depend on 'local' conventions and in general on the professional group's 'culture'. Talking about European harmonization of these codes hardly makes sense.
51. Which type of model is more relevant, however, is an open issue. If SR is introduced when the professional group is already in place, it is possible that quality levels were chosen a long time ago, so that at the time when SR begins they are given. Thus, the real question mark is to what extent quality choices of already established producers may or may not be changed.
52. A precondition for mobility is repeated purchase.

# 3. Advertising restrictions in professional services

## Chiara Fumagalli and Massimo Motta

*There are some 15 Organization for Economic Cooperation and Development (OECD) countries where advertising professional services is completely or partially restricted. The main market failure in markets for professional services is that information is asymmetric between the professionals on the one side and the consumers on the other. Both economic theory and empirical evidence support the view that advertising restrictions in the market for professional services are detrimental to welfare. Advertising restrictions further limit the information available to consumers and thus widen the information gap, rather than correct the externalities and market failures in this industry.*

*Three arguments are made repeatedly to justify advertising restrictions in professional services markets: that advertising would be unethical; that deceptive, untruthful advertising is really unethical; and that the spread of information which would occur if professionals could advertise would be undesirable. The economist's reply to these arguments is: if advertising prohibitions are otherwise against the public interest, ethical concerns do not provide a reason that restrictions on advertising should be permitted; that consumer protection laws against deceptive advertising are already in place; and that the spread of information from advertising might even go in the direction of further protecting consumers.*

*Two other arguments are also made to justify advertising restrictions: that advertising would decrease the quality of the services provided, and that advertising would increase concentration, and therefore harm market structure. The logic of the first argument follows only if price advertising alone is used, and consumers are unable to distinguish the good from the bad. However, minimum quality standards would provide a preferable solution. The second argument applies mainly with respect to persuasive advertising for consumer products, rather than informative advertising of professional services. Empirical evidence shows that advertising professional services seems to favour entry and reduce concentration.*

*Empirical studies show that advertising increases welfare: it appears to reduce prices, but not quality, and it tends to promote entry. Advertising restrictions have anticompetitive effects: theory and empirical evidence show that they are welfare detrimental. There is a strong case to remove all advertising restrictions.*

## INTRODUCTION

Advertising restrictions exist in different countries. They might take different forms, such as prohibitions of price advertising, advertising bans, limitation of advertising to certain media, and limitation of advertising of only certain types of products and services. By and large, however, we can identify two broad categories of activities in which advertising restrictions have been imposed: (i) the professional services sector (for example, services provided by lawyers, doctors, engineers, architects and so on), and (ii) manufacturing sectors, where consumption of the goods produced is deemed to be harmful for consumers or gives rise to negative externalities (for example, alcoholic beverages and tobacco). The rationale, objectives and likely effects of advertising restrictions in these two categories are entirely different. Thus, analysis of advertising restrictions in the two categories must be approached from different perspectives. This chapter focuses mainly on advertising regulations in professional services; it will only briefly describe some issues related to advertising bans in the sector for hazardous products.

Markets for professional services are typically heavily regulated. Regulatory instruments include licensing, qualification requirements, quality standards, price controls, entry restrictions and advertising restrictions. The rationale for such regulation should be the protection of customers who would otherwise suffer from information asymmetries, and in particular, from their inability to judge the quality of the services they are purchasing.

Theoretical and empirical evidence will be used here to argue, however, that advertising bans in these markets are not only redundant but also welfare detrimental. This is because consumer protection is achieved more efficiently by licensing and qualification requirements, which directly establish minimum quality standards (MQSs) applicable to the services offered. In contrast, advertising bans (as well as price regulations, such as minimum or recommended fees) have little economic justification. In particular, truthful and non-deceptive advertising in markets for professional services reduces prices and search costs for customers, aids entry, facilitates a better matching of consumers' needs with services offered, and therefore ultimately leads to an increase in consumer welfare.

Advertising increases the amount of relevant information available to consumers (such as information related to specialization of the providers of services, their locations, and possibly the prices they charge), which in turn leads to an increase in competition among professionals. Advertising also facilitates entry of new professionals, who currently have difficulty establishing a clientele in all the countries where advertising is forbidden. In short, advertising benefits customers and new entrants, but increases competition for incumbent professionals.

Obviously, allowing advertising does not mean allowing individuals to make unsubstantiated and deceptive claims. Consumer protection laws, which currently prevent manufacturers from making deceptive and misleading announcements, should also be applied to professional advertising.

The remainder of this chapter is organized as follows. Section A introduces the issue of advertising restrictions in professional services, briefly describing such regulations in the main western countries, and critically discussing the main rationale for such regulations. Section B reviews the main theoretical contributions in the economics literature regarding the effects of informative advertising. Section C reviews the empirical studies that have measured the effect of advertising restrictions (or of removing such restrictions) on prices, entry and quality of services. Section D briefly addresses advertising bans in sectors other than professional services, clarifying that such bans are inspired by policy objectives which have little to do with competition policy and therefore cannot be evaluated in terms of their impact on consumer welfare. Finally, in light of the arguments developed by theory and confirmed by empirical studies, the last section draws the conclusion that advertising restrictions applicable to professional services are likely to be welfare detrimental and that truthful advertising should therefore be allowed.

## A. ADVERTISING RESTRICTIONS IN PROFESSIONAL SERVICES: AN OVERVIEW

This section considers restrictions on advertising in markets for professional services, such as services provided by doctors, pharmacists, lawyers, architects and engineers. It first describes the current legal status in the main industrialized countries, then discusses the possible rationale for such restrictions.

### Restrictions to Advertising in the Main Industrialized Countries

In many countries, professionals may not advertise in almost any form. In Italy, for instance, lawyers are prohibited from advertising their services, because it is viewed as contrary to the dignity and honour of the profession. The code of conduct established by the professional association of lawyers also prohibits any type of advertising, except indication of specialization in the lawyer's letterhead or in the lists of lawyers prepared by the association. Lawyers should also avoid use of their relationship with the media as a means of advertising.[1] Similar rules banning lawyer advertising also exist in Spain, and for barristers in the UK. They have the effect of keeping potentially useful information away from consumers. Other countries, such as Germany, Belgium and France, also forbid lawyer advertising, but allow lawyers to publish information about their main areas of activity and specialization.[2] Complete or partial lawyer advertising restrictions exist in some 15 OECD countries.[3] In other countries, including Sweden, Denmark, the US and solicitors in the UK, lawyers are allowed to advertise, provided that their advertised messages respect some basic rules, such as truthfulness and non-deceptiveness, and that they do not make comparisons.[4]

A similar situation exists with respect to other professions. Doctors, for instance, face strict advertising restrictions in many countries. In Italy, doctors are permitted only to indicate their area of specialization (for example, pediatrician, gynaecologist, dermatologist and so on) in the telephone directory and in a plate outside the building in which patients are received.[5] Similar restrictions exist in many other European countries, although some countries (for example, Austria, Denmark, Ireland, Luxembourg, Portugal, Sweden and the UK) also allow indication of specialization in newspapers.[6]

Many countries are now rethinking the role of regulation in markets for professional services, and eliminating many regulatory barriers to competition, including advertising restrictions.[7] In Europe, national reforms will be influenced by decisions taken at the European Union level. The European Commission has already ruled that Article 81 applies to professional services, and that collective price fixing and advertising restrictions (including restrictions on comparative advertising) imposed by a professional order are violations.[8] It has also established a clear distinction between rules of a deontological nature (which guarantee impartiality, competence, integrity and responsibility of professionals), versus rules that might distort competition in the market for professional services and should therefore be avoided.[9]

**Possible Rationale for Advertising Restrictions**

Advertising restrictions are one form of regulating markets for professional services. Other forms include minimum educational requirements and minimum practice requirements, as well as other quality standards. For instance, to practise as a lawyer, regulations might require a law degree, a period of apprenticeship under the supervision of an established lawyer, and that certain basic rules be respected, such as keeping oneself informed, and respecting the privacy of clients.

Other forms of regulation encountered in many countries include restrictions on entry (for example, rules limiting the number of notaries that can exist in a certain city, or requiring a minimum distance between one pharmacy and another); regulations limiting fee competition (for example, minimum or recommended prices, and more rarely, maximum prices); limits on forms of practice (for example, rules prohibiting creation of a corporation, as well as association with non-professionals), usually to ensure that a professional is personally responsible to the client.

The existence of such regulations in markets for professional services can be justified because such markets are characterized by a very particular situation: asymmetric information between the professional, who usually knows the quality of the service he/she can provide clients, and the clients, who are unable to judge the quality of such a service, both before and after having consumed the service.[10] For instance, one might visit a doctor because of a pain in the left shoulder. The patient, however, does not know whether this is due to heart problems or to some other cause. The patient might have surgery, pleased to have a nice and reassuring doctor, who says there is nothing to worry about, and discover only after a heart attack that the diagnosis was incorrect. The same is true for other professional services. The care, knowledge and ability of lawyers, engineers, architects, accountants and professionals in general are very difficult for a layperson to verify.

As a result of information asymmetries, the professional is at an advantage *vis-à-vis* the client, and may abuse that advantage. To ensure that consumers are protected, regulations are needed in markets characterized by information asymmetries. The MQS is one such regulatory tool.[11] As noted above, in markets for professional services, an MQS might take the form of a qualification requirement. For instance, to practise as a cardiologist, one must have a degree in medicine and have passed all examinations in the specialization of cardiology. This does not guarantee the competence of the cardiologist, but it makes competence more likely than it would be with respect to a charlatan who has never followed a course in a medical school!

Given that some form of regulation is required in these markets, it does not appear that all regulatory instruments currently in use are necessary to increase efficiency. For instance, minimum fees for some services do not benefit consumers, but they do benefit professionals who are subject to them. Likewise, as shown below, the rationale for advertising restrictions is not clear.

Justifications for such strict restrictions are difficult to find. In markets characterized by information asymmetries, laws that prevent professionals even from disclosing their area of specialization appear to be without justification. If anything, the amount and quality of information available to the consumer should be increased, not decreased. Publicizing information about the studies carried out by professionals, their diplomas, their rate of success, their previous work experience, their location and possibly the prices they charge should all help reduce the ignorance of consumers, and therefore help balance the information asymmetry. For instance, a person seeking a lawyer to assist him/her in purchasing real property should have access to information about which lawyers are specialized in property transactions, where they are located, how many cases they have handled and so on. If such information is not available, the consumer must rely on word of mouth, with the danger that the lawyer selected does not have the required expertise.

Accordingly, it is not obvious why advertising restrictions should be imposed in markets characterized by information asymmetries. Three reasons are normally invoked to support the existence of restrictions in such circumstances. The first, and most often cited, reason is that advertising by professionals is unethical, as professionals should not endeavour to attract clients by means which do not respect the dignity of the profession.[12] This argument is difficult to discuss in economic terms, as it has less to do with economics, and more to do with professional ethics. However genuine and in good faith such ethical concerns might be, they have little to do with welfare of the population at large. Professional codes should not have a negative impact on other groups, such as consumers. Accordingly, rules in professional codes prohibiting professionals from competing on prices or from advertising should be deemed illegal whenever they are against the public interest.[13]

Moreover, it is not clear why public disclosure of a professional's area of specialization, education or professional record should be considered against the prestige of the profession. Deceptive advertising and unsubstantiated claims would be unethical, and should not be permitted. Laws already exist, however, protecting consumers from false statements made in advertising messages.

Paradoxically, publicity might even have the side-effect of protecting consumers from charlatans. In Italy, the print media have recently disclosed that hundreds of people who never met the necessary requirements have held themselves out as doctors and dentists, and have practised undisturbed and undetected for years. If these groups had been allowed to advertise, it may have contributed to the diffusion of information, and thereby facilitated efforts by consumers to check whether such claims were truthful. In short, it does not seem that advertising restrictions would protect the public against incompetents, as some professionals claim; the reverse might even be argued.

The second argument often cited to justify advertising restrictions is that the quality of services offered might decrease. This argument can be expressed in economic terms as follows. Assume that advertising consists mainly of price advertising, and that some doctors are well educated ('good' doctors), while others are less well educated ('bad' doctors). The former have invested more than the latter in their education, have accumulated loans during their years of medical education, and therefore want to charge a higher hourly fee. Assume further that consumers are not able to distinguish good doctors from bad doctors – that is, that no information is available to consumers about doctors' qualifications, so that they base their choice only on prices. In such circumstances, consumers might be lured to demand the services of bad doctors, which would then drive the good doctors out of the market.[14]

The above reasoning, however, is based on a number of assumptions.[15] As shown below, neither economic theory nor empirical research supports the view that advertising decreases the quality of goods and services offered. Even if this were the case, the existence of licensing regulations (MQSs) would already ensure that doctors are providing services of acceptable quality. Accordingly, even the bad doctors would have been to medical school and would have had the basic training necessary to practise the profession at an acceptable level. Moreover, if good doctors could publicize their higher level of education, price advertising would not drive them out of the market, as long as some consumers were willing to pay more to receive higher-quality services.

The third argument invoked to justify advertising restrictions is that advertising might increase concentration, thereby reducing consumer welfare.[16] Assuming that some professionals have better financial resources than others, they will be able to afford more advertising, which will, in turn, attract consumers and give them an even stronger financial position. Professionals who do not advertise would lose market share, while professionals who advertise would gain market share. Market power and prices would rise, and consumer welfare would decrease.

Escalation of advertising expenditures is a typical phenomenon of consumer goods industries, and processes of the type described are not uncommon in many manufacturing industries.[17] However, it is unlikely that similar processes would occur in markets for professional services. Escalation of advertising usually involves persuasive advertising, which aims to shift the tastes of consumers and make them more willing to pay for a certain brand that conveys a certain image. This is not the type of advertising that professionals are likely to employ.[18] Moreover, if information on education, specialization, and past professional record could circulate freely, but unverifiable claims could not be made, consumers would be likely to base their choices on such simple facts, rather than on an expensive advertising campaign. Since publicizing such facts is relatively simple and inexpensive, it is unlikely that advertising might be accessible to only a few, well-endowed individuals.[19]

As shown below, advertising would facilitate entry and *reduce* concentration. Markets for professional services are currently characterized by enormous difficulties of access, due not only to licensing and entry restrictions but also to the impossibility for entrants to make themselves known. It is difficult for a new entrant to build a clientele in a market where clients can only rely on friends, relatives, or word of mouth to obtain information about service providers. The spread of information brought about by advertising would thus facilitate entry and increase competition. Accordingly, older and established professionals are likely to favour advertising restrictions, which protect them from competition, and younger prospective entrants to favour advertising. Since only established professionals are members of the professional associations, they are the strongest voices against advertising.

In summary, the arguments often asserted to support advertising restrictions applicable to professional services do not seem well founded. The sections that follow will rely upon economic theory and empirical evidence to show that the abolition of such restrictions would be likely to improve consumer welfare, and to decrease the market power profits of established professionals.

## B.   ECONOMIC THEORY ON THE EFFECTS OF ADVERTISING

Economic theory suggests that advertising can have effects on consumer welfare and firm profits. These effects operate through different channels according to the informational content of advertising. Advertising can provide consumers with information about prices, helping them to find the firms that charge the least, and reducing the time and energy that they must spend in costly search activity. This helps effective competition to work, as firms know that consumers will not patronize them if they do not price competitively.

Even when it does not convey price information, advertising can provide other important information about the existence of products and services, the firms that sell them, and their relevant characteristics. This not only helps consumers to find a good or service suited to their taste, but also exerts competitive pressure on firms.

This can be illustrated by an example. Assume that a consumer has skin problems but is aware of only one doctor, a general practitioner, in his/her home town. The consumer may be willing to go to this GP and pay a high price, even though the latter is not a dermatologist. If more information were available, the consumer might learn that there is also a dermatologist in the town. In this case, information would have a twofold effect: it would allow for a better fit between the patient's needs and the doctor; and it would help contain the prices requested by doctors. More generally, if consumers are aware of the spectrum of goods and services available, they will be more sensitive to price changes. This limits the ability of firms and professionals to exert market power. Moreover, richer information about the goods and services on the market benefits consumers by allowing them to identify the variety and quality of products best suited to their needs.

The main economic models that have formally and rigorously dealt with these issues are set forth below. They fall into three broad categories: price advertising, advertising with respect to the existence and characteristics of goods in the market, and advertising about experience goods, which allows firms to send signals to consumers about the quality of the products they offer.

## Price Advertising

In markets where consumers are not perfectly informed about the prices firms charge and where the acquisition of information is costly, two results are possible. The first is that each firm will act, at equilibrium, as a complete monopolist over its usual customers[20] and equilibrium prices will be set at the monopoly level. The second is that there may be permanent price dispersion in the range between the perfectly competitive price and the monopolistically competitive price.[21] In this setting, if advertising is possible, firms that set low prices have an incentive to inform consumers about their prices. Price advertising makes consumers aware of low prices without bearing search costs. Hence, advertising fosters competition among firms, and significantly affects the equilibrium outcomes of markets where consumers have little information about prices *ex ante*.

A paper by Robert and Stahl,[22] which introduces price advertising into an *optimal sequential search model*, is representative of this category. A priori, consumers are uninformed about prices charged by different firms for a homogeneous good. They must visit a store to learn about a price, which is costly, unless they are reached by an advertisement quoting a price. Their optimal strategy is to search sequentially for lower prices if they find the observed or advertised price unattractive. In equilibrium, firms either charge a high price, which they do not advertise, or charge a low price, which they advertise intensively. As advertising costs fall, firms advertise more intensively. When advertising costs are sufficiently low, consumers become fully informed and the equilibrium outcome converges to the perfectly competitive one. Accordingly, removing an advertising ban on professional fees (that is, decreasing advertising costs from a prohibitively high level) should induce a procompetitive effect and improve welfare through lower prices and reduced costly search activity.

Bester and Petrakis[23] also find that price advertising fosters competition. They assume that a priori, consumers are informed only of the price offered by the neighbourhood store (or most preferred store), and must pay a switching cost to visit distant sellers. However, they can learn the price charged at the other location if the distant seller advertises price. If the cost of advertising is prohibitively high, each seller charges the monopoly price without advertising. Undercutting the competitor is not profitable, since this is feasible only through advertising. If advertising costs are sufficiently low, with positive probability sellers will advertise to attract customers from distant locations; with the remaining probability they post a high price and serve only local customers. Again, by making consumers aware of attractive price offers at other locations, price advertising enhances competition, induces lower prices and improves consumer welfare. Sellers find themselves in a 'Prisoner's Dilemma': an agreement not to advertise prices would generate higher profits, but such an agreement cannot be sustained as a 'non-cooperative equilibrium'. If the firms in the industry agree not to advertise but do not have the means to make such an agreement binding (for instance, because this is against competition laws), each seller could gain by deviating and advertising a lower price. The agreement would thereby collapse.

Accordingly, while advertising restrictions applicable to professional fees damage consumers, they benefit professionals. Not surprisingly, professional associations lobby for advertising restrictions in many countries. Without rules that have the force of law, informal agreements asking members to refrain from advertising would not succeed.

### Advertising the Existence of Products

In the previous group of models, consumers are aware of the availability and the characteristics of products; only price information is imperfect. If, however, consumers are not informed of the existence of a product and/or its distinguishing features, advertising can convey this kind of information. For instance, advertising could make consumers aware of a nearby lawyer or of a lawyer's area of specialization.

Grossman and Shapiro[24] investigate the role of informative advertising about the existence, price and characteristics of products. They assume that goods are horizontally differentiated, that consumers have heterogeneous tastes, and that each consumer is unaware of the existence of a particular brand unless he/she sees an advertisement describing it. Advertising helps make the market more competitive because it makes available information about the brands in the market, thereby increasing product substitutability. Hence, it raises the elasticity of demand faced by each firm and thereby reduces prices. The lower the cost of advertising, the more intensively firms will use it, the better informed consumers will be, and the lower the equilibrium price will be. Moreover, higher advertising intensity implies a further positive effect: by improving the level of information available to consumers, advertising improves their matching with brands and hence their welfare. This reinforces the result that if advertising costs decrease, consumer welfare increases. It is, however, possible that as the price of advertising decreases, firms' profits decrease. The direct effect of a reduction of advertising costs is to increase profits. However, there is also an indirect effect: the cost reduction will raise advertising intensity and decrease informational product differentiation. This induces firms to lower prices and reduces profits.[25] This provides a further reason why producers favour advertising restrictions. In summary, this model emphasizes that removing bans on professional advertising will benefit consumers not only through lower fees, but also through richer information about the types of professional services provided in the market, thereby allowing them to demand the services of the professional who best fits their needs. Conversely, professionals would generally benefit from maintaining such restrictions, which protect them from competitors and allow them to command higher prices.

Consumers may know the prices of all existing products, but may ignore which product offers the best match for their needs. In such a case, advertising provides information about the quality of matches. Meurer and Stahl[26] assume the existence of two products and two types of buyers, each type of buyer ideally matched to one of the products. Without advertising, consumers perceive the two goods as homogeneous, and Bertrand competition will lead prices down to marginal cost. As advertising increases, a larger fraction of consumers becomes aware of their preferred good, and they are willing to pay more for it. Firms face a tradeoff when consumers are partly informed and partly uninformed: they can charge a high price serving only informed customers, or they can charge a low price losing revenues from informed customers[27] but gaining revenues from additional sales to uninformed customers. With little advertising, the share of informed customers is small, and firms find it profitable to compete for the large fraction of uninformed customers with low prices. As the amount of advertising increases, firms have more loyal customers and compete less for the uninformed ones.

In contrast to the previous models, advertising increases product differentiation and creates more market power. Once brand loyalty is sufficiently high, firms find it more profitable to serve only informed customers and charge the monopoly price. In this case, consumer welfare is not monotonic with respect to advertising levels. As the level of advertising increases, prices rise and the fraction of uninformed customers who are served declines. These negative effects more than offset the positive effect of better matches. When only informed customers are served, increasing advertising does not affect prices, but it does improve matches and consumer welfare. Accordingly, if customers are aware of all the professionals providing services in the market, but are unable to assess which one can best satisfy their needs, advertising can have two opposite effects: it can educate customers about the quality of matches, but it will thereby increase their willingness to pay for the service of a particular professional and that professional's ability to charge higher prices. When the second effect prevails, removing advertising bans can be harmful.

Some crucial assumptions, however, play a role in this model by making the effects of advertising less beneficial than in most other models. For instance, professionals are perceived, *ex ante*, to be perfectly homogeneous, and their existence or location is assumed to be perfectly known. As information increases, matching improves, but this does not lead more consumers away from demanding the services of professionals. They always purchase, even if they do not find the right match.

### Advertising Signalling Quality

The previous models deal with 'search goods', which are goods whose quality or other relevant characteristics are evident before purchase, although after costly search. Products whose quality can be evaluated only after consumption, however, are denoted as 'experience goods'. Advertising cannot credibly convey much direct information about the quality of experience goods. For instance, a seller's claim to be offering high-quality goods is unverifiable and might well be false and misleading. Thus, the rational consumer would ignore such claims. But the fact that a good is advertised might be a signal that the brand is of high quality. In particular, Milgrom and Roberts[28] show that high prices and advertising expenditures can be efficiently used by a firm providing a high-quality good to distinguish its product from that of a low-quality producer. The high-quality firm chooses prices and quality that the low-quality firm has no incentive to mimic. Moreover, for a high-quality producer, signalling with both price and advertising is cheaper than with price changes alone. The assumption that repeat sales increase with quality is crucial for this result. Price increases imply that the high-quality firm, whose fraction of repeat purchasing is larger, loses customers at a greater rate than does the low-quality firm. Therefore, the high-quality firm prefers to resort to advertising. If advertising were banned, the high-quality firm might continue to signal, but it would do so by adopting even higher prices. This represents a Pareto-inferior situation: profits fall for the high-quality producer, and consumers have the same information as they did before the ban, but they pay higher prices.

In summary, this model suggests that removing restrictions on professional advertising benefits consumers, because it allows them to infer information about professional competence in a less costly manner. It also benefits more-qualified professionals, because they can distinguish themselves from less-qualified ones at a lower cost.

### Conclusion

The theory discussed above does not support the conclusion that allowing professionals to advertise would damage consumers. On the contrary, and provided that appropriate regulatory tools such as qualification requirements or MQSs guarantee the quality of services, it indicates that informative advertising will generate gains for consumers. The models discussed above, which represent work at the frontier of economic research, suggest that advertising will induce lower prices, improve the consumer's ability to identify the services he/she desires, and provide richer information about the qualification of service providers.[29] Since competition in the market may, however, intensify as the result of allowing advertising, professionals may lose profits from removing such restrictions. This suggests why they often oppose this possibility.

## C.    THE EFFECTS OF ADVERTISING: EMPIRICAL STUDIES

This section will review the empirical literature on the effects of advertising in markets for professional services. The evidence generally supports the argument that advertising would be beneficial. The first group of articles, focusing on the effect of price advertising, concludes that less-restrictive rules governing professional advertising lead to lower professional fees. The second group of papers, which deal with the effect of advertising on quality, does not support the claim that advertising lowers the quality of professional services. On the contrary, some evidence reveals that advertising might help professionals to signal the quality of services. Finally, studies investigating the impact of advertising on entry into professional markets indicate that less-experienced professionals are more likely to advertise, and that advertising promotes entry by allowing entrants to make themselves known to consumers. The general conclusion is, therefore, that empirical evidence confirms the theoretical insights: advertising benefits consumers by making a market more competitive and thus lowering fees. Worries about quality deterioration and barriers to entry due to advertising are unfounded.

**Empirical Evidence on the Effects of Advertising on Prices**

Benham[30] and Benham and Benham[31] analyse the impact of advertising restrictions on the price of eyeglasses in the US. Advertising of eyeglasses and eye examinations was prohibited in some states but allowed in others, which made it possible to study the impact of advertising on prices. In the first paper, higher prices for eyeglasses are found to be associated with restrictions on advertising. Estimates of eyeglass prices suggest that advertising restrictions cause a 25 per cent to more than 100 per cent increase in the price paid by consumers. Moreover, in states prohibiting only price advertising, prices are slightly higher than in states with no restrictions, and considerably lower than in states prohibiting all advertising. This estimate suggests that even non-price advertising plays a role in lowering prices. Finally, no specific evidence was found to support the claim of systematic differences in quality of products between states that allowed and states that prohibited advertising.

The second paper explores the price consequences of more general constraints on information in the retail market for eyeglasses. Again, there exists a considerable diversity across states in the strength and uniformity of professional control over the types and quantity of information that can be transmitted. The authors find a sizeable positive correlation between professional control and prices paid for eyeglasses. A common explanation for this correlation is that in states where professionals are numerous and hence exert substantial control, optometrists and physicians supply a larger proportion of the output than do commercial firms. The services of the former are of higher quality and are more costly than the services of the latter. However, a highly significant correlation is found between the extent of professional control and selling price for each group of providers. Therefore, in states where professional control is weaker, lower prices do not simply result from a shift in the source of care, but also demonstrate the strong incentives that optometrists have to increase professional control over information, since both their selling prices and their market shares increase with this control.

Love et al.[32] and Stephen[33] focus on the market for legal services (in particular for conveyances) in the UK. There, since the early 1980s, there has been a consistent effort to deregulate the legal profession. Accordingly, in 1984, advertising by solicitors was permitted for the first time in England and Wales. Revised practice rules permitting more individual advertising by solicitors were introduced in Scotland in 1985. These works explore the effect of the elimination of the advertising ban on the fees charged by solicitors. Love et al. consider 27 geographical markets in England and Wales, and find that marketwide price advertising reduces the conveyancing fees charged in the relevant market. Some evidence also suggests that this effect can be obtained from other combinations of advertising activity, such as non-price media advertising and enhanced Yellow Pages entries. Stephen estimates the impact of advertising on the level of conveyancing fees charged by a sample of Scottish solicitors. His study confirms that non-price media advertising combined with enhanced Yellow Pages entries make the demand faced by the individual firm more elastic, thereby lowering fees.

Finally, although it does not refer to the market for professional services, evidence gathered in a controlled experiment by a Canadian agency in the 1970s also confirms the theoretical finding that information decreases prices.[34] The experiment involved two cities: Ottawa-Hull, where the experiment was conducted, and Winnipeg, the control city. The experiment was made in three stages. In the first stage (17 weeks), prices charged by grocery stores for food products in two cities were collected. In the second stage (five weeks), consumers in Ottawa-Hull received information (advertisements in local newspapers and, for some consumers whose purchase decisions were to be closely monitored, notices by mail) on the prices charged by stores during the first stage. In Winnipeg, no information about prices was released. In the third stage (six weeks), price information was collected by the researchers but not distributed to consumers. The result was that prices decreased by 6.5 per cent in Ottawa with respect to prices in Winnipeg during the second stage and the first week of the third stage. However, prices began to increase again almost as soon as information was not disclosed to consumers, and arrived at the pre-experiment level by the end of the whole experiment. Observation revealed that 43 per cent of the sample of consumers in the experimental city who were closely monitored had changed store as a result of the comparative price programme, to the benefit of stores charging lower prices. This controlled experiment, as well as similar ones carried out subsequently in Canada and the US,[35] reveals that disclosure of price information unambiguously decreases market prices.[36]

## Quality and Advertising

Few studies have addressed the effect of informative advertising upon the quality of professional services. These studies compare quality of services in states of a federal country where advertising is allowed with states where advertising is not allowed. The results do not suggest that advertising lowers the quality of services offered.[37]

Kwoka[38] is an exception. He tests the price and quality effects of advertising in the US optometry profession. He identifies cities where an advertising ban is in effect, as well as those where it is allowed. For the latter, he defines four categories of providers according to the chosen advertising tool: practitioners using storefronts with prominent signs or display; optometrists affiliated with small local firms who advertise in the Yellow Pages and/or newspapers; large optical firms who are heavy media advertisers; and non-advertising optometrists practising in 'professional-looking' offices. His estimates suggest that advertising causes substantial and significant declines in the prices of eye examinations offered by all types of optometrists. Even non-advertisers in advertising markets are forced to lower prices to compete. Moreover, he measures the quality of the optometric service as the time (in minutes) spent in the examination. Advertisers are estimated to give shorter examinations, but non-advertisers in advertising markets give higher-quality examinations than their counterparts in non-advertising markets. Moreover, the mean time spent in advertising markets is actually longer than in non-advertising markets. Time spent in examination is perhaps a crude proxy of quality levels. Nevertheless, these results are certainly inconsistent with the view that advertising endangers high-quality service.[39]

### Advertising and Entry

Empirical evidence does not confirm the argument that removal of advertising restrictions might deter entry[40] of young professionals, increasing market power of established ones. For instance, Folland's[41] study of the English market for physician services presents evidence indicating that less-experienced physicians are more likely to advertise. Advertising allows young physicians to gain visibility and reputation. Accordingly, advertising should make entry easier and promote competition. Similarly, Rizzo and Zeckhauser[42] consider advertising practices of American physicians. They confirm that less-experienced physicians, together with women and foreign medical graduates, are more likely to advertise.[43]

To conclude, even if scant, the empirical evidence does not suggest that advertising might represent a barrier to entry. Rather, it seems to help young professionals to build a clientele and ultimately to enter the market.

## D.  ADVERTISING RESTRICTIONS IN OTHER MARKETS

Advertising restrictions of a different type and strength have been introduced in markets for goods whose consumption is supposed to be harmful to individual consumers and possibly, through negative externalities, to society at large. The best examples of such products are alcoholic drinks and cigarettes, for which advertising is in most industrialized economies either partially or completely banned.[44] The rationale for introducing such bans lies in the belief that by prohibiting advertising, consumption of such goods will decrease. The public policy objective in such circumstances is unusual: the reduction of aggregate consumption of products considered to be 'bad'. A similar objective underlies certain environmental policies that heavily tax consumption of polluting substances to reduce their use. However, advertising bans may not help attain this policy objective. Empirical analyses of markets where such bans have been imposed show an ambiguous impact on aggregate consumption. Some studies even find that after a ban is imposed, consumption might have increased.[45]

Little economic research on the subject has been done, but a possible explanation for the ambiguous effect of advertising restrictions on consumption is explained by Motta.[46] First, as discussed above, a professional's advertisement would usually be of the 'informative' type, normally announcing in a local newspaper or magazine (or on a personal web page) the location of his/her office, his/her specialization and professional record and perhaps the price for a typical visit. In contrast, advertising in markets for alcoholic drinks and tobacco products would mostly be of the 'persuasive' type, designed not to increase the level of information available to consumers with respect to the characteristics of the goods for sale (as is likely in the case of professional services), but to enhance their willingness to pay and to increase their brand consciousness. Such advertising may attempt to persuade the potential consumers that smoking its cigarettes would increase their pleasure and possibly improve their image in society. Far from having the effect of increasing competition, this type of advertising – usually done at the national level, on a large scale, rather than at the local level – increases product differentiation and allows producers to charge higher prices.

Such advertising for consumer products has two likely effects: for given prices, it might increase demand, as for an individual who has never consumed the product before but buys it after having seen an advertising campaign; and for given demand, it would tend to increase prices that consumers already purchasing the product are willing to pay. But through this latter effect, such advertising might reduce total demand. Overall, therefore, it is not clear whether advertising would increase aggregate demand, and therefore whether an advertising ban would decrease consumption.[47]

Other reasons might also explain the lack of success of advertising bans in decreasing total consumption of alcohol and tobacco products. For instance, in one country, firms have been able to circumvent the ban by advertising other goods bearing the same brand, thereby keeping the brand consciousness of consumers high. Tobacco companies have commercialized clothing, sunglasses and several other products under the same name as their cigarettes, whose direct promotion is forbidden. Therefore, the empirical findings that advertising prohibitions do not decrease consumption might simply be due to ineffectiveness of the prohibitions.

Another possible explanation for the US market is the 'Fairness Doctrine', a regulation that, for every tobacco advertisement broadcast, obliged TV channels to give equivalent free time on the air for anti-smoking campaign commercials. When TV advertising for tobacco products was later forbidden, anti-smoking advertising also fell. Since the latter seemed to be particularly effective in deterring individuals from smoking, this might explain why the tobacco TV advertising ban did not result in decreased consumption (and perhaps, paradoxically, had the opposite effect).[48]

The objective of decreasing consumption is better attained through other instruments, such as massive educational campaigns that explain the harmful effects associated with the consumption of the products, and the use of taxes that discourage demand through a price increase.[49]

The US Supreme Court established a test to determine whether restrictions of commercial speech should be allowed.[50] If applied to advertising bans applicable to tobacco, alcohol and other possibly harmful products, the test suggests that a ban should be permitted as long as it directly advances a substantial government interest and it is not more extensive than necessary to serve that interest. Advertising bans on tobacco and alcohol products would be likely to fail this test, since such bans may not advance the government objective of reducing consumption, and since there are probably other means by which that objective could be reached without distorting the market.

Competition concerns are not a priority of public policies that aim at decreasing consumption of harmful or unhealthy products. Higher prices or difficult entry in the market might be considered as a necessary price to pay to obtain desirable health policy effects. Such competition distortions are, however, justified only if the objective of reducing total demand for such products is likely to be advanced and it is not possible to use other regulatory tools that could reach the same objectives without distorting the market.

## CONCLUSIONS

Professional services are characterized by considerable asymmetric information between professionals and consumers. The latter not only may be unable to verify the quality of services before purchase, but they also may be unable to determine quality after consumption. This justifies regulation in such markets through such mechanisms as licensing, qualifications requirements and other MQSs. However, once consumer protection is guaranteed by these regulatory tools, prohibiting professionals from disclosing information through advertising is unlikely to be welfare improving.

Indeed, both economic theory and empirical evidence support the opposite view. By *truthfully* advertising their prices, location, area of specialization, rate of success and previous experience, professionals can provide very useful information to consumers. This information will help consumers identify the services and professionals best suited to their needs (in terms of quality, price and other characteristics), thereby reducing time and energy spent in search activity. In turn, professionals would operate in a more competitive environment, which would decrease prices. Advertising might also help less-experienced professionals to form a clientele. This should promote entry and exert additional competitive pressure.

Finally, there is no evidence supporting the claim that advertising would cause quality to decrease. Advertising might help professionals to signal the quality of their services and to be compensated accordingly. Again, consumers would have a better choice as a result.

Accordingly, there is no economic reason why truthful informative advertising should be prohibited in the market for professional services. Deceptive and unsubstantiated claims are already punished by consumer protection laws. The effort exerted by professional orders to maintain such legal restrictions appears to be motivated by the intention to weaken competition rather than benefit consumers. Therefore, professional associations should limit themselves to deontological rules that guarantee that advertised messages are consistent with the impartiality, competence, integrity and responsibility of professionals. However, they should refrain from any restrictions on advertising, which are likely to distort competition in the market for professional services.

## NOTES

1. Autorità Garante della Concorrenza e del Mercato, *Indagine conoscitiva nel settore degli ordini e collegi professionali* (On the professional services sector) 98–99, Supp. N. 1, Boll. N. 40, Anno VII (Rome, 1997) (providing a complete description of advertising restrictions in all markets of professional services).
2. *Id.* at 102–3.
3. OECD, *Roundtable on Competition in Professional Services* 35 (Paris: OECD, 1999).
4. *Id.* at 10–14; AGCM, *supra* note 1, at 103–4.
5. AGCM, *supra* note 1, at 168–70.
6. *Id.* at 179.
7. For an overview of such developments, see OECD, *supra* note 3 (discussing national reforms in various OECD countries). Further, the Italian Competition Authority makes a number of sensible suggestions on how the regulation of professional services should be modified. AGCM, *supra* note 1. The reform currently being discussed in the Italian parliament is a first step in this direction, but seems far too conservative.
8. CNSD (Consiglio Nazionale degli Spedizionieri Doganali), 1993 *Official Journal* (L 203) 27; COAPI (Colegio Oficial de Agentes de la Propriedad Industrial), 1995 *Official Journal* (L 122) 37; see Maria José Bicho, *Professions libérales: aspects essentiels de l'action de la Commission en matière d'application de la concurrence*, in 2 *Competition Policy Newsletter* 2 (European Commission, 1999).
9. EPI Code of Conduct, 1999 *Official Journal* (L 106) 14.
10. In economic jargon, goods of this type are called 'credence goods'. 'Search goods' are goods whose quality can be judged upon inspection, but require a costly search activity to be identified; 'experience goods' are goods whose quality can be judged after having bought and used them. See Philip Nelson, 'Advertising as Information Once More', in *Issues in Advertising: The Economics of Persuasion* (David Tuerck, ed., Washington, DC, 1978); Philip Nelson, 'Advertising as Information', 81 *Journal of Political Economy* 729 (1974); Philip Nelson, 'Information and Consumer Behaviour', 78 *Journal of Political Economy* 311 (1970) (distinguishing search goods from experience goods). Information asymmetries are stronger for experience and credence goods, for which inspection prior to purchase is not sufficient to establish the quality of the good.
11. The use of MQSs in markets characterized by lack of information for consumers has been supported by formal economic theory since the article of Hayne Leland, 'Quacks, Lemons and Licensing: A Theory of Minimum Quality Standards', 87 *Journal of Political Economy* 1328 (1979). For a critical view of MQS, see the chapter by Carlo Scarpa in this volume (Chapter 2).
12. See, for example, AGCM, *supra* note 1, at 58.
13. Rules included in professional codes which eliminate competitive behaviour resemble calls for 'fair competition' in the US and some European countries at the beginning of the 1900s. At that time, entrepreneurs and even some economists advocated rules against 'cut-throat

competition'. In that case, however, the policy objective was not 'prestige', but economic stability.

14.  This example is a simplified version of the adverse selection argument first made by George Akerlof, 'The Market for Lemons: Quality Uncertainty and the Market Mechanism', 84 *Quarterly Journal of Economics* 488 (1970). Adverse selection might also lead to the complete disruption of the market. For instance, if people did not want to go to bad doctors and formed correct expectations about the quality of doctors in the market, when the good doctors leave the market, the bad ones are left without patients.

15.  The assumptions are that advertising is limited to price advertising, consumers have no information on the education and training of doctors, and good doctors must charge higher prices than bad doctors. The last assumption need not be true, as good doctors have higher fixed costs, not higher variable costs. If anything, good doctors might have lower variable costs at any given level of quality of service.

16.  See, for example, AGCM, *supra* note 1, at 58.

17.  See, for example, John Sutton, *Sunk Costs and Market Structure* (Cambridge, MA: MIT Press, 1991). This pathbreaking book shows that in some food and drinking industries, firms which have engaged in massive advertising campaigns have been able to increase the willingness to pay of the consumers for their brands, thus getting the leadership of the market and increasing their market shares remarkably. Higher market concentration is often a result of this process.

18.  In any event, professionals should only be allowed to make truthful, verifiable statements.

19.  The means that could be employed to advertise specializations and past record might include a web page, an announcement in a local newspaper, or an entry in a telephone directory and the Yellow Pages. Professionals are likely to be able to finance such minor expenses.

20.  See Peter Diamond, 'A Model of Price Adjustment', 3 *Journal of Economic Theory* 156 (1971).

21.  See Dale Stahl, 'Oligopolistic Pricing With Heterogeneous Consumer Search', 14 *International Journal of Industrial Organization* 243 (1996); Rafael Rob, 'Equilibrium Price Distribution', 52 *Review of Economic Studies* 457 (1985); Hal Varian, 'A Model of Sales', 70 *American Economic Review* 651 (1980); Jennifer Reinganum, 'A Simple Model of Equilibrium Price Dispersion', 87 *Journal of Political Economy* 851 (1979); Louis Wilde and Alan Schwartz, 'Equilibrium Comparison Shopping', 46 *Review of Economic Studies* 543 (1979); Bo Axell, 'Search Market Equilibrium', 79 *Scandinavian Journal of Economics* 20 (1977); Steven Salop and Joseph Stiglitz, 'Bargains and Ripoffs: A Model of Monopolistically Competitive Prices', 44 *Review of Economic Studies* 493 (1977); George Stigler, 'The Economics of Information', 69 *Journal of Political Economy* 213 (1961). In these models, price dispersion is obtained by assuming either that consumers are heterogeneous in terms of their search technology or that producers are heterogeneous.

22.  Jacques Robert and Dale Stahl, 'Informative Price Advertising in a Sequential Search Model', 61 Econometrica 657 (1993).

23.  Helmut Bester and Emanuel Petrakis, 'Price Competition and Advertising in Oligopoly', 39 *European Economic Review* 1075 (1995).

24.  Gene Grossman and Carl Shapiro, 'Informative Advertising with Differentiated Products', 51 *Review of Economic Studies* 63 1984); see also Gerard Butters, 'Equilibrium Distributions of Sales and Advertising Prices', 44 *Review of Economics* 465 (1977).

25.  In the model of Grossman and Shapiro, *supra* note 24, and in other similar models, it is assumed that consumers will buy a good independently of the price and specification of the products available. However, a reasonable alternative assumption is that total demand increases when information improves – that is, the consumer might decide not to buy if uncertain of whether the product matches his need, whereas he/she would buy if he/she knew the product's features and price. This effect might be beneficial to firms, as they would face higher demand when information spreads.

26.  Michael Meurer and Dale Stahl, 'Informative Advertising and Product Match', 12 *International Journal of Industrial Organization* 1 (1994).

27.  Price discrimination is ruled out.

28. Paul Milgrom and John Roberts, 'Price and Advertising Signals of Product Quality', 94 *Journal of Political Economy* 796 (1986). For other models in which advertising signals quality, see Kyle Bagwell and Gary Ramey, 'Advertising as Information: Matching Products to Buyers', 2 *Journal of Economic Management* 199 (1994); William Rogerson, 'Advertising as a Signal When Price Guarantees Quality' (Northwestern University Center for Mathematical Studies in Economics and Management Science Discussion Paper No. 704, 1986); Richard Kihlstrom and Michael Riordan, 'Advertising as a Signal', 92 *Journal of Political Economy* 427 (1984); Richard Schmalansee, 'A Model of Advertising and Product Quality', 86 *Journal of Political Economy* 485 (1978). Advertising can also be used to signal *low* quality.

29. Many papers have been written on a slightly different subject: whether the level of advertising arising at a market equilibrium will be efficient – that is, the level that a social planner would choose. No clear conclusion can be drawn from this literature. According to the particular specifications of the models, the level of advertising chosen by firms at the market equilibrium might be excessive or insufficient with respect to the social optimum. Allowing advertising is preferable to forbidding it, even if the level of advertising may not be at exactly the socially efficient level.

30. Lee Benham, 'The Effect of Advertising on the Price of Eyeglasses', 15 *Journal of Law and Economics* 337 (1972).

31. Lee Benham and Alexandra Benham, 'Regulating Through the Professions: A Prospective on Information Control', 18 *Journal of Law and Economics* 421 (1975).

32. James Love, Frank H. Stephen, Derek G. Gillanders and Allan A. Paterson, 'Spatial Aspects of Deregulation in the Market for Legal Services', 26 *Regional Studies* 137 (1992).

33. Frank Stephen, 'Advertising, Consumer Search Costs and Prices in a Professional Service Market', 26 *Applied Economics* 1177 (1994).

34. See Grant Devine, 'A Review of the Experimental Effects of Increased Price Information on the Performance of Canadian Retail Food Stores in the 1950s', 26 *Canadian Journal of Agricultural Economics* 24 (Glenview, IL and London: Scott Foresman, 1978); Grant Devine and Bruce Marion, 'The Influence of Consumer Price Information on Retail Pricing and Consumer Behaviour', 61 *American Journal of Agricultural Economics* 228 (1979). We have not been able to consult the original source. We report here the description of the method and result as it appears in Dennis Carlton and Jeffrey Perloff, *Modern Industrial Organization* 581–6 (1994).

35. *Id.*

36. A number of empirical studies in a variety of sectors (drugs, liquor, toys and gasoline) also show that price advertising decreases average market prices. See *id.* at 602–3.

37. See OECD, *supra* note 3, at 15. The OECD Roundtable includes a review of the literature on the subject made by the US Federal Trade Commission. This review 'found that, out of eleven comparative studies, six found the quality effect to be neutral or mixed, two found the restraints improved quality, and three found they actually decreased it'. *id.*

38. John Kwoka, 'Advertising and the Price and Quality of Optometric Services', 74 *American Economic Review* 211 (1984).

39. Data analysed by Kwoka, *id.*, also show a strong positive association between price and time-quality. The price of additional examination time is higher in advertising environments, even though total price is less. Practitioners in advertising markets are apparently more successful in differentiating their services, and in getting compensated accordingly. Conversely, restrictive markets cause a levelling of price despite the existence of quality diversity. This supports the view of advertising as a device to signal quality. Finally, the average price in advertising markets is lower than in restrictive markets, holding quality constant.

40. A wide empirical literature, based on the 'structure–conduct–performance' paradigm used by industrial economists in the 1970s, considers the link between advertising and concentration. Under this paradigm, advertising was seen as a barrier to entry. It held that in sectors with high advertising–sales ratios, a firm cannot enter unless it engages in costly advertising expenditures. This reasoning was, however, applied to consumer products rather than professional services. Further, the empirical results demonstrated little or no effect of advertising upon concentration ratios. Recent theory has clarified that advertising cannot be seen as an exogenous barrier to entry, as advertising outlays are an endogenous variable for firms. See

Sutton, *supra* note 17 (discussing the theoretical issues, an empirical analysis and presenting case studies conducted in the light of modern industrial organization theory).

41. Sherman Folland, 'Advertising by Physicians: Behaviour and Attitudes', 25 *Medical Care* 311 (1987).

42. John Rizzo and Richard Zeckhauser, 'Advertising and Entry: The Case of Physician Services', 98 *Journal of Political Economy* 476 (1990).

43. However, experienced physicians seem to benefit more, in terms of annual earnings, from advertising. Experienced physicians apparently refrain from advertising for reasons other than financial considerations. They are more likely to adhere to the traditional canons of the medical profession, which oppose advertising. Hence they resort less to advertising even though they would draw a large benefit from it.

44. For instance, some restrictions on tobacco advertising exist in all OECD countries, and at least six of them have a complete advertising ban. M. Stewart, 'The Effect on Tobacco Consumption of Advertising Bans in OECD Countries', 12 *International Journal of Advertising* 155 (1993).

45. Regarding the effects of advertising prohibitions on tobacco consumption, see, for example, Martyn Duffy, 'Advertising and the Inter-product Distribution of Demand: A Rotterdam Model Approach', 31 *European Economic Review* 1051 (1987); Badi Baltagi and Dan Levin, 'Estimating Dynamic Demand for Cigarettes Using Panel Data: The Effects of the Bootlegging, Taxation and Advertising Reconsidered', 6 *Review of Economics and Statistics* 148 (1986); Nehran Radfar, 'The Effect of Advertising on Total Consumption of Cigarettes in the UK', 20 *European Economic Review* 225 (1985); Jack Johnston, 'Advertising and the Aggregate Demand for Cigarettes: A Comment', 14 *European Economic Review* 117 (1980); Tony McGuinness and Keith Cowling, 'Advertising and the Aggregate Demand for Cigarettes', 6 *European Economic Review* 311 (1975), and 14 *European Economic Review* 127 (1975); James Hamilton, 'The Demand for Cigarettes: Advertising, the Health Scare and the Cigarette Advertising Ban', 54 *Review of Economics and Statistics* (1972). Regarding the effects of advertising prohibitions on alcohol consumption, see Jon Nelson and John Moran, 'Advertising and US Alcohol Beverage Demand: System-wide Estimates', 27 *Applied Economics* 1225 (1995); Jon Nelson and David Young, 'Advertising Bans, Alcohol Consumption and Alcohol Abuse: An International Comparison' (unpublished mimeo 1999).

46. Massimo Motta, 'Advertising Bans', Centre for Economic Policy Research (Discussion Paper no. 1613, 1997).

47. This distinction in the type of advertising is crucial. Informative advertising would certainly increase demand, as it either increases demand for given prices, or decreases price for given demand, which in turn would raise demand.

48. See James Hamilton, *supra* note 45.

49. However, raising taxes on harmful products beyond a certain threshold might have the effect of increasing smuggling from neighbouring countries rather than decreasing consumption. The experience of Canada and Sweden in recent years has been instructive, and calls for co-ordination of tax policies among neighbouring countries whenever possible.

50. See *Central Hudson Gas & Electric v. Public Service Commission of New York*, 447 US 557 (1980) and the discussion in Laudati (see Chapter 4 in this volume).

# 4. Reading Adam Smith into the First Amendment: the US Supreme Court doctrine of commercial speech

## Laraine L. Laudati

*This chapter discusses the evolution of the Supreme Court decisions under the commercial speech doctrine of the First Amendment of the US Constitution, scrutinizing regulations and provisions of professional codes that place limitations on advertising and solicitation of business, and largely addressing professionals.*

*The Supreme Court's rationale for granting protection to commercial speech was recognition of the important role played by the free flow of commercial information from seller to buyer in a free enterprise system. The Court deemed it very important that price, quality and availability of information should be freely obtainable, because this would help ensure that economic decisions are made in a sound, informed manner, which would aid competition and the optimal allocation of resources. Thus, the rationale for applying the First Amendment in this area is based on economic analysis.*

*Through the years, the Court has developed a four-part test for addressing cases involving advertising, particularly advertising by professionals: the activity that is the subject of the advertisement must be lawful, and the advertisement must not be misleading; a substantial state interest must be protected through the restraint on advertising; the regulation in question must directly advance the substantial state interest that has been identified; and there must be no less-restrictive means available.*

*The Supreme Court's four-part test differs in an important respect from the guidelines established in Australia for their regulatory review, and from the recommended legislation of the US National Commission to Review the Antitrust Laws. Unlike the other tests, the Supreme Court test requires that a nexus be established between the substantial state interest (the objective of the regulation at issue) and the means embodied in the regulation to advance that interest. This, combined with the final element that no less-restrictive means be available, provides a powerful tool for eliminating rules that impede the First Amendment's protection of commercial speech. In all commercial speech cases considered by the Court where an advertising ban is involved, the state has been unable to show that the ban directly advances the substantial state interest. It has reasoned that other, more effective ways exist to ensure that the public is protected against poor-quality professional services. For instance, licensing requirements and other types of qualifications are seen by the Supreme Court as the best way to achieve protection of the public. A modified version of the Supreme Court test, including this nexus requirement, might also be included in a guideline for the review of anticompetitive regulation.*

## INTRODUCTION

Commercial speech has been defined as speech that communicates only commercial information, proposes nothing more than a transaction, and relates solely to the economic interests of the speaker and its audience.[1] The United States Supreme Court has ruled that advertising,[2] solicitation of business,[3] and labelling of products[4] all constitute commercial speech, and as such has provided them with protection under the First Amendment of the United States Constitution since 1975.[5] The Court's rationale for affording First Amendment coverage to commercial speech was the need to protect the flow of information to the consumer making economic decisions in a free market economy. Thus, the Court recognized the important role that commercial speech has long played in the functioning of the free market system.

The law has evolved to ensure that state regulation that imposes limitations on commercial speech does not unnecessarily impede the provision of accurate information about the availability, price, quality and so on of goods and services to consumers. Over the nearly quarter century since commercial speech was first deemed protected, the Court has developed a framework for analysing the constitutionality of state regulation limiting the dissemination of commercial speech, which it has applied in a variety of factual settings. In these cases, diverse facets of the benefits and burdens of various regulations, and some of their anticompetitive effects, have been brought to light. Many of the cases have involved regulation of the professions.

The commercial speech jurisprudence is directly relevant to the present exercise of establishing a legal framework for analysis of the anticompetitive effects of regulation, and specifically of advertising restraints. Our focus in the Round Table on the Anticompetitive Impact of Regulation is basically the same as the Supreme Court's has been in its commercial speech decisions: we would like to ensure that regulation of advertising (and regulation in general), which is meant to advance a socially beneficial policy, does not impede the proper functioning of a free market economy any more than necessary.[6] Thus, the Court's jurisprudence can provide us guidance in the present exercise, especially in constructing a legal framework for analysis of the anticompetitive effects of regulation and for establishing appropriate legal presumptions and burdens of proof.

It is regrettable that no caselaw analysing the anticompetitive effects of government regulation directly under the antitrust laws is available in the United States. The reason for this gap is that in 1943, the Supreme Court established in *Parker v. Brown* that the federal antitrust laws are not applicable to regulations adopted by the states, because they constitute 'state actions'.[7] In *Parker*, the Court observed that under the dual system of government in the United States, the Constitution establishes that the states are sovereign 'save only as Congress may constitutionally subtract from their authority, [and] an unexpressed purpose to nullify a state's control over its officers and agents is not lightly to be attributed to Congress'. The Sherman Act, however, makes no mention of the state as such, and nothing in the Act or its legislative history would support a purpose to restrain a state or its officers or agents from activities directed by its legislature.[8]

The remainder of this chapter is organized as follows. Section A sets forth in greater detail the notion of commercial speech, distinguishing it from other speech protected under the First Amendment, and explaining how the First Amendment has placed limits on the power of the states to enact laws and regulations that restrict commercial speech. It also addresses the nature of the interest protected under the commercial speech doctrine, which provides the basis for establishing its relevance to a competition analysis of state regulation. Section B sets forth the four-part test established by the Supreme Court in *Central Hudson Gas & Electric v. Public Service Commission of N.Y.*[9] to analyse the constitutionality of restraints on commercial speech. It also evaluates the difference in treatment of the two main categories of restriction on commercial speech: blanket bans and 'time, place, and manner' restrictions. Section C discusses the Court's special considerations when commercial speech restraints involve the professions. Section D compares the *Central Hudson* test to review standards designed to eliminate the anticompetitive effects of regulation that have been developed in two other fora. Finally, Section E derives the lessons to be learned from the commercial speech jurisprudence that are useful in establishing a legal framework for analysing the anticompetitive effects of regulations of various types controlling private businesses and the professions.

## A.   THE FIRST AMENDMENT AND COMMERCIAL SPEECH: THE NATURE OF THE INTEREST PROTECTED

The First Amendment of the US Constitution provides that 'Congress shall make no law ... abridging the freedom of speech, or of the press'.[10] The freedom of speech is constitutionally protected because it is a fundamental democratic principle. Although the Supreme Court has interpreted the First Amendment to protect commercial speech, it has consistently recognized a 'common sense distinction' between such speech, which occurs in an area traditionally subject to government regulation, and other varieties of protected speech.[11] The greater 'hardiness' of commercial speech, which is inspired by the profit motive, likely diminishes the chilling effect that may attend its regulation.[12] Commercial speech has been afforded a lower level of protection under the First Amendment than other constitutionally guaranteed expression. However, the state retains less regulatory authority in cases where a restriction on commercial speech strikes at the substance of the information communicated rather than the commercial aspect of the speech, such as by depriving citizens of information in order to influence their behaviour.[13] Thus, in such cases, the stricter standard of review used in non-commercial speech First Amendment cases applies.[14]

The Court's basis for affording First Amendment protection to commercial speech is the important informational function such speech has in a free market economy. It serves not only the economic interests of the speaker, but also those of the consumer and society in general as it informs the public of the availability, nature and prices of products and services. Accordingly, it promotes informed economic decision making and thereby performs an indispensable role in the efficient allocation of resources in a free market system.[15]

The Supreme Court elaborated the importance of this function in *Virginia Pharmacy Board v. Virginia Consumer Council*.[16] There, a state law declared that a pharmacist was guilty of 'unprofessional conduct' and subject to professional discipline if he/she advertised prescription drug prices. The pharmacist in question desired to advertise: 'I will sell you the X prescription drug at the Y price'. The plaintiffs, a consumer group and a consumer, claimed that the First Amendment entitled them, as users of prescription drugs, to receive price and other information that pharmacists wished to communicate through advertisements. The Court recognized the significance of the consumer's concern for the free flow of information:

> [T]hat interest may be as keen, if not keener by far, than [the consumer's] interest in the day's most urgent political debate. ... Those whom the suppression of prescription drug price information hits the hardest are the poor, the sick, and particularly the aged. A disproportionate amount of their income tends to be spent on prescription drugs; yet they are the least able to learn, by shopping from pharmacist to pharmacist, where their scarce dollars are best spent. When drug prices vary as strikingly as they do, information as to who is charging what becomes more than a convenience. It could mean the alleviation of physical pain or the enjoyment of basic necessities.[17]

The Court also identified the 'significant societal interests' that are served by commercial speech:

Advertising, however tasteless and excessive it sometimes may seem, is nonetheless dissemination of information as to who is producing and selling what product, for what reason, and at what price. So long as we preserve a predominantly free enterprise economy, the allocation of our resources in large measure will be made through numerous private economic decisions. It is a matter of public interest that those decisions, in the aggregate, be intelligent and well informed. To this end, the free flow of commercial information is indispensable. And if it is indispensable to the proper allocation of resources in a free enterprise system, it is also indispensable to the formation of intelligent opinions as to how that system ought to be regulated or altered. Therefore, even if the First Amendment were thought to be primarily an instrument to enlighten public decision-making in a democracy, we could not say that the free flow of [commercial] information does not serve that goal.[18]

The Court reiterated these thoughts about the economic significance of commercial speech in various subsequent decisions.[19]

Thus, the Court has repeatedly made clear that First Amendment protection of commercial speech is motivated by the objective to protect the flow of information regarding the availability, price, quality and so on from seller to buyer. This will ensure that economic decisions are made in an informed manner, thereby aiding competition, the proper functioning of the free market system and an optimal allocation of resources. The motivation for protecting commercial speech is therefore similar to the underlying policy objective of the antitrust laws. For this reason, the Supreme Court's commercial speech decisions are relevant to the present exercise of deriving a framework for analysing regulation to eliminate its anticompetitive effects.

## B. THE *CENTRAL HUDSON GAS & ELECTRIC* FOUR-PART TEST

Under the First Amendment, the interest of society, the consumer, and the seller of a product or service in the free flow of commercial information is not absolute. Rather, that interest must be balanced against the state's interest in protecting consumers from commercial harms. Thus, the degree of protection available for commercial speech depends on the nature of the expression and of the government interests advanced by the regulation that inhibits such speech.[20] 'The entire commercial speech doctrine ... represents an accommodation between the right to speak and hear expression about goods and services and the right of government to regulate the sales of such goods and services'.[21]

After several years of decisions in commercial speech cases, the Court developed a four-part test in *Central Hudson Gas & Electric v. Public Service Commission of N.Y.* for determining whether a given restraint on such speech violates the First Amendment:

At the outset, we must determine whether the expression is protected by the First Amendment. For commercial speech to come within that provision, it at least must concern lawful activity and not be misleading. Next, we ask whether the asserted governmental interest is substantial. If both inquiries yield positive answers, we must determine whether the regulation directly advances the governmental interest asserted, and whether it is not more extensive than is necessary to serve that interest.[22]

Each of these criteria is discussed in further detail below. Discussion of these criteria as they have been applied in cases involving regulation of the professions appears in Section C below.

### Not False or Misleading

Since First Amendment protection of commercial speech is based on the informational function of advertising, that protection extends only to commercial messages that accurately inform the public about lawful activity. Accordingly, the state is free to ban forms of communication more likely to deceive the public than to inform it, such as false and misleading advertising, or commercial speech related to illegal activities.[23]

### Substantial State Interest

The state must prove that it has a 'substantial interest' to be achieved by any regulation that restricts commercial speech. This requires an analysis of the strength of the government's interest in restricting speech.[24] The interest proffered by the state for purposes of the matter before the Court need not be the same as the original interest of the state at the time the legislation was enacted. Rather, the insufficiency of the original motivation for enacting a law does not diminish other more current and more relevant motivations.[25]

The Court has recognized a substantial state interest in a variety of circumstances, often providing scant reasoning for why the interest was deemed substantial, or accepting the judgment of a state legislature without further examination. For instance, with respect to regulation of the health, safety and welfare of citizens, the following were deemed substantial state interests: reducing the demand for gambling;[26] reducing the consumption of alcoholic beverages,[27] preventing brewers from competing on the basis of alcohol strength (which could lead to greater alcoholism and its attendant social costs);[28] aiding parents' efforts to discuss birth control with their children.[29] With respect to the regulation of a public utility, energy conservation[30] and a concern that fair and efficient rates are charged[31] were deemed to constitute substantial state interests. In contrast, the Court held that shielding recipients of mail from printed advertisements they are likely to find offensive does not constitute a substantial state interest, as recipients of objectionable mailings could avoid them 'simply by averting their eyes'.[32]

## Restriction Directly and Materially Advances a State's Interest

The third element of the *Central Hudson* test is that the regulation in question must directly and materially advance the substantial state interest. The Court views this element to be critical, otherwise 'a State could with ease restrict commercial speech in the service of other objectives that could not themselves justify a burden on commercial expression'.[33]

The burden of proof is on the state to establish that the link between its interest and the contested regulation is present. The state cannot satisfy this burden by 'mere speculation and conjecture; rather, a governmental body seeking to sustain a restriction on competition must demonstrate that the harms it recites are real and that its restriction will in fact alleviate them to a material degree'.[34] The connection between the regulation and the interest concerned must be direct and material, not speculative or tenuous. 'Conditional and remote eventualities' are not sufficient.[35]

If the state satisfies this burden, the burden shifts to the party asserting rights under the First Amendment to refute the state's showing, which requires more than conclusory assertions that the rule lacks a factual basis.[36]

Two major categories of regulations imposing restraints on commercial speech have been recognized by the Court: blanket bans and time, place and manner restrictions (including disclosure requirements). In *44 Liquormart, Inc. v. Rhode Island*, the Court summarized the standard of review to be applied to the two categories:

> When a state regulates commercial messages to protect consumers from misleading, deceptive, or aggressive sales practices, or requires the disclosure of beneficial consumer information, the purpose of its regulation is consistent with the reasons for according constitutional protection to commercial speech and therefore justifies less than strict review. However when a State entirely prohibits the dissemination of truthful, nonmisleading commercial messages for reasons unrelated to the preservation of a fair bargaining process, there is far less reason to depart from the rigorous review that the First Amendment generally demands.[37]

### Blanket bans

Blanket bans on commercial speech are prophylactic rules that entirely prevent the speech from being uttered. They constitute the most restrictive form of regulation of commercial speech, and the most threatening form from the standpoint of the First Amendment, as they 'all but foreclose alternative means of disseminating certain information'.[38] Such rules are generally based on the assumption that the state can protect the public by keeping it in ignorance, because the public will respond irrationally to the truth.[39]

Blanket bans are often designed to serve an underlying government purpose unrelated to consumer protection. The Court has stated that 'special care' should attend the review of blanket bans designed to pursue non-speech related policy, or state interests that do not relate to consumer transactions.[40] In such cases, blanket bans could screen the underlying government policy from public view and should be subject to the more rigorous review applied under the First Amendment in non-commercial speech cases.[41] Thus, the mere fact that a message proposes a commercial transaction does not dictate that the more limited level of constitutional protection afforded commercial speech should apply.[42]

The Court's reasoning was not always clear with respect to what the state must show to satisfy its burden that a blanket ban directly and materially advances a substantial state interest, but it has evolved over time to a very strict requirement. In its earlier decisions, no clear requirements were specified. For instance, in *Central Hudson*, decided in 1980, the Court upheld the advertising ban simply asserting that 'the State's interest in energy conservation is directly advanced' by the ban on promotional advertising because 'there is an immediate connection between advertising and demand for electricity' and 'Central Hudson would not contest the advertising ban unless it believed that promotion would increase its sales'.[43] It did not, however, point to any record evidence that caused it to draw these conclusions. In contrast, in *Bolger v. Youngs Drugs Products Corp.*,[44] decided in 1983, it struck down the federal government's blanket ban on mailing of unsolicited advertisements for contraceptives, on the ground that the ban provided only a 'marginal degree of protection' to aid parents' efforts to discuss birth control with their children. It reasoned: '[w]e can reasonably assume that parents already exercise substantial control over the disposition of mail once it enters their mailboxes', and 'parents must already cope with the multitude of external stimuli that color their children's perception of sensitive subjects'.[45]

A very permissive approach based on speculation about the legislature's reasoning for enacting a rule was again taken by the Court in its 1986 decision in *Posadas de Puerto Rico Assoc. v. Tourism Co.*[46] There, it upheld a blanket ban on advertising of casino gambling, reasoning that a direct and material link had been established between the ban and the state's interest in limiting gambling on the tenuous ground that the 'Puerto Rico Legislature obviously believed, when it enacted the advertising restrictions at issue here, that advertising of casino gambling aimed at the residents of Puerto Rico would serve to increase the demand for the product advertised', which it found to be a 'reasonable' belief, and that this would hurt the state's interest in limiting gambling.[47] The Court rejected appellee's argument that a direct and material link had not been established because the legislature had not barred advertising of other types of gambling, such as horse racing, cockfighting and the lottery. The Court reasoned that the legislature felt that the risks associated with casino gambling were significantly greater than those for the other forms of gambling. The Court overruled its *Posadas* decision, and adopted a stricter approach with respect to the direct and material link requirement, in its 1996 decision in *44 Liquormart, Inc. v. Rhode Island*.[48] There, a state regulation banned the advertisement of retail prices of alcoholic beverages, for the purpose of promoting 'temperance'. The Court ruled that the state's burden of establishing a material link between the regulation and promotion of temperance was 'particularly great given the drastic nature of its chosen means – the wholesale suppression of truthful, non-misleading information'. It then established an elevated burden: that the state would have to show that the price advertising ban would *significantly* reduce alcohol consumption. Finding that the state had presented no evidence to this effect, the Court invalidated the regulation.[49]

The Court has also adopted a stricter approach with respect to another aspect of direct and material link requirement in *Rubin v. Coors Brewing Co*.[50] There, it focused on the regulatory context of the blanket ban, and whether the ban was part of an irrational and inconsistent regulatory scheme. In *Rubin*, the Court ruled that the overall irrationality of the government's regulatory scheme was ground for concluding that the regulation in question could not directly and materially advance the asserted interest. There, the challenged regulation prohibited the disclosure of alcoholic content of beer on labels (unless required by state law), and the interest asserted by the state was to suppress the threat of 'strength wars' among brewers, which would lead to greater alcoholism and attendant social costs. The scheme was deemed irrational because (i) although the regulation prohibited disclosure of alcoholic content of beer on *labels* unless required by state law, federal regulations applied a contrary policy to beer *advertising* (which the court viewed as a more influential weapon in any strength war), prohibiting disclosure of alcoholic content only in states that affirmatively prohibit such advertising; (ii) federal regulations allowed the disclosure of alcoholic content on the labels of distilled spirits, and required it for wines with more than 14 per cent alcohol; and (iii) federal regulations permitted brewers to signal high alcohol content through use of the term 'malt liquor'. The Court held:

> To be sure, the Government's interest in combating strength wars remains a valid goal. But the irrationality of this unique and puzzling regulatory framework ensures that the labeling ban will fail to achieve that end. There is little chance that [the contested regulation] can directly and materially advance its aim, while other provisions of the same act directly undermine and counteract its effects.[51]

Thus, the 1995 holding of the *Rubin* Court requiring an overall rationality and consistency of the regulatory scheme differs considerably from the *Posadas* Court's allowance of a blanket ban of one type of gambling, in an overall regulatory context where advertising of other forms of gambling was still permitted.

## Time, place and manner restrictions

As stated above, for commercial speech to come within the protection of the First Amendment, it must concern lawful activity and not be misleading. Accordingly, '[w]hen a state regulates commercial messages to protect consumers from misleading, deceptive, or aggressive sales practices, or requires the disclosure of beneficial consumer information, the purpose of its regulation is consistent with the reasons for according constitutional protection to commercial speech and therefore justifies less than strict review'.[52] The Court has been far less demanding on the state to meet its burden to establish a direct and material link when a time, place or manner restriction, rather than a blanket ban, is at issue.

Since the main cases where time, place and manner restrictions were considered involve the legal profession, they will be discussed in Section C below.

## Restriction Narrowly Drawn

The fourth element of the four-part test requires that the regulation at issue is not more extensive than it needs to be to advance the state's substantial interest. In *Central Hudson*, conservation was the state interest that the Court had deemed substantial. The Court questioned 'whether the Commission's complete suppression of speech ordinarily protected by the First Amendment is no more extensive than necessary to further the State's interest in energy conservation'.[53] In rejecting the arguments of the state on this element and invalidating the regulation, the Court stated:

> The Commission's order reaches all promotional advertising, regardless of the impact of the touted service on overall energy use. But the energy conservation rationale, as important as it is, cannot justify suppressing information about electric devices or services that would cause no net increase in total energy use. In addition, no showing has been made that a more limited restriction on the content of promotional advertising would not adequately serve the state's interest.

\* \* \*

> The Commission also has not demonstrated that its interest in conservation cannot be protected adequately by more limited regulation of appellant's commercial expression.

... In the absence of a showing that more limited speech regulation would be ineffective, we cannot approve the complete suppression of Central Hudson's advertising.[54]

Accordingly, *Central Hudson* appears to require the state to show (i) that the regulation in question is not more extensive that it needs to be, and (ii) that a more limited restriction would be ineffective. In a subsequent decision, the Court elaborated upon the showing required:

> What our decisions require is a 'fit' between the legislature's ends and the means chosen to accomplish those ends, a fit that is not necessarily perfect, but reasonable; that represents not necessarily the single best disposition but one whose scope is 'in proportion to the interest served,' that employs not necessarily the least restrictive means but ... a means narrowly tailored to achieve the desired objective.[55]

Most cases in which the Court has found against the state on this element involved blanket bans because they are generally a more extensive speech restriction than necessary to accomplish the state's legitimate regulatory objective. For instance, in *44 Liquormart*, the Court concluded that rather than banning advertising on liquor prices, the state could advance its interest in promoting temperance by direct regulation of prices, increased taxation, limitations on per capita purchases, or educational campaigns focused on the problems of excessive, or moderate, drinking.[56] Similarly, in *Rubin v. Coors Brewing Co.*, the Court agreed with Coors' argument that several alternatives, such as directly limiting the alcohol content of beers, prohibiting marketing efforts emphasizing high alcohol strength, or limiting the labelling ban only to malt liquors (the segment of the market threatened with strength wars), would all be less intrusive of its First Amendment rights than the ban on disclosure of alcohol content on beer labels.[57]

## C.   SPECIAL CONSIDERATIONS FOR RESTRICTIONS ON THE COMMERCIAL SPEECH OF PROFESSIONALS

The majority of cases where the constitutionality of restrictions on commercial speech has been challenged involved regulation of professionals, including lawyers, pharmacists, physicians and certified public accountants. The provisions of professional codes, generally administered by professional associations under the authority of the states, placing limitations on advertising and solicitation of clients have thereby been subjected to First Amendment scrutiny. Since the earliest commercial speech decisions, the Court has recognized that special considerations might apply in such cases because professionals, particularly lawyers and physicians, are engaged in providing services in which professional judgement is a large component. This gives rise to a greater state interest in regulating the professions as compared with business in general, which does not involve the dispensation of professional judgement.[58] The Court has also indicated that differences among professions might bring different constitutional considerations into play, and that the state may have a stronger interest in regulating some professions than others.[59]

This section will discuss special considerations for cases involving the professions with respect to each of the four *Central Hudson* criteria.

### Not False or Misleading

In the light of the information gap between professionals and consumers of professional services, the Court has been especially concerned that commercial speech of professionals can be false or misleading. For instance, physicians and lawyers do not dispense standardized products; rather, they render professional services of almost infinite variety and nature. Consequently, the possibility of confusion and deception from certain types of commercial speech is greater.[60] Concern over the potential to mislead has been addressed by the court in several cases involving advertising and solicitation of clients.

#### Advertising

The Court has ruled that banning advertising by attorneys outright is a violation of the First Amendment. It has, however, acknowledged the danger that lawyer advertising could be misleading in some circumstances, which should be addressed by imposing limitations on what services a lawyer can advertise, and by requiring that certain disclosures be made in advertisements.

*Bates v. State Bar of Arizona*[61] was the seminal decision in which the Court ruled that lawyer advertising could not constitutionally be banned. In attempting to justify its advertising ban, the state bar association had argued, among other things, that advertising by lawyers would be inherently misleading for several reasons. First, such services are highly individualized with regard to content and quality and therefore not capable of informed comparison on the basis of an advertisement. Second, the consumer of legal services is unable to determine in advance what services he/she will need. Third, lawyer advertising would highlight irrelevant factors and fail to demonstrate the relevant factor of skill. The Court rejected these arguments, holding that advertising by attorneys would not be inevitably misleading because of an inherent lack of standardization in legal services. Routine legal services, such as uncontested divorces, simple adoptions, uncontested personal bankruptcies, and name changes, are the only ones that lend themselves to advertising. These were precisely the services that appellants had advertised. If the state bar was concerned that the exact services included in the package would not be clear, it could define the services that must be included. Moreover, even though the precise services required in each case might vary slightly, this does not make the advertisement inherently misleading, as long as the attorney does the necessary work at the advertised price. The Court acknowledged that advertising would not provide a complete foundation for selecting an attorney, but reasoned that it would make little sense to deny the consumer at least some of the relevant information needed to make an informed decision on the ground that the information was incomplete. The preferred remedy would be more, rather than less, disclosure to correct an inaccurate picture. In dictum, the Court indicated that advertisements by lawyers that contain claims as to the quality of legal services would raise serious difficulties, as such claims are probably not susceptible to precise measurement or verification, and under some circumstances, might be deceptive, misleading, or false.[62]

In *Zauderer v. Office of Disciplinary Council*,[63] an attorney had advertised, among other things, his availability to represent clients in cases alleging injury from use of the Dalkon Shield intrauterine device. The advertisement contained an illustration of the device and stated that this device had generated a large number of lawsuits, that readers should not assume that their claims for personal injury from use of this device were time-barred, and that appellant was handling such cases on a contingent fee basis, such that 'if there is no recovery, no legal fees are owed by our clients'. The state disciplined appellant on the ground that the advertisement violated its prophylactic rules against self-recommendation and accepting employment resulting from unsolicited legal advice. In attempting to justify application of the rule to this advertisement, the state claimed that absent the rule, it would have great difficulties in distinguishing deceptive from non-deceptive legal advice in advertisements. The Court disagreed, holding that the problem of distinguishing deceptive from non-deceptive advertisements containing legal advice was no different from, and no more complex than, doing so with respect to advertisements for other goods and services. Moreover, it found the appellant's statements regarding Dalkon Shield litigation were easily verifiable and accurate, stating:

> Were we to accept the State's argument in this case, we would have little basis for preventing the government from suppressing other forms of truthful and nondeceptive advertising simply to spare itself the trouble of distinguishing such advertising from false or deceptive advertising. The First Amendment protections afforded commercial speech would mean little indeed if such arguments were allowed to prevail. Our recent decisions involving commercial speech have been grounded in the faith that the free flow of commercial information is valuable enough to justify imposing on would-be regulators the costs of distinguishing the truthful from the false, the helpful from the misleading, and the harmless from the harmful. ... An attorney may not be disciplined for soliciting legal business through printed advertising containing truthful and nondeceptive information and advice regarding the legal rights of potential clients.[64]

As to the rule banning the use of illustrations in advertising, the Court rejected the state's 'unsupported assertions' that the use of illustrations would be deceptive, and that such deception would be especially difficult to police. The Court held:

> We are not persuaded that identifying deceptive or manipulative uses of visual media in advertising is so intrinsically burden-some that the State is entitled to forgo that task in favor of the more convenient but far more restrictive alternative of a blanket ban on the use of illustrations. ... Given the possibility of policing the use of illustrations in advertisements on a case-by-case basis, the prophylactic approach taken by Ohio cannot stand; hence, appellant may not be disciplined for his use of an accurate and non-deceptive illustration.[65]

In contrast, the statement in the advertisement that appellant was willing to represent clients in Dalkon Shield personal injury cases on a contingent fee basis, and that '[i]f there is no recovery, no legal fees are owed by our clients', but failing to disclose that clients may be liable for significant litigation costs even if their lawsuits were unsuccessful, was held to be deceptive:

> The advertisement makes no mention of the distinction between 'legal fees' and 'costs,' and to a layman not aware of the meaning of these terms of art, the advertisement would suggest that employing appellant would be a no-lose proposition in that his representation in a losing case would come entirely free of charge. The assumption that substantial numbers of potential clients would be so misled is hardly a speculative one: it is a commonplace that members of the public are often unaware of the technical meanings of such terms as 'fees' and 'costs' – terms that, in ordinary usage, might well be virtually interchangeable. When the possibility of deception is as self-evident as it is in this case, we need not require the State to 'conduct a survey of the ... public before it [may] determine that the [advertisement] had a tendency to mislead'. The State's position that it is deceptive to employ advertising that refers to contingent-fee arrangements without mentioning the client's liability for costs is reasonable enough to support a requirement that information regarding the client's liability for costs be disclosed.[66]

The Court noted the significant differences between blanket bans and disclosure requirements:

> In requiring attorneys who advertise their willingness to represent clients on a contingent-fee basis to state that the client may have to bear certain expenses even if he loses, Ohio has not attempted to prevent attorneys from conveying information to the public; it has only required them to provide somewhat more information than they might otherwise be inclined to present. ... The State has attempted only to prescribe what shall be orthodox in commercial advertising, and its prescription has taken the form of a requirement that appellant include in his advertising purely factual and uncontroversial information about the terms under which his services will be available. Because the extension of First Amendment protection to commercial speech is justified principally by the value to consumers of the information such speech

provides, appellant's constitutionally protected interest in not providing any particular factual information in his advertising is minimal. Thus, in virtually all our commercial speech decisions to date, we have emphasized that because disclosure requirements trench much more narrowly on an advertiser's interests than do flat prohibitions on speech, 'warning[s] or disclaimer[s] might be appropriately required ... in order to dissipate the possibility of consumer confusion or deception.'[67]

## Solicitation

Two Supreme Court decisions have addressed the dangers that commercial speech by professionals in the form of in-person solicitation of clients could be misleading. One of the cases involved a ban on in-person solicitations by lawyers, and the other, by certified public accountants. In the former, the Court ruled that the dangers of overreaching and undue influence justified the ban; in the latter, it ruled that they did not.

The case concerning lawyers was *Ohralik v. Ohio State Bar Association*.[68] There, appellant, an attorney, had engaged in in-person solicitation of two clients in the immediate aftermath of a car accident, in violation of a disciplinary rule of the state bar association banning such solicitations. In upholding the disciplinary rule, the Court acknowledged that in-person solicitation by a lawyer, 'a professional trained in the art of persuasion', of 'an unsophisticated, injured, or distressed lay person' is rife with possibilities of overreaching, invasion of privacy, exercise of undue influence, and outright fraud. 'The aim and effect of in-person solicitation may be to provide a one-sided presentation and to encourage speedy and perhaps uninformed decision-making; there is no opportunity for intervention or counter-education by agencies of the Bar, supervisory authorities, or persons close to the solicited individual'. The lay person 'may place his trust in a lawyer, regardless of the latter's qualifications or the individual's actual need for legal representation, simply in response to persuasion under circumstances conducive to uninformed acquiescence', and the plight of the person 'makes him more vulnerable to influence' and makes 'the advice all the more intrusive'.[69] The Court distinguished lawyer advertising from in-person solicitation, observing that the latter is not visible or otherwise open to public scrutiny. This renders it difficult or impossible to ascertain what occurred, especially if the solicitation is of a distressed lay person.

In contrast, the Court invalidated the state Board of Accountancy's rule banning direct, in-person solicitation of clients by accountants in *Edenfield v. Fane*.[70] There, the Court held that CPA (Certified Public Accountant) solicitations in a business context are not inherently conducive to overreaching and other forms of misconduct.[71] Unlike lawyers, accountants are not trained in the art of persuasion and advocacy, but in a way that emphasizes independence and objectivity. Moreover, unlike the unsophisticated prospective client of the lawyer, the typical prospective client of the CPA is a sophisticated and experienced business executive who has an existing professional relationship with a CPA, who selects the time and place for the meeting, and who has no expectation and exerts no pressure to be retained on the spot. Thus, the dangers of overreaching, misrepresentation and fraud that the Court found present in *Ohralik* were not present in *Edenfield*.

The two decisions make clear that a determination of whether commercial speech in the form of in-person solicitation by professionals can subject potential clients to a danger of overreaching or possible fraud depends on the type of professional making the solicitation, the type of client likely to be solicited, and the circumstances underlying the solicitation.

## Substantial State Interest

In cases involving the professions, the Court has generally recognized that the state has a substantial interest in the maintenance of professionalism in order to protect consumers. It has ruled:

> States have a compelling interest in the practice of professions within their boundaries, and ... as part of their power to protect the public health, safety, and other valid interests they have broad power to establish standards for licensing practitioners and regulating the practice of professions.[72]

Moreover, the Court has recognized the greater interest of the state in regulating the professions than other types of business because the former involve the dispensation of professional judgement. Accordingly, states have broad powers to establish standards for licensing practitioners and to regulate the practice of the professions, thereby protecting consumers of professional services from various potential abuses by professionals.

### Advertising cases

A state interest in maintaining professionalism was recognized in some way in all cases where a blanket ban on advertising by professionals was at issue. Some of these cases were decided before the *Central Hudson* four-part test was established, and therefore do not directly address state interest as a separate criterion. For example, in *Bates v. State Bar of Arizona*, the Court did not specify a substantial state interest, but it 'recognized' and 'commended' the 'spirit of public service with which the profession of law is practiced and to which it is dedicated'.[73] In *Virginia Pharmacy Board*, the state interest in maintaining a high degree of professionalism of licensed pharmacists was deemed substantial.[74] Indeed, there the Court acknowledged that the state had a very broad interest in regulating pharmacists, based on its concern for maintaining professionalism: 'Virginia is free to require whatever professional standards it wishes of its pharmacists; it may subsidize them or protect them from competition in other ways'.[75]

In *Zauderer v. Office of Disciplinary Council*,[76] the state had maintained that its prophylactic rules against the use of illustrations in advertisements by lawyers was justified by its interest in preserving the 'dignity' of attorneys. The Court rejected this as an interest substantial enough, and held that determining when an illustration would be undignified was too subjective to abridge the appellant's First Amendment rights. Moreover, it was not persuaded that undignified behaviour was likely to recur frequently enough to justify a prophylactic rule.

### Solicitation cases

In *Ohralik*, the Court recognized a substantial state interest in the maintenance of standards among members of the licensed professions, and especially lawyers since they are essential to the primary governmental function of administering justice and have historically been viewed as officers of the courts. Accordingly, the state had a substantial interest in protecting consumers, regulating commercial transactions, and shielding individuals from harmful in-person solicitation by lawyers whom it has licensed.[77] In *Edenfield*, the state interest of controlling various aspects of the professionalism of certified public accountants, including maintaining their independence, protecting consumers from fraud or overreaching, and ensuring against conflicts of interest, was judged substantial.[78]

Another case involving solicitation of clients by lawyers also identified the substantial state interest as the maintenance of professionalism. In *Florida Bar v. Went For It, Inc.*, a disciplinary rule barred attorneys for a period of 30 days following the occurrence of an accident from singling out accident victims or their families in order to solicit their business. The state's interest in protecting the privacy and tranquillity of personal injury victims and their loved ones against intrusive, unsolicited direct mail contact by lawyers in the wake of accidents was deemed substantial.[79]

### Restriction Directly and Materially Advances a State's Interest

Although the Court has repeatedly recognized a substantial state interest in maintaining professionalism, states have had great difficulties in establishing a direct and material link between that interest and a commercial speech restraint. As in the cases involving the regulation of business, the Court has been especially reluctant to find a direct and material link when the restraint was a blanket ban on commercial speech of professionals. The decisions make clear that the Court's reluctance to accept the state's arguments on this criterion relates to its suspicion that the organized professions have used professional rules as a vehicle to shield themselves from competition.

**Advertising cases**

The state was unable to satisfy its burden to establish a direct and material link in any of the cases involving a ban on advertising by professionals. In *Virginia Pharmacy Board*, the state claimed that its interest in maintaining the professionalism of pharmacists was advanced by a statute that banned them from advertising prescription drug prices. In support of the rule, the state Pharmacy Board argued that advertising would create price competition that might cause the pharmacist to economize at the customer's expense, reducing or eliminating the truly professional portions of his/her services. Customers would price-shop, thereby undermining the pharmacist's effort to monitor the drug use of a regular customer to ensure that the drug would not provoke an allergic reaction or be incompatible with another medicine that the customer was taking. The Board also argued that advertising would reduce the professional image of the pharmacist as a skilled and specialized craftsman, which attracted talent to the profession and reinforced the good habits of its members.

The Court invalidated the rule, concluding that no direct link between the statute and maintaining professionalism had been established:

> [O]n close inspection it is seen that the State's protectiveness of its citizens rests in large measure on the advantages of being kept in ignorance. The advertising ban does not directly affect professional standards one way or the other. It affects them only through the reactions it is assumed people will have to the free flow of drug price information. There is no claim that the advertising ban in any way prevents the cutting of corners by the pharmacist who is so inclined. That pharmacist is likely to cut corners in any event. The only effect the advertising ban has on him is to insulate him from price competition and to open the way for him to make a substantial, and perhaps excessive, profit in addition to providing inferior service. The more painstaking pharmacist is also protected but, again, it is a protection based in large part on public ignorance.[80]

In *Bates v. State Bar of Arizona*, the Court rejected various claims by the state that the advertising ban advanced its interest in professionalism: that advertising would impede the sense of pride that the legal profession generates, bring about commercialization, and undermine the attorney's 'sense of dignity and self-worth'; that the hustle of the marketplace would adversely affect the profession's service orientation; and that advertising would erode the client's sense of trust in his/her attorney. It held:

> [W]e find the postulated connection between advertising and the erosion of true professionalism to be severely strained. At its core, the argument presumes that attorneys must conceal from themselves and from their clients the real-life fact that lawyers earn their livelihood at the bar. We suspect that few attorneys engage in such self-deception. And rare is the client, moreover, even one of modest means, who enlists the aid of an attorney with the expectation that his services will be rendered free of charge. In fact, the American Bar Association advises that an attorney should reach

'a clear agreement with his client as to the basis of the fee charges to be made,' and that this is to be done '[a]s soon as feasible after a lawyer has been employed.' If the commercial basis of the relationship is to be promptly disclosed on ethical grounds, once the client is in the office, it seems inconsistent to condemn the candid revelation of the same information before he arrives in the office.

Moreover, the assertion that advertising will diminish the attorney's reputation in the community is open to question. Bankers and engineers advertise, and yet these professions are not regarded as undignified. In fact, it has been suggested that the failure of lawyers to advertise creates public disillusionment with the profession. The absence of advertising may be seen to reflect the profession's failure to reach out and serve the community: Studies reveal that many persons do not obtain counsel even when they perceive a need because of the feared price of services or because of an inability to locate a competent attorney. Indeed, cynicism with regard to the profession may be created by the fact that it long has publicly eschewed advertising, while condoning the actions of the attorney who structures his social or civic associations so as to provide contacts with potential clients.

It appears that the ban on advertising originated as a rule of etiquette and not as a rule of ethics. Early lawyers in Great Britain viewed the law as a form of public service, rather than as a means of earning a living, and they looked down on 'trade' as unseemly. Eventually, the attitude toward advertising fostered by this view evolved into an aspect of the ethics of the profession. But habit and tradition are not in themselves an adequate answer to a constitutional challenge. In this day, we do not belittle the person who earns his living by the strength of his arm or the force of his mind. Since the belief that lawyers are somehow 'above' trade has become an anachronism, the historical foundation for the advertising restraint has crumbled.[81]

Two other claims by the state in its effort to establish a direct and material link in *Bates* could also be said to relate to the interest in maintaining professionalism. First, lawyer advertising would 'stir up litigation', causing harm to the administration of justice. The Court rejected the notion that the administration of justice is necessarily harmed by use of the judicial machinery:

Advertising is said to have the undesirable effect of stirring up litigation. The judicial machinery is designed to serve those who feel sufficiently aggrieved to bring forward their claims. Advertising, it is argued serves to encourage the assertion of legal rights in the courts, thereby undesirably unsettling societal repose. There is even a suggestion of barratry ...

But advertising by attorneys is not an unmitigated source of harm to the administration of justice. It may offer great benefits. Although advertising might increase the use of the judicial machinery, we cannot accept the notion that it is always better for a person to suffer a wrong silently than to redress it by legal action.

Second, the state claimed that lawyer advertising would increase overhead costs of the profession, which would be passed on to the consumer, thereby creating entry barriers and entrenching the position of the bar's established members. This, too, was rejected:

The ban on advertising serves to increase the difficulty of discovering the lowest cost seller of acceptable ability. As a result, to this extent attorneys are isolated from competition, and the incentive to price competitively is reduced. Although it is true that the effect of advertising on the price of services has not been demonstrated, there is revealing evidence with regard to products; where consumers have the benefit of price advertising, retail prices often are dramatically lower than they would be without advertising. It is entirely possible that advertising will serve to reduce, not advance, the cost of legal services to the consumer.

The entry-barrier argument is equally unpersuasive. In the absence of advertising, an attorney must rely on his contacts with the community to generate a flow of business. In view of the time necessary to develop such contacts, the ban in fact serves to perpetuate the market position of established attorneys. Consideration of entry-barrier problems would urge that advertising be allowed so as to aid the new competitor in penetrating the market.[82]

Finally, in *Zauderer*, the Court ruled that no direct and material link had been established between maintaining professionalism and a rule against accepting employment resulting from unsolicited legal advice as applied to the appellant's print advertisement concerning the Dalkon Shield (described above). The Court observed that the print advertisements at issue there were not on equal footing with in-person solicitations at issue in *Ohralik* (discussed below):

> Our decision in *Ohralik* was largely grounded on the substantial differences between face-to-face solicitation and the advertising we had held permissible in *Bates*. ... [Print advertising] poses much less risk of over-reaching or undue influence. Print advertising may convey information and ideas more or less effectively, but in most cases, it will lack the coercive force of the personal presence of a trained advocate. In addition, a printed advertisement, unlike a personal encounter initiated by an attorney, is not likely to involve pressure on the potential client for an immediate yes-or-no answer to the offer of representation. Thus, a printed advertisement is a means of conveying information about legal services that is more conducive to reflection and the exercise of choice on the part of the consumer than is personal solicitation by an attorney. Accordingly, the substantial interests that justified the ban on in-person solicitation upheld in *Ohralik* cannot justify the discipline imposed on appellant for the content of his advertisement.[83]

The Court also rejected a claim that preventing lawyers from 'stir[ring] up litigation' by advertisements constituted a justification for applying the blanket ban on solicitation to the appellant's Dalkon Shield advertisement in *Zauderer*.[84] The Court stated:

> Nor does the traditional justification for restraints on solicitation – the fear that lawyers will 'stir up litigation' – justify the restriction imposed in this case. In evaluating this proffered justification, it is important to think about what it might mean to say that the State has an interest in preventing lawyers from stirring up litigation. It is possible to describe litigation itself as an evil that the State is entitled to combat: after all, litigation consumes vast quantities of social resources to produce little of tangible

value but much discord and unpleasantness. '[A]s a litigant,' Judge Learned Hand once observed, 'I should dread a lawsuit beyond most anything else short of sickness and death.'

But we cannot endorse the proposition that a lawsuit, as such, is an evil. Over the course of centuries, our society has settled upon civil litigation as a means for redressing grievances, resolving disputes, and vindicating rights when other means fail. There is no cause for consternation when a person who believes in good faith and on the basis of accurate information regarding his legal rights that he has suffered a legally cognizable injury turns to the courts for a remedy: 'we cannot accept the notion that it is always better for a person to suffer a wrong silently than to redress it by legal action' [citing *Bates v. State Bar of Arizona*]. That our citizens have access to their civil courts is not an evil to be regretted; rather, it is an attribute of our system of justice in which we ought to take pride. The State is not entitled to interfere with that access by denying its citizens accurate information about their legal rights. Accordingly, it is not sufficient justification for the discipline imposed on appellant that his truthful and non-deceptive advertising had a tendency to or did in fact encourage others to file lawsuits.

### Solicitation cases

The state has been successful in establishing a direct and material link in two of the cases involving the regulation of solicitation of clients by professionals, and unsuccessful in one. In *Ohralik*, the court upheld a ban on in-person solicitation of clients by lawyers. Since the case was decided before *Central Hudson*, it did not follow the four-part analysis. Instead, it upheld the ban because it was a prophylactic measure whose objective was the prevention of harm before it occurs, and it was not 'unreasonable' for the state to assume that in-person solicitation is 'more often than not' injurious to the person solicited. The reasons for the injury all related to overreaching, invasion of privacy, the exercise of undue influence, and outright fraud, and have been discussed above.

In *Florida Bar v. Went For It, Inc.*,[85] the Court held that a direct and material link between the rule creating a 30-day blackout period and the interest in protecting the privacy and tranquillity of accident victims had been established because the state bar had submitted a 106-page summary of a two-year study of lawyer advertising and solicitation. It contained both statistical and anecdotal evidence that 'the Florida public views direct mail solicitations in the immediate wake of accidents as an intrusion on privacy that reflects poorly upon the profession'.[86] Further, in response to an argument raised in the dissenting opinion that the evidence did not establish the statistical significance of the study, the majority opinion stated that 'we do not read our case law to require that empirical data come to us accompanied by a surfeit of background information'.[87]

In contrast, a ban on in-person solicitation of clients by certified public accountants was invalidated in *Edenfield v. Fane* on the ground that the State Board of Accountancy had 'present[ed] no studies that suggest personal solicitation of prospective business clients by CPAs creates the dangers of fraud, overreaching, or compromised independence that the Board claims to fear'.[88] Nor had the record disclosed 'any anecdotal evidence, either from Florida or another State, that validate[d] the Board's suppositions'.[89] Moreover, the Court noted that unlike lawyers, who are trained as advocates, CPAs are trained in a way that emphasizes independence and objectivity; and the clients of CPAs are likely to be sophisticated and experienced business executives who have an existing professional relation with the CPA, who select the time and place for the meeting, and for whom there is no expectation or pressure to retain the CPA on the spot.

## Restriction Narrowly Drawn

The Court has been reluctant to hold that broad prophylactic rules are needed to achieve the state's substantial interest in cases involving regulation of professions, as it was in the cases involving regulation of business. Beginning with *Virginia Pharmacy Board*, it has made clear that it prefers time, place and manner restrictions that do not completely suppress commercial speech.

The state has not been successful in satisfying its burden on this element in the cases where advertising bans were imposed on professionals. The hostility to blanket bans for their overbreadth is evident in the Court's decisions. For instance, in *Virginia Pharmacy Board*, rejecting the price advertising ban applicable to pharmacists, the Court observed:

> Virginia is free to require whatever professional standards it wishes of its pharmacists; it may subsidize them or protect them from competition in other ways. But it may not do so by keeping the public in ignorance of the entirely lawful terms that competing pharmacists are offering.[90]

Similarly, in *Bates*, the Court held that although the suppression of attorney advertising constituted a violation of the First Amendment, the state was free to impose alternative forms of regulation on the time, place and manner of attorney advertising.

The Court also rejected the use of a prophylactic rule in *Zauderer*, where it did specifically address the issue of whether the regulation was broader than necessary. As to the ban on solicitation as applied to the Dalkon Shield advertisement, the Court held that the prophylactic rule was 'in tension with our insistence that restrictions involving commercial speech that is not itself deceptive be narrowly crafted to serve the state's purpose'. Similarly, as to the ban on illustrations in lawyer advertising, it held that the state had failed to meet its burden because it had cited 'no evidence or authority of any kind for its contention that the potential abuses associated with the use of illustrations in attorneys' advertising cannot be combated by any means short of a blanket ban'.[91]

Finally, in *Florida Bar v. Went For It, Inc.*, the Court analysed more precisely the fit between the regulation and the state's interest, considering whether the 30-day blackout regulation was unconstitutionally overinclusive to the extent that it banned targeted mailings even to citizens whose injuries or grief were relatively minor. It rejected this claim, on the ground that it could not readily imagine less-restrictive alternatives, and that it found the Bar's rule to be reasonably well tailored to the stated objective. Moreover, the rule left open for lawyers numerous alternative channels for communicating with potential clients.[92]

## D.   COMPARISON OF THE CENTRAL HUDSON TEST TO REVIEW STANDARDS DESIGNED TO ELIMINATE ANTICOMPETITIVE EFFECTS OF REGULATION

The *Central Hudson* test bears a resemblance to tests that have been proposed for use in reviewing new and existing regulation to determine its anticompetitive effects in the US and Australia. This section will compare the *Central Hudson* test with these other tests.

### NCRAL Legislative Proposal

In 1979, a US National Commission to Review the Antitrust Laws (NCRAL) studied the anticompetitive effects of regulation in five sectors. Based on the evidence from these case studies, it proposed legislation that would have imposed on federal agencies a requirement that they apply a uniform standard before promulgating new regulations, designed to require them 'to focus on the economic effects of their actions, and to maximize competition as a regulatory tool'. The proposed legislation, which was never enacted, contained a three-part test for agencies to apply to any action 'the effect of which may be substantially to lessen competition, to tend to create a monopoly, or to create or maintain a situation involving a significant burden on competition'. The agency could not approve such action unless it found:

a) Such action is necessary to accomplish an overriding statutory purpose of the agency;
b) The anticompetitive effects of such action are clearly outweighed by significant and demonstrable benefits to the general public; and

c) The objectives of the action and the overriding statutory purpose cannot be accomplished in substantial part by alternative means having less anticompetitive effects.

The structure and substance of the NCRAL proposal are similar to the *Central Hudson* test, notwithstanding the different contexts in which they were meant to apply: the former, with regard to proposed federal regulations; the latter, with regard to existing federal or state restrictions on commercial speech. The basic requirement in the NCRAL proposal that the action be necessary to accomplish an 'overriding statutory purpose' is similar to the *Central Hudson*'s 'substantial state interest' requirement. However, use of the term 'overriding' in the NCRAL proposal, which is stronger than 'substantial', suggests that the Committee believed it was appropriate to place a very strict burden on the government with respect to this element.

As to the second element of the NCRAL proposal, again the terminology seems stronger than that of the analogous provision of the *Central Hudson* test, and the focus is different. The former requires that significant and demonstrable benefits to the general public must *clearly outweigh* anticompetitive effects, which again is strong language that appears to place a very high burden on the agency. This element makes no reference, however, to the 'overriding statutory purpose' of the first element of the NCRAL test. In contrast, the analogous provision of the *Central Hudson* test is that the regulation must directly and materially advance the state's substantial interest. Its focus is on the relationship between the substantial state interest and the regulation. The Court has never suggested that the state must quantitatively assess the benefits of the legislation against the costs resulting from harms to the free flow of commercial information, perhaps because of the difficulties of gathering the evidence needed to make such a showing. However, the stricter requirements that the Court has imposed with respect to blanket bans suggests that it does, in effect, perform a sort of balancing.

The third element of the NCRAL proposal, that the objectives 'cannot be accomplished in substantial part by alternative means having less anticompetitive effects', again appears to impose a stricter standard than that of *Central Hudson*. The latter requires only that the regulation at issue is not more extensive than necessary to accomplish the state's substantial interest. Thus, the NCRAL proposal suggests that if it is possible to achieve only a substantial part of the government's overriding statutory purpose by less-anticompetitive means, then the regulation is overbroad. In contrast, the *Central Hudson* standard has been interpreted as a requirement only for a reasonable fit between the regulation and the state's interest, and not necessarily the single best fit (with the caveat that blanket bans are generally found to be overbroad.)

In summary, the NCRAL approach appears stricter than the *Central Hudson* test, placing a higher burden on the government to justify its regulation, with respect to all elements.

## The Australian Regulatory Review Standard

The Council of Australian Government (COAG) has designed a standard for use in its review to modify or eliminate laws, regulations and so on that are restrictive of competition, initiated in 1995:

> Legislation (including Acts, enactments, Ordinances or regulations) should not restrict competition unless it can be demonstrated that:
> a) the benefits of the restriction to the community as a whole outweigh the costs; and
> b) the objectives of the legislation can only be achieved by restricting competition.

A review should:

> a) clarify the objectives of the legislation;
> b) identify the nature of the restriction on competition;
> c) analyse the likely effect of the restriction on competition and on the economy generally;
> d) assess and balance the costs and benefits of the restriction; and
> e) consider alternative means for achieving the same result including non-legislative approaches.

Unlike the NCRAL proposal and the *Central Hudson* test, the COAG standard of review does not consider the substantiality of the government's interest underlying the legislation under review. Rather, it only requires that the objectives of the legislation be clarified. Nor is there any requirement of a direct link between the legislation and the achievement of its objectives. Rather, the COAG standard focuses on a balancing of benefits and costs of the restriction. In comparison with the NCRAL balancing requirement (anticompetitive effects clearly outweighed by significant and demonstrable benefits to the public), the COAG standard seems lenient.

Moreover, as to consideration of less-restrictive alternatives, the COAG standard seems the most lenient of the three, requiring only 'consideration' of alternative means. It does not, however, require any showing that the objectives of the legislation cannot be achieved by means having less-anticompetitive effects, nor that there is even a reasonable fit between the legislation and achievement of the objectives. Thus, this standard seems to leave greatest room for flexible interpretation and, perhaps, political manipulation.

# E.  LESSONS TO BE LEARNED FROM SUPREME COURT DECISIONS ON COMMERCIAL SPEECH: DEVELOPING A LEGAL FRAMEWORK FOR ANALYSING ANTICOMPETITIVE EFFECTS OF REGULATIONS AFFECTING PRIVATE BUSINESSES AND PROFESSIONALS

This final section will be devoted to deriving from the above analysis of Supreme Court commercial speech jurisprudence, and its comparison with the NCRAL and COAG review standards, a legal framework for performing a review of regulations to eliminate their anticompetitive effects. The *Central Hudson* test can be adjusted and supplemented for use as a legal framework for a regulatory review designed to eliminate the anticompetitive effects of regulation. We recommend the following framework.

## Does the Regulation Potentially Have an Anticompetitive Impact, and if so, What Is It?

An initial question must be added to the *Central Hudson* test: does the regulation potentially have anticompetitive effects? The reviewing body should have the burden to identify the potential anticompetitive effects of the legislation. The reviewing body must be capable of applying such competition-based criteria to each regulation to determine whether the danger of anticompetitive effect is present. This suggests that at least some members of that body should be economists. If the reviewing body concludes that this danger is present, the state should have the opportunity to rebut by showing that as applied, the regulation does not have an anticompetitive effect. Those charged with implementing the regulation should be involved in preparing this rebuttal.

The Australian National Competition Council (NCC) has provided a list of the types of regulations that are likely to have anticompetitive effects. In addition to regulations that restrict advertising and promotional activities, the NCC has identified the following:

1. Those that govern the entry and exit of firms or individuals into or out of markets;
2. Those that control prices or production levels;
3. Those that restrict the quality, level or location of goods and services available;
4. Those likely to confer significant costs on businesses; or
5. Those that provide advantages to some firms over others by, for example, sheltering some activities from the pressure of competition.[93]

Perhaps further categories of regulations that should be added to this list will be revealed, and will lead to the development of a set of economic criteria to assess and measure the anticompetitive effects of regulation.

## Does the State Have a Substantial Interest to be Achieved by the Regulation, and if so, What Is It?

Assuming that a regulation does potentially have anticompetitive effects, the next question should be whether the state has a substantial interest to be achieved by the regulation. It does not seem possible to define, *ex ante*, a set of criteria for determining when a state's interest will be substantial. This determination will, to some extent, depend on subjective judgement, and will be affected by each nation's own criteria. The burden of proof should be on the state to establish its substantial interest. It will be crucial to ensure that the reviewing body is impartial, objective and motivated to protect the public interest.

As shown above, the commercial speech cases have not provided any clear guidance for determining whether a state's interest is 'substantial'. It has been generous in recognizing as substantial a state interest related to protection of the health, safety and welfare of citizens. It has also validated a broad interest of the state in maintenance of professionalism, since professional services involve the dispensation of professional judgement, and given the information gap between professionals and consumers of professional services. Its interest in regulating lawyers has been deemed even more substantial, given that they are officers of the court. However, the Court has been unwilling to credit a state's interest as substantial when the interest asserted has been overly subjective, such as protecting the 'dignity' of attorneys.

## Does the Regulation Directly and Materially Advance the State's Interest?

The third element of the *Central Hudson* test, which analyses the relationship between the state's interest and the regulation, should also be applied in a regulatory review. The burden of proof that a direct and material link exists should be placed on the state. If it fails to meet this burden, the reviewing body should recommend to the legislature that the regulation should be modified or repealed.

With respect to advertising restrictions, blanket bans should be disfavoured because they completely block the free flow of commercial information and thereby impede the competitive process. The Supreme Court subjected them to a very strict standard of review, even in cases involving professionals, where more regulation is justified (as explained above). Thus, some actual scientific proof of the link should be required. The Court has specifically rejected arguments as to the evils of competition in the professions (for example, causes pharmacists to economize on services at customers' expense, reduces professionalism; reduces the image of the professional; increases overhead costs of lawyers, which are passed on to their clients, creating entry barriers and entrenching the position of established lawyers), to justify blanket bans presented by the state. The Court has been highly suspicious of regulations that focus on the assumed reactions of customers to the advertised information, rather than on the professional standards. As to the legal profession, the court has rejected arguments that advertising would impede the attorney's sense of pride and self-worth, or that advertising is undignified; or that it will stir up litigation, harming the administration of justice. It has allowed blanket bans on in-person solicitation of clients by lawyers (but not by CPAs), given the dangers of overreaching and the impossibility of control by the bar. It has indicated that a blanket ban on lawyer advertising might be permissible where a lawyer makes claims of quality of service or other claims that are not susceptible of measurement or verification, which may be false or misleading. With respect to time, place, and manner restrictions on advertising, a lower standard of proof could be imposed. These criteria established by the Supreme Court could be considered by a reviewing body confronted with similar advertising/solicitation restrictions.

### Do the Benefits of the Legislation Significantly and Demonstrably Outweigh the Costs from Its Anticompetitive Effects?

This criterion was absent from the *Central Hudson* test, but included in the NCRAL standard. It should be included as a criterion for a regulatory review because, even if a direct and material link is established, but the anticompetitive effects are so costly that they outweigh the benefits, the regulation should not be allowed to remain in force. Experience with cost/benefit analysis should provide some scientific basis for how this analysis should be performed. The burden of proof should be on the state to establish that the benefits outweigh the costs. If it fails to meet this burden, the reviewing body should be authorized to invalidate the regulation, or to require a modification, or to send a recommendation to the legislature to the effect that the regulation should be modified or repealed.

### Are There Any Means to Achieve the State's Substantial Interest that Would Have Less-anticompetitive Effects?

Finally, the regulatory review should assess whether any means exist to achieve the state's substantial interest that would have a less-anticompetitive effect. The burden of proof should again be on the state to show that no less-restrictive means exists. As to advertising restraints, blanket bans will be highly suspect as to their overbreadth. Perhaps the reviewing body could seek input from those subject to the regulation, or from the public, as to possible less-restrictive alternatives. If the state disagrees with a suggested less-restrictive alternative, it should be obliged to provide reasons that such alternatives would not be acceptable.

## NOTES

1. *Central Hudson Gas & Electric v. Public Serv. Comm'n*, 447 US 557, 561–2 (1980).
2. *Va. Pharmacy Bd. v. Va. Consumer Council*, 425 US 748, 770 (1976).
3. *Edenfield v. Fane*, 507 US 761 (1993); *Ohralik v. Ohio State Bar Assn*, 436 US 447 (1978).
4. *Rubin v. Coors Brewing Co.*, 514 US 476 (1995).
5. First Amendment protection of commercial speech was first established in *Bigelow v. Va.*, 421 US 809, 811 (1975).
6. Although the Court's focus in commercial speech cases is primarily the significance of such speech to the proper functioning of a free market economy, its decisions have occasionally referred to the importance of the freedom of speech as a democratic principle. The latter is the focus of the First Amendment's protection of speech in general, as distinguished from commercial speech.
7. 317 US 341 (1943). In *Parker*, a raisin producer challenged a state regulatory programme designed to restrict competition among growers and thereby maintain prices in the raisin market.
8. *Id.* at 350–51. Compare *Goldfarb v. Va. State Bar*, 421 US 773 (1975). In *Goldfarb*, the Court held that a minimum fee schedule published by a county bar association constituted classic price fixing in violation of Section 1 of the Sherman Act. The antitrust rules were held applicable in that case because the county bar association was a 'purely voluntary association of lawyers' with no formal powers to enforce the fee schedule; enforcement had been provided by the state bar, the administrative agency through which the state supreme court regulates the practice of law in the state.

    State bars generally are the organized bar operating under the code of ethics approved by the state's supreme court pursuant to statutory authority, and have responsibility for assuring compliance with professional ethics and standards by lawyers whom they license. Here, the state bar had never taken disciplinary action to compel adherence to the fee schedule, but it had published reports condoning fee schedules, and it had issued two ethical opinions saying that fee schedules could not be ignored. The Court held that *Parker v. Brown* was not applicable because the state supreme court had not required publication of the fee schedule: 'It is not enough that, as the County Bar puts it, anticompetitive conduct is "prompted" by state action; rather, anticompetitive activities must be compelled by direction of the State acting as a sovereign'. *id.* at 791.
9. *Supra* note 1, 447 US 557 (1980).
10. First Amendment, US Constitution. Although the First Amendment does not mention the states, it has been held to apply to the states under the Due Process Clause of the Fourteenth Amendment. See *Bd of Ed., Island Trees Union Free School Dist. No. 26 v. Pico*, 457 US 853, 855 n. 1 (1982); *Bigelow v. Va., supra* note 5, 421 US at 811; *Schneider v. State*, 308 US 147, 160 (1939).
11. For example, *Ohralik, v. Ohio State Bar Ass'n, supra* note 3, 436 US 447. In a concurring opinion in *Rubin v. Coors Brewing Co., supra* note 4, 514 US 476, 491–8, Justice Stevens challenges the distinction made in the Supreme Court caselaw between commercial speech and other forms of protected speech. He argues that the only distinction that should be made is 'the importance of avoiding deception and protecting the consumer from inaccurate or

incomplete information'. *id.* at 493. He believes that this narrowing of the distinction would be appropriate because 'the borders of the commercial speech category are not nearly as clear as the Court has assumed, and its four-part test is not related to the reasons for allowing more regulation of commercial speech than other speech'. *id.* at 493, and that 'whether or not speech is "commercial" has no necessary relationship to its content'. *id.* at 494. He concludes that 'economic motivation or impact alone cannot make speech less deserving of constitutional protection, or else all authors and artists who sell their works would be correspondingly disadvantaged'. *id.*

A somewhat stronger position was taken by the concurring justices in *Central Hudson Gas & Electric v. Public Serv. Comm'n, supra* note 1, 447 US at 574, who stated that they, 'doubt whether suppression of information concerning the availability and price of a legally offered product is ever a permissible way for the State to "damper" the demand for or use of the product'.

12.   *Va. Pharmacy Bd. v. Va. Consumer Council supra* note 2, 425 US at 771 n. 24.
13.   *Linmark v. Willingboro*, 431 US 85, 9697 (1977). In Linmark, the town had banned the use of 'for sale' signs on residential property in order to further its goal of promoting stable, racially integrated housing – that is, to prevent residents from selling their homes and leaving town. This rule was held unconstitutional and invalidated.
14.   *Id.*
15.   *Va. Pharmacy Bd. v. Va. Consumer Council, supra* note 2, 425 US 748. Even the commercial speech of a monopolist is protected. In *Central Hudson Gas & Electric v. Public Serv. Comm'n, supra* note 1, 447 US 557, the Court ruled that when the party uttering the commercial speech is a monopoly, protection is still afforded by the First Amendment. The Court stated:

> Monopoly over the supply of a product provides no protection from competition with substitutes for that product. Electric utilities compete with suppliers of fuel oil and natural gas in several markets, such as those for home heating and industrial power. ... Each energy source continues to offer peculiar advantages and disadvantages that may influence consumer choice. For consumers in those competitive markets, advertising by utilities is just as valuable as advertising by unregulated firms.
>
> Even in monopoly markets, the suppression of advertising reduces the information available for consumer decisions, and thereby defeats the purpose of the First Amendment.

   *Id.* at 567 (citations omitted).
16.   *Supra* note 2, 425 US 748.
17.   *Id.* at 763–4.
18.   *Id* at 765.
19.   For instance, in *Bates v. State Bar of Arizona*, 433 US 350, 364 (1977), the Court again elaborated the importance of the free flow of commercial speech to the consumer:

> The listener's interest is substantial: the consumer's concern for the free flow of commercial speech often may be far keener than his concern for urgent political dialogue. Moreover, significant societal interests are served by such speech. Advertising, though entirely commercial, may often carry information of import to significant issues of the day. And commercial speech serves to inform the public of the availability, nature, and prices of products and services, and thus performs an indispensable role in the allocation of resources in a free enterprise system. In short, such speech serves individual and societal interests in assuring informed and reliable decisionmaking.

\* \* \*

Advertising is the traditional mechanism in a free-market economy for a supplier to inform a potential purchaser of the availability and terms of exchange.

Similarly, in *Edenfield v. Fane, supra* note 3, 507 US at 767, a rule of the Florida Board of Accountancy prohibited accountants from engaging in direct, in person, uninvited solicitation of business. In striking down the rule as an unconstitutional limitation of commercial speech, the Court stated:

> The commercial market place, like other spheres of our social and cultural life, provides a forum where ideas and information flourish. Some of the ideas and information are vital, some of slight worth. But the general rule is that the speaker and the audience, not the government, assess the value of the information presented. Thus, even communication that does no more than propose a commercial transaction is entitled to the coverage of the First Amendment.

20. *Central Hudson Gas & Electric v. Public Serv. Comm'n, supra* note 1, 447 US 557.
21. L. Tribe, *American Constitutional Law*, Secs. 12–15, p. 903 (2d edn 1988), quoted in *44 Liquormart, Inc. v. R.I.*, 517 US 484, 134 L.Ed. 2d 711 (1996).
22. *Central Hudson Gas & Electric v. Public Serv. Comm'n, supra* note 1, 447 US at 566.
23. The Court has observed that greater 'objectivity' of commercial speech as compared with other speech protected under the First Amendment justifies affording the state greater freedom to distinguish false advertisements from true ones. *Va. Pharmacy Bd. v. Va. Consumer Council, supra* note 2, 425 US at 771, n. 24.
24. *Posadas de Puerto Rico Assoc. v. Tourism Co.*, 478 US 328, 341 (1986) overruled on other grounds, *44 Liquormart, Inc. v. R.I., supra* note 21, 517 US 484.
25. *Bolger v. Youngs Drug Products Corp.*, 463 US 60, 71 (1983).
26. *Posadas de Puerto Rico Assoc. v. Tourism Co., supra* note 24, 478 US 328. The Court noted that the legislature's belief underlying its law prohibiting advertising of casino gambling was that '[e]xcessive casino gambling among local residents ... would produce serious harmful effects on the health, safety and welfare of the Puerto Rican citizens, such as the disruption of moral and cultural patterns, the increase in local crime, the fostering of prostitution, the development of corruption, and the infiltration of organized crime'. *id.* at 341.
27. *44 Liquormart, Inc. v. R.I., supra* note 21, 517 US 484. Although the decision in *44 Liquormart* does not clearly address the issue of substantial state interest, the Court appears to assume that reducing the consumption of alcoholic beverages is a substantial interest. The Court noted that in an earlier Rhode Island Supreme Court case in which the same statutes were at issue, the state supreme court had found that the asserted government interests, 'the promotion of temperance and the reasonable control of the traffic in alcoholic beverages', to be substantial. It then stated that it accepted 'the State Supreme Court's identification of the relevant state interest served by the legislation'. *Id.*, 134 L.Ed. 2d at 720, n. 4.
28. *Rubin v. Coors Brewing Co., supra* note 4, 514 US at 485. The Court stated: 'Both panels of the Court of Appeals that heard this case concluded that the goal of suppressing strength wars constituted a substantial interest, and we cannot say that their conclusion is erroneous. We have no reason to think that strength wars, if they were to occur, would not produce the type of social harm that the Government hopes to prevent'.
29. *Bolger v. Youngs Drug Products Corp., supra* note 25, 463 US at 73 ('Parents have an important "guiding role" to play in the upbringing of their children ... which presumptively includes counseling them on important decisions', quoting *Bellotti v. Baird*, 443 US 622, 637 (1979).)
30. *Central Hudson Gas & Electric v. Public Serv. Comm'n, supra* note 1, 447 US at 568–9. The Court simply stated: 'In view of our country's dependence on energy resources beyond our control, no one can doubt the importance of energy conservation. Plainly, therefore, the state interest asserted is substantial'. *Id.* at 568.
31. *Id.* at 568–9.
32. *Bolger v. Youngs Drug Products Co., supra* note 25, 463 US at 73. In *Bolger*, the Court rejected the claim that shielding recipients of mail (at home or elsewhere) from advertising by the manufacturer of contraceptive devices that the recipients were likely to find offensive constituted a substantial state interest. There, the Court stated that 'offiensiveness was "classically not [a] justificatio[n] validating the suppression of expression protected by the First

Amendment. At least where obscenity is not involved, we have consistently held that the fact that protected speech may be offensive to some does not justify its suppression". We specifically declined to recognize a distinction between commercial and noncommercial speech that would render this interest a sufficient justification for a prohibition of commercial speech'. *Id.* at 70, quoting *Carey v. Population Services Int'l*, 431 US 678, 701 (1977). The Court reasoned that the First Amendment would permit the government to prohibit offensive mailings only if the 'captive' audience were unable to avoid the objectionable speech.

33. *Edenfield v. Fane, supra* note 3, 507 US at 771.
34. *Rubin v. Coors Brewing Co., supra* note 4, 514 US at 487, quoting *Edenfield v. Fane, supra* note 3, 507 US at 770–71. In *Bolger v. Youngs Drug Products Co., supra* note 25, 463 US 60, decided two years before *Zauderer v. Office of Disciplinary Council*, 471 US 626 (1985), the Court recognized that the federal government's blanket ban on mailing of unsolicited advertisements for contraceptives provided only a 'marginal degree of protection' to aid parents' efforts to discuss birth control with their children, based on common-sense reasoning rather than studies. (Held that the law in question 'provides only the most limited incremental support for the interest asserted', because '[w]e can reasonably assume that parents already exercise substantial control over the disposition of mail once it enters their mailboxes', and 'parents must already cope with the multitude of external stimuli that color their children's perception of sensitive subjects'.)
35. *Central Hudson Gas & Electric v. Public Serv. Comm'n, supra* note 1, 447 US at 569.
36. See *Florida Bar v. Went For It, Inc.*, 515 US 618 (1995).
37. *44 Liquormart, Inc. v. R.I., supra* note 21, 134 L. Ed. 2d at 726.
38. *Id.*, 134 L. Ed. 2d at 727.
39. *Linmark v. Willingboro, supra* note 13, 431 US at 96–7.
40. *Central Hudson Gas & Electric v. Public Serv. Comm'n, supra* note 1, 447 US at 566 n. 9.
41. For instance, in *Linmark v. Willingboro, supra* note 13, 431 US at 96–7, a ban on 'For Sale' signs in front of houses was ruled unconstitutional because it was 'content based' and did not leave open alternative channels of communication.
42. *44 Liquormart, Inc. v. R.I., supra* note 21, 134 L. Ed. 2d at 726.
43. *Supra* note 1, 447 US at 569.
44. *Supra* note 25, 463 US 60.
45. *Id.* at 73.
46. *Supra* note 24, 478 US at 341–2.
47. *Id.*
48. *Supra* note 21, 517 US 484.
49. *Id.*, 134 L. Ed. 2d at 729. The opinion stated:

> We can agree that common sense supports the conclusion that a prohibition against price advertising, like a collusive agreement among competitors to refrain from such advertising, will tend to mitigate competition and maintain prices at a higher level than would prevail in a completely free market. Despite the absence of proof on the point, we can even agree with the State's contention that it is reasonable to assume that demand, and hence consumption throughout the market, is somewhat lower whenever a higher, noncompetitive price level prevails. However, without any findings of fact, or indeed any evidentiary support whatsoever, we cannot agree with the assertion that the price advertising ban will significantly advance the State's interest in promoting temperance.

50. *Supra* note 4, 514 US 476.
51. *Id.* at 489.
52. *44 Liquormart, Inc. v. R.I., supra* note 21, 134 L. Ed. 2d at 726; see *Va. Pharmacy Bd. v. Va. Consumer Council, supra* note 2, 425 US at 772 n. 24 (the state can freely impose regulation requiring that commercial messages 'appear in such a form, or include such additional information, warnings, and disclaimers, as are necessary to prevent its being deceptive').
53. *Central Hudson Gas & Electric v. Public Serv. Comm'n, supra* note 1, 447 US at 569–70.
54. *Id.* at 570–71.

55. *Board of Trustees of State University of N.Y. v. Fox*, 492 US 469, 480 (1989) (citations omitted).
56. *44 Liquormart, Inc. v. R.I.*, *supra* note 21, 134 L. Ed. 2d at 730.
57. *Rubin v. Coors Brewing Co.*, *supra* note 4, 514 US at 490–91. In *Bolger v. Youngs Drug Products Co.*, decided in 1983, the Court did not discuss less-restrictive alternatives. It merely stated that the federal government's blanket ban on advertisement of contraceptives was overbroad because '[t]he level of discourse reaching a mailbox simply cannot be limited to that which would be suitable for a sandbox', *Supra* note 25, 463 US at 74.
58. See *Va. Pharmacy Bd. v. Va. Consumer Council*, *supra* note 2, 425 US at 773 n. 25 and 773–5 (concurring opinion); *Bigelow v. Va.*, *supra* note 5, 421 US at 825 n. 10.
59. *Goldfarb v. Va. State Bar*, *supra* note 8, 421 US at 792.
60. *Va. Pharmacy Bd. v. Va. Consumer Council*, *supra* note 2, 425 US at 773 n. 25.
61. *Supra* note 19, 433 US 350.
62. *Id.* at 366.
63. 471 US 626 (1985).
64. *Id.* at 646.
65. *Id.* at 649.
66. *Id.* at 652–3 (citations omitted).
67. *Id.* at 651 (citations omitted).
68. *Supra* note 3, 436 US 447.
69. *Id.* at 464–5.
70. *Supra* note 3, 507 US 761.
71. *Id.* at 774–5.
72. *Goldfarb v. Va. State Bar*, *supra* note 8, 421 US at 792.
73. *Supra* note 19, 433 US, 350. This case predated *Central Hudson*, and therefore did not analyse the record according to the four-part test.
74. *Va. Pharmacy Bd. v. Va. Consumer Council*, *supra* note 2, 425 US at 766.
75. *Id.* at 770.
76. *Supra* note 34, 471 US 626 (1985).
77. *Ohralik v. Ohio State Bar Assn*, *supra* note 3, 436 US at 464–5.
78. *Edenfield v. Fane*, *supra* note 3, 507 US at 769–70.
79. *Florida Bar v. Went For It, Inc.*, *supra* note 36, 515 US at 625.
80. *Va. Pharmacy Bd. v. Va. Consumer Council*, *supra* note 2, 425 US 769.
81. *Supra* note 19, 433 350.
82. *Id.* at 377–8.
83. *Zauderer v. Office of Disciplinary Council*, *supra* note 34, 471 US at 642.
84. *Id.* at 643 (citations omitted). See *Bates v. State Bar of Arizona*, *supra* note 19, 433 US at 375.
85. *Supra* note 36, 515 US 618.
86. *Id.* at 626.
87. *Id.* at 628.
88. *Supra* note 3, 507 US at 771.
89. *Id.*
90. *Va. Pharmacy Bd. v. Va. Consumer Council*, *supra* note 2, 425 US at 770.
91. *Zauderer v. Office of Disciplinary Council*, *supra* note 34, 471 US at 648.
92. *Florida Bar v. Went For It, Inc.*, *supra* note 36, 515 US at 632–4.
93. NCC, *Legislative Review Compendium* (Melbourne, Australia, April 1997).

# 5.   Occupational regulation[1]

## Allan Fels, David Parker, Blair Comley and Vishal Beri

*Regulation is an important part of the legal and institutional fabric of a country. However, governments have become increasingly concerned that inappropriate regulation may lead to adverse growth, efficiency and distributional outcomes. This chapter considers possible rationales for occupational regulation, including information limitations with respect to professional services; 'non-voluntary' transactions, which may follow from a professional's ability to misrepresent costs and potential benefits of services; and distributional considerations for regulations such as price caps.*

*Occupational regulation can take various forms, including entry barriers (for example, registration, licensing, negative licensing, certification and accreditation), and control of transaction content (for example, information requirements and restrictions on the conduct of business). It can also apply economywide or be sector specific, raising problems of complexity for reformers.*

*The chapter recognizes that regulatory failure will occur if occupational regulation is not well targeted to achieve its legitimate objective, or if it has unintended consequences. Thus, it urges reformers to focus on the general question: 'What are the appropriate objectives of regulation, and how can we design regulations to best achieve these objectives, without producing unintended consequences?' The chapter concludes with a set of principles to guide the design of quality regulations.*

## INTRODUCTION

The appropriate level of regulation should be addressed in reform of occupational regulation, irrespective of whether the direction of reform is towards more or less regulation. Formal legal structures that create, codify and limit rights can be general to an economy or specific to particular trade sectors. Occupational regulation is usually sector specific and typically has evolved as a way of codifying previous practices and customs where the pace of change or scope of transactions has demanded it. The appropriateness of general or specific regulation will depend upon the objective of the regulation and whether the problem addressed is isolated or systemic.

The regulation applying to an occupation can be complex, usually involving many layers and different institutional structures. Specifically, there is the general law, sector-specific law and general custom and practice. There may be general or sector-specific regulators, and professional bodies may also undertake self-regulatory functions. The interrelationship between these different layers and institutions can be problematic.

The general trend in addressing these issues has been to find new ways to regulate occupations that avoid unjustified restrictions on competition and encourage best practice and innovation. This should be done such that important social goals are promoted.

The remainder of this chapter is organized as follows. Section A considers both legitimate and illegitimate rationales for occupational regulation. Section B examines the various ways that regulation can achieve its objectives and illustrates the types of regulation that are likely to be most efficient. Section C considers general versus sector-specific regulation, and Section D addresses regulatory failure. Section E sets forth some ideas for regulatory reform, and some brief conclusions follow.

## A. THE RATIONALE FOR OCCUPATIONAL REGULATION

Law, custom and practice all set the environment in which market transactions take place. Regulation of market activity may be necessary where additional sets of rights, or qualifications of rights, are required to assist the market to operate in a manner that is efficient and equitable for participants. Promoting competition is often useful to encourage both an efficient and equitable operation of a particular market. Competition provides a discipline that balances the interest of sellers and buyers. This can be particularly important if one group may otherwise have the ability to capture all the benefits of economic activity through limiting competition. However, unfettered market activity, and unfettered competition, do not always promote the most desirable outcome.

The regulation of occupations generally arises out of recognition that there may be a set of circumstances under which competition and unconstrained transactions do not produce optimal outcomes. Such constraints include barriers to entry (such as qualification requirements) or regulation of transactions themselves (such as price or other content controls). Three potentially legitimate rationales often given for regulating individual market transactions in occupational services, as well as inappropriate justifications, are discussed below.

## Information Limitations

A purchaser of goods or services must assess quality. The consequences of making incorrect judgements (that is, the risk) for a relatively simple good with few characteristics are likely to be small, as consumers are likely to be able to form a reasonably accurate estimate of the value of the good. The ability of consumers to estimate accurately is most likely when consumers can assess the quality of the goods after consumption, and they undertake repeat purchases.

However, professional services are significantly more difficult for consumers to assess. Five key characteristics of professional services tend to magnify the information asymmetry and its consequences. First, services are generally not observable before they are purchased in the same way as goods are. Second, professional services are, by nature, complex, and often require considerable skill to deliver and tailor to the consumer's needs. Therefore, it can be difficult for the consumer to assess the quality of the service before it is purchased. Third, the quality of many professional services can be difficult to assess even *after* the service has been purchased. For example, if a consumer hires a lawyer to represent him/her in litigation, and the litigation is ultimately unsuccessful, it is difficult for the consumer to know whether the legal services were poorly delivered or the case was inherently difficult to win. Fourth, consumers often are infrequent purchasers of professional services. Therefore, they do not have repeat purchases to assess quality. Fifth, the consequences of purchasing poor professional services can be significant. For example, the service may represent a large expenditure for the consumer, and a defective service (for example, a heart bypass operation) can risk serious and irreversible harm.

These characteristics can be used to justify regulation aimed at quality assurance. Such schemes are intended to provide a guaranteed level of service quality to consumers, and therefore reduce risks associated with purchasing professional services. To some extent, these schemes substitute search and information gathering by individuals with information gathering and assessment through a regulatory mechanism, thereby reducing the transaction cost for consumers and helping the market to function efficiently.

All professional services should not necessarily be regulated in the same way. Different services have different complexities and risks. In some markets, consumers may be able reasonably to assess quality and risk through word-of-mouth reputation or branding.

## Non-voluntary Transactions

Non-voluntary exchange may not be mutually beneficial. Concern about coercion can be used to justify laws that invalidate contracts entered under duress. Societies generally have laws, customs and practices that limit the ability of individuals to coerce others. In markets for professional services, there may be a case for special protection because of greater opportunity for subtle coercion. For example, professionals may have significant opportunities to misrepresent the costs and benefits of taking a particular course of action. There may also be cases where relationships of trust between the professional and the client can be abused.

## Distributional Considerations

Distributional considerations are often used to justify regulations that set the terms on which services are provided. These can include price caps, which are intended to provide services at lower cost to low-income earners. Whether distributional concerns should be addressed through such direct occupational regulation or through a more direct redistribution mechanism is debatable, and may depend on the stage of development of the economy.

Several problems with such regulation should be considered. First, attempting to redistribute through such regulatory mechanisms is often not transparent. It can be difficult to know whether those whom the government intends to assist are actually assisted by the policy. Second, a regulatory approach to redistribution may not be well targeted. Such indirect regulations cannot differentiate among income groups. Therefore, high-income groups will also benefit, funded from a cross-subsidy from other consumers. The total redistributive benefit would thus be less than the total cost imposed on other consumers. Third, a more-efficient method may be to target the distributive issue directly through the tax/transfer system. However, if the redistribution would otherwise not take place, it may be best to undertake some, albeit imperfect, redistribution via regulation.

In summary, economists are generally sceptical about the desirability of using occupational regulation tools to achieve distributional objectives. Such regulations can lead to non-transparent outcomes, benefit some recipients in unintended ways, and be less efficient than redistributing through the tax/transfer system.

## Inappropriate Justifications

Regulations that have the objective of merely increasing returns to regulated groups are not generally considered appropriate, given the arguments about distributional considerations discussed above. In particular, redistribution to regulated groups is likely to involve negative distributional consequences for relatively poor consumers. Occupational regulation in fact often has this effect. For example, restrictions on entry to a profession can be expected to limit supply and raise prices and incomes of those providing the service. The restriction on entry may arguably be justified on the basis of consumer protection, and the resulting increase in price represents the cost to the consumer of that protection. But where restrictions on entry to an occupation are justified on safety grounds, they should be no tighter than necessary, and there should be no better, more direct mechanism, to achieve that objective. The consumer would otherwise be forced to overpay for the protection. The unintended effect of the regulation will be to redistribute wealth from consumers to the regulated profession. Therefore, regulatory reform of occupations should ensure that regulations that have the effect of increasing the returns to incumbents are justified.

To determine whether an asserted justification is valid, policy analysts must determine what problem the regulation is meant to address, and why it is necessary to address this problem by regulation. In particular, it is important that the objective of the regulation be thoroughly assessed, and that the various ways in which that objective can be achieved, as well as the likely outcome of proposed regulations, are analysed. To avoid the distributional problems discussed above, regulations should be assessed from an economywide perspective as opposed to the perspective of only the regulated group.

Good-quality regulation is that which achieves appropriate objectives in the most efficient way. Poor-quality regulation can have either inappropriate objectives, inefficiently achieve appropriate objectives or have unintended consequences. Moreover, experience in many countries has shown that substantial compliance costs can give rise to an increased incidence of non-compliance.

## B.   FORMS OF OCCUPATIONAL REGULATION

The various types of sector-specific occupational regulations commonly imposed by governments are discussed in this section.[2] Occupational regulations can take the form of entry barriers, transaction regulation and redress mechanisms, and can vary in their degree of restrictiveness.

### Entry Barriers

Many occupations are subject to regulations imposing barriers to entry, which can take a variety of forms. Five types of entry barrier regulations are discussed here: registration, licensing, negative licensing, certification and accreditation.

### Registration
Registration schemes require practitioners to register before they can provide their service.[3] Such regulation may impose educational requirements and/or require membership in professional bodies. Candidates for registration may also be required to pass probity tests or satisfy the 'fit and proper' criteria. Reg-

istration schemes can be run by government agencies or by self-regulating industry bodies.

## Licensing

Granting a licence to practice an occupation is often dependent on formal qualifications, approved training periods, or general probity tests.[4] However, licensing can restrict entry into an occupation and restrict the range of permitted activities. Licences can be issued by government agencies or industry licensing boards.

## Negative licensing

These regulations generally recognize the entitlement of individuals to practise, but provide that they can be prohibited from practising if they have committed an offence deemed sufficiently serious to warrant exclusion from the industry. Negative licensing imposes lower barriers to entry than licensing.

## Certification

Whilst not strictly restricting market entry, certification and information regulations are also aimed at ensuring that acceptable standards of conduct in practice are maintained. A certification body responsible for keeping a list of practitioners who have reached a certain level of competency or who meet other standards usually administer such regulations. These schemes are usually non-legislative, and fostered by industry bodies. However, while certification indicates the achievement of a certain level of expertise or competency, a non-certified practitioner may also be able to provide services. For example, certified practising accountants (CPAs) are distinguished from those accountants who have not completed the additional study required to become a CPA.

## Accreditation

Accreditation is similar to certification. For example, under an agricultural and veterinary chemicals accreditation scheme, manufacturers, distributors and retailers who are not accredited with necessary training in the appropriate handling and storage of chemicals can be prevented from trading in chemicals.

## Transaction Content Regulation

## Information regulations

Designed directly to address information asymmetries, information regulations may require government warnings or provision of specific guidance to potential consumers. They are generally considered to be the least-intrusive form of regulation.

**Transaction regulations**

Regulations that broadly address transactions may include provisions on price and other forms of regulation. Occupational regulation may thus be included in the broader mosaic of regulation. For example, building codes and legal procedures provide a range of regulations to ensure quality standards.

**Performance-based regulation**

Performance-based regulation, which focuses on outputs, is generally preferable to prescriptive regulation, which controls inputs, as the latter tend to impose greater restrictions on innovation and competition. For example, environmental regulations that specify permissible emission levels, in contrast to those that require the use of specific pollution-control technology (that is, input control), are generally deemed preferable. Performance-based regulation allows firms to discover the best, or invent a better, means to achieve the emission target, which may not be the technology that the regulator would have chosen.

Occupational regulations that impose entry barriers tend to include input controls rather than performance-based criteria. This may be justified if performance-based criteria did not provide adequate protection to consumers. For instance, if unqualified persons were unable systematically to provide services meeting reasonable performance criteria, and the risk of harm to consumers from substandard service is very high, input control regulation may be preferable.

## C.   SECTOR-SPECIFIC AND GENERAL REGULATION

The regulatory structure applicable to an occupation is often complex. This complexity can pose a challenge for reformers, as analysis of and agreement on appropriate regulatory objectives or on how best to achieve them may not be straightforward.[5] Sector-specific occupational regulation may be justified when issues require a tailor-made solution, or the consequences of inappropriate behaviour are so serious that more stringent safeguards are required than those generally imposed. The various approaches to regulation need not, however, be mutually exclusive. The approach adopted is often a combination of the approaches described above and reliance on general law. Moreover, some laws allow specified professional associations to establish standards for entry into the occupation, conduct rules for practitioners, and other consumer safeguards. Safeguards usually include redress mechanisms, should inappropriate behaviour be detected. Accelerated dispute settlement procedures may be made available to aggrieved consumers, in addition to general legal processes.

The decision whether to regulate will depend on the nature of the transaction to be regulated, the seriousness of the consequences that would flow from inappropriate behaviour, and the likely effectiveness of different regulatory mechanisms. Serious consequences do not always dictate that a regulatory solution should be adopted. In many cases, government action will not be the most effective solution as the government may lack information and capacity to enforce regulations. Dispersed information, held by groups and individuals closer to the industry, may be more reliable and a better basis for action. In such situations, standards of practice developed and implemented by the profession may be preferable to government-prescribed regulation. The cultural context and general mores of social behaviour may impose significant sanctions for inappropriate behaviour through loss of reputation within the community.

Alternatively, economywide laws (including competition law, fair trade law, and common law principles of contract, tort and equity) and institutional structures may be sufficient to control behaviour. The extent to which specific regulation should displace the general law is an important issue in occupational regulation, and is discussed further in the section that follows.

In general, the principle that minimum feasible regulation targeted directly at the identified objective offers some guidance on whether general or sector-specific regulation should be adopted. An issue of general concern, such as the potential for misleading conduct, is normally best addressed through generally applicable legislation. Addressing such a general issue on a sector-by-sector basis can invite problems if all sectors are not covered. On the other hand, an issue specific to a sector, such as the need for lawyers to observe a higher than normal standard of care, should be addressed by sector-specific regulation. Departures from minimum feasible regulation threaten to give rise to unintended consequences.

## D. REGULATORY FAILURE

Broadly speaking, the rationale for regulation is to address a market failure. Regulation does not, in practice, always achieve its objective, and can have undesirable side-effects. Three key questions should be considered in this context. First, is the regulation well targeted to address the identified problems? Second, are all consequences of the regulation intended? Third, is the regulation better equipped than other policy instruments to address the problems? If the answer to any of these questions is no, then there is 'regulatory failure'. Policy makers must be acutely aware of the possibility of regulatory failure. In addressing a market failure, regulators risk substituting a regulatory failure, which may have even worse consequences than the initial market failure. The risk of regulatory failure is minimized if the processes of establishing and reviewing regulation follow sound principles. Accordingly, regulations should address a clearly stated objective, be analysed from an economywide perspective, be the minimum feasible regulation, and be periodically reviewed by appropriate bodies.

Even regulations that are appropriately targeted when established may, over time, become inappropriate through the evolution of their context and application. To this end, two issues should be considered: regulatory capture and regulatory drift. Regulatory capture occurs when a regulator's decisions are biased in favour of the regulated industry. This threatens to occur when professional associations are responsible for setting standards of entry, and for carrying out registration, licensing and/or certification functions. Professional bodies may be keen to maintain the incomes of existing practitioners, and can do so by restricting the supply of practitioners through high entry standards.[6]

Although entry standards may be necessary to ensure consumer protection, regulatory capture may lift standards above the necessary level. This may create skilled, high-priced services, and eliminate lower-quality, lower-priced services from the market. If so, consumers who cannot afford high-priced services, but may be adequately served by a less-qualified practitioner, tend to be marginalized or even excluded from the market. Where this occurs, governments may feel obliged to intervene further in the market to subsidize particular consumers, thereby allowing them access to the necessary services. This is an additional layer of regulation with the objective of counteracting the effect of the regulatory failure. A more direct means of addressing the issue would be directly to attack the regulatory failure.

The regulatory failures outlined above can be minimized by two safeguards. First, self-regulatory actions of professional bodies should be subject to competition law or, if competition law is not applicable, to some other means of control. In the absence of such control, the likelihood of regulatory capture is high. Second, members of the regulated group should not dominate professional governing bodies. For example, restrictions may be placed on the number of board members who have a pecuniary interest in the regulated industry. In setting such restrictions, the need to have members with specialist expertise must be considered.

Finally, even if regulations are appropriate when adopted, they can cease to be appropriate over the passage of time. Such regulatory drift can result from structural modification of the economy due to changing technology or consumer preferences. The required level of consumer protection may rise (if services become more complex) or fall (if consumers become more sophisticated). This suggests that, from time to time, regulations should be reviewed to ensure that they remain fit for their purpose.

## E.   REFORM OF OCCUPATIONAL REGULATION

Regulatory reform has two distinct elements, one substantive and one procedural. The reform of substantive regulation applying to a sector is often called 'deregulation', which can be misleading, since reforms are normally aimed at better-quality regulation. This may, in some circumstances, imply more regulation. Moreover, substantive reform can often involve an easing of the prescriptiveness of regulation, rather than a strict reduction in the number of regulations. Reform should generally aim at maintaining necessary consumer protection mechanisms while increasing flexibility for providers of goods and services. The first step is normally to assess the costs and benefits associated with a regulation, followed by pursuit of more cost-effective forms of regulation where necessary. Thus, prescriptive regulation could be replaced by performance-based regulation, where the quality of services provided by an occupation is regulated by standards and performance measures. Governments, industry bodies and consumer groups could participate in the development of standards and performance indicators so that the priorities of each are accommodated, where possible, by regulation. This kind of regulatory practice enables all participants in the market to take advantage of changing circumstances and to adjust their priorities accordingly, without undermining the purposes of regulation.

Governments can reform their own internal regulatory processes with the objective of improving the quality of new regulation. This could involve using a range of regulatory quality mechanisms, such as: including provisions within a law for its own periodic review and regulations promulgated under it; enacting provisions for more general reviews to determine anticompetitive effects and avenues of reform; requiring government proposals for new regulations or amendments to existing rules to be accompanied by regulatory impact statements; and enacting sunset provisions. Regulatory quality mechanisms can help reduce and avoid the regulatory inflation that many countries have experienced over recent decades.

## CONCLUSION

The underlying rationale of occupational regulation is protecting the consumer, which is legitimate in light of the complexity of the services in question. However, regulation may not be well designed to achieve this objective, and may be captured by and confer inappropriate benefits upon regulated groups. Governments have become increasingly aware of potential problems with regulation, and have initiated a range of review processes and ongoing accountability mechanisms to make regulation more effective.

The discussion in this chapter has raised a number of questions regarding appropriate regulatory policy. The following principles attempt to capture the essence of this discussion.

- The objective of a regulation should be clearly identified and the need for a regulatory solution should be demonstrated.
- The merits of a regulation should be assessed from an economywide perspective that includes an analysis of the interests of the regulated (including compliance costs) as well as of those whom the regulation is intended to benefit. Where feasible, this should include consultation with affected parties.
- Minimum feasible regulation, which minimizes restrictions on competition, should be used to ensure that regulations are well targeted and to lower the possibility that the regulation will have unintended consequences.
- The effects of various options (including non-regulatory options) should be analysed, including direct and secondary effects and implementation issues, to determine the net costs and benefits of the options.
- Where possible, regulatory standards should be consistent with international standards to minimize barriers to international competition.
- Competition law or some other controls should apply to self-regulatory activities of professional associations to ensure that they do not bring about unjustified restrictions on competition.
- Jurisdictions should ensure that regulatory bodies are composed of members that strike an appropriate balance between the need to have regulations set and administered by individuals with sufficient expertise, and the need to ensure that representatives of an occupation do not have inappropriate control over entry and conduct in a profession.
- Regulations should be subject to an ongoing review process to ensure that the rationale for their existence remains relevant, and that the regulation remains the best way of addressing any underlying problem.

## NOTES

1. Originally delivered at APEC (Asia-Pacific Economic Cooperation) Regulatory Reform Symposium, Duantan, Malaysia, 5–6 September 1998.
2. In Australia, many occupations have some form of sector-specific regulation. Such regulations are generally the responsibility of state governments, as the Commonwealth government does not have specific constitutional power to regulate occupations.
3. In Australia, registration schemes regulate entry into a range of occupations such as law, accounting and health services.
4. In Australia, licences have traditionally been required to practise many occupations, including construction and manufacturing, engineering trades and agricultural industries as well as

lawyers, accountants and other service professionals. For most occupations, the licence to practise has been valid only within the jurisdiction in which the licence was granted; an additional licence has been required to practise in another state or territory.

5. The Australian experience in some regulatory reform exercises is that the staff members of the regulator are not in agreement as to their objectives.

6. For example, the 1994 Baume Report, commissioned by the Australian Commonwealth government, found that the Royal Australasian College of Surgeons and other associations of specialist surgeons exercised an exceedingly high level of control over the supply of qualified general and specialist surgeons. The control of supply by these medical bodies is reflected in the fees and charges surgeons are able to command. A range of other studies have made similar links between the control of supply and high costs in relation to legal and accounting services.

# 6. Regulation, competition and the professions

## Frederic Jenny

*Consumers face information asymmetries and difficulties in evaluating quality of services, either* ex ante, *or sometimes even* ex post. *In addition, consumers do not even know where their demand curve lies because they do not know what services they need. As a result, in many professions, the consumer asks two things of the provider of the service: a prescription of where his/her demand curve lies, and the type of service and price offered by the professional to meet the consumer's demand. Since the consumer has no ability to assess the value of the prescription of the services offered, the provider of the service is able to induce either overconsumption or underconsumption – that is, to pretend that the demand curve is higher than it actually is.*

*Moreover, consumption of many services, such as medical or legal services, is urgent and nearly compulsory. Thus, the consumer cannot defer or refuse to buy the service. In such circumstances, consumers have no mobility across service providers, no possibility of comparing their respective services. Thus, even if there are no anticompetitive restrictions due to self-regulation, competition cannot work in a meaningful way or in a way that will lead to efficiency in the professions.*

*Traditional microeconomic theory suggests that if certain restrictions are eliminated, competition will follow, leading to a better allocation of resources. However, this theory is based on the assumption that consumers know where their demand curves lie and have perfect information. Since these assumptions are not true with respect to professional services, it is not obvious that efficiency will follow when anticompetitive practices are eliminated. For services used repeatedly, business consumers can overcome these problems through innovative contractual arrangements and vertical integration. However, such solutions are not available for individual consumers.*

*A recent development in France lies at the heart of one part of the problem. Markets for professional services would function more effectively if the diagnosis could be separated from the provision of the service. In a number of professions, firms have emerged whose function is to assess the proposals made by the providers of the service. The emergence of this new profession raises the question of how to assess the value of the firm that assesses the value of the other firms. This emergence has been met with considerable resistance by many professions. In several cases, the profession boycotted any person who would resort to such a firm.*

*Finally, the chapter suggests that if this assessment function cannot be done privately because there is no quality control on the firm making the assessment, perhaps the state should provide such a service to consumers.*

## INTRODUCTION

In France, a variety of professional services (such as services of medical doctors, dentists, pharmacists, lawyers, accountants and so on) are either regulated by public authorities or subject to self-regulation elaborated by the professionals themselves. When such sectors are not publicly regulated or subject to some form of officially sanctioned self-regulation, the professionals involved tend to establish private collective agreements to regulate their members' behaviour. Typically, these professional regulations contain provisions establishing conditions of entry into the profession, the scope of permissible activity of the professionals, and the duties of the professionals *vis-à-vis* their clients and other professionals of the same sector.

Collective anticompetitive behaviour resulting from compliance with public regulatory professional codes is legally exempt from French competition law.[1] However, the French competition authority (*Conseil de la concurrence*) may be called upon to decide whether professionals have restricted competition above and beyond these regulations. The legal exemption does not, however, apply to professional services that have no officially recognized public regulation, but only self-regulation or an ethical code. The *Conseil de la concurrence* must sometimes consider whether anticompetitive conduct resulting from the provisions of the ethical code contribute to economic progress and can thus be exempted from antitrust law through an efficiency defence.

In recent years, the *Conseil de la concurrence* has examined the effects on competition of public regulation or private self-regulation in a number of professional sectors. The publicly regulated professions include: pharmacists;[2] medical doctors;[3] dental surgeons;[4] architects;[5] lawyers;[6] accountants;[7] and surveyors.[8] The professions that are not publicly regulated but have a private self-regulation code include advertising agencies;[9] optometrists;[10] private detectives;[11] operators of ambulance services;[12] real estate agencies;[13] construction experts;[14] and art experts.[15]

Public codes or self-regulations are found in the professional services sector much more frequently than in the industrial goods sector. From an economic standpoint, how can the proliferation of such codes in the professional services sector be explained? Are these sectors subject to specific market failures that could justify a restriction of competition among professionals?

## A.   THE NATURE OF THE COMPETITIVE PROCESS

The ultimate goal of competition policy is to promote an efficient allocation of resources.[16] Standard economic analysis suggests that competition will lead to an efficient allocation of resources only if a number of conditions are met, including perfect information of economic agents. This condition applies both to the providers and consumers of goods and services. Providers must have perfect information on, for instance, available technologies and factor costs; consumers must have the information needed to know their preferences and the position and shape of their demand curves as well as the characteristics or qualities of the goods or services offered by the different suppliers.

Assuming that suppliers are profit maximizers, they will automatically choose to provide the goods or services that maximize their profits. These are the goods and services for which the difference between the price per unit that consumers are willing to pay (a measure of the utility that consumers attach to the units of the good or service given their tastes, the opportunities available to them and their budgetary constraints) and the cost of production of these units (a measure of the social cost of production) is the largest. Competition among producers of a particular good or service will thus force them to minimize their costs of production and sales prices. The competitive market mechanism will thereby maximize the surplus of the economy. The position of consumers' aggregate demand curves for various goods and services will indicate to producers what to produce, and will contribute to the efficient allocation of factors in the economy.

In this classical and simplified explanation of how competitive markets work, no strategic role is assigned to intermediaries, such as retailers. The market is characterized as a direct confrontation between supply and demand without any need for intermediaries.

In the real world, the assumption of perfect information of economic agents is never fully satisfied. Indeed, the role of assumptions in social science models is not to describe real-life conditions, but to provide a simplified (and therefore partly inaccurate) representation of reality. An assumption is justified only if it does not contradict other assumptions, and if it allows derivation of results that are not contradicted by empirical analysis. A consequence of the assumption that consumers have perfect information in market theory is that, when confronted with competing suppliers of a good or service, consumers will tend to switch to the supplier who offers the best quality–price ratio. Thus, in the competitive model, poor performers (that is, those charging a higher price than their competitors for a given level of quality or those offering a lower quality for a given price) must either improve their performance or face the risk of being eliminated from the market.

The assumption that economic agents have perfect information seems acceptable (that is, seems to lead to predictions consistent with empirical tests) with respect to common standardized industrial goods subject to repeated buying. Through various channels, including experience developed over time, advertising and the press, among others, consumers reward the suppliers who offer them the best quality–price ratio for such goods. Ample empirical evidence indicates that inefficient firms tend to lose market share over time, and must eventually improve their performance or face elimination from the market.

However, as goods become more complex and more differentiated, the assumption that consumers have perfect information as to what is available on the market becomes more problematic. With imperfect information, consumers rely less on their experience and more on external advice or sources of information to determine where their demand curve lies for particular products or particular brands of a product, or to assess the respective characteristics and quality of competing branded goods. This is why retailers in the real economic world play a more proactive role in the market mechanism than the basic economic model assumes.

Beyond playing a passive role of delivering the goods that consumers want to buy, retailers play a prescriptive role by selecting brands, displaying the products that they offer for sale, demonstrating the respective qualities of the goods they have selected and advising the consumer. This can help consumers establish where their demand curve lies for various products. Thus, the strategy of retailers becomes a crucial factor in shaping the market equilibrium. Manufacturers of industrial branded goods recognized this phenomenon long ago, and developed cooperative mechanisms with their retailers so that their products would be 'pushed'. This directly contradicts the assumption that consumers, knowing their preferences and having perfect information on the available goods, know precisely where their demand curve lies. The cooperation sought by manufacturers is frequently obtained through a reduction in the level of competition among their retailers, such as through selective or exclusive distribution systems. This makes it difficult for competition authorities to assess the consequences of such cooperation mechanisms on intrabrand and interbrand competition, and to assess their welfare effects.

## B.   PROFESSIONAL SERVICES AND MARKET FAILURE

When examining the limitations of applying the traditional, simplified microeconomic model of competitive markets in the area of professional services, two distinct features should be considered. First, consumers (particularly individual consumers) often do not know what their needs are. This violates one of the conditions necessary for competitive processes to lead to an efficient allocation of resources. Consumers usually have limited means to assess independently where their demand curve lies, and must therefore rely on the prescriptions of service suppliers. Accordingly, suppliers can behave strategically and manipulate consumer demands, which thus can no longer be considered a constraint to which suppliers adjust by channelling resources to their most socially efficient use. 'Moral hazard' is also a problem when consumers do not know where their demand curve lies and must rely on service providers to prescribe the appropriate level of service. For example, in countries where doctors are paid for each medical act performed, they tend to prescribe many more medical acts than do doctors in countries where their revenue is independent of the number of medical acts performed.

Second, professional services are often customized rather than standardized, making it extremely difficult to compare features of competing offers *ex ante*, or the value of the service provided *ex post*. For example, when an architect is paid a percentage of the cost of a building or a house, it can be exceedingly difficult for the consumer to determine whether the construction options selected were the most economical. It is also difficult for a car owner to judge whether the garage to which his/her car has been towed has provided an accurate assessment of necessary repairs *ex ante*, or whether all the repairs undertaken were justified *ex post*.

The combination of consumers' inability to know where their demand curve lies and their inability to assess the quality of the services provided by different professionals has several implications: that even in a competitive environment, too much or too little of a service may be provided compared to where the consumer's demand curve would lie if he/she had perfect information; and that the price paid for the service may be higher than it would have been if the consumer had perfect information, due to the impossibility of assessing the quality–price ratio of competing service providers' offers.

## C.   REGULATION AND SELF-REGULATION OF THE PROFESSIONS

Corporate clients of professional services can sometimes avoid, at least partially, the transaction costs implied by the moral hazard problem. For example, a corporation with a large fleet of trucks can vertically integrate and repair its own trucks, rather than be overcharged or face the cost of unnecessary repairs by independent garages. Moreover, for both corporate and individual consumers, leasing contracts can, where feasible, substantially eliminate the moral hazard cost related to repair services for complex machines such as computers or automobiles, since the equipment owner must make repairs and has no incentive to overcharge him/herself or to undertake unnecessary repairs.

In most cases, however, vertical integration is not an option for individual consumers. Moreover, the innovative contractual arrangements mentioned in the preceding paragraph may not be applicable to a wide range of professional services, such as the services of medical doctors or lawyers. Where they are applicable, they give rise to another externality: users of the leased complex machines have no incentive to use them carefully, since they do not have to pay for repairs. Such contracts, therefore, do not guarantee an optimal allocation of resources.

In addition, individuals are often especially vulnerable to the strategic behaviour of suppliers of professional services because they cannot choose not to consume the service. In contrast, goods consumers usually can either defer or abandon the purchase of a good, and are thus in a better position to exert pressure on suppliers. For example, a consumer considering the possibility of buying a television or a computer can defer his/her purchase to explore the options available to him/her more thoroughly. In contrast, an injured or sick patient urgently requiring the services of a medical doctor often does not have either the time or the mobility necessary to explore the market. Similarly, the owner of a damaged car often cannot avoid having his/her car repaired. In some cases (for example, services provided by lawyers and public notaries), legal requirements may compel the consumer to find a service provider. For example, a person who is sued may be forced to find a lawyer to represent him/her.

The vulnerability of consumers from these combined factors has given rise to a variety of derogatory terms commonly used by the general public to describe some service providers (for example, 'quack' doctors, 'crooked' lawyers, 'cheating' automobile repairmen). In the best of cases, public authorities believe they should regulate a number of professions to protect unsuspecting consumers. Regarding professions that are not publicly regulated, attempts at self-regulation may be motivated by the desire of professionals to protect their collective reputation by limiting the amount of abuse that can be imposed on inherently vulnerable clients. For instance, in France, numerous professional regulations require members of the profession to behave in ways that will not bring ill repute to the profession.

Professional groups (for example, associations of lawyers, doctors, pharmacists, architects, surveyors) often argue that limiting entry in a profession through qualification requirements assessed by incumbent professionals will ensure that unsuspecting consumers do not suffer from poor-quality or inadequate service, and will prevent overconsumption (particularly in the case of medical doctors). They argue further that limiting competition among providers will benefit consumers by protecting them against deceptive tactics or false or misleading claims. In France, for example, self-regulation of 'building managers' (*gestionnaires d'immeubles*) not only prohibited a building manager from aggressively seeking the clientele of a competitor, but also required him/her to notify a competitor whenever the owner of a building had spontaneously decided to change from a competitor to him/her. Another example is the French medical doctors' regulatory code of ethics, which prohibits doctors from advertising and precisely specifies the information allowed on a letterhead or appearing on their office door. Doctors are also prohibited from practising in a building in which another doctor practising in the same field is already established, unless the latter agrees to the opening of another practice in the same building. This provision is often justified on the ground that it protects patients from confusion between doctors and from the risk of being treated by a doctor not familiar with their medical background. Another provision of this code requires that when a patient consults a doctor who is not his/her regular doctor, the consulted doctor must forward his/her diagnosis to the regular doctor and not give it directly to the patient. The alleged purpose of this requirement is to ensure that the diagnosis of the consulted doctor is accurate given the medical history of the patient.

It is also argued that limiting price competition among professional service providers by establishing a concerted tariff will protect consumers against abusively high prices and the temptation of certain suppliers to offer more competitive prices by lowering quality. For instance, the self-regulation of French advertising agencies required them to charge a uniform fee of 10 per cent of the value of the advertising space purchased by the client. A number of professional groups, including those of architects and lawyers, make collective price recommendations.

The self-regulation of the three main French professional associations of art experts and appraisers provides an excellent, albeit extreme, example of anti-competitive self-regulation. Art appraisers advise potential buyers or sellers as to both the authenticity and value of a piece of art. Courts may also call upon them to testify in judicial proceedings. It is notoriously difficult for clients to assess the quality of the services rendered in these professions. Aware of the suspicion in which they are held by consumers, art appraisers have created three professional associations, each with a private professional code of conduct, the stated purpose of which is to guarantee the quality of the services offered by their members. An examination by the *Conseil de la concurrence* in 1998 revealed:

- In one of these organizations, new members could be admitted only if they passed a professional examination administered by the incumbents, or if they were co-opted by the other members of the organization. In the other two organizations, a new member could be admitted only with the recommendation of two members, one of whom should be in the same or a closely related field to that of the applicant, and only if the applicant had more than eight years of practice in the field in one case, or more than ten years in the other case. It was explicitly provided that the ruling councils of the professional associations need not motivate their decisions regarding the admission of new members.

- In all three associations, experts could practise only in a limited number of fields, irrespective of their professional qualifications. They were required to cooperate with other members of the same association if they were called upon to assess the authenticity and value of collections of objects falling in more than the three categories for which they were listed.

- The behavioural section of the codes required the experts to abstain from 'unbecoming' pricing or commercial behaviour, such as overcharging or lowering their fees in the hope of attracting clients, or using commercial techniques to attract the clients of a competitor.

- One of the codes required that whenever a member was to intervene in an auction, he/she should enquire whether another member of the organization had assessed the authenticity or the value of the objects being auctioned during a period of three years preceding the time of the auction. If so, he/she should share his/her fees with the other member.

- The same code required that if a member was called upon to assess the authenticity or value of an object, he/she should determine whether the owner of the object usually called on another expert. If so, the member was required to warn the other expert with a view to either collaboration or compensation.

- Finally, all three organizations published recommended tariffs and exchanged information on the names of members they had expelled for non-compliance with their self-regulations.

It is highly doubtful whether any of these provisions was useful in guaranteeing the quality of the expert work undertaken by members.

## D. THE CASE AGAINST REGULATION AND SELF-REGULATION IN THE PROFESSIONS

Competition authorities tend to view unfavourably the provisions typically found in professional codes or self-regulations, recognizing that they are often used as vehicles for unwarranted protectionism. They lobby for deregulation of the professions whose anticompetitive professional codes result from a public law or a regulation, and sanction privately established professional codes of ethics or self-regulations with anticompetitive effects. The main reason for their scepticism is that they doubt whether the restrictions to competition embedded in such codes and self-regulations can have the positive effects of eliminating or alleviating the moral hazard problem. For example, a provision limiting entry or price competition does not guarantee that each supplier will not induce consumers to overconsume, and may result in a higher average price than would be obtained if competition prevailed. Similarly, a provision limiting the ability of doctors or architects to open a practice may result in less choice for consumers, and therefore a more limited scope for competition than would exist if entry were not constrained.

Most professional regulatory codes or self-regulations are, at best, crude instruments to alleviate the problem of information asymmetry faced by consumers, because they assume that competition will lead professionals to behave in a strategic fashion with regard to consumers. They assume that without regulatory intervention, professionals would deceive consumers, clients or patients to entice them away from competitors. Specifically, professionals would allegedly make false claims, offer shoddy quality, oversell services or charge abusively high prices. However, as profit maximizers, professionals will do so, if they can, irrespective of whether they are faced with competitive pressure. If anything, the elimination of competitive pressures may exacerbate the tendency of professionals to behave strategically. For example, the provision of the French medical code, described above, which makes it difficult for patients to obtain a second opinion, facilitates overtreatment. The patient has little possibility of assessing the accuracy of the diagnosis, leaving him/her little recourse but to comply with the doctor's orders.

Since professionals usually draft the professional codes to which they will be subject, either alone or with the relevant governmental authorities, such codes are subject to regulatory capture. For instance, provisions which require a period of traineeship for entry in a profession, but which do not establish a mechanism which guarantees that a traineeship can be obtained by all aspiring candidates, can act as barriers. Similarly, provisions conditioning entry on the presentation of two or three recommendations by established professionals are also problematic.

## E.   THE LIMITS OF COMPETITION IN THE SECTOR OF PROFESSIONAL SERVICES

Removing the most blatant anticompetitive provisions of regulatory codes or self-regulations will promote free entry and increase competition among the providers of a particular service. However, it may not promote competition sufficiently to lead to an efficient allocation of resources. As discussed above, some professionals have an incentive to behave strategically by manipulating the information they provide to potential clients. As long as consumers cannot get an independent assessment of where their demand curve lies, and of the quality of service provided by competing suppliers, competitive market mechanisms may not function properly. Under such circumstances, market mechanisms will not fully guarantee that the information disseminated, or the diverse contractual arrangements available, will allow consumers to make informed decisions. However, only informed decisions are consistent with economic efficiency. Just as restricting competition constitutes an inadequate tool for solving the moral hazard problem, restoring competition without addressing the consumer's need for information will usually not lead to the expected positive result.

In certain cases, elimination of anticompetitive practices in the professional service sector is likely to increase the dispersion of both prices and the quality of services offered. This could be a positive development, allowing freer choice by consumers. If, however, they remain dependent on the prescriptions of service providers, the increased uncertainty that risk-averse consumers face regarding price and quality of services offered may partially offset the benefits from freer competition. This may explain the scepticism (or even outright hostility) that French consumer organizations have shown towards decisions prohibiting price fixing by certain professions, such as lawyers and architects.

## F.   A NECESSARY COMPLEMENT TO COMPETITION IN THE PROFESSIONS

The key to promoting efficiency in the professions is to alleviate the information problem faced by consumers, thereby enabling them to determine where their demand curve lies and to know what options are open to them.

In France, a new form of activity is emerging with respect to some professions: the auditing of prescriptions or services furnished by service providers. This is similar to the role played by independent experts working for insurance companies who assess the actual damage to a car that has been in an accident, and the true cost of repairs (although the independence of the experts from the insurance companies for which they work is questionable). Over the last ten years, firms have also emerged that specialize in auditing advertising agencies' proposals to clients. French advertising firms traditionally receive fees based on the amount of advertising space bought by their clients. The demand for auditors arose because clients suspected that advertising agencies behaved strategically, either by recommending the purchase of too much advertising space or by overcharging for the advertising space. Similarly, auditing services are now also available with respect to the budgets of advertising films used by clients to promote their products or their company. Advertising film auditors emerged because most commercial firms wanting to use film advertisement know very little about the film industry, and felt that the producers of such films could behave strategically and overcharge them. Auditors would also be useful with respect to architectural, medical or legal services.

Independent auditing, either by commercial firms or free clinics, of the prescriptions made by service providers may not be a perfect solution, since the independence and quality of service provided by the auditors may also be difficult to assess. However, it can impede members of the professions from strategic use of their dual role as the one who prescribes and provides the services. Auditors are a necessary complement to the elimination of the most blatantly anticompetitive provisions of regulatory codes and self-regulation used by the professions.

If this assessment function cannot be done privately because there is no quality control on the firm making the assessment, perhaps the state should provide such a service to consumers. It could, for instance, establish free or public clinics to provide an assessment of diagnosis before the consumer sees the service provider. This would be a useful complement to the antitrust authority to eliminate unjustified anticompetitive practices.

## NOTES

1. Decision No. 86–1243 of 1 December 1986 regarding the freedom of pricing and competition.
2. See Decision of the *Conseil de la concurrence* of 4 February 1998 regarding an action and demand for injunction presented by Mrs Slamon Evrard, 1988 Annual Report of the *Conseil de la concurrence*, p. 852; Decision No. 98-D-56 of the *Conseil de la concurrence* of 15 September 1998 regarding business practices in the pharmacy sector of Val d'Yerres dans l'Essonne, 1998 Annual Report of the *Conseil de la concurrence*, p. 652; Decision No. 97-D-26 of 22 April 1997 regarding business practices detected in the sector of delivery of medication to residences, *BOCCRF* (*Bulletin officiel de la Concurrence, de la Consommation et de la Répression des frauds* – Official bulletin of competition, consumer protection and repression of fraud) (8 July 1997); Decision No. 97-D-18 of 18 March 1997 regarding business practices in the sector of delivery of medication to residences, *BOCCRF* (29 April 1997); Decision No. 90-D-08 of 23 January 1990 regarding business practices with respect to setting opening hours for pharmacies, *BOCCRF* (22 February 1990).
3. See Decision No. 96-D-49 of 3 July 1996 regarding business practices in the organization of doctors on duty in Grand Amiens, *BOCCRF* (27 July 1996); Decision No. 95-D-8 of 19 December 1995 regarding business practices in the sector of prosthesis of joints, *BOCCRF* (15 May 1996).
4. See Decision No. 97-D-25 of 22 April 1997 regarding business practices of unions of dental surgeons in Indre and Loire CNSD 37 and of Rhône CNSD 69, *BOCCRF* (8 July 1997); Decision No. 89-D-36 of 7 November 1989 regarding business practices in the market of dental prostheses, *BOCCRF* (1 December 1989).

5. See Decision No. 96-D-18 of 26 March 1996 regarding business practices of the regional council of the order of architects of Auvergne and of architects' offices on the occasion of a public market, *BOCCRF* (27 July 1996); Opinion No. 95-A-19 of 7 November 1995 regarding a request for opinion presented by the regional council of the order of architects of the Aquitaine region on the professional services by the Pact-Arim. Associations, *BOCCRF* (12 February 1996); Decision No. 95-D-35 of 10 May 1995 regarding business practices in the sector of distribution of pharmaceuticals in the valley of Arve, *BOCCRF* (25 July 1995).

6. See Opinion No. 90-A-02 of 4 January 1990 concerning the draft law relative to the exercise of liberal professions for which the title is protected by legislation or regulation, *BOCCRF* (22 February 1990).

7. See Opinion No. 97-A-12 of 17 June 1997 regarding a request for opinion presented by the order of accountants, the professional unions IFEC (Insititut Français des experts comptables – French Institute of Accountants), ECF (Federation des experts comptables de France – Federation of French Accountants) and the union to promote accountants, regarding the restriction of the exercise of their professional activities in the legal domain, *BOCCRF* (18 November 1997).

8. See Decision No. 98-D-28 of the *Conseil de la concurrence* of 21 April 1998 regarding an action and demand for injunction presented by Mr Seguin, geometry expert, 1988 Annual Report of the *Conseil de la concurrence*, p. 399.

9. See Opinion No. 87-A-12 of 18 December 1987 regarding the advertising sector, *BOCCRF* (26 December 1987).

10. See Opinion No. 89-A-12 of 12 September 1989 regarding a proposal for the preamble of statutes of the union of opticians in the Rhône-Alpes region, *BOCCRF* (30 September 1989).

11. See Decision No. 92-D-39 of 16 June 1992 regarding business practices in the sector of private researchers, *BOCCRF* (15 August 1992).

12. See Decision No. 95-D-6e of 24 October 1995 regarding business practices of transport enterprises working with the hospital centre Robert-Boulin de Libourne, *BOCCRF* (24 January 1996).

13. See Decision of 9 April 1996 regarding business practices in the sector of management and expertise in real estate, *BOCCRF* (3 September 1996).

14. See Decision No. 97-MC-01 of 4 February 1997 regarding a question of injunction presented by the Finance and external commerce minister in the sector of technical control of builders, *BOCCRF* (11 June 1997).

15. See Decision No. 98-D-81 of the *Conseil de la concurrence* of 21 December 1998 regarding business practices in the sector of art and art collection experts, 1998 Annual Report of the *Conseil de la concurrence*, p. 829.

16. See generally *European Competition Law Annual 1997: The Objectives of Competition Policy* (Claus Dieter Ehlermann and Laraine Laudati, eds, Oxford: Hart, 1998).

# 7.  Panel discussion

**Prof. Jenny**   With respect to Mrs Bruzzone's chapter, I would like to make the following point. I was recently in Australia, and I met with Dr Hilmer to discuss my concern about an issue unrelated to the subject of this conference – competition at the multilateral level. Because there is no constituency for this, I asked him, 'In Australia, how did you create a constituency for the changes in regulation? What was your recipe?'. His reply was that initially they looked at sectors where there were regulations that were very obviously anticompetitive. They rapidly realized that going the sectoral route was going to generate resistance from each and every lobby. So they decided not to do this, and to look at the general picture, and thereby get at a higher level of abstraction. He said that this was a very useful approach.

Second, the Motta/Fumagalli chapter mentions that advertising restrictions have an anticompetitive effect, and therefore should be eliminated. If we start from that standpoint, any kind of restriction on the strategy of a firm is always going to have an anticompetitive effect and should always be eliminated. But this seems short-sighted – we must consider what the alternative would be. In the case of advertising allowed for good and bad doctors, what I fail to see is, if advertising is allowed, would not the bad doctors just increase their prices to pass off as good doctors, since patients are unable to distinguish bad from good doctors? If they *are* able to distinguish bad from good doctors, then we have a different logic. This is for further discussion. Let us have a look at the US on the question of advertising.

**Dr Laudati**   I should like to begin with a comment regarding the European Commission's recent decisions in the area of advertising by professionals. The Commission has issued three decisions, the first in 1993 (customs agents in Italy), the second in 1995 (industrial property agents in Spain), and the third in April 1999 (professional patent agents before the European patent organization). All three held that Article 81 is applicable to the code of conduct of the professional association involved, and that agreements made through these codes of conduct constituted a restriction of competition. The logic was as follows: the members were deemed to be undertakings; the professional associations were deemed to be associations of undertakings; the codes of conduct were deemed to be decisions of associations of undertakings; and therefore the provisions of the codes of conduct which set maximum and minimum fee schedules were deemed to be appreciable restrictions of competition, in violation of Article 81(1). The 1999 case also involved a professional code provision that placed a limit on comparative advertising, and on solicitation of the clients of another patent agent. The Commission decided that these provisions were also in violation of Article 81(1), although it granted a short-term exemption under Article 81(3). It thus allowed these latter provisions to continue in effect until some time in the year 2000, in order to ease the transition between a situation where no advertising had been allowed, to one where there will be no restriction on advertising. It is very encouraging that the Commission has decided that Article 81 applies to advertising by professionals. It is still case law in its infancy, and it will be very interesting to see what further use will be made of it.

The difference between the Commission's interpretation of its role with respect to professional codes, versus that of the US, is noteworthy. In the Commission, the decision was made that Article 81 applied even though member state authorities may approve the professional codes (in the case of customs agents, the code was approved by the authorities; in the case involving industrial property agents, the agents had received national authorization to create a professional code). In contrast, in the US, the state action doctrine established in the Supreme Court decision of *Parker v. Brown* holds that the federal antitrust laws do not apply when an action is deemed to be one of the state. Thus, all state regulations are outside of federal antitrust scrutiny. This is, however, something that the Supreme Court has found a way around because, as my chapter makes clear, it has interpreted the First Amendment to protect commercial speech and its analysis under the commercial speech doctrine of advertising has been very similar to antitrust analysis.

Professional codes of conduct by associations of lawyers are generally deemed to be state action, because the state supreme courts generally approve them. In the *Goldfarb* case, however, the federal antitrust laws were applied to invalidate the fee schedule of a professional association of lawyers, based on the technicality that a county bar association had established this fee schedule. The Court held that since the county bar association was a separate and voluntary organization, it fell within the coverage of the antitrust laws.

Second, the Motta/Fumagalli chapter has discussed a list of reasons used to justify advertising restrictions. Each of these can be illustrated by cases that the Supreme Court has decided. First is the idea that lawyer advertising would be unethical. In several of the cases, the Court has explicitly rejected this argument, based on the economic realities of the situation, that lawyers earn their livelihood from the practice of law. Second is that advertising would cause the quality of services to decrease. In a case involving a ban on price advertising by pharmacists, the Court ruled that this was absolutely not the case, and all that the ban did was to insulate all pharmacists, both good and bad, from competition, but did nothing to ensure quality of service. Third is that advertising might result in an increase in concentration. In one case, the Court held that lawyer advertising would absolutely not increase concentration and that the opposite was, in fact, the case. Established lawyers benefit greatly from not having advertising, whereas new lawyers trying to enter have a great deal of difficulty because they are not able to advertise.

**Prof. Fels**   Regarding self-regulation, we deal with that in Australia in a manner that does not differ greatly from how other countries do. I agree with Professor Scarpa's analysis, that self-regulation tends to be driven by self-interest. Therefore, I do not have strongly positive feelings about self-regulation, but I do have some positive feelings: self-regulation is usually well informed, by people who know what to do, and sometimes it is well motivated. Australian law condemns any self-regulation that is the result of private agreement in a profession and is anticompetitive, or is otherwise likely to violate the antitrust laws, unless the profession comes forward to the Commission and seeks authorization on the ground that a sufficient public benefit is present.

We have dealt with several hundred cases of regulations by occupations, professions and businesses. For instance, several years ago, locksmiths wanted to form a master locksmiths' association. Becoming a member would have great value, because it would be well known that the members had particularly good locks. They came to the Commission with the proposal to form this association, and to exclude some people from it. That sounded anticompetitive. We asked them to justify this terribly anticompetitive arrangement, and to explain who would be excluded from membership. They replied, for a start, that anyone with a criminal record should be excluded. That sounded not totally unreasonable. They also wanted to exclude anyone who was unethical in their behaviour, which meant that they cut prices. We decided not to uphold that restriction. Typically, the better self-regulation schemes have anticompetitive elements, and sometimes it must be quite anticompetitive to work well. In this case, they wanted to have disciplinary powers to exclude certain people. They need independent procedures, including independent tribunals, to ensure that any expulsions from an association are for legitimate reasons. There is an issue of how to harness the best elements of self-regulation, but at the same time protect the public interest against abuse.

I shall turn to several issues of politics and practical experience. Professor Jenny asked why the lobbies are successful. Economics tends to rely on the public choice theory, which, although not without some value, is a limited and poor explanation of many political phenomena. There are élite theories of regulation. For instance, the central role of lawyers in politics has an important effect on self-regulation. The medical profession is intimately involved, and disproportionately influential, in the making of health policy. The government is dependent on the medical profession for the success of its health policy. As a byproduct, they get some anticompetitive bonuses. The public choice theory of Stigler has some excellent ideas, but is totally ahistorical. Stigler's theory suggested that industry wanted regulation at a time when exactly the opposite was happening: there was a wave of regulation that industry did not want.

Finally, as to what might be done, I suggest the following. First, we must establish some general principles and criteria of professional regulation and self-regulation, and get the central agencies of government involved. Typically, regulatory capture is a problem. For instance, there have been countless crusading attorneys general and lawyers in Australia who have argued in favour of reform of the legal profession. The matter is then sent back to the legal profession to sort out. What is really needed is for the central agencies, the treasuries, the finance ministers, the prime ministers, the presidents and so on to take control of how the regulation works rather than leaving it to the professions themselves. Law and health are primary examples of where this is needed.

Second, sanctions should be imposed to ensure that reforms come about. For instance, in Australia, we are attempting to impose some financial sanctions on the state governments to ensure that they implement the reforms.

Third, publicity is needed. For instance, in the medical area, regulation is often justified as being there to protect the public or the sacred character of the relationship between doctors and patients. In the US and Australia, market power is crudely exercised in this area to raise medical incomes at the expense of the public, with no broader ethical issues. When doctors boycott a hospital to get their pay increased, or when they have a price-fixing agreement, we should perhaps take advantage of the public prejudice against the medical profession.

Fourth, regulation should be subject to transparent, public, independent periodic scrutiny from outside the profession. Competition law should be fully applied, with no exceptions for the professions.

Fifth, competition advocacy has an important role. Competition advocacy is usually a sign that the competition people have been left out. Professor Amato quite correctly stated that there has been a change in public perception and understanding over time. People are starting to become aware that major competition issues exist in many areas. However, the political system has not responded by giving power to the procompetition lobby to bring about the changes. Rather, competition agencies are usually not terribly important in the political scheme of things, but are allowed only to go along and give a speech at a public hearing on a regulation, or to submit comments. To bring about the needed changes, competition policy should instead be injected into the central areas of government decision making, through the most powerful agencies and ministers, from the prime ministers down.

**Prof. Jenny**   The French Competition Authority deals extensively with regulation of the professions, and strives to eliminate anticompetitive restrictions of all types. Yet, I am not completely satisfied with our job performance, or with the impact of our work, although we keep doing it and I think we should keep on doing it. The reason for my dissatisfaction is that once the most obvious competition restrictions in the professions have been eliminated, competition should work in a meaningful way and lead to an efficient result, but I am not convinced that it does. More competition will differentiate prices and services, resulting in a wider spectrum of possible individual transactions. However, if there is no appreciation of the fair price or the fair quality of service, consumers may pay more or have a lower quality of service than they would if they could appreciate price and quality. A wider diversity of outcomes is possible with more competition.

Thus, risk-averse consumers may feel satisfied that public regulation or self-regulation of doctors, limiting their number and imposing at least some kind of constraint on their performance, is better than no regulation. How many divorces must one experience before finding the right divorce lawyer? One often hears talk about 'crooked lawyers'. No one complains about 'crooked steel makers'. What is the reason for this difference of perception? It may be the inability of consumers to assess quality, and their awareness of this inability. Even if we eliminate some of the anticompetitive provisions, we still do not have a market that works very well.

In light of the above, I query whether we are doing something that is useful, and that will make a significant difference with respect to how markets work. In France, the competition authority's decisions to open up professions, or eliminate seemingly anticompetitive self-regulation, have been met with considerable hostility on the part of consumer organizations. They have systematically argued that it is fine to tell consumers to try to make comparisons about things for which they have no understanding, but this is not a very useful proposition.

Some of the chapters have discussed liability rules or diligence rules, suggesting that this is one way that abuses might be eliminated. Such rules, however, are not a perfect solution. First, they are *ex post* solutions, used after the damage has been done. The damage normally imposes a heavy cost. Second, consumers must rely on the courts to determine diligence or malpractice. Then we are back to the problem of how to assess the quality of the service. Medical malpractice is extremely difficult to establish.

My chapter discusses a new activity that has been emerging in France to address this problem: independent auditing of services. Such auditing may impede professionals from strategic use of their dual role as the one who prescribes and provides services.

**Dr Hilke**  Professor Jenny's chapter and comments raise the question of what actually constitutes a consumer protection regime. To talk about it in terms of truthful advertising policing is not, in our opinion, a sufficient view of what this function constitutes. We also see consumer protection as the role of identifying pieces of information that consumers can use to do comparative shopping. The Federal Trade Commission has created many trade rules that require the publication of information that consumers can use to compare products. For instance, an 'R' rule has been promulgated with respect to insulation, which means that anyone who is selling thermo pane windows or insulation must reveal the insulation quality. A scale is provided, and the manner of testing for purposes of the scale is set. The same was used in conjunction with tobacco products to get a nicotine reading, which was required to be revealed at each sale. Consumers could use this information to aid in comparison shopping. The combination of truthful advertising and a standard that consumers can use to make comparisons seems like a better and fuller definition of what consumer protection ought to consist of.

We have been discussing how consumers are not able to assess lawyer quality. Can any of us provide an objective definition of what lawyer quality is? If no engineering-based comparison of quality is possible, the problem is greater than it is for something like insulation, where a technical definition can be used. I suspect that the possibility of assessing quality for various goods and services lies along some sort of gradient, and as we think about remedies, a clear distinction ought to be maintained between those for which quality can be scientifically established, and those for which it cannot.

**Prof. Siniscalco**  I have two comments. First, with respect to advertising, a clear distinction must be made between information, commercial speech (as defined in the chapter by Dr Laudati), persuasive advertising and comparative advertising.

Second, I believe we should analyse matters in a dynamic context, rather than in a static context as we are now doing. In the area of cultural evolution, one analyses social and legal norms as norms that evolve through a process. The two key questions are why do they change, and why are they so slow to change? Social and juridical norms typically evolve very slowly given the needs of a certain society.

The existing restrictions on advertising are typical of low geographical mobility. In a world of high mobility, the need for information grows. If I live in my town and travel infrequently, then the advertising restriction may be appropriate. But if I travel often, and I have a car accident in France, or need a dentist in Barcelona, and I am not from those areas then information is necessary. This seems like another case where the institution is adapting too slowly to the needs.

**Mr Heimler**    The politics of how to introduce competition is a very important aspect of our work, and of the work of other antitrust authorities concerned with competition advocacy. The problem with liberalization is that it should be multidimensional: each element on which firms compete should be taken into account for the reform to be successful. For instance, if we partially liberalize an industry, freeing enterprises regulated on many dimensions of their activity to charge the price they like, then we would not expect competition to produce all the benefits we expect, provided that other dimensions of competition, such as entry, hours of work, or innovation, are still strictly regulated. Since our goal is to benefit the consumer, liberalizing one aspect without completely opening up a market would not maximize consumer surplus. In fact, companies may raise, rather than reduce, prices. Thus, such partial liberalization may give rise not only to consumer disadvantages, but also to the broader disadvantage that the public would believe that competition is not beneficial, but instead creates advantages only for market incumbents. It is difficult to convey to politicians and the public that competition is a multidimensional problem, and that it involves not just freeing one single characteristic of the competitive game enterprises play, but freeing all aspects. Trade liberalization in manufacturing has been successful because once trade is liberalized, imports come in immediately. In contrast, trade liberalization is not the solution in services because markets are generally local. In these cases, a competition-orientated regulatory reform is the solution.

**Prof. Schwartz**    I want to start with a general observation. It is sometimes forgotten that there is value to having choice, such as a lower-quality product at a lower price. In the US, there are orange growers and other agricultural groups that prohibit the sale of small oranges or other 'unsuitable' products on the ground that they do not meet the standard. But someone may like a smaller orange at a lower price. So it should be made clear that we are discussing potential efficiency reasons for quality standards only for cases where there are significant information problems and spillover on the reputation of other providers – such as blaming all doctors for a problem with one doctor.

I agree with Professor Jenny that there is a genuine issue of asymmetric information, and that competition is not always going to solve the problem. But, I also agree with Dr Hilke that we must always remind ourselves of the limits of the government's information – does anyone know the quality of the lawyers?

I shall give several examples where market institutions arise to attempt to solve these issues, and allowing competition can help in this endeavour. First, with respect to the quality of lawyers, corporations in the US have started benchmarking the performance of lawyers. Corporations used to hire a single law firm; now they hire two or three of them and they benchmark – for this kind of legal brief, how much is one firm charging versus the other?

Second, there is something to Professor Jenny's point that maybe there should be government providers to give a diagnosis, because their incentives are not to maximize profit, and therefore they are more trustworthy. We now see department stores explicitly advertising that their sales team is not operating on commission, precisely to assure the customer that a salesperson is not going to say 'it fits fantastically' when it is three inches too short.

Third, to protect consumers against their perceived inability to bargain particularly well – everyone dislikes bargaining with car dealers because they do not believe themselves to be good at bargaining – some companies have now implemented a policy of no haggling, telling the dealers that there must be a uniform price, and bargaining is not permitted. This is a market response to demand by consumers for a policy that reduces their harm from their informational disadvantage.

Fourth, becoming a member of an automobile association can solve the example given of travelling and not knowing the local providers. Associations do the monitoring for you. They find the approved dealers and they decide with whom to go.

A final example of trying to find out the prices and quality of different offerings is long-distance prices – I do not know if anyone can figure out who charges the cheapest price. It is too complicated, and there are incentives by the long-distance companies to make it complicated, to hamper the ability to comparison shop. But, there are also strong forces by competitors to disrupt this system. For example, Sprint, which had the smallest market share among the three majors, AT&T and MCI being the biggest, came out with '10 cents anytime anywhere'. Sprint's simple and transparent offer cut through the clutter, and that has made a huge difference.

While competition will not be perfect, it is important to remember that the ability to get a second opinion, an alternative voice, is a powerful instrument. We should think twice before we constrain it through quality standards or other restrictions.

**Prof. Joerges** Regarding the minimum quality problem, usually when producers impose vertical restraints on their dealers, they prefer to defend such measures by characterizing them not as quality requirements, but as safety requirements. Does your analysis help to distinguish quality from safety? Second, the functioning of markets often seems to presuppose the setting of standards. How is it possible to discriminate between compatibility objectives and minimum quality requirements? Similar difficulties are present in the harmonization of laws.

**Mr Wise**  I have spent much of my career writing comments defending the expansion of competition law to its maximum extent in the professions. Several years ago I wrote the piece for the OECD that came close to saying that. But the more I hear Professor Jenny talk about this, the more I wonder whether I have been on the right side on behalf of my clients all these years.

I offer a response to the comment about the co-evolution of social conditions and norms. In the US, the practice of letting the lawyers advertise has perhaps gone farther than anywhere else, and no doubt farther than it should have. I was struck in Dr Laudati's chapter by the faith that lawyers would engage in informative advertising. It reminds me of a regulatory problem that I dealt with several years ago, in which the issue was whether the Bar Association could apply rules that, in effect, required only informative advertising, because the lawyers who wanted to advertise most aggressively did not want to use informative advertising. They wanted to use persuasive advertising. They did not want the lawyer in question talking to the camera about legal issues. They wanted to have commercially made background tracks of car crashes, and big headlines screaming 'You need me now!'. I am not quite sure where this comes out. It makes me believe that Professor Jenny is correct about the likelihood of contract and other institutional forms evolving to deal with this.

I believe that we shall see a bipolar distribution – many lawyers will go with large organizations that will advertise and sell reputation by brand. This will perhaps result in a kind of entry barrier. Good lawyers, who cannot afford to advertise for themselves in a way that they think is sensible, will join up with a big firm rather than practise on their own, and the fee will be that of the larger firm. This will solve the information problem across jurisdictions, just as businesses do now. Because they are repeat purchasers and sophisticated purchasers, they can rate the lawyers. At the other end will be the lawyers showing the television advertisement with the car crashes. I am not quite sure what the effect will be. Already, I think a number of consumers look at advertisements like that and say 'That guy is a quack, I wouldn't hire him, if he has to advertise, he cannot be good'. They filter out the ones they will deal with in terms of whether or not they advertise. On the other hand, some consumers watch television all day, and that may be all they know about. Maybe the low-quality lawyer is the one appropriate for them. Maybe this needs to exist, and they would not have had a lawyer at all before. I do not know the answer, but it will be very complex, and may not look like we think it will in the long run.

**Dr. Laudati**  In the commercial speech decisions of the Supreme Court discussed in my chapter, there was a distinction made between lawyer advertising of strictly factual matters, and persuasive advertisements, which Mr Wise has discussed. The commercial speech decisions only protect the factual type of lawyer advertising. But the example points out the great difficulty that there is in making rules that will safeguard the integrity of professional advertising. There is a very great danger of abuse, in exactly the type of situation illustrated by Mr Wise's example.

**Dr Mehta**   The chapters and the discussion bring more focus on the points that Professor Fels and Professor Jenny have made. More competition is allowed, and more market solutions are used for many of the problems. But there are many situations where leaving it strictly to the market does not bring about a solution. For the competition authorities, a crucial issue arises. Dr Laudati has summarized some of the cases where the European Commission has acted, and has found a restriction to be present in violation of Article 81. In the future, this will incite professionals to ask about the lawfulness of their code provisions. This presents a big challenge to economists to suggest how the remedies can be crafted. That is not at all clear in the situations mentioned regarding information asymmetries, where the solution is not simply to allow more entry; there may be too much entry. This is sometimes also a problem. Improving the information does not provide the entire answer, because there is no real engineering definition of what we are looking for. Professor Fels, you mentioned that you had hundreds of these notifications, and gave your benediction to some. How did you decide when to give your benediction?

**Prof. Fels**   I can comment on how we deal with them. For example, we had a case involving farm and veterinary chemicals. There are many explosions of these chemicals on farms, many accidents. This was damaging the reputation of the industry. The more respectable members of the industry decided to form an association. A chemical manufacturer could only be a member and advertise that it was a member of this good association if it observed certain minimum safety standards. To make it work, they needed to expel various manufacturers that did not meet these criteria. We saw that as a partial improvement, but there was also a lot of self-interest in excluding smaller players, new entrants, and other companies that wanted to do things differently. None the less, the underlying scheme had some merits. We struck a kind of compromise, under which they could form this association and advertise, so that chemicals purchased from them would likely comply with the best safety requirements. We overturned some of their exclusionary practices, had an independent body looking at them, and so on. That is a typical case of how we deal with it.

I wanted to reinforce something that Mr Dutz said about lawyer advertising. In the health sector, there are very serious advertising problems. Advertising is aimed particularly at gullible people, who believe anything about health and cures. A particular part of the population is especially vulnerable: sick people, old people, people who have subnormal intelligence, or are culturally or in other ways disadvantaged. All of these can be exploited by advertising that does not actually breach the truth in advertising laws, but comes close to doing so. For example, in Australia, where the advertisement restriction has been lifted, the outbreak of advertising of cosmetic surgery is massive, and has involved a huge exploitation of vulnerable consumers. It is difficult to tackle it. As part of our ideal competition reforms, it seems that we must look not only at laws that very directly restrict competition. In addition, we should include the consumer protection laws.

In terms of tackling the big problems of the professions and so on, we should not get too far ahead of the game. It is fair to know that competition is not the perfect solution alone to all of these problems, but if we get to the priorities, then it seems that there are many other things we need to solve before we get on to these side-effects of the reforms. In other words, there is a lifetime of work ahead in tackling just the gross anticompetitive restrictions in the professions – the entry restrictions, the price fixing, the self-regulation and many other things. In my view, they are the first things on the agenda.

Also, I know what Mr Heimler is getting at when he says that competition has many dimensions, and it can at times be a mistake to get partial deregulation because it may not produce benefits. But there is a real policy issue: is it better to get some partial deregulation than nothing, and to wait for the perfect solution? It can be argued either way. Sometimes partial deregulation is not so good. Other times, it paves the way for later regulation. There are instances where it has been good to get partial deregulation. For example, with respect to shopping hours, it has been far better to adopt the partial solution of deregulation in shopping hours in certain sorts of shops, because this will probably bring the whole system tumbling down. You start to generate initiatives and anomalies that will create pressure for the whole system to come to an end. That is not always the case, but sometimes partial regulation is a necessary step, even a political step, towards getting the ideal outcome.

In terms of the priorities in the professions, it seems that the biggest and most difficult is the health sector. That is where the greatest resources are involved, but it is also very difficult to tackle. There are profound questions about how the whole system is run. Then it is always worth kicking the lawyers around a bit. After that, the other areas of professional regulation, I am not so sure about – the engineers, the architects, the accountants and those areas.

**Prof. Jenny**   I would like to make two comments. First, I was not arguing that we should not do what we are doing; I was arguing that something else should be done as well. I would feel more certain of what we do if it were always obvious that welfare would increase if we eliminate a price restriction imposed by a profession, and as a result there would be increased price differentiation, given that risk-averse consumers would have no way of comparing the different services offered by the different members of the profession. If it is obvious that welfare will increase at least marginally, then we would know that we are going in the right direction even if we are not going very far. However, I suspect that this is not so, in which case there is a real problem.

Second, I question the distinction between persuasive and objective advertising. What objective advertising is possible in professions in which services are tailor-made, not duplicable, and in which there is no reference? For instance, what kind of objective information could help me choose a divorce lawyer? I just cannot conceive of it. I think we are kidding ourselves by saying there can be such a thing as objective information that will help consumers. It may help consumers to understand something, but nothing that will be relevant to the particular service that they need in relation to a particular provider of the service. I know you could disagree, but I am just putting this on the table to see what the reaction is. Sitting as the vice-chairman of the French Competition Authority and having specialized lawyers in front of me all the time, sometimes we go overboard because the lawyers have been so terrible that we feel obliged not to find the defendant guilty because otherwise he/she will have been a victim of such a lawyer, sometimes from a rather reputable law firm.

**Prof. Scarpa**  I would first like to respond to Professor Joerges' comments. I believe that standardization is a completely different issue. I agree that standardization can sometimes foster competition, because it forces firms to make very comparable products, so that they must compete more aggressively on prices. Indeed, sometimes there are cases where the refusal to standardize the product is an attempt to differentiate it, more or less artificially, from another firm's products. We know that product differentiation is a way to relax price competition between firms, which could certainly be a reason to encourage standardization, although there are always gains and losses. An increase in price competition will occur at the expense of product differentiation. In a case-by-case discussion, we might say that one thing or the other is better, but these two aspects will always be there.

Safety is an important issue. The key question is, whose safety is involved? If it is my own safety, I care, but why should anyone else care? If a person buys a product that might negatively affect his/her safety without imposing social costs, then that person's evaluation of the relevance of safety is nothing but another component of his/her evaluation of quality. It is a subjective judgement on which I have little else to say. When it is someone else's safety, the story is different. For instance, if I make windows that are to be used in doors in a large block of flats, then those windows must be very resistant, otherwise a child may kill himself riding his bicycle into this glass. Then we are in a different field, which is – broadly defined – the same as public health.

I have the impression from the discussion that there are some areas where public worries about quality, not necessarily regulation, are very justified, in two fields: health and law. But being somehow worried does not necessarily mean asking for regulation. We all agree that certain basic rights must be safeguarded, such as the right to health, the right to be defended in court in an appropriate way and so on. We agree further that we should look at what happens in these markets. However, we can *talk* about quality standards in these markets, but often we are not imposing quality standards on a product; we are simply regulating *inputs*. For instance, with respect to licensing or certification, as professors we have received our certification quite a few years ago, and what we have done since is our business. Have we studied? Have we not? No one is checking. This does not have a devastating effect on students, who survive the worst lecturers. But for doctors, it might be different. As in these two cases, any regulation we can hope to put in place in the field of professions typically refers to things that are only vaguely related to actual output quality, and we cannot expect much from them.

**Prof. Siniscalco**     With respect to the information-sensitive sectors that we have been discussing, such as health, law and so on, are there examples of information provided by third parties? I am thinking of a Standard & Poor's rating of lawyers in New York, or *Guide Michelin* – meaning not only the list, but also the stars. Would it be possible? It could solve many incentive problems that we have been discussing. There is a problem of the extent of the market, but with the Internet, the fixed cost of producing such a list is not prohibitive.

**Dr Nicoletti**     I shall make two points. First, even if the consumer understands quality, and is able to distinguish between bad and good quality, it is not always easy to find out who is responsible for bad quality. This difficulty may occur whenever the responsibility for the quality of a service is shared by several operators because the service is provided in the context of networking with other professions. For instance, in the health sector, if something goes wrong with the medical services, is it the doctor who sold the services who is responsible? Or are there ancillary services that went wrong? Another example is airport services: who is responsible for a delay in take-off or landing, or in delivering luggage? This raises the issue whether competition and reputational mechanisms would solve the problem of choice for the consumer, and would allow for enforcement of minimum quality standards by the government regulator or the self-regulated profession. To this end, mechanisms must be found to allocate the sanctions between the responsible parties so as to maximize their incentives to deliver good quality.

Second, I have a question for Professor Jenny regarding risk aversion. I am not sure how risk aversion can be invoked as an argument that competition would not necessarily bring welfare improvements. To do so, one must assume that competition would increase risk. But we do not know whether this would be the case.

**Prof. Amato**   If you are going for oranges, it makes more sense than if you are sick and looking for a doctor. You are not ready to run risks when you are sick, when you are seeking someone to treat your cancer.

**Dr Nicoletti**   I agree with that. But I am asking whether the consumer is better insured against the risk of getting a bad doctor when entry and fares are regulated by the government or when more competitive mechanisms are at work.

**Prof. Jenny**   I did not mean this. I meant the elimination of a price restriction imposed by the profession, where the consumer would have no reference to the normal price to pay for that service. We found that consumers like to have a professional tariff, because at least they are satisfied that they are not charged an abusive price. You are right on the quality, it does not say much.

**Dr Dutz**   I wanted to briefly share with the group a policy proposal that was put forward by the Mexican federal office of regulatory reform. Dr Hilke talked about metrics and the 'R' rule for insulation, and Professor Schwartz talked about the power of getting a second voice. The policy proposal has to do with public policy professionals, civil servants and policy makers. The idea was that the federal regulatory reform agency in Mexico only had jurisdiction at the federal level, but there were many anticompetitive regulations at the state level that they could not tackle. They thought they should introduce a transparent metric, which need not be engineering related, for anticompetitive deregulation or improvement in regulatory reform at the state level. In this case, businesses and consumers would do comparative shopping. States wanting to attract business to their state would want to appear better according to this transparent metric. Perhaps, in the European case, it would be published on the front page of the *Financial Times*. It is a suggestion to introduce competition in regulatory reform as well.

**Prof. Motta**   The comment made by Dr Hilke regarding consumer protection was very important. In markets characterized by asymmetric information between consumers and professionals, it is important to reduce this information gap. Publishing information and making it available to consumers goes in the right direction, while restricting advertising does not. Whether this is enough to solve the market failure in professional services markets, I am not sure. My impression is that some minimum quality standards or licensing requirements might still be needed in some markets. I would not care about minimum quality standards for hairdressers, while in health, it is extremely important. The cost of having someone who is not qualified to practise as a doctor is too high. I think this distinction should be made. The important problem remains of where to set the standard, as both Dr Hilke and Professor Schwartz stated. I think for doctors and health services, some sort of standards should be in place.

**Dr Laudati**   I shall make a brief remark in response to Professor Jenny's comment about lawyer advertising. I think there is a very clear distinction to be made between factual advertising and quality advertising. In the cases, the Supreme Court gives the examples of uncontested divorces, simple adoptions, uncontested personal bankruptcies and name changes, all of which involve a very standard package of services. If a price is given for providing this package of services, there can be price comparisons. Quality is not so much of a question when such a standard and simple filing of papers is involved. When quality is important, however, that is a different matter. That is where the problems really arise.

**Dr Hilke**   This is in response to a question about whether people were comparing information. Most of you must know about *Consumer Report*, a magazine published in the United States that compares all sorts of products. Its publishers make up their own tests to make these comparisons. A number of national magazines have been developing grading systems for major hospitals, for different illnesses. One area that is really fascinating, and has become an entire industry, is comparison of educational institutions. They are ranked on 85 different criteria, and published in a book that recounts the student's perspective on the experience there, faculty contributions and so on. So these things are being done, some on a commercial basis, and not just a non-profit basis.

**Mr Wise**   I would like to attack the legal profession here on two points. First, I agree that it is difficult to advertise objectively anything that is relevant. The kinds of examples that Dr Laudati gave are things that lawyers should not even be doing. The defining quality of a professional's service is that it is not routine tasks like those, but the difficult tasks that cannot be compared. Second, lawyers do compare one another, but the only criteria are how much money they are making and whether they are going to reimburse each other. I am aware of no third party grading for lawyers in terms of quality of professional services.

**Prof. Amato**   Considering this discussion, I go back to one of my initial points – that we must consider alternatives. We cannot say that something is anticompetitive, therefore. ... *Vis-à-vis* which alternatives? We must be very simplistic. Market failures exist. Sometimes markets take care of themselves, but sometimes they do not. We must accept this cruel fact of life. Therefore, sometimes regulations are needed. Sometimes, a bad regulation cannot be substituted with no regulation at all, leaving the entire matter to general antitrust rules. Sometimes we must find substitutes in the area of better regulation. This is my problem. I would not have raised this issue, should I start from the conclusion that whenever I meet an anticompetitive regulation that is inefficient, the only alternative is the general antitrust rules, and no special regulation at all. My issue is what alternatives exist. Whenever possible, the general antitrust rules, but I must be aware that this, in the end, may turn out to be ideological, and it does not function. It might also be inefficient. Professor Jenny was bold, as the vice-chairman of an antitrust authority, to make this point repeatedly, but this is an important point to consider.

I remember a case in the Italian Competition Authority having to do with taxi drivers in Rome. We had quite a hard discussion in the Authority. Some of us were ready to drop any limit to entry, except the licence. In the end, we decided we needed more competition inside the regulated framework because the nightmare of Santiago was there, because we are all aware of disruptive competition and so on. But this is not the only nightmare that we must be aware of. There are also other nightmares. In the health sector, there is not even the possibility of 'repeating your divorce', because you are dead before you can have a second chance. We must be well aware of this. Therefore, in this case, minimum quality standards apply. That is why I am not convinced that the framework given by Mr Heimler applies; competition is a sort of universe. One cannot introduce an element of it without calling for all of the others, until the final outcome is reached – the perfect competitive market. This is something that can be done with some sectors, but cannot be done with others. Therefore, we must be very market specific. I am convinced that Professor Scarpa should accept what Professor Motta said, not to give a general statement about minimum quality standards. It really depends on the market and the alternatives. Once a regulation has been assessed as both anticompetitive and inefficient, is the only alternative the perfect market, or is it better to envisage a different kind of regulation? What Professor Siniscalco was proposing makes sense. We have Standard & Poor's for financial institutions, because the need for stability in financial markets probably was an incentive for this independent countervailing power. Can there be something similar also for other markets? This is part of the answer, which is certainly more procompetitive than other forms of regulation. I am convinced that in many instances, just spreading around information is enough. But this is not always so. Other forms of protection are sometimes needed. The research of better forms of consumer protection by regulation remains an important mission.

PART II


Regulations Affecting Structurally
Non-Competitive Industries: The Provision
of Public Services

# Introduction

## Alberto Heimler

This part addresses regulations affecting the provision of public services, an area that in Europe has witnessed very important reforms over the last decade. In particular, starting in the late 1980s, the European institutions have intervened quite extensively in the liberalization process with a number of legislative tools aiming at promoting competition and preventing the segmentation of national markets. The instruments that the Community used are differentiated according to their legal basis and to the degree by which they constrain national governments. *Harmonization directives* issued by the Council of Ministers are usually based on the principle of mutual recognition. They derive their legality from the articles in the Treaty aiming at the creation of a unified market. These directives have led to the opening up of domestic markets traditionally closed to (foreign) competition, such as public procurement, banking, insurance, electricity, gas, rail, airport services and so on. Council directives cannot be appealed. *Competition-driven directives* are based on Article 86 (and on competition law), and are imposed on member states directly by the Commission, without any intervention from the Council of Ministers. These directives, particularly frequent in telecommunications, can be appealed to the Court of Justice. *Commission communications* are issued on a number of specific issues, such as universal service obligations, interconnection charges and so on. They have completed directives with non-binding instructions to member states on specific regulatory matters.

The Community has had more than ten years' experience with the liberalization of public utilities. However, it is still quite difficult clearly to identify the circumstances in which one instrument is preferred to another. Article 86 directives have been common in telecommunications, where a widespread consensus among member states was found for the need to liberalize. On the other hand, in areas such as electricity where a common view among member states was far more difficult to attain, the relevant directives have been issued by the Council of Ministers. The directives do not cover all sectors, nor do they impose a given structure on the liberalized markets. They leave member states free to go beyond the minimum level of competition that they impose, or to liberalize markets that are not yet European Union (EU) concerns. Moreover, directives are neutral with respect to private or public ownership.

In telecommunications, the EU began to liberalize the terminal equipment market in 1988. Ten years were needed after this initial act to introduce full competition also in voice telephony. In electricity, the Council directive approved in June 1996 does not fully liberalize the electricity market, and represents a compromise among those that favoured a centralized system of electricity supply and those that opted for a market-orientated structure. The same occurred with respect to postal services, gas and rail, where the EU directives did not go as far as fully liberalizing the industry.

In all of these sectors, the directives have introduced a minimum degree of competition in member state markets. Therefore, even after the EU has issued a directive, there is much room for further opening public utility markets to competition based on domestic decisions. In particular, national governments should address major structural questions, such as how to deal with public service obligations, vertical integration and privatization, and major behavioural questions, such as the efficient way of pricing access to essential facilities, the role of regulation and antitrust, and whether government should provide public services itself or contract them out.

Great care must be taken in designing proper regulatory instruments. Mark Armstrong, with examples from the United Kingdom, provides an assessment of the possible distortions of competition originating from regulation that is badly designed or enforced. He shows that some policies of protecting the incumbent (granting a monopoly franchise, giving the monopolist a subsidy, not introducing a regulatory regime for access), protecting new entrants (placing limits to further entry, introducing asymmetric regulation, imposing market-share ceilings on the incumbent) and protecting consumers (prohibiting price discrimination by the incumbent, maintaining distorted tariffs) may all create very important distortions of competition that, in the end, are detrimental to consumers, as they lead to inefficient entry, high prices and low-quality services.

Addressing more structural issues, and in particular the scope for a thorough restructuring of vertically integrated monopolies before privatization, Darryl Biggar argues that unless there are strong economies of scope, vertical separation can efficiently eliminate the incentives for an integrated monopolist to refuse to competitors access to the essential facility it controls. Such separation facilitates the achievement of a competitive industry, strongly reducing the incentives for the incumbent to reintroduce by private behaviour the same restrictions of competition that were in place when the industry was characterized by special and exclusive rights. Along the same lines, Marius Schwartz provides an assessment of the vertical separation decision that in 1984 led to the break-up of AT&T in the US, and to the creation of the seven regional Bell operating companies. He shows that no Bell operating company has yet been allowed to enter into long distance because competition at the local level has not yet been considered sufficient, as the 1996 Telecommunications Act requires for lifting the ban to operate in the long-distance markets. None the less, the simple possibility that the Bell operating companies could eventually be allowed to enter into long distance has made them more accommodating in allowing access to the local loop than they would have been had they been vertically integrated.

Domenico Siniscalco with his co-authors provides an assessment of the privatization operations of electric utilities. Analysing a large number of privatizations of electric utilities, he argues that, contrary to *a priori* beliefs that treasury ministers would prefer to privatize a monopoly, the data reveals that it is in their best interest to liberalize first and privatize later. In fact, liberalization reduces the uncertainty of investors over the regulatory structure and leads to higher proceeds from privatizations.

Mark Dutz and Alberto Heimler address the regulatory challenges related to the liberalization of services other than public utilites, such as trucking and local services. Mark Dutz, presenting a chapter written with Aydin Hayri, shows that in Mexico, where thorough liberalizing reform occurred in trucking, the industry was significantly rationalized, leading to a very strong increase in efficiency to the benefit of consumers. Furthermore, the Mexican trucking industry case shows the importance of the antitrust agency in ensuring that private behaviour does not reintroduce the competition restrictions prevalent under strict regulation. Alberto Heimler addresses the question of whether local services should be supplied competitively, contracted out or subject to a process of competition for the market. Since local conditions differ, as do the types of services local governments supply, it is essential to induce local governments to act efficiently. This can best be achieved by ensuring that local governments face a strict budget constraint and are responsible for local receipts and revenues. They would then choose to act in the best interest of their citizens. Other solutions, such as imposing an auction mechanism from the centre, can lead to efficient solutions only when sunk investments are negligible.

Finally Giuseppe Nicoletti performs a micro and macro analysis showing the positive effects that competition-based regulatory reform has on efficiency and growth in OECD countries. His results provide the general framework for assessing the need for reform.

# 8. Regulation and inefficient entry: economic analysis and the British experience

**Mark Armstrong**

---

*This chapter discusses some problems encountered in the British regulatory experience in its attempts to introduce competition into regulated industries. It provides a partial taxonomy of what can go wrong when regulation and competition interact. The dangers of regulatory policy for inefficient entry are considered under three main headings: the protection of incumbents; the protection of entrants; and the protection of consumers.*

*With respect to the protection of incumbents, three subcategories of anti-competitive regulation are identified. First, granting the incumbent a monopoly franchise is the clearest category of anticompetitive practice. The chapter discusses examples of how such regulation has impeded competition in the gas, electricity and postal service industries in Britain. The second subcategory is asymmetric regulation of incumbents and entrants. One example is the BBC, which is funded by a licence fee, something that acts as a tax on all consumers. That implies that all other broadcasters must compete against this subsidy when trying to attract their own subscribers. The third subcategory is the lack of regulation of access charges, which can lead to no entry taking place. For instance, British Gas was a vertically integrated firm, controlling the pipelines to which others need access in order to supply gas competitively. British Gas was left free to set the price for transmission of rival gas in its pipeline. After seven years of legal liberalization, the result was minimal competition.*

*With respect to the protection of entrants, five subcategories of anticompetitive regulation are considered. First is regulation that places limits on further entry. For instance, telecommunications was subject to the 'duopoly policy' for seven years, under which only one firm was licensed to act as a (fixed link) competitor with the incumbent, BT. Second, new entry has been encouraged through a regulatory policy of asymmetric treatment of entrants and incumbents. For instance, line-of-business restrictions are placed on incumbents, but not on entrants. In Britain, to induce entry of cable television firms, BT has not been allowed to provide television or entertainment services over its network, whereas the cable firms are encouraged jointly to provide television and telephony. Competition can seriously be impaired if the incumbent is prevented from participating in some important sector of a market. Third, market-share targets have been imposed on incumbents. This is a poor way to run a market because the incumbent firm can reduce its market share only by behaving less, rather than more, competitively. Fourth, premature deregulation of a market when substantial market power is still present implies that retail prices will be high, which may, in turn, induce a high degree of potentially inefficient entry. Fifth, entrants have been granted generous terms of access to the incumbent's essential network facilities. Again, the result could be excessive and inefficient entry.*

*With respect to the protection of consumers, three subcategories of anti-competitive regulation are identified. First, price regulation often takes the form whereby the average price of a basket of the incumbent's services is controlled, but the firm has some leeway in choosing the pattern of its relative prices within the basket. This can give rise to incentives to react particularly aggressively to entry where it occurs, or even to act in a 'predatory' manner, and thereby to deter efficient entry. Second, the incumbent may be prohibited from engaging in price discrimination. The incumbent is then required to offer the same tariff to different consumer groups, even when the scope for competition is greater for some groups than for others. If the incumbent lowers its price in response to entry in one market, it must also lower its prices in other markets. Such policies blunt the incumbent's incentive to compete in markets where entry occurs, thus inducing potentially inefficient entry. Third, cross-subsidies built in to an incumbent's regulated tariffs can induce an inefficient pattern of entry. In particular, with* laissez-faire *entry there is a danger of inefficient entry into artificially profitable markets, a danger of a lack of efficient entry into loss-making markets, and difficulties in funding the loss-making services if widespread entry occurs.*

## INTRODUCTION

This chapter explores some unpleasant interactions between policies for regulating firms with market power and policies for achieving efficient entry. These anticompetitive effects of regulation can take many forms, and it is clear that different policies will have different effects. Sometimes the 'wrong' kind of entry will take place, and sometimes the 'right' kind of entry will not take place. In this chapter some examples of such problems are taken from the British experience of regulation and liberalization.[1]

It could, at times, be a deliberate – and justified – policy to sacrifice productive efficiency for some wider goal. Nevertheless, a careful analysis should be made of the costs involved, which is the purpose of this chapter. The discussion is carried out under three headings: the problems for productive efficiency associated with (A) the protection of incumbents, (B) the protection of entrants, and (C) the protection of consumers. It is not always easy to separate out policies neatly under these three headings, especially as regulators often justify their policies as being in the 'interests of consumers'. For instance, universal service obligations are there ostensibly to protect certain vulnerable consumer groups, but act also as a justification for protecting incumbents (for example, against cream-skimming entry). These social obligations also act in practice, however, to *assist* entry into profitable markets.

It is easy to criticize existing policies. The interaction of regulation and liberalization is particularly complex, and it is inevitable – especially in a country like Britain, a pioneer of utility regulation – that early policies will be flawed. However, this chapter does not attempt to go beyond this remit. Except at the end, where some policies for access charges that ensure efficient entry are briefly discussed, there is little analysis of what the policies should be.

## A. PROBLEMS ASSOCIATED WITH THE PROTECTION OF INCUMBENTS

Some of the most flagrant examples of anticompetitive policy making are concerned with protecting incumbents from the full rigours of competition. These policies are discussed under the following headings.

### Monopoly Franchises

One policy is to grant an incumbent firm a monopoly franchise, perhaps for a temporary period. This is a clear-cut example of anticompetitive regulation, but it remains surprisingly common. Recent examples of this in Britain include:

- gas and electricity supply to residential customers were legal monopolies until 1998; and
- postal service (currently for letters costing under £1) is still a legal monopoly.

The argument usually given for *temporary* monopoly is that incumbents require a 'transitional' period to prepare for full-blown competition.[2] But the evidence demonstrates that a more effective way for inefficient incumbents to become competitive is to face competition. A more cynical explanation is that such policies are part of the 'privatization contract', a kind of bribe paid to the incumbent (comprising both the employers and employees) to persuade it to support the privatization process.

Another argument against competition is that it may undermine various politically desirable cross-subsidies built into the incumbent's tariff (for instance, tariffs favouring residential customers at the expense of businesses). For instance, the argument is used to justify the ban on competing postal services in Britain (and most of the rest of the world). It is, indeed, virtually impossible to combine cross-subsidies with *laissez-faire* competition in the long term. Perhaps the chief negative aspect of universal service obligations is that they provide incumbents with a reasonable-sounding argument for entry restrictions. However, Section C will examine the problems caused by universal service policies, and show that if it is desired to maintain the cross-subsidies, better ways than banning entry can be found to accomplish this.

**Unequal Tax Treatment of Entrants and Incumbents**

Another example of public policy being used to protect incumbents from competition is the method of funding the BBC in Britain. From a purely economic point of view, the current funding arrangements for the BBC are dramatically anticompetitive. Anyone wishing to watch any kind of television programming (other than via a video machine) is required to pay the BBC licence fee – around £100 per year – even if they do not wish to watch the BBC's output. As a result, for those who watch television at all, the BBC's output is free at the margin. Other broadcasters must attract viewers whilst at the same time funding their output by more conventional means (advertising or subscription). The result is likely to be that even superior rivals will find it difficult to compete against the BBC for viewers.[3] It is difficult to imagine such an arrangement being tolerated for any other industry. The asserted justification is that the BBC is a 'public service' broadcaster, producing more socially desirable output than that produced by purely commercial broadcasters. However, this old argument has been given a new twist: the latest controversy is a plan for the BBC to levy an additional 'digital' licence fee on all who subscribe to new digital services, such as BSkyB's, in order to fund the BBC's own entry into these new markets.[4]

**Unregulated Access to the Incumbent's Facilities**

The final way that lenient treatment of incumbents will lead to anticompetitive effects is a *laissez-faire* attitude towards access by entrants to the incumbent's network facilities. Without regulation, a network monopoly will usually inhibit competition in services provided over its network by setting high network access charges, especially if it is vertically integrated. For instance, soon after its privatization, British Gas was required by its licence to allow third-party access to its pipeline, but the level of access charges was left free for the incumbent to choose. The result was that for the first seven years after its privatization, British Gas faced no rivals in gas supply. A Monopolies and Mergers Commission (MMC) investigation in 1987 recommended, among other things, that British Gas be required to publish information about its access charges, rather than negotiate terms bilaterally. This reform, however, did nothing to reduce the *level* of the firm's access charges, which remained uncontrolled. As a result, little opportunity existed for entrants who were more efficient than the incumbent in providing services over the incumbent's network to compete effectively.[5]

## B. PROBLEMS ASSOCIATED WITH THE PROTECTION OF ENTRANTS

It is common regulatory practice to 'assist entry', especially in the early stages of liberalization.[6] A large number of entry barriers and incumbency advantages exist in the network industries, related to sunk costs, customer inertia and so on. A natural question is whether potential entrants should be given special assistance. Economic theory has not generated any clear-cut general principles in this regard. Entry assistance might stimulate beneficial future competition that otherwise would not exist, but might also damage productive efficiency and distort competition. However, remaining agnostic about the merits of such assistance, the drawbacks of the various *methods* of providing assistance should be considered. This section will do so, while Section C will discuss entry assistance related to the incumbent's universal service obligations and other pricing restrictions.

### Limitations on Further Entry

A common policy is to license only one or two firms to compete with the incumbent. For instance, in the UK, under the 'duopoly policy' in fixed link telecommunications which existed from 1984 to 1991, only Mercury (as it was then known) was permitted to offer a nationwide service in competition with British Telecom (BT). Protecting one or more entrants by raising legal barriers to the entry of other firms is a curious means with which to assist entry. The idea is presumably that no entry at all would occur unless there is a guarantee against further entry, and a little entry is better than none. Three arguments against this policy are:

- If a second entrant would make the first entrant unprofitable, it is unclear whether the second firm would enter (unless it was much more efficient than the first, in which case it would be good to have this entrant in any event).

- A ban on further entry is likely to make collusive behaviour between the two firms more tempting.
- The likely main effect of the policy is to benefit the incumbent rather than the entrant. If entry assistance is desired it can surely be better targeted.

## Asymmetric Treatment of Incumbents and Entrants

Entrants are often freed from restrictions placed on incumbents, such as universal service obligations and prohibitions on cross-market entry. Allowing an entrant to pick and choose the markets and customers it wants, while the incumbent is forced to serve all customers at a distorted tariff, is a major source of entry assistance. This is discussed below.

Incumbents are often prevented from serving a related market as a means to encourage entry into that market. Recent examples in Britain include the following.

- From 1991 to 2001, BT has been banned from providing television and other entertainment services over its telecommunications network, whereas the cable companies have been encouraged to provide both television and telecommunications services jointly over their networks. The policy was designed indirectly to aid the cable companies in their entry into the telecommunications market, by making their entry into providing television services more profitable, with the long-run aim of providing viable rival infrastructure to BT's network.[7] Since the cost of local network duplication is several hundred pounds per line, the long-run benefits of having several competing telecommunications networks must be substantial to justify this policy.
- Historically, Oftel has been unwilling to require BT to offer 'equal access' to rivals in the long-distance and international call markets. Oftel has now been required by the European Commission to provide equal service by the year 2000, although Oftel is seeking a small deferral of this requirement.[8] This policy benefits local entrants such as the cable companies, because many subscribers switch to cable companies largely because they provide less-costly long-distance and international calls. These services are *not* conveniently available from BT's network when equal access is not in place. This policy leads to the possibility that efficient entry by indirect long-distance firms is forestalled, as well as the danger of inefficient entry into the local market.

- BT is not allowed to use 'fixed-wireless' technology in its local loop, except in specified rural areas. This policy was partially intended to assist the entry of Ionica, a purely fixed-wireless entrant, which has since gone bankrupt.
- In the pay-TV market, BSkyB's satellite distribution platform is treated quite differently from the cable industry's, even though each platform has broadly comparable subscriber numbers. For instance, BSkyB is required to provide third-party access to its platform for rival retailers, whereas the cable platform is 'closed'. Moreover, BSkyB cannot retail its channels directly to cable subscribers and must instead sell its programmes at the wholesale level to cable firms, who then price and market these channels themselves.

Competition can seriously be impaired if the incumbent is prevented from participating in some important aspect of a market. The choice between 'conduct' and 'structural' remedies is difficult. British regulatory policy in this regard has been extremely mixed: some privatizations have been accompanied by vertical restructuring and some have not. However, the most recent policies have involved a more lenient attitude towards vertical integration. For example, the strict separation between electricity generation and supply in Britain has been relaxed. This trend has the procompetitive advantage of keeping incumbents in all the markets.

## Explicit Market-share Targets for Incumbents

A superficially desirable policy for regulators keen to ensure effective competition in their industry is to aim at a specified market-share reduction by the incumbent firm. Achieving such a target may provide an easy way to demonstrate how effectively regulators are doing their job. However, even ignoring the well-known drawbacks of using raw market-share data as an indicator of competitiveness, such a policy is bound to be anticompetitive. This is because the incumbent is required by regulation to compete *less* effectively (for instance, by increasing its prices). The likely result is that inefficient entrants will prosper.

The gas industry provides a good example of such a policy in the UK:

- In its 1988 report on gas competition, the MMC recommended that British Gas be allowed to contract for no more than 90 per cent of the new gas coming to market.
- More drastically, in 1992, the Office of Fair Trading recommended that British Gas reduce its market share in the business market (excluding that used for electricity generation) to 40 per cent by 1995. British Gas's market share in the business market fell. By 1996 its share of the market

for consumption greater than 2500 therms per annum was just 29 per cent. As a result, it was left seriously exposed in its long-term contract commitments with gas fields.[9]

## Premature Deregulation

An inverse link exists between the tightness of regulation and the amount of entry. If a market is deregulated when substantial market power is still present, prices will be high. This may, in turn, induce a high degree of entry. Given that there is a price/cost margin due to market power, this entry may not be the most efficient. In Britain, the clear example of this is electricity generation. Two generation firms historically have largely set wholesale electricity prices. As a result of high prices there, a large amount of entry into generation has occurred, largely using gas generators, arguably leading to inefficient excess capacity in the sector.[10]

## Favourable Terms of Access to the Incumbent's Facilities

Finally, granting entrants generous terms for access to the incumbent's facilities (such as gas pipelines, the electricity grid, or the local lines connecting the incumbent's subscribers in telecommunications) is common practice. The effects of a low *level* of access charges is discussed here (inefficient *structure* of access charges is discussed in the next section). In telecommunications, a major policy dilemma for access charges exists. If the incumbent is forced to cover the fixed costs of local network provision partly out of call charges (there is an 'access deficit'), and if rivals had access to the incumbent's network at marginal cost, then this could over time lead to inefficient cream skimming. The result is that the incumbent would be unable to cover its fixed costs. On the other hand, in the early stages of liberalization, competition is bound to be limited, and perhaps in danger of being stifled altogether. In the early days of the duopoly policy in Britain, Mercury was explicitly granted favourable access to BT's network, and in particular was exempted from contributing to BT's access deficit:

> [I]t is reasonable to exempt a new competitor ... from the [access deficit] contribution in the early stages of its business development, in the interests of helping it get started. If this were not done, the ability of the newcomer to compete might be inhibited because of the economies of scale available to the incumbent and competition might never become established.[11]

In terms of its effect on entry, the effect of subsidized access prices is similar to allowing the incumbent to charge high retail prices, as discussed above.

Entrants care largely about their available *margin* between retail prices and access charges, not the absolute value of these prices. The difference between the two policies is that with high retail prices, consumers pay for entry assistance, whereas with low access charges, the incumbent pays. Either way, though, the likely result will be inefficient entry. Oftel now believes that this policy should not be followed: 'Oftel does not favour using interconnection charges to provide entry assistance but will continue to tackle barriers to entry directly'.[12]

## C.　PROBLEMS ASSOCIATED WITH THE PROTECTION OF CONSUMERS

A number of problems for efficient entry are caused by policies designed to protect consumers. In particular, the retail tariff that the regulated incumbent is permitted or required to offer will significantly affect the pattern of entry that occurs. This issue is subdivided into three parts: (i) the effects of average price regulation (which means that there is a *negative* relationship between prices in competitive markets and prices in monopolized markets); (ii) the effects of prohibiting price discrimination (which means that there is a positive relationship between prices in competitive markets and prices in monopolized markets), and (iii) the effects of the incumbent's tariff not reflecting its underlying costs. The implications of (i) and (ii) are contrasting. Roughly speaking, with the former, there is too little entry, and with the latter, there is too much. In practice, policies (ii) and (iii) are usually combined. This is evident, for instance, with respect to universal service policies that require the incumbent to offer geographically uniform tariffs even when costs differ. For the sake of clarity, the two effects will be separately analysed. Problem (iii) is quite complex, especially when access to the incumbent's facilities is an issue. We discuss the problems with cost-based access pricing and local loop unbundling under this heading.

### Average Price Regulation

Price cap regulation often takes the form whereby a measure of the *average* price of a basket of the incumbent's prices is controlled, but the firm has some leeway in choosing the pattern of its relative prices within the basket. Such a system has good features in terms of allowing the firm to make its tariff reflect costs, especially as relative costs change over time. It can, however, also give rise to incentives to react aggressively to entry, a feature that may deter efficient entry.

A good example is the balance between local and long-distance call charges in the early years of competition in British telecommunications. BT initially faced competition almost entirely in the long-distance market (for residential subscribers at least). Other than the usual healthy incentive to compete fairly with rivals, its average price cap gave it an additional incentive to cut prices in the more competitive market. This was that price cuts in the long-distance market enabled it to raise prices in its captive market for local calls. Indeed, such incentives might be so great as to cause its prices to fall below the associated cost of providing the long-distance service, which is one of the usual tests for predatory pricing. As a result, competition from rivals might be thwarted even if they are more efficient than the incumbent. From 1984 to 1992, BT's basket of regulated services fell on average by 43 per cent in real terms. However, its peak-time long-distance charges fell by 65 per cent over the period, while local call charges fell by less than 20 per cent and fixed charges actually rose a little in real terms. Naturally, much or all of this might be justified by cost-based tariff rebalancing. Mercury, the competitor, complained vociferously to Oftel, however, that BT's behaviour was anticompetitive (a charge not upheld by Oftel at the time).[13]

**Constraints on Price Discrimination**

Policy often involves prohibitions on the incumbent engaging in price discrimination. The incumbent is thereby required to offer the same tariff to different consumer groups, even when the scope for competition is greater for some groups than others. This is roughly the opposite policy to average price regulation: here, if the incumbent lowers its price in response to entry in one market, it must then *lower* its prices in other markets. Such policies will blunt the incumbent's incentive to compete in markets where entry occurs. In particular, less-efficient rivals may well succeed in their chosen markets because the incumbent cannot afford to compete aggressively with them. The usual rationale for such policies has recently been re-stated by Oftel:

> As part of the last Price Control Review Oftel set out the principle that those basic elements of telecoms service would be provided at geographically averaged prices so that they are available to all consumers at the same price throughout the country. ... It has the benefit of ensuring that the benefits of competition in areas of the country where BT faces strong competition are extended throughout the country.[14]

This argument has some appeal, as prices are then lower in monopolized markets than they otherwise would be. This benefit comes with the cost, however, of perhaps excessive entry in competitive markets. Consumer protection in the captive markets in any event could be better targeted by direct price regulation. Such a policy also has the effect of assisting entry (see previous section), but it is a blunt and ill-focused instrument for doing so.

Both average price regulation and constraints on price discrimination are policies that link, in opposite ways, the price an incumbent can charge in one market to the prices it charges in others. Such policies will surely distort entry incentives. A good principle is that, where practicable, the incumbent's prices in more-or-less captive markets should be de-linked from those in more competitive markets, as this policy targets price control where it is needed most, and allows undistorted competition elsewhere.

### Incumbent's Tariff Not Cost-reflective

An incumbent's retail tariff can be out of line with its underlying costs in numerous ways. For instance, in telecommunications there may be:

- a requirement that the incumbent offers a geographically uniform tariff even when its costs of providing services differ around the country;
- a requirement that the incumbent offers a balance between fixed and usage dependent charges better suited to lower-usage residential subscribers than higher-usage business subscribers;
- a requirement that the incumbent charges for calls on a per minute rather than a per call basis, when the cost of providing a call relates largely to call set-up rather than ongoing, time-dependent costs.

Tariffs that do not reflect costs are one of the most potent sources of regulation-induced problems with competition. All else equal, a tariff that involves large positive margins in some markets and large negative margins in others will attract an undesirable pattern of entry.

A simple example of geographically uniform tariffs illustrates some of the problems. Assume an incumbent firm (for example, a postal or telecommunications firm) is required by regulation to offer a *uniform* price $P$ for providing a specified service anywhere in the country. The country is divided into two broad kinds of region, urban and rural, and the incumbent incurs costs for providing service in an urban area of $C_{urban}$ and in a rural area of $C_{rural} > C_{urban}$. Suppose that $C_{urban} < P < C_{rural}$, and that overall the incumbent makes a reasonable profit. However, profits from the urban sector, where it has a positive margin of $P - C_{urban}$ per unit, are used to cross-subsidize the rural market, where it makes a loss of $C_{rural} - P$ per unit. Assume further that the two services yield the same level of gross utility to people in both regions, so that the concept of universal service applies to service quality and not just to price, where this utility is denoted $U$. Therefore, the *net* utility for people in either region is $U - P$.

This system of cross-subsidy leads to several problems with *laissez-faire* competition:

1. *Cream skimming*  Assume an entrant has unit cost for the urban service of $c_{urban}$ and provides a service with gross utility $u_{urban}$. Therefore, it can charge $P + (u_{urban} - U)$ for its urban service and still attract customers. It will find it profitable to enter that market provided this price is above its costs, that is, if

$$P + (u_{urban} - U) \geq c_{urban}.$$

On the other hand, entry is socially desirable in this market if and only if

$$u_{urban} - c_{urban} \geq U - C_{urban}.$$

Therefore, whenever

$$U - C_{urban} > u_{urban} - c_{urban} > U - P,$$

entry will take place when this is not efficient. This problem can occur when the entrant offers a substandard service ($u_{urban} < U$), or when its costs of providing the service are higher ($c_{urban} > C_{urban}$), or both. In particular, if both firms offer the same quality of service, so that $u_{urban} = U$, then the above condition becomes $C_{urban} < c_{urban} < P$. Alternatively, if costs are the same, so that $c_{urban} = C_{urban}$, then inefficient entry occurs whenever $P - C_{urban} > U - u > 0$, that is, when the entrant offers a substandard (but not too substandard) service. Therefore, there is ample scope for inefficient entry in the profitable markets.

2. *Lack of efficient entry in loss-making markets*  Assume an entrant has cost for the rural service of $c_{rural}$ and provides a service that gives gross utility there of $u_{rural}$. Then, using the above style of argument, if

$$U - C_{rural} < u_{rural} - c_{rural} < U - P,$$

entry will *not* take place even though it is efficient. This problem of insufficient entry can occur when the entrant offers a superior service ($u_{rural} > U$) or when its costs of providing the rural service are lower ($c_{rural} < C_{rural}$). In particular, if both firms offer the same quality of service, then the above condition reduces to $C_{rural} > c_{rural} > P$. Therefore, there is ample scope for a lack of efficient entry in the loss-making markets.

3. *Funding problems* If widespread cream-skimming entry takes place in urban markets, then the incumbent will not be able to fund its loss-making rural service.

In sum, when the incumbent's tariff does not reflect its costs, with *laissez-faire* entry distortions are expected in the form of too much entry in the artificially profitable markets, and too little in the loss-making markets. Issue (3) is not the focus of this chapter, but will be an important issue for regulators to address, and tends to be the problem that is their greatest concern.[15] Some proposed solutions to the above problems include:

- Ban entry, as is the case with basic postal service in most countries, including Britain. This deeply unimaginative policy obviously eliminates all potential benefits from competition. (See Section A above.)
- Rebalance the incumbent's tariff to reflect its underlying costs, so that instead of a uniform price, the incumbent's price in the urban market is $P_{urban} = C_{urban}$ and its price in the rural market is $P_{rural} = C_{rural}$. This would solve all three of the problems (1)–(3) at once, and in particular, entry would take place in either sector if and only if an entrant is more efficient than the incumbent. However, this policy is alleged to be politically unacceptable in industries such as post and telecommunications, though this is rarely put to the test. Other goods and services are non-uniformly priced in terms of urban and rural locations, most notably housing. Why should post be so different? Also, in Britain, as a result of the regional structure for firms in the electricity and water industries, these services are not uniformly priced across the country. There may be good economic arguments for subsidizing the communication services for rural areas, such as to 'bring the country together' in some sense. This does not, however, imply that geographically *uniform* tariffs are desirable.
- Even if full-blown rebalancing is ruled out, it seems a good principle, as in the section above discussing problems to do with entry assistance, to de-link the profitable from the loss-making markets. Thus, even if the incumbent's prices are not fully brought into line with its costs, a partial move in that direction would still yield significant gains for both productive and allocative efficiency.
- Create a 'universal service fund', so that, for instance, the uniform tariff remains in place but all firms, both entrants and the incumbent, pay a tax (on turnover, for instance) which is used to fund the loss-making sector. This would most likely be provided by the incumbent. This policy is sometimes followed in the telecommunications sector. However, while it overcomes the funding problem caused by cream-skimming entry, it does not help the inefficient entry problems (1) and (2) above. In

particular, there will most likely be no significant entry into the loss-making areas, and the efficiency or otherwise of the incumbent there will never be tested. In Britain, Oftel currently believes that the incumbent, BT, incurs little or no net cost in providing universal services, and hence does not believe it to be necessary to set up a universal service fund.[16]

- Impose similar tariff and social obligations on entrants as well as the incumbent. In practice, this will be hard to achieve. For instance, in telecommunications, an entrant could put all its marketing effort into attracting profitable subscribers, and none into the loss-making subscribers. This behaviour is hard to control. Even if possible, though, it is not obviously desirable, as an entrant may be particularly good at serving just one kind of market, but would be forced to serve all markets.

- Use public funds to subsidize the loss-making sector, and leave the profitable sector to manage itself. In Britain, loss-making rail services are funded directly out of government funds. As a result, distortions need not be imposed on profitable routes in order to fund social obligations. The right to run these loss-making services could be auctioned off to the firm that requires the lowest subsidy for a specified level of service. This would add a desirable degree of competition for the provision of these services. This scheme has the major advantages that (i) it does not distort profitable markets unduly (although of course additional distortions are imposed throughout the economy in order to fund the subsidy), and (ii) it makes explicit the level of subsidy required, and politicians may find it hard to justify high subsidies, targeted to small groups of people, to the wider electorate. On the other hand, it may be difficult to combine this kind of policy with EU policies aimed at preventing state aids.

- Finally, if keeping the unbalanced retail tariff in place is desired, a more complex solution would be to impose a tax/subsidy scheme that brings the entrant's private incentives to enter into line with those of overall efficiency. Assume that the entrant must pay a tax of $A_{urban}$ per unit in the urban market, and a tax of $A_{rural}$ (which may be negative) in the rural market. Then the above analysis shows that entry will occur if and only if it is efficient for the entrant to do so provided that:

$$A_{urban} = P - C_{urban} > 0; A_{rural} = P - C_{rural} < 0. \qquad (8.1)$$

For instance, with this tax, entry into the urban market will occur if and only if

$$P + (u_{rban} - U) \geq c_{urban} + A_{urban},$$

which is precisely when it is efficient, that is, when $u_{urban} - c_{urban} > U - C_{urban}$. Thus, these entry taxes and subsidies bring entry incentives into line with overall efficiency. It is optimal to discourage entry into profitable markets (in the sense of requiring a positive tax for entry there), and to encourage entry into loss-making markets (in the sense of subsidizing entry there). Moreover, the scheme has the additional benefit that if entry takes place in the profitable market, there are still sufficient funds from taxation for the incumbent to continue to serve the rural market. In economics jargon, this tax system is an example of what is known as the 'efficient component pricing rule', and has the feature that the entrant pays a tax (or subsidy) equal to the incumbent's profit margin (or opportunity cost) in the relevant market. This system, which implies that entrants face the same implicit tax regime as the incumbent, therefore solves at once all the three problems (1)–(3) listed above.

Related issues arise when entrants need access to an incumbent's network facilities in order to provide their own services. An obvious point, but one that is rarely tackled effectively by regulators, is that when the retail tariff is out of line with its costs, allowing entrants access to the incumbent's network facilities at cost (in some sense) will be likely to lead to the problems discussed in the example above – that is, too much entry in profitable markets, too little entry in loss-making markets, and if cream-skimming entry takes place, the incumbent may be unable to fund its loss-making obligations.

Oftel has been reasonably sensitive to this issue, and has sometimes imposed surcharges on to cost-based access charges.[17] For telecommunications at the EU level, however, there has been greater emphasis on 'cost-based' interconnection charging than on retail tariff rebalancing (about which EU policy is currently vague). This issue will become particularly problematic if 'local loop unbundling', which involves an incumbent providing many of its network elements to rivals at cost, is mandated throughout Europe.

The Annex to this chapter discusses the problem of how to price network elements in the context where the incumbent's retail tariff is regulated. In general, an entrant (in telecommunications) has two ways to enter a market: it can build its own infrastructure and be independent from the incumbent, or it can rely on the incumbent's investments by leasing/buying some of the incumbent's network elements. The problem for policy is then twofold: the regime should (i) ensure that entry occurs if and only if this is efficient, and (ii) if entry occurs, the entrant should have the correct 'make-or-buy' incentives, so that it builds its own infrastructure if and only if this is more efficient than using the incumbent's facilities. The Annex argues that:

- In order to ensure that entry occurs (in whatever form) only if it is efficient, it is necessary to levy an entry tax (or subsidy) of the form in expression (8.1) above, and this is levied regardless of whether the entrant makes use of the incumbent's network. Otherwise, there will be too much entry in profitable markets and too little in loss-making markets.
- In order to ensure that when entry *does* take place the correct investment decision is made by the entrant, it is necessary to make the incumbent's network elements available at (forward-looking) cost. Otherwise, productive inefficiency will result.

Thus, a policy that mandates that the incumbent's network be available to entrants at cost is half-correct. The correct make-or-buy decision is then made, *given* entry. However, when the incumbent's retail tariff is forced to be out of line with its costs, as with most universal service policies, such a policy will, on its own, lead to inefficient patterns of entry.

## CONCLUSION

This discussion has been too brief to sustain firm conclusions. However, it is clear that many policies designed to help incumbents, entrants or consumers (or all three) can act to encourage inefficient entry or discourage efficient entry. The broad lesson is that for any proposed policy designed to protect one group, for instance some form of price control placed on an incumbent, the regulator should think hard about the possible side-effects in terms of inefficient entry, and about how the policy could be modified to lessen these negative aspects. A theme that appeared more than once was that, where an incumbent firm faced competition (or the threat of it) in some markets but not in others, it seemed desirable to de-link these markets as far as possible. For instance, if, as seems likely, some consumer groups deserve special protection (that is, a subsidized service), then direct funding of this policy, such as through a well-designed and competitively neutral universal service fund, is likely to be superior to a policy that distorts competition in the other, less-problematic, sectors.

## NOTES

1. This chapter was written in July 1999. Britain is the focus of this chapter not because it has an especially poor record in enabling efficient entry, which it does not, but because (i) it is the country with which the author is most familiar, and (ii) it has a longer record of attempting liberalization of network industries than most other countries in Europe.
2. Another argument, especially in less-developed or transitional economies, is that the profit generated by enforced monopoly enables a higher degree of investment. For some tentative

arguments along these lines, see Mark Armstrong and John Vickers, 'Regulatory Reform in Telecommunications in Central and Eastern Europe', 4 *Economics of Transition* 295 (1996). This argument seems to require the economy to be in such a bad state that funds neither from taxation nor from private lenders are forthcoming, and most investment funds can only be generated internally by the firm.

3. This artificial advantage is offset to some extent by the ban on the BBC using advertising as a source of funds. However, public support for the BBC being funded by the licence fee rather than through advertising is apparently mixed.

4. For more details on this proposal, see Department for Culture, Media and Sport, *Davies Report on the Future Funding of the BBC* (London: HMSO, July 1999).

5. See Mark Armstrong, Simon Cowan and John Vickers, *Regulatory Reform: Economic Analysis and British Experience* Section 8.4.2 (Cambridge, MA, 1994).

6. See *id.*, Sections 4.2.2 and 7.2.2; Mark Armstrong, 'Local Competition in UK Telecommunications', in *Regulating Utilities: Understanding the Issues* (Michael Beesley, ed., London, 1998).

7. For further details, see Department of Trade and Industry, *Competition and Choice: Telecommunications Policy for the 1990s* (London, 1991).

8. For further details about this policy, see Oftel, *Implementation of Carrier Pre-Selection in the UK: A Statement* (London, 1999).

9. Armstrong, et al., *supra* note 5, Section 8.4.3; George Yarrow, '*Progress in Gas Competition*', Section 2, in Beesley, ed., *supra* note 6.

10. Armstrong, et al., *supra* note 5, Section 9.4.1; Richard Green and David Newbery, '*Competition in the Electricity Industry in England and Wales*', 13 *Oxford Review of Economic Policy* 27 (1997).

11. Department of Trade and Industry, *supra* note 7, at 70.

12. Oftel, *Pricing of Telecommunications Services from 1997: A Consultative Document*, para. 5.10 (London, 1995).

13. See Armstrong et al., *supra* note 5, sections 4.3.3 and 7.5.4.

14. Oftel, *Universal Telecommunications Services: A Consultative Document*, para. 3.27 (London, 1999).

15. For instance, in its recent consultative document on universal service in telecommunications (Oftel, *supra* note 14), Oftel makes virtually no mention of the problems for efficient entry caused by these kinds of uniform tariffs, and instead focuses on the funding issue.

16. See Oftel, *supra* note 14.

17. See Armstrong et al., *supra* note 5, Section 7.5.6 (providing more details about how early policy towards access pricing in telecommunications included significant elements of 'efficient component pricing', and thus may have partially corrected various distortions then present in BT's retail tariff).

# TECHNICAL ANNEX ON THE PRICING OF NETWORK ELEMENTS

Assume the incumbent (in the telecommunications market) already has a network in place.[1] The incumbent has operating costs $C$ for providing services to any given subscriber, has regulated price $P$ for providing these services, and these services provide each of its subscribers with gross utility $U$ (so that their net utility is just $U - P$).

**Infrastructure Entry**

Assume first that an entrant buys no network elements (such as local loops) from the incumbent, and therefore builds its network from scratch. Assume that in doing this, it incurs costs $c$ per subscriber, which is likely to be substantially above $C$ since the latter only involves operating costs and not the sunk costs of construction. This new network gives subscribers gross utility $u$, which may be higher than $U$ if a newer technology (for example, broadband) is being used. Therefore, the entrant can charge a price up to $P + (u - U)$ and still attract subscribers.

Assume that the entrant has to pay a tax of $A$ for each subscriber it attracts. As in Section C above, entry will take place if and only if

$$P + (u - U) \geq c + A.$$

On the other hand, such entry is desirable (compared to no entry at all) if and only if

$$u - c \geq U - C.$$

Therefore, if the entrant is required to pay a fee for each subscriber it attracts equal to

$$A = P - C, \tag{8.2}$$

that is, equal to the incumbent's 'forward-looking opportunity cost', entry will occur if and only if this is efficient. (This is again just an instance of the so-called efficient component pricing rule as in expression (8.1) above.) To the extent that $P$ allows the recovery of the incumbent's sunk costs, it is likely to exceed the operating costs C, and hence the 'access charge' $A$ is likely to be positive (even though the entrant purchases no network services from the incumbent). For many reasonable parameter values (that is, unless $u$ is particularly high or $c$ is particularly low), there will be no infrastructure entry under the above optimal entry fee regime, for the reason that the entrant has to compete against an incumbent whose network investment has already been sunk.

## Entry by Using the Incumbent's Network Elements

Assume that the entrant is given the opportunity to buy/lease some part of the incumbent's network (for example, its local loops). It costs the incumbent $C_A$ per subscriber to provide this access service to the entrant (which may be close to zero since its network is already sunk). Given that it has access to the incumbent's network, it costs the entrant an additional amount $\hat{c}$ per subscriber to supply its retail service, which then generates utility $\hat{u}$ to its subscribers. ($\hat{u}$ may differ from $u$ if using the incumbent's network degrades or enhances the entrant's own service.) Entry by using the incumbent's network elements is desirable (compared to no entry at all) if

$$\hat{u} - (\hat{c} + C_A) \geq U - C,$$

whereas such entry is privately profitable for the entrant if

$$P + (\hat{u} - U) \geq \hat{c} + a,$$

where $a$ is the charge for using the incumbent's network elements. Therefore, private and social incentives are brought into line provided that

$$a = C_A + (P - C),$$

that is, if the access charge is equal to the direct cost of access plus the incumbent's lost profit in the retail sector (which is again a version of the efficient component pricing rule: ECPR). In particular, unless the incumbent's retail price is close to its operating cost (that is, the cost not including the sunk cost that has already been invested), which is unlikely, pricing network access at cost seems undesirable if the aim is to achieve (static) efficiency. The above expression is more illuminatingly written as

$$a = C_A + A,$$

where $A$ is as given in expression (8.2) above. Written this way, the charge for the incumbent's network elements is decomposed into (i) the direct cost of providing access and (ii) the ECPR tax $A$ designed to induce efficient entry.

**Giving the Entrant the Correct 'Make-or-Buy' Incentives**

In this framework, welfare with no entry is $U - C$, with infrastructure entry it is $u - c$, and with entry via the incumbent's network it is $\hat{u} - (\hat{c} + C_A)$. Assume the regulator is unsure which mode of entry (if any) is desirable, that is, that it does not know the values of $u$, $\hat{u}$, $c$ or $\hat{c}$ and hence cannot be sure which of these three values for welfare is highest. Is there an access pricing regime that decentralizes the decision to the entrant and ensures that the correct form of entry (if any) is pursued?

The answer, in this simple setting, is Yes. Assume that whenever the entrant supplies service to a subscriber (either by building its own infrastructure or leasing the incumbent's network elements), it pays the incumbent its opportunity cost $A = P - C$. In addition, it may choose to use the incumbent's network elements if it pays the actual cost $C_A$ for the service. Then this induces the correct make-or-buy decision by the entrant. It is easily calculated that the entrant's profits under the three possibilities are zero if it does not enter,

$$(u - c) - (U - C)$$

if it builds its own infrastructure, and

$$(\hat{u} - \hat{c} - C_A) - (U - C)$$

if it uses the incumbent's network elements. These profits are welfare in the three cases (minus a constant), and so with this access pricing regime the entrant will make the entry decision that maximizes welfare, and efficiency is ensured.[2]

Thus, in the simple model, allowing the entrant access to the incumbent's network at (forward-looking) cost is correct, since it gives the entrant accurate signals about what to build for itself and what to lease. This is true, however, only if the incumbent's opportunity cost is also paid whenever the entrant attracts subscribers away from the incumbent.

## NOTES

1. In the following, abstractions are made from other interconnection services, such as call termination payments between rival local operators. This permits the analysis to focus on the provision of correct incentives for efficient entry and infrastructure construction.
2. More generally, if there are several different network elements that could be used by an entrant, for example, switching as well as local loops, then the same argument would suggest that each of these elements be charged at incremental cost, and that the entrant also pay the incumbent's opportunity cost.

# 9. When should regulated companies be vertically separated?

## Darryl Biggar[1]

*Many regulated or state-owned utility industries, such as telecommunications, electricity, railways, postal services, ports, airports and so on, feature a non-competitive component vertically integrated with a competitive component. Competition in the competitive component can enhance the quality of the regulation in these industries and deliver benefits to users and consumers. A key issue in such industries is whether separating the ownership of the competitive and non-competitive components, supported by line-of-business restraints that prevent reintegration, would enhance the level of competition in the competitive component, and the overall quality of regulation.*

*Regulatory policy in the last ten years has been directed towards introducing competition in the competitive segment of those industries. Competition can be introduced by leaving the firm integrated and relying on access regulation, or by a form of separation. The primary argument for integration is vertical economies of scope, which arise from efficiencies that firms enjoy when they are vertically related. They cannot be captured through an arm's-length vertical contract to a separated downstream firm.*

*Several arguments favour separation. First, when a firm is vertically integrated, it has an incentive to keep competition out of downstream markets, which the regulator must continuously fight against. Once separated, the upstream firm no longer has the incentive to fight against the regulator to restrict competition downstream. Second, a regulated entity should not be allowed simultaneously to operate a non-regulated entity, because that will blur the cost structure of the firm. It will always attempt to shift costs away from the regulated component to the non-regulated component, and may be able to engage in predatory pricing in the competitive component by shifting some of its costs in the other direction. Third, good policy making must take account of the cost of policy errors. It is far easier to reintegrate a separated firm through merger, than to separate a firm. Given the irreversibility of integration, there should be a bias in favour of separation. Fourth, separation, especially when it enhances competition, is likely to be opposed by a large coalition of forces, including the incumbent firm, the finance ministry, the industry regulator, the industry unions and suppliers, and the subsidized consumers.*

*The chapter concludes that there should be a presumption in favour of separation and the burden of proof should be on the advocates of integration. It advocates a case-by-case approach, rather than a blanket rule, because economies of scope and the quality of access regulation differ in each case, in each industry, and in each country. The national competition authority should have a substantial role in decisions affecting the industry structure, and should weigh the efficiency benefits against the effects on competition in the course of its review of merger proposals or proposals to relax the line-of-business restraints on the incumbent.*

## INTRODUCTION

Many industries, especially traditional utility industries, have a structure in which a non-competitive component is vertically integrated with a competitive component or activity. Examples of this structure arise in railways, postal services, telecommunications, electricity and many other regulated industries. In the past, most regulatory regimes did not seek to introduce competition into the competitive components of these industries. Policy makers were therefore faced with regulating an often large, vertically integrated firm providing services in many different markets.

One of the most important developments in regulatory thinking in the past two decades has been the recognition of the role that competition can play as a tool for enhancing the quality of the regulation of such sectors. Introducing competition has three significant advantages: it enhances efficiency and innovation in the competitive activities; it minimizes the scope and therefore the opportunity for distortions arising from traditional forms of regulation; and it focuses the regulatory interventions on the non-competitive 'core' or the 'kernel' of the underlying market failure.

In order to introduce and maintain competition in the competitive activities, it is necessary to somehow regulate the terms and conditions of access by rivals to the non-competitive activity. The primary question that this chapter addresses is whether to go further, and separate the ownership of the competitive and the non-competitive activities. It sets out the principles and factors to be taken into account by policy makers as they seek to make decisions as to whether vertical separation is desirable.

## A.  THE BASIC PROBLEM: VERTICAL INTEGRATION BETWEEN NON-COMPETITIVE AND COMPETITIVE ACTIVITIES

### Non-competitive Activities

A 'sector' of the economy is not a single homogeneous economic activity, but consists of a number of separate activities or 'components', many of which produce intermediate goods or services for use in other activities within the sector. Where two intermediate goods or services are complements in the production of the final good or service, these two intermediate goods are in a *vertical* relationship. Where the two intermediate goods are substitutes in the production of the final goods, the activities are in a *horizontal* relationship. For example, the services of train and track are complements in the delivery of rail transportation services and therefore are in a vertical relationship. The services of two ports which both may be used as a transfer point en route to a final destination are substitutes and therefore are in a horizontal relationship.[2]

Each individual component or activity has its own cost and demand conditions. For some activities, the cost and demand conditions may be such that the component or activity cannot sustain competition. On the cost side, an activity may not sustain competition when there are economies of scale – that is, when an increase in the scale of operation does not increase costs proportionately (at least up to the total market demand).[3] Activities that exhibit substantial economies of scale can only sustain a single firm. The activity is said to feature a 'natural monopoly'. If there are two or more firms operating in the market, one will eventually emerge as the largest, and will be able to drive out the others.[4]

There are many examples of economies of scale, particularly in network industries. In the rail sector, for example, once a line is constructed, the capital cost of running an additional train is negligible, until the line reaches its capacity. In the postal sector, the cost of adding an additional letter to an existing delivery round is negligible provided the total weight of the mail bag is not more than the delivery person can carry. In the telecommunications sector, the cost of an additional telephone call is negligible, provided the network is not already full.[5] In each case, a single firm can supply the market demand at lower cost than could two or more firms.

An activity also may not be able to sustain competition for demand reasons. In some markets, the demand for a good or service increases with the number of purchases of the same good or service. These markets are said to exhibit 'network externalities' or 'network effects'. Network externalities often arise in information technology and communications industries. There are often benefits to being on a larger network, or on a more widely adopted standard, as it increases the number of people with whom one can interact or conduct economic transactions. Provided there are costs of being connected to (or compatible with) two or more networks (or standards), consumers will pay more for the benefit of being on a larger network.[6] Markets that exhibit sizeable network externalities can only sustain a single firm. Where there are two or more firms, one will eventually emerge as the largest, and will be able to drive the others out.[7] Recent examples of battles for standards include the battle between Sony and VHS for the home video cassette standard, and the battle between Microsoft and Apple for the PC operating system standard.

There is a fundamental underlying similarity between the cost and demand-side effects. The cost conditions that determine when a market cannot sustain competition have a direct counterpart in demand conditions. It is well known that a market cannot sustain competition when there are increasing returns to scale or (equivalently) marginal cost is below average cost. Similarly, a market cannot sustain competition when an increase in the scale of output more than proportionally increases the revenue accruing to the firm, or (equivalently) when marginal revenue is above average revenue. This chapter will refer to activities that cannot sustain competition (that is, those activities for which competition would lead to a single provider) as non-competitive activities, whether the activity cannot sustain competition for cost or demand reasons.

In addition to these cost and demand reasons, an activity may also be non-competitive when regulatory restraints on competition have been imposed with respect to that activity. Such restraints are imposed for various reasons including, most commonly, to permit the incumbent firm a source of revenue to fund mandated non-commercial services. In many industries, it is politically and administratively convenient to fund non-commercial services in a non-transparent manner, through internal cross-subsidization from other services which are priced above cost. Those prices for other services can only be maintained above cost if they are protected from competition. For instance, postal operators are protected from competition with respect to standard letter mail, on the ground that this is necessary to protect the cross-subsidization of letter delivery in high-cost or rural areas. This chapter will include within the set of non-competitive activities those that are non-competitive as a result of regulatory restraints.[8]

## Vertical Integration

In many sectors, especially in traditional utility industries, non-competitive activities are provided within the same firm as complementary competitive activities. In other words, the non-competitive activity is vertically integrated with a competitive activity, as illustrated in Figure 9.1.

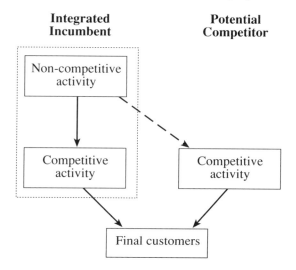

*Figure 9.1   An industry with an integrated non-competitive component*

Many examples of this structure can be found, such as trains and rail infrastructure, which are complements in the provision of rail transport services. The operation of trains is a potentially competitive activity, while the provision of rail infrastructure is not. Generation and transmission are complements in the provision of electricity, but the provision of generation services in electricity is competitive, while the provision of high-power transmission lines to carry the resulting electricity is not.[9] (See Table 9.1.)

Vertical integration and vertical arrangements between firms do not give rise to the same competition concerns as horizontal integration and horizontal arrangements. A profit-maximizing unregulated firm may choose to integrate vertically and exclude competition for a variety of efficiency-enhancing reasons. The question, therefore, is under what if any circumstances might a firm's decision to vertically integrate and eliminate downstream competition be inefficient from the perspective of the wider society?

Privately owned profit-maximizing firms should be distinguished here from regulated or state-owned firms. Economists have debated the incentives of privately owned profit-maximizing firms to restrict competition in vertical markets. Such firms may have incentives to restrict competition inefficiently, depending on the market structure, the instruments the firm can use to control competition downstream and the information available to the firm.[10]

However, in the case of regulated or state-owned firms, the incentive to restrict competition downstream is clearer. A regulated firm may seek to

*Table 9.1   Industries featuring both competitive and non-competitive components*

| Sector | Non-competitive component(s) | Competitive component(s) |
|---|---|---|
| Railways | Track and signalling infrastructure[†] | Operation of trains. Maintenance facilities |
| Electricity | High-voltage transmission of electricity[†]<br>Local electricity distribution[‡] | Electricity generation |
| Postal services | Door-to-door delivery of non-urgent mail in residential areas[‡] | Transportation of mail<br>Delivery of urgent mail or packages<br>Delivery of mail to high-volume business customers, especially in high-density areas |
| Telecommunications | Local residential and business telephony[‡][*] | Long-distance services<br>Mobile services<br>Value-added services<br>Local loop services to high-volume business customers, especially in high-density areas |
| Gas | High-pressure transmission of gas[†]<br>Local gas distribution[‡] | Gas production |
| Air services | Airport services such as take-off and landing slots | Aircraft operations<br>Maintenance facilities<br>Catering services |
| Waste management | Door-to-door collection of residential waste[‡] | Waste processing and disposal<br>Collection of waste from high-volume business customers, especially in high-density areas |
| Water | Distribution of water and wastewater | Water collection and treatment |
| Maritime transport | Port facilities (in certain cities) | Pilot services, port services |

*Notes*

[†]  Scope for competition varies depending on geography and nature of demand, among other things.

[‡]  Services in lower-density, lower-volume residential areas are less likely to be competitive than services to high-density, higher-volume commercial areas.

[*]  In the case of telecommunications, demand-side or network effects are as important as the underlying cost structure in limiting the number of firms providing local services that could be sustained in the absence of regulation.

integrate as a way of expanding its capital base or reducing the information available to the regulator. If the non-competitive component is regulated, while the competitive component is not (or is less heavily regulated) the integrated firm has an incentive to monopolize the downstream unregulated competitive market in order to capture some of the monopoly profits that it is not allowed to capture upstream. Furthermore, in an industry characterized by rapid technological change, restricting entry downstream may protect the integrated firm from technological developments that threaten its monopoly upstream. Finally, if the firm is not profit maximizing, but employment or revenue maximizing, it may have an incentive to limit entry downstream in order to weaken the cost-efficiency pressures of competition.

In other words, with certain caveats, vertical integration and elimination of downstream competition are primarily of concern in regulated or state-owned industries.[11] These industries will be the focus of this chapter.[12]

## B.  VERTICAL SEPARATION VERSUS VERTICAL INTEGRATION

A firm that owns a non-competitive component can exercise market power and must be subject to some form of price regulation, notwithstanding whether the non-competitive component is integrated with the competitive component. In other words, some form of 'access' regulation is inevitable. The key question that this chapter addresses is whether the regulator should allow the incumbent firm to remain integrated, or whether it should take the additional step of vertical separation of the competitive and non-competitive activities (supported by some form of line-of-business restraints to prevent reintegration or entry by the owner of the non-competitive activity into the competitive market).[13]

The choice between vertical separation and vertical integration involves a choice between a structural approach to regulation and a behavioural approach. Vertical separation is a structural approach, involving the loss of any economies of scope. It reduces, however, the incentive and ability of the incumbent firm to restrict competition in the competitive component. Allowing the incumbent firm to remain vertically integrated, on the other hand, requires a more restrictive form of behavioural regulation to offset the incentive and ability of the firm to restrict competition in the competitive component. In addition, as shown below, separation yields additional benefits that are not available under integration.

### Separation Forces Loss of Economies of Scope

The primary disadvantage of vertical separation is that it may involve the loss of economies of scope from integration. These include: enhanced flows of information (allowing more efficient incentive contracts); reduction of transaction costs and improved investment in relationship-specific assets as a result of overcoming hold-up problems; and reduction of distortions associated with market power at one or both of the two levels.

Many of these potential cost efficiencies can be at least partially exploited through contractual arrangements between separate firms. An understanding of the costs of separation therefore requires a comparison between the cost efficiencies achievable under integration versus those achievable through contractual arrangements. Where there are vertical contractual arrangements that can achieve the same efficiencies as integration, economies of scope are negligible.

One source of cost efficiencies should be highlighted: enhanced transaction costs arising from technological innovation. Important innovations in the services offered to final consumers may require investments in both the services provided by the competitive and non-competitive activities. For example, where a rail spur serves a coalmine, innovations in coal transportation might involve changes to the rail infrastructure. These could be more easily achieved when infrastructure and train operations are integrated. Contractual arrangements could, in principle, specify the procedures to be followed in the event of certain innovations. In practice, however, the uncertainty in the nature, timing and scope of innovation make such arrangements impractical.

If the price of the non-competitive component is greater than marginal cost (despite regulation), integration is justified on efficiency grounds, as explained in Box 1, below. Raising the marginal price for access to the non-competitive activity above its marginal cost induces distortions that the upstream firm would like to avoid. For example, when the competitive activity can substitute for other inputs, in a circumstance known as 'variable proportions', pricing the non-competitive service above marginal cost induces the downstream firm inefficiently to substitute away from the use of this input. When the downstream market is imperfectly competitive, the downstream firms add an additional mark-up (a 'double marginalization') to the final product, reducing output and increasing the total welfare loss. A regulator might try to overcome these efficiency losses using vertical contractual arrangements such as two-part tariffs or price discrimination. Either approach ensures that marginal price does not exceed marginal cost. However, these arrangements are feasible only when it is possible to prevent resale among downstream customers.[14] When resale cannot be prevented by either the firm or the regulator,[15] vertical integration allows the firm to capture the efficiency benefits by selling to its downstream subsidiary at marginal cost, without fear of resale.

In contrast, when the upstream firm or the regulator can prevent resale among downstream customers, the efficient outcome can be achieved through vertical arrangements. Thus, integration would yield no additional cost benefits. For example, the problem of double-marginalization can be overcome through a contractual arrangement that requires the downstream competitive firm to purchase a minimum quantity (or equivalently, imposes a price ceiling on the final good, equivalent to final price regulation). As another example, a 'tie-in' or 'bundling' strategy can solve the distortion highlighted in the 'variable proportions' problem. By requiring the downstream firm to also purchase other inputs from the upstream firm, the upstream firm can ensure that these inputs are priced to prevent distortion in their relative consumption downstream.

In practice, assessing the magnitude of economies of scope is difficult. As shown below, the regulated firm often has a strong incentive to inflate claims of efficiency benefits of integration. In this context, as in consideration of the efficiency benefits in mergers, it is appropriate only to accept efficiency claims that can be verified by reasonable means. The *US Horizontal Merger Guidelines* provide a very clear statement of this principle:

> Efficiencies are difficult to verify and quantify, in part because much of the information relating to efficiencies is uniquely in the possession of the merging firms. Moreover, efficiencies projected reasonably and in good faith by the merging firms may not be realized. Therefore, the merging firms must substantiate efficiency claims so that the [US Department of Justice] can verify by reasonable means the likelihood and magnitude of each asserted efficiency, how and when each would be achieved (and any costs of doing so), how each would enhance the merged firms' ability and incentive to compete, and why each would be merger-specific. Efficiency claims will not be considered if they are vague or speculative or otherwise cannot be verified by reasonable means.[16]

### Separation Avoids Difficult and Costly Regulation

Having considered the benefits of vertical integration, the advantages of separation will now be discussed. The primary advantage of vertical separation is that it reduces the incentive and ability of the provider of the non-competitive activity to restrict competition in the competitive activity. This is important because it lessens the regulatory burden and the problems that arise from the asymmetry of information between the regulator and the regulated firm.

Vertical separation, by reducing the incentives for discriminatory behaviour, allows the regulator to rely on a lighter-handed form of regulation, allowing the incumbent firm efficiently to exploit any informational advantage that it enjoys. For example, the regulated firm may have better information than the regulator on:

1. *Factors influencing the setting of prices*  Efficient pricing of access to the non-competitive activity may involve complex schemes, including multipart pricing, peak-load pricing, and discrimination between different classes of

## BOX 1:   WHY INTEGRATE? ECONOMIC EFFICIENCY BENEFITS FROM VERTICAL INTEGRATION

This box highlights some of the economic efficiency benefits that arise from vertical integration. Economists point to three types of incentives for vertical integration: (1) reduction of transactions costs that arise when there is relationship-specific investment; (2) improvement of the information and therefore the efficiency of arm's-length incentive contracts between the two firms; and (3) reduction of the distortions arising from the exercise of market power at one or both levels.

A classic example of relationship-specific investment is a coal-fired power station located at the mouth of a coalmine. The transactions costs lead, in practice, to either long-term vertical contracts or vertical integration. An example of vertical integration to improve incentive contracts arises when the downstream firm must make an effort to promote the upstream firm's products. In this case, vertical integration eliminates the need for an incentive contracting arrangement between the upstream and downstream firms.

This box focuses on the last case: vertical integration as an attempt to eliminate the distortion that arises from the exercise of market power or, more generally, when the price for the non-competitive component is above marginal cost, even when the firm is regulated. A regulated price might be above marginal cost, for example, when there are increasing returns to scale in the non-competitive sector and the regulator is prevented from directly subsidizing the fixed cost of the regulated firm, so that the efficient regulated price is equal to average cost. When a price differs from its underlying marginal cost, an economic distortion occurs which can lead to a loss in overall welfare.

When the downstream customers are firms (rather than final consumers) who are buying the input for use in their own production process, charging above marginal cost induces distortions that do not arise when selling directly to final consumers. When the downstream production process is not perfectly competitive, it adds its own mark-up, leading to a situation of 'double marginalization'. The final price will be even higher than that which would be set by an integrated firm (and possibly higher than the monopoly price). Moreover, when the downstream production process can substitute other inputs, it will be induced to do so by an input price above marginal cost, even though such substitution is inefficient. Finally, when the downstream firm must make an effort that increases the quality or the demand for the final product, it will have a smaller incentive to do so when its margins and sales are lower as a result of the higher cost of the input.

A firm with market power will seek to eliminate these distortions when it can capture some of the resulting gains in welfare. One way to eliminate the distortion is to use two-part tariffs. Provided the marginal part of the tariff is equal to marginal cost, the distortion from the exercise of market power is eliminated. The firm can then use the fixed part of the tariff to extract some of the resulting welfare gains. Two-part tariffs, however, are not always feasible. If the downstream customers can trade among themselves, it will be less costly to buy from an existing customer of the monopoly firm rather than to buy directly from the monopolist. Where two-part tariffs are not feasible, the incumbent firm is forced to use simple linear prices, which inevitably result in a marginal price above marginal cost.

Even if the firm were forced to use linear prices, it might still be able to reduce or eliminate the distortion arising from pricing above marginal cost if it could perfectly discriminate between classes of downstream customers, so that marginal customers were charged no more than marginal cost. Again, however, if the downstream customers can trade among themselves, a price discrimination strategy is not feasible.

By granting the monopoly firm greater control over resale, vertical integration can assist it to reduce the distortion brought about by its exercise of market power. By vertically integrating, the firm can 'sell' to its downstream subsidiary at a price equal to marginal cost, ensuring that the monopoly service is used efficiently in its downstream applications. Partial vertical integration can also assist a price discrimination strategy. By integrating with the downstream firms which have elastic demand, the monopoly firm can 'sell' the monopoly service at a lower internal transfer price, while simultaneously selling the monopoly service at a high price to downstream firms with inelastic demand.[17] Vertical integration can also improve the information that the firm has about demand elasticities by giving it direct access to the final consumers.

customers and demands. An external regulator may not have the necessary information to enforce such arrangements, thereby limiting the pricing efficiency possible under vertical integration. With vertical separation, the regulator can allow the non-integrated firm some discretion to use the information it has to set its prices efficiently. Oversight of the prices of the non-competitive activity can be limited to ensuring that the firm does not earn monopoly rents overall.

2. *Capacity*    The provider of the non-competitive activity will typically have better access than the regulator to key information, such as the capacity of the non-competitive activity. An integrated provider may seek to misrepresent the available capacity, or misuse the capacity in a way that denies its availability to competitors. King notes that if the regulator cannot verify the 'surplus capacity' of an integrated firm, that firm will have:

> every incentive to either design the facility so that there is no surplus capacity or to waste that capacity so as to reduce end market competition. In the case of gas, it is even possible that it will pay a pipeline operator to use the surplus capacity themselves and burn-off excess gas at the end of the pipe rather than to sell access.[18]

3. *Quality*    Similarly, if the regulator cannot verify the quality of the services provided by the non-competitive activity, the integrated firm has an incentive to lower the quality of services provided to competitors.[19] In contrast, a separated firm has no incentive to discriminate on quality.

In practice, regulatory interventions are slow and imperfect. Imposing controls on a firm's behaviour is time consuming and subject to inertia. Moreover, such controls are not always perfectly obeyed. These imperfections have different effects under vertical integration as opposed to vertical separation. Under the former, such imperfections in regulatory processes operate largely to the benefit of the incumbent.[20]

An integrated firm will use all regulatory, legal, political or economic mechanisms in its power to restrict access to the non-competitive activity in order to maintain (or gain) market power in the competitive activity. Regulation can limit the ability of an integrated firm to use access prices or terms and conditions as a tool for restricting access to the non-competitive activity. However, the incumbent firm may be able to use other mechanisms, such as obfuscation, strategic delay, legal processes or regulatory processes as tools for restricting the timeliness or quality of access. Because the regulated firm has strong incentives to innovate in regulatory evasion, the regulator will find that it is constantly 'catching up' with new strategies by the incumbent in restricting access. Access regulation is likely to become more detailed and intrusive over time.

In most countries, the competition authority will also have a role in controlling the ability of the incumbent to restrict competition in the non-competitive activity. For the same reasons (the information advantage of the incumbent, the slowness and imperfection of competition law enforcement processes, the incumbent's incentives to innovate in anticompetitive behaviour, the incumbent's incentives to use legal processes to delay enforcement decisions, and the competitive disadvantage of the new entrants in the face of delay and imperfect enforcement), antitrust enforcement is unlikely to be able to offset completely the advantage of the incumbent relative to the new entrants.

The effects of integration on access regulation were explored in a recent study comparing access arrangements with the US Bell regional operating companies (which are vertically separated) and GTE (a vertically integrated, rival telecommunications company). As set out in Box 2, below, access negotiations with integrated GTE took longer and were less likely to be successful. GTE's negotiating stance was systematically more aggressive than the Bells', and despite the access regulatory regime, entry was systematically lower in regions serviced by GTE.

The US Federal Trade Commission (FTC) Competition Bureau Director has summarized the tradeoff as follows:

> A behavioural approach has several drawbacks. First, it does not eliminate the incentive and opportunity to engage in exclusionary behaviour. Rules can try to limit the opportunity, but few rules are invulnerable to evasion. Second, detection of violations can be difficult. For example, discrimination in access could take the form of a subtle reduction in quality of service, whose effects could be difficult to identify and measure. Third, behavioural rules can require long-term monitoring of compliance, which can be a costly process. A structural approach minimizes the cost of monitoring compliance with the order. With a divestiture order, for example, that usually is a short-term requirement because the principal monitoring function is to make sure that the divestiture takes place in the manner required by the order. ... We also recognise, however, that a purely structural approach to certain problems, requiring a complete separation of business functions, may be costly or difficult to implement, and it may require a sacrifice of integrative efficiencies.[21]

In summary, effective regulation of an integrated firm increases the demands on the regulator and the regulatory regime, requires a tighter control on the behaviour of the integrated firm and is unlikely to be fully successful at offsetting the incentives of the incumbent to act anticompetitively. With vertical integration, the regulator requires considerably more information, stronger remedies and more robust regulatory processes than with vertical separation. Vertical separation lightens the demands on the regulator, allows a lighter, more efficient control of the behaviour of the incumbent and is likely to be more successful at introducing competition.

# BOX 2:   COMPARING GTE AND BELL CONDUCT

In the US, the 1983 antitrust decision which vertically separated AT&T did not apply to its smaller rival in local telephony services, GTE. As a result, unlike the Bell regional operating companies, GTE provides both local and long-distance telephony services. A recent study by Mini compares AT&T's negotiations to enter local markets served by GTE with those by the local Bell companies in the 22 states in which both GTE and a Bell company offer service.[22] The results give an indication of the enhanced difficulty of obtaining access (even where that access is mandated and regulated) when the incumbent is vertically integrated.

First, Mini's results suggest that access agreements are more likely to be reached, and to be reached more quickly, under vertical separation. As of March 1999, AT&T had failed to obtain approved interconnection agreements with the Bells in only two of the 22 sample states, but failed with GTE in ten of these states. In the 12 states where agreement was reached with both GTE and the local Bell, it was reached first with the Bell in 11 cases, and only once with GTE. In addition, the average delay in reaching agreement is 70 per cent longer with GTE (457 days with the Bells and 781 days with GTE).

Second, the incumbent is systematically more aggressive in negotiating under vertical integration. Mini compares the prices demanded by the incumbent for resale of local service, and finds that when going into arbitration, GTE offers a higher price for residential service in 15 out of 18 states and a higher price for business service in 13 of 18 states. On average, GTE offers a discount off the retail price of residential service of $1.20, whereas the Bells offer a $1.98 discount. This represents 8 per cent of the average monthly bill for GTE and 13 per cent for the Bells.

Finally, despite access regulation, entry is systematically lower in regions served by the integrated incumbent. In the states in which both Bell and GTE data were reported, the Bell had a higher percent of resold lines 12 times out of 15 in the case of residential lines, and 14 out of 14 for business lines. The proportion of resold residential lines was, on average, three times higher with the Bells (0.53 per cent against 0.15 per cent for GTE). The Bells' average proportion of resold business lines (1.32 per cent) was 18 times larger than GTE's.

These results demonstrate the increased difficulty of ensuring access and the reduced effectiveness of the resulting competition under vertical integration.

## Separation Improves Information and Eliminates Cross-subsidization

Some arguments in favour of separating regulated and unregulated firms apply more generally, and not just to the vertical industry structure which is the focus of this chapter. In any regulatory process, obtaining reliable cost information about the regulated entity is difficult. When the regulated firm is integrated with a non-regulated entity, the regulated firm may be able to shift costs from the non-regulated to the regulated component, inflating its costs and therefore, indirectly, its regulated prices. Obtaining accurate cost information about the non-competitive activity may be facilitated when it is separated into an independent firm, under distinct ownership. Separation reduces the opportunities for, and makes more transparent the practice of, using internal transfer prices to shift costs and profits around within the firm. Thus, it may be easier to regulate efficiently the non-competitive activity when it is vertically separated.[23]

In addition, a regulated or state-owned firm, because it does not necessarily operate under a strict profit-maximizing objective, may be able to engage in anticompetitive cross-subsidization even when it would not be strictly profitable in the long run to do so. Whenever a regulated firm is integrated with a firm that operates in a competitive market, there is a danger that the firm will use some of the profits from the non-competitive segment to subsidize its competitive segment, thereby restricting competition. The blurring of the costs between the regulated and non-regulated components makes this cross-subsidization difficult to detect. Vertical separation prevents cross-subsidization from occurring.[24]

Such considerations explain why it is common for regulated firms to be subject to line-of-business constraints that prevent them from entering unrelated markets.

## C.   BALANCING SEPARATION AND INTEGRATION: IS A PRESUMPTION IN FAVOUR OF SEPARATION APPROPRIATE?

Neither access regulation nor vertical separation is systematically preferred over the other. The choice between the two approaches will depend upon characteristics of the relevant market. These characteristics will differ from sector to sector and country to country, and will change as the legal environment, regulatory structures, technology and competition evolve. It is not possible to state in general what a consideration of separation on its merits alone would yield in any specific case.

However, there are arguments in favour of adopting a stance in favour of separation. That is, to adopt a policy that separation would be adopted unless clear evidence to the contrary can be demonstrated by the advocates of integration. This approach is consistent with merger policy, under which anticompetitive mergers are typically prohibited unless the advocates of the merger can demonstrate that the efficiency gains would be sufficiently large. For example, the FTC and the courts 'have placed the burden of proof of efficiency claims on the proponents of a merger and require substantial and convincing proof of significant economies' before allowing an anticompetitive merger to proceed.[25] The advantage of such a stance is that it provides strong incentives to the interested parties to reveal key information, which they otherwise would have an incentive to conceal. Adopting a stance in favour of separation provides incentives for those parties which hold key information to make it known.

In addition, a stance in favour of separation may be necessary to counterbalance the political and social interests that might be allied against separation. The liberalization of a formally regulated and/or state-owned sector is seldom straightforward politically. Incumbent stakeholders, including incumbent unions, suppliers and management usually have an interest in maintaining existing rents. These interests are concentrated and usually extremely vocal in their opposition to reform. Divestiture, especially where it is likely to enhance competition significantly, will probably be strongly opposed by the incumbent stakeholders. In contrast, as in many other competition issues, the broader public and consumer interests in favour of competition and reform are diffuse and less well organized.

Separation, especially when it is likely to foster downstream competition, will probably face opposition from a formidable alliance of actors, including:

- the regulated firm, which directly faces the costs of lost economies of scope and increased competition, without sharing in the benefits of competition to consumers;
- consumers, who are currently the beneficiaries of subsidized service, when those subsidies are threatened by the introduction of competition;
- unions and suppliers, who face the loss of their share of the rents through competition;
- government finance ministries, which directly incur the cost (in terms of reduced proceeds from the privatization) of a reduction in market power from competition and any lost economies of scope;[26] and
- the industry regulator, who stands to gain more from the interventionist, active role of the regulator under vertical integration.

In the face of such opposition, separation policies are less likely to succeed on their merits. This strengthens the argument that in the course of a major liberalization, it is appropriate to start with a presumption in favour of separation.

Who should make the decision whether to separate or not? The national com-petition authority is well placed to make judgements over the appropriate structure for an industry in the process of liberalization. Indeed, one of the primary reasons for the existence of an independent competition agency is to allow it to make such sensitive decisions in a controversial environment in a non-political manner. Competition agencies have, over time, built up signifi-cant experience and jurisprudence in balancing the economic benefits of a merger (or divestiture) against a potential loss to competition. They have a mandate to represent the broader public interests in competition against the concentrated interests favouring concentration or integration. They also have experience in doing so.

There are a variety of ways in which competition authorities could be involved in structural decisions, such as:

- providing the competition authority with the possibility of having a public voice in the separation decision. In Australia, the National Competition Policy reforms include a requirement to hold a public consultation on structural questions as part of the reform process, embedding an oppor-tunity for the competition agency to have its say;
- adopting separation as the default alternative for liberalization, then allowing the competition authority to scrutinize recombination proposals in the same manner as it supervises other horizontal and vertical mergers in the economy; and
- granting the competition authority the power to divest firms in the process of liberalization.

Whichever approach is adopted at the initial phase of a liberalization, the com-petition authority should be responsible for scrutinizing proposals that would lead to the reintegration of the incumbent firm. This would include oversight of merger proposals (which most competition authorities are mandated to do) and of requests for relaxation of the line-of-business restraints. In the US, for example, the Department of Justice has an important and explicit role in the decision whether to allow the local telephone companies (the 'RBOCs') into the long-distance telephony market.

Table 9.2 summarizes the factors to be considered when choosing between vertical separation and vertical integration. Broadly speaking, vertical integra-tion requires that the regulator have access to considerably more information (about costs, quality, capacity and the actions of the incumbent) than under vertical separation. A decision between integration and separation involves balancing economies of scope and other economic benefits of integration against the difficulty of obtaining sufficient information to make access regulation effective. When economies of scope are small and little information is available

Table 9.2 Summary of factors influencing choice between separation and integration

| | Factors favouring vertical separation | Factors favouring vertical integration |
|---|---|---|
| Economies of scope | Weak or no economies of scope between the competitive and non-competitive activities | Strong economies of scope between the competitive and non-competitive activities |
| Boundary of the non-competitive activity | Clear, well-defined boundary, stable with respect to changes in technology and demand | Unclear; changes with demand and technology |
| Ability to prevent resale between downstream customers | Incumbent can prevent resale. Thus, can adopt two-part or multipart pricing schemes | Incumbent cannot prevent resale. Thus, incumbent is restricted to simple linear price for access |
| Ability to price discriminate on the basis of demand elasticities | Incumbent and/or regulator can obtain information on final demand elasticities without integration | Obtaining information on final demand elasticities requires integration |
| Degree of competition in competitive activity | A high level of competition is expected downstream, reducing double marginalization problem | Limited competition is expected downstream, exacerbating double marginalization problem |
| Nature of downstream technology | Downstream technology uses non-competitive activity in 'fixed proportions'; thus, there is no distortion from monopoly pricing upstream | Downstream technology uses non-competitive activity in 'variable proportions'; thus, there is a potential distortion from monopoly pricing upstream |
| Regulated firm has private information about costs and demand elasticities | Efficient pricing requires use of private information of incumbent, which it can conceal, efficient pricing requires auctions of the capacity of the non-competitive component | Access prices can be reasonably efficient using easily available information |

| | | |
|---|---|---|
| Regulated firm has private information about capacity or quality | Incumbent can conceal capacity, or quality of service provided by incumbent is not verifiable | Capacity and quality are readily verifiable |
| Institutional and legal context | Incumbent firm has wide scope for using legal and regulatory processes to delay or obfuscate | Institutions are effective at controlling the incentives on the incumbent to delay or obfuscate |
| Information about costs on the competitive component | Difficult to obtain, making the prevention of anticompetitive cross-subsidization difficult | Easy to obtain, and can be used to prevent anticompetitive cross-subsidization |
| Information about costs on the non-competitive component | Difficult to obtain because internal transfer prices used to shift costs and profits around an integrated firm | Readily available |

regarding costs, demand and so on, vertical separation is preferred. In contrast, when economies of scope are large and key information is readily verifiable, vertical integration is preferred.[27]

Finally, even though vertical separation and integration cannot be simultaneously adopted in the same market, they are not necessarily mutually exclusive across an industry serving many markets. It may be possible to adopt vertical separation for some non-competitive activities and vertical integration for others. For example, vertical separation of the local loop for residential telecommunications customers might be combined with vertical integration in the service to business customers.

## D.   OTHER FORMS OF SEPARATION

This chapter has focused on the polar cases of full separation and full integration. Other forms of separation have occasionally been proposed, with the intention of obtaining some of the benefits of separation without the loss of economies of scope. Some of these approaches are summarized in Table 9.3, which shows that they do not address the incentive on the owner of the non-competitive component to restrict competition. Thus, they amount to different forms of behavioural regulation. The use of the term 'separation' to describe these forms is therefore somewhat misleading.

Accounting separation, in particular, has been heavily criticized as not overcoming the fundamental problems associated with integration. For example, Hardt comments:

> Theory predicts that ... accounting separation has no effect on the dominating firm's behaviour, accounting separation does not effectively prevent discrimination of a competing network user, and accounting separation cannot effectively be used to promote entry, either. ... [A]ccounting separation is not equivalent to structural separation. Although they look equivalent at first sight, their ways of functioning economically and their implications (in terms of access prices, output levels and prices, and entry possibilities for potential competitors) differ considerably. ... It is important for regulators to be fully aware of the economic implications of the measures adopted in a policy aimed at non-discriminatory access pricing. An incorrect assessment of the effect of accounting separation will lead to higher consumer prices and lower welfare.[28]

Similarly, Hilmer notes:

> It is important to stress that mere 'accounting separation' will not be sufficient to remove the incentives for misuse of control over access to an essential facility. Full separation of ownership and control is required. In fact, failure to make such separation despite deregulation and privatisation is seen as a major reason why infrastructure reform in the UK has been disappointing.[29]

'Functional separation' or 'functional unbundling' goes further than accounting separation by requiring separation of the personnel and assets of the two activities. The ability of functional separation to overcome the incumbent's incentives is questionable. For example, in Italy, Telecom Italia was required to keep its Internet access provider functionally separate from the rest of its operations. Nevertheless, in July 1998, the Italian Competition Authority opened an investigation into allegations by an association of Internet access providers that Telecom Italia discriminated in favour of its own Internet access provider. The discrimination allegedly took the form of pricing, use of information about telecommunications customers to solicit their Internet access business, and use of information received when other Internet access providers 'did the paperwork' to solicit their Internet access business.

A form of functional separation has been common in the US electricity industry. Nevertheless, this appears not to have prevented all abuses. In March 1998, the Electricity Consumers Resource Council (a group of large electricity consumers, representing 6 per cent of all electricity consumption in the US), in a petition to the Federal Energy Regulatory Commission (FERC), provided 13 pages of 'examples of common ongoing forms of transmission provider discrimination', including:[30]

- exploitation of the different regulatory treatment of power for 'native load' (demand that is traditionally served by a utility) so that access to transmission by other generators is blocked;
- withholding transmission capacity under the claim that it is needed for reserve in order to maintain reliability or to provide network service;
- inaccurate or unreasonable delays in reporting available transmission capacity;
- granting access to information from the transmission part of a utility to its affiliate's marketing personnel in advance of that information being available to competing firms;
- sharing information about a rival's request for transmission capacity to a utility's own downstream affiliate; and
- confirming requests for transmission capacity faster for a utility's affiliate than for rival firms.

In place of functional separation, a form of 'operational separation' has been advocated for the US electricity industry. Under operational separation, the ownership of the non-competitive component is separated from its control, which is given to an independent entity. Control over the transmission grid is handed to an 'independent system operator' (ISO), which plays the role of a regulator. Thus, operational separation can be viewed as a detailed form of behavioural regulation, with the same advantages and disadvantages. In some

*Table 9.3  Different forms of separation*

| Form of separation | Description | Comment |
|---|---|---|
| Accounting separation | Does not require any structural or operational changes to the firm. Merely requires that the firm prepare accounts that identify the revenues and costs of certain specified activities. Detailed rules often describe how the firm is to allocate costs between the specified activities, and how the firm is to handle transactions between the specified activities and the other parts of the firm | This form of separation has no effects on the firm's incentives. It may assist the regulator in obtaining cost information. However, given the opportunities of the firm to influence the disclosed information, the resulting information is of questionable value |
| Corporate separation | Requires that the firm adopt a particular legal structure, with specific activities carried on in specific places within the structure. There may also be detailed rules about how transactions between the different legal entities are to be handled | This form of separation has no effect on the firm's incentives. As with accounting separation, it may assist in obtaining cost information, but has the same drawback that given the opportunities of the firm to influence the disclosed information, the resulting information is of questionable value. |
| Functional separation (or functional unbundling) | This term has been used in the electricity industry in the US.* It refers to a stronger form of access regulation in which rivals are also guaranteed non-discriminatory access to information about the activities of the non-competitive component (and may require separation of personnel) | This is not a structural approach and does not address the incentive of the owner of the non-competitive component to restrict competition |

| | | |
|---|---|---|
| Operational separation (or operational unbundling) | The integrated firm's owners retain ownership of the assets, but control over the assets passes to a third party who makes decisions on prices, quantities, marketing and so on. The decisions can, in principle, also extend to decisions over new investments | This is not a structural approach but a form of behavioural regulation, where the regulator is deeply involved in the operation of the integrated firm and has access to necessary information. It does not address the incentive issue, but offsets its effects through a very detailed form of regulation |
| Joint ownership | The players in the competitive market share ownership of the non-competitive component | This approach is a midpoint between full separation and full integration. Under certain circumstances, it may lead to higher welfare than either of the other choices. However, there is a serious risk that the joint owners will prevent new entry |
| Full ownership separation | The competitive and non-competitive parts of the firm are placed in different firms with distinct ownership and arm's-length interaction | Ownership separation can reduce the incentive and the ability of the non-competitive component to restrict competition in the competitive component |

*Note:* * See OECD, *Regulatory Reform in the United States* (Paris: OECD, 1999), p. 283

cases, competing firms appear to have a direct input into the operation of the ISO, making this approach similar to that of the 'joint ownership' approach.

It remains to be seen whether operational separation will be successful. The OECD report on Regulatory Reform in the US Electricity Industry commented:

> The institutional structure of ISOs is still evolving in response to actual experience in the United States markets. While some of the limits of the possible institutional structure have been identified on the basis of analysis of incentives of participants, no ISO has yet operated for a sufficiently long time that it is clear that this new institution will deliver on its promise, in practice. Hence, even where a reform does not require divestiture of generation from transmission, it is important that reforms contain the option to require divestiture in the event that an ISO does not, in practice, deliver the appropriate operational and investment outcomes.[31]

Even in the unlikely event that regulatory controls on behaviour are successful, they may negate the effects of integration:

> [T]he open network rules often implemented to deal with potential vertical foreclosure problems may end up requiring the incumbent to behave as if it is not vertically-integrated – for example, by mandating that it separate the operations and accounts of its competitive and regulated monopoly businesses, and restricting private communications between the regulated operator of the 'bottleneck' network and its unregulated affiliates. In this case, it is not clear that the potential benefits of vertical integration can be realised in the end as a result of these restrictions, since they effectively require the firm to behave as if they are not vertically integrated.[32]

## CONCLUSION

Many regulated industries have an industry structure that involves a non-competitive activity vertically integrated with a competitive activity. Policies that seek to enhance the level of competition in the competitive activity can improve the overall effectiveness of regulation in such industries. Two broad approaches for enhancing competition in the competitive activity involve a choice between vertical separation and vertical integration. Both integration and separation have advantages and disadvantages. Neither approach emerges as clearly preferable in all circumstances.

This chapter has sought to derive a set of principles governing the decision for separation compared with integration. At the broadest level, vertical separation has the disadvantage of forcing the loss of any efficiency benefits from integration. However, it has the advantage of reducing the incentive of the provider of the non-competitive activity to restrict competition in the competitive activity. Separation also enhances the transparency of the regulated firm's costs, and reduces its ability to engage in anticompetitive cross-subsidization.

In summary, the quality of competition and regulation will be enhanced by a policy of restricting regulated or state-owned firms to operating only in non-competitive markets, except where the advocates of integration can demonstrate that there are clear efficiency benefits from allowing the firm also to compete in a vertically related market. The national competition authority should have a substantial role in decisions affecting industry structure, weighing the efficiency benefits against the effects on competition in the initial liberalization, and in the course of its review of merger proposals or proposals to relax the line-of-business restraints on the incumbent.

## NOTES

1. This chapter follows from work the author has been doing for the Organization for Economic Cooperation and Development (OECD) Committee on Competition Law and Policy. Although he hopes that something coming from this work will eventually be endorsed by the Committee, this chapter presents his own views.
2. In the context of a network, it may not always be possible to label a specific separation as vertical or horizontal, as the various parts of the network may be combined by consumers in ways which are sometimes complementary and sometimes competing. For example, assume a rail network involves links from two coastal towns A and C to an inland town, B. In this case, the routes A–B and B–C may be combined to obtain rail transport from A to C. Alternatively, the routes A–B and C–B may compete in the transport of goods from the coast to the inland town.
3. This often arises when capacity must be installed in 'lumps' and when the smallest lump of capacity that can be added exceeds the total market demand.
4. More than one firm may be sustainable in the market when they provide sufficiently differentiated products. Products are differentiated when each firm provides unique features that some customers value.
5. A natural monopoly can also arise where substantial investment or 'start-up costs' are necessary to commence operations. For example, in industries where reputation is of critical importance, it may take many years to build up the necessary reputation to become profitable.
6. In some industries, firms can influence these costs of being 'connected to' or 'compatible with' more than one network. In these industries, the size of these switching costs becomes a strategic decision of the firm. If the firm believes it can become large enough to benefit from the network effects, it may seek to raise the switching costs as a way to gain a competitive advantage over its rivals. Examples of this arise in the airline industry. Airlines use loyalty programmes such as frequent flyer plans to discourage switching between airlines.
7. As before, more than one firm may be sustainable in the market when they produce sufficiently differentiated products.
8. This assumes that the regulatory restraints limit competition to the smallest extent possible, consistent with the achievement of the objectives of the regulation.
9. See Martin Cave, Peter Crowther and Leigh Hancher, *Competition Aspects of Access Pricing, Report to the European Commission* (Luxembourg: Office for Official Publications of the European Communities, 1996).
10. With certain provisos, in the context of the simple market structure set out in Figure 9.1, a profit-maximizing, unregulated firm has no incentives inefficiently to restrict competition in the downstream market. Restricting competition in the downstream market has potential cost, as competition in that market provides incentives for efficiency and innovation. A profit-maximizing unregulated firm has the incentive to balance the costs of these competition restrictions against the efficiency benefits of integration, and has incentives to allow just as

much competition in the downstream market as is efficient. Armstrong et al. state: 'If endowed with full information and commitment power, and enough instruments of control, a monopolist in one activity would have nothing to gain from inefficiency in a vertically-related activity because maximising profit would entail maximising efficiency. In particular, it would be neither privately nor socially desirable to exclude a more efficient competitor from the related activity'. Mark Armstrong, Simon Cowan and John Vickers, *Regulatory Reform: Economic Analysis and British Experience* 147 (Cambridge, MA and London: MIT Press, 1994).

11. In a study of vertical integration between mobile telephone companies and local exchange carriers in the US, Reiffen et al. find evidence of both discrimination against rivals (referred to above as restriction of competition in the downstream market) and enhanced efficiency from the vertical arrangements. David Reiffen, Laurence Schumann and Michael R. Ward, 'Discriminatory dealing with downstream competitors: evidence from the cellular industry' 48 *Journal of Industrial Economics* 253 (September 2000). Since inefficient restriction of downstream competition is another example of an undesirable implication of regulation and state ownership, this strengthens the argument for deregulation and privatization where it is feasible.

12. This focus on regulated and non-profit-maximizing firms is also found in the Australian Hilmer report: 'While it is difficult to define precisely the nature of the facilities and industries [for which access regulation would apply], a frequent feature is the traditional involvement of the government in these industries, either as owner or extensive regulator'. Frederick Hilmer, *National Competition Policy: Report by the Independent Committee of Inquiry* 251 (Canberra, Australia: Government Publishing Service, 1993).

13. As used in this chapter, vertical separation refers to the full separation of ownership of the parts of the integrated firm. Other forms of separation are discussed later in this report.

14. Or, more strictly, it must be possible to prevent resale to downstream firms that have not paid the 'fixed' part of a two-part tariff.

15. In general, the instruments available to the regulator are even more limited than those available to the firm. If the firm is unable to use two-part tariffs, the regulator will not be able to do so. The only exception arises when the regulator can subsidize the incumbent firm, because the regulator can set the marginal price equal to marginal cost and use subsidies to cover the incumbent firm's losses.

16. US Department of Justice and Federal Trade Commission, *US Horizontal Merger Guidelines* (8 April 1997) <http://www.usdoj.gov/atr/public/guidelines/horiz_book/4.html>. Other countries also place the burden of proof on merging firms to demonstrate efficiency benefits. For instance, in New Zealand 'The onus of proof lies on the applicant to provide sufficient and credible evidence to support its public benefit claims' (OECD, *Competition Policy and Efficiency Claims in Horizontal Agreements*, OCDE/GD(96)65, p. 32 (Paris: OECD, 1996)).

17. This analysis highlights a flaw in a common argument: that a monopolist can capture all of the monopoly rents without integrating. This is summarized, for example, in Brennan:

> Leveraging theories, then and now still have to overcome the well-known argument that if a firm has a monopoly in one market, particularly one which provides an input on a 'fixed proportions' basis to downstream suppliers, it can capture all of the monopoly profits that could be extracted after vertically integrating. If so, the only reasons to integrate vertically would be to realise cost reductions or other operating efficiencies that, while increasing profits, represent gains to the economy as a whole. (Timothy Brennan, 'Is the Theory behind U.S. v. AT&T Applicable Today?', 1995 *Antitrust Bulletin* 459)

This argument fails to recognize that by integrating the monopolist, it may be able to overcome the distortions that arise from pricing above marginal cost.

   A further reason for integration is that the downstream activity may provide a complementary input, the benefit of which cannot be wholly captured by the downstream firm. The downstream activity would then have an incentive to free ride on the inputs provided by competing firms. Too little of this input will therefore be provided. The effect is analogous to the 'double marginalization' problem, where the downstream firm provides too little output. In the present case, the downstream firm provides too little of a complementary input, such as advertising. Vertical integration is a solution in this case; an exclusive territory for the downstream firm would also be a solution.

18. Stephen King, 'Access Pricing: A Discussion Paper', Government Pricing Tribunal, NSW, Research Paper No. 3, p. 2 (February 1995).
19. Since many personal services involve quality elements that cannot be verified, access cannot be easily mandated with respect to such services.
20. Regulatory processes may also favour integration. In general, it is easier to change a regulatory decision regarding the services to which access must be provided than it is to change the boundaries of a firm. The appropriate boundary of the non-competitive segment may change over time as cost, technology and demand conditions change. When the incumbent firm is integrated, access regulation can be more flexible in responding to changes in the boundary of the non-competitive segment than it can when the incumbent firm is separated.
21. 'William J. Baer, Director, Bureau of Competition, US Federal Trade Commission, Speech entitled 'FTC Perspectives on Competition Policy and Enforcement Initiatives in Electric Power' (4 December 1997); see also US Federal Trade Commission, 'Promoting Wholesale Competition Through Open Access: Non-discriminatory Transmission Services by Public Utilities, Recovery of Stranded Costs by Public Utilities and Transmitting Utilities' (7 August 1995).
22. Federico Mini, 'The Role of Incentives for Opening Monopoly Markets: Comparing GTE and RBOC Cooperation with Local Entrants', Georgetown University Department of Economics Working Paper 99-09 (July 1999) (www.georgetown.edu/departments/economics/wk-paper/wp_list.htm).
23. A related argument is against 'bigness' *per se*: that large firms may be able to exercise an inappropriate level of political influence, and that separation can reduce the size of the firm to a level whose political influence is more reasonable.
24. See Brennan, *supra* note 17, at 463. Brennan focuses on the effects on cross-subsidization as one of his two key reasons for the vertical separation of AT&T (the other being the effect on the local exchange company's incentives to restrict access to the long-distance market).
25. OECD 1996, *supra* note 16, at 42.
26. These arguments are weak for several reasons. Privatizing a monopoly firm essentially allows the government to capitalize a stream of monopoly rents. That monopoly rent amounts to a form of a 'tax' on the product in question, raising the question whether a tax on this product is an appropriate means of raising revenue. Even if it is an appropriate means to raise revenue, privatizing the monopoly may not be an efficient mechanism for raising the tax as the purchasing firm will discount the stream of revenues (possibly fearing further regulation in the future) at a higher rate than the government. In addition, the government may not be able to capture all of the revenue by privatizing a monopoly because some of the rent will be dissipated in what is known as 'x-inefficiency'.
27. Unfortunately, easy cases are unlikely to arise in practice, as it is precisely when economies of scope are strong that accounting information regarding key cost variables is difficult to obtain.
28. Michael Hardt, 'Rejoinder: The Non-equivalence of Accounting Separation and Structural Separation as Regulatory Devices', 19 *Telecommunications Policy* 69 (1995).
29. Hilmer, *supra* note 12, at 241.
30. Electricity Consumers Resource Council, 'Petition for a Rulemaking on Electric Power Industry Structure and Commercial Practices and Motion to Clarify or Reconsider Certain Open-Access Commercial Practices' (25 March 1998), http://www.elcon.org/public_pdf/ferc_filings/1998/petition.pdf>.
31. OECD, *Regulatory Reform in the Electricity Industry: The United States* (Paris: OECD, 1999).
32. Paul Joskow, 'Regulatory Priorities for Reforming Infrastructure Sectors in Developing Countries' (unpublished mimeo 1998).

# 10. Conditioning the Bells' entry into long distance: anticompetitive regulation or promoting competition?[1]

## Marius Schwartz

*The US Telecommunications Act of 1996 seeks to open local telephone markets to competition and authorizes the Bell companies to offer long-distance services only after they have taken certain steps to open up their own local markets to competition.*

*The Act imposes obligations on incumbents to facilitate the development of three forms of local competition: through the entrant building its own networks; through the entrant building some of its own facilities, and leasing unbundled network elements from the incumbent; and through the entrant buying the incumbent's existing retail services, at a wholesale discount, and reselling them. The Act obliges incumbents to cooperate extensively.*

*The question of when the Bells should be allowed to offer long-distance services is one of the most important, and one of the most contentious, in the Act. The Bells have been kept out of long distance since 1982, under a court decree. Section 271 of the Act provides that the Bells can provide long-distance services after they have implemented a 'competitive checklist', consisting of 14 items. There are two main reasons for linking the entry of the Bells into long distance to the opening of their local markets: to prevent a threat to long-run competition in long distance; and to help open the Bells' local markets to competition.*

*Critics argue that the Section 271 standard needlessly prevents the Bells from competing, constitutes excessive regulation, that the standard is so tough that no one can meet it and therefore no one will try to, and that the Bells should be allowed to enter the long-distance market now. The chapter contends that the incentives that this standard creates will advance the Act's competitive goals more efficiently and rapidly than other standards, and with less regulation. The standard already is having positive effects in opening local markets, even though no Bell company has yet satisfied the standard, three years after the Act took effect.*

# INTRODUCTION

More than three years have passed since the enactment of the Telecommunications Act of 1996, and no regional Bell operating company has yet been authorized to offer long-distance services originating in a state where it offers local service. The reason is that none has met the Act's requirements of taking the actions necessary to facilitate local competition in that state. Some have criticized the Bell entry conditions as superfluous and anticompetitive regulation, urging their relaxation or elimination. Although it is disappointing that the conditions have not yet been met, these criticisms are misplaced. Adhering to the current process ultimately should produce less-intrusive regulation, and foster competition.

This chapter will begin by summarizing the logic for conditioning a Bell company's entry on the opening of its local market to competition. It then explains why the conditions for approving Bell entry should not be softened, and discusses suggestive evidence that these conditions have already usefully influenced the Bells' conduct. Finally, after taking brief stock of developments since the Act, the chapter suggests that there is now a basis for cautious optimism.

## A. THE TELECOMMUNICATIONS ACT OF 1996 AND THE ECONOMIC LOGIC FOR CONDITIONING THE BELLS' ENTRY

### The Act's Objectives and Key Requirements

The passage of the 1996 Telecommunications Act[2] marks a turning point in US policy towards competition in telecommunications. Beyond its specific provisions, the Act embodies a congressional commitment to open *all* telecommunications markets to competition, and to move away from a regime of regulated local monopoly and of geographic or type-of-service restrictions on firms' permissible activities.[3]

### Local competition

Of particular significance is the commitment to open the 'local market' – the local exchange networks and their associated services, historically the domain of regulated franchise monopolists. Section 253 of the Act takes the major step of striking down legal or regulatory barriers imposed by states or local authorities. In addition, the Act targets artificial entry barriers stemming from incumbents' installed-base advantages, a legacy from the franchise monopoly era. The Act lays out an ambitious agenda for local competition. It envisages entry not only by *facilities-based* competitors building their own networks, an entry mode which requires relatively modest cooperation from incumbents, notably, interconnection to exchange traffic. The Act also aims to facilitate entry by competitors that use some or all of the incumbent's *unbundled network elements* (such as unbundled loops); and entry by competitors that *resell* the incumbent's existing retail services ('resale') in fact understates the entrant's role, because the entrant takes over all retailing functions for the customers it acquires. Accordingly, the Act mandates all incumbents to extend to local competitors the cooperation needed for entry through any of the three paths. Any incumbent must make available to competitors: interconnection with and access to unbundled elements of its local networks, at rates based on these facilities' cost; and its retail services, at discounted wholesale rates, for resale by entrants.[4]

### Bell entry

The Act also permits the regional Bell operating companies to offer, under suitable circumstances, long-distance (interLATA) services. The Bells were barred from such services by the 1982 antitrust court order that separated AT&T from the local Bell companies.[5] The Act authorizes the Bells immediately to offer long-distance services that originate in a state where the Bell does not offer local service (hence does not control local networks). But to offer long-distance services originating in any state where it does offer local service (local exchange and exchange access), a Bell must first obtain approval for that state from the Federal Communications Commission (FCC). The relevant conditions are described in Section 271 of the Act: (a) the Bell must have fully implemented a 14-point competitive checklist, which largely parallels the obligations imposed on all incumbents (including non-Bells) under Section 251, or, in certain limited circumstances, offer all the items in a statement of generally available terms;[6] (b) its long-distance services will be provided in compliance with the separate subsidiary and non-discrimination requirements of Section 272; and (c) the FCC must find that approving the Bell's application is in the public interest. In making its overall determination, the FCC must consult with the Department of Justice (DOJ) and accord its evaluation 'substantial weight'.

### The Economic Logic for Conditioning the Bells' Entry

The Bells account for about three-quarters of the revenues of all local phone companies nationwide, and about the same fraction of all long-distance minutes originate in their service areas. Consequently, the Section 271 process is quite important. A threshold question raised by critics of Section 271 is, why link at all the Bells' entry into long distance and the opening of their local markets? The main basis for keeping the Bells out of long distance originally was to prevent them from discriminating in access arrangements against competitors that depend on the Bells for local access. But, critics maintain, these access arrangements are by now well established, so there is no risk that the Bells could degrade these arrangements, even if they had an incentive to do so once allowed into long distance. Delaying Bell entry, critics argue, merely prevents enhanced competition in long distance, and the realization of efficiencies from the Bells' provision of integrated services (both cost savings, and the value to consumers of obtaining one-stop shopping from a single provider).

While there are indeed potential costs of delaying the Bells' entry until the local market is opened, there are also substantial benefits from requiring such linkage – benefits which comfortably outweigh the costs. The benefits fall into two broad categories: preventing longer-run harm in long distance, and expediting the opening of the local market.[7]

**Safeguarding longer-run competition in long distance**
It is certainly true that regulation can do a considerably better job of preventing the degradation of established arrangements than of securing the development of new ones. However, it is wrong to claim that Bell entry cannot pose any threat to competition in long distance solely because those access arrangements are well established. As technology and demand conditions change, access arrangements also will require adaptation. If allowed into long distance before the local market is opened – and hence, without a realistic prospect that local competition will take root over a reasonable horizon – the Bells could, over time, pose a serious threat to the cost and quality of local access for their non-integrated long-distance rivals, by denying them efficient and timely upgrades to new arrangements.

**Opening the local market**
The second concern – which was not present at the time of the MFJ – is with opening the local market to competition. Allowing premature entry by a Bell into long distance can reduce the Bell's incentives to cooperate in opening its local market. An obvious reason is the loss of the so-called 'carrot effect' – that having secured its desired long-distance authority, a Bell has less to gain from continuing cooperation that facilitates local competition.

Another reason why a Bell's premature entry into long distance will make it less cooperative in offering wholesale local services is the magnified incentive to impede competitors from providing *integrated services*. The logic is as follows. A provider's ability to offer both local and long-distance (as well as other) telecommunications services is believed to be competitively important: it can deliver cost savings enabled by joint provision (for example, economizing on billing); and it allows the provider to offer one-stop shopping, which is valuable to many consumers. A Bell might try to impede a competitors' ability to offer integrated services (i) by degrading their *established* access arrangements in long distance, which regulation may be able to prevent in the short run; or (ii) by denying them the new wholesale *local* services needed for local competition (such asUnbundled Network Elements (UNEs) and discounted retail services for resale). A Bell's authority to sell long-distance services at substantially unregulated retail rates increases its gain from impeding competitors' ability to offer integrated services (by denying them local services) in two ways. First, since competitors are denied cost savings from joint provision, they can put less pressure on the Bell's retail prices. Second, the Bell can capture a disproportionate share of the business of customers who value one-stop shopping. Thus, authorizing a Bell to offer long-distance services before its local market is open implies that the Bell will have more to lose from *local* competition, so the Bell's resistance to opening its local markets will magnify.[8]

Producing worse incentives for a Bell to cooperate in opening the local market will make it significantly harder to foster local competition. The ambitious model of local competition envisaged in the Act rests on extensive 'network sharing' with competitors, and this will require establishing a panoply of complex new technical systems, protocols and business arrangements. Because these wholesale local services are complex and new, a policy of relying solely on regulatory mandates to foster their development and deployment is especially problematic, as there is no established norm for what is feasible and how fast. Authorizing premature Bell entry into long distance would, therefore, spawn a considerably greater need for intrusive regulation to compel the Bells to implement the new local competition arrangements, relative to securing these arrangements at the beginning, with greater Bell cooperation harnessed through the Section 271 incentives. Section 271 is thus designed ultimately to reduce the need for intrusive regulation.

Two final points support the argument that the cost of delaying a Bell's long-distance entry until it opens its local market, as mandated by Congress, is outweighed by the benefits. First, the local market is much larger, with revenues about twice those from long-distance net of access payments (which the Bells already collect). Second, the local market is far less competitive than is long distance, leaving more unexploited gains from competition.

## B.   DO THE 271 INCENTIVES MATTER?

### Why the Bar Is *Not* Too High

The more extreme criticisms of Section 271 maintain that it cannot affect the pace at which local markets are opened, because its conditions merely duplicate similar cooperation obligations already imposed on all incumbents by other provisions in the Act (principally, Sections 251 and 252). Thus, critics argue, Section 271 is superfluous, and needlessly delays Bell entry. This argument defies common sense in holding that regulatory enforcement of obligations is so effective that any incentive effects created for the Bells by Section 271 necessarily become irrelevant.

More reasoned critics concede that a *properly structured* Section 271 standard can elicit fruitful cooperation from the Bells, but claim that the Section 271 bar has been set too high, as evidenced by the Bells' refusal or inability to meet it. They argue that the bar should be lowered, because sticking to the current standard is counterproductive: it will delay Bell entry, without helping to open the local markets. A legal response is that the DOJ's and FCC's interpretation of the Section 271 standard merely tracks the Act. Two responses based on economic reasoning are the following.

**Commitment and credibility**

First, and most important, is the issue of commitment and credibility. To have any chance of ensuring that the local market is truly open before Section 271 approval, it is crucial that there be a known commitment to the articulated Section 271 standard. Bell company posturing and testing the waters are inevitable in a process such as this, and an initial reluctance to 'deal' may reflect no more than a desire to extract better terms – to force down the bar. A commitment to hold firm to the Section 271 standard, barring major unforeseen developments, is therefore crucial.

Conceivably, some Bells were willing to extend the requisite cooperation, but believed they could instead secure long-distance entry by mounting legal challenges to the Act and by pressuring the FCC and the DOJ. For this very reason, efforts to soften the Section 271 standard because it is allegedly unproductive can make it so. They can discourage the Bells from meeting the standard even when they would be willing to meet it if convinced that this was their only way to gain long-distance entry.

**Bells' tradeoff changes over time**

Assume, *arguendo*, that until now, the Bells have been genuinely unwilling to accept the terms of the Section 271 standard. However, merely because a Bell finds the 'terms of trade' of Section 271 unacceptable today does not imply it would continue to refuse them in the future. As a result of fairly predictable changes in market conditions, one might expect a Bell's posture to change, leading the Bell to meet the Section 271 standard in the future even if it refuses to meet it initially.

There are at least two reasons why the Bell's resistance will soften. First, local competition is developing in any case to serve the Bells' more profitable customers, such as large businesses.[9] Entrants serving such customers are often less dependent on Bell cooperation, because they rely more heavily on their own facilities. Such entry diverts from the Bell some of these lucrative customers, and therefore reduces what the Bell stands to lose by opening *all* its local markets as required by Section 271. Second, the Bells' inability to offer long-distance services (including international) will become a growing disadvantage in competing to serve large business customers, who demand one-stop shopping from a single provider, and who may be able to obtain this from other vendors such as the major long-distance companies. This is likely to be of particular concern to those Bells who have national or international aspirations.

Sophisticated critics might attack the argument that the Section 271 standard will be met eventually, by claiming that its logic is incomplete: if a Bell agrees to cooperate because some local competition will have developed in any event, then the remaining procompetitive benefits from securing the Bell's cooperation at that point also are lower. This, critics may argue, implies that the delay in long-distance approval will have been undesirable, because the benefits forgone in long distance outweigh the residual benefits from securing cooperation in the local market – benefits which must be small, as revealed by the Bell's willingness to accept the Section 271 terms at that point.

The last step, however, does *not* follow. Local competition may develop without Bell cooperation sufficiently to erode much of the Bell's profit from large business customers and other lucrative markets, thereby altering the Bell's Section 271 calculus. Yet securing the Bell's cooperation in opening up remaining market segments to competition can still deliver substantial benefits to consumers. In particular, while the residential market contributes a relatively small share of a Bell's profit (largely because residential rates are more heavily regulated than rates to large business customers), considerable efficiency gains can be expected from bringing competition to the residential (and small business) market and easing the need for intrusive regulation.[10] It is therefore incorrect both logically and factually to presume that if selective entry has eroded local market profit sufficiently for the Bell to accept the Section 271 terms, then the value to society from attaining the Bell's cooperation also must have diminished correspondingly. Such a zero-sum presumption overlooks the substantial, and well-recognized welfare gains from shifting to competition and away from regulation as the main guardian of consumers' interests.[11]

## Evidence of Section 271's Impact

Some critics have argued that Section 271, as interpreted by the agencies, is asking for the impossible; thus, the Bells will simply abandon all hope of complying and resist cooperating, both now and in the future. This contention is flawed on two counts: meeting the Section 271 requirements is well within the Bells' ability; and the Bells themselves recognize this, as revealed by the beneficial impact that Section 271 already appears to be having.

Because the value to a Bell of obtaining long-distance authority, relative to the Bell's loss from opening the local market, will vary across states (for example, with the relative amount of long-distance traffic), one would expect a Bell to find the Section 271 tradeoff acceptable sooner in some states than others. It is therefore revealing that the states in which the Bells have been most serious about undertaking the steps needed to open their local markets are also those where the Bells have most aggressively sought long-distance authority.

In addition, suggestive evidence comes from comparing the overall behaviour of the Bells with that of GTE. Like other non-Bell incumbents, GTE does not require Section 271 authority to offer long-distance services, and therefore should normally be less inclined than the Bells to cooperate in opening its local markets.[12]

The findings in a study by Mini[13] are consistent with those of a recent FCC study for the issues that both studies examined.[14] Mini tests whether the Bells have been relatively more cooperative with local entrants than has GTE. This should be viewed as a 'one-sided' test. A finding of no difference could mean either: (a) that the Section 271 incentives are redundant, because the Section 251 obligations already induce maximal cooperation by all incumbents – an implausible interpretation; or (b) that the Section 271 mechanism has not yet influenced the Bells' conduct, but will do so in the future. Thus, a finding of no difference would not prove that Section 271 is forever irrelevant; but a finding that the Bells have been more cooperative indicates that Section 271 incentives *are* relevant.[15] Mini finds that the Bells have been more cooperative than GTE according to various measures, and his tests show that the differences are statistically significant.

Mini compares AT&T's negotiations to enter local markets served by GTE and by a Bell in the 22 states where both GTE and a Bell offer service and where all the relevant data is available. Focusing on states where AT&T negotiated with both GTE and a Bell permits comparisons while controlling for the potentially important role of the particular state regulatory commission. AT&T is chosen because it has been one of the most active firms seeking access to incumbents' networks in order to become a local competitor, and because it provided data on its negotiations.[16] GTE is chosen because it is by far the largest non-Bell incumbent, accounting for approximately 11 per cent of access lines nationally at the end of 1996, and because AT&T did not pursue negotiations with the other major non-Bell incumbents, including Cincinnati Bell, Frontier and Sprint.[17]

## Litigation

To expedite the negotiations for access and interconnection between entrants and incumbents, Section 252 allows parties to file challenges only in federal (not state) court, and only after a state commission has issued an order on an (arbitrated or negotiated) agreement. Mini accordingly classifies litigation as 'premature' if it was filed prior to a final commission order (challenging the arbitrator's decisions, or the commission's interlocutory order). In the 22 common states, AT&T filed three premature challenges against GTE and three against the Bells. The Bells filed three premature challenges against AT&T, while GTE filed 16. Mini notes that GTE's premature litigation is likely to have caused only modest delay directly, but might have significant indirect effects. For instance, by flagging a wide-ranging set of issues that the incumbent intends to challenge, it signals an aggressive posture towards entrants.

## Delay

As of March 1999, AT&T had failed to obtain approved interconnection agreements with the Bells in only two of the 22 sample states, but failed with GTE in ten of these states. In the 12 states where agreement was reached with both GTE and the local Bell, it was reached first with the Bell 11 times, and only once with GTE. Mini also compares the average delay in reaching an agreement. He constructs this average by computing the interval between AT&T's initial request and either (a) the date when the state commission approved a final agreement, or (b) March 1999, if no agreement had been approved by that date. Step (b) understates the true delay, and the overall bias this creates is greater for GTE than for the Bells, because GTE failed to reach an agreement ten times to the Bells' two. Even with this bias in GTE's favour, Mini finds that the average delay (equally weighted across all the states) is 457 days with the Bells, and 781 days with GTE – 70 per cent longer with GTE.

## Pricing: parties' requests and arbitrators' awards

An especially telling measure of GTE's tougher posture compared to the Bells' is the difference in their pricing *requests*, going into arbitration, for providing access to their networks and services. Mini compares the initial requests for resale discounts and for prices to lease unbundled network elements. The results for resale discounts are discussed here; the findings for UNEs are substantially similar.

The Act requires incumbents to offer their retail services to entrants for resale, at wholesale prices discounted from the retail prices because the incumbent avoids retailing costs. These avoided retailing costs are unlikely to differ significantly between GTE and the Bell (unlike the costs of facilities, which do differ significantly).[18] Thus, a natural measure to compare is the dollar discount offered by GTE versus that offered by the Bell in that state.[19] A lower discount benefits the incumbent and harms the entrant. In the 18 states for which all the necessary data were available, AT&T's request is not systematically different as between GTE and the local Bell. In contrast, GTE's resale discount offer for residential customers was lower than the local Bell's offer in 15 of the 18 states, and for business customers GTE's offer was lower in 13 of the states.

Regarding magnitudes, Mini estimates the average residential discount (across states) offered by GTE at $1.20, and that offered by the Bells at $1.98. This difference is economically significant: relative to their average monthly bills, the discount offers are 8 per cent for GTE and 13 per cent for the Bells, and it is well known that the resale business operates on very narrow margins. The results were similar for business discounts.[20]

Interestingly, GTE does not seem to receive more favourable arbitration awards as a result of its tougher requests than do the Bells, perhaps because state commissions are reluctant to award very different prices to two incumbents in the same states. However, GTE does appear to benefit from its tougher posture and to harm entrants, since a tougher GTE request is associated with higher awards to both it and the Bell company in the respective state relative to other states.[21]

### Entry record

The above comparisons of wholesale prices do not capture differences between GTE and the Bells in their cooperation with entrants on *non-price* dimensions, such as the quality and timeliness with which new arrangements needed by competitors are made available (for example, operations support systems). Such new arrangements are critical for the success of local competition. Yet measuring incumbents' cooperation in developing and deploying them is hard for an investigator; and imposing such cooperation is hard for regulators. This is why it is important to provide better incentives for incumbents to cooperate, as the Section 271 process attempts to do for the Bells. In an attempt roughly to estimate the 'total impact' of Bell versus GTE cooperation, Mini analyses FCC data on the extent of competitive entry (by all firms, not only AT&T). The data come from voluntary responses to a survey.[22] Although they should be interpreted with caution, they are nevertheless suggestive.

Mini first reports raw measures of entry. (Entry reflects the joint influence of many factors, including price and non-price cooperation by incumbents and the relative interest of entrants.) One entry measure is the number of lines resold to local competitors as a percentage of the incumbent's total lines in the state. In states where both Bell and GTE data were reported, the Bell had the higher percentage of resold residential lines 12 times out of 15, and 14 out of 14 times for resold business lines. The figures for the Bells were considerably higher than for GTE. The highest residential percentage for GTE was 0.8 per cent, while the highest Bell was 2.1 per cent. The averages (equally weighted across states) were three times larger for the Bells: 0.15 per cent for GTE and 0.53 per cent for the Bells. The disparity is even greater for resold business lines. GTE's maximum is 0.5 per cent, while the Bells' maximum is 9.3 per cent, followed by 3.2 per cent and 2.3 per cent. The Bells' average of 1.32 per cent is 18 times larger than GTE's average.

Mini also tests whether the significantly lower level of entry into GTE's territories, according to the above measure and others, can be explained by variables that proxy for market conditions affecting the profitability of entry, such as customer density and incumbents' price–cost ratio. Controlling for the effect of such factors, he consistently finds that the GTE effect (dummy variable) remains negative and highly significant.[23]

Finally, the fact that Mini detects significantly greater cooperation by the Bells over his sample period is a somewhat unexpected result. Until recently, the Bells mounted vigorous legal challenges to Section 271; thus, the Bells are likely to have discounted their need to open their local markets as a condition for entering long distance. As explained below, this legal uncertainty is finally being resolved. In the future, therefore, the incentive effects of Section 271 on the Bells' conduct should be even more pronounced.

## C.   MEETING THE BELL ENTRY CONDITIONS: GROWING PAINS AND FUTURE PROSPECTS

As stated above, the Act vests authority over Bell applications with the FCC, and directs the FCC to accord 'substantial weight' to the competitive evaluation of the DOJ. The DOJ articulated its standard early in the process and fairly explicitly. As a result, the DOJ analysis has strongly influenced the FCC's decisions, which have generally agreed with the DOJ assessments in turning down the five applications to date.[24]

This section will first discuss the DOJ standard, then briefly summarize the DOJ and FCC assessments of the rejected applications. It concludes that, despite these unsuccessful applications, the future of the Section 271 process appears to be promising.

### The DOJ's Competitive Standard: Local Market Is Irreversibly Open

The Act does not specify a standard that the DOJ must use in making its evaluation of a Bell's application. The DOJ adopted a standard that it believes reflects the logic of the statute and will help attain its goal of promoting competition as efficiently and expeditiously as possible. The standard requires an applicant to show that the Bell's local market in the state for which long-distance approval is sought is fully and *irreversibly open* to competition, through all three entry modes envisaged in the Act: construction of new networks interconnected with the Bell's networks ('facilities-based' entry), use of the Bell's unbundled network elements, and resale of its discounted retail services.[25]

## The standard's requirements and logic

The standard does *not* require the presence of ubiquitous facilities-based local competition that is fully effective in eliminating the Bell's market power. Insisting on this would contradict the Act's philosophy that market forces should determine the extent and type of competitive local entry.[26] For this reason, the Act requires that all three entry modes be made available, but does not express a preference among them (for example, facilities-based competition in some instances may be less desirable than relying, in whole or in part, on the incumbent's facilities).

Moreover, conditions have changed markedly since the time of the MFJ regarding the risk that the Bells' presence in long distance would lead to their discriminating in local access against long-distance competitors. There are now major established competitors in long distance, and the access arrangements have long been in place. A combination of regulation and some local competition can do a reasonable job of protecting these *established* access arrangements, at least in the near term. On the benefits side, opting for the DOJ standard rather than the stricter standard of fully effective local competition both avoids unduly delaying the competitive gains that can arise from Bell entry, and provides the Bells with better incentives to cooperate in opening their local markets.

The DOJ standard requires that the Bells have extended the cooperation needed to ensure that local markets are fully *open*, and that the opening is *irreversible* – that is, it cannot be undone once the Bell obtains long distance authority and thus becomes less inclined to continue cooperating.

Securing the Bells' cooperation in opening the market is so important in large measure because local competition will require the development and deployment of a host of new and complex systems and arrangements to enable efficient network sharing. It is much harder for outside enforcers to mandate the creation of such new systems than it is to prevent degradation of existing ones. For complex new systems, outsiders' information of what is feasible and at what speed will be far inferior to that possessed by the firm (here, the Bell). This factor makes it difficult both to know what to request and to impose sufficient penalties, creating considerable scope for delays by the incumbent. By conditioning a Bell's entry on the opening of its local market, the DOJ standard improves the Bell's incentives to cooperate in developing and deploying these systems much more efficiently and expeditiously than can be achieved through regulatory fiat alone.

The second element of the DOJ standard – the market opening is irreversible – requires that performance benchmarks for these new arrangements be in place before authorizing Bell entry. Establishing these benchmarks entails developing performance measures, agreeing on reporting procedures and performance standards, and creating a sufficient track record of performance against which any future degradation can be reliably detected. Once such benchmarks have been established, they help regulators, courts, and competitors to prevent backsliding by the Bell. In short, the DOJ standard seeks to prevent both delay and backsliding, and is met by ascertaining that any significant artificial impediments to competition have been durably removed.

**Factual inquiry**

Determining whether the DOJ standard is met follows a sensible system of shifting presumptions. The most reliable evidence that the market has been opened is a record of significant entry through all three entry modes. The more widespread and diverse the competition, the greater is one's confidence that the various inputs needed by competitors are available on commercially viable terms with respect to quality, functionality and pricing. Moreover, competitors' willingness to invest in the market signals their confidence that the market opening is irreversible. Finally, the presence of competitors with a significant stake in the market will itself make it harder for an incumbent to roll back the process. In short, evidence that significant competition has taken root establishes a presumption that the market is irreversibly open.

Evidence of significant competition, however, does not entail a minimum market-share test for competitors. Specifying a high or even moderate market-share threshold that local competitors must reach before the Bell may enter long distance would risk creating perverse incentives for certain potential local entrants to scale back their own entry plans. In particular, the large long-distance carriers, which arguably are the most capable of local entry on a large scale, might be induced to pull their punches in order to delay the Bells' entry into long distance. More importantly, the market may be open even if little or even no entry is observed, as this could merely reflect lack of interest by entrants.

In the absence of significant competition, however, the Bell must produce persuasive alternative evidence to show that the lack of competition is not due to significant remaining artificial impediments. This involves showing three main elements:

• The new inputs needed by local competitors are meaningfully available, and their provision could be scaled up to meet growth in demand and extended to additional geographic regions. Performance *benchmarks* must also have been established, as discussed above, preferably via commercial utilization or, if this is not an option, through rigorous testing.

- These inputs are available at prices reasonably close to costs, and competitors can have sufficient confidence that prices will remain reasonable in future to justify their investments in entry.[27]
- No significant other barriers remain, such as regulatory barriers or barriers arising from exclusionary private conduct.

The DOJ believes that its standard provides the Bells with a reasonable roadmap of what they must do in order to establish that their markets are open. The standard's substantive requirements can be met with the right effort and commitment.

**Unsuccessful Bell Applications**

In the five applications decided through October 1999, the DOJ concluded that the applicant Bell's local market was not fully and irreversibly open to competition. The FCC rejected these applications, one on the ground that the threshold requirements of Track A had not been met, and the rest on the ground that they did not satisfy the threshold competitive checklist requirements. Thus, the FCC has not yet had to reach its public interest test,[28] although the test could properly become outcome determinative in future applications.

Meaningful implementation of the checklist requires a two-part showing, neither part of which has been satisfied to date. First, *all* checklist items must be provided to competitors, *without undue restrictions* on how they can be used or combined. Second, access must be provided through *wholesale support processes* that allow efficient and rapid interaction between competitors and the incumbent's wholesale arm.

First, regarding unencumbered access to all checklist items, some of the applicant Bells made elements available only in a way that materially impeded competitors' ability to use them,[29] or simply refused to provide certain items.[30] An especially important and contentious issue has been whether incumbents must provide the so-called UNE 'platform' – all the elements of the network, in their pre-existing combination, at cost-based prices, or whether competitors must supply some of their own elements in order to qualify for these cost-based prices. Incumbents argued that the platform is merely a backdoor way to obtain retail services for resale, but at lower prices.[31] They sought to break up existing combinations of unbundled elements sought by competitors. Competitors countered that: (a) the Act does not require them to provide their own elements in order to qualify for UNE pricing; and (b) the platform enables them not only to qualify for a different pricing methodology, but also to provide services not available through resale. Most notably, these services include exchange access for long-distance carriers (such access is sold by incumbents only to long-distance carriers, not end users, hence is not a 'retail service' eligible for resale).

Potentially, new services could be generated from the existing capabilities of the incumbent's network but have not yet been offered by the incumbent.

Second, even if the incumbent places no explicit or technical restrictions on access to UNEs and to retail services for resale, such access must be provided in a manner that allows competitors to compete effectively with the incumbent's own retail arm. The FCC thus requires that a competitor must receive parity compared to the incumbent's retail arm in service dimensions such as obtaining items in large quantities, expeditiously, and without encountering quality problems. (If there is no retail analogue to a particular wholesale service, the FCC has said that the access must be sufficient to allow an efficient competitor a meaningful opportunity to compete.)

Incumbents, however, have traditionally operated as retailers (and as wholesalers of a limited set of services, notably, local access for long-distance carriers), and were not set up to operate as large-scale wholesalers of various inputs to local competitors. In order for incumbents to become efficient wholesale providers of such inputs, as sought by the Act, it will therefore be necessary to develop and deploy new systems, which the DOJ has termed *wholesale support processes*. These systems must enable smooth and timely communication and interaction between competitors and the incumbent's wholesale operations. In many cases, this involves procedures for granting competitors non-discriminatory access to the incumbent's internal *operations support systems* (OSS). These are the systems used by the incumbent for functions such as obtaining pre-ordering information about a customer or about available services, ordering, installation, repair and maintenance, and billing. Providing competitors efficient access to OSS requires, among other things, the development of electronic interfaces between competitors and the incumbent, because manual processing is both inherently slower and much more prone to error. In other cases, the functionality needed by a competitor may not yet exist, so the issue of parity is moot. However, adequate new arrangements would be needed. None of the applications submitted to date has demonstrated adequate access to OSS.

**Hopeful Signs**

The absence of a successful application to date has, understandably, bred frustration and disappointment. Some critics have decried the Section 271 process as dysfunctional and a failure, urging the DOJ and the FCC to eliminate it. Perhaps acknowledging that the agencies are merely following the roadmap laid in the Act, some critics have called for revising the Act itself. Although the failure thus far to satisfy the Section 271 conditions is disappointing, departing from the current process would be a serious mistake. Attaining the vision of local competition articulated in the Act is difficult, and the incentives created by Section 271 can play a substantial role in inducing the Bells to do what does not come naturally to any incumbent.

While there can be no guarantees, promising signs indicate that adhering to the current process will help advance the Act's goals of promoting competition in all markets in a reasonably timely manner. There are two bases for this optimism: the cloud of legal uncertainty over the Act is clearing, and real progress is being made to resolve the difficult technical challenges of creating the new systems needed to allow efficient network sharing by local competitors.

### Clarifying the legal rules

A major reason for the relatively slow progress thus far has been the Bells' understandable reluctance to open up their markets before they have explored what they perceived as promising legal challenges to the mandates of the Act. Like any other company, a Bell does not wish to act against its own interest by facilitating competition. This is precisely why mechanisms such as Section 271, and the obligations on all incumbents contained in the other sections of the Act, are necessary.

Given the enormous stakes involved, and perceived ambiguities in the Act, it was predictable that incumbents would litigate to test the limits of these obligations. The issues taken to the courts include the terms of particular agreements between incumbents and new entrants, the meaning of various provisions of the Act, the reasonableness of the FCC's implementing regulations, and the scope of the FCC's regulatory authority. Some even challenged the constitutionality of the Act, as bill of attainder, on the grounds that the Section 271 obligations single out the Bells versus other incumbents.[32]

Fortunately, the courts have now resolved most of the fundamental disputes and have upheld the Act and most of the FCC's implementing regulations. In January 1999, the Supreme Court affirmed the FCC's broad authority to adopt regulations implementing all substantive provisions of the 1996 Act and upheld on the merits all but one of the specific regulations whose validity was at issue.[33] The Court's decision in this unusually complex case reinstated the FCC's vital and central role in telecommunications regulation.

The DC Circuit and Fifth Circuit have now held that the Act's restriction on the Bell companies' provision of in-region long-distance services is constitutional,[34] and the Supreme Court denied *certiorari*. The United States Court of Appeals for the DC Circuit, which hears all challenges to the FCC's rulings on Bell applications under Section 271, also upheld the FCC in both appeals from its decisions denying Bell applications.[35] In addition, the DC Circuit has upheld the Commission and the Act in several cases addressing the scope and interpretation of the Section 271 prohibition, holding, for example that certain so-called 'marketing' arrangements between Qwest and the Bells violated that prohibition.[36]

The vast majority of federal district courts and all of the courts of appeals that have entered judgments in cases seeking review of state agency decisions under Section 252(e)(6) of the Act also have upheld the Act and the FCC's regulations. The courts have rejected state agency contentions that the constitutional prohibition on suits against the states in federal courts bars such review, and they have required states to conform with agreements to the Act and the FCC's regulations.

Some significant issues do remain, and litigation will surely continue.[37] However, the major legal overhangs are finally being resolved. This is a key reason for believing that the Bells become more willing to cooperate in meeting the Section 271 requirements for their long-distance entry.

**Implementing the complex new systems**
It would be quite unfair, however, to blame the slow progress solely on recalcitrance by the Bells. The framework for local competition required by the Act places heavy demands for complex network sharing with competitors. Even with the best intentions, it would take considerable expense, effort and time to develop the myriad of complex new systems called for by the Act, and to eliminate the kinks.

However, significant progress is being made. In particular, serious efforts have been under way in some states, such as New York and Texas, to develop and test the new systems of providing access to OSS, with the close involvement of state commissions and participation by third-party testers.

## CONCLUSION

The task of opening to competition certain traditionally monopolized utility markets, such as local telephony, gas and electricity, is never easy. Incumbents in such markets typically control important bottleneck facilities to which even efficient competitors would require access in order to compete effectively. Using regulatory 'sticks' alone to try and secure incumbents' cooperation in offering such access is likely to be difficult, costly and slow. Providing incumbents with better incentives to cooperate can help greatly, and one way to provide such incentives is to condition a regulatory concession desired by the incumbent on the latter's cooperation in providing access for competitors. As long as delaying the particular concession is not itself too costly, the linkage can be beneficial, because of its role in promoting competition in the incumbent's market and in closely related markets.

An important example of such a policy in the US is Section 271 of the 1996 Telecommunications Act, which requires the regional Bell companies to open their local markets to competition as a condition for being allowed to enter long-distance services. In general, economists are properly wary of restricting entry into any market by an unregulated firm that controls no bottleneck facilities. The case of conditioning the Bells' entry into long distance, however, is fundamentally different. The Bells control important bottleneck facilities – their ubiquitous local networks and customer bases – to which both long-distance providers and local competitors would require certain access, and have incentives to use this control to impede competitors.

The Section 271 process can greatly assist in securing from the Bells the measures needed to open their local markets and permit competition to evolve with minimal artificial impediments; in so doing, the process can thereby ultimately also minimize the need for intrusive regulation. Predictably, there have been bumps in the road, but promising signs are emerging. To paraphrase Mark Twain, rumours of Section 271's death are greatly exaggerated.

# NOTES

1. The views expressed in this chapter are those of the author, and are not purported to represent those of the Department of Justice.
2. Pub. L. 104–104, 110 Stat. 56 (1996) (codified at 47 U.S.C. § 151 *et seq.*).
3. For a broader discussion of the Act, see Timothy Brennan, 'Making Sense of the Telecommunications Act of 1996', 5 *Industrial and Corporate Change* 941 (Berlin, Heidelberg, New York: Springer-Verlag, 1996); Marius Schwartz, 'Telecommunications Reform in the United States: Promises and Pitfalls', in *Telecommunications and Energy in Systemic Transformation* (Paul Welfens and George Yarrow, eds, 1997).
4. Section 251 of the Act lists these obligations, while Section 252 establishes procedures for negotiations between incumbents and local entrants and for arbitration and oversight by state regulatory commissions. In imposing the unbundling and resale obligations, the Act reflects a view that entrants should not be required to enter on a fully vertically-integrated basis, because competition that relies (partially or wholly) on the incumbent's facilities can still yield significant benefits by enabling entrants to share in the efficiencies of incumbents' established, ubiquitous networks. The benefits can include direct efficiency gains in the entered vertical segments (such as retailing functions, in the case of resale entry); or indirect gains, by allowing an entrant to acquire customers before fully building out its own network, thereby facilitating a transition to facilities-based competition.
5. *Modification of Final Judgment* (MFJ), *U.S. v. AT&T*, 552 F. Supp. 131 (D.D.C. 1982).
6. The FCC must consult with the state commission to verify compliance with the checklist. The Act provides for two tracks, A and B. Track A requires the Bell to have a binding access and interconnection agreement with one or more competitors which are operational, employ exclusively or predominantly their own facilities, and which (individually or between them) serve business and residential customers. The agreement(s) must cover all checklist items, and the FCC must determine that all are in fact being provided (not merely promised on paper). Track B provides a limited exception to the requirements of Track A, to guard against cases where Track A is not implemented solely due to lack of interest by entrants (as evidenced by their failure to request an agreement) or bad faith on their part. To satisfy Track B, when applicable, the Bell must provide a statement of terms and conditions under which it generally offers the checklist items. The statement must be approved or permitted to take effect by the state commission.
7. A more complete discussion of these issues is provided in the Affidavit of Marius Schwartz, 'Competitive Implications of Bell Operating Company Entry into Long-Distance Telecom-

munications Services' (14 May 1997), <www.usdoj.gov/atr/statements/Affiwp60.htm> (Schwartz 1st affidavit). This affidavit was filed with the FCC in support of the DOJ's evaluations. See, for example, United States Department of Justice, In the Matter of Application of SBC Communications Inc. et al. Pursuant to Section 271 of the Telecommunications Act of 1996 to Provide In-Region, InterLATA Services in the State of Oklahoma, FCC, CC Docket 97–121 (16 May 1997) <http://www.usdoj.gov/atr/public/comments/sec271/sbc/sbc.htm> (DOJ Oklahoma Evaluation).

8.  Accordingly, it is misleading to argue, as have some critics of Section 271, that a Bell's long-distance entry can pose no competitive risk, and to characterize the Section 271 authority as merely a 'hostage' used to pry open a Bell's local market (the traditional 'carrot' effect). Authorizing a Bell's entry before its local market is open will magnify its incentives to deny competitors key wholesale local services, as well as its incentives to try and degrade their long-distance access arrangements over time.

9.  Useful documentation of the pattern and scope of competitive entry is offered in President's Council of Economic Advisers, 'Progress Report: Growth and Competition in U.S. Telecommunications 1993–1998' (Washington, DC, 8 February, 1999).

10. As an indicator of the Act's concern with the residential market, Track A of the Section 271 conditions requires an applicant Bell to have an approved agreement with a competitor serving both business and residential customers.

11. These welfare gains derive from several sources, including: enhanced responsiveness to consumer choice, stronger incentives to cut costs and to innovate, and reduced direct costs associated with the regulatory process and, more importantly, reduced indirect costs due to intrusive regulation (such as delay and the setting of an inefficient structure of retail prices). See, for example, Joseph Farrell, 'Creating Local Competition', 49 *Federal Communications Law Journal* 201 (1996).

12. Other incumbents were not barred from long distance, as were the Bells, under the terms of the MFJ.

13. Federico Mini, 'The Role of Incentives for Opening Monopoly Markets: Comparing GTE and RBOC Cooperation with Local Entrants', Georgetown University Department of Economics Working Paper 99-09 (July 1999) <www.georgetown.edu/departments/economics/wk_paper/wp_list.htm>. Mr Mini is a doctoral student in economics, completing his dissertation under the supervision of the author.

14. FCC Industry Analysis Division, Common Carrier Bureau, 'Local Competition: August 1999', www.fcc.gov/ccb/stats.

15. It is conceivable that the difference between GTE and Bell conduct reflects idiosyncratic GTE characteristics rather than the differential incentives created by Section 271. Mini reports, however, that GTE was not more aggressive in regulatory proceedings prior to the Act, based on his discussions with industry experts and regulators.

16. Obtaining such data without the company's assistance would be difficult, as the data is often confidential and comes from disparate, idiosyncratic sources. Indeed, assembling Mini's data proved quite laborious even with AT&T's assistance, as it required combing manually through numerous contracts and other lengthy documents.

17. AT&T did negotiate with SNET, which provides local service only in Connecticut (SNET has since been acquired by SBC). AT&T's delay in reaching an agreement with SNET is far longer than the average delay Mini finds for the Bells, and therefore is consistent with the pattern he finds when comparing GTE vs. the Bells.

18. For UNEs, especially for loops, the costs vary considerably between incumbents, according to factors such as customer density and terrain. Mini uses estimates (from the Hatfield Model) of the cost to each company in each state of providing loops and end-office switching, and expresses GTE's and the Bell's pricing request in a state relative to that company's estimated cost. He compares the requested price–cost margins. Combining the data on loops and switching, GTE's request was higher in seventeen of the 23 cases where all data were available.

19. Resale discount offers are always expressed as a percentage of the retail prices, prices which differ between GTE and the Bells and which are not consistently reported. To compare the *dollar* discounts, Mini constructs estimates of the average monthly residential and business

revenues per line, for each incumbent by state, and applies the reported percentage offers to these estimates.

20.  The average residential bill across states is $14.85 for GTE and $15.41 for the Bells. For business customers, the corresponding average bills are $51.70 for GTE and $48.49 for the Bells, and the discounts offered are $4.11 by GTE (8 per cent off the bill) and $6.06 by the Bells (12.5 per cent off the bill).

21.  Econometric regressions show that GTE's request appears as positive and significant in explaining both the award to it and to the local Bell, whereas the Bell's request is positive and significant in explaining its award, but *insignificant* in explaining the award to GTE. In the regression explaining awards for *loops* (for which the dependent variable is the price–cost ratio awarded), GTE's request is again positive and significant throughout, while the Bell's request is insignificant in explaining its award (as well as GTE's). A possible interpretation is that the state commission is more sensitive to GTE, realizing that, unconcerned with Section 271 repercussions, GTE is more willing to press its case.

22.  FCC, Common Carrier Bureau, *Local Competition* (December 1998), <http://www.fcc.gov/ccb/stats>.

23.  The FCC's Local Competition study, *supra* note 14, obtains similar statistical findings concerning entry patterns: 'we find that 'controlling for demographics, new firms are more likely to enter BOC [Bell operating company] regions than ... independent (that is, non-BOC incumbent) regions ... This empirical evidence lends credence to the view that the BOC long distance prohibition [the need for Section 271 approval] *is* effective in facilitating competitive entry into BOC local telephone markets' (p. 6).

24.  The five applications, and the accompanying DOJ Evaluations and FCC Orders, are as follows: (1) SBC in Oklahoma: Application of SBC Communications, Inc., et al. Pursuant to Section 271 of the Telecommunications Act of 1996 to Provide In-Region, InterLATA Services in the State of Oklahoma, CC Docket No. 97–121 (11 April 1997) ('SBC Oklahoma Application'); DOJ Oklahoma Evaluation, *supra* note 7; Memorandum Opinion and Order, In re: SBC Oklahoma Application, 12 FCC Rcd 8685 (1997); (2) Ameritech in Michigan: Application of Ameritech Michigan Pursuant to Section 271 of the Communications Act of 1934, as amended, to Provide In-Region, InterLATA Services in Michigan, CC Docket No. 97–137 (21 May 1997) ('Ameritech Michigan Application'; Evaluation of the United States Department of Justice, In re: Ameritech Michigan Application, CC Docket No. 97–137 (25 June, 1997); Memorandum Opinion and Order, In re: Ameritech Michigan Application, 12 FCC Rcd 20543 (1997); (3) BellSouth in South Carolina: Application by BellSouth Corporation, BellSouth Telecommunications, Inc., and BellSouth Long Distance, Inc., for Provision of In-Region, InterLATA Services in South Carolina, CC Docket No. 97–208 (30 September 1997) ('BellSouth South Carolina Application'); Evaluation of the United States Department of Justice, In re: BellSouth South Carolina Application, CC Docket No. 97–208 (4 November 1997); Memorandum Opinion and Order, In re: BellSouth South Carolina Application, 13 FCC Rcd 539 (1997); (4) BellSouth in Louisiana I: Application by BellSouth Corporation, BellSouth Telecommunications, Inc., and BellSouth Long Distance, Inc., for Provision of In-Region, InterLATA Services in Louisiana, CC Docket No. 97–231 (6 November 1997) ('First BellSouth Louisiana Application'); Evaluation of the United States Department of Justice, in re: First BellSouth Louisiana Application, CC Docket No. 97–231 (10 December 1997); Memorandum Opinion and Order, In re: First BellSouth Louisiana Application, 13 FCC Rcd 6245 (1998); (5) BellSouth in Louisiana II: Second Application by BellSouth Corporation, BellSouth Telecommunications, Inc., and BellSouth Long Distance, Inc., for Provision of InRegion, InterLATA Services in Louisiana, CC Docket 98–121 (9 July 1998) ('Second BellSouth Louisiana Application'); Evaluation of the United States Department of Justice, In re: Second BellSouth Louisiana Application, CC Docket No. 98–121 (19 August 1998); Memorandum Opinion and Order, In re: Second BellSouth Louisiana Application, 13 FCC Rcd 20599 (1998).

25.  This standard is articulated and its logic is explained in the DOJ's Oklahoma Evaluation, May 1997, *supra* note 24. See also Schwartz I[st] affidavit, *supra* note 7, and Affidavit of Marius Schwartz, The 'Open Local Market Standard' for Authorizing BOC InterLATA Entry: Reply to BOC Criticisms (3 November 1997), <http://www.usdoj.gov/atr/statements/1281.htm>

(Schwartz 2nd affidavit). This 2nd affidavit was first filed in support of the DOJ's South Carolina Evaluation, cited above.

26. It also would contradict the intent of Congress, as indicated by the fact that a provision in an early bill which required the Bell to face a facilities-based competitor of 'comparable scope' was ultimately dropped.

27. The Act requires an incumbent's rates for interconnection and access to unbundled network elements to be 'just, reasonable, and nondiscriminatory', and 'based on the[irl cost'. The FCC has applied this language and adopted rules requiring costs to be estimated based on the methodology of forward-looking total element long-run incremental cost (TELRIC). The Supreme Court's *Iowa Utilities* decision affirmed the FCC's authority to establish a pricing methodology that states must follow. *AT&T Corp. v. Iowa Utilities Board*, 119 S. Ct. 721 (1999). The TELRIC methodology, if reasonably applied, would satisfy the DOJ's open market standard with regard to the incumbent's prices.

28. The FCC gave some indication of its thinking on the public interest test in its Order turning down Ameritech's application in Michigan, *supra* note 24, but has not been required to comment further on the subject since then.

29. For example, the DOJ and FCC found that in South Carolina, BellSouth's statement of generally available terms (used under Track B) failed to describe adequately what elements it will provide, the method in which it will do so, or the terms. BellSouth South Carolina Application, *supra* note 24. Such vagueness naturally hampers competitors.

30. For example, the DOJ and FCC found that Ameritech in Michigan refused to provide shared local transport, and provided trunking facilities whose quality was insufficient to ensure non-discriminatory interconnection with competitors (as compared to the interconnection quality between its own networks). Ameritech Michigan Application, *supra* note 24.

31. Prices can be lower because the Act requires different methodologies to calculate prices for UNEs and for resale. UNEs are to be priced 'bottom up' – based on the incumbent's costs of providing these elements. In the case of resale, wholesale prices are calculated 'top down' – starting from the existing retail prices and discounted by the estimated costs that the incumbent can avoid as a result of delegating these retailing functions to the reseller entrant. If retail prices exceed the incumbent's overall costs (including both facilities and retailing expenses), the top-down methodology will produce higher prices for competitors than the bottom-up methodology.

32. This argument seems strained, considering that the Bells alone were subject to the MFJ and its line of business restrictions, and that the Bells generally supported the Act because it voided the MFJ and replaced it, *inter alia*, with the Section 271 obligations. Thus, it is strange that such a fundamental challenge was mounted a year and a half after the passage of the Act. in any event, the courts have rejected these arguments.

33. *AT&T Corp. v. Iowa Utilities Board*, *supra* note 27, 119 S. Ct. 721. The FCC's Local Competition Order of August 1996, among other things: (a) required prices of unbundled elements to be based on the forward-looking TELRIC methodology, and not on 'historic' costs; (b) specified the network elements that incumbents must provide; and (c) prohibited an incumbent from separating network elements that it then combined, over the objection of a new entrant requesting access to combinations of network elements (to avoid unnecessary costs for entrants and consumers). Federal Communications Commission, First Report and Order (1996) ('Local Competition Order'). 'In the Matter of Implementation of the Local Competition Provisions in the Telecommunications Act of 1996', CC Docket No. 96–98. Many incumbent phone companies and states filed petitions for judicial review of the FCC Order; the cases were consolidated in the US Court of Appeals for the Eighth Circuit. In a 1997 ruling, the Eighth Circuit held that the FCC lacked jurisdiction to promulgate pricing rules and therefore vacated the pricing rules without considering their substance. *Iowa Utilities Board v. Federal Communications Commission*, 120 F.3d 753 (8th Cir. 1997). The court also addressed various arguments concerning unbundled elements, ruling for the FCC on some issues and for the incumbents on others. The government and many of the private parties asked the Supreme Court to review the Eighth Circuit's rulings.

In its *Iowa Utilities* decision, the Supreme Court held that the FCC's general jurisdiction to implement the Communications Act extends to the local competition provisions added by the 1996 Act. The state commissions' authority to 'establish rates' under Section 252 does not displace the FCC's authority to promulgate pricing rules; rather, state commissions are to apply the FCC's rules in setting specific prices. (The issue of the substantive propriety of the FCC's pricing rules, which was briefed but not decided in the Eighth Circuit, was not presented to the Supreme Court, and is now before the Eighth Circuit on remand.)

On unbundled elements, the Supreme Court held that the FCC has broad discretion in interpreting and implementing the requirements of the Act and that the regulations, with one exception, reasonably interpret and apply the Act. Accordingly, the Court affirmed the Eighth Circuit's holdings that the FCC properly construed and applied the statutory definition of 'network element', and that the FCC reasonably declined to impose a requirement that carriers seeking to use the incumbent's unbundled elements must also own some facilities. The Court also upheld Rule 315(b), which prohibits incumbents from separating already-combined network elements. Reversing the Eighth Circuit, the Court held this important rule to be a reasonable interpretation of the statute, consistent with generally accepted definitions of 'unbundled' and rationally based on the Act's non-discrimination requirement. The Court also addressed challenges to the FCC's Rule 319 rejected by the Eighth Circuit. This rule requires an incumbent to provide requesting carriers with access to a minimum of seven specified network elements. The Court held that the FCC failed adequately to consider the Act's 'necessary' and 'impair' standards when it identified the network elements that must be made available to requesting carriers. Accordingly, the FCC must reconsider Rule 319 and articulate and apply a standard rationally related to the goals of the Act.

34.  *SBC Communications, Inc. v. FCC*, 154 F.3d 226 (5th Cir. 1998); *Bell South Corp. v. FCC*, 162 F.3d 679 (DC Cir. 1998).

35.  *SBC Communications, Inc. v. FCC*, 138 F.3d 410 (DC Cir. 1998); *Bell South Corp. v. FCC*, 162 F.3d 678 (DC Cir. 1998). (Ameritech did not appeal the denial of the Michigan application; BellSouth voluntarily dismissed its appeal from the denial of its Louisiana application, No. 98–1087 (DC Cir).)

36.  *US West v. FCC*, 177 F.3d 1057 (DC Cir. 1999).

37.  On remand from the Supreme Court's decision upholding the FCC's authority to adopt pricing rules, the Eighth Circuit is now considering challenges to the substance of those rules. Specifically, it will determine whether the FCC's decision that access to unbundled network elements and interconnection should be priced on the basis of forward-looking costs using the TELRIC methodology is reasonable and consistent with the Act. The Eighth Circuit also is considering arguments as to the effect, if any, of the Supreme Court's decision on the FCC's requirement that the incumbents provide shared transport, which the court of appeals previously upheld. *Southwestern Bell v. FCC*, 153 F.3d 597 (8th Cir. 1998). Also on remand from the Supreme Court, the FCC is reconsidering its Rule 319, which specifies the unbundled network elements incumbents must provide, in light of the Court's holding that in adopting the rule it had failed appropriately to consider certain statutory standards. The Commission is expected to reissue a UNE rule in the near future; various parties are likely to seek further court of appeals review.

# 11. Regulation and privatization: the case of electricity

## Domenico Siniscalco, Bernardo Bortolotti and Marcella Fantini[1]

*This chapter explores the relationship between sound regulation and privatization, setting forth an empirical analysis of privatization in the electricity sector. The literature and statements by the finance ministries provide two principal reasons why electricity monopolies are privatized: to raise revenues, which is the 'finance minister's argument', and to promote efficiency and market liberalization. A tradeoff must be made between the public sector budget constraint on the one hand, and liberalization and efficiency on the other, because liberalization introduces competition and reduces profits of the monopolist. If the utility is first liberalized and then privatized, shareholder value (that is, treasury value at the time of privatization) decreases – which means that the treasury collects less money.*

*The findings in this study suggest that this argument is false, at least with reference to the electricity sector, and that there is a strong reason to liberalize first, and then to privatize. This conclusion is important in itself because in many countries, privatization seems to slow down liberalization. When a big electrical company is being privatized, the liberalization process seems to become more difficult.*

*The study focuses on electricity at the worldwide scale, covering the period from 1977 to 1997, considering 38 countries, 19 of which have privatized their electricity utility (which is almost the universe of privatized companies in electricity). Two market-structure variables are built: a vertical integration index, which takes the value of one when the company is vertically integrated in electric power generation, transmission and distribution, and zero otherwise; and a market regulation index, which attempts to measure the quality or pervasiveness of regulation. The empirical test is a regression analysis that explores whether the decision to privatize is related to the vertical integration and market regulation indexes. The dependent variable is the number of privatizations, and the independent variables are government revenues and share value of stock sold.*

*The study makes three major findings. First, a negative relationship exists between privatization and the vertical integration index. Privatization is likely only after restructuring a vertically integrated firm. Second, a positive relationship exists between privatization and the regulation index. There is an implicit discount related to regulatory risk: the amount of revenues raised through privatization will be higher if the industry is fully regulated because a reasonable investor will assume that at some point, an unregulated monopoly will be regulated. If it is not fully regulated at the time of privatization, investors are willing to pay only a lower price. Third, the percentage of the stock sold is related to these variables. If the government has not yet completely regulated the industry, or if the monopoly has not yet been separated into the three phases, only partial privatization is likely to occur.*

*The study concludes that good regulation on the product market spills over to the capital market. To have a complete privatization, where the state actually withdraws from public ownership, and real competition in the capital market, with many owners, quality regulation in the product market is required. Thus, regulation matters in the decision to privatize: it allows for more and better privatization. This implies that a minister of finance should liberalize first, and privatize second.*

## INTRODUCTION

Privatization began in the early 1960s with German Chancellor Adenauer's privatization of Volkswagen and Weber, which came to a halt almost immediately when problems emerged. Margaret Thatcher reinitiated privatization in the late 1970s, and it then became a worldwide phenomenon. Typically, privatization starts with small-scale operations in non-strategic sectors (namely, agriculture, industry, banking and so on) that did not require regulation to substitute for public ownership. At a second stage, privatization spreads into utilities and network industries (gas, electricity, telecommunications (TLC), transport and so on), often sold piecemeal due to the size of corporate assets.

On a worldwide scale, privatization appears to follow a common pattern, although substantial differences exist in the scale of state sell-offs among geographical areas. In virtually all major regions, however, including Western Europe, Latin America, Australasia, the former Soviet Union, the Middle East, North Africa and Asia, the percentage of revenues from the sale of utilities appears to be increasing over time (see Figures 11.1–7).[2]

Despite this common trend, privatization processes evolve at different speeds. Only a few countries have entered the second stage, fully privatizing strategic sectors such as energy, telecommunications or transport. The UK went furthest in privatization in the shortest time. The Thatcher government started in 1977

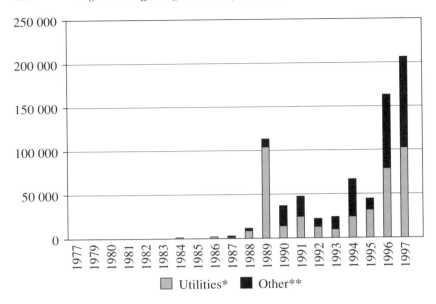

*Notes*
\*   *Utilities include*: Airport, bus and taxi services; electricity, gas transmission and distribution; postal services; rail service; roads; seaports; telecommunications; transport; water and sewerage.
\*\*  *Other includes*: Agriculture; airlines; airspace; banking; broadcasting; catering and bars; chemicals and allied products; construction; construction materials; electrical and electronic equipment; engineering; financial miscellaneous; food and beverage manufacturing; forestry and fishing; hotels; insurance; machinery; metals and metal products; mining; miscellaneous manufacturing; miscellaneous services; motor vehicles, multiple; oil and gas; paper and board; pharmaceuticals; postal services; printing and publishing; rail equipment; real estate; retailing; roads; rubber and plastics; science and engineering; scientific instruments; clocks; photographic equipment; shipbuilding; shipping; telecommunications equipment; textiles; tobacco; tourism.

*Figure 11.1   Distribution of revenues in the world*

with British Petroleum (BP), the national oil company, followed by companies of the industry sector. By the end of the 1980s, the process experienced an abrupt acceleration, with privatization of water and sewerage, electricity, TLC and, more recently, railways. Similarly, Argentina has rapidly entered the second stage. The privatization process started in 1990 with important sales in utilities. From 1990 to 1996, 88 per cent of sales occurred in strategic sectors, mainly in the electricity and gas distribution sector.

Some ambitious privatization programmes experienced an abrupt interruption despite a promising start. For instance, French privatization started in 1986–87 in the financial and banking sector (Saint Gobain, Paribas, Sogenal, Banque du Bâtiment and Travaux Publiques, Crédit Commerciale de France).

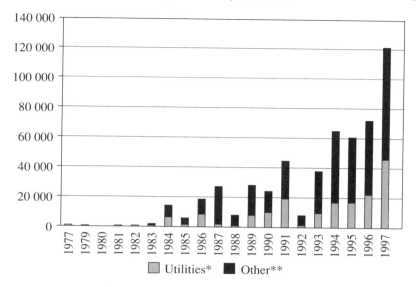

*Figure 11.2    Distribution of revenues in Western Europe*

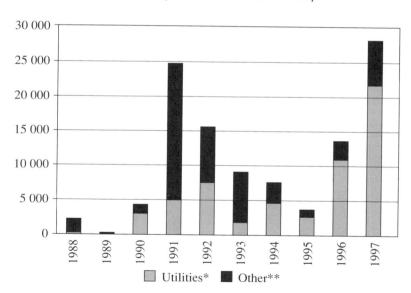

*Figure 11.3    Distribution of revenues in Latin America*

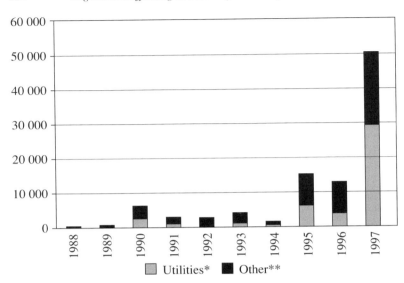

*Note*:    *, **, see note to Figure 11.1.

*Figure 11.4    Distribution of revenues in Australasia*

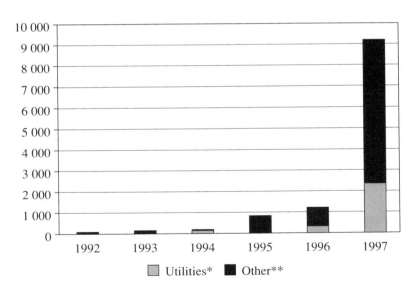

*Note*:    *, **, see note to Figure 11.1.

*Figure 11.5    Distribution of revenues in the former Soviet Union*

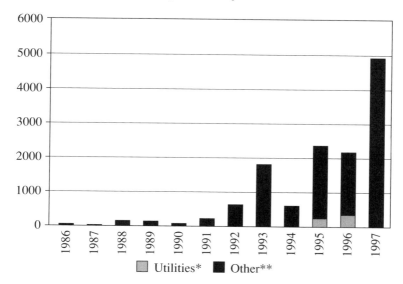

*Figure 11.6  Distribution of revenues in the Middle East and North Africa*

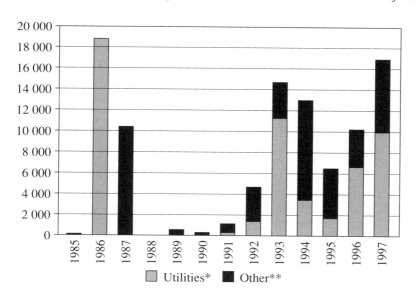

*Figure 11.7  Distribution of revenues in Asia*

The first sale in the energy sector took place in 1992 with the partial sale of Elf Aquitaine and Total. After a long interruption, the process regained momentum in 1997 with the sale of France Telecom. Notwithstanding some recent announcements, the majority of assets in strategic sectors are still publicly owned.

The Italian experience is similar. The privatization process started in 1985 with partial sales of SIRTI and Alitalia. From 1985 to 1995, sales involved mainly the industry and banking sectors. The first large floatation in the utility sector took place a decade after the start of privatization, with the first divested piece of Eni, the national oil company. In the last years, some significant sales have occurred in the utilities (Eni and Telecom Italia). However, privatization of electricity has been only partial, and privatization of railways is still wishful thinking.

Is there anything special about privatization of utilities? What factors determine the speed of privatization, or the frequency of sales in strategic sectors? Why have some governments raised substantial proceeds when selling infrastructure while others have substantially underpriced the shares? Why have some governments decided to transfer ownership and relinquish control of utilities while others have only partially privatized them?

An earlier study by the present authors,[3] which started from the seminal work by La Porta, Lopez-de-Silanes, Shleifer and Vishny,[4] conjectured that institutional and legal factors help explain the diversity of privatization processes around the world. It presented evidence that investors' legal protection (shareholders' rights and their enforcement) allows governments to sell higher stakes. French civil law countries were shown to bypass capital markets, more often opting for private placements than common law countries. These results suggested that genuine privatization is easier to accomplish where appropriate legal institutions exist.

This chapter argues that legal institutions, particularly regulation, may be even more important in the divestiture of monopolies. The privatization process can smoothly enter the second stage involving utilities only if governments have injected competition into the market and structured a clear regulatory framework *before privatization*. A well-defined regulatory framework is key in privatization since it provides a substitute for public ownership, avoiding the pitfalls of private ownership of natural monopolies. It should allow governments to sell more companies in the utility sector and, more importantly, to transfer the majority of stock.

Regulation may also determine the success of privatization in terms of proceeds. Conventional wisdom suggests that regulation decreases the expected profitability of the investment, given that firms will be forced to operate in a competitive environment post-privatization. Given rational expectations by investors, future profitability will be perfectly anticipated at the time of the sale. Governments may therefore face a tradeoff between revenue maximization and efficiency. On the other hand, regulatory risk also affects value. In the absence of regulation, the contract struck by investors and a government privatizing a utility will necessarily be incomplete. It is prohibitively costly to specify *ex ante* all possible actions that should be taken if the government decides to renegotiate the previous agreement and regulate the market *ex post*. Contract incompleteness typically generates underinvestment in specific assets, which will be reflected in the price agreed upon in the initial contract. A clear regulatory setting can reduce transaction costs and generate a premium on privatization proceeds.[5]

Regulation is not the only factor explaining the pace of divestiture in network industries. An additional factor is market structure, as privatization may prove particularly difficult in vertically integrated systems. Selling a vertically integrated business is not efficient, since cross-subsidies are possible. As demonstrated by the BP and British Gas experience, when governments attempt to increase the competitiveness of the market after privatization, the integrated incumbent is typically able to subsidize the competitive side of the business and stifle entry.[6] These concerns lead benevolent governments and regulators to recommend unbundling of the activities before privatization. Unbundling and liberalization is difficult, however, where a powerful player dominates the market, since it can exert pressure at the legislative stage to maintain the status quo.

This chapter attempts to assess the effect of market structure and regulation on privatization in a typically regulated sector, electricity. When analysing market structure, national markets dominated by vertically integrated players have been singled out. Legal documents have been used to assess the extent of regulation of the electricity sector in 38 jurisdictions, taking into account institutional features related to enforcement. The empirical analysis shows:

- The speed of privatization in electricity is partially determined by market structure. The frequency of sales is significantly reduced when the system exhibits a high degree of vertical integration.
- Regulation appears to be the key to state asset divestiture in the electricity sector. In highly regulated settings, more sales are made and larger stakes are sold.
- Revenues appear to be positively correlated to regulation. When privatizing utilities, governments may not face a tradeoff between revenue maximization and efficiency. The empirical data suggests that setting a clear institutional framework may allow governments to reduce uncertainty about future policy, with the consequence that the auctioning of the shares will be more successful in terms of proceeds.

To conclude, Friedman[7] once lamented that there is unfortunately no good solution for technical monopoly. There is only a choice among three evils: private unregulated monopoly, private monopoly regulated by the state, and government operation. Our results suggest that at the privatization stage, the second option is perhaps the lesser evil.

The link between regulation and privatization of utilities has been the focus of a wide theoretical literature that is not surveyed here.[8] This literature includes neither reliable regulatory indicators for the electricity sector in a cross-section of countries, nor a systematic statistical analysis of the economic effects of market structure and regulation in privatization. This chapter provides tentative results in that direction.

The chapter is organized as follows: Section A presents the data, describing the variables and the predictions tested and Section B presents the empirical results; a conclusion follows.

## A.   DATA AND VARIABLES

The source used for data at the company level is Privatisation International. It reports 135 sales and $107.8 billion in revenues in the energy sector (80 per cent of both figures in electricity and 20 per cent in oil and gas) in 26 countries for the 1977–97 period. The present study is restricted to electricity for two main reasons: first, sales in this sector account for the largest proportion of the revenues in power; second, oil and gas includes regulated as well as unregulated segments. This analysis is further restricted to sales in power generation, excluding transmission and distribution mainly because more countries have been involved in privatization of the upstream segment of the industry. It considers companies involved in generation alone, and excludes partially integrated operators, such as distributors with some generation capacity or generators that own segments of the transmission network. Sales are listed in Table 11.1.

The choice of the sample is mainly determined by the availability of reliable data about the electricity industry and regulation, beginning with the 49-country sample used by La Porta et al.[9] and Bortolotti et al.[10] From that sample, regulatory and market structure indicators were retrieved for 38 countries, mainly drawn from Lewington[11] (a leading source for institutional and legal materials concerning regulated sectors). For the countries not included in that source, original national documents were relied upon.[12]

The analysis at the company level is based upon data for 48 generators in 19 countries. The description of the variables appears in Table 11.2.

## Quantity and Quality of Privatization

The quantity and quality of privatization in the electric sector are the dependent variables in the present analysis. Quantity refers to two variables: (i) the total number of sales in electricity generation in a given country (*ELSALES*); (ii) the per country aggregate proceeds from total sales in US dollars 1996 (*ELREVENUES*).[13] Quality is defined as the stake privatized at the firm level (*ELSTOCK*), taking into account multiple issues, if any.

### Vertical integration

The structure of the electricity sector varies greatly around the world, ranging from high concentration and vertical integration to more competitive and separated regimes. At one end of the spectrum, electricity is mainly provided by a single vertically integrated company operating nationwide. Many European countries fit this model: ENEL in Italy, EdF in France, the Electricity Supply Board in Ireland and PPC in Greece all operate in generation, transmission and distribution, under public ownership. In the Belgian and Austrian systems, different companies appear to be involved in different market segments, but a closer look at the ownership structures reveals a high degree of concentration of activities within a single entity. In Belgium, until October 1996, Tractebel owned a majority stake in Powerfin and a solid controlling position in Electrabel, which in rum owns the majority of stock in the 'mixed' intermunicipal companies that provide nearly 80 per cent of electricity distribution. In Austria, several companies are responsible for generation, transmission and distribution. Nevertheless, VG, the interstate interconnection transmission company, owns a majority stake upstream in eight generators and downstream through direct or indirect holdings in the several regional or municipal distribution companies. In both cases, vertical integration is completely replicated by ownership.

In other countries, there is less horizontal concentration of activities within a single firm or through shareholdings. However, a number of vertically integrated players often operate on a regional scale. For instance, Germany is horizontally decentralized, but the generation and transmission (and to some degree distribution) activities are regionally integrated in nine main utilities. A similar structure is also found in Denmark and Scotland, where supply consists of two vertically integrated regional systems.

At the other extreme of the spectrum are vertically separated and often more competitive settings. Vertical separation and liberalization are often the outcome of a process of deep restructuring of the industry via unbundling. These liberalization processes are particularly important for the scope of the present analysis, as they form a part of a well-designed privatization package.

*Table 11.1    Privatization in electricity generation, 1977–1997*

| Country | Company | Date | Type | Revenues (US$ bn) | Stock |
|---|---|---|---|---|---|
| Argentina | Segba (Puerto) | 01/03/92 | Private sale | 0.09 | 60 |
| | Segba (Costanera) | 01/05/92 | | 0.09 | 60 |
| | Alto Valle | 01/09/92 | Private sale | 0.02 | 90 |
| | Dock Sud | 01/09/92 | Private sale | 0.03 | 90 |
| | Guemes | 01/09/92 | Private sale | 0.09 | 60 |
| | Segba (Pedro de Mendoza) | 01/09/92 | Private sale | 0.01 | 90 |
| | Alicura | 01/07/93 | | 0.39 | 59 |
| | Cerros Colorado | 01/07/93 | | 0.18 | 59 |
| | El Chocon | 01/07/93 | | 0.53 | 59 |
| | Hidroelectrica Piedra del Aguila (Hidronor) | 01/12/93 | Private sale | 0.27 | 59 |
| | Ameghino | 01/06/94 | | 0.02 | 59 |
| | Futaleufu | 01/04/95 | Private sale | 0.23 | 98 |
| | Direccion Provincial de Energia | 10/07/96 | Private sale | 0.05 | 60 |
| | Luis Piedrabuena de Bahia Blanca plant (Eseba) | 31/07/97 | Private sale | 0.03 | 100 |
| Australia | Loy Yang B power station | 01/01/93 | Private sale | 1.01 | 40 |
| | Yallourn Energy | 05/03/96 | Private sale | 1.88 | 100 |
| | Hazelwood | 01/08/96 | Private sale | 1.83 | 100 |
| | Loy Yang B | 01/04/97 | Private sale | 0.78 | 49 |
| | Loy Yang A | 22/04/97 | Private sale | 3.80 | 100 |
| | Southern Hydro | 21/11/97 | Private sale | 0.27 | 100 |
| Austria | Verbund (Oesterreichische Elektrizitaetswirtschaft) | 01/11/88 | Public offer | 0.44 | 49 |
| | EVN Energie-Versorgung Niederosterreich | 17/11/89 | Public offer | 0.13 | 25 |
| Brazil | COPEL | 17/01/97 | Public offer | 0.09 | 8.27 |
| | Cachoeira Dourada | | | 0.71 | 100 |
| Canada | Nova Scotia Power | 12/08/92 | Public offer | 0.68 | 100 |
| Chile | Colbun-Machicura | 01/01/96 | | 0.41 | 44.2 |
| | Tocopilla | 01/11/96 | Private sale | 0.18 | 51 |

| | | | | | |
|---|---|---|---|---|---|
| Colombia | 499MW Betania hydroelectric plant | 19/12/96 | Private sale | 0.30 | 99 |
| | 1000 MW Chivor hydroelectric plant | 20/12/96 | Private sale | 0.64 | 100 |
| England and Wales | National Power (Gencos 1) | 06/03/91 | Public offer | 1.40 | 60 |
| | PowerGen (Gencos 1) | 06/03/91 | Public offer | 2.28 | 60 |
| | National Power (Gencos 2) | 01/03/95 | Public offer | 2.81 | 40 |
| | PowerGen (Gencos 2) | 01/03/95 | Public offer | 1.87 | 40 |
| | British Energy | 10/07/96 | Public offer | 2.18 | 87.73 |
| Finland | Kemijoki Oy | 01/02/97 | | 0.43 | 25 |
| Germany | Rhein-Main-Donau (RMD) | 05/07/94 | Private sale | 0.45 | 75.5 |
| | Neckar | 31/12/95 | Private sale | 0.10 | 99 |
| Northern Ireland | Ballylumford power station (Northern Ireland Electricity) | 01/04/92 | Private sale | 0.22 | 100 |
| | Coolkeeragh power station (Northern Ireland Electricity) | 01/04/92 | Private sale | 0.01 | 100 |
| | Kilroot, Belfast West power stations (Northern Ireland Electricity) | 01/04/92 | Private sale | 0.35 | 100 |
| New Zealand | Mangahao Hydro Power Station | 30/11/97 | Private sale | 0.03 | 100 |
| Pakistan | Kot Addu power station | 03/04/96 | Private sale | 0.22 | 26 |
| Peru | Cahua | 25/04/95 | Private sale | 0.04 | 60 |
| | Edegel | 17/10/95 | Private sale | 0.52 | 60 |
| | Ventanilla | 12/12/95 | Private sale | 0.12 | 60 |
| Portugal | Pego Power | 28/11/93 | Private sale | 1.16 | 90 |
| Scotland | Scottish Hydro Electric | 12/06/91 | Public offer | 1.72 | 100 |
| | Scottish Power | 12/06/91 | Public offer | 3.67 | 100 |
| Spain | Empresa Nacional de Electricidad (ENDESA) | 26/05/94 | | 1.05 | 6.7 |
| | ENDESA | 21/10/97 | | 4.56 | 25 |
| United States | Milwaukee County power plant | 01/12/94 | Private sale | 0.06 | 100 |
| Thailand | Electricity Generating Public Company (EGCO) | 09/11/94 | | 0.18 | 49 |

*Source*: Privatisation International.

*Table 11.2    Description of the variables*

| Variable | Description |
| --- | --- |
| *ELSALES* | Total number of operations by Public Offer (PO) and Private Sales (PS) in electricity generation per country 1977–97<br>Source: Privatisation International |
| *ELREVENUES* | Aggregate revenues from total operations in electricity generation per country 1977–97 (million US dollars 1996)<br>Source: Privatisation International |
| *ELSTOCK* | Cumulative stake sold in electricity generators at the firm level<br>Source: Privatisation International |
| *RIGHT* | Dummy taking the value 1 if the majority of sales is implemented by a right-wing party and 0 otherwise<br>Source: Privatisation International and Arthur S. Banks, Alan J. Day and Thomas C. Mueller (eds), *The Political Handbook of the World* (Binghamton, 1997) |
| *CREDIBILITY* | Average of scores on the rule of law, risk of expropriation, and risk of contract repudiation by government<br>Source: International Country Risk Guide |
| *VINT* | Dummy taking the value 1 when a vertically integrated electric system is present<br>Source: Lewington (1997) |
| *AGENCY* | Dummy taking the value 1 when an independent agency as regulatory institution is present<br>Source: Lewington (1997) |
| *POOL* | Dummy taking the value 1 when a wholesale electricity market ('pool') is operational<br>Source: Lewington (1997) |
| *TPA* | Dummy taking the value 1 when regulated third-party access is granted by law<br>Source: Lewington (1997) |
| *REG* | Regulatory index taking the value 3 when *AGENCY*, *POOL* and *TPA* dummies are present<br>Source: Lewington (1997) |
| *FLOAT* | Total value of trades on the major stock exchange/GDP<br>Source: World Development Indicators |
| *TURNOVER* | Total value of trades on the major stock exchange/market capitalization<br>Source: World Development Indicators |
| *CONS* | Average consumption of electricity in KwH 1977–96<br>Source: International Energy Agency |
| *GROWTH* | Average annual percent growth of GDP per capita for the period 1970–93<br>Source: World Development Indicators |

England and Wales represent a blueprint for liberalization and restructuring in the electricity sector. Since the reform set forth in the 1988 White Paper was strictly implemented, the market has experienced horizontal and vertical separation. The Central Electricity Generating Board (CEGB) has been broken up into two generators (National Power and PowerGen), and the National Grid company. The regional electricity boards were privatized as the regional electricity companies (RECs) with responsibilities for the distribution and supply businesses.[14]

Some countries have followed the British model. In the early 1990s, Argentina experienced 'one of the most drastic, comprehensive and rapid sets of changes ever observed in the electricity services in a modern democracy'.[15] Until 1992, the electricity industry was publicly owned and mainly consisted of three vertically integrated operators (SEGBA, AyE and Hidronor). The 1992 privatization law required that competition and market mechanisms be introduced and promoted whenever possible, which involved unbundling of activities. The recommendations of the law have been implemented through a split of the three companies into 21 generation companies, three distribution companies, and through a merger of high-voltage transmission into a newly incorporated company, Transener.

Following its 1992 legislative reform, Peru has to some extent implemented a radical horizontal and vertical separation of electric supply. The generation activity of Electroperu and Electrolima was split into various entities, while the regional companies kept distribution as their sole activity. Similar processes also occurred in Chile, Australia and Spain.

For present purposes, the existence of a vertically integrated system within a given country must be quantified. The relevant information concerning the industry structure is captured by the dummy *VINT*, taking the value one where the market is dominated by a single player, by various vertically integrated players or by a single entity owning controlling stakes in the upstream and downstream electricity business.

Vertical integration may hinder privatization. As stated above, sale of a vertically integrated business may not be efficient, since cross-subsidies are possible. It appears that to achieve efficiency, issue of the shares of the electric companies is required, separating out the natural monopoly side of the business. But this splitting is problematic when vertically integrated incumbents dominate the market. We therefore expect a negative correlation between the *VINT* dummy with our first quantity variable, *ELSALES*.

Vertical integration could also have a negative impact on aggregate proceeds. Indeed, market structure affects profitability, as investors anticipate that they will have to compete in the generation business with vertical integrated players. If the regulatory regime is limited, the network owner retains substantial market power, and can grant access at more favourable conditions to its own generators.

The presence of a vertically integrated incumbent may therefore discourage entry, with negative consequences on proceeds. To test this conjecture, the *VINT* dummy is introduced in the *ELREVENUES* regressions.

## Market regulation

Regulation is a key element in infrastructure privatization. A well-designed regulatory framework protects consumers from monopoly abuses and investors from arbitrary political action, and provides incentives for efficient operation and investment.[16] But how can the quality of regulation be measured? Is it possible to rank the intensity of regulation across jurisdictions using objective indicators? Comparative study of different institutional arrangements is intrinsically a difficult task, but with appropriate restrictions of the field, the experiment yields some useful results.

In the cross-section of countries studied here, with very few exceptions (Ireland, Thailand, the Philippines, Venezuela, Austria), the electricity market is typically subject to some form of public control. This means that at least a legal document involving the companies operating in the sector has been adopted and in place since January 1997. However, the mere existence of a law involving electricity provides little information; more details are needed on what has been regulated and the institutions designed to enforce the existing regulation.

The more interesting aspects of regulation in electricity generation and distribution involve: (i) entry conditions; (ii) access to the network; (iii) prices. The regulation of market access varies greatly around the world. In most countries, producers must meet certain requirements to obtain a licence, such as capacity, safety, environmental protection and so on. These requirements are often allocated on the basis of competitive bidding or other procedures.

While licences or the imposition of some standard upon generators are common features of entry regulations almost everywhere, countries differ systematically in the way the access to the network is regulated. The two sides of electricity supply – generation and local distribution – are linked through the network. For competition to be effective, access to natural monopoly bottlenecks should be guaranteed by law, and access rates suitably regulated. In some jurisdictions, network access is guaranteed to all producers and all eligible customers under objective and non-discriminatory conditions (regulated Third-party access or TPA). In others, however, it is left to the benevolence of the network owner. An intermediate case is negotiated TPA, under which generators have granted access to the network, but on conditions that depend on the agreement with distributors.

The TPA model is explicitly indicated in the European Directive for the Internal Electricity Market. Member states that have liberalized network access via regulated TPA include Denmark, Finland, Sweden, England and Wales, and the Netherlands. Negotiated TPA has been adopted in Austria, Portugal and Germany.[17]

Another important institutional aspect of the functioning of the electricity market is the presence of a 'pool' or a regulated wholesale electricity market. The pool is an organized market for trading in electricity: generators compete to supply power to the grid. The existence of a pool is an element of regulation because, in most circumstances, it has been introduced by law and is a good indicator of the effectiveness of regulation in fuelling competition among generators.

A wholesale market for electricity was first established in Chile in the 1980s, in the United Kingdom in 1990 and in Argentina in 1992. Competitive pools are also operational in Scandinavia (the Nordpool, which has linked Norway and Sweden since 1992, and the EL-EX in Finland since 1996), in Spain since 1996, and in parts of the US, Australia and New Zealand.

Finally, the price formation mechanism is also regulated at various levels, typically in transmission and distribution. Excluding more exotic solutions, prices of the network owner are subject to RPI-X or rate of return regulation. Control of the price formation mechanism is crucial for the efficiency of the system. Virtually all countries that have a regulation concerning the electricity market somehow regulate prices. Since no proxy for the 'quality' of price regulation across countries is available (that is, the X in RP1-X), it is excluded from this analysis.

Economists often neglect the institutional aspects of regulation. Nevertheless, they warrant attention, since they provide valuable information as to how regulation is enforced. This analysis attempts to establish whether the law in a given jurisdiction foresees an independent regulatory agency that is not merely advisory. Here, 'independent' means that the agency it is not a branch of a ministry, and is engaged only in arm's-length relationships with regulated firms and political authorities, facing low risks of being captured by firms or governments. 'Not advisory' means that the agency is endowed with decision-making powers to set and enforce tariffs, to establish regulations concerning security and quality standards, interruptions and reconnections, and metering and billing.

In most countries, a ministry (Energy, Industry, Development and so on) is directly charged with regulatory functions. In some cases, a regulatory agency exists but is not independent from government and political interference. For instance, the Spanish agency (*Comision del Sistema Electrico Nacional*), while formally independent, is mainly a consultative body attached to the Ministry of Industry and Energy. Independent regulators endowed with decision-making powers are frequent in the Anglo-Saxon world, in some Latin American countries such as Brazil and Chile, and in several European countries that are committed to introducing institutional innovation in the regulation of electricity.

From this preliminary description of the regulatory settings around the world, a regulatory index (*REG*) has been constructed for each country (see Table 11.2). *REG* takes the value three when a country's regulatory setting entails: (i) regulated TPA; (ii) a 'pool' or a regulated wholesale market for electricity; and (iii) an independent regulatory agency. The higher the index, the more pervasive the regulation and the more competitive the electricity market is likely to be.

Next, the relationship between a country's regulatory index and the quantity and quality of its privatization is determined. This is done by statistically testing various hypotheses about the effect of regulation on privatizing utilities. The first hypothesis is that a more regulated environment should facilitate state sell-offs, because players operate under more competitive regimes in well-regulated settings. Efficiency losses due to natural monopolies are considerably reduced, which increases the political feasibility of infrastructure privatization. A positive correlation between *REG* and *ELSALES* is therefore expected.

Second, the regulation index is correlated with aggregate proceeds from privatization in the electricity market (*ELREVENUES*). Conventional theory suggests that regulation decreases the expected profitability of investment in a privatized firm, given that the firm will operate in a more competitive environment post-privatization. If regulation curbs above-normal profits, investors should insist on paying less for corporate assets in highly regulated settings. But a correlation in the opposite direction cannot be excluded, since clearly established rules reduce uncertainty about future regulatory intervention. Regulatory risk is particularly important for investors in the electric sector, where stranded assets and long-term contracts are common characteristics of firms and transactions.[18]

Finally, regulation can serve as a substitute for public ownership of a natural monopoly. The public provision of infrastructure is reasonable, given the possible negative consequences for the taxpayer of private ownership of natural monopolies. This is precisely the reason why government ownership is often recommended by constitutions. But effective regulation may avoid the distributive effects of privatization, allowing governments to privatize larger stakes and eventually relinquish control. To test the effect of regulation on corporate governance in privatized firms, the regulation index was correlated with the quality measure, the cumulative percentage of privatized stock (*ELSTOCK*).

**Controls**
Several variables have been used in the empirical analysis to control for country-specific effects. The average annual consumption of electricity in Kwh for the period from 1977 to 1996 (*CONS*) was used to control the size of demand in a given country. Consumption is highly correlated with GDP (correlation 0.95). Thus, *CONS* was also used to control for the size of the country. This variable is spurious as a measure of the supply side of the market, given that many

countries import electricity. Nevertheless, given that in larger countries the electricity sector may also be larger, inclusion of this variable allows account to be taken of the supply-side effects of privatization.

The analysis also includes the political orientation of a country's privatization by the dummy *RIGHT*, the institutional credibility index, given by scores in terms of rule of law, risk of expropriation and contract repudiation by government (*CREDIBILITY*), and the financial market liquidity indicators (*FLOAT* and *TURNOVER*). Variables used in the current authors' earlier work are used to explain the quantity and quality of privatization, and to determine whether they also have an impact in the electricity sector.

## B.   EMPIRICAL RESULTS

Tables 11.3–6 display the empirical results. Since many countries did not privatize electricity generation, the dependent variable contains many zeros. Even in these cases, market structure or weak regulation may help interpret the absence of privatization. Under these circumstances, ordinary least squares (OLS) regressions would probably yield downward-biased results. Tobit models were therefore used in the empirical analyses at the country level. In contrast, the quality variable at the company level, that is, the cumulative stake sold in electricity generators (*ELSTOCK*), is always positive and assumed continuous. OLS estimation is therefore more appropriate. Tables 11.3 and 11.4 show the results for the *ELSALES* regressions with vertical integration and regulation as independent variables, respectively. Estimation using the two variables in the same equation is impossible due to co-linearity problems.

Table 11.4 shows that vertical integration is strongly negatively correlated with the number of sales in the electricity sector. The coefficient of the *VINT* variable is significant and relatively stable in different specifications, controlling for country-specific effects. This evidence confirms that the presence of a vertically integrated system is a considerable obstacle to electricity privatization.

As stated above, vertically integrated operators should be separated before privatization to avoid the distortions of private ownership of a natural monopoly. Separating generation, which is the potentially competitive part of the business, from transmission and distribution should reduce the likelihood of cross-subsidization within the company. This explains why frequency of sales is lower in electricity markets dominated by a single vertically integrated player. In several circumstances, the incumbent, with its large corporate assets, is powerful and can invest resources in the political market to avoid liberalization. Thus, only a government strong enough to counterbalance this pressure to keep the status quo can implement unbundling. Accordingly, vertical integration is an important determinant of the speed of a privatization process.

*Table 11.3    Privatization in the electricity sector, regulation and vertical integration*

| Country | EL SALES | EL REVENUES | Agency | Pool | TPA | Regulation | Vertical integration |
|---|---|---|---|---|---|---|---|
| Argentina | 14 | 2011.12 | 1 | 1 | 1 | 3 | 0 |
| Australia | 6 | 9570.29 | 1 | 1 | 1 | 3 | 0 |
| Austria | 2 | 564.94 | 0 | 0 | 0 | 0 | 1 |
| Belgium | 0 | 0 | 0 | 0 | 1 | 1 | 1 |
| Brazil | 2 | 803.54 | 1 | 0 | 0 | 1 | 1 |
| Canada | 1 | 674.94 | 1 | 0 | 0 | 1 | 1 |
| Chile | 2 | 538.76 | 1 | 1 | 1 | 3 | 0 |
| Colombia | 2 | 936.93 | 0 | 1 | 1 | 2 | 0 |
| Denmark | 0 | 0 | 0 | 0 | 1 | 1 | 1 |
| England and Wales | 3 | 9547.12 | 1 | 1 | 1 | 3 | 0 |
| Finland | 1 | 429.97 | 1 | 1 | 1 | 3 | 0 |
| France | 0 | 0 | 0 | 0 | 0 | 0 | 1 |
| Germany | 2 | 548.95 | 0 | 0 | 0 | 0 | 1 |
| Greece | 0 | 0 | 0 | 0 | 0 | 0 | 1 |
| India | 0 | 0 | 1 | 0 | 0 | 1 | 1 |
| Indonesia | 0 | 0 | 0 | 0 | 1 | 1 | 1 |
| Ireland | 0 | 0 | 0 | 0 | 0 | 0 | 1 |
| Israel | 0 | 0 | 1 | 0 | 0 | 1 | 1 |
| Italy | 0 | 0 | 1 | 0 | 0 | 1 | 1 |
| Japan | 0 | 0 | 0 | 0 | 0 | 0 | 1 |
| Malaysia | 0 | 0 | 0 | 0 | 0 | 0 | 0 |
| Mexico | 0 | 0 | 1 | 0 | 1 | 2 | 0 |
| Netherlands | 0 | 0 | 0 | 0 | 1 | 1 | 0 |
| New Zealand | 1 | 33.5 | 0 | 1 | 0 | 1 | 0 |
| Northern Ireland | 3 | 575.95 | 1 | 0 | 1 | 2 | 0 |
| Norway | 0 | 0 | 1 | 1 | 1 | 3 | 0 |
| Pakistan | 1 | 214.98 | 0 | 0 | 0 | 0 | 0 |
| Peru | 3 | 685.94 | 0 | 0 | 1 | 1 | 0 |
| Philippines | 0 | 0 | 1 | 0 | 0 | 1 | 1 |
| Portugal | 1 | 1162.9 | 1 | 0 | 0 | 1 | 1 |
| Scotland | 2 | 5384.48 | 1 | 0 | 1 | 2 | 1 |
| Singapore | 0 | 0 | – | – | – | – | – |
| South Africa | 0 | 0 | 1 | 0 | 0 | 1 | 1 |
| South Korea | 0 | 0 | 0 | 0 | 0 | 0 | 1 |
| Spain | 1 | 5609.55 | 0 | 1 | 1 | 2 | 0 |
| Sri Lanka | 0 | 0 | – | – | – | – | – |
| Sweden | 0 | 0 | 1 | 1 | 1 | 3 | 0 |
| Switzerland | 0 | 0 | 0 | 0 | 0 | 0 | 0 |
| Thailand | 1 | 179.98 | 0 | 0 | 0 | 0 | 1 |
| USA | 1 | 55.99 | 1 | 1 | 1 | 3 | 0 |
| Venezuela | 0 | 0 | 0 | 0 | 0 | 0 | 1 |

*Source*:    Calculation on Privatisation International Database; Lewington (see note 11).

*Table 11.4    Privatization in the electricity sector (Tobit)*

| Independent variable | Dependent variable: *ELSALES* | |
|---|---|---|
| Constant | −3.65** | −0.12 |
| | (1.50) | (1.34) |
| Vertical integration | | −3.70** |
| | | (1.39) |
| Regulation | 1.82** | |
| | (0.57) | |
| Consumption | −0.32E–06 | 0.45E-06 |
| | (0.13E-05) | (0.14E–05) |
| Right | 2.02 | 2.67* |
| | (1.34) | (1.50) |
| σ | 3.32** | 3.54*** |
| | (0.58) | (0.62) |
| Nobs | 37 | 37 |
| Log. likelihood | −60.47 | −61.75 |

*Notes*
\*      Statistically significant at the 10% level.
\*\*     Statistically significant at the 5% level.
\*\*\*    Statistically significant at the 1% level.
Standard errors in brackets.

Table 11.4 provides evidence of the effects of regulation on the variable *ELSALES*.

The regulatory index *REG* is highly significant, positive and stable in different specifications. The regression presented is representative of many others. The frequency of sales in the electricity sector is therefore highly positively correlated with the extent of regulation. This result is easily explained. If a well-defined regulatory framework is in place at the time of the sale, privatization will be easier for governments; if the market is liberalized in the segments where competition is viable and appropriately regulated where natural monopoly-type bottlenecks exist, supernormal profits will be curbed. A well-designed privatization package, including liberalization and regulation, will therefore be more politically acceptable. If clear rules exist, privatization can smoothly enter the second stage involving utilities such as electricity.

The control variable *CONS* is not significant in either the regression in Table 11.3 or that in Table 11.4. This indicates that the scope of a country's privatization in the electricity sector is virtually independent of electricity demand. In contrast, the political dummy *RIGHT* is significant and positive. The results in the earlier work of the present authors suggested that conservative majorities appear to be more involved in the privatization of strategic sectors such as electricity.

It is not surprising that vertical integration and regulation have an impact on the speed of divestiture of state assets. The countries that have successfully privatized have also deeply restructured and liberalized the electricity sector before privatization. The economic effects of vertical integration and regulation upon the proceeds from sales in the electricity sector is more controversial.

As stated above, some argue that liberalization and regulation reduce the expected profitability of the investment, so that bidders should not be willing to pay as much for assets in the electricity business in highly regulated settings. Others contend that regulatory risk also has an impact at the time of the sale. Investors may discount the possibility of unexpected regulation or government decisions by policy makers, as happened in the case of the Monopolies and Mergers Commission intervention in the BP case.

The results shown in Table 11.5 provide some tentative answers to these important questions. In all regressions presented here, the higher the regulatory index, the higher the aggregate proceeds from sales in the electricity sector. In particular, a one point increase in the index raises revenues of an amount of approximately US$1.8 billion. Regulatory risk therefore seems to have a substantial impact. No statistically significant relation is present either with respect to the turnover ratio or the institutional credibility variable (*CREDIBILITY*). The second financial market development indicator (*FLOAT*) is, instead, positively related to the privatization proceeds, indicating a possible role for liquidity on the financial success of the issues.

These results with respect to the effects of regulation on privatization proceeds can be interpreted within the framework of incomplete contracting.[19] Buying a utility is akin to signing a contract with the government. In the privatization transaction, parties are called upon to strike this contract with limited information concerning future contingencies. Under these circumstances, regulation reduces uncertainty and therefore transaction costs. Clear rules appropriately enforced help bidders to gauge more precisely the expected profitability of the investment, which increases their willingness to pay. In contrast, the absence of a well-defined regulatory framework increases transaction costs, because rational investors will discount for the possibility that government may change the rules of the game *ex post*. The consequences of such an act can be particularly severe in electricity, where long-term investment and stranded assets are intrinsic characteristics of the market.[20]

The introduction suggested that the quality of a privatization process can be evaluated based on the size of the stake sold. The current authors' previous analysis demonstrated the relevance of legal institutions and their provision of investor protection for this variable. In utilities, and particularly electricity, an important issue is whether regulation affects the willingness of government to transfer ownership and relinquish control to privatized firms.

*Table 11.5  Revenues in the electricity sector (Tobit)*

| Independent variable | Dependent variable: *ELREVENUES* | |
| --- | --- | --- |
| Constant | −3578.33** | 39.93 |
|  | (1238.28) | (1210.67) |
| Vertical integration |  | −2526.88** |
|  |  | (1419.47) |
| Regulation | 1830.89** |  |
|  | (541.47) |  |
| Consumption | −0.18E–02 | −0.82E–03 |
|  | (0.13E–02) | (0.15E–02) |
| Float | 7970.38* | 6109.54 |
|  | (4116.34) | (4721.75) |
| σ | 3093.21** | 3661.78** |
|  | (542.63) | (649.12) |
| Nobs | 35 | 35 |
| Log likelihood | −179.95 | −183.49 |

*Notes*
\*   Statistically significant at the 10% level.
\*\* Statistically significant at the 5% level.
Standard errors in brackets.

In Table 11.6, a regression for *ELSTOCK* has been run using the regulatory index of the country in which the privatized company operates, and some control variables at the country level. A major flaw in these estimates is that due to the lack of data, there is no control of firm-specific fixed effects. Although preliminary, the results in Table 11.6 indicate a clear positive and statistically significant correlation between the regulatory index and the stake sold. The coefficient remains stable and significant when account is taken of country-specific effects, whereas the controls are never significant.

Regulation not only influences the quantity of state assets sold in the electricity industry, as confirmed by the results from the sales and revenues estimates, but may also shrink the residual stake held by government. This evidence has strong implications for corporate governance in utilities. Regulation may be a substitute for public ownership: benevolent governments will privatize larger stakes if shareholders will not reap surpluses via excessive dividends at the expense of consumers. But privatization is by no means perfectly equivalent to public ownership, since privatization exposes companies to the discipline of capital markets. The takeover threat in the market for corporate control compels managers to operate utilities efficiently, reducing costs to preserve profitability. Such competition will be severely limited if governments retain golden shares or other legal devices in order to transfer ownership but retain control.[21]

*Table 11.6   Privatized stock in the electricity sector (OLS)*

| Independent variable | Dependent variable: *ELSTOCK* | |
| --- | --- | --- |
| Constant | 63.7*** | 29.53* |
|  | (9.61) | (16.10) |
| Regulation | 5.71 | 6.62* |
|  | (3.79) | (3.64) |
| Consumption |  | 0.60E-05 |
|  |  | (0.10E-04) |
| Credibility |  | 4.27** |
|  |  | (1.78) |
| Nobs | 48 | 48 |
| Adj. $R^2$ | 0.04 | 0.14 |

*Notes*
\*      Statistically significant at the 10% level.
\*\*     Statistically significant at the 5% level.
\*\*\*    Statistically significant at the 1% level.
Heteroskedastic-consistent standard errors in brackets.

## CONCLUSIONS

This chapter attempts to single out some critical influences affecting the privatization of infrastructure. It focuses upon two factors that may influence the pace of divestiture in network industries: vertical integration and regulation. The results are straightforward. First, vertical integration of a system substantially reduces the frequency of utility sales. Second, regulation appears to be crucial for the success of privatization in the utility sector. The regulatory indicators correlate strongly with the quantity of sales of electricity, the size of the stake sold and the revenues from sales. As theory suggests, the public-monopoly-turns-into-private-monopoly argument does not apply in well-regulated settings. Consequently, an important rationale for public ownership of natural monopolies loses relevance. This reasoning explains not only the low number of sales and percentage of stock sold in poorly regulated electricity markets, but also why sales are less frequent where vertical integrated players dominate the market.

Regulation does not appear to decrease the revenue generated by the sale of public enterprises, although it can reduce the expected profitability of the firm curbing supernormal profits. However, it provides clear rules and a framework in which investments and business opportunities can be more effectively gauged. The regressions in this study indicate that the latter factor dominates the former in investors' decision making. Governments should therefore not be wary of regulating first and *then* privatizing.

## NOTES

1. We thank Carlo Scarpa for very useful discussions, Alessandro Lanza for data, William Baumol, Richard Green and Frank Stephen for comments. Claudia Panseri provided excellent research assistance. The usual disclaimer applies.
2. Worldwide proceeds from privatization since 1977 total $700 billion, the market capitalization of the privatized firm has doubled to $1.5 trillion, and world GDP originating from state-owned companies has decreased from 9 to 6 per cent (although it is higher than that in many European countries). William Megginson and Robert Netter, 'From state to market: a survey of empirical studies of privatization', Fondazione Eni Enrico Mattei Note di Lavoro, forthcoming in *Journal of Economic Literature*.
3. Bernardo Bortolotti et al., *Privatisation and institutions: A Cross-country Analysis*, 67 Fondazione Eni Enrico Mattei Note di Lavoro (Milan, 1997).
4. Rafael La Porta et al., 'Legal Determinants of External Finance', 52 *Journal of Finance* 1131 (1997); Rafael La Porta et al., 'Law and Finance', 106 *Journal of Political Economy* 1113 (1996).
5. Oliver Williamson, *The Economic Institutions of Capitalism* (1985); Oliver Hart and John Moore, 'Incomplete Contracts and Renegotiation', 56 *Econometrica* 755 (1988); Benjamin Klein, Robert G. Crawford and Armen A. Alchian, 'Vertical Integration, Appropriable Rents, and the Competitive Contracting Process', 21 *Journal of Law and Economics* 297(1978).
6. Dieter Helm and Tim Jenkinson, 'Introducing Competition into Regulated Industries', in *Competition in Regulated Industries* (Oxford, 1998).
7. Milton Friedman, *Capitalism and Freedom* 128 (Chicago: University of Chicago Press, 1962).
8. For a cross-country empirical analysis of the effects of institutional credibility on electric utility investment, see Mario Bergara, Witold J. Henisz and Pablo Spiller, 'Political Institutions and Electric Utility Investment: A Cross-nation Analysis' (unpublished mimeo 1998); see also Jean Jacques Laffont and Jean Tirole, *The Theory of Procurement and Regulation* (Cambridge, MA: MIT Press, 1993); John Vickers and George Yarrow, *Privatization: An Economic Analysis* (Cambridge, MA: MIT Press,1988).
9. *Supra* note 4.
10. *Supra* note 3.
11. Ilka Lewington, *Utility Regulation, Privatisation International* (London, 1997).
12. The UK has been disaggregated into England and Wales, Scotland and Northern Ireland, mainly because market structure differs substantially in the three regions. England and Wales are separated systems, with a high degree of competition in generation, given the existence of a wholesale electricity market (the 'pool'). In contrast, in Scotland, there are two vertically integrated operators (Scottish Power and Scottish Hydro). In Northern Ireland, a single company operates in both transmission and distribution (Northern Ireland Electricity), but three generators are present. Furthermore, a separate regulator (Ofreg) has responsibility for both gas and electricity.

13. This is consistent with how quantity was defined in the earlier work of the present authors, *supra* note 3.
14. Richard Green and David Newbery, 'The Electricity Industry in England and Wales', in *Competition in Regulated Industries*, Dieter Helm and Tim Jenkinson, eds, (Oxford, 1998).
15. Carlos Bastos and Manuel A. Abdala, *Reform of the Electric Power Sector in Argentina* 21 (Buenos Aires, 1996).
16. Richard Braeutigam, 'Optimal Policies for Natural Monopolies', in *Handbook of Industrial Organization*, Richard Schmalansee and Robert Willig, eds, (Amsterdam: North-Holland, 1989); Laffont and Tirole, *supra* note 8.
17. Regulation of grid access in Germany is enforced by the competition authority.
18. Helm and Jenkinson, *supra* note 6.
19. Ronald Coase, 'The Nature of the Firm', 4 *Economica* 386 (1937); Hart and Moore, *supra* note 5.
20. Auction theory provides a normative interpretation of this result. The government typically enjoys superior information about the regulatory environment in which the firm will operate. Adoption of regulation makes it publicly accessible and verifiable. If the bidders' valuations are correlated, expected revenues for governments will increase in all standard auctions. Paul Milgrom and Robert Weber, 'A Theory of Auctions and Competitive Bidding', 50 *Econometrica* 1081; Klaus Schmidt and Monica Schnitzer, 'Methods of Privatization: Auctions, Bargaining and Giveaways' (Center for Economic Policy Research Discussion Paper No. 1441, 1997).
21. It may be argued that endogeneity problems may affect these results. The degree of privatization could determine market structure, as a deintegrated regime can be the outcome of privatization. The variable *VINT* is none the less defined as a dummy for the presence of a vertically integrated system. It is less evident that vertical integration is endogenous to the degree of privatization. Similarly, it may be argued that liberalization, regulation and privatization are all parts of a structural reform package and simultaneously implemented. This is seldom true. Rather, the results show that in the electricity sector, with few exceptions (for example, Spain), regulation is typically followed by the privatization decree. Hausman tests have been used to check for possible simultaneity, and the results were mixed. Nevertheless, the results are more supportive of the hypothesis of exogeneity of the variables of interest.

# 12. Inappropriate regulation and stifled innovation in the road freight industry: lessons for policy reform

**Mark Dutz and Aydin Hayri**[1]

*This chapter addresses the importance of domestic competition after trade lib-eralization in developing and transition economies. Focusing on the Mexican trucking industry, the study asked whether more competition in essential business services leads to increased innovation, new goods, and new products in downstream markets by users of the services, and if so, to what extent.*

*During the 1980s in Mexico, road freight transport was subject to very restrictive regulation. Licences were difficult to obtain, specified particular classes of service, and required affiliation with an established company. The country was divided into a number of corridors in which capacity was controlled, ensuring rigid market segmentation. Freight centres decided which carrier would carry each shipper's load, preventing direct negotiations between carriers and shippers, and destroying carriers' incentives to invest in reputation. Loading and delivery were subject to fixed terms. Finally, fixed prices were established for five categories of products, uniform for all seasons and regions of the country, with penalties for charging above or below the authorized rate. The regulation prevented any truck owner from having more than five trucks, but the market was highly concentrated because a limited number of partici-pants controlled the freight centres. Small truckers attempted to evade this control, but stiff penalties were imposed.*

*The universal service argument was the main justification for this regulation. Road transport had the character of a public service, which required a concession granted by the federal government. Open competition threatened to disrupt economic activity through high price variability and uncertain service availability, especially to less-accessible regions of the country.*

*Reforms were introduced between 1989 and 1993, which brought about free entry into trucking on all routes, and into container and cargo handling. The study revealed that after reform, substantial changes occurred in the trucking industry: an increase in both quantities and distances of freight hauled, a fall in price, a decrease in delivery times, an increase in reliability (in terms of both timeliness and transit losses), fleet modernization, computerization on the Internet, satellite and cellular-based tracking services, and provision of comprehensive logistic solutions to individual firms. In downstream industries, shippers benefited from reduction in trucking costs, reduction of inventory holdings, innovations pertaining to standardization of lot sizes and containerization, outsourcing of trucking (rather than maintaining a fleet of trucks) and from the introduction of new products that improved road freight services allowed and spurred.*

*The study reaches several policy conclusions. First and foremost, that regulatory reform and enhanced provision of certain infrastructure services can lead to increased innovation and competition in downstream user industries, with substantial economywide benefits from these effects. Second, that successful reform requires careful planning and high-level political support. Third, a competition authority can have an important role as advocate, helping to build reform constituencies, especially when downstream business interests that will benefit from reform are only potential. Ex post, the competition agency must play a critical enforcement role, to ensure that private behaviour does not mimic the previous cartelized behaviour under regulation.*

## INTRODUCTION

Discussions of the benefits of competition and regulatory reform typically focus on price and quantity effects in the market under consideration. However, improvements in certain infrastructure services also can stimulate entry and competition in downstream user industries, allowing new firms to enter, incumbent users to offer new products in new markets, and rivalry to intensify.[2] To the extent that reform spurs innovation in infrastructure services, and these innovations in turn generate substantial new downstream activities, the economywide benefits of regulatory reform are likely to be substantially greater.

Mexico provides an ideal example of such downstream benefits from increased competition in an essential business service, and conversely of the forgone benefits under pre-reform regulation. From a particularly extreme degree of rigid regulation with a high degree of government interference, in 1989 Mexico established a new policy framework for the road transport industry based on free entry and market-based price setting. In addition to expected gains from reductions in trucking prices, there have been a number of other sources of downstream gains. All of these gains could have been realized earlier if inappropriate regulation had not been in place. In particular, the benefits forgone did not depend on state-of-the-art technology that would not have been available during the preceding decade. Rather, the benefits followed from simpler innovations such as faster and more reliable trucking. These benefits have, in turn, allowed user companies to offer new goods, both introducing previously unavailable products as well as making it possible for existing products to reach new areas. Less-costly and more-customer-responsive trucking services have also led to a number of other logistics-related innovations within user firms. Finally, instead of continuing to invest and maintain a private own-account fleet of trucks, some user firms have outsourced these functions to now more-efficient trucking companies. Outsourcing converts the potentially large fixed cost of building a fleet of trucks into a variable cost. It thereby eases entry barriers created by large capital requirements, which could be substantial in countries with less-well-functioning capital markets such as Mexico.

This chapter reviews the experience of the Mexican road freight industry as a case study of the anticompetitive impact of regulation. Following an overview of policy objectives and regulations, it sets forth the measurements of changes in firm performance, including downstream benefits from innovation and new products – a good proxy for forgone benefits under the previous regime of regulation – using the improvement in constructed operating margin directly attributable to road freight innovations. This gain could be as high as 10 per cent for a representative fertilizer company. The chapter concludes by highlighting, among other policy implications, the role that competition authorities should play in minimizing the anticompetitive effects of regulation.

## A.   WHAT HAPPENED IN MEXICAN INTERSTATE TRUCKING?

### Context

Government regulation of the trucking industry in Mexico extends back to the late 1940s. Regulations have been gradually increased under the tutelage of the Mexican Ministry of Communication and Transport (Secretaria de Comunicaciones y Transportes: SCT) Programme of Development for Federal Trucking, with an increasing involvement of trucking leaders in the design of governmental policy.

Trucking deregulation was undertaken in the context of general reform rather than as an isolated action. In 1983, Mexico began a process of macroeconomic and structural reforms to increase the reliance on market forces. This programme included an important opening to international trade, which led to Mexico becoming a GATT (General Agreement on Tariffs and Trade) member in 1986. Combined exports and imports roughly tripled between 1980 and 1990, resulting in a substantial increase in cargo volume on routes connected with international trade, while volume on other routes stagnated.[3] On the one hand, industry linked to international trade was being strangulated by the antiquated trucking system. On the other hand, truckers locked into unprofitable routes wanted to get a piece of the profitable international trade-linked trucking routes, and therefore emerged as strong supporters of trucking deregulation.

The Ministry of Finance (SHCP) and the Office of Economic Deregulation within the Ministry of Industry and Trade (SECOFI) took advantage of these changes and the dynamics created with Mexico's then-forthcoming participation in NAFTA (North American Free Trade Agreement) to push forward the deregulation of interstate trucking through a three-step plan. In their first step, SHCP and SECOFI secured the cooperation of the National Trucking Association (Camara Nacional de Autotransporte de Carga: CANACAR) by emphasizing modernization of the trucking fleet, rather than deregulation, as their primary policy goal. They supported their rhetoric with sweeteners such as subsidized loans for truckers who wanted to renovate their fleets. The second step was to eliminate route restrictions by a presidential decree that allowed truckers to operate on any interstate route. In the third step, after waiting for another six months or more for competition to take hold on many of the important trucking routes, another presidential decree eliminated all price regulations.

Regulation was implemented by presidential decree. The new law was not published until late 1993. This delay generated substantial uncertainty among carrier companies, as many were not clearly informed of the new rules, or they expected an eventual reversal. The signing of NAFTA in 1992 apparently cleared the uncertainty. Until then, the reformers decided not to push the legislation, at least in part because CANACAR had close connections with representatives in Congress who could have stalled the reform. It was therefore deemed more expedient to initiate reforms through decree (under executive authority), carefully choosing the wording of texts in order not to contravene existing constitutional pronouncements. The period from 1989 until 1993 was seen as a test period by the government, during which it could have retreated had it faced excessive resistance. In spite of the uncertainty created by ambiguous rules, this approach was pragmatic in that it minimized the risk of a reversal.

At present, any trucking company can carry interstate cargo between any two points without price regulation. As discussed below, neither the strength of competition nor the prevalence of innovations has been uniform among geographic regions and industry segments. Restrictions on intrastate trucking remain in certain states that did not follow the federal government's lead for deregulation.[4]

With respect to international competition, foreign carriers are still not permitted to use federal roads for international transport. NAFTA established a schedule of liberalization of the transportation sector in three, five and ten years. However, integration of systems between the US and Mexico has been slowed by a unilateral US decision to postpone the implementation of NAFTA with respect to trucking.[5] Foreign carriers are not allowed to own Mexican trucking companies until 2004. However, changes implemented in January 1990 permit the *maquiladoras* to transport their own products in their own trucks across the border.

## What Changed?

### Licensing
Old regulations required truckers to obtain route-specific trucking concessions from SCT, in addition to a general trucking licence. The administrative process for granting these concessions required existing service providers to approve new applicants. Moreover, incumbent firms had both preferential treatment whenever it was necessary to increase the number of trucks, as well as the right to object to future increases in installed capacity. These procedures strengthened the position of existing firms and led to the formation of cartels. Many owner–operators preferred to operate illegally rather than apply for a licence.

Today, only a general trucking licence is required, and truckers can operate on any interstate route. The current Regulation for Federal Cargo Trucking establishes the following requirements for obtaining a permit: (i) complete the registration form that SCT issues (although the regulation does not specify what it must include); (ii) show evidence of third-party damage insurance; (iii) declare the vehicle characteristics; and (iv) show the certificate of low-pollution emissions. The authorities' response to the application must be provided within 30 days.

### Routes
The old regulations established a fixed route system, with 11 corridors radiating out of Mexico City. This prevented spatial diversification of industry and led to inefficiencies, as it was not always possible to match loads for backhauling or to arrange cross-corridor shipments. Today, truckers are free to set their own routes.

### Freight centres
Under the old system, truckers could load and unload cargo only at specified freight centres (*centrales de carga*). Shippers were required to channel their requests through these centres. While originally motivated by economies in provision of common services (such as provision of spare parts, insurance and paperwork), many freight centres facilitated the enforcement of restrictive trucking rules and regulations, as well as cartelization. Moreover, freight centres drove a wedge between shippers and carriers because freight centres, not shippers, selected the trucker. Today, cargo traffic flows independently of freight centres and shippers can freely select their own trucking company.

## Containers

In 1981, SCT created Multimodal, a semi-public company, with an exclusive monopoly franchise to provide door-to-door multimodal services. Collusion between Multimodal and the freight centres led to a system of surcharges and unofficial payments that often far exceeded the stated tariffs. Service standards were low and deliveries often delayed, resulting in a tendency for container traffic to be confined to port areas (and thereby forgoing the benefits of door-to-door delivery). In addition, customs regulations did not permit import-bearing containers that were temporarily brought into the country to transport domestic cargoes, resulting in empty outbound movement of containers. Today, any company can engage in container handling, and there are no restrictions on the use of international containers for domestic transportation.

## Handling

SCT used to grant exclusive concessions for cargo handling in certain federal areas, such as railroad stations, ports, custom areas and border crossings. New regulations annulled all exclusive licences to handle cargo in federal areas, for handling cargo movements at railroad stations and border customs facilities, as well as for the drayage services to cross the border.

## Private operators

Under the old system, private own-account carriers needed permission to haul their own goods and, except for extraordinary and temporary circumstances, were not allowed to carry cargo of third parties. Today, there are no restrictions on their activities other than the general licensing requirement.

## Pricing

SCT used to set official trucking tariffs, uniform for all seasons and regions of the country, presumably above the competitive level and high enough to balance, on average, both fixed and variable costs and yield 'reasonable' profits. Trucking companies provided the cost information that the authorities evaluated and used as a reference for setting rates, but rates often bore little or no relationship to the costs of a specific shipment. Concessionaires were not allowed to charge prices above or under the authorized rates.[6] The reform abolished official rates. Article 65 of the current regulation explicitly establishes that truckers must freely determine rates. These amendments fostered quality differentiation of the service, as rates reflecting differing quality were now freely negotiable directly between trucking service providers and users.

## Insurance

Under the old regulations, trucking companies' responsibilities for damaged or missing freight were uniformly established for all varieties of cargo and were explicitly limited to very reduced quantities, unless the shipper paid an additional fee in proportion to the declared value of the good. The government had fixed the ceiling on the trucker's responsibility for cargo loss or damage to only US$0.31/ton. A further regulation prevented negotiation of incremental insurance by fixing the rate at which shippers could insure their cargo irrespective of the product-specific shipping risks (at 3 mills per declared value). As a result of these rules, trucking companies paid little or no attention to limiting transit losses. Article 84 of the new regulations protects shippers from cargo loss or damage by requiring trucking companies to pay damages equivalent to the declared value by the shipper.

**Taxation**
While overall road costs were being recovered, there were important cross-subsidies between automobiles and trucks. By 1989, trucks were only paying for approximately 15 per cent of the costs that they caused to the highway network. This was essentially due to the relatively low Mexican price of diesel fuel, which in late 1989 was roughly US$0.65/gallon, insufficient to allow adequate cost recovery, coupled with the absence of significant licence fees or direct taxes levied on truckers.[7] On 1 December 1989, the price of diesel was increased and trucks now pay about 50 per cent of highway costs.

## B.   PERFORMANCE IMPACT

It is difficult to isolate the impact of a specific policy reform from other changes in the economic environment, such as concomitant regulatory changes in related sectors, a drastic trade opening with Mexico's most significant trade partners, important related tax changes, and a severe economic downturn in 1995. None the less, the authors conducted in-depth interviews with carefully selected, representative shippers and trucking companies in mid-1998, after deregulation had been completed. These interviews were used to supplement and corroborate the more general trends in official statistics.[8] In assessing downstream impact, this chapter reports the maximum benefits for selected downstream users directly attributable to key road freight logistics innovations as an indication of the forgone gains under the previous regulatory regime.

### Impact on the Road Freight Industry

### Output and prices
*Significant increases in output levels*   Between 1989 and 1995 the traffic volumes in ton-kilometres of domestic public road freight transport increased

by 52 per cent, from 107,243 to 162,827 million ton-kilometres, while real GDP grew by only 13 per cent. The average annual increase per year since reforms began, at 8.6 per cent per year, is more than double that during the 1980 to 1989 pre-reform period (3.4 per cent per year). The average distance carried increased by almost 30 per cent after having been roughly constant for the previous nine years since 1980. A similar picture arises based on the volume of freight hauled. Between 1989 and 1995, there was an 18 per cent increase in domestic road freight transported. The average annual increase since reforms began, at 3 per cent, is also greater than during the pre-reform period (at 2.5 per cent per year).[9] In comparing these two series of output-related statistics, although both increased significantly more during the post-reform period, distances travelled increased substantially more than volumes carried, in effect longer trips to new and further locations. Trucking companies also increased their national reach: most survey respondents indicated that they opened offices in states where they did not operate before the reforms.

*Fall in prices*     Rate analysts in SCT found that between 1987 and 1994, nationwide trucking rates declined 23 per cent in real terms. One SCT official estimated that in 1994, general trucking cargo rates on the major route between Laredo and Mexico City were approximately 30 per cent lower in real terms than the prevailing rates in 1987.[10] Another study concludes that while there is only incidental and anecdotal evidence on changes in truck tariffs, the evidence indicates a 25 per cent reduction in real terms.[11]

The substantial reduction in overall tariff levels documented in available nationwide studies is corroborated by the present survey. Almost all downstream users of trucking services interviewed reported that the cost of hiring a truck had fallen in real terms since 1989. Estimates of the size of the decline generally ranged between 5 and 15 per cent. More careful probing of additional exogenous factors confirms that real prices of trucking services have declined significantly, although the magnitude of the price change is difficult to quantify given the variations in the actual service provided. For instance, one shipper estimated that an additional 20 per cent price fall for the originally-available service should be attributed to the higher-quality levels now available, including newer trucks, faster delivery, and more-reliable shipping facilitated by more sophisticated tracking systems. Another shipper estimated that the price fall would have been even more substantial if it did not incorporate the effect of new toll roads, which he estimated added 6 per cent to the cost of a typical trip.

## Innovations and productivity

*Large trucking firms adopt innovations*     Survey results indicate that a substantial amount of innovation in the industry has occurred, with almost all 'better-practice' logistics improvements introduced only after 1990. Importantly, sophisticated technological innovations have been almost exclusively adopted by larger firms. All large trucking companies have modernized their fleet, with most buying new trucks with electronic combustion systems to minimize the use of fuel. Over 80 per cent of the firms adopting a standardized process for the purchase, maintenance and resale of trucks were larger carriers. Most large companies also have taken advantage of computer systems to improve administrative controls and to upgrade their communications systems with customers through Internet use.

*Small trucking firms struggle to survive*   The contrast with small firms is extremely stark. Some small firms reported that they have not introduced any innovations since 1989, while others have introduced limited innovations, such as radio communications or limited improvements in office equipment.[12] Only two out of the six small firms interviewed have been able to invest in fleet modernization and computer systems. Their planned innovations are more modest in scope, limited to modernization of existing equipment.

*Greater client responsiveness*   Perhaps even more important than operational innovations, trucking companies introduced significant innovations in their responsiveness to the needs of downstream users. This has been the most widespread new practice, instituted by over two-thirds of all carriers surveyed in the years 1993, 1995 and 1997. Again, over two-thirds of the carriers introducing these innovations were larger firms.

*Productivity on the rise*   These innovations appear to have had a significant impact on productivity in the industry. Nationwide statistics indicate that productivity as measured by output per employee increased substantially. Traffic volumes measured in ton-kilometres increased by 8.6 per cent per year since 1989, and measured in tons, by 3 per cent per year. As shown below, employment increased at less than 1 per cent per year. Another measurable dimension of productivity change, the average age of the entire nationwide power units fleet (tractors for pulling trailers and integrated tractor-trailers, including an overwhelming majority of older owner-operated vehicles) has also improved, though only slightly. The average age fell from roughly 14 years in 1990 to 13 years in 1997. Purchases of new, more technologically advanced equipment fell drastically during the debt crisis years of 1995 and 1996, but have again begun to increase. Projections of future purchases and renovations anticipate the average fleet age falling to roughly six years over the next decade.[13]

## Profits, wages and employment

*Sharp falls in profit margins especially by smaller firms*    Survey results indicate that profits (defined as pre-tax operating income as a percentage of revenues) fell substantially in the industry. Between 1989 and 1997, five out of six small carriers experienced profit declines, generally in the order of 50 per cent. In contrast, three out of eight large firms experienced profit declines, generally in the order of 30 per cent; three out of eight large firms reported no change in profit levels; and one reported an increase in profit margins.[14] These results suggest that in general, small firms were forced to sacrifice to stay in the market, while aggressive large firms responded to stiffer competition by offering differentiated quality of service.

*Labour reallocation in favour of larger firms*    Between 1989 and 1995, nationwide road freight statistics indicate a 5.2 per cent (or roughly 0.9 per cent per year) employment increase in the industry, from 509.5 to 536.1 thousand average annual remunerated employees. This masks a surprising 9 per cent increase during the first two years of reform, between 1989 and 1991, followed by relative stagnation between 1991 and 1993, an upturn in 1994, and then a sizeable decline in 1995 alongside the general macroeconomic downturn associated with the debt crisis.[15] The survey results suggest that there was a substantial reallocation of employment in the industry. Incumbent small firms generally remained small, either contracting or expanding by a few workers. Among large firms, the less-agile ones substantially decreased their workforce. One firm reduced its workforce by three-quarters, from 1000 to 250 workers. More-aggressive large firms expanded substantially. One such firm grew from 150 to 720 workers and another from 180 to 447.

### Impact on Downstream Industries

The survey of users of trucking services focused on three broad types of industries as representative of different types of common users in Mexico: agro-industrial, electronics and auto-parts firms. In addition, two companies that specialize in the import and distribution of general goods were also interviewed. The anticompetitive impact of the old regulations on downstream firms was particularly severe, with adverse effects on inventory levels held by user firms, forgone revenues from new products and forgone cost savings from outsourcing, and more generally obstacles to intense rivalry in downstream markets.

### Costs

Many factors affect the inflation-adjusted cost of trucking services faced by downstream user firms. Substantial improvements in quality following regulatory reform, including reductions in delivery times and transit losses, have positively affected the basic product provided, especially for intensive users. This complicates the assessment of cost impact.

Six of seven intensive users reported that delivery times have decreased substantially, on average 40 per cent, with the impact directly linked to trucking deregulation. The key factors cited as responsible for the decrease were better equipment and fewer stops taken by drivers. Among the eight non-intensive users, delivery times decreased for two and remained unchanged for four.

Five of seven intensive users reported that transit losses have also decreased substantially, on average 35 per cent. Improved equipment and better security provided on federal roads (especially on toll roads) were cited as the main reasons. Transit-related losses also declined for three non-intensive users, and remained unchanged for four.

Reduced inventory levels have led to cost savings for four out of 12 responding firms, all four being intensive users. More reliable and rapid transport services permit users to use more intensively both just-in-time delivery of raw materials, parts and components, and build-to-order manufacturing for outbound shipments. One agro-industry firm reported that in spite of increased sales, inbound inventory levels have fallen on average from 45 to 18 days, while inventories of finished goods have fallen from seven to three days.

Four of the users reported that direct trucking costs fell in real terms, three of which were intensive users. Reported cost decreases related to trucking ranged from 33 to 15 to 5 per cent. However, even users reporting increases of 5 or 15 per cent in real terms acknowledged the importance of reversing factors such as increases in the cost of toll roads or higher-quality trucking services, as reflected in more rapid delivery times and significantly lower transit losses.

### Innovations and new products

Since the onset of regulatory reform, a number of intensive users have reported that as a direct result of lower-cost or higher-quality trucking services, they can now deliver new products to market. 'New' products include those that were not previously available on the market due to prohibitively high cost or inflexible transportation services, as well as existing products that can be shipped to new areas or can be delivered in new forms (direct to customer rather than via wholesalers or retailers).

An expanded range of products has been offered by eight of 13 respondents, including four of the seven intensive users. For instance, a fertilizer producer reported that it had increased the number of products sold from 12 to 32, with sales of new products accounting for 30 per cent of total current sales. Seventy per cent of this increase was directly attributable to lower-cost and higher-quality trucking services; the remainder was attributable to growth in demand due to the higher level of fertilizer use in Mexican fields. Another example is that faster delivery times have helped a tequila producer expand its number of separate brands from three to 45, with average delivery times falling by 20 per cent. Half of this decline in delivery time is directly attributed to faster trucking services, while the other half is attributed to faster loading and unloading at warehouses and ports.

The main impact of improvements in trucking services for four of 12 survey respondents has been increased sales of existing products to new areas. A large Mexican producer of time-sensitive electronic components used by other downstream firms attributes 30 per cent of expanded sales (which account for 50 per cent of current total sales) to higher-quality trucking services. Other explanatory factors behind the increase in new clients are NAFTA-related tax changes and additional internal logistics-related changes, such as the intro-duction of bar code tags and computerized systems for faster and more reliable documentation handling. Another example is that for a company specializing in the production and distribution of Mexican peppers, 90 per cent of total sales is sales in new areas. Improvements in the quality of trucking services have resulted in a reduction in losses from transit-related problems from 5 to 4 per cent of now-higher total sales, and a 10 per cent reduction in delivery times. This has reportedly played a significant role in generating expanded sales.

Direct delivery to retailers or end-users has allowed some user companies to realize higher net margins. For instance, an agro-industry firm experienced an improvement of approximately 0.4 per cent in its operating margin, which it attributed to direct delivery. The benefit followed from the joint impact of new end-user customers receiving direct deliveries and higher net margins on such direct sales (after controlling for other factors that could also have accounted for increased direct deliveries).

**More-efficient logistics systems**

Less-costly, more-customer-responsive trucking services have led to a number of other logistics-related innovations within user firms, such as concentrating manufacturing and warehousing in fewer locations, which has led to cost savings. Controlling for other factors such as changes in demand and rail shipping, the joint impact of these changes was in the order of a 0.6 per cent improvement in a specific intensive user's operating margin.

Rationalizing loads, both through adopting standard lot sizes and container-ization, has led to further cost savings for some user firms. Containerization, in turn, contributes both to less-costly transport and decreased damages and losses during transit. A number of firms reported cost savings from these logistics-related changes, which have generally been introduced in the post-deregulation period.

A third logistics-related innovation is the emergence of two large integrated logistics companies, each with about one million square feet of warehousing space.

### Additional Economywide Impacts

#### Outsourcing and enhanced rivalry
The absence of a well-functioning market in a variety of infrastructure services essential for entrepreneurial activity requires firms to establish in-house capabilities or forgo production. The alternative to purchasing road freight transport services responsive to specific user needs on the open market is to invest and maintain a private own-account fleet of trucks. From an industrywide perspective, the high fixed costs of doing so may be prohibitive for cash-starved new entrepreneurs. Although such costs are not largely sunk, tapping capital markets may not be an option for prospective entrants lacking reputation. An important additional benefit of a more-competitive trucking market, therefore, is to allow firms to outsource their transport requirements, in effect converting a fixed cost into a variable cost. The benefits from enhanced new entry and rivalry for markets which make intensive use of trucking services are likely to be substantial.

#### Other benefits
As a result of reductions in truck tariffs, SECOFI has estimated that between 1987 and 1994, the overall distribution costs of commodities in Mexico has declined by approximately 25 per cent in real terms. Deregulation of trucking has also had an impact on the once publicly owned railway company, Ferrocarriles Nacionales de Mexico (FNM). The reduction of trucking rates after 1989 enabled truckers to compete more effectively with FNM. This caused a diversion from rail to truck transport, particularly during the 1989–91 period, when rail traffic declined significantly.

## C.  POLICY LESSONS FOR REFORM

Following deregulation and Mexico's entry into NAFTA, the Mexican trucking sector has been experiencing a radical transformation. Regulatory reform has increased competition. It has had the least impact on small shippers, whose market was already competitive, and included a large number of illegal owner–operators. Medium-size and large-size shippers, however, could take advantage of regulatory reform to reduce their trucking costs. The overall decrease in trucking prices has caused inefficient operators with inadequate equipment to exit the market. Regulatory reform has also impacted large shippers, who are willing to pay higher prices for the faster and more-reliable service that they require. Under the former rigid regulation regime, no carrier had the incentive to offer high-quality services. NAFTA has affected this market segment most significantly, as closer trading ties to the US has caused Mexican firms to upgrade their logistics operations. Large carriers, often as partners of US trucking companies, have begun to offer improved services.

The main policy lessons from Mexico's experience in deregulating this sector include:

- Increased competition in the road freight industry has played a positive role in fostering economywide innovation and growth. In addition to gains from lower trucking prices, the removal of access barriers to transport infrastructure generates substantial downstream benefits, facilitating entry and new products. Delivery times and transit losses have decreased substantially. More reliable and rapid transport services have permitted user companies to reduce inventory levels and make more intensive use of both just-in-time delivery of raw materials, parts and components, as well as build-to-order manufacturing for outbound shipments. More importantly, faster and more-reliable trucking has allowed user companies to offer 'new' goods, both previously unavailable products as well as existing products reaching new areas. More customer-responsive trucking services have reportedly also led to a number of other logistics-related innovations within user firms, such as centralizing manufacturing and rationalizing loads. Finally, some user firms have outsourced their transport requirements, in effect converting a fixed into a variable cost and thereby lowering entry barriers significantly.

- Successful reform requires careful planning, execution and high-level political support. To bring about reform of existing regulations and to introduce increased competition, a strategy is needed which takes account of key interested stakeholders, both supporters and opponents. In the late 1980s, transport regulation in Mexico was viewed with growing disdain, particularly as a result of studies documenting the high economic costs associated with the prevailing system. The concurrent general programme of structural reform was a favourable context for regulatory reform of the trucking industry. Given the potential for blockage of reforms by the trucking chamber and its members, who had been benefiting from the officially-sanctioned cartel, certain key planning and implementation steps were taken. First, the initial reform was planned by a small group independent from the oversight ministry (where some officials who traditionally had client relations with truckers or feared losing their positions could have sabotaged the initiative). Second, the reforms were presented to recalcitrant truckers as a 'modernization' effort, rather than as an effort to eliminate oligopoly and promote competition. Soft loans for fleet modernization were offered in exchange for the chamber's non-opposition. Third, deregulation was sequenced, with entry restrictions eliminated first, followed by tariff ceilings. This was designed to prevent a possible consumer backlash if the forces of competition had been too weak initially to prevent sharp price rises. Finally, unconditional support was secured from the highest political levels, in this case directly from the president.

- The competition agency has a critical role to play in any regulatory reform initiative, both in terms of *ex ante* advocacy and *ex post* enforcement. The national competition agency should play a critical role to help lay the groundwork for reform. It should make a strong case that the costs of the pre-reform regime are excessive, and the expected benefits of reform are high. It can do so through media relations and systematic relationships with representatives of consumer and producer interests, including chambers of commerce, small business and entrepreneurship organizations, consumer protection institutions, consumer groups, local training and research institutes and other relevant interested parties. Following reform, the competition agency should strictly enforce competition laws to ensure that cosy cartel-like behaviour stimulated by tight entry restrictions does not persist. Public policies of segmentation and price and quantity controls naturally leave a strong imprint on post-reform market conduct. The competition agency must ensure that inefficient, anticompetitive public regulation is not replaced by socially inappropriate anticompetitive interfirm agreements. The experience of Mexico is instructive in this regard. At least three separate strong interventions were required by the Mexican Federal Competition Commission to discipline attempted anticompetitive practices by the trucking industry in the years following the initial regulatory reforms.

## NOTES

1. The materials are based on work prepared under funding from the World Bank research preparation grant 'Competition and barriers to entrepreneurship' (RPO-682–57), as reported in Mark Dutz, Aydin Hayri and Pablo Ibarra, 'Regulatory Reform, Competition and Innovation: A Case Study of the Mexican Road Freight Industry', (Policy Research Working Papers No. 2318, World Bank, Washington, DC, 2000). This research reflects the work of the authors and does not reflect the views and policies of the World Bank or the countries it represents.
2. Aghion and Schankerman explore analytically how improved infrastructure availability affects the intensity of downstream competition by facilitating entry, expansion and restructuring of more-efficient relative to less-efficient firms. Philippe Aghion and Mark Schankerman, 'Competition, Entry and the Social Returns to Infrastructure in Transition Economies', 7 *The Economics of Transition* 79 (1999).
3. See Arturo Fernandez, 'Trucking Deregulation in Mexico', in *Regulatory Reform in Transport: Some Recent Experiences* 105 (Jose Carbajo, ed., Washington, DC: World Bank, 1993).

4. See 'Report and Recommendation of the President – Mexico: Road Transport and Telecommunications Sector Adjustment Project 14', World Bank Report No. P-5254-ME (1990). Discussion of intrastate trucking is outside the scope of this chapter.
5. This decision was based on arguments of divergent coordination in standards, lack of security in Mexican main highways and low technology of Mexican carriers. See Alejandro Ibarra-Yunez, 'Dominant Firm and Company Integration: The Case of Transportation in Mexico and the US', 2 *Latin American Business Review* 6 (1999).
6. Some specific products such as corn, wheat, rice, sorghum, sugar, salt, cement, coarse sand, gravel, sulphur, coal, raw oil and gasoline were subject to an 8 per cent discount that functioned as a cross-subsidy.
7. World Bank 1990 Report, *supra* note 4, at 19.
8. For a description of the methodology, data and more detailed results, see Dutz et al., *supra* note 1.
9. See *Manual Estadistico del Sector Transporte 1995* (Statistical manual of the transport sector 1995), Tables 4.1.1–2, Instituto Mexicano del Transporte, Secretaria de Communicaciones y Transportes (1997).
10. 'Performance Audit Report – Mexico: Road Transport and Telecommunications Sector Adjustment Loan 29', World Bank Report No. 14400 (1995).
11. 'Mexico: The End of Transition – A Review of the Transport Sector 8', World Bank Report No. 12654–ME (1994).
12. This finding of low or no investment in technological upgrading by smaller firms is consistent with the findings of an earlier survey by Ibarra-Yunez, *supra* note 5, at 21, which concludes: 'reputation, differentiation of service or quality were not evidenced by the survey from the residual carriers of short hauls'.
13. This estimate is based on information elaborated by CANACAR from historical 1990–97 data from SCT and ANPACT (Asociacion Nacional de Productores de Autobuses, Camiones y Tractores: National Association of Producers of Buses, Trucks and Tractors).
14. These findings of low profits even for large firms may be at least in part driven by deterioration in macroeconomic conditions as a result of the 1995 debt crisis. Prior to that downturn, an earlier survey of 13 carriers found an average pre-tax profitability of 17 per cent between 1993 and 1994. In contrast, average profitability in the US sector of large carriers was close to 21 per cent between 1989 and 1994. A similar substantial variation in profitability between large firms was found in that survey, with the leading carrier showing 12 per cent growth in profitability between 1993 and 1994, while the poorest performer registered a fall of 25 per cent. See Ibarra-Yuncz, *supra* note 5, at 18.
15. See IMT, *supra* note 9, Table 1.1.4.

## OTHER REFERENCES

Capalleja, Dávila, 'El tratado Trilateral de Libre Comercio en Materia de Transporte de Carga' (The trilateral treaty of free trade in road transport), in *Lo Negociado del TLC* (Mexico City, 1995).

Capalleja, Dávila and Enrique Rafael, 'La Reglamentación del Autotransporte de Carga en México' (The regulation of road transport of cargo in Mexico), in *El Efecto de la Regulación en Algunos Sectores de la Economía Mexicana* (The effect on the Mexican economy of regulation in several sectors) (Francisco Gil Díaz and Arturo Fernández, eds, ITAM-CINDE-FCE: Lecturas de El Trimestre Economico No. 70, Mexico City, 1994).

Comisión Federal de Competencia (Federal Competition Commission), *Informe Annual de Competencia Económica 1995–1996* (Annual report of economic competition) (1996).

Giermanski, James, 'Texas to Mexico: A Border to Avoid' (unpublished mimeo on file with Texas A&M International University, US, 26 September, 1995).

Islas, Victor, *Estructura y Desarrollo del Sector Transporte en Mexico* (1990).

Martinez, Gabriel and Guillermo Farber, *Desregulacion Economica (1989–1993)* (1994).

Rico, Oscar, 'Algunos Indicadores de la Evolución de las Empresas de Autotransporte de Carga en Mexico, 1988–1993', in 31 *Notas* (1996).

Secretaría de Comunicaciones y Transportes, *Estadísticas Básicas del Autotransporte Federal* (1996).

Sempe Minvielle, Carlos, *Tecnica Legislativa y Desregulacion* (1997).

US Department of Transportation, *Census Surface Trade Flow Data* (1996).

# 13. Local public services in Italy: make, buy or leave it to the market?

## Alberto Heimler

*This chapter focuses on how to assure efficiency (that is, high quality and low cost) in the provision of local public services. Local governments should intervene in the marketplace whenever the competitive system is unable to satisfy requirements of general interest that the government intends to pursue, both with respect to public goods (for example, street lighting, street cleaning, traffic control, local police service, fire protection and the sewer system) and non-public goods (for example, local transport, health services, waste disposal, baker services, cemeteries, recreational services, nursing homes, water, gas and electricity). Some of these services are already supplied by the market, although perhaps not at the desired level of price or quality. Local governments must decide whether they should directly provide them, contract them out, allow them to be supplied competitively by the market, or provide them in competition with the private sector.*

*In a world of perfect information, internal provision and contracting out lead to the same outcome. However, information is not perfect because the government is never able to write a complete contract, and many goods or services have characteristics, such as quality, that are not verifiable* ex post. *Public provision of services is preferable when the cost from unverifiable reduction in quality is high, the probability of innovation is limited, the establishment of a reputation as high-quality provider is not important, competition is weak and consumer choices are ineffective.*

*In Italy, it is difficult to induce public firms to maintain quality and minimize costs, because local taxes are generally administered centrally, and the effects of any savings at local level are felt nationally rather than locally. Consequently, cost efficiency is not an issue in local elections or local government actions. Rather, attention is more likely to be paid to quality of services. Under the classical theory of fiscal federalism, giving local governments responsibility for their budget is the best way to induce them to behave efficiently, because the democratic process disciplines local politicians. This would enable them to choose which services the local government should provide, and which it should contract out.*

To enhance efficiency in the provision of local services, the Italian government has recently proposed to auction the right to provide local services for a specified period of time. Auctions would create competition for the market, which can be an effective substitute for competition in the market whenever regulation is unnecessary after a firm wins the auction. They are most appropriate when a long-term contract is offered, as the firm will make verifiable investments in factors such as machinery or rolling stock. At the end of the licence period, the firm is unlikely to make investments because they will be lost when the contract ends. Accordingly, auctions are the preferred solution for services with low sunk investments, especially if companies can move and provide the service elsewhere if they lose the licence (for example, waste disposal and local transport). In contrast, privatization would be the preferred solution for services with considerable sunk investments (for example, electricity and gas distribution, water supply).

## INTRODUCTION

Local governments provide the population with a number of services that are or could be paid by each consumer according to the quantity consumed, such as public transport, waste disposal, health services, day-care services, water supply, cemeteries and, in some cases, gas and electricity. They also supply public goods, such as street lighting and cleaning, traffic control, local police services, fire protection, sewage systems and so on, and they perform administrative functions both for individuals and enterprises. Which of these services should be provided directly by the government, assigned to a licensee or supplied by private firms in competition with each other is an open question that has, in the past, received many different answers.

For example, 50 years ago, economists were suspicious when they observed any form of externality or monopoly power, and they invariably thought it necessary for governments to intervene. In both such circumstances, they generally advocated nationalization and public ownership.[1] Simons, a free market economist who none the less accepted and promoted public ownership of public utilities, believed that nationalization would, by itself, eliminate the profit motive from managers' actions, turning natural monopolies into companies that would maximize consumer welfare. Starting from the 1950s, economists in the US began slowly to convert to a free market ideology, believing that private firms would achieve an efficient allocation of resources also in circumstances where monopolistic conditions prevailed. In such cases, if the market power originated from a natural monopoly, the solution would be regulation.

In contrast, in Europe, the best form of control of market power by natural monopolies was still considered to be nationalization, the benefits of which were accepted without proof. In many countries, this led to a production structure where the role of the state was quite substantial in the provision of both private and public goods. Only with the collapse of the communist economies did the case for nationalization weaken, and the number of advocates for privatization of public enterprises has increased geometrically in recent years. Government and markets are not necessarily substitutes. For example, certain public goods (such as roads) clearly facilitate the operation of markets. More generally, there is a tradeoff between private and public ownership in terms of costs and benefits, which depends on the specific characteristics of the product being supplied. Efficiency in the functioning of government institutions should also be taken into account.

The issue is not whether a market should be regulated, but given that the government intends to finance the provision of certain services, what the best way is for the government to achieve its goals. Should it contract the service out or provide the service itself? The problem is similar to the one addressed by Coase with respect to the boundaries of the firm.[2] In the case of public services, the questions asked by Coase could be restated in the following manner: What services should the local government itself provide? For natural monopolies, should there be state production or a regulated private monopoly? Should central or local governments decide on how local services are to be organized? These are the general questions this chapter will address.

## A.   WHAT LOCAL SERVICES SHOULD PUBLIC FIRMS PROVIDE?

Local governments, like central governments, should intervene in the market only to the extent that the competitive system is unable to satisfy public requirements that the government intends to pursue. The government must supply public goods, because the amount otherwise supplied by the market would be less than socially optimal.[3] For example, police services, street cleaning and lighting, road services, traffic control, fire protection and sewer systems all fall within this category.[4] Local governments must decide whether they should provide these services directly or license them out to the private sector.

Local governments supply other services that are not pure public goods, such as local transport, health services, waste disposal, day-care services, cemeteries, recreational services, nurseries, water, gas and electricity. In principle, the market should supply some of these services. Others have a natural monopoly component, such as the distribution network in water, gas, electricity and local rail services, that would allow only for a partial opening up to competition. For these, local governments must decide whether to provide the services directly or to regulate a private firm (that is, purchase the services from the private sector).

For services that have no natural monopoly component, government intervention (such as licensing) may be justified when local governments are pursuing goals that the market would be unable to attain on its own. For example, by introducing competition, the regularity of local bus transport services could be disrupted,[5] or a negative externality from waste disposal or cemetery services could cause social harm, or universal service may not be provided. Should this group of services be supplied directly by the local government or contracted out to the private sector? If the latter, should there be one or a number of licences?

A final category of services is those provided by local governments in competition with the private sector, such as health-care services, nurseries, day-care centres, recreational services and swimming pools. In contrast to the other local services mentioned above, the market already supplies these services, although maybe not at the desired price or quality level. Whether local governments should provide these services directly, or whether the local governments' goals should be attained through specific subsidies, leaving actual production to the market, is a problem that is certainly relevant for local governments, but will not be addressed in this chapter.

## Models of Government Behaviour

The various models of how governments behave may help determine what local services governments should provide. The 'helping hand' model is based on the assumption that governments maximize social welfare, and therefore intervene in order to eliminate alleged market failures. Experience has shown the falsity of this premise. It is now clear that governments intervene in order to pursue their political agenda, which only occasionally coincides with social welfare.

In contrast, under the '*laissez-faire*' model, scepticism of governments' ability to pursue social welfare leads to almost complete reliance on markets. Government intervention is justified under this model only with respect to law, order and national defence.

Recently, the 'grabbing hand' model has been defined by Schleifer and Vishny,[6] based on earlier work by Olson[7] and Becker.[8] Like the *laissez-faire* model, it is sceptical of the benefits of government intervention. However, it 'focuses more constructively on the design of reforms'.[9] Based on the political economy of decision making, it focuses on the day-to-day activities of government. It seeks to ensure that in practice, taking into account all possible constraints on decision making, decisions lead to efficient solutions.

## Ownership of Assets

In a world of perfect information, it would not matter whether the provision of services were carried out directly by government or contracted out to the private sector. The local government would either enter a contract that fully covers the provision of the service with an outside producer, or instruct the appropriate local government branch to provide the service. Accordingly, the question of who should provide the service would be irrelevant.

Public versus private ownership of assets becomes an important issue when the government is unable to write and enforce a complete contract. The government may know exactly what is needed, but it may be impossible to verify some dimensions of the service *ex post*. If contracts are incomplete (which in fact is always the case), the ownership of assets becomes important because it determines who benefits from *ex post* bargaining over situations not covered by the contract.[10] For example, property rights are important for ensuring that innovation is carried out. As Shleifer[11] states: '[O]wnership strengthens the owner's incentives to make investments that improve or reduce the costs of using the assets, because the owner has the power to reap more of the rewards on these innovations'.

Government ownership of enterprises is problematic because the ultimate ownership is diffuse, which weakens the incentives for cost minimization and innovation. Often, government enterprises dissipate rents with other participants in the production process, such as workers, managers and suppliers, so that profits do not accrue to the owners (the public). Thus, in the absence of concentrated ownership, the incentive for innovation and cost minimization is strongly reduced.

Contracts are often incomplete in that they do not specify an objective and verifiable minimum quality standard, leaving regulators with problems of enforcing such minimum standards. If a contract cannot assure a required level of quality, a private firm would always have the incentive to cut costs by reducing the quality of service provided. For example, with respect to nursing homes and prisons, private employers subject to price regulation would reduce the quality of services, serving food of lower quality or employing low-wage personnel who would mistreat the elderly or prisoners.

One possible solution is to eliminate the private firm's incentive to cut costs through a contract that provides that the firm will be compensated for all its costs. Under such a contract, the firm would have low incentives for both cutting costs and enhancing quality. It would, however, always have the incentive to increase costs, leading to monopolistic rents. In such circumstances, the government would have the incentive to monitor all expenditure decisions. Private ownership would then acquire all the characteristics of public ownership.

It is not always the case that when a contract does not effectively specify a minimum quality standard, the private supplier will provide low-quality services. If it is possible to introduce competition in the market, then suppliers will have an incentive to improve quality in order to attract more customers. Thus, competition among private suppliers is one solution to the quality reduction problem. Furthermore, even without direct competitors, a private firm may be motivated to maintain or improve quality because this might enhance their reputation as a high-quality service provider. If the incentives are correctly established, firms with a good reputation for high-quality services may be in a better position to win additional contracts, or have their contract renewed when it expires.

Finally, private provision of services may be preferable because it will enhance the possibilities of innovation. If there is a potential for innovation, a private firm will have the incentive to do so. A government-owned firm, in contrast, will be more reluctant, because it will be unable directly to enjoy the benefits from the innovation.

As Schleifer has suggested,[12] these considerations imply that public provision is superior to private provision of local services only when: (a) the opportunity for cost reduction stemming from a decrease in non-contractible quality is high; (b) the probability of product or process innovation is limited; (c) gaining reputation as an efficient service provider is unimportant; and (d) competition is weak and consumer choice is ineffective. Not many services fulfil all of these prerequisites.

## B. ENSURING EFFICIENCY IN THE PROVISION OF LOCAL SERVICES

The democratic process is designed to ensure that voters reward local politicians for the benefits they receive in return for their vote, such as lower taxes, better services, less corruption, a cleaner environment, less disorder in urban development and so on. If voters are rational and well informed, they will reward efficiency in the provision of local services if this has a positive effect on their taxes, and local politicians will be motivated to minimize costs and achieve balanced budgets in these circumstances. However, local services are often financed through the national budget rather than the local budget, and local governments often do not control the level of local taxation. In such circumstances, voters will not see themselves as benefiting from efficiency in the provision of local services. Rather, they will see themselves as benefiting only from improvements in quality.

The classical theory of fiscal federalism holds that in order to induce local governments to behave efficiently in the provision of local services, they should be given responsibility for their budget. This principle of subsidiarity, or 'the locals know best' rule, is applicable only when the benefits are concentrated at the local level. If there are wider effects, higher levels of government should have decision-making authority. Indeed, the level of government responsible for decision making should be defined in relation to the geographic extension of the benefits originating from public services. A study by Lopez de Silanes, Shleifer and Vishny demonstrated that in the US, local governments face a tradeoff between the political benefits of in-house provision of services, and the pressure to curb government spending, originating from 'clean government' state laws.[13] The higher this pressure, the more frequently they decide to contract out. This implies that if central government decides that efficiency should be improved at all levels of government, it should make each government level responsible not only for spending, but also for revenues, to the extent this is possible. Local governments (and their voters) would then decide how to allocate scarce resources in the best possible way, in accordance with local characteristics. Discipline must otherwise be imposed centrally, which is less effective, and is sometimes at the expense of local autonomy and local consensus.

In a recent draft law on local services presented to the Italian parliament, the Italian government was unable or unwilling to give local governments greater independence in spending and taxation. Rather, it has attempted to require that the right to provide major local public services should be subject to competitive tendering, irrespective of local specific conditions and voter preferences. In 1985 in the UK, local authorities were subjected to a competitive tendering requirement for a number of activities or services.[14] As Figure 13.1 demonstrates, Italy and the UK are two of the countries where municipalities have the lowest fiscal autonomy among OECD countries. Thus, it is not surprising that they chose to impose discipline in spending centrally.

It would be more efficient to give local governments greater discretion over the make-or-buy decision. The local authorities' low level of control over their budget makes it unlikely, however, that local governments, in the tradeoff between political patronage and efficiency, would opt in favour of efficiency. The lower the fiscal responsibility of local governments, the more important it is for central governments to impose efficiency as the objective. But a rule to contract out the provision of local services is a partial measure that does not necessarily lead to overall efficiency in local government behaviour.[15]

The lack of financial responsibility by local governments in Italy can be explained by analysing the proportion of costs covered by revenues for major public local services. Only in the case of gas and electricity distribution do revenues exceed costs (which does not necessarily imply that production is carried out efficiently, but only that pricing is cost orientated). Most other

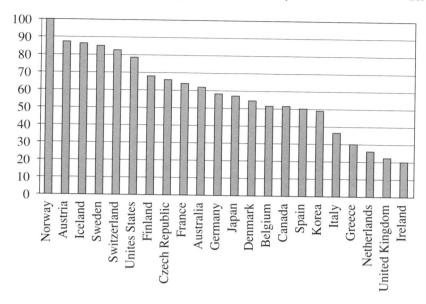

*Note*:  Total receipts minus transfers from other levels of government. All data for 1996 except Spain, Italy, Greece, Ireland (1995) and the Czech Republic (1994).

*Source*:  National Accounts. Countries omitted where information is not available. Taken from Biggar, see note 14.

*Figure 13.1*   *'Own receipts' at the local level as a percentage of total local receipts, 1996*

services are run with a huge loss, suggesting that political patronage is more important than efficiency. For services that are financed through taxation, such as waste disposal, revenues only represent approximately 90 per cent of costs. For others, such as local transport, revenues cover less than 25 per cent of costs. The difference between revenues and costs for local services is for the most part covered by general taxation, administered at the national level. The local voter is not involved and would not gain anything (indeed would lose) from an increase of the coverage ratio. (See Table 13.1.)

The existing system of local government financing in Italy is geared towards political patronage, enhancing the propensity of local administrators to spend, while not rewarding financial responsibility. This must be reversed, and the system should be reformed to promote efficiency and financial responsibility, increasingly shifting the expense of local services to the local communities.

*Table 13.1     Major local public services in Italy, 1994*

| Services | Diffusion (population share %) | Total expenditure (billions of lire) | Coverage ratio (revenues/ costs %) |
|---|---|---|---|
| Water supply | 100 | 4432 | 86 |
| Cemeteries | 100 | 691 | 35 |
| Sewage system | 100 | 1267 | 50 |
| Street lighting | 100 | 1478 | 0 |
| Waste collection | 100 | 7000 | 92 |
| Local transports | 90 | not available | 24 |
| Funeral services | 63 | 116 | 124 |
| Day-care centres | 61 | 1050 | 33 |
| Gas distribution | 47 | 5003 | 116 |
| Theatres, museums | 38 | 332 | 30 |
| Hotels and nursing-homes | 31 | 828 | 68 |
| Electricity | 17 | 2076 | 122 |

*Source*:   Enea-Nomisma, *Rapporto sui servizi pubblici locali in Italia* (Report on local public services in Italy) (Rome, 1999).

## C.   AUCTIONS, PRIVATIZATION AND EFFICIENCY

The auction system that the proposed new legislation would introduce in Italy would eliminate the possibility that local governments would directly provide services such as waste disposal, local transport, gas and electricity distribution, and water supply. Auctions would replace decisions by administrators, even in cities where services might already be efficiently provided. Although in some (rare) cases, auctions might not lead to greater efficiency, this proposal is generally sound, given the country's institutional structure and the difficulties involved in achieving a decentralized fiscal discipline. It is questionable, however, whether auctions are the right solution or whether other instruments could have been used. In any event, under present circumstances it would be far more difficult to give financial autonomy to local governments than to impose efficiency considerations from the centre.

Local services are not all equal. Some involve non-contractible sunk investments while others do not. If non-contractible sunk investments are important but the services do not have the characteristics described in Section A (Ownership of assets) above (as in gas and electricity distribution, water supply and local rail transport), then these services could still be contracted out. Policy makers must then decide whether the licence should have an infinite time horizon or be for a fixed term. The crucial issue in this regard is the extent to which inefficiencies might appear near the end of the licence term. In particular, such inefficiencies result from a company's failure to make efficiency-improving investments (in capital goods, training, restructuring and so on) whenever necessary. Whatever the length of the licence term, near its end, the incentive to invest (even in maintenance) will substantially decrease, leading to distortions and disadvantages for consumers. The possibility of a payback by the new entrant is generally not sufficient to eliminate the distortions. A new entrant would be unable to pay especially for the non-capital investments, which are probably even more important than the capital investments,[16] given the difficulties involved in determining the exact amount. This is why when sunk investments are substantial, permanent licences (and the possibilities they provide for expansions, mergers and acquisitions) are more efficient than fixed-term licences. In such circumstances, privatization of the local government-owned company, accompanied by regulation, is more efficient than an auction.

In contrast, if there are no sunk investments, fixed-term licences are efficient because the danger of distortions in the propensity to invest around the end of the licence term would be minimal. Competition for the market can thus be effectively introduced. For instance, an auction to provide waste removal or local transport services would lead to efficient results if the outside contractor providing the services could easily take his/her know-how, equipment and workforce to the next town if he/she does not win the next auction. The possibility of quality reductions due to lack of maintenance at the end of the franchise period would be minimal. The contract should be granted to the bidder that offers to supply the service with the minimum subsidy, and it should have a short time duration. The shorter the licence term, the greater the probability that circumstances will not change, which would necessitate a renegotiation of the level of subsidies or the price. Sunk costs should not be contractually introduced, for example constraining the use of the capital equipment to services provided in a given town.

An auction system may present problems during the franchise period, as the franchisee may threaten the municipality that it cannot guarantee the quality of services as agreed unless subsidies or prices are increased. Given the essential nature of the services (for example, waste disposal or local transport), it is unlikely that a local government (especially one without financial autonomy) would decide to re-tender, given the problems that an interruption of such services would cause. Given this pressure to accommodate any request by an incumbent franchisee, a short-term licence is preferable.[17]

In general, competition for the market is a substitute for competition in the market. In both cases, regulation is unnecessary. If the auction is organized so that the price of the service is fixed and competitors bid for the minimum subsidy required to accept the contract, then there is no need for further regulation. The same is true if the auction is organized so that competitors bid to supply the service at the lowest price, with no subsidy.

The presence of an information asymmetry on the part of potential bidders makes competition for the market less efficient. At the end of its licence period, the incumbent that bids on a new contract may use internal information on the relevant market's cost structure. Other potential bidders may be unwilling to underprice the incumbent, leading to a structural reduction in the number of participants in the tendering process, especially for contracts of a special and unique nature.

The solution is to create local markets that are similar to each other, so that a company operating in one location would have enough information to participate in the tender offer of another location. This is particularly important for large cities, which represent a very small percentage of all municipalities in most countries. If scale economies are not important, a solution would be to divide the city into smaller sections for which separate tenders could be made. This would increase the number of bidders, because even small companies could take part.

If there are sunk investments and municipal companies are privatized, a regulator will be needed to prevent the monopolist from exploiting its market power. To reduce the danger of capture, distance should be created between the regulator and the regulated company. Centralized regulation is therefore preferable, especially when voters do not benefit from cost savings achieved in the provision of local services. Local governments that favour political patronage over efficiency will continue to do so as regulators. Moreover, should local governments eventually be given financial autonomy so that efficiency considerations matter to them, it is preferable that regulators do not exist in every municipality. To guarantee skilful regulatory institutions, the small size of the regulated municipal market may require that such functions be carried out at the regional level, if not centrally.

## D.   LOCAL SERVICES AND COMPETITION

Not all local services are characterized by natural monopoly characteristics. Moreover, some aspects of a given service may be exercised under competitive conditions, while others are intrinsically monopolistic.

Exclusive franchises are normally granted not only to assure protection to a natural monopolist, since it is extremely rare for a competitor efficiently to enter a market that is 'naturally' monopolistic. They are also granted to ensure that a service provider remains profitable should prices be regulated and service obligations be imposed. If tariffs are not designed to cover the costs of the service being provided, but instead are an average of total costs of the service provider, then it is likely that some services will be priced below their incremental costs and other services will be priced above their stand-alone costs. A new entrant, competing away the profits gained on the most profitable service, might prevent the incumbent from continuing to cover its costs at the given prices. In such circumstances, opening the service to competition without a thorough reform of the tariff structure may disrupt universal service. Such a tariff reform is at times politically and technically feasible. In such cases, competition could be an efficient solution. However, should it be impossible to rebalance tariffs, the monopolist must be protected from outside entry.

Even if the service provider is protected from outside entry for its main mission, some of its activities could be opened to competition. For example, although the distribution of electricity, gas and water cannot be opened to competition (a single pipe enters each residence), supply can easily and efficiently be opened to competition. The identification of potentially competitive activities for each local public service must be done on a case-by-case basis. Any competitive activities identified should be liberalized.

It is questionable whether a company that has been granted a special and exclusive right should be allowed to continue supplying a complementary competitive activity and, if so, whether separation should be required.[18] Competition law provisions that prohibit abuse of a dominant position are not always effective in eliminating any possible abuse. A natural monopolist subject to cost-plus regulation might have the incentive artificially to increase costs of the regulated service, in order to cover some of the costs of the competitive activity. The regulated company could thereby supply the potentially competitive activity at prices below average incremental costs, and competitors would be kept out of the market. Predation is not the reason for such a strategy, because it is not directed at gaining monopoly profits when all competitors are eliminated. Government-owned firms (or firms that are completely dependent on a government decision, such as renewal of a licence) very seldom maximize profits. Lott argues that pricing below costs is more likely with government-owned enterprises that are not profit maximizing, but output, employment or revenue maximizing.[19] In such cases, vertical separation eliminates the possibility of such pricing behaviour.

Vertical separation is also necessary to prevent a regulated natural monopolist controlling an essential facility from refusing access to competitors based on objective reasons (such as the absence of capacity), but with anticompetitive effects. Such refusals would be justifiable from a competition policy perspective, but may be the result of strategic decisions by the company controlling the essential facility. For example, an electricity transmission company that is vertically integrated with a generation facility may decide not to enlarge transmission capacity in order to impede entry. In such cases, vertical separation would eliminate the anticompetitive incentives.

On the other hand, if economies of scope are important, then separating the two activities would lead to inefficiencies. Thus, an analysis of the importance of economies of scope is necessary for deciding whether to separate. If significant economies of scope are present, it would be inefficient to separate the competitive activity, and it would be unlikely that a 'competitive' activity would indeed exist, since a firm would be unable to compete successfully without being able to exploit those economies.

## CONCLUSIONS

Local governments supply public and private goods and services, for some of which they operate in competition with private firms, while for others the local government firm is the only supplier.

In the case of natural monopolies, the choice between public or private property is relevant because the structure of managers' incentives is not the same in the two systems. Public firms are less likely to pursue efficiency, instead favouring political patronage. If governments are interested in efficiency, they should encourage private firms to supply local public services. Only when the effect on costs of a reduction of quality is high and quality is non-contractible are public firms more efficient than private ones. If reputation of being a high-quality service provider is important, then a private firm would not have the incentive to reduce quality.

In many countries, municipalities themselves usually supply local public services because the system of incentives is such that for local governments, the tradeoff between political patronage and cost minimization generally favours the former. When local taxes are administered centrally, any savings at the local level produce their effects nationally as opposed to locally. Consequently, cost efficiency in local services is not an issue in local elections, nor in local government actions. Prices and quality are all that matter. In such cases, the optimal solution is as follows:

- Local governments should be given financial autonomy and required to balance their budget. Then, local governments would take the decisions that benefit their citizens, freely choosing which service they should provide themselves and which service they should contract out. Should citizens not be satisfied with the choices local politicians make, they would oust these politicians through the democratic process. If political patronage is pushed to the extreme, local governments may not even be able to ensure the desired level of quality. In such circumstances, some reaction in favour of efficiency is likely, both locally and centrally. Locally, citizens, unsatisfied with the low quality of local services, would demand higher quality. This, in turn, could lead local governments to demand higher transfers from the centre. At the centre, if local fiscal autonomy is difficult to introduce, a possible response is to force some discipline on local governments in order to improve both quality and efficiency. This is what occurred in the UK in 1985 with a law that imposed a tendering process for local services on local governments. The same is happening now in Italy, with a law the government has presented to parliament.

• In these two countries, the chosen solution for local services that cannot be opened up to competition was to introduce competition for the market, which is equivalent to competition in the market. Both lead to productive and allocative efficiency and, in principle, do not require any behavioural regulation. The longer the licence term, however, the greater the need for regulation because unexpected events can occur and the firm may need to renegotiate the terms of providing the service. The shorter the licence term, the more the results of a process of competition *for* the market resemble a competitive system (*in* the market). When there are large, non-contractible sunk costs, it is preferable to give the company a permanent licence. Otherwise, the incentives to invest and to maintain the efficiency of the firm will be strongly distorted close to the end of the licence term and remedies will be difficult to introduce. When there are no sunk costs (and contracts are easily written), competition for the market (and short-term licences) can eliminate the need for regulation. If the local service provider is either privatized or is given a long-term licence, it becomes necessary to regulate.

• If local governments are not given financial autonomy, the regulation of local services should be undertaken from the level of government where efficiency considerations matter most. If local governments are given financial autonomy, regulation can be undertaken locally, choosing a higher level of government only to gain economies of scale in the controlling function. In any case, if a local service or an activity within a local service can be provided under competitive conditions, it should be opened to competition.

• The monopolist should not be allowed to provide the liberalized activity for a number of reasons. First, when it is likely that its objective is not profit, but revenue or employment maximization, anticompetitive cross-subsidization becomes more likely. More-efficient producers may be kept out of the market by having captive consumers pay indefinitely for the difference between costs and revenues in the liberalized activity. Furthermore, a natural monopolist may refuse access to an essential facility based on objective reasons, such as the absence of capacity, that are justifiable from a competition policy perspective. However, such reasons may result from strategic decisions by the company controlling the essential facility. Vertical separation is efficiency enhancing only if the complementary activities do not enjoy significant economies of scope. Otherwise consumers are better off if both activities are supplied by the same concern.

- If economies of scope are present and are of significant magnitude, then the monopolist should be allowed to operate as an integrated concern. The antitrust authority should intervene if prices in the liberalized activity are set below average incremental costs.

## NOTES

1.  See, for example, James Meade, *Planning and the Price Mechanism: The Liberal Socialist Solution* (London: Allen & Unwin 1948); Henry C. Simons, 'A Positive Program for Laissez Faire', in Henry C. Simons, *Economic Policy for a Free Society* (Chicago: University of Chicago Press, 1948).
2.  Ronald Coase, 'The Nature of the Firm', 4 *Economica* 386 (1937).
3.  Pure public goods have the following characteristics: (i) it does not cost anything for an additional individual to enjoy the benefits of that public good; (ii) it is difficult to exclude individuals that have not paid from the enjoyment of a public good.
4.  But see Ronald Coase, 'The Lighthouse in Economics', 17 *Journal of Law and Economics* 357 (1974). Coase shows that the lighthouse system in the UK was set up by private enterprises, and the threat of free-riding did not impede the system from developing. However, Coase did not show that the number of lighthouses actually introduced was sufficient to satisfy demand.
5.  See Claude Henry, 'Competition and the Regulation of Public Utilities in the European Union' (1997) (Laboratoire d'économétrie, École Polytechnique, Paris Working Paper No. 469). Henry cites the report by the Transport Committee of the House of Commons on 'The consequences of bus deregulation' in support of his claim that the effects of competition between bus companies was not satisfactory.
6.  Andrei Shleifer and Robert Vishny, *The Grabbing Hand: Government Pathologies and their Cures* (Cambridge, MA: Harvard University Press, 1998).
7.  Mancur Olson, *The Logic of Collective Action* (Cambridge, MA: Harvard University Press, 1965).
8.  Gary Becker, 'A Theory of Competition Among Pressure Groups for Political Influence', 98 *Quarterly Journal of Economics* 371 (1983).
9.  Shleifer and Vishny, *supra* note 6, at 3.
10. Oliver Hart, *Firms, Contracts and Financial Structure* (Oxford: Oxford University Press, 1995); Gene Grossman and Oliver Hart, 'The Cost and Benefits of Ownership: A Theory of Vertical and Lateral Integration', 94 *Journal of Political Economy* 691 (1986).
11. Andrei Shleifer, 'State Versus Private Property', 12 *Journal of Economic Perspectives* 133 (1998).
12. Id.
13. Florencio Lopez de Silanes et al., 'Privatization in the United States', 8 *Rand Journal of Economics* 447 (1997).
14. Darryl Biggar, 'Promoting Competition in Local Services: Solid Waste Management' (1999) (Background to meeting of OECD Competition Law and Policy Committee, Working Party 2, Competition and Regulation). This obligation was lifted in 1998 because the system of

mandatory tendering was considered too rigid and unable to address the quality of services question.

15. If the contracted-out spending accounts for a sufficiently large proportion of local expenditure, the gains could be significant.
16. See Richard R. Nelson and Howard Pack, 'Asian Miracle and Modern Growth Theory', 109 *Economic Journal* 416.
17. In Phoenix, Arizona, the local government, after having split the city in a number of zones each auctioned out to different contractors, assigned one zone to itself to enable itself to resist any possible hold-up by one of the private contractors.
18. For a thorough analysis of vertical separation versus integration, see the chapters by Darryl Biggar (Chapter 9) and Marius Schwartz (Chapter 10) in this volume.
19. John Lott, *Are Predatory Commitments Credible? Who Should the Courts Believe?* (Chicago: University of Chicago Press, 1999).

# 14. Cross-country regulation patterns and their implications for macroeconomic and sectoral performance[1]

## Giuseppe Nicoletti

*This chapter draws together the results of recent OECD-based research aimed at (i) constructing an international database on economywide and industry-specific regulations and market structures; (ii) creating summary indicators for comparing the friendliness to competition of regulatory and market environments across countries; and (iii) finding empirical evidence on the effects of regulatory reform on performance, at both the sectoral and macro levels, with a focus on labour market performance.*

*The OECD International Regulation Database was constructed from replies to a questionnaire sent to all OECD governments and data from other sources. It is multidimensional, encompassing several aspects of regulation in a given regulatory area, includes both quantitative and qualitative data, and covers both economywide and industry-specific regulation.*

*The summary indicators of regulation and market structure have a pyramidal structure, going from specific regulatory features to overall regulatory environments. Comparison of indicators across countries at different levels of this pyramid reveals the sources of differences in overall indicators. The indicators cover product markets and labour markets, focusing on employment protection legislation. A striking result is the strong correlation between the restrictiveness of product and labour market regulations across countries. This has several implications for the way regulation affects labour market performance in the OECD.*

*At the macro level, indicators of product and labour market regulation were related to the rate and composition of employment. Multivariate analysis revealed that countries with regulatory environments unfriendly to competition tend to have lower employment rates and a distorted employment composition. Moreover, wage premia in manufacturing are also positively correlated to the restrictiveness of regulations.*

*At the sectoral level, the economic effects of regulatory reform in the telecommunications, electricity supply and air passenger travel industries were explored using cross-country/time-series data. Regression results suggest that in telecommunications, efficiency, prices and quality of service are affected by the market share of new entrants and the time remaining to liberalization; in electricity supply, performance is affected by industry structure (for example, the degree of unbundling of transmission and generation) and regulations governing access to the grid; and in air travel, industry efficiency is affected by the overall regulatory and market environment, while load factors and fares are affected by route-specific regulations and market structures (including airport dominance at route ends).*

*This type of analysis allows policy makers to perform regulatory 'bench-marking' against best-practice countries, to gauge the qualitative impact of regulatory reform on performance and, ultimately, to help them build support for regulatory reform.*

## INTRODUCTION

Economic regulation can be defined as the use of the government's coercive power to restrict the decisions of economic agents.[2] It may include restrictions on firm decisions over entry, exit, the use of inputs, the quantity and the type of output produced, and prices. These restrictions are likely to affect significantly (in intended or unintended ways) the functioning of labour and product markets, since outcomes in these markets will generally be driven by the interplay of market forces with the regulatory framework. Therefore, regulation can be expected to have important repercussions on overall allocative and productive efficiency.

In the past two decades, an increasing number of countries have been reviewing and updating regulatory policies in both the labour and product markets. This reform process has differed (sometimes widely) in timing and scope across countries, but it has generally been characterized by a move towards a more market-orientated approach. This involved the elimination of regulations where they are no longer needed, the softening of regulations that appear to be excessively restrictive of market mechanisms and the shift from 'command-and-control' to 'incentive-based' regulatory schemes. In many countries, the reform process was partly driven by 'peer pressure' originating from the policies implemented and the results obtained by their main commercial partners.

The historical experience with regulatory reform has been relatively long and widespread. This suggests that it should be possible to check whether the expectation of economists that regulatory reform brings about improvements in economic performance is corroborated by the empirical evidence. While country-specific evidence on the economic benefits of market and regulatory changes exists, however, surprisingly few studies have attempted to look at these effects from a comparative, cross-country perspective. Two main factors explain the prevalent focus on the experience of single countries. First, there is a dearth of systematic and internationally comparable data on regulatory and market structures. Second, meaningful comparisons of the outcomes of regulatory reform in different countries are difficult because these outcomes depend on a host of country-specific factors often unrelated to regulation.

This chapter describes the effort made by a team of OECD economists to (a) collect and format data on regulation and market structure at the international level; (b) summarize this data parsimoniously enough to be used in cross-country comparisons; and (c) investigate the linkages between cross-country differences in regulatory and market environments and performance in a way that controls for country-specific factors. Specifically, it reports the progress made along three axes of research:

- the construction of a database of internationally comparable data on economywide regulations, and industry-specific regulations and market structures;
- the estimation of indicators of regulation and market structure that summarize (at different levels of detail) the information on the regulatory and market environments characterizing OECD countries; and
- the investigation (based on these data and indicators) of the empirical evidence concerning the effects of regulatory reform on economic performance at the macroeconomic level as well as in three industries: telecommunications, electricity supply and air passenger transport.

From the policy point of view, the chapter is not meant to offer specific suggestions on regulatory design or on the anticompetitive effects of particular regulations.[3] However, by summarizing the results of several empirical studies, it provides useful background information for policy makers to the extent that the reported results can (i) offer an analytical framework, basic data and indicators for benchmarking countries against examples of best regulatory practice in the OECD; (ii) reassure that the therapy followed for reforming regulatory regimes has been successful; (iii) give supporting arguments to push forward with the overhaul of regulatory regimes; and (iv) help gauge the potential economic impact of regulatory reform at the industry and macroeconomic levels.

The chapter is organized as follows. Section A briefly describes the data collection and formatting effort. Section B illustrates the approach taken and the results obtained in comparing regulatory environments across countries by means of summary indicators of regulation. Sections C and D report the main results of the analysis of the effects of (i) economywide regulations on employment and wages and (ii) industry-specific regulations and market structures on efficiency and prices in telecommunications, electricity supply and air passenger transport.

## A. THE OECD INTERNATIONAL REGULATION DATABASE

Comparing regulation across countries can help policy makers to situate their country across the range of possible regulatory policies, and economists to infer the economic consequences of different regulatory choices. For this reason, the OECD has constructed a database containing detailed information about regulatory environments in the OECD area. But comparing regulations is arduous because (i) information about single regulatory provisions can hardly be analysed in isolation from the wider regulatory environment and (ii) this information is usually scarce and qualitative in nature. To address some of these comparability problems, the data collected was multidimensional, attempting to cover most relevant aspects of a regulatory area. Also, the data collection methodology was uniform across countries, relying as much as possible on a multiple-choice questionnaire.[4]

The information collected concerned both economywide and industry-specific regulations. At the industry level, data on market and industry structure was also collected, providing the bridge between regulation, which may influence market structure, and economic performance, which may be affected in different ways by regulatory interventions and their repercussions on product market competition.

Economywide regulations were defined as regulations that affect all or most sectors of the economy equally, while industry-specific regulations concern only particular activities or markets (such as price caps or limitations on the number of competitors in fixed telephony). At the economywide level, the focus was set on those regulations that are likely to influence economic activity most pervasively, such as trade and competition policies, and administrative burdens. A large amount of industry-specific information was also used to infer the economywide regulatory stance in areas such as state ownership or control of business enterprises and legal limitations on the number of competitors allowed in business activities. At the industry level, analysis of service activities was emphasized, since they have traditionally been highly regulated, many of them remained relatively sheltered from international competition and are frequently undergoing significant liberalization.

The OECD International Regulation Database contains (for each country) approximately 1000 basic indicators of economywide and industry-specific regulations, as well as information on the market structure and performance of six service industries in or around 1998:[5] telecommunications (fixed and mobile), electricity supply, road freight, railway transport, air passenger transport and retail distribution (Table 14.1). These data are both qualitative (for example, descriptions of regulatory provisions) and quantitative (for example, number of days needed to obtain a licence or market shares). The information was mainly drawn from the answers of OECD governments to an *ad hoc* questionnaire, although other sources were also used.[6] The resulting data have been thoroughly reviewed by government or OECD experts.

*Table 14.1    Number of basic data points in the International Regulation Database (by type of data and source)*[*]

| Type of data | Number of data points | Source |
|---|---|---|
| General policies | 146 | Questionnaire; OECD; Economic Freedom of the World 1997; Centre Européen des Entreprises Publiques; European Commission |
| Competition policies | 473 | Questionnaire |
| Electricity | 30 | Stelner (2000)[**]; International Energy Agency |
| Telecommunications | 71 | Questionnaire; OECD |
| Transportation (road freight, railways, passenger air travel) | 136 | Questionnaire; OECD; European Commission; European Conference of Ministers of Transport; International Civil Aviation Organization |
| Retail distribution | 91 | Questionnaire; European Commission |
| Public procurement | 39 | Questionnaire; OECD |
| Total | 986 | |
| *of which: Regulation* (%) | 88.5 | |
| *Market structure* (%) | 7.5 | |
| *Performance* (%) | 4.0 | |

*Notes*
[*]    As of May 2000.
[**]    Faye Steiner, 'Regulation, Industry Structure and Performance in the Electricity Supply Industry', OECD Economics Department Working Paper No. 238 (Paris: OECD).

## B. THE REGULATORY AND MARKET STRUCTURE INDICATORS

The regulatory indicators are cardinal measures that summarize economywide and industry-specific regulations by regulatory domain.[7] The regulatory and market structure indicators can be used for comparing regulatory and market environments across countries and/or investigating the impact of cross-country differences in regulation and market structure on economic performance. They are all designed to express the stringency of regulations, from least to most restrictive (generally along a 0–6 scale), as regards their impact on market competition. Indicators of economywide regulations were largely derived from the data contained in the regulation database and, therefore, are only available for a single (recent) period. Product market indicators were supplemented with indicators of labour market regulations, with a special focus on employment protection legislation (EPL). EPL indicators, which cover regulatory developments over the past decade, were constructed using detailed information on laws and procedures concerning workers holding temporary or permanent contracts.[8]

Industry-specific indicators generally have the same structure as economywide indicators. However, their precise definition changes according to the characteristics of the sector and they are supplemented by indicators of market structure. In addition, in some industries the time dimension was covered as well. This was essential in order to study the effects of sectoral regulatory reforms on performance. The precise definitions of the industry-specific indicators constructed for the telecommunications, electricity supply and air passenger travel industries are described in the next section.[9]

Economywide regulatory indicators have a pyramidal structure, established according to the taxonomy shown in Figure 14.1. Indicators at the top of the pyramid summarize the overall regulatory environment in the product market. At the next level, they summarize information about broad classes of regulatory interventions, such as product market regulations concerning resident or foreign operators (inward- and outward-orientated interventions). At the intermediate and lower levels, they summarize information about types of interventions within these broad classes (for example, state control of business sector activity) as well as their specific modalities (for example, public ownership or involvement in private firms). At the bottom, they coincide with more specific features of the regulatory regimes (for example, scope of the public enterprise sector or use of command-and-control regulations). These specific features are often derived as combinations of the basic information on regulation obtained from the questionnaire or other sources.

For example, the summary indicator of state control includes the responses to a number of questions in the questionnaire and information coming from

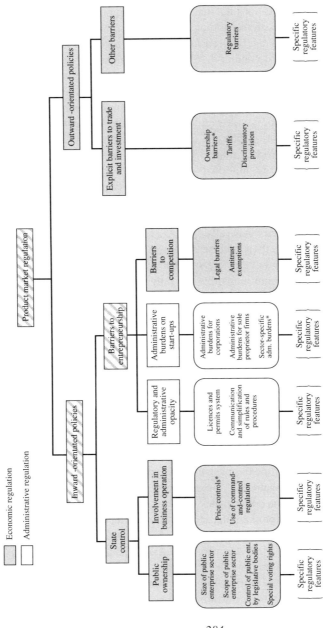

*Note:* * Includes sector specific information on road freight, air transport, retail distribution and some telecommunications services.

*Source:* Giuseppe Nicoletti, Stefano Scarpetta and Olivier Boylaud, 'Summary Indicators of Product Market Regulation with an Extension to Employment Protection Legislation', OECD Economics Department Working Paper No. 226, 1999.

*Figure 14.1  Taxonomy of regulations*

two independent external sources. The questions concern (i) the percentage of business industries in which the state controls enterprises; (ii) the existence of special voting rights; (iii) the control of the business decisions of state-controlled enterprises by the legislature; (iv) the use of command-and-control regulatory instruments by national governments; and (v) the existence and scope of price controls in inherently competitive industries (such as retail distribution). The external sources are used to construct an indicator of the share of state-controlled enterprises in the non-agricultural business sector.[10]

The construction of the indicators involved several steps:

- preparation of the *basic data* (which are contained in the OECD International Regulation Database or obtained from external sources) and classification of the data into two broad sets, inward- and outward-orientated policies, and several *regulatory domains* (for example, state control or barriers to entrepreneurship);
- definition of the *detailed indicators* (often specified as combinations of the basic data), which constitute the basis for subsequent aggregations;
- identification of the *regulatory sub-domains* (for example, public ownership, administrative burdens on start-ups) and construction of the corresponding *summary indicators*, which summarize the various dimensions of regulation described by the detailed indicators; and
- construction of the *overall indicator* of product market regulation, which summarizes the features of the various regulatory domains and provides the most synthetic measure of regulation.

To minimize subjective judgement in summarizing the information provided by the detailed indicators, factor analysis was used to construct the summary and overall indicators. Factor analysis reveals, within each regulatory domain, families of detailed indicators that are associated with different underlying (unobserved) factors (the regulatory sub-domains), and weights each of the detailed indicators according to its specific contribution to the cross-country variance of the factor it is mostly associated with. As a result, countries can be 'scored' on each of these latent factors using the estimated weights. Each factor generally contributes to a different extent to the explanation of the overall cross-country variance of the data, and it is usually sufficient to focus on only a few factors whose combined contributions explain a significant proportion of this variance. The relative contributions of each of the retained factors to the explanation of their overall variance are used as weights in further aggregating the (factor-specific) scores on regulatory sub-domains into summary indicators of regulation by domain and the summary indicators by domain into an overall product market indicator. Up to 50 indicators on specific regulatory features were used in the construction of the overall product market indicator.

This procedure ensures that the identification of the regulatory sub-domains and the aggregation of the detailed indicators are data based, with the resulting summary indicators accounting for a large part of the variance of regulations across countries. Factor analysis assigns the largest weights to the regulatory indicators that have the largest variation across countries, independently of prior views on their likely impact on performance. Therefore, the summary indicators are constructed without pre-empting the conclusions of the analysis, and focus only on those dimensions of regulation that are potentially useful for explaining cross-country differences in performance (regulations that are similar across countries cannot explain differences in performance). These properties are particularly desirable both for benchmarking countries and for exploring the linkages between regulatory environments and economic performance.

Figure 14.2 shows the estimates of the overall indicator of economywide product market regulations for a subset of OECD countries. Countries are ranked by increasing level of anticompetitive restrictions. Although all countries are placed well below the theoretical top value of the scale, the indicators suggest that the friendliness of regulatory environments to product market com-

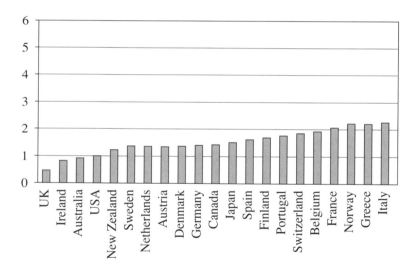

*Note*:     * The scale of indicators is 0–6 from least to most restrictive.

*Sources*:     Giuseppe Nicoletti, Stefano Scarpetta and Olivier Boylaud, 'Summary Indicators of Product Market Regulation with an Extension to Employment Protection Legislation', OECD Economic Department Working Paper No. 226, 1999.

*Figure 14.2     Summary indicator of economywide product market regulations[*] (increasingly anticompetitive)*

petition still varies substantially across the OECD.[11] The United Kingdom, Ireland, Australia, the United States and New Zealand are estimated to have the least-restrictive overall regulatory environments. By contrast, the regulatory environment appears to be the least friendly to competition in Italy, Greece and Norway.

To put these results in perspective, a number of qualifications are necessary. First, the indicator only covers formal regulations, leaving out other kinds of regulatory interventions such as administrative guidance or self-disciplinary measures of professional associations. In addition, no attempt was made to measure the quality of product market regulations and the extent to which they are enforced. Also, a market-orientated regulatory environment is only a necessary condition for enhancing product market competition, because in many markets competition could be stifled by anticompetitive behaviour of private businesses (for example, cartels or abuses of dominant position). Since the effectiveness of competition policies or different approaches to regulating network industries are not assessed, our indicator is unable to tell whether competitive pressures are actually operating in the economies under consideration. As a result, the ranking of countries provided by the summary indicators should be considered only as an approximation of the anticompetitive stance of product market regulations across the OECD.

The picture emerging from the overall indicator can be analysed in more detail by regulatory domain.[12] The highest cross-country variations are found in state control and, to a lesser extent, in barriers to entrepreneurship, whose most variable component concerns administrative burdens on business start-ups. State control and barriers to entrepreneurship are also significantly correlated across countries (the correlation coefficient is 0.5 and is significant at the 5 per cent level), with countries having tight entry regulations also tending to impose burdensome administrative procedures on business enterprises. Other significant cross-country and cross-sector correlations are found between the degree of state control and the scope of legal barriers to entry. This suggests that these two types of regulatory interventions often go hand in hand and, hence, their restrictive effect on market mechanisms is compounded. By contrast, with few exceptions, countries are more homogeneous in their attitudes towards trade policies, due to the rounds of trade negotiations and the widespread participation in multilateral agreements and/or supranational institutions.

Differences in labour market regulations are equally significant. These regulations are still determined essentially at the domestic level even in the European Union, and Nicoletti et al.[13] argue that market pressures originating from rising economic integration are unlikely, by themselves, to bring about convergence of labour market regulations across countries. Nonetheless, the evolution of indicators of EPL for permanent and temporary workers during the past decade suggests that, broadly speaking, there has been a tendency for a significant deregulation of temporary contracts, while only modest changes have been recorded for permanent contracts.[14]

In general, relatively restrictive product market regulations are matched by analogous EPL restrictions.[15] There is a strong statistical correlation between the overall indicator of product market regulation and the indicator of EPL across countries (the correlation coefficient is 0.7 and is significant at the 1 per cent level). A possible explanation is that restrictive product market regulations may make it less urgent for entrepreneurs to lobby for and for workers to accept an easing of EPL. In turn, by increasing the speed of labour market adjustment, less-restrictive EPL may make regulatory reform in the product market easier to implement.[16] The strong correlation between regulatory regimes in the labour and product markets also suggests that their influence may have compounded effects on labour market outcomes, making regulatory reform in only one market less effective than simultaneous reform in the two markets.

Considering both product market regulations and EPL, four clusters of countries can be identified:[17]

- The first includes most Southern European countries (France, Italy, Spain and Greece), which combine relatively strict regulations on both the labour and product markets.
- The second includes continental European countries, which share relatively restrictive product market regulations, but can be further split in two subgroups according to the EPL stance: Germany, the Netherlands, Finland, Austria and, especially, Portugal being more restrictive than Denmark and Belgium.
- The third group includes common-law countries, which are characterized by a relatively liberal approach in both the labour and product markets (the US, the UK, Canada, Ireland, Australia and New Zealand).
- Finally, Japan and Sweden are outliers in the sense that they combine relatively restrictive labour market regulations with relatively few (formal) restrictions in the product market.

## C.   THE EFFECTS OF REGULATION AND MARKET STRUCTURE ON MACROECONOMIC AND INDUSTRY PERFORMANCE

Regulatory provisions in the labour and product markets are generally motivated on public interest grounds. For instance, employment protection legislation may improve worker–employer relationships, encourage investment in human capital and internalize the social costs of worker dismissal, with potentially beneficial effects on labour productivity and the production process.[18] Similarly, product market regulations may be justified by natural monopoly conditions, the existence of externalities or asymmetric information and, more generally, as a means to improve the allocation of resources and consumer welfare in the presence of market failures.[19] However, the effects of regulatory provisions in the product and labour markets often drift away from the original public interest aims, resulting in the protection of special interest groups, which are better organized and gain more from regulatory interventions.[20] In addition, product and labour market regulations and their implementation are sometimes likely to involve costs that exceed their expected benefits.[21] Finally, technical progress and the evolution of demand can render the design of existing product market regulations obsolete in a number of instances, while the progress in regulatory techniques may facilitate the fine tuning of regulation, for example, by separating potentially competitive and inherently imperfect product markets. As a result, in the absence of regulatory reform, existing regulations are often likely to become ineffective and unnecessarily restrictive of market mechanisms in both the product and labour markets, potentially bringing about static and dynamic inefficiencies and losses in social welfare.[22]

The toolkit of regulatory indicators described in the previous section has a natural empirical application in the analysis of the effects of cross-country differences in regulation on economic performance. Initial investigations have concerned (i) the combined impact of product and labour market regulations on labour market performance and (ii) the impact of sectoral regulations and regulatory reform on the performance of the telecommunications, electricity supply and air travel industries.

## Regulation and Labour Market Performance

Product market regulations may affect firm behaviour in three main ways: by increasing the costs of producing any given level of output (for example, compliance or avoidance costs); by affecting market structure (for example, legal limitations on the number of competitors); and by changing the incentive structure (for example, public ownership). The inhibition of product market competition has immediate consequences for labour demand and wage determination, both at the firm level and in the aggregate. In general, the wage elasticity of demand will be reduced and the labour demand schedule will shift inwards.[23] In addition, the existence of rents induced by the lack of competition will generally prompt employees to ask for wage premia, especially if they are unionized.[24] *Ceteris paribus*, this will induce firms to choose capital–labour ratios higher than in a competitive situation, causing lower employment and additional productive inefficiencies. Therefore, except in some cases of natural monopoly, entry restrictions will generally negatively affect economic efficiency and labour market equilibrium relative to a competitive benchmark, having important effects on both the overall level of employment and its composition. The level may be negatively affected by distortions in labour demand, upward pressures in wage rates and reduced rates of enterprise creation and survival, and the composition by the differential effects of regulatory and administrative provisions on different kinds of enterprises (such as sole proprietor versus corporate firms). While the nature and the intensity of these effects will depend also on the features of labour market institutions (such as degree of unionization and centralization of bargaining mechanisms), their sign will generally remain the same across different institutional settings.[25]

Empirical studies of the effects of regulatory reforms on labour market performance have generally focused exclusively on the impact of certain labour market regulations, largely ignoring the role of product market regulations and the interactions between regulatory interventions in the two markets.[26] Based on the cross-country regulatory indicators described in the previous section, companion papers by Boeri et al.[27] and Nicoletti et al.[28] provide empirical evidence on the effects of product market regulations on the level of employment, wage premia and the composition of employment, after controlling for EPL and other institutional features of labour markets.[29] A detailed account of the econometric results is outside the scope of this chapter. Their essence, however, can be caught by a few graphs and tables drawn from the above studies, showing the bivariate correlations between selected indicators of product market regulation and measures of employment and wage premia.

## Countries with Restrictive Labour and Product Market Regulations Tend to Have Lower Employment Rates

Figure 14.3 plots the non-agricultural business employment rates of OECD countries (in 1995) against the summary indicators of product and labour market regulation.[30] The lower panel suggests that a significant negative correlation exists between the employment rate and the stance of EPL. The relationship between product market regulation and non-agricultural business sector employment is even stronger (top panel): tight regulatory regimes tend to be associated with a lower proportion of employment in the non-agricultural business sector.

Given the close cross-country correlation between the regulatory indicators of the product and labour markets (see above), it is hard to identify empirically their separate effects on employment. However, econometric results suggest that the negative relationship between employment rates and product market regulation persists even after filtering out the effects of EPL and other policies

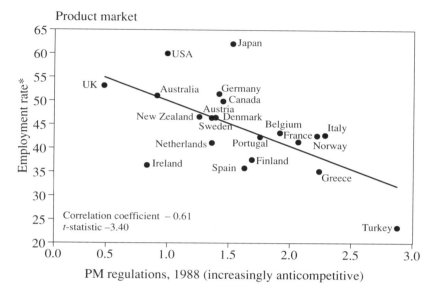

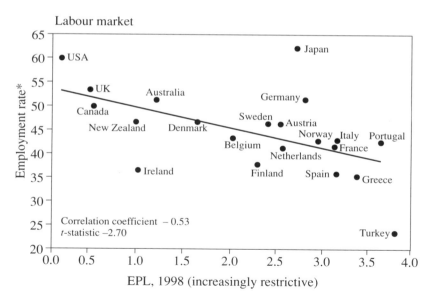

*Note:* * Non-agricultural business sector.

*Figure 14.3   Product and labour market regulations and non-agricultural employment rate*

and institutions directly affecting employment, such as the generosity of the unemployment benefit system, the tax wedge, union density and the bargaining system.[31] Specifically, employment appears to be negatively and significantly correlated with the degree of state control and administrative burdens on business start-ups.

**Strict Product Market Regulations Tend to Lead to Higher Wage Premia**

Table 14.2 describes the results of bivariate correlations between the regulatory indicators and wage premia in manufacturing industries.[32] The summary

*Table 14.2    Regulations and wage premia*

| Regulations | Positive correlation | Negative correlation |
|---|---|---|
| Product market regulation | Paper and printing Non-metallic mineral products Fabricated metal products | |
| State control | Paper and printing Fabricated metal products | Non-metallic mineral products |
| Legal barriers to entry | Food and beverages Paper and printing Non-metallic mineral products Fabricated metal products | |
| Administrative burdens on corporations | | Non-metallic mineral products |
| Licensing and permits system | | Wood products |
| Communication and enforcement of administrative procedures | Other manufacturing products | |
| Regulatory and tariff barriers to trade | Food and beverages Other manufacturing products Textile products | |
| Non-tariff barriers | | Food and beverages Non-metallic mineral products Fabricated metal products Textile products Other manufacturing products |
| Employment protection legislation | Fabricated metal products Other manufacturing products | |

*Source*:    Giuseppe Nicoletti, Robert C.G. Haffner, Stephen Nickell, Stefano Scarpetta and Gylfi Zoega, 'European Integration, Liberalisation and Labour Market Performance', in Tito Boeri, Giuseppe Bertola and Giuseppe Nicoletti (eds), *Welfare and Employment in a United Europe* (Cambridge, MA: MIT Press, 2000).

indicators of product and labour market regulation and several of their components are positively and significantly correlated with unexplained cross-country differences in sectoral wages. As expected, among product market regulations, the most frequent correlations are found with legal barriers to entry and regulatory and tariff barriers to trade. Legal barriers to entry exert a strong effect on wage premia in both fragmented industries, such as food and non-metallic mineral, and segmented industries, such as paper and printing. Regulatory and tariff barriers to trade are positively associated with wage premia in high-import/high-product differentiation industries, such as food and other manufacturing. Surprisingly, some regulatory provisions display a significantly negative correlation with the estimated wage premia: non-tariff barriers seem to be associated with lower wage premia in almost all sectors, while adminis-trative burdens are associated with lower wage premia in the wood and non-metallic mineral industries. As shown below, in fragmented industries, administrative burdens and opacities may favour the development of individual enterprises for which costs and procedures are often lower, thereby lowering industry wages. On the other hand, the result concerning non-tariff barriers seems harder to explain.

### Biases in the Regulatory Environment Tend to Distort the Composition of Employment

Figure 14.4 plots the share of self-employment in total non-agricultural business employment against a measure of regulatory distortions discouraging the creation of corporations. This measure is defined as excess regulatory burdens falling on corporations, that is, the difference between the indicators of admin-istrative burdens for the start-up of corporations and sole proprietor firms.[33] The self-employment rate appears to be positively related to excess burdens, safe for Belgium where self-employment is boosted by fiscal distortions despite the relatively high administrative burdens falling on start-ups of sole proprietor firms. Econometric analysis confirmed this result in a multivariate context con-trolling for the structural characteristics of the economy (such as income levels and the output mix) and labour market regulations (such as EPL).[34]

## D. REGULATION, MARKET STRUCTURE AND SECTORAL PERFORMANCE

Regulation affects economic performance mainly through its impact on product market competition. Therefore, the regulation–performance nexus is likely to be clearest at the disaggregated level, where market structure characteristics

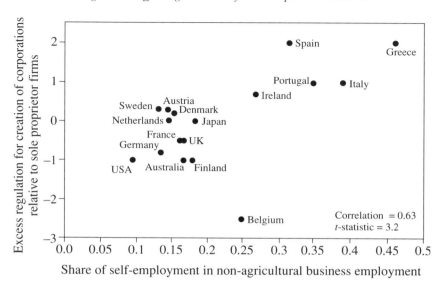

*Note*:   *The difference between the indicators of administrative burdens on the creation of corporations and sole proprietor firms.

*Source*:   Tito Boeri, Giuseppe Nicoletti and Stefano Scarpetta, 'Regulation and Labour Market Performance', in Giampaolo Galli and Jacques Pelkmans (eds), *Regulatory Reform and Competitiveness in Europe* (Cheltenham, UK: Edward Elgar, 2000).

*Figure 14.4    Share of self-employed and product market regulations*

can best be approximated. Of particular interest are industry-specific studies aimed at evaluating the effects of regulatory reform on dimensions of industry performance that are relevant for allocative efficiency and consumer welfare. Here, the main results of cross-country analyses concerning telecommunications, electricity supply and air passenger transport are reported. These industries were chosen on the basis of three main criteria: economic relevance, variability of the market and regulatory environments across countries and availability of comparable data on regulation, market structure and performance. In collecting the data, particular attention was devoted to the microeconomic and/or the time dimension of regulation and market structure.[35]

To the extent possible, a common approach has been maintained for the three industries. The effects of regulatory reform on performance are inferred by relating the variation in regulatory regimes and market structures across countries and (where possible) over time to a set of performance measures (generally productive efficiency and prices) after controlling for other non-regulatory effects potentially explaining the observed variation in market outcomes. The precise definition of the performance measures varies according to the specificities of each industry. For instance, efficiency in long-distance telecommunications has been defined in terms of mainlines or minutes of conversation per employee, while electricity efficiency has been defined in terms of output per unit of total capacity, and air transport efficiency (at the route level) in terms of passenger-kilometres per available seat-kilometres (so-called load factors). In each sector, explanatory variables include: (i) a set of variables controlling for economic structure and technology; (ii) indicators of regulation focusing on market access (as legally defined), pricing and ownership structure; (iii) indicators of industry and market structure focusing on the organization of the industry and/or the role of new entrants. The final aim of the analysis is to draw conclusions about both the sign and the relative intensity of the effects of regulation and market structure on the selected measures of performance. For illustrative purposes, Table 14.3 describes the indicators of performance, regulation and market structure used in each of the sectoral analyses.

## Telecommunications

Boylaud and Nicoletti[36] look at the economic effects of changes in regulation that increase the role of market mechanisms in the telecommunications industry by eliminating barriers to entry and/or the role of public enterprises.[37] The analysis accounted for both the *status* of the regulatory framework at each point in time and expected *changes* in the framework at a future date, which are likely to spur changes in the behaviour of incumbents. It focuses on three broadly-defined services that have undergone significant changes in regulation, market structure and/or performance in recent years: domestic long-distance fixed telephony ('trunk'), international long-distance fixed telephony ('international'), and cellular mobile telephony ('mobile'). These services are also pooled in order to infer the overall effects of regulatory and market developments on the performance of the telecommunications industry.

To make cross-country/time-series analysis possible, several service-specific indicators of liberalization, privatization and market structure were established. Figure 14.5 shows the clustering of countries over the period from 1993 to 1997 obtained by summarizing this information through factor analysis. Three underlying factors were identified: (i) the market and regulatory environment in fixed telephony; (ii) the market and regulatory environment in mobile telephony; and (iii) the timing of the liberalization process. The figure plots the (period) averages of the country scores in the first factor against the scores in the third factor (Panel A) and the second factor (Panel B). In Panel A, two broad groups of countries can be identified:[38] the 'liberal' countries, in which trunk and international telephony have been liberalized early on and new entrants

Table 14.3   *Indicators of performance, regulation and market structure used in empirical analysis*

| Period | Telecommunications 1991–1997 | Electricity 1986–1996 | Air travel 1996/1997 | |
|---|---|---|---|---|
| | | | National level | Route level |
| **Disaggregation** | Trunk, International, Mobile | Generation | | |
| **Regulation** | Time to liberalization<br>Time to privatization<br>Liberalization index<br>Index of state control of public telecom operator | Time to liberalization<br>Time to privatization<br>Liberalization index<br>Privatization index<br>Index of state control of incumbent<br>Index of pricing regulation<br>Threshold for consumer choice of supplier | Openness of domestic market to competition<br>Openness of international market to competition<br>Index of state control of incumbent<br>Presence of special voting rights<br>Loss make-ups by government<br>Presence of public service obligations<br>Index of state control on route carriers | Carrier designation rules<br>Capacity regulation rules<br>Price regulation rules<br>Charter flights rules |
| **Market and industry structure** | Market share of new entrants<br>Number of foreign telecom operators in domestic market | Index of unbundling (generation/transmission)<br>Index of unbundling (all industry segments)<br>Existence of an electricity spot market | Number of major airlines<br>Market share of incumbent in domestic market<br>Market share of incumbent in international market<br>Number of 100 busiest routes serviced by more than 3 carriers<br>Herf. Index on domestic market<br>Herf. Index on international market | Number of major airlines<br>Number of limited-size incumbents<br>Number of third-party carriers<br>Number of alliances<br>Herf. Index of capacity<br>Congestion in departure and arrival airports<br>Incumbent's share of slots in departure and arrival airports |

| Performance | | | | |
|---|---|---|---|---|
| Productivity | Outgoing MITT* total employment (international) <br> Number of mainlines/total employment (trunk) <br> Number of mobile subscribers/mobile employment (mobile) | Utilization rate: electricity produced divided by total capacity <br> Deviation of reserve margin from optimum | Overall efficiency index (computed using Data Envelope Analysis) | Average load factor (adjusted for stage length) <br> Highest load factor (adjusted for stage length) |
| Prices | International collection charges <br> Revenue from international service/outgoing MITT <br> Tariff basket for trunk communications <br> Revenue from mobile service/number of subscribers <br> Basket of national leased lines charges | Industrial end-user electricity price <br> Ratio of industrial to residential end-user electricity prices | | Business fare (adjusted for stage length) <br> Economy fare (adjusted for stage length) <br> Discount fare (adjusted for stage length) |
| Quality | Answer seizure ratio <br> Service reliability | | | |

*Note:* * MITT = minutes of international communications.

Panel A. Fixed telephony and liberalization*

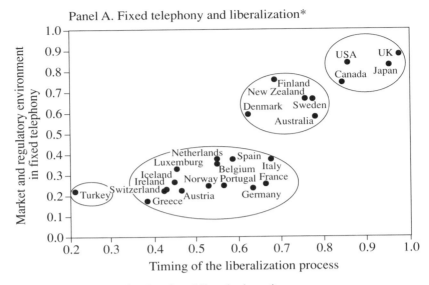

Panel B. Fixed and mobile telephony*

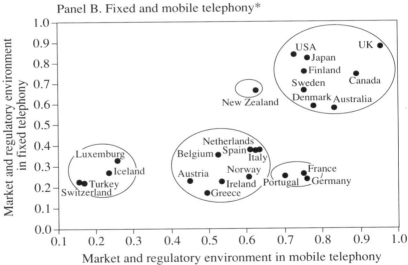

*Note*:    * Fixed telephony includes only domestic and international long-distance services.

*Source*:    Olivier Boylaud and Giuseppe Nicoletti, 'Regulation, Market Structure and Performance in Telecommunications', OECD Economics Department Working Paper No. 237 (2000).

*Figure 14.5    Grouping countries according to estimated factors, 1993–1997 (increasingly competitive)*

have significant market shares (the common-law countries, Japan and some Nordic countries); and the 'middle-of-the-road' countries, in which trunk and international telephony had undergone little liberalization over the sample period, but committed to liberalize soon (basically the continental European countries). In the first group, the United Kingdom, Japan, the United States and Canada have the most competitive environments. Turkey stands on its own since liberalization has been postponed to a more distant date. In Panel B the situation is complicated by the different stages of development of mobile telephony across the OECD and the influence of the internationalization indicator on country scores along the mobile telephony factor. Due to a relatively low degree of internationalization and a low number of competitors in the mobile market, New Zealand is isolated from the group of liberal countries and Switzerland, Iceland and Luxembourg are isolated from the group of middle-of-the-road countries. Moreover, a subset of countries with particularly liberal environments in mobile telephony but restrictive fixed telephony environments (including Germany, France and Portugal) can also be identified.

The comparative experience of 24 OECD countries over the 1991–97 period (analysed by means of panel data techniques) provides empirical evidence that liberalization of the telecommunications industry and the development of effective competition in telecommunications services generally lead to higher productivity, lower prices and better quality. By contrast, there is no clear evidence as to the effects on performance of privatization *per se*, maybe due to the relatively aggregate level at which the analysis was performed.[39] A summary of the empirical results obtained in the regressions pooling trunk, international and mobile services (focusing for simplicity only on the regulation and market structure variables) is provided in Table 14.4.

From the policy point of view, these results suggest that the economic benefits of liberalization and regulatory reform in the telecommunications industry are large and relatively quick to come about. Significant benefits derive from adjustments triggered by the mere perspective of liberalization (proxied in the empirical analysis by the time remaining to the liberalization date), but their depth and scope depend on the establishment of effective competition in telecommunications markets. Therefore, final and intermediate users of telecommunication services are likely to gain substantially from liberalization initiatives.

## Electricity

Steiner[40] looks at the economic effects of changes in ownership, industry structure and entry regulation of electricity supply in 19 OECD countries over the 1986–96 period. The focus is set on regulatory reform in the generation segment of the industry, since this is where most of the technological innova-

*Table 14.4    The effects of regulation and market structure on performance in the telecommunications industry (summary of results of pooled panel regressions, 1991–1997)[1,2]*

| Dependent variable[3] | International, trunk and mobile | | International and trunk |
|---|---|---|---|
| | Productivity | Prices | Quality |
| Number of observations | 446 | 406 | 335 |
| | Fixed effects | Fixed effects | Random effects |
| Market share of new entrants[4] | 0.01 | –0.01 | 0.02 |
| | *4.17* | *–3.27* | *0.74* |
| Time to liberalization | 0.17 | –0.17 | 1.08 |
| | *7.19* | *–6.24* | *6.83* |
| State ownership index | 0.12 | –0.07 | –0.44 |
| | *0.65* | *–0.35* | *–0.24* |
| Time to privatization | –0.10 | 0.03 | 0.03 |
| | *–3.88* | *1.11* | *0.19* |

*Notes*
1. Other explanatory variables include: for efficiency and quality – economic structure, technology; for prices – economic structure, technology, tariff rebalancing indicator. The sample period is 1993–97 for mobile services.
2. For random effects: $z$-statistic in *italics*; for fixed effects: $t$-statistic in *italics*.
3. Performance variables were standardized in the pooled regressions.
4. Liberalization index for mobile services.

*Source*:    See Figure 14.5.

tions and reform initiatives were implemented. However, regulatory changes affecting other segments of the industry (such as transmission and distribution) are also taken into account. The analysis attempts to control for cross-country differences in exogenous factors (such as natural resource availability) and policy preferences that led to the adoption of different generation technologies, as well as for the different cost characteristics of these technologies.

Using several sources, cross-country/time-series indicators of regulation and industry structure were constructed. These indicators summarize information about (i) the degree of liberalization of entry into generation as well as its timing; (ii) the ownership structure and the timing of privatization of incumbent utilities; (iii) the degree of unbundling of the various segments of the industry, with a special focus on the separation between generation and transmission; (iv) the features of the rules governing access to the national grid by third parties (that is, producers that do not own the grid); (v) the existence of a spot market for electricity; and (vi) the degree of consumer choice of the electricity supplier.

Patterns of regulation and market structure were summarized by means of factor analysis, which scored countries according to two main factors: the degree of liberalization (including reforms in both the legal framework and the organization of the industry) and the degree of privatization. The resulting country clusters are shown in Figure 14.6. Over the whole period (top panel), five groups of countries emerge: the United Kingdom has the highest liberalization score and a high privatization score; Norway scores high on liberalization but low on privatization; the United States and Japan form a group with a high degree of privatization but a low degree of liberalization; Belgium scores high on privatization but low on liberalization; and the remaining countries form a group with low scores on both liberalization and privatization. These groups reflect the different nature of regulatory reforms in the United Kingdom and Norway, the history of investor-owned, regional, integrated utilities in the United States and Japan, and the integrated but privately-owned national monopoly in Belgium. The lower panel positions countries according to scores for 1996, the final year in the sample. Comparison of the two panels illustrates the historical movement of countries along the two reform axes. In 1996, Australia joins the United Kingdom to form a group with a high degree of both liberalization and privatization. Sweden, Finland and Denmark join Norway in the group characterized by a high degree of liberalization, but a low degree of privatization. The United States remains in a group with Japan, as before. The United States appears to have a lower liberalization score than some countries in the remaining group which is characterized by both low liberalization and privatization scores; this is because the variables associated with the liberalization factor are predominantly measures of vertical integration, and the US utilities remained integrated in 1996.

Competition in electricity generation is likely to affect the productive efficiency of generation plants, and retail electricity prices (which largely reflect the cost of generation). Using data collected by the International Energy Agency, these two dimensions of performance were measured, respectively, by (a) the average utilization of capacity (as measured by electricity production over total capacity) and the appropriateness of reserve margins (that is, the ability of capacity to handle peak load), as measured by the deviation of reserve margins from their 'optimal' level;[41] and (b) the industrial end-user prices and the price differentials between residential and industrial consumers. The expectation is that, over time, competition will tend to increase utilization rates, reduce price levels and price differentials (due to reduced room for price discrimination), and bring reserve margins closer to their 'optimal' levels (by reducing over- or underinvestment).

The results of panel data econometric analysis, which are summarized in Table 14.5 (focusing for simplicity on the regulatory and industry structure variables), provided some support to this expectation. Although the significance

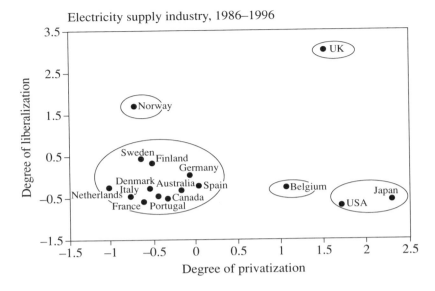

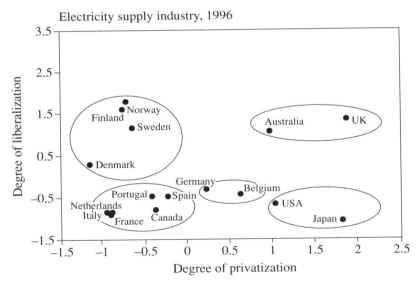

*Source*:   Faye Steiner, 'Regulation, Industry Structure and Performance in the Electricity Supply Industry', OECD Economics Department Working Paper No. 238 (2000).

*Figure 14.6*   *Grouping countries according to estimated factors (increasingly competitive)*

of individual coefficients is affected by multicollinearity between several of the regulation and industry structure variables, the following conclusions can be drawn:

- The unbundling of generation and transmission, expansion of Third Party Access (TPA), and introduction of electricity markets reduce both industrial end-user electricity prices and the ratio of industrial to residential prices.
- Unbundling of generation and transmission and private ownership each serve to improve the utilization of capacity in electricity generation.
- Unbundling of generation and transmission and private ownership each bring reserve margins (the ability of capacity to handle peak load) closer to their optimal level.

*Table 14.5   The effects of regulation and industry structure on performance in the electricity supply industry (summary of results of random effects panel regressions, 1986–1996)*[*]

| Dependent variable | Efficiency | | Prices | |
|---|---|---|---|---|
| | Utilization rate | Reserve margin deviation | Industry price | Industry/ residential price ratio |
| Number of observations | 209 | 209 | 209 | 209 |
| Unbundling of generation from transmission | 3.E–05 *2.912* | –0.104 *–3.520* | –0.001 *–0.659* | –0.051 *–2.425* |
| Private ownership | 1.E-05 *1.804* | –0.033 *–1.442* | 0.003 *2.70* | 0.035 *2.786* |
| Third-party access | –1.E–05 *–0.769* | 0.040 *1.484* | –0.003 *–1.357* | –0.035 *1.755* |
| Wholesale pool | – – | – – | –0.005 *–2.306* | –0.114 *–3.861* |
| Time to liberalization | – – | – – | 0.001 *2.814* | – – |
| Time to privatization | – – | – – | 0.001 *1.510* | – – |

*Note*:   [*] *z*-statistic in *italics*. Other explanatory variables include: for efficiency – preferences for nuclear and coal technologies, urban density; for prices – hydro and nuclear shares in generation, GDP.

*Source*:   See Figure 14.6.

- However, a high degree of private ownership and imminence of both privatization and liberalization tend to increase industrial end-user prices. The positive relationship between private ownership, privatization and prices perhaps reflects significant market power of private or privatized utilities (and failure to regulate it) as well as the wish of governments to maximize revenues from asset sales. A possible explanation for the positive relationship between time to liberalization and prices is that high prices act as an incentive for liberalization (that is, reverse causality).

## Air Transport

Gonenc and Nicoletti[42] used detailed information about state control, regulation and market structure of air passenger transport by scheduled airlines flying on domestic and international routes to infer the impact on performance of cross-country differences in the regulatory and market environment at both the national and route levels. Performance, state control, regulation and market structure were measured at the level of domestic industries for 27 OECD countries and route by route for around one hundred busiest international routes connecting the 12 largest OECD countries.[43] The analysis accounts for interactions between the national and route levels. For instance, route performance is related to the combined influence of state-controlled carriers on the route. Conversely, the performance of the domestic industry is related to the exposure to competition of domestic carriers on international routes. The detailed treatment of domestic and international regulatory provisions and market structures makes it possible to analyse not only the generic influence of competition on performance, but also the relative effects of different regulatory and market arrangements, such as domestic liberalization, openness of international routes, presence of challenger airlines and airport dominance.

At the national level, performance is measured by an overall indicator of productive efficiency of the domestic industry (computed using a representative sample of airlines).[44] State control takes into account ownership and governance factors (such as special voting rights) and state involvement in business operation (such as loss make-ups and service obligations) of domestic companies. Regulation includes openness to competition of the domestic and international routes served by domestic carriers, and market structure includes information on the number and market shares of companies operating on domestic routes as well as the number of international routes (originating from the reference country) served by more than two carriers. At the route level, performance is measured by capital productivity (as expressed by load factors) and economy, business and discounted fares (both load factors and fares are adjusted by stage length).[45] State control includes (combined) state interference in the corporate governance of carriers operating on the route. Regulation includes route-specific provisions concerning carrier designation, capacity regulation, authorization of charter flights and pricing. Market structure is measured by the number and shares of carriers operating on the route as well as slot congestion and the share of slots controlled by incumbent airlines in (origin and destination) airports.

Summarizing national patterns of state control, regulation and market structure by means of factor analysis, countries can be scored along three main factors: (i) the market environment, including the number of competitors and market concentration at home and on international routes served by domestic carriers; (ii) the entrenchment of a flag carrier, including the degree of government control, the special rights and the market share (on both domestic and international routes) of the flag carrier (if any); and (iii) the openness of regulations on international routes served by domestic carriers. Figure 14.7 shows the resulting summary indicator of the regulatory and market environment at the national level, as well as its three components. Similar indicators were computed at the route level.

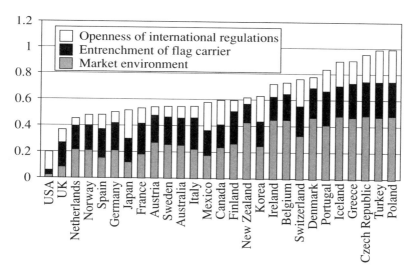

*Source*: Rauf Gonenc and Giuseppe Nicoletti, 'Regulation, Market Structure and Performance in Air Passenger Transport', OECD Economics Department Working Paper No. 254 (Paris: OECD, 2000).

*Figure 14.7    Summary indicator of regulatory and market environment at national level (increasingly anticompetitive)*

The indicator suggests that the US has by far the most liberal air transport environment in the OECD, followed at a distance by the UK and the Netherlands. By contrast, the most anticompetitive environments are found in some southern European and transition countries. The three components of the overall indicator show that the primacy of the US depends mainly on its relatively fragmented market structure (with several competing carriers at home) and the absence of an entrenched flag carrier. However, the US does not compare well with other countries on regulations affecting international routes because, although it has established a number of Open Sky air agreements, it is not part of any fully-liberalized regional aviation market. In each of the continental European countries, the market environment is generally more concentrated than in the US and, in most countries, the flag carrier is still dominant and protected. However, EU-wide liberalization of cabotage makes for a potentially more competitive international environment than in the US.

The bivariate correlations between the summary indicators obtained at the national and route levels and some measures of efficiency and prices are suggestive of the link between regulation, market structure and performance in the air travel industry. At the national level, the summary indicator of regulatory and market environment was related to the overall productive efficiency of the domestic air travel industry, as measured by the Data Envelope Analysis estimates. Figure 14.8 suggests that there is a strong positive corre-

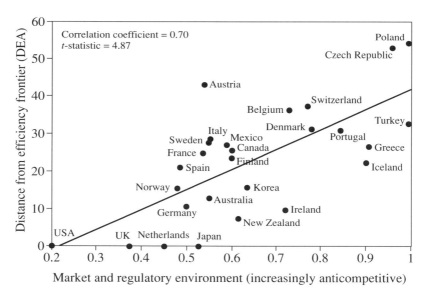

*Source*:   See Figure 14.7.

*Figure 14.8   Regulation, market structure and efficiency in air passenger transport (national level)*

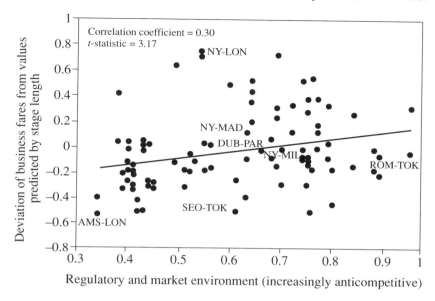

*Source*:   See Figure 14.7.

*Figure 14.9    Regulation, market structure and air fares (Route level)*

lation between industry efficiency and the friendliness to competition of the regulatory and market environment in domestic routes and international routes served by domestic carriers.

Figure 14.9 shows that, at the international route level, a positive correlation exists across routes between business fares (adjusted for stage length) and the restrictions to carrier competition determined by bilateral (or multilateral) agreements between origin and destination countries. Economy fares, discount fares and load factors display similar correlations with regulation and/or market structure on international routes. However, the three types of fares and load factors are affected in different ways by the regulatory and market characteristics considered in the analysis. These suggestive results are corroborated by multivariate analysis, in which the influence on performance of factors unrelated to regulation and market structure is controlled for and the separate impacts of different variables are better identified. Table 14.6 summarizes some of the preliminary regression estimates at both the national and route level, focusing on the coefficients of the regulatory and market structure indicators. The results suggest that restrictive regulatory and market environments (at home and on international routes) tend to reduce the efficiency of the air travel industry both

Table 14.6   The effects of regulation and market structure on national and route-level performance in the air passenger travel industry (summary of results of OLS cross-section regressions[1,2])

| Dependent variable | Efficiency[3] — National level — Distance of domestic industry from efficiency frontier (DEA measure) | Efficiency[3] — National level — Average inoccupancy factor on international routes served by national carriers[4] | Route level — Inoccupancy factor of best performing carrier on route | Prices[3] — Business class fare | Prices[3] — Route level — Economy fare | Prices[3] — Route level — Discount fare |
|---|---|---|---|---|---|---|
| Observations | 26 OECD countries | 26 OECD countries | 96 international routes | 99 international routes | 99 international routes | 99 international routes |
| **Explanatory variables[5]** | | | | | | |
| Strictness of overall regulatory and market environment (at national or route level) | 0.53 *5.18* | 0.49 *2.78* | 0.27 *2.43* | 0.33 *3.38* | 0.21 *2.25* | 0.18 *2.17* |
| Strictness of overall market environment in industry at route ends | | | 0.28 *2.55* | −0.36 *−3.80* | 0.02 *0.22* | 0.33 *3.90* |
| Difficulty in accessing infrastructure at route ends (airport dominance and congestion) | | | −0.03 *−0.25* | 0.22 *2.21* | 0.18 *1.79* | −0.05 *−0.51* |
| Government control over route carriers | | | −0.09 *−0.80* | 0.27 *2.88* | 0.04 *0.40* | −0.11 *−1.30* |

*Notes*
1.  The reference periods for the cross-sections are 1996/1997 for regulation, market structure and efficiency indicators, and 1999 for prices.
2.  *t*-statistics in italics.
3.  Adjusted for stage length.
4.  The inoccupancy factor is the complement to the load factor (number of seats occupied in a plane).
5.  Other explanatory variables include: in national regressions – propensity to air travel, average size of fleet, average age of fleet; in route regressions – propensity to air travel at route ends, purchasing power at route ends, average size of fleet at route ends.

*Source:*   See Figure 14.7

308

at the aggregate and route levels, and increase international air fares. Especially in business, time-sensitive travel, this effect is compounded by government control of route carriers and airport dominance phenomena.

## CONCLUSIONS

Cross-country comparisons of regulatory environments and the analysis of their impact on the economy have traditionally been hampered by the dearth of internationally comparable data on regulation and market structure. This chapter described a new set of data and methodologies for constructing indicators summarizing economywide regulatory environments, industry-specific regulations and market structures for a large set of OECD countries. Given the complexity of regulatory systems, quantifying regulations by means of summary indicators runs the risk of oversimplifying reality. For this reason, the usefulness of the data and indicators proposed should be assessed on the basis of three criteria: Do the indicators depict cross-country patterns of regulation that are plausible in view of the policies followed by OECD countries in the past two decades? Do the indicators have any power to explain cross-country differences in economic performance? Do the indicators suggest linkages between regulation and performance that are intuitively appealing and justifiable?

The evidence summarized in this chapter suggests that these criteria are likely to be satisfied. Based on the pyramidal structure of the regulatory indicators, the position of each OECD country along a scale measuring the restraining influence of regulations on market mechanisms and the distance of market structures from competition can generally be explained by referring to the countries' score on the more detailed components of the summary indicators. The resulting patterns of regulation and market structure appear to reflect the cross-country differences in the implementation of regulatory reforms. When the indicators are used to analyse the linkages between regulation, market structure and performance, the results are encouraging at both the macroeconomic and industry levels. Measured differences in economywide regulations help to explain the cross-country dispersion of employment levels, wage premia and employment composition. Measured disparities in the implementation of regulatory reform at the sectoral level and the resulting differences in market structures are found to affect efficiency and prices in the telecommunications, electricity supply and air passenger travel industries. Overall, the regression results suggest that there are significant efficiency gains to be reaped from a thorough implementation of regulatory reform at both the macroeconomic and industry levels.

The analysis provides broad empirical support for the presumption of a positive impact of entry and price liberalization, administrative simplification and product market competition on economic performance. However, at a finer level of analysis, the issues of regulatory design that are of high interest to policy makers, such as assessing which reforms are most likely to result in increased competition and which institutional and regulatory arrangements are best suited to lead to rapid improvements in performance, need to be addressed. This is a matter for future empirical research.

## NOTES

1. Special thanks to the other members of the regulation team at the Organization for Economic Cooperation and Development (OECD) Economies Department – Olivier Boylaud, Rauf Gonenc and Faye Steiner – and Stefano Scarpetta. Their substantial contribution to the work on regulatory indicators and the effects of regulation on performance made this chapter possible. Of course, I remain entirely responsible for errors and omissions. The project has also benefited from comments by many other colleagues within the OECD and the support of Ignazio Visco, Mike Feiner and Jørgen Elmeskov. Part of the work described in this chapter has been financed by the European Commission. As regards the linkages between regulation and employment, the support of Centre for European Policy Studies-Confindustria and the Fondazione Rodolfo DeBenedetti, as well as useful comments by Tito Boeri, are also acknowledged. The opinions expressed in the chapter are those of the author and do not engage the OECD or the European Commission.
2. W. Kip Viscusi, J. Vernon and J.E. Harrington, *Economics of Regulation and Antitrust* 307–11 (Cambridge, MA: MIT Press, 1997).
3. These issues are discussed in Rauf Gonenc, Maria Maher and Giuseppe Nicoletti, 'The Implementation and the Effects of Regulatory Reform: Past Experience and Current Issues', OECD Economics Department Working Paper No. 251 (Paris: OECD 2000).
4. The multiple-choice format shifts the burden of interpreting the answer on the countries themselves, reducing the scope for discretion by the analyst. However, it does not eliminate comparability problems because countries may interpret the questions in different ways.
5. The database can be found on the OECD website (www.oecd.org). For the telecommunications and electricity supply industries it contains also time-series information on the evolution of regulation in the past 15 years.
6. In May 1997, ministers of OECD countries asked the OECD to conduct reviews of regulatory reform in member countries beginning in 1998, based in part on self-assessment. As part of these reviews, the OECD developed a questionnaire designed to provide essential information on the regulatory frameworks and on industry-specific regulations in member countries. It was distributed to all member countries in March 1998.
7. An analysis of the cross-country patterns of regulation highlighted by the economywide indicators, as well as details on sources and methodologies used for their construction can be found in Giuseppe Nicoletti, Stefano Scarpetta and Olivier Boylaud, 'Summary Indicators of Product Market Regulation with an Extension to Employment Protection Legislation', OECD Economics Department Working Paper No. 226 (Paris: OECD, 1999).
8. This information was assembled by the OECD and its accuracy was verified by member governments. See OECD, *OECD Employment Outlook* (Paris: OECD, 1999).
9. The OECD International Regulation Database was also used to construct cross-country regulatory indicators for the road freight and retail distribution industries (see Olivier Boylaud, 'Regulatory Reform in Two Competitive Industries: Road Freight and Retail Distribution', OECD Economics Department Working Paper No. 255 (Paris: OECD, 2000)), and, to a more limited extent, for the railway industry (see Gonenc et al., *supra* note 3).
10. The indicator was based on the index covering all OECD countries published in James Gwartney and Robert Lawson, 'Economic Freedom of the World', *The Fraser Institute Annual*

*Report*, 1997. The index was adjusted using the data published in Centre Européen des Entreprises à Participation Publique, *Annales Statistiques* 1997, which measures the share of public enterprises in non-agricultural business value added, employment and capital formation for the 15 EU member states, and data on privatizations proceeds from OECD, 72 *Financial Market Trends* (1999).

11. The range of values taken by the summary indicator is smaller than the 0–6 scale along which individual regulatory provisions were ranked due to aggregation effects. This is because, in general, countries are ranked differently on different individual provisions.

12. Nicoletti et al., *supra* note 7.

13. Giuseppe Nicoletti, Robert C.G. Haffner, Stephen Nickell, Stefano Scarpetta and Gylfi Zoega, 'European Integration, Liberalisation and Labour Market Performance', in *Welfare and Employment in a United Europe* (Tito Boeri, Giuseppe Bertola and Giuseppe Nicoletti eds, Cambridge, MA: MIT Press, 2001).

14. See generally Nicoletti et al., *supra* note 7.

15. *Id.*; Nicoletti et al., *supra* note 7.

16. A lax EPL regulation may, however, make workers' resistance to regulatory reform fiercer in so far as insiders would be less protected in the event of redundancies.

17. For details, see Tito Boeri, Giuseppe Nicoletti and Stefano Scarpetta, 'Regulation and Labour Market Performance', in *Regulatory Reform and Competitiveness in Europe* (Giampaolo Galli and Jacques Pelkmans, eds, Cheltenham, UK: Edward Elgar, 2000).

18. By reinforcing job security, EPL may create a more cooperative environment for the development of the production process. George A. Akerlof, *An Economist Theorist's Book of Tales* (Cambridge: Cambridge University Press, 1984). By ensuring long-lasting work relationships, it encourages employers' investment in training, also enhancing internal flexibility. Michael J. Piore, 'Perspectives on Labour Market Flexibility', in 25 *Industrial Relations* 146 (1986). To the extent that the costs of EPL are borne by all workers (in terms of lower overall wages), the costs of insuring against the social consequences of dismissals are pooled. Assar Lindbeck and Dennis J. Snower, *The Insider–Outsider Theory of Employment and Unemployment* (Cambridge, MA: MIT Press, 1988).

19. For a discussion of theories of regulation and the related empirical evidence, see, for example, Roger G. Noll, 'Economic Perspectives on the Politics of Regulation', in 2 *Handbook of Industrial Organization* 1253 (Richard Schmalensee and Robert D. Willig, eds, Amsterdam: North-Holland, 1989); Roger G. Noll, 'The Economic Theory of Regulation After a Decade of Deregulation: Comments', in *Brookings Papers on Economic Activity: Microeconomics* 48 (1989); Clifford Winston, 'Economic Deregulation: Days of Reckoning for Microeconomists', 31 *Journal of Economic Literature* 1263 (1993); Clifford Winston and Robert W. Crandall, 'Explaining Regulatory Policy', in *Brookings Papers on Economic Activity: Microeconomics* 1 (1994).

20. Special interest groups are usually composed of a relatively small number of producers whose individual marginal gains from regulatory interventions are large, as opposed to the large audience of consumers who are typically dispersed and poorly organized, and whose marginal gains are individually small. Sam Peltzman, 'The Economic Theory of Regulation after a Decade of Deregulation', *Brookings Papers on Economic Activity: Microeconomics* 1 (1989). In the labour market, the insiders (holding permanent contracts generally characterized by stricter EPL) enjoy a higher level of job security, bringing about an increase in wage pressure at the expense of job-seekers and overall employment levels. Samuel Bentolila and Juan J. Dolado, 'Labour Flexibility and Wages: Lessons from Spain', 9 *Economic Policy* 53 (1994).

21. For instance, the cost of US federal regulations was estimated to range from 4 to 10 per cent of GDP. US Office of Information and Regulatory Affairs, Office of Management and Budget, 'Draft Report to Congress on the Cost and Benefits of Federal Regulations', Washington, DC (1998). The costs of regulation for the Dutch economy were estimated to range from 11 to 14 per cent of net national income. Peter A.G. Van Bergeuk and Robert C.G. Haffner, *Privatisation, Deregulation and the Macroeconomy* (Cheltenham, UK: Edward Elgar, 1996). In the labour market, labour turnover may be curbed by excessively strict EPL. Giuseppe Bertola, 'Labour Turnover Costs and Average Labour Demand', 10 *Journal of Labor Economics* 389 (1992). Employment levels may be reduced if hiring and firing costs are not transferred into

lower wages. Jørgen Elmeskov, John Paul Martin and Stefano Scarpetta, 'Key Lessons for Labour Market Reforms: Evidence from OECD Countries' Experience', 5 *Swedish Economic Policy Review* 205 (1998).

22.  For a review of the rationale, the status and the potential effects of regulatory reform in OECD countries, see *The OECD Report on Regulatory Reform* (Paris: OECD, 1997).

23.  John Hicks, *The Theory of Wages* (London: Macmillan, 1932).

24.  For a survey of theory and evidence on the effects of product market competition on wages, see Stephen J. Nickell and Richard Layard, 'Labour Market Institutions and Economic Performance', in *Handbook of Labour Economics* (forthcoming).

25.  Stephen J. Nickell, 'Product Markets and Labour Markets', 6 *Labour Economics* 1 (1999).

26.  Labour market regulations can have a powerful impact on labour market outcomes by changing the set of constraints under which labour demand and supply decisions are taken. Elmeskov et al., *supra* note 21.

27.  *Supra* note 17.

28.  *Supra* note 13.

29.  The focus is on a subset of OECD countries (excluding Korea, Mexico and the Central and Eastern European members, for which time-series data was lacking or unreliable) over the 1982–95 period. The analysis of wage premia is based on 11 manufacturing and non-manufacturing industries (at the two-digit level) and four service industries (at the one-digit level).

30.  Focus on the business sector is justified because this is where regulations are most likely to affect employment decisions. Agricultural employment is excluded because (i) the regulatory indicators do not include provisions (such as those contained in national and supranational agricultural policies) that are most relevant for explaining employment in this sector; (ii) the sensitivity of employment to economywide regulations is likely to have peculiar features in agriculture due to the predominant presence of self-employment; (iii) the exclusion of agriculture eliminates a potentially spurious relationship between employment and regulations in so far as, over the sample period, the largest declines in agricultural employment have been experienced by countries with relatively low GDP per capita, which are also characterized by restrictive regulatory environments.

31.  Boeri et al., *supra* note 17; Nicoletti et al., *supra* note 13.

32.  Nicoletti et al., *supra* note 13. Wage premia are defined as sectoral differences in wages which cannot be explained by differences in observable worker characteristics.

33.  These indicators summarize several kinds of administrative requirements to be fulfilled in order to create the two kinds of firms: number of procedures (for example, registration, licence and so on) necessary before and after the establishment of the firm; number of levels of government to be contacted; minimum capital requirements; direct administrative costs and so on.

34.  Nicoletti et al., *supra* note 13.

35.  The time dimension was incorporated into the analysis of telecommunications and electricity. The analysis of air passenger transport accounts for the microeconomic dimension by looking at the linkages between regulation, market structure and performance at both the national and the route levels.

36.  Olivier Boylaud and Giuseppe Nicoletti, 'Regulation, Market Structure and Performance in Telecommunications', OECD Economics Department Working Paper No. 237 (2000).

37.  However, it would be incorrect to consider telecommunications as 'unregulated' and perfectly competitive in countries that reduced these forms of state involvement. Most often, they will be simply subject to a form of regulation that deals with the characteristics of the industry in a different way. For example, 'deregulation' of entry in mobile communications generally consists in replacing legal monopolies by a system of multiple franchises that are assigned at the discretion of the government.

38.  The grouping of countries was done by applying cluster analysis separately to the two sets of factor scores plotted in the figure.

39.  At the firm level, evidence of a positive influence of privatization on performance was recently found by Juliet D'Souza and William L. Megginson, 'The Financial and Operating Performance of Privatized Firms During the 1990s', 54 *Journal of Finance* 1397 (1999). See also the survey of empirical studies in Gonenc et al., *supra* note 3.

40. Faye Steiner, 'Regulation, Industry Structure and Performance in the Electricity Supply Industry', OECD Economics Department Working Paper No. 238 (Paris: OECD, 2000).

41. The optimal reserve margin used in this analysis was 0.15, following estimates of 0.15–0.20 in Southern Company Services in Richard J. Gilbert and Edward P. Kahn, *International Comparisons of Electricity Regulation* (Cambridge: Cambridge University Press, 1996).

42. Rauf Gonenc and Giuseppe Nicoletti, 'Regulation, Market Structure and Performance in Air Passenger Transport', OECD Economics Department Working Paper No. 254 (Paris: OECD, 2000).

43. The data refer to 1996 or 1997 for industry efficiency, bilateral air service agreements, the domestic regulatory environment and market structure at home and on international routes (including airport slots). Route fares refer to 1999.

44. Overall efficiency is measured by means of Data Envelope Analysis, a non-parametric procedure that estimates the distance from the production efficiency frontier based on observations concerning the complete set of input and (possibly multiple) output choices by different decision units. The present analysis has total passengers transported and total passenger-kilometres as outputs, and total personnel, capacity, fleet, kilometres flown and average stage length as inputs.

45. The price variables used in the regressions are defined as deviations of standard (business and economy) fares and discount fares of the leading carrier on a route from the benchmark prices expected for each stage length. Benchmark prices are estimated by regressing observed prices on stage lengths. Load factors are adjusted in the same way.

# 15. Panel discussion

**Prof. Amato**   Dr Biggar, you listed finance ministers among the forces likely to oppose separation. Why do you include finance ministers?

**Dr Biggar**   Finance ministers, who are primarily concerned with the government's bottom line as opposed to public welfare, will prefer to privatize a monopoly because revenues will generally be higher from the privatization of a monopoly. In addition, the losses of economies of scope are a direct loss to the owner, which is the finance ministry, while the benefits of competition are shared by all consumers. Thus, an integrated firm may be more valuable than the separated parts, even though competition and overall welfare is enhanced from separation.

**Prof. Fels**   Usually, the bottom line interests of finance ministers are in conflict with the procompetitive wishes one has with regard to public utilities that have pre-existing market power. It is very good to have former competition regulators in charge of finance ministries, who understand these things!

**Dr Biggar**   Competition authorities have a role to play to offset that coalition of interests which includes the incumbent firm, the finance minister, the industry regulator, industry unions and suppliers, and subsidized consumers.

**Mr Heimler**   Separation is also desirable because it stimulates innovation. I agree with Dr Biggar that separation decisions are rare, both in antitrust policy and as a structural decision by regulators.

**Prof. Amato**   This question is directed to Professor Schwartz. What are the general conclusions of your study? May I conclude that whenever regulation of entry can be effectively used as an incentive for opening entry in a connected market, it is a sound regulation and it is not anticompetitive?

**Prof. Schwartz**   I do not want to say that it is a general conclusion, as there is an important 'if' – if you think that the benefits you will get outweigh the costs. But the general point is that relying on sticks alone to try to force monopolists to do what they do not want to do is very difficult. Any kind of incentive device, if it is not too costly, can help.

**Mr Heimler**   There is a problem of independence of the variables in the study by Professor Siniscalco et al. It may be that when a state decides to privatize, it first decides that it should install a regulatory structure. This means that the decision to separate vertically is actually a decision to privatize, and so is the decision to regulate.

**Prof. Siniscalco**   That is true. Whenever we observe a vertically separated electricity company, it was separated because of the privatization. Moreover, without vertical separation, privatization will be very poor.

**Dr Biggar**   Why was the regression for vertical integration separate from the regression for regulation?

**Prof. Bortolotti**   The specification is common, but the two variables could not be put together. Mr Heimler's point was very important, addressing the issue of potential endogeneity of the regulatory variables with the privatiza-tion. We have tried to address this point, first, by attempting to identify an objective value or proxy for the quality of regulation at the time of the issues. In many cases, regulation was in place before the time of the issues. Thus, the potential endogeneity problem is perhaps less relevant in these circumstances. As a technical matter, we have also implemented some Nausmann tests to check for this possible simultaneity between privatization and regulation. We are in the position to accept the exogeneity of this variable.

**Prof. Fels**   I would like to distinguish between clear, well-established, and well-understood regulatory regimes, and regulatory regimes that are pro-consumer. In a number of privatizations where the regulatory regime is extremely clear for five or ten years before privatization occurs, the government has greatly benefited from higher share value at the time of sale. However, the rules have deliberately been extraordinarily generous in the interest of investors in order to maximize sales revenue. For instance, pricing regulations have locked in extremely high prices for many years, to be charged to ordinary consumers, far above any economically justified price. This has been the area of conflict, because this great opportunity to get better prices, more efficiency and so on, is missed.

**Dr Nicoletti**   I understand well the argument in Professor Siniscalco et al.'s study as to why quality regulation will increase the value of the firm, and lead to higher revenues. It is less clear why vertical separation would raise the value of the firm.

**Prof. Siniscalco**     We are making a political argument.

**Prof. Amato**     You are probably repeating the previous argument that partial privatization is undesirable, and therefore privatization requires vertical separation for political reasons. Politicians want to keep parts of the operation, such as transmission, in public hands.

There is another reason why vertical separation is important. For instance, as an initial part of Italy's privatization of electricity, we are selling generation plants. A company that is competing to purchase these generation plants told me that it is ready to buy as long as it feels assured that access to transmission facilities will be truly impartial. Thus, there is a purely financial reason for separation: if I do not separate, they are not ready to buy because they do not feel guaranteed in their future business.

**Prof. Siniscalco**     That is a perfectly sound argument. We should integrate this notion of guaranteed third-party access as a sub-argument of our argument for quality regulation. Without a guarantee, the purchaser puts its neck into the guillotine.

**Dr Nicoletti**     This argument is only correct if you do not unbundle the whole generation capacity. But my question is what is the rationale for your conclusion that revenues are higher when you privatize if you have first vertically separated?

**Prof. Siniscalco**     I could not yet carry out the exact test needed to answer the question you are asking, because we are still collecting the data on book value. In order to evaluate regulatory risk, the difference between the value of the company and its book value must be calculated.

**Mr Heimler**     Companies are probably now in a position to discuss the rules on privatization of generation. They may have purchased even if they were not in that position. This might be a way to influence the rules if they can make a credible threat of not buying. But it is possible that they will buy in any event. In fact, Professor Schwartz was telling me that in the US, generation facilities are purchased even though the transmission line is in the hands of the incumbent.

**Dr Hilke**     The reason for that is the entry restrictions, which make the value of the generation facilities far higher than the value of the current plant.

**Prof. Amato**   That is the point. The market can price everything.

**Prof. Jenny**   With respect to Dr Dutz's study, we have studied trucking deregulation and other regulatory reform in Mexico. There was a general issue of how to build a constituency for reform, not specifically with respect to trucking, which is an issue that Dr Dutz addressed. The Mexican answer at the federal level was clear – it deregulated without bothering to build up a constituency. They felt that if they had tried to build up a constituency, they would never have succeeded in introducing reforms. This is slightly different from Dr Dutz's perception.

Second, in the trucking industry, the most important states of Mexico were reinstating the regulations that had been eliminated at the federal level. Was your data collected during a period when nothing had yet been reinstated, or does it take into account the reinstatement of some of those regulations? If the latter, there may be a bias. Assuming there is no contamination of the data, because you looked at a period when nothing had been reinstated at the state level, how do you account for the push for the reinstatement of these regulations? It does not seem logical given what you perceive as very important visible benefits to the users of the trucking industry. I would be sceptical if your answer is that the trucking industry was able to bribe the politicians to reinstate at the local level, because it would seem that the users should have been able to bribe the politicians not to reinstate the regulation. Since this case involves sizeable economies, this is more incredible.

**Dr Dutz**   On the first question, we looked as carefully as possible into the actual process of regulatory reform in Mexico in the late 1980s. The actual process did, in fact, take place in a commander-like fashion, by a small group within the Ministry of Finance who drafted the initial reform regulation, then followed through in stages. However, this reform took place within the context of NAFTA. Although they were not actively courted at the time, strong support constituencies developed among all the outward-looking industries that wanted to export. A number of background studies had been done highlighting the benefits of reform for them. It was not clear at the time how powerful the trucking union was.

On the second question, regulatory reform was limited to the federal highways, since they fell within the jurisdiction of the federal authorities. State level rules varied greatly. Some states also introduced substantial reforms, others did not. Some that introduced reforms are now backtracking. We did not explicitly control for different progress at the state level. Our question was what were the most positive aspects of innovation that could potentially follow deregulation, had they actually been realized, and if so, what was their size? Much work remains to be done in terms of variation across states, and in terms of the dynamics at the state level.

**Mr Heimler**     At the local level in Rome, there are 6000 taxi drivers. If each household where a family member is a taxi driver is composed of at least three voters, altogether there are 18 000 people who can vote with one single objective – keep the taxi drivers' income high and oppose liberalization. There is no possibility that consumers would be able to exercise a countervailing power so as to neutralize such concentrated interests. In fact, the rest of the population has many other objectives and does not care very much about taxi rates. Lobbies at the local level become so important precisely because they can vote with one single objective.

**Prof. Amato**     The Italian road freight area is an incredibly crowded economic sector – 160 000 small owners, with no more than a couple of trucks each. There is wide competition among them, but at the same time, it is a very protected sector on the whole, which opposes new entry and receives tax incentives and state aid on fuel. Several problems must be overcome to build a constituency for reform in this area. The most innovative and generally the weaker companies and their clients do not care, because they have their own logistic. Most of the country, including consumers, small retailers, and others, entirely depend on these 160 000 truckers, who have an enormous blackmail power in the country. If their demands are not satisfied, they threaten to stop serving the country, as they do in France. The taxpayer thus suffers the burden, and no one complains. Reform efforts that have been undertaken through the years are typically political efforts based on faith in competition, but they have no constituency.

**Prof. Jenny**     I do not want to belabour the point, but there seems to be an asymmetry. The answer which was given was that at the time of NAFTA, somehow the exporters were able to lobby –

**Prof. Amato**     It is a different case.

**Prof. Jenny**     But it seems illogical that at one point the exporters would be able to overcome the lobby of the small truck companies, which resists change, and then at some other point, that lobby is most powerful to prevent change. Have I understood correctly that at the time of NAFTA, the users were the lobbying force that somehow was the constituency for change, and prevailed?

**Dr Dutz**     To clarify, the situation in Mexico was very close to that which Professor Amato described in Italy, with respect to the political efforts of a small group who had faith in competition. The NAFTA context provided a positive background for this type of regulatory reform, but the reforms did not come about because of the strong or active lobbying of the exporters. The impetus came from Salinas and a small group of his advisors. The Mexican authorities were quite clever in how they sequenced the reform process, putting forward a few proposals to win over key trucking interests up front in order to make the whole policy thrust palatable to them.

**Prof. Schwartz**   My question relates to Mr Heimler's study. Is there a simple explanation why local authorities in Italy do not raise the funds themselves, as opposed to getting them from the centre?

**Prof. Amato**   In the early 1970s, major structural revenue reforms were adopted, under which revenue collection was centralized due to widespread corruption and inefficiencies in local collection of revenues. This is now in the process of being reversed. I have introduced a property tax on houses, which was the first stone of reconstruction of local revenue responsibility. Since then, an increasing share of revenues is collected locally.

I understand the distinction between services that require sunk investments, and those that do not. Mr Heimler's solution is that we should privatize the monopolies from now to eternity. I am not sure whether it really works, because if a firm has been the provider of a service for 20 years and has made considerable investment to do so, then there is an auction, this firm will have an interest in the renewal of its licence. If it stops making investments, another firm is likely to be selected. The firm cannot move from place to place, abandoning ruins of previous services, because its reputation would fall dramatically. A regulation always governs a local service, and will typically require part of the returns to go to investments, training of personnel, antipollution and so on. I do not see how the provider of the service could drop investments simply because it is close to the end of its licence.

**Mr Heimler**   An important distinction should be made between verifiable quality and unverifiable quality. I argue that these services often involve unverifiable quality. For these, at the end of the licence period, the quality of service may decline. For instance, the bus company may randomly begin to disrupt services at certain times, which is very difficult to monitor and verify, *ex post*. Reputation is normally difficult to verify for the auction participants, and it is difficult to determine what weight should be attributed to reputation in the decision of whether to allocate a licence to one or another. For a fixed term licence, the concern is much lower.

**Prof. Amato**    I do not see the alternative. Assuming that what you say is correct, that there is a lack of sufficient incentives to renew, to innovate, by the end of the time period of a licence. Does the licensee of an alternate service have incentives to innovate?

**Mr Heimler**    That is a problem. It depends on the system of regulation. People say that price cap regulation would induce innovation in any event.

**Prof. Meny**    This problem was a concern at the beginning of the century in France. Local companies were licensed to provide gas-powered light. Subsequently, electricity appeared and became more efficient, cheaper and so on. The licensed companies resisted the shift from gas to electricity, arguing that they had been licensed for 20 years to provide lighting through gas, not electricity. This can happen when technological changes make the previous licence obsolete and inadequate. The licensee can still claim that it has no obligation to update its technology.

**Prof. Siniscalco**    Many local services with sunk costs have a network, such as gas, electricity, water and so on. I believe the solution for these is separation. The local grid should be separated, and competition should be promoted on the grid itself. Then competition and innovation take place, and it becomes a matter of investing simply in the grid. The grid operator, who must make investments, should be adequately compensated for those investments through access charges. This is apparently in the scheme of liberalization of local services even in Italy.

**Mr Kohl**    Regarding innovation, I believe that transferability of the licence is a solution, because the non-innovating incumbent can be bought out by an innovative challenger.

**Mr Heimler**    I agree, but transferability is like privatization.

**Prof. Jenny**    Dr. Biggar had a neat transparent balance. On one side there was one item, economies of scope; on the other side, there were five items. I am uncertain what to get from this, but five items are not necessarily more important than one item. To the extent that competition authorities have an advocacy role to play, for example, in questions of vertical integration, it would be useful if economists gave them better tools to assess the probability or the extent of those economies of scope. In my experience, a competition authority trying to decide whether to advocate vertical separation has difficulties making the analysis. The companies have all kinds of arguments about how separation will destroy their economies of scope. However, the competition authority normally lacks serious tools to assess the importance of those economies of scope, and then balance them with the competitive disadvantages. Much revolves around an estimate of the importance of those economies of scope. When Dr Biggar ended his talk, he said there should be a presumption in favour of separation, but I am not sure.

**Dr Biggar** Of course, one item does not balance three or five or however many. It depends on the weights. A case-by-case analysis is needed, which suggests a presumption in favour of separation, especially since a decision to separate at the beginning is perhaps more reversible. But I agree that perhaps it is a question of the instruments that a competition authority needs to obtain the information. I have no answer to that.

In the earlier discussion, in relation to Professor Siniscalco's study, there was no inconsistency between my statement that vertical separation would reduce the proceeds from privatization, and Professor Siniscalco's study, which shows that the countries that have chosen vertical separation have, on the whole, greater revenues from privatization. Those two things are not inconsistent because the decision to privatize is not independent of the structure. It could be that only the countries that are vertically separated have privatized. The countries that have separated have higher privatization revenues and the countries that have integrated have zero. There is really no conflict.

PART III


Reform, Regulatory Institutions and
the Role of Competition Authorities

# Introduction

## Allan Fels

This part addresses reform, regulatory institutions and the role of competition authorities. The chapters and discussion in this part cover two major areas. First, what is the appropriate government unit to promulgate and administer regulation? Under this heading, we should also discuss whether to have industry-specific regulation, or general regulation; whether regulation should occur at the local, state, regional, national or supranational levels; whether Europe should have a general regulator in areas like telecommunications; what the relationship is of technical regulation in an industry to the general economic regulation, and whether one body should be responsible for both, or they should be separated.

Second, what is the appropriate institution to be responsible for review and reform – the antitrust authority, the Directorate General for Competition in Europe, or some other body? If the latter, should it be a general or industry specific body? These issues are so central to good government these days that perhaps this task should be performed by the most powerful agencies at the very core of government with the strongest commitment to economic reform, such as the finance or treasury ministry, or the economic institutions. For instance, the Australian Competition and Consumer Commission (ACCC), which I head, was originally attached to the Attorney General's department. It was later moved into Treasury, which did not know much about the legal issues that would arise, but had a much better perspective of what the priorities in competition reform should be. It also had far more power to support the ACCC on competition issues than did the much more marginal Attorney General's department. The change allows Treasury to benefit from our presence when microeconomic issues arise, which is especially useful to help them understand and be better informed about market realities.

Third, we have set forth the first two questions as two distinct ones. But perhaps one body should promulgate regulation *and* be responsible for review and reform. We might also consider whether the enforcement of the law should be separated from its fundamental review and reform. In Australia, it was politically too much to ask that the enforcement agency also get the job of determining whether there should be some changes in the law, so the latter responsibility was delegated to the National Competition Council (NCC).

One final issue addressed by this part is who should be responsible for competition advocacy. The panel was asked to focus on the competition advocacy role of competition agencies, which is surely an important topic. It is, however, a subset of the broader issue of competition advocacy. It reflects the political history that competition agencies have had the greatest interest in this issue, and that competition regulators around the world have played an important role in competition advocacy. However, one reason they have had this role is that they have tended to be left out of governments' core decision making about competition issues. Competition agencies have then had to exercise influence through intervention, public submissions, interventions at public hearings and so on. Thus, we should consider whether other instruments and power locations in government should also be responsible for competition advocacy.

The chapters in this part cover various aspects of these issues. My chapter about Australia reports on an intellectually sophisticated attempt to set out and adopt a coherent and comprehensive approach to national competition policy. The chapter by Laraine Laudati also reports on this attempt, as well as several other attempts that governments have made to eliminate anticompetitive regulation. The chapter by Manuel Ballbe and Carlos Padros is a perceptive study of the key role of independence of the regulatory agency, a matter of great importance, and particularly challenging in the early days of the recent attempted adoption of a serious competition policy by Spain. The Spanish chapter also raises important questions about the relationship of competition policy and regulation, suggesting that this relationship needs to be much closer.

Then follow two chapters about competition advocacy. John Hilke's chapter is a case study of competition advocacy by the US Federal Trade Commission in relation to the electricity policy industry debate at the state level. Michael Wise's chapter is a general survey of Organization for Economic Cooperation and Development (OECD) country experiences with advocacy. The lessons to be learned about how to do this well are discussed in the two chapters. These relate mainly to the role of competition regulators in trying to argue for changes in laws, regulations and regulatory practices that restrict competition and harm consumers, even though these are outside the jurisdiction of competition regulators.

The chapter by Kirti Mehta also addresses these issues, but from a different perspective. This is because the European Commission's Directorate General for Competition has an effective voice at the table of all European Commission policy making. The competition commissioner sits at the table along with all the other commissioners when decisions are made in any sector of the European economy. Thus, the competition commissioner has an important input. The enforcement agency is thus also a policy maker in this instance.

The final chapter, by Michael Kohl, considers matters from a different perspective. Recognizing that the promotion of competition is important for the welfare of the Community, it asks whether there is a constitutional basis for scrutinizing anticompetitive regulation, and whether this is worthwhile as a constitutional aim. It thus tackles the issues from another dimension, that is, the use of constitutional safeguards to protect competition.

# 16. Australia's comprehensive review of anticompetitive laws

## Allan Fels

*This chapter analyses Australia's unique experiment to review and reform anti-competitive laws and regulations, which is one aspect of the reforms introduced by its comprehensive National Competition Policy (NCP) in 1995. The regulatory review requires that over the five-year period ending in 2000, all laws and regulations at all governmental levels (federal, state and local) be subjected to an independent, transparent review to determine whether they restrict competition in any way, in any sector. The criteria for review are: whether the law is in the public interest, given its anticompetitive effect; and if so, whether the same objective could be achieved in a less anticompetitive manner. Accordingly, repeal or reform of anticompetitive laws should follow the review.*

*To implement the reform programme, a new agency, the National Competition Council (NCC), was created. The state and territory governments, which initially embraced the idea of the review, retained the power to review their own laws and regulations, in a public, independent, and transparent manner. The Commonwealth did not, however, fully trust the long-term commitment of the states and territories to carry out the review. Thus, the NCP provided for the payment of substantial sums to those states and territories that carried out their reviews properly. The NCC was empowered to determine whether they had done so, and thus whether they were entitled to receive their payments. The NCC was also empowered to conduct an initial review, from which it determined that over 2000 laws at every level of government should be analysed in greater detail.*

*The review, until now, presents a mixed picture. Many reviews that would not have occurred (since there is normally substantial resistance when review of a single piece of legislation is proposed) were made possible by this procedure. The easier reviews have been completed first, and generally on time, with some positive results. Some reviews have not been conducted in a satisfactory manner, and some reforms are inadequate. The NCC has temporarily withheld some payments, and threatened to withhold them permanently if the reviews are not completed properly. But the final outcome is still not determined.*

*The chapter concludes that Europe should give high priority to adopting a similar comprehensive legislative review designed to eliminate the countless anticompetitive laws and regulations in all the member states.*

## INTRODUCTION

Most countries accept that competition plays a central role in the achievement of high living standards and the provision of economic opportunities for individuals. Free, competitive markets are the most likely to achieve an efficient, technologically progressive and internationally competitive economy. The ultimate economic goal of competition policy is therefore to achieve economic efficiency.

In some instances, however, it is inappropriate to pursue competition for its own sake. For example, in some industries, economies of scale can be maximized only by a monopoly. Moreover, society has some non-economic goals that clash with the pursuit of economic goals. These may include various social goals such as a fair distribution of wealth and income, environmental goals, safety and health goals and so on.

This chapter discusses legislation and other forms of government regulation that limit competition. It begins with a review of the economic factors that influence the degree of competition in a market. It will then consider government policies that influence competition, and processes that may be adopted to minimize anticompetitive legislation. The final section reviews the developments in Australia to this end.

## A.    THE FACTORS THAT INFLUENCE THE DEGREE OF COMPETITION IN A MARKET

To understand the effect of government policies upon competition, it is first useful to set forth the factors that influence the degree of competition in a market. The traditional structure–conduct–performance (SCP) paradigm is relevant to understanding the determinants of competition and the role of competition policy. The *structure* of a market includes:

- technical and economic characteristics, such as capital intensity, demand conditions, and product substitutes;

- entry conditions, such as entry restrictions imposed by governments through licensing laws, trade restrictions and so on;
- number and size distribution of participants in the industry;
- nature of import competition; and
- other factors such as vertical integration, product differentiation and so on.

The *conduct* or behaviour of an industry includes:

- production, selling and pricing policies of firms;
- provision of information to the market by firms, such as through advertising; and
- arrangements among firms, such as cartels.

The *performance* of an industry includes:

- efficiency; and
- technological progress.

The structure of an industry has traditionally been viewed as the most important determinant of the state of competition, and as having a key effect upon conduct. In recent years, however, this view has changed, as it has been recognized that the conduct of firms can affect entry conditions and other factors relevant to structure. Whatever the exact importance of structure, it is a variable that is especially likely to be influenced by government policies, such as those that restrict entry. Traditional antitrust and competition laws, in contrast, mainly affect conduct.

## B.  GOVERNMENT POLICIES THAT AFFECT COMPETITION

A wide range of government policies can affect competition, either positively or negatively. Competition policy has traditionally been equated with antitrust, competition or trade practices law. A comprehensive competition policy, however, must address *all* government policies that affect competition. A comprehensive competition policy therefore involves:

- prohibition of anticompetitive conduct through traditional antitrust and competition laws;
- liberal policies regarding international trade and the free movement of all factors of production, including labour and capital, across international borders;

- liberal policies regarding free trade and the free movement of all factors of production across internal borders;
- repeal of laws and removal of government regulation that unjustifiably limits competition, such as legislation creating entry barriers of all kinds, including professional licences, minimum price laws, restrictions on advertising;
- reform of inappropriate monopoly structures, especially those created by governments;
- appropriate access to essential facilities;
- removal of unjustified state aids;
- 'competitive neutrality' for government businesses, such that they do not trade at an artificial net competitive advantage over private sector competitors by virtue of being government owned;
- separation of industry regulation from industry operations (for example, dominant firms should not set technical standards for new entrants); and
- a level playing field for all participants.

Government laws and regulations can affect competition in numerous areas. Some of the areas include legislation and regulation about the legal system, foreign and domestic investment, intellectual property, taxation, public and private ownership, small business policy, licensing, contracting out and bidding for monopoly franchises. The policies extend across all sectors, including agriculture, mining, construction, manufacturing, and all forms of services, including health, education and social security. They apply at all levels of government: supranational, national, state, regional and local.

The modern economy is based on various forms of competition policy. Nearly every sector has its own competition policy, some of which is good while some is not, and some of which is explicit, some implicit. Many are sectoral policies that have not been seriously analysed as to their consistency with the general principles underlying (or that should underlie) national competition laws and policies.

The laws affecting competition can take many forms. They may be embodied in constitutions, statutes and/or regulations. They may be general laws affecting all businesses, such as taxation laws, or industry specific, such as telecommunications laws, or they may range across a number of markets, such as laws limiting shopping hours, licensing laws and so on.

Legislation affecting competition may directly or indirectly:

- govern the entry and exit of firms or individuals into or out of markets;
- control prices or production levels;
- restrict the quality, level or location of goods and services available;
- restrict advertising and promotional activities;

- restrict price or type of inputs used in the production process;
- confer significant costs on businesses; and
- provide advantages to some firms over others by, for example, sheltering some activities from the pressures of competition.

## C.   AUSTRALIA'S NATIONAL COMPETITION POLICY

In recent years, Australia has sought to adopt a comprehensive national competition policy. Three factors have been especially important. First, there is increasing acknowledgement that Australia is, for all practical purposes, a single integrated market. The economic significance of state and territory boundaries is diminishing with advances in transportation and communication. Second, while trade policy reforms have markedly increased the competitiveness of the internationally traded sector, many goods and services provided by public utilities, professions and some areas of agriculture are sheltered from both international and domestic competition. Legislation has protected some of these important parts of the Australian economy from competition. Third, procompetitive reforms implemented domestically in recent years have progressed sector by sector, without the benefit of a broader policy framework or process. Reforms undertaken in this way are typically more difficult to achieve, as the ground rules (including the respective roles of the national, state and territory governments) must be negotiated on a case-by-case basis. A national competition policy has enabled policy makers to achieve reform more broadly, to promote nationally consistent approaches and to avoid the costs of establishing diverse industry-specific and subnational regulatory arrangements.

Such considerations led commonwealth, state and territory governments to agree on the need for development of a national competition policy, which would give effect to the following principles, first articulated in 1991:

- no participant in the market should be able to engage in anticompetitive conduct against the public interest;
- as far as possible, universal rules of market conduct should be uniformly applied to all market participants, regardless of the form of business ownership;
- conduct with anticompetitive potential said to be in the public interest should be analysed by an appropriate, transparent assessment process, with provision for review, to demonstrate the nature and incidence of public costs and benefits claimed;
- changes in the coverage or nature of competition policy should be consistent with, and support, the general thrust of reforms;

- an open, integrated domestic market for goods and services should be developed by removing unnecessary barriers to trade and competition; and
- in recognition of the increasingly national operation of markets, complexity and administrative duplication should be reduced.

**The Hilmer Report**

To determine how to give effect to these principles, the governments commissioned a report by the Independent Committee of Inquiry into National Competition Policy. The report, chaired by Professor Fred Hilmer (then Director of the Australian Graduate School of Management at the University of New South Wales) was completed in August 1993. The Hilmer Report concluded that the greatest impediment to enhanced competition in many key sectors of the economy was the restrictions imposed through government regulation, whether in the form of statutes or subordinate legislation, or government ownership. Examples cited included legislative monopolies for public utilities, statutory marketing arrangements for many agricultural products and licensing arrangements for various occupations, businesses and professions.

The Committee noted that neither government imposition of an anticompetitive regulation nor compliance by a business (private or public) with such a regulation is prohibited by the Trade Practices Act, however anticompetitive the consequences. Thus, application of the Trade Practices Act is not sufficient to overcome regulatory arrangements that establish monopolies, provide for the compulsory acquisition of crops, regulate prices, restrict the performance of certain activities to licensed occupations or a host of other regulatory restrictions on competition.

The Committee concluded that a new mechanism was required to ensure that regulatory restrictions on competition did not exceed what was justified in the public interest. It recommended that all Australian governments adopt a set of principles aimed at ensuring that statutes and regulations do not restrict competition unless the restriction is justified in the public interest. This would involve:

- accepting the principle that any restriction on competition must be clearly demonstrated to be in the public interest;
- subjecting new regulatory proposals to increased scrutiny, with the requirement that any significant restrictions on competition lapse within a period of no more than five years unless re-enacted after further scrutiny through a public review process;
- subjecting existing regulations that impose a significant restriction on competition to systematic review to determine whether they conform with

the first principle, and requiring them to lapse within five years, unless re-enacted after scrutiny through a further review process; and
* reviewing regulations taking an economywide perspective, to the extent practical.

While the Committee concluded that implementation of these principles could be left largely to individual governments, it envisaged the establishment of a National Competition Council (NCC), the composition of which would be settled by all governments, with the objective to provide a high-level, independent, analytical advisory body in which all governments would have confidence.[1] The NCC could be given references to undertake and/or coordinate nationwide reviews in specified areas, and to provide guidance on any transitional issues. It could also assist governments in developing more detailed principles for individual sectors, and contract out analytical work to other bodies such as the Productivity Commission, the Australian Bureau of Agriculture and Resource Economics, or state or private bodies.

Another institutional option was to call upon the established antitrust regulator, the Australian Competition and Consumer Commission (ACCC), to play the role ultimately assigned to the NCC. The ACCC is an established, substantial body with a good knowledge of the markets needing reform, which is indispensable for effective reform. The ACCC was also accustomed to dealing with powerful interest groups. However, Professor Hilmer (with the support of the ACCC) rejected this possibility, because the ACCC is already regarded as powerful, and would have been seen by politicians as too powerful if assigned these additional functions. It also would have entered into major conflicts with every government in Australia, in addition to the conflicts it typically experiences with the private sector. Moreover, it was being assigned important new roles at that time, including taking over the work of the Prices Surveillance Authority, regulating the communications, energy and transport industries, administering much of the new access law regime, and facing new challenges in the enforcement of the Act, which had been extended to additional areas, such as the professions, public utilities and agricultural marketing boards.

The Industry Commission (now known as the Productivity Commission) was also rejected for the role. Originally called the Tariff Board, its initial task was to set tariff rates for various Australian industries. It became a fervent critic of protectionism, producing numerous independent reports identifying the high costs of trade protection to the Australian economy, and critically assessing the case for particular protections for each industry. As protections were reduced, the Commission shifted its attention to other areas needing microeconomic reform, such as the energy sector, and produced major reports outlining possible reform patterns. The Industry Commission's work, however, was circumscribed because it depended on the Commonwealth government for references, which was often reluctant to refer controversial areas (unless they fit the wishes of the government at the moment). The Commission had a well-deserved reputation for relying upon high-level, hard-line economics and for its independence. It was unacceptable to the states, which preferred to assign these functions to a body like the new NCC, which would be partially composed of representatives whom they nominated. The Commission continues, however, to conduct reviews that are part of the national competition policy.

The Hilmer Report suggested that the NCC should both study the need for reform and act as broker to implement the reform. The state and territory governments accepted the principles of the Hilmer Report on the whole, and they agreed that the legislative reviews were necessary and should occur. However, they did not want the NCC to perform the central brokering role, and instead desired to control the reviews themselves. They accepted the general principles that all forms of regulation should be reviewed, that competition principles should govern the findings, and that the reviews should be public, independent and transparent. At that time, the states and territories were reasonably keen on the idea of the review. However, given the states' and territories' reservations about the NCC, the Commonwealth was somewhat doubtful of their real willingness to persist with support for competition reforms over a five-year period. Thus, as described below in greater detail, the Commonwealth stated that it would pay the states and territories several billion dollars as long as they did the job properly, and the NCC was empowered to make that determination.

**The Review**

The elements of the review programme are described in the Introduction to Part III, and will therefore only be briefly summarized here. In 1995, the Council of Australian Governments (COAG) (which is made up of the prime minister and the state premiers and chief ministers of the two territories) committed to perform the review. It signed a competition policy agreement (CPA), which provided for the review and reform of all laws that restrict competition.

One of the NCC's first tasks was to identify the laws that affected competition and were in need of review. Well over 2000 such laws were identified, covering a broad array of sectors: agriculture, mining, construction, manufacturing, distribution and all services, including financial, health, communications, transport and personal (such as hairdressing). The scope and variety of coverage is demonstrated by the following partial list of the legislation which has been considered as part of the assessment of 'second tranche' progress (see below):

- regulation of the dairy industry;
- domestic marketing arrangements for rice;
- shop trading regulations;

- liquor licensing;
- third-party motor vehicle insurance;
- workers' compensation arrangements;
- professional indemnity insurance for legal practitioners;
- regulation of Australia Post;
- agricultural statutory marketing arrangements;
- pharmacy regulation;
- regulation of professions;
- employee choice and public sector superannuating;
- gaming regulation;
- taxi licensing and regulation;
- animal welfare legislation;
- food legislation;
- resource development agreement legislation; and
- digital television.

Another list is set out in Table 16.1, which is a selection of legislation scheduled for review over the remaining period of the national competition policy (NCP) legislation review programme.

The principles underlying the reviews were that legislation and regulations should not restrict competition unless it could be demonstrated that the benefits of the restriction to the community as a whole outweigh the costs, and the objectives of the legislation can only be achieved by restricting competition. The states retained substantial freedom as to how to proceed with the reviews, but they were required to submit by 1996 a timetable for reform that would allow for completion of the legislative reviews by the year 2000.

The agreement required that reviews be comprehensive, bona fide examinations of the effects of restrictions on competition and on the economy generally; that they be conducted in an open and rigorous manner, with maximum provision for public consultation or involvement; and that membership of review panels be independent and impartial and be viewed as such. As for new legislation, each state was required to satisfy the underlying principles of the review and to demonstrate that it was doing so. The states further agreed that anticompetitive legislation that survived review should be systematically reconsidered every ten years.

The NCP provided financial incentives to the states to meet their review and reform obligation in the form of three tranches of 'competition payments' worth billions of dollars. These payments were to be made by the Commonwealth to the states and territories in return for satisfactory progress in meeting NCP obligations, including deadlines for regulatory review. However, it insisted that this money would only be given if the reviews were judged by the NCC to have been conducted properly. Thus, the NCC is responsible for assessing the

*Table 16.1    Selective list of legislation scheduled for NCP legislative review*

| Jurisdiction | Legislation |
| --- | --- |
| Commonwealth | Dairy industry legislation |
| Commonwealth | Financial Corporations Act |
| Commonwealth | Intellectual property protection legislation |
| New South Wales | Professional Standards Act 1994 |
| New South Wales | Classification (Publications Films and Computer Games) Enforcement Act 1995 |
| New South Wales | Rail Safety Act 1993 |
| Victoria | Architects Act 1991 and Regulations 1994 |
| Victoria | Conservation Forests and Lands Act 1987 |
| Victoria | Fisheries Acts and Regulations |
| Queensland | Environmental Protection Act 1994 and Regulations |
| Queensland | Consumer Credit Legislation Amendment Act |
| Queensland | Invasion of Privacy Act 1971 and Regulations |
| Western Australia | Dental Act 1939 and Regulations |
| Western Australia | Grain Marketing Act 1975 and Regulations |
| Western Australia | Taxi Act 1994 and Regulations |
| South Australia | Hairdressers Act 1988 |
| South Australia | Meat Hygiene Act 1994 |
| South Australia | Landlord and Tenant Act 1939 |
| Tasmania | Door to Door Trading Act 1986 |
| Tasmania | Land Use Planning and Approvals Act 1993 |
| Tasmania | Shop Trading Hours Act 1984 |
| Australian Capital Territory | Education/schooling legislation |
| Australian Capital Territory | Prostitution Act 1992 |
| Australian Capital Territory | Motor Traffic Act 1936 |
| Northern Territory | Retirement Villages Act |
| Northern Territory | Agent's Licensing Act |
| Northern Territory | Housing Act |

*Source*:   NCC Annual Report 1997–1998.

progress of state and territory reviews and for making recommendations to the federal treasurer as to whether payments should be made. The NCA did not, however, require that the NCC assess the Commonwealth's progress in meeting these requirements. Thus, very large amounts of money are at stake, and the NCC can only recommend that they be paid to states that have conducted their reviews properly. While there is some credibility to this threat, it is unclear how far it will ultimately be pursued.

The NCC has recently published its second tranche assessment of governments' progress in implementing national competition policy and related reforms. A somewhat mixed picture emerges. Most of the reviews have been completed on time and in accordance with the proper processes, but the most difficult areas for review have been left until last. Although reviews have been concluded in a number of areas, government action in response to the reviews is still inconclusive. Some payments have already been held back, and more holdbacks are threatened for next year. The NCC has indicated to some governments that if the competition payments are to be made in full, more radical change will be required by the year 2000. For example, in the agricultural sector, some serious anticompetitive restrictions have been reviewed but not removed. Monopoly marketing board arrangements, under which all produce or output in a given industry is supplied to the board, which then sells it in Australia and abroad, has been partially reformed. The supply to the domestic market has been freed, but the export monopoly remains. However, the export arrangement accounts for a very large part of the industry's output. The monopoly over the marketing of exports continues, and significant inhibitors have been imposed on anyone seeking to behave in competitive fashion in the domestic market. The NCC has flagged a number of areas in which it will re-review the state of progress in certain reform areas with a view to making possible financial deductions in the year 2000.

## D.   REACTIONS TO THE REVIEW

Following its adoption, the NCP has been subject to a significant degree of opposition and resistance by directly affected groups. There is a tendency to blame it for any economic change in the community. For example, the NCP has been unduly blamed for a decline in economic activity in rural areas, which was caused by structural change having little to do with the adoption of the NCP.

Moreover, state governments have also resisted where there have been adverse effects on government revenue. The state governments did not fully understand what they were committing themselves to with the NCP review. On the whole, politicians initially favoured the idea of a national competition policy. In some ways, proclaiming it is the easy part, but implementation is far more difficult.

The NCC has replied by stressing that the ultimate criterion by which laws should be judged is whether they benefit the public, not whether they limit competition. Criteria such as social and environmental benefits, for example, have not been abandoned, as some critics have alleged. If laws that promote these benefits clash with economic goals, however, governments must explicitly determine that such social and environmental goals are supreme and must be achieved in a way that limits competition.

Moreover, the Australian economy has been doing well recently. Australia has weathered the Asian financial crisis very well. By OECD standards, its economic performance in recent years has been quite good, in part because the flexible structure of the economy has been able to cope with shocks from the rest of the world better than in the past. This is, to some extent, attributable to the effects of the NCP and a number of other reforms, such as those adopted in earlier years with respect to the financial sector. As a result, the unfavourable press that the NCP had been receiving has eased.

The enthusiasm of governments for the review has waned somewhat, although not totally. Once the reforms had been enacted in 1995, the attention of the crusaders who brought about the reforms moved on to other areas. The Commonwealth government and the state governments have tended to believe that with enactment of the reforms in 1995, the matter has been addressed. This attitude is incorrect, as the process of competition reform is ongoing and requires continual pressure to resist the efforts of adversely affected interest groups to prevent or slow down progress. To some extent, these problems can be addressed by the establishment of permanent institutions whose task is to press for the implementation of the reforms. A degree of ongoing political leadership from the top is, however, still required.

Reform of competition policy is different from other types of economic reform, such as trade policy. In order to bring about a trade policy reform, the government must undertake a difficult political battle. However, once a reform has been enacted removing a trade protection or lowering the rate of protection, there is no need for further government action. The market goes to work and reallocates resources. In contrast, enactment of a competition policy reform is the beginning rather than the end of the battle. In some ways, enactment of the general reform law is the easiest part of the process, which may be helped because its implications are not fully understood. The more difficult part is implementation, which brings about numerous battles in the different sectors of the economy as the reforms are applied to them. The groups affected by the reforms will typically go back to governments in an effort to have them reverse the commitment to reform in their sector. The actual processes, including investigations, reports, court cases, determinations, appeals, repeal of legislation and so on, are lengthy and time consuming.

There is also scope for criticism of the reforms on the ground that factors other than economics are more important. Those who hold the privileged position free from competition are usually well placed to lobby and argue publicly against the reforms. To counter such efforts, strong independent institutions are needed, with a commitment to implementing the reforms and a willingness to argue for them publicly.

The business community has welcomed the reforms, and their support has been very important. They feel that it is unfair that the competition laws target them, and ignore the areas of big government monopoly, and all the government acts that are anticompetitive. They also feel that it takes a bit of the 'heat' off them if competition authorities are preoccupied with these other areas. Although some businesses stand to lose from the reforms, the majority of the business community has much to gain from the repeal of anticompetitive laws: it will receive supplies more efficiently and competitively, and it will gain new opportunities.

## CONCLUSION

It is too early to judge the success of the Australian review programme. Most scheduled reviews have been concluded, which is an achievement in itself. The governments' decision to review every area of anticompetitive legislation automatically has opened numerous topics for review. Most reviews have at least led to some progress in a procompetitive direction. To date, however, the reviews have not achieved a fully competitive outcome.

The Australian review has implications for Europe, which should give high priority to adopting a comprehensive, vigorously applied competition policy. Europe's macro policy seems to be progressing satisfactorily, with the adoption of the euro and the progress on the internal market. However, it seems important to have flexible, competitive product markets, partly in relation to the employment problem, but also more generally, to enable the European economy to adapt to changes such as those that will follow from the euro.

Europe should place high priority on adopting a review agenda similar to Australia's, covering all the countless laws in every sector in every member state that restrict competition, the structures of the public utilities that are unduly anticompetitive, and other laws of this sort. It would need support and leadership at the highest levels in Europe, at the Commission, and among some national leaders and finance ministers, as well as from the business community. This process might be initiated by having a high-profile inquiry by an independent commission of important people, with a commitment to and some knowledge of competition policy. It should probably be serviced by the Directorate General for Competition. It would study this problem, gaining support for the idea, and setting up a plan of action.

Every country, every continent has its own institutional issues and culture, among other things. I do not know if this proposal would succeed in Europe, but it would be well worth discussing.

# NOTE

1. Australia has had a long tradition of establishing independent bodies to report on the need for economic reform. For example, several independent committees produced numerous reports that paved the way for financial deregulation in the 1980s.

# 17. Introduction to existing programmes addressing the anticompetitive impact of regulation

## Laraine L. Laudati

*This chapter reviews recent efforts to eliminate the anticompetitive effects of regulation. Four major efforts are discussed, as follows:*

- *The Australian legislative review project, initiated in 1995. This is an extraordinary effort to analyse all existing legislation to determine whether it has anticompetitive effects, and if so, to modify the legislation in order to eliminate those effects.*
- *The US National Commission for the Review of Antitrust Laws and Procedures (NCRALP) Report. Approximately 20 years before the Australians undertook their review, NCRALP prepared a report that focused, in part, on the anticompetitive effects of regulation. It recommended the enactment of legislation that would have instituted a screening device to eliminate anticompetitive provisions in new legislation, and a review of existing legislation with an eye to making revisions where necessary to eliminate anticompetitive provisions.[1]*
- *The OECD regulatory reform project. The overall goal of this project is improving regulation, one aspect of which is to address its anticompetitive effects.*
- *National competition advocacy programmes. Some governments have relied on their competition authorities to act as guardian of competition through competition advocacy programmes. These programmes have been a useful vehicle for making regulators aware of competition issues.*

## INTRODUCTION

This chapter sets forth the major efforts that have been undertaken to date designed to reform or eliminate anticompetitive regulation. The most significant effort has been that of the Australians, which is discussed in detail below.

Other efforts discussed are that of the US National Commission for the Review of Antitrust Laws and Procedures, the Organization for Economic Cooperation and Development (OECD) Regulatory Reform Project, and national competition advocacy programmes. These programmes provide useful input for the current effort to design guidelines on the elimination of anticompetitive regulation for the European Union (EU).

## A.   THE AUSTRALIAN REGULATORY REVIEW PROJECT

In 1992, the prime minister of Australia commissioned an independent study of national competition policy. The Independent Committee of Inquiry, chaired by Professor Frederick G. Hilmer, conducted an extensive investigation, involving submissions from numerous public and private entities, and considered all aspects of what the national competition policy should encompass. One section of the Committee's Report dealt with regulatory restrictions on competition.[2] Recognizing that all government interventions, at some level, affect the competitive position of firms, the Report found that the pervasiveness of interventions was harmful to the economy. Examples of such restrictions were found in a broad range of sectors of the economy, including agriculture, the professions, transport and government monopolies.

The Report recommended that a central plank of the new national competition policy should be to devise a mechanism to facilitate the reform of government regulation that unjustifiably restricts competition. Under this scheme, all existing and proposed legislation should be subject to analysis for anticompetitive effects.

Hilmer suggested that two forms of regulation were of particular concern because they had the most direct impact on competition. The first of these was regulation that creates barriers to market entry,[3] including licensing regimes regulating the number of producers or the volume of production (often in conjunction with price regulation), and regulations that set standards or qualifications, which may be more restrictive than necessary to protect the public interest, or may be enforced in a manner that discriminates in favour of incumbents.[4] The second area of special concern was regulation that restricts competitive conduct, such as price controls, restrictions on advertising, and ethical standards.

The Hilmer Report recommended that the guiding principles of the national policy with respect to reform of regulation should be the following:

1.  There should be no regulatory restrictions on competition unless clearly demonstrated to be in the public interest. Governments that restrict the ability

of consumers to choose among rival suppliers and alternative terms and conditions should demonstrate why this is necessary in the public interest.

2. Proposals for new regulation that has the potential to restrict competition should include evidence that the competitive effects of the regulation have been considered, that the benefits of the proposed restriction outweigh the likely costs, and that the regulation is no more restrictive than necessary in the public interest. Where a significant restriction on competition is identified, the relevant regulation should be subject to a sunset provision deeming it to lapse within a period of no more than five years unless re-enacted after further scrutiny in accordance with Principle 3.

3. All existing regulation that imposes a significant restriction on competition should be subject to regular review to determine conformity with Principle 1. The review should be performed by an independent body, involve a public inquiry process and include a public assessment of the costs and benefits of the restriction. If retained after initial review the regulation should be subject to the same requirements imposed on new regulation under Principle 2.

4. To the extent practicable and relevant, reviews of regulation undertaken pursuant to Principles 2 and 3 should take an economywide perspective of the impact of restrictions on competition.

No specific recommendations as to how to measure the magnitude of either the public benefits of regulation or of its anticompetitive impact were provided.

The Hilmer Report recommended that each Australian state should be responsible for implementing the reform principles within its jurisdiction. It also urged the creation of a new, independent, nationally-focused institution, the National Competition Council (NCC), which would: (i) coordinate reforms among the states and facilitate the cooperative process, (ii) make economywide reviews of particular regulatory restrictions, and (iii) develop more detailed principles for analysing regulatory restrictions, based on the principles set forth above.

The Report suggested options for dealing with regulations the costs of which exceeded the benefits to the community. The options were: a national law creating a 'right to compete' or a 'right to buy' that would override the state regulation; or retention by the states of powers to handle such situations. It urged a cooperative approach, with the possibility of enacting a national law at a later time, should the cooperative approach not function effectively.

The Australian government embraced the recommendations of the Hilmer Report in the overhaul of its national competition law. It adopted the concept of 'competition policy in the wider sense', which encompasses not only traditional antitrust law, but also the removal of government-imposed impediments to competition, and proactive steps to promote competition. Specifically, in April 1995, the Council of Australian Governments (COAG) signed the Competition Policy Agreement (CPA), providing, among other things, for the review and reform by the year 2000 of all laws that restrict competition.[5] The review was expected to render substantial benefits across the economy by reducing regulatory compliance costs, increasing the scope for business innovation, and making markets more responsive to the needs of consumers.[6]

The CPA established the following guiding principle for the review:

> [L]egislation (including Acts, enactments, Ordinances or regulations) should not restrict competition unless it can be demonstrated that:
> (a)  the benefits of the restriction to the community as a whole outweigh the costs; and
> (b)  the objectives of the legislation can only be achieved by restricting competition.[7]

The Agreement required that reviews be comprehensive, bona fide examinations of the effect of restrictions on competition and on the economy generally, and that they include genuine assessments of the costs and benefits of the restrictions. It stated that a review should:

> (a)  clarify the objectives of the legislation;
> (b)  identify the nature of the restriction on competition;
> (c)  analyse the likely effect of the restriction on competition and on the economy generally;
> (d)  assess and balance the costs and benefits of the restriction;[8] and
> (e)  consider alternative means for achieving the same result including non-legislative approaches.[9]

The NCC, which was created as part of the overhaul of national competition policy, subsequently provided further guidance as to the type of legislation that is likely to restrict competition:

> Legislation affecting competition may directly or indirectly:
>
> •  govern the entry and exit of firms or individuals into or out of markets;
> •  control prices or production levels;
> •  restrict the quality, level or location of goods and services available;
> •  restrict advertising and promotional activities;
> •  restrict price or type of inputs used in the production process;
> •  be likely to confer significant costs on businesses; or
> •  provide advantages to some firms over others by, for example, sheltering some activities from the pressures of competition.[10]

The NCC has also indicated that an analysis of the impact of the legislation on different groups, and of alternatives, should be a part of the review.[11]

The CPA left each state with substantial powers and discretion for implementing the regulatory review in its own jurisdiction. It required only that by

1996, each state submit a timetable for reform, which would allow for completion of the legislative review by the year 2000.[12] It also established that each state must require proposals for new legislation to be accompanied by evidence that the legislation is consistent with the guiding principle. Finally, it provided that anticompetitive legislation should be systematically reviewed every ten years.

Initially, no criteria were established for the composition of review panels. Thereafter, in its 1996–1997 Annual Report, the NCC stated:

> [R]eviews should be conducted in an open and rigorous manner. As part of this, members of review panels should be impartial in relation to the issues under review. In this respect, the Council considers that industry representatives should not be appointed to review panels, and is cautious of situations where the government bodies responsible for promulgating particular regulations are represented on review panels. The Council also considers that reviews should generally make provision for public consultation or involvement. At a minimum, terms of reference should be made publicly available.[13]

The national competition policy (NCP) provided financial incentives to the states to meet their review and reform obligations, in the form of three tranches of 'competition payments'. These payments would be made by the Commonwealth to the states and territories in return for satisfactory progress in meeting NCP obligations, including deadlines for regulatory review. The NCC is responsible to assess state and territory progress, and make recommendations to the federal treasurer as to whether payments should be made. The NCA did not, however, require that the NCC assess the Commonwealth's progress in meeting these requirements.

Assessment of progress on implementation has proved difficult, since the NCP agreements are broad statements of intent rather than specific requirements against which progress can be readily assessed.[14] Nonetheless, progress on the review has been reported in the annual reports for 1995–1996, and 1996–1997.

The Annual Report for 1996–97 stated that approximately 100 reviews had been completed by March 1997. The early findings indicated that reform was needed in certain areas. For instance:

- pharmacy legislation was found to afford significant protection from competition to industry incumbents and to impose costs and restrictions on pharmacists and their practices. For example, pharmacists are limited to owning no more than three outlets, and a new pharmacy cannot locate within two kilometres of an existing approved pharmacy without losing the benefits of certain subsidies;

- significant overlap and unnecessary regulation was apparent with respect to business licences; and
- restrictive and discriminatory trading hours legislation was repealed in one territory, when analysis revealed that the costs exceeded the benefits.

A number of reforms have followed from the reviews that have already been completed, including the repeal of legislation, the removal of specific provisions, the development of replacement legislation, and the streamlining of administrative arrangements and licensing. For instance:

- restrictive trading hours legislation was repealed when review revealed that its costs exceeded its benefits;
- a large number of licences are expected to be abolished or consolidated and simplified;
- redundant legislation is being abolished; and
- on several occasions, reviews recommended that anticompetitive legislation be retained because it yielded substantial public benefits.[15]

In several instances, however, the review led to the retention of anticompetitive arrangements.[16] For instance:

- Some jurisdictions determined, without review, that the benefits outweigh the costs of an anticompetitive restriction, or have sought to exempt certain classes of anticompetitive regulation from review.[17] The NCC reported that little justification exists for exempting a class of anticompetitive legislation from review, even though there might be a case for exempting certain such legislation from reform.
- In certain instances, the review carried out by the states has been deemed deficient because it prejudged anticompetitive legislation to be in the public interest,[18] or recommended, without sufficient justification, the retention of anticompetitive legislation.[19] Even the assessment of the Commonwealth's legislative review has revealed that it has retained anticompetitive legislation in the health-care area.[20]
- Several external parties have complained to the NCC with respect to the composition and method of operation of the reviews, and the scope and availability of review terms of reference.
- There have also been problems with respect to the outcomes of some specific reviews. In several instances, a government chose to retain a restriction on competition when the review had recommended that reform would be in the public interest.[21]

- In several instances, new legislation likely to restrict competition substantially has been allowed to take effect by the responsible state government.[22]
- Finally, there have been problems where recommended reforms have not been implemented, notwithstanding the government's efforts to do so, because opposition parties in state parliaments have opposed their implementation. The NCC has indicated that it considers the NCP as a 'national commitment by all parties, binding not only the government but also the parliament'.[23]

In July 1997, the NCC recommended that all 'first tranche' payments should be made, notwithstanding its finding that several states had fallen short of their obligations, because it viewed its role as encouraging reform rather than penalizing non-compliance.[24] In a supplementary assessment, however, the NCC recommended that Aus$10 million be withheld from New South Wales for its failure to comply with obligations to reform its regulations related to domestic rice marketing.[25]

After several years of experience with implementation of the legislative review, and in recognition of the need for robust processes for the success of the review, the NCC commissioned a private economics consulting firm to develop guidelines which would reflect best practices for legislation reviews. The 'Guidelines for NCP Legislation Reviews'[26] recognized that good-quality reviews required comprehensive terms of reference reflecting competition principles, appropriate review mechanisms, consultation with the community, recommendations consistent with the evidence, and implementation of review recommendations. The Guidelines thus set forth best practices with respect to the three phases of conducting a review: establishing a review, undertaking a review, and implementing review recommendations, each of which consisted of a number of separate tasks.

As to Phase I, establishing a review, the Guidelines recognized a number of hurdles that reviewers face, including: resistance from vested interests, lack of data for analysis, lack of independent analysis, lack of resources and consistent economic framework for conducting analysis, inability clearly to demonstrate benefits of change against apparent benefits of regulation, and insufficient incentive to comply with reforms. To address these hurdles, the Guidelines placed considerable emphasis on the importance of a well-designed review mechanism. This should include a review team and a steering committee. The former should be made up of independent individuals, familiar with competition policy, economic concepts and the legislation under review. The latter should be headed by a representative from a government department with an economywide perspective, and possibly a representative of the department responsible for implementation of the legislation and one from the jurisdiction's competition policy unit. Interest group representatives should have no advisory role. Different types of review should be used, ranging from full independent public review to departmental review, depending on the importance of the legislation and the potential for misunderstanding. The reviewers should work according to publicly available, detailed terms of reference.

As to Phase II, undertaking a review, the Guidelines followed the five steps set forth above from the CPA. Regarding objectives of the legislation, which may be explicit in the legislation or legislative history or implied, the review should assess them according to priority, consistency and contemporary relevance. It should then determine whether the objectives should be modified, reprioritized, deleted, augmented or accepted. Regarding restrictions of competition, the Guidelines suggest that they be categorized (following the categories identified by the NCC, set forth above) and prioritized according to degree of restrictiveness. Next, the review must establish a framework for comparing the current situation with the legislation to a hypothetical commercial environment without the legislation, which is very difficult. This must then be quantified, in order to tally benefits and costs. The Guidelines specify how the problems of dealing with unreliable data should be addressed in making the cost–benefit analysis. Finally, when the net benefits of the restriction are positive, a further analysis is required to determine whether more procompetitive alternatives exist. A list of procompetitive alternatives to each category of restriction is provided.

As to Phase III, implementation of the review, the Guidelines observe that this is the business of the government once it has received the recommendations from the review. Necessary reform legislation should be drafted and passed in order to meet NCP commitments. Payment or withholding of commonwealth funds should follow. However, obstacles to effective implementation include political issues, poor quality reviews, the complexities of bringing about change, and legal obstacles that may transcend jurisdictional borders. The Guidelines make suggestions for dealing with these obstacles, including educating the electorate, increasing transparency and engaging experts.

The Guidelines reflect the kinds of difficulties that the Australian review has met to date, and are a positive effort to make the remaining reviews more effective.

## B.   THE REPORT OF THE US NATIONAL COMMISSION FOR THE REVIEW OF ANTITRUST LAWS AND PROCEDURES

In 1979, a report was issued by the National Commission for the Review of Antitrust Laws and Procedures (NCRALP) in the United States. This

Commission had been appointed to address a number of questions regarding the US antitrust laws, including the large number of statutory exemptions from those laws, and the concomitant economic regulation created to replace the forces of competition in the affected industries. NCRALP reviewed the immunities and economic regulations in five areas, which it deemed to be the highest priorities at that time: surface transportation, insurance, agriculture, ocean shipping and export trade. The fundamental conclusion was that 'regulation should eliminate competition only when truly essential to the achievement of articulated public objectives and ... the regulatory techniques chosen should operate in the least anticompetitive manner possible'.[27]

The Commission identified a number of problems that follow from the use of economic regulation. First, it expressed a basic distrust of such regulation, because it 'cannot supply the constant discipline, the spur to improved performance, the immediate rewards for successful innovation, and the rapid punishment for waste and inefficiency, that are provided by the free market'.[28] This concern was reinforced by numerous academic studies, which had concluded that economic regulation tends to be protectionist, and thereby to discourage input cost control and to decrease efficiency. Second, there is often a mismatch between asserted legislative purposes and actual industry conditions (such as the use of entry and price regulation, suitable for natural monopolies, in conjunction with industries that were not natural monopolies). Third, it noted that economic regulation is often an indirect way of subsidizing certain consumers at the expense of others, which is highly inefficient and causes costly dislocations.

The Commission recommended that an industry-by-industry inquiry should be made, following a consistent analytical approach, at both federal and state levels, to combat anticompetitive regulatory activities in order to eliminate the high economic costs of regulation that have no corresponding social benefits. It developed the following framework for analysis:

> First, evaluation of particular immunities should begin by considering the historical and economic context in which the immunity was created. When the immunity in question was enacted, what did the policy-makers believe to be the costs or ill effects of relying on free competition? In short, what was this immunity supposed to do?
>
> Second, compared with these original beliefs and expectations, what have been the results? Have the regulatory goals been achieved? Or have changed conditions or new learning undermined the assumptions on which the regulatory structure was first justified?
>
> Third, what costs or benefits have been associated with the immunity and its attendant regulatory scheme? ... A general understanding of economic regulation can also suggest a number of less formal, but nonetheless revealing factual inquiries to help determine the existence of significant social costs with respect to particular immunities or regulatory controls. Commissioner Kahn suggested several specific questions of this sort to the Commission:

(1)  Has the monopoly value of regulatory restraints and immunized collective action been capitalized into the high cost of entry licenses?
(2)  Are innovators and innovations being excluded?
(3)  Are the customers of the industry working to escape or eliminate the regulations?
(4)  Do input prices appear to be inflated?
(5)  Can we compare the performance in the regulated industry in question to that in some unregulated market?

Finally, if removal of the antitrust immunity and deregulation appears justified based on changed economic conditions or unacceptably high social costs, questions relating to methods of transition should be considered: Would increased competition create unacceptable dislocations? Are disruptions likely to be short-term or long-term? Are the interests of consumer benefits and equity best served by a relatively brief or relatively long transition?[29]

The Commission suggested that this industry-by-industry inquiry should be coupled with adoption of mechanisms to focus attention on competitive issues within existing regulatory programmes, and endorsed a Senate bill to this end. The bill established a three-part test for all federal agencies to apply to any action 'the effect of which may be substantially to lessen competition, to tend to create a monopoly, or to create or maintain a situation involving a significant burden on competition'. Such an action would be approved only if:

(1)  such action is necessary to accomplish an overriding statutory purpose of the agency;
(2)  the anticompetitive effects of such action are clearly outweighed by significant and demonstrable benefits to the general public; and
(3)  the objectives of the action and the overriding statutory purpose cannot be accomplished in substantial part by alternative means having less anticompetitive effects.[30]

The legislation was never enacted. However, the Carter administration undertook deregulatory initiatives discussed in the Report with respect to various sectors, including trucking and airlines. Thereafter, the Reagan administration embraced deregulation as an official policy of the executive branch, which was aggressively implemented. Thus, the Report is viewed retrospectively as an important part of the process by which public consciousness of the effects of harmful regulation was increased.

Presently, there is no US law requiring that new regulations be tested for anticompetitive impact. However, as described below, the US antitrust authorities screen legislation for its anticompetitive effects through their competition advocacy programmes. Moreover, in specific sectors (such as telecommunications), deregulation has required such testing. In addition, the principles of administrative review applied by US courts impose some marginal limits on regulatory discretion to restrict competition. Most federal regulatory statutes employ a 'public interest' standard, and the courts have recognized that preservation of competition is in the public interest.

Notwithstanding all of these efforts, some experts believe that the problem of anticompetitive regulation is still pervasive in the US at federal, state and local levels. However, this problem is not a priority in the present timeframe, given the current state of economic prosperity in the US.

## C. THE OECD REPORT ON REGULATORY REFORM

In 1997, the OECD issued a report on regulatory reform.[31] Although not specifically focused on curing the anticompetitive effects of regulation, the Report includes 'improving economic performance' as one of the main goals of reform, which it defines as promoting competition, market openness, technological innovation, structural adjustment and other dimensions important to economic growth. Further, it observes that reform that enhances competition and reduces regulatory costs can boost efficiency, reduce prices, stimulate innovation and improve the ability of economies to adapt to change and remain competitive in global markets.

The Report found that economic regulations that reduce competition and distort prices are pervasive. Such regulations can take various forms, such as restrictions on starting up and operating businesses (quotas on business licences and shop opening hours). The report concluded: '[I]n the absence of clear evidence that such regulations are necessary to serve public interests, governments should place a high priority on identifying and removing economic regulations that impede competition'.

Studies of regulatory reform in several specific sectors (professions, telecommunications, and electricity, among others) were also made as part of this project. Of special significance to the present work is the chapter addressing the professions. Various types of restrictions on competitive practices (for example, on price competition, such as fixing minimum or maximum fees; truthful advertising; use of non-deceptive trade names; and relationships with other kinds of businesses) traditionally have been justified as preventing market failures that harm consumers. However, such restrictions are not necessary to assure quality; rather, they are correlated with higher prices and less innovation. Consequently, regulations that unjustifiably prevent entry, fix prices, or prohibit truthful, non-deceptive advertising should be rescinded, and new regulations that provide the public with protection while permitting competition should be adopted.[32]

In its effort to devise a programme for regulatory reform, the Report reviews the history over the last 20 years of the regulatory reform movement in OECD countries. Beginning in the early 1980s, governments focused on *deregulation* as they became aware that government intervention was needlessly restricting competition. However, as a result of the backward-looking nature of deregulation and its failure to provide guidance with respect to new regulation, governments began to focus on *improving regulatory quality* – that is, creating more efficient, flexible, simple and effective regulations.[33]

Accordingly, the Report identified three main tasks as essential to the process of improving regulatory quality: (i) building a regulatory management system, (ii) reforming processes for developing new regulations, and (iii) upgrading the quality of existing regulations. Apropos of the first (building a regulatory management system), the Report emphasizes the importance of establishing support for a reform programme at the highest political levels, and of creating open communication with affected interests and the public with respect to the programme. It also states that establishment of explicit standards for regulatory quality is crucial to the reform process.

Apropos of the second (improving the quality of new regulation), the Report observes that regulation is often made with too little understanding of its consequences in terms of both direct costs and benefits, and indirect effects, such as impact on innovation, competition and trade. Accordingly, it recommends the institution of regulatory impact analysis (RIA), in order fully to understand the consequences of new regulation, thereby avoiding regulations that are less effective and more costly than they should be.[34] RIA is an empirical method of decision making, to the extent that decisions are based on fact finding and analysis that defines the parameters of action according to established criteria. Thus, it widens and clarifies the relevant factors for decision making. It is a method of '(i) systematically and consistently examining selected potential impacts arising from government action and of (ii) communicating the information to decision-makers'.[35]

By 1996, 18 OECD countries (and the EU) had adopted RIA programmes.[36] The analytical methods used for RIA in these countries vary considerably, with nine countries imposing a general requirement to assess all important aspects (known as 'consequence analysis'), three focusing only on fiscal costs, two on compliance costs to businesses, and four requiring cost–benefit analysis. RIA is implemented by the regulators themselves, although the institutions responsible for overseeing these programmes vary: some are specialized bodies with only that responsibility, others are at the centre of government or a part of other government agencies, such as budgeting, and others are within outside bodies. The OECD Report concludes that RIA will fail if it is left entirely to regulators, as well as if it is too centralized.[37] Finally, the development of written guidance is an indicator of the effectiveness of the programme.

The Report makes seven major policy recommendations for regulatory reform, to be seen as an integrated package, and to apply broadly across sectors and policy. The recommendations are as follows:

- adopt at the political level broad programmes of regulatory reform that establish clear objectives and frameworks for implementation;
- review regulations systematically to ensure that they continue to meet their intended objectives efficiently and effectively;
- ensure that regulations and regulatory processes are transparent, non-discriminatory and efficiently applied;
- review and strengthen where necessary the scope, effectiveness and enforcement of competition policy;
- reform economic regulations in all sectors to stimulate competition, and eliminate them except where clear evidence demonstrates that they are the best way to serve broad public interests (in particular, review as a high priority those aspects of economic regulations that restrict entry, exit, pricing, output, normal commercial practices and forms of business organization);
- eliminate unnecessary regulatory barriers to trade and investment by enhancing implementation of international agreements and strengthening international principles; and
- identify important linkages with other policy objectives and develop policies to achieve those objectives in ways that support reform.

In related OECD work, the Public Management Service (PUMA) has issued a checklist of ten principles for producing efficient, flexible and transparent regulations:

- Is the problem correctly defined?
- Is government action justified?
- Is regulation the best form of government action?
- Is there a legal basis for regulation?
- What is the appropriate level (or levels) of government for this action?
- Do the benefits of regulation justify the costs?
- Is the distribution of effects across society transparent?
- Is the regulation clear, consistent, comprehensible and accessible to users?
- Have all interested parties had the opportunity to present their views?
- How will compliance be achieved?

The second and sixth questions in the checklist have particular relevance here. Apropos of the second, PUMA has indicated that when considering whether government action is justified, 'markets should always be considered as an alternative to government action, and the capacity of the private sector and individuals to deal with the problem should be assessed'. Moreover, PUMA notes that most OECD countries do not consider economic costs of new regulations. To do so, it suggests that various kinds of market analyses of effects on competition, international competitiveness or technological innovation can be used, particularly with respect to regulations with larger economic effects.

## D.  COMPETITION ADVOCACY PROGRAMMES

### Competition Advocacy in the United States (Department of Justice and Federal Trade Commission)

In the United States, the two antitrust enforcement agencies, the Antitrust Division of the Department of Justice (DOJ) and the Bureau of Competition of the Federal Trade Commission (FTC), have competition advocacy programmes. Formal advocacy activities include providing Congress with testimony on competition issues raised in legislation, and providing regulatory agencies with written comments and testimony on proposed regulations. The agencies also provide informal input, through participation in executive branch task forces and committees, informal advice on congressional matters, speeches, and participation on panel discussions. The agencies also engage in advocacy activities where enforcement jurisdiction is lacking as the result of some form of antitrust immunity. Advocacy activities of both agencies have focused on regulated private price fixing and government ratemaking, limitations on entry, access to essential facilities, and output restrictions; interventions have been in a variety of sectors (for example, telecommunications, financial services, transport, energy, agriculture and the professions).

Through its programme, the DOJ seeks to achieve four objectives: (i) the elimination of unnecessary and costly existing regulation; (ii) preventing the growth of unnecessary new regulation; (iii) minimizing competitive distortions caused by necessary regulation by promoting the least anticompetitive form of regulation consistent with the valid regulatory objectives; and (iv) ensuring that regulation is properly designed to accomplish legitimate regulatory objectives.[38]

The competition advocacy functions of the DOJ are performed by the section of the DOJ that has enforcement responsibility for the sector involved. The major competition advocacy effort is submitting comments and intervening in the proceedings of federal regulatory agencies to cause them to focus on competition issues. A large number of regulated industries are covered, but the issues raised tend to be the same: 'whether competition is feasible, whether an industry is naturally monopolistic, whether cross-subsidies exist and, if so, whether they are desirable, whether economies of scale are substantial, whether domestic regulation inhibits US firms from effectively competing against their foreign counterparts in foreign markets, and whether particular regulations are likely to accomplish their stated objectives'.[39]

More specifically, analysis of new and existing regulation by the DOJ focuses on whether the benefits to the public of regulation outweigh its anticompetitive effects; whether the benefits can be achieved by some less-anticompetitive alternative; and where regulation is needed, whether it is crafted to achieve its objectives with no unintended consequences. In addressing these issues, the DOJ must consider several basic questions:

- What are the costs or disadvantages of free competition in the market or industry at issue?
- As to existing regulation, has it fulfilled its purpose, and do the underlying economic and social conditions that originally justified market interference still exist?
- What costs and benefits are associated with the existing or proposed regulatory scheme? (In particular, to what degree does it stifle innovation? Has the monopoly value of regulatory restraints and immunized collective action been capitalized into the high cost of entry licences? Do industry customers seek to eliminate regulation? Are input prices inflated? How does the performance of the regulated industry compare with that of an unregulated market?)[40]
- If existing regulation is to be eliminated, what are the necessary elements of a transition from a regulated to a competitive, unregulated market?
- If regulation is appropriate, is the regulatory scheme well tailored to achieve its purpose?

A second aspect of the DOJ's competition advocacy programme involves testimony on legislative matters (that is, proposed new laws). Competition advocacy constitutes one aspect of the 'interagency clearance process' for generating administration views on proposed legislation, which is coordinated by the US Office of Management and Budget (OMB).[41] Legislation, or comments/testimony of the executive branch on pending legislation that is to be transmitted to Congress, is circulated for clearance by the OMB to the agencies likely to have an interest in the matter. When a competition policy issue is raised in proposed legislation, the OMB seeks input from the DOJ/FTC. The DOJ and FTC can also initiate their own comments on pending legislation.

Similarly, the FTC's advocacy programme seeks to 'prevent or reduce possible consumer injury caused by laws, regulations or self-regulatory standards that interfere with the proper functioning of the marketplace'.[42] Its advocacy activities include filing enforcement cases, rulemaking and advising government agencies and self-regulatory organizations on the competitive effects of proposed legislation or rules. For instance, in the area of professional licensing, it has filed lawsuits against medical, dental and other professional associations, and state boards responsible for regulating such professionals, to halt the illegal suppression of truthful advertising and solicitation, to prevent price fixing, and to challenge ethical guidelines and membership requirements of professional associations that restrict contractual or commercial practices of their members.

The agencies' advocacy efforts have, at times, met with opposition from groups attempting to shield themselves from competition, and government bodies sharing their views. Accordingly, the agencies have viewed their advocacy efforts to include persuading lawmakers of the greater benefits of the competitive approach.

## Competition Advocacy in the European Union (DG Comp)[43]

As the Directorate General of the Commission in charge of competition, DG Comp is responsible for ensuring that the competition provisions of the Treaty are respected. One aspect of fulfilling this responsibility is competition advocacy within the Commission. To this end, DG Comp engages in an array of activities, including policy debate and negotiation, with other DGs of the Commission that are responsible for a broad array of sectors.

At a general level, DG Comp presents its annual report to the Parliament, the Economic and Social Committee, and the Council of Ministers, in reply to which the latter bodies submit comments to DG Comp. This creates a regular interinstitutional dialogue regarding competition policy. The Competition Commissioner and DG Comp also participate regularly in meetings of parliamentary committees and of those of the Economic and Social Committee where issues of competition policy are being discussed.

The internal procedures of the Commission require that before taking a formal decision, an Interservice Consultation, which is a systematic consultation of all concerned Directorates General of the Commission, must be made. Accordingly, DG Comp is formally consulted by all other services of the Commission regarding draft regulations, directives, decisions, communications or other documents of the Commission that raise competition issues. This consultation process allows DG Comp to play an essential competition advocacy role. Under this procedure, DG Comp can ensure that competition policy is considered with respect to texts adopted by the Commission or the Council in all areas for which the Commission has authority to act (for example, commercial policy, industrial policy, creation/promotion of the internal market, research and environment).

DG Comp believes that its advocacy efforts have been most influential in four sectors: telecommunications, transport, financial services and energy. At times, other services of the Commission have not agreed with DG Comp when the latter has advocated deregulation and opening up of certain sectors to competition. In such situations, the role of DG Comp as guardian of competition policy has been essential.

# CONCLUSION

A systematic review of all existing laws to eliminate their anticompetitive effects has only been attempted in Australia. The Australian review is commendable for attempting to cover all sectors in all states and the national government. It has made an important contribution in establishing the substantive questions that should be asked in a review, and in recognizing the types of legislation that are most likely to have a harmful effect on competition. Moreover, because this review is actually occurring, it has been forced to address the difficult issue of appropriate institutional arrangements for conducting a review, and for implementing the reforms that the review reveals to be necessary.

However, it remains to be seen whether the Australian review will be effective. Evidently, the guidelines originally provided to the states were not sufficiently detailed to ensure that consistent standards were being applied by all reviewers. Initial reports indicated reluctance by some states to pursue the review vigorously in all sectors. It is not clear whether institutional arrangements have been appropriate to guarantee an impartial, rigorous and transparent review. Moreover, the annual reports do not provide a complete picture of how effective the reviews have been to date. Rather, they give a small number of examples of instances in which reforms have been implemented, or problems with implementation have been experienced. It is unclear whether the reviewing bodies in each of the Australian states are well designed to accomplish the task at hand. However, the resistance of some states to perform reviews, to carry out high-quality and professional reviews, or to make changes that appear to be needed indicates that the review may have problems of an institutional nature. The 1999 'Guidelines for NCP Legislation Reviews', prepared by a private consulting firm, should be helpful in dealing with these problems.

Although the legislation that it recommended was never enacted, the US NCRALP Report has played an important role, both in the US and outside. The Report identified several key questions that should be answered in a legislative review, including the need to consider the original goal of the regulation, whether the legislation has achieved the goal and if not, whether the goal is still relevant. It also suggested that cost–benefit analysis that focused specifically on competition issues be employed. It did not, however, address the key issue of what institutional arrangements should be made to implement a legislative review. As noted above, the NCRALP Report was an important element leading to the major deregulation movement in the US. It has provided a useful analytical framework for determining when reform is needed. However, the Report has not led to a systematic review of laws and regulations in the US, and the concerns of anticompetitive effects of regulation appear not to play an important role in the present administration's public policy.

Competition advocacy programmes, such as those in the US and the EU, can have the beneficial effect of increasing the awareness of competition concerns in the legislative and regulatory rulemaking process. However, in the absence of substantive and procedural guidelines for review, it is likely that the quality of review is variable. Moreover, the US antitrust agencies resort to advocacy in areas where they have no enforcement authority. In the EU, competition concerns articulated during the advocacy process must be balanced against a number of other concerns. Thus, there is no guarantee that competition advocacy programmes will actually protect the interests of competition.

This review of existing programmes should be helpful to the Round Table in defining a framework for substantive analysis, institutional issues, and procedures for a programme designed to eliminate the anticompetitive effects of regulation.

## NOTES

1.  Other competition authorities have engaged in more limited reviews. For instance, the Italian competition authority has reviewed the anticompetitive effects of regulation in some sectors.
2.  Commonwealth of Australia, *National Competition Policy: Report by the Independent Committee of Inquiry* (August 1993) (hereinafter 'the Hilmer Report').
3.  The Report discussed a number of entry barriers created by public ownership or funding of services. *Id.* at 192–5. These, however, are not the subject of the present chapter.
4.  The Report also identified several barriers that are not directly relevant in the present discussion: barriers to the interstate movement of goods and to the importation of foreign goods. Under Community law and various international provisions, these types of barriers are already being addressed.
5.  COAG entered three agreements establishing a national competition policy, one of which was the Competition Policy Agreement.
6.  NCC, Annual Report 1996/97, at 58.
7.  Council of Australian Governments, Competition Principles Agreement (11 April 1995).
8.  With respect to the analysis of benefits and costs of legislation, the NCC has indicated by way of illustration that the following might be considered with respect to legislation supporting an agricultural statutory marketing authority or licensing arrangement:

    - Public benefit considerations could encompass, among other things, an assessment of increased returns to producers, stabilised prices, production and incomes, reduced marketing costs and increased demand in the short-term in terms of economic and regional development, including employment and investment growth.
    - Public cost considerations could encompass, among other things, an assessment of acquisition, production and pricing controls which adversely affect the efficient allocation of resource use both within the agricultural sector and the wider economy. For example, minimum prices that are set above competitive levels can insulate producers from market disciplines, inhibit productivity improvements, and encourage production at a level which cannot be absorbed. Furthermore, the inefficiencies of higher domestic prices for agricultural commodities may be passed on to end-use industries affecting the competitiveness of Australian business, and ultimately the interests of consumers generally, through higher prices.

9.  NCC, Competition Principles Agreement, *supra* note 7, para. 5(9).

10. NCC, 'Legislation Review Compendium' (April 1997). Some of the states, such as Queensland and South Australia, have developed their own guidelines. For instance, Queensland developed guidelines for identifying restrictive legislation that should be reviewed, including legislation that prohibits or restricts activity through licensing agreements, quantitative entitlements, technical standards or price controls. *Id.* at 66. Similarly, South Australia established that the restrictions which should be identified for review could have one or more of the following effects:

   - Create a monopoly;
   - Restrict entry by limiting the number of producers or the amount of product;
   - Restrict entry based on the qualifications or standards of providers of goods and services or on the quality or standard of the product;
   - Restrict entry of goods or services from interstate or overseas thus providing a competitive advantage to local producers;
   - Limit competitive conduct in a market by restricting ordinarily acceptable forms of competitive behaviour such as advertising, competition on the basis of price, use of efficient equipment or hours of operation;
   - Provide for administrative discretion such as favouring incumbents, treating public and private sector providers differently or setting technical standards only available from a single supplier.

11. NCC, 'Considering the Public Interest Under the National Competition Policy' (November 1996).
12. In some instances, the NCC has concluded that a review of a specific industry should be carried out at the national level rather than the state level. For instance, it supported a national review of pharmacy legislation due to the interlinkages between various levels of regulation of the pharmacy sector. The Annual Report 1996/97, *supra* note 6, at 62 states: '[P]harmacy legislation affords industry incumbents significant protection from competition and imposes costs and restrictions on pharmacists and their practices. For example, pharmacists are limited to owning no more than three outlets, and a new pharmacy cannot locate within two kilometres of an existing approved pharmacy without losing the benefits of certain subsidies provided under the Pharmaceutical Benefits Scheme'.
13. NCC, Annual Report 1996/97, *supra* note 6, at 28.
14. *Id.* at 52.
15. NCC, 'The NCP Legislation Review Program', speech (1996).
16. NCC, Annual Report 1996/97, *supra* note 6, at 63.
17. NCC Annual Report 1995/96, p. 18.
18. For instance, the NCC's 1997 'Legislative Review Compendium', *supra* note 10, at 34, 66, states that New South Wales had failed to include its Casino Control Act 1992 in its review on the ground that this Act's exclusive licensing arrangements provide the strong public benefit of minimizing the risk of criminal influence and exploitation of gambling. However, the NCC argued that since this Act contains exclusive licensing arrangements, it should be reviewed, and failure to do so constituted a violation of the state's obligations under the NCA. The NCC did not, however, withhold financial benefits, instead allowing an additional period for the state to correct this deficiency. Similarly, Queensland had failed to list various casino agreement acts for review, on the ground that they legitimate existing contracts. The NCC followed a similar approach to that which it had followed with respect to New South Wales.
    In its supplementary assessment, the NCC decided that these arrangements should be addressed outside of the first tranche assessment process. NCC, 'National Competition Policy and Related Reforms: Supplementary Assessment of First Tranche Progress' 4 (30 June 1998).
19. For instance, a 1996 review of the Queensland sugar industry recommended, *inter alia*, continuance of the domestic marketing monopoly and the single export test, and a ten-year moratorium on further review of the arrangements. Although the recommendations were accepted by the Queensland and Commonwealth governments, the NCC questioned the recommendations. NCC, Annual Report 1996/97, *supra* note 6, at 25.

Similarly, notwithstanding the 1995 recommendation of an independent review group that reform and deregulation would benefit the community, New South Wales decided not to reform its domestic rice marketing arrangements. Following extensive discussions with the NCC, New South Wales offered no justification for this decision. As a result, the NCC recommended that part of the first tranche payment to New South Wales be withheld if the problem were not resolved by 31 January 1999. Further efforts are currently under way to resolve the problem. NCC, 'Supplementary Assessment of First Tranche Progress', *supra* note 18, at 7.

20. NCC, 'Assessment of First Tranche Commonwealth Progress with Implementing National Competition Policy' 3 (August 1998). The anticompetitive legislation was the National Health Act 1953, the Health Insurance Act 1973, the Quarantine Act 1908, and legislation related to Medicare.

The latter involved 1996 legislation that limits Medicare provider numbers available annually to new doctors, which was deemed to restrict competition by restricting entry to private medical practice. The Commonwealth neither justified the restriction, nor demonstrated that it had examined alternative non-restrictive means of achieving the objectives of the legislation consistent with the CPA. *Id.* at 19.

The Health Insurance Act 1973 regulates and restricts the allocation of licensed pathology collection centres. This affects competition between pathology laboratories.

21. NCC, 'Assessment of State and Territory Progress Implementing NCP and Related Reforms' 21 (1997). A 1995 review of the domestic rice marketing arrangements in New South Wales recommended that deregulation would provide net community benefits. Notwithstanding this recommendation, the NSW government retained anticompetitive vesting arrangements available to the New South Wales Rice Board. The NCC expressed its concern with this decision, and the New South Wales government indicated a willingness to resolve the matter with the Council. NCC, Annual Report 1996/97, *supra* note 6, at 25.

22. *Id.* at 25.

23. *Id.* at 28.

24. *Id.* at 54.

25. NCC, 'Supplementary Assessment', *supra* note 18.

26. Centre for International Economics, 'Guidelines for NCP Legislation Reviews Prepared for the National Competition Council' (February 1999).

27. National Commission for the Review of Antitrust Laws and Procedures, 'Report to the President and the Attorney General' 243 (22 January 1979).

28. *Id.* at 178.

29. *Id.* at 187–9.

30. *Id.* at 309.

31. OECD, 'Report on Regulatory Reform, Thematic Studies and Sectoral Studies' (Paris: OECD, 1997).

32. For instance, such regulations may take the form of insurance, bonding, client restitution funds or disciplinary controls.

33. OECD, 'Thematic Studies', *supra* note 31, at 203.

34. OECD, 'Regulatory Impact Analysis: Best Practices in OECD Countries' (Paris: OECD, 1997).

35. 'Meeting on Regulatory Impact Analysis: Best Practices in OECD Countries' (29–31 May 1996) <http://www.oecd.org/puma/regref/summary.htm>.

36. The EU member states that have adopted RIA are: Austria, Finland, France, Germany, Italy, Sweden and the UK. Non-EU countries include Australia, Canada, Japan, Mexico, New Zealand and the United States.

37. OECD, 'Meeting on Regulatory Impact Analysis', *supra* note 35.

38. United States Department of Justice, *Antitrust Division Manual*, Ch. 5 (3rd edn February 1998).

39. *Id.*

40. *Id.*; NCRAL Report, *supra* note 27.

41. Executive Order 12866 specifies that the OMB shall carry out the function of review of agency rulemaking to ensure that regulations are consistent with applicable law, the President's

priorities, and the principles specified in that Executive Order. The Executive Order states that agencies should assess all costs and benefits of available regulatory alternatives, including the alternative of not regulating, before promulgating a regulation. Moreover, among the principles that it requires agencies to abide by are: that they assess the alternatives to direct regulation; that they design regulations in the most cost-effective manner, considering, among other things, incentives for innovation and costs of enforcement and compliance; that they base decisions on the best reasonably obtainable economic and other information concerning the need for and consequences of the intended regulation; and that they should specify performance objectives rather than the behaviour or manner of compliance that regulated entities must adopt. It also requires agencies to analyse existing regulations to determine whether they are consistent with the principles set forth therein.

42. FTC, 'Regulatory Reform Case Study (FTC): Professional Services' (unpublished paper).
43. The following discussion is mainly based on the submission of DG Competition to the OECD in response to the 'Questionnaire sur les actions de plai doyer des autorités de la concurrence' (Questionnaire on pleadings of competition authorities) (21 August 1996).

# 18. Spanish independent authority and its role in a new competitive environment

## Manuel Ballbe and Carlos Padros

*In Spain, economic transition from a controlled to a free market economy has proceeded far more slowly than the democratic transition. This is largely because institutional arrangements in this post-monopoly period, combined with anticompetitive regulation, are not conducive to advancing the economic transition. This chapter analyses some of the difficulties of overcoming these problems. It focuses on the institutional shortcomings of the Spanish competition system; problems with the dual enforcement system and decentralization; problems with leaving sectoral regulators in charge of competition law enforcement in their respective sectors; and infrastructure problems that impede the process of liberalization.*

*The institutional set-up of the Spanish competition authorities has left the government with extensive power to control competition policy. The Competition Tribunal is structurally independent from the government, but it is a weak institution, lacking powers to investigate or prosecute competition cases (although it has some powers of decision with respect to private litigation). These were placed in the hands of the Competition Service, which is a part of the Ministry of Economy. Moreover, the government has retained the power to pass anticompetitive legislation, as the Competition Tribunal can merely provide its opinion to the government that a given regulation will produce anticompetitive effects. The judiciary branch offers little control, as ordinary judges with little or no expertise in economic issues or competition law adjudicate competition cases. There are also significant problems with transparency, with the result that the reason for decisions on competition matters are often obscure.*

*The Spanish competition authority, as well as most other national competition authorities in Europe, tends to foster the creation and protection of national champions. The result is a robust national oligopoly. The subsidiarity principle could be relied upon to centralize competition enforcement in such cases. The European Commission should be empowered to evaluate anticompetitive regulation in member states.*

*In Spain, sectoral regulators tend to have broad powers, including initiating competition litigation and liberalizing the industry through the prohibition of anticompetitive practices. These sectoral regulators are subject to political interference. Authority over competition matters should be removed from these regulators and placed in the hands of a strengthened independent general competition authority.*

*Finally, in Spain, infrastructures are a hidden obstacle to competition. The introduction of competition into industries that were formerly state monopolies leads to a decrease in prices. The former monopolist seeks to hold onto its former privileges, and has taken advantage of the opportunities provided by political control of infrastructures. Limiting infrastructure capacity allows monopolists to prevent competition from functioning properly, and to keep prices at non-competitive levels.*

## INTRODUCTION

The Spanish regulatory system is based on a model of strong government intervention, deeply rooted in the Spanish Catholic culture and values, which favour monopoly.[1] Spain's first Competition Act dates back only to 1963, but its effective implementation did not begin until 1989, with the passage of the current Competition Act (*Ley de Defensa de la Competencia*) (LDC).[2] The 1963 competition law was enacted as the result of external pressures demanding economic liberalization following the Second World War.[3] However, as is typical of countries in the Mediterranean Rim, the legal and economic implications of the Competition Act were not understood in Spain.

The Mediterranean countries have systematically marginalized competition, and devaluated it as a modern tool of economic policy.[4] This lack of receptivity to competition in the Southern European tradition results from a narrow understanding of the concept, emphasizing its economic dimension. Accordingly, neither territorial fragmentation of power nor effective competition has developed. The monopolistic culture remains a strong obstacle to the development of competitive markets in Southern Europe.

The implications of a competitive system go far beyond economics. The competition principle has its origins in the history of democracy and the rule of law in a constitutional state. Coke's judgment in 1602 explicitly recognizes antitrust as a constitutional construct, in reaction to the Crown's nearly 700 monopolies. Coke declared that 'all monopolies are against this great Charter because they are against freedom and liberty of the subject and against the law of the land'.[5] Moreover, the construction of a democratic system in Europe has followed from a struggle against the concentration of economic power. In 1656, Harrington already perceived that an economic structure favouring concentration would imperil the political system. He introduced the general principle that the fragmentation of economic power (landowners) is a decisive factor needed to prevent concentration of political power and authority.[6] Similarly, nearly 100 years later, Trenchard and Gordon stated that monopolies are equally dangerous in commerce, in politics and in religion, and that free trade, a free government and a free mind are the rights and the blessing of mankind.[7]

Thus, competition is primarily a political, legal and constitutional principle rather than an economic one,[8] whose adoption and acceptance resulted from the fight against monopoly, absolutism and concentration of power in other non-economic areas of social organization. The current debate on competition law as a legal tool for a market economy is simply the final stage in a strong anti-monopoly tradition.

This tradition of anti-monopoly as a political value has been obscured in Europe, but was revitalized in the United States. The constitutions of 13 American states include this principle in their declaration of rights. For instance, Maryland's 1776 constitution establishes that monopolies are odious and contrary to the spirit of free government and to the principles of trade, and therefore should be avoided. More than 100 years later, this principle was federalized and explicitly recognized by Senator Sherman in his brilliant discourse:

> If power is entrusted to a single man, this is a royal prerogative which is inconsistent with our form of political government and should be subject to firm opposition from State and National authorities. ... If we do not tolerate an absolute monarch as a political power, we should not tolerate an absolute monarch in the production, transportation and sale of what we need for living.[9]

Europe is slowly recovering the tradition that it exported and that clearly influenced EC Treaty Articles 81 and 82, abandoning a strong monopolistic culture.

The democratization of Spain two decades ago has not been accompanied by a clear understanding of the relationship between democracy and competition. The economic transition has proved to be much slower than the democratic one. Resistance and lack of understanding of the value of pluralism and fragmentation of economic power have seriously impeded modernization of Spain's economic structure. Although Spain has enacted a competition law and created competition authorities, these authorities must focus primarily on public regulations and governmental activities that ignore competition. In some markets where European legislation has required liberalization, Spanish competition authorities have had to build a market where it did not exist. The role differs substantially from that of competition authorities in jurisdictions with a long antitrust tradition, such as the United States.

This chapter is organized as follows. Section A explores the institutional structure of the Spanish competition authorities. It describes some of their formal characteristics, such as independence from government, but shows that in practice, such characteristics have not functioned as originally intended. Section B considers how European competition policy has influenced the attitude towards competition in Spain. It shows that rather than promoting a competitive market structure and innovation, the European approach has fostered creation of national champions in order effectively to compete in a regional-blocs scenario. This has led to a state-based industrial structure. Jurisdictional competition between the two levels should be encouraged as an incentive to enforcement effectiveness. Section C analyses the recent emergence of sectoral bodies entrusted with the regulation of energy and telecommunications. Although initially empowered to enforce competition law, this power was soon removed and attributed to the Competition Tribunal (*Tribunal de Defensa de la Competencia*) (TDC). Section D analyses how infrastructure has operated as a hidden element frustrating effective competition. Examples of anticompetitive regulations in the Spanish economy are given in the Annex.

## A. 'INDEPENDENCE' OF THE SPANISH COMPETITION AUTHORITIES

The lack of effective enforcement of the LDC is largely attributable to the institutional structure of the competition authorities that it created. The LDC failed to establish real independence of the competition authorities from a government that never truly believed in the benefits of competition law as a tool to regulate a healthy economy. The dictatorship regime had never enforced competition rules, instead favouring corporatism and regulatory capture.

Article 20 of the 1989 Democratic Act stated that the TDC: 'exercises its functions with complete independence and only defers to the judicial order'.[10] The system for appointing members of the TDC was designed to ensure their independence. As Cases observed:

> The Tribunal is composed of a president and eight members recommended by the Ministry of Economics and Finance and appointed by the government, from among lawyers, economists and other experts with more than fifteen years' professional experience. Accordingly, this constitutes a pure system of governmental appointment that eliminates intervention by other bodies such as Parliament. Tribunal members are appointed for a six-year term, renewable for three years. This is potentially significant for the independence of the Tribunal, since it implies that the term of its officials could last beyond the term of the government that has appointed them. Thus, the provision could cause a break of the bond that results from appointment of Tribunal officials by the government. Indeed, it is possible that the bond will never be formed because the Tribunal operating at a given time is not appointed by the government in power at that time.[11]

Thus, the intent was to prevent government from controlling how competition law would be enforced, and to free the TDC from political debate.

Notwithstanding this feature, one of the most critical institutional short-comings in the Spanish system is the division of authority between the TDC and the Competition Service (*Servicio de Defensa de la Competencia*) (SDC). While the TDC is independent, the SDC is dependent on the Ministry of Economy. But it is the SDC that has exclusive power to initiate investigations and act as public prosecutor in competition cases. The SDC's record in performing these functions has been abysmal. For instance, it has initiated investigations of only four industrial concentrations since the LDC took effect. This number is astonishingly low in comparison with other European competition authorities, such as the Italian authority, which initiates nearly 100 cases per year.

This division of authority between the two bodies prevents the TDC from functioning independently for an additional reason. Resolutions of the SDC may be appealed to the TDC, which consumes most of the latter's resources. For instance, in 1998, more than 60 per cent of the TDC's workload involved review of SDC decisions.

Finally, the TDC's ability effectively to enforce the competition law is undermined by the power of government to pass anticompetitive legislation. Pursuant to Article 2 of the LDC, government intervention in the market is exempt from the competition rules. This provision must be narrowly constructed, but viewed together with the government's power to grant individual exemptions, little remains within the jurisdiction of the TDC.

It seems that the TDC has been deliberately weakened. Structurally, the most important enforcement instruments are in the hands of the SDC. Although the TDC is formally an independent administrative body, its lack of power to initiate investigations implies that it is vaccinated against activism. As the TDC itself has stated: 'Certainly, the functional independence of the Tribunal will be strengthened if steps were taken to attribute it with the power to open and conduct proceedings and to convert the SDC into one of the Tribunal's components'.[12]

### Enforcement of Competition Law Against Anticompetitive Regulation

The TDC is not empowered to enforce competition law with respect to governmental regulation. It can merely refer such a case to the government, indicating that the regulation at stake produces anticompetitive effects, but it is left up to the government to reform the regulation.

Competition is, however, a constitutional principle in Spain. Accordingly, administrative judges could determine that an anticompetitive regulation is unnecessarily restrictive or discriminates in favour of some producers. Unfortunately, Spanish judges, like judges in other member states, have no understanding of competition law and its enforcement mechanisms. As Hutchings and Levitt have observed:

> It is still the case that very few judges in national courts have received any academic or practical training in EC law and no doubt even fewer in competition law or economics. Indeed Italy has had a national competition law regime only since October 1990 and Spain only since August 1989. The result is that the national courts' analysis tends to be legalistic and formalistic, and devoid of economic analysis.[13]

Thus, the record of invalidation of regulation by Spanish courts on this ground is virtually nil.

**Transparency**

Transparency is one of the most effective tools to foster competition, as it helps build a culture of respect for competitive industry behaviour. In Spain, transparency in important government processes affecting competition is sorely lacking. For instance, there are no public hearings concerning processes as crucial as the establishment of electricity prices.[14]

The TDC has a research sub-directorate, which has published various studies regarding the most anticompetitive practices of Spanish industries. Three such studies focused on anticompetitive regulation and its possible remedies. These studies generated debate regarding such practices, and have helped raise the public's consciousness of competition issues. In recent years, however, the TDC has prepared other studies, but the government has not permitted their publication.

# B.  DUAL ENFORCEMENT OF COMPETITION LAW

European integration and the formation of a single market have resulted in substantial changes in the markets of most European industries. Notwithstanding the existence of a single market, national competition authorities still have concurrent jurisdiction with the European Commission on most issues. Although enforcement decentralization is desirable, caution is in order for several reasons.

First, national competition authorities tend to foster creation of national champions as a way to protect national industries.[15] For instance, in the Spanish banking industry, a wave of banking mergers occurred in the late 1980s, and more recently *Banco Santander* merged with *Banco Central Hispano*. These mergers were inspired by the need to rationalize the domestic bank base in order to withstand the competitive shock resulting from opening the Spanish market to competition. Similar tendencies can be observed throughout Europe.

Far more merger activity occurs at national level rather than European level. The reason is that mergers between companies located in distant markets, where each company has imperfect knowledge of the other's strengths and weaknesses, are likely to make essential management decisions more difficult.[16] Moreover, banks that were large in their home markets are much smaller and more vulnerable in an international context, and prefer to remain large in their national markets through domestic mergers. Hoschka has observed:

> While official statements of both regulators and public authorities cite economic efficiency as the main rationale for increasing domestic concentration, an equally plausible economic interpretation is that domestic authorities attempt to raise barriers to cross-border entry activities by foreign banks. Such entry barriers may result from the fact that a more concentrated oligopoly is able to coordinate strategies. Alternatively, regulators may merge banks which are particularly 'vulnerable' to foreign takeovers into bigger institutions which are more difficult to acquire.[17]

Consequently, the justification for domestic bank mergers seems not to be economic rationality, but a desire to maintain a robust national oligopoly which will defend market share of home institutions and prevent cross-border takeovers. Therefore, competition authorities must prevent the balkanization of markets under the false image of economic restructuring.

Flynn has observed: '[t]he overall goal is that a competitive process not the quantitative concept of competition, be the rule for big and small'.[18] National champions enjoy greater economies of scale and scope, but the long-run effect of protecting them from cross-border competition is predominance of economic operators' interests rather than consumer welfare.

Second, the European Commission should have expanded powers to enforce competition law and to evaluate anticompetitive national regulation. European pre-emption of national regulatory powers as the result of ineffective competition law enforcement by national authorities would be desirable. Although the subsidiarity principle is normally analysed from the perspective of devolution of central powers to the member states, it also implies centralization of powers when Community goals are not effectively pursued at member state level. This construction introduces effectiveness as the criterion to be used to attribute shared competencies, and would create a strong incentive to foster regulatory proficiency.[19] Ineffective enforcement by national regulators would imply that Community-level enforcement is required. This theory explains the birth of the European Agency for Medicines, as no national mechanism for securing free movement of authorized medicines throughout the Community was effective.

In the US, the growth of federal regulation was initially based on the poor record of state enforcement of antitrust legislation. This provoked a reaction on state level to recapture the lost powers.

Many States have adopted statutes mirroring the Federal Trade Commission Act or the Sherman and Clayton antitrust acts. Until the 1970s antitrust law was generally left to the federal government. But as federal enforcement of antitrust law became the subject of presidential campaigns and federal enforcement became more erratic, states have become active in developing their own statutes and enforcement policy.[20]

Paradoxically, more power at European level to enforce competition law would provide a greater stimulus for national competition authorities that would be forced to act in accordance in order to retain their powers. Regulatory competition or enforcement competition among authorities should be encouraged.

Finally, European institutions should not act through the state's administration. When a system of indirect administration is used to enforce Treaty Articles 81 and 82, the incentive for a national administration to develop a cooperative structure mirroring that of the National Association of Attorney General (NAAG) in the US disappears. Although at first sight this system might be seen as more respectful of state interests, in the end, it prevents its own development through integrated coordination.

This type of integrated policymaking by state attorneys general can seriously threaten federal control over important areas of regulation. In 1985, for instance, in a challenge to the Reagan administration's antitrust law enforcement posture, 50 states adopted a uniform set of antitrust enforcement guidelines for non-price vertical restraints ... When uniformly enforced, coordinated state law enforcement policies such as NAAG's antitrust guidelines establish a *de facto* system of national law having the effect of pre-emption in reverse.[21]

Accordingly, Europe must ensure the existence of a dual system of enforcement of competition law, which fosters vertical competition. Alternative supervision mechanisms are much more likely to produce positive results.

## C.  NEW SPECIALIZED SECTORAL BODIES: THE CSEN

An issue has developed as to whether competition in previously regulated sectors should be introduced and controlled by a general national competition authority like the TDC, or by specialized industry regulators. In Spain, many independent sectoral regulators exist, such as the Energy Commission and the Telecommunications Commission. Although regulation can be a specialized field, it is preferable to have a general competition authority in charge of the regulation of competition. Specialization might raise problems, such as the unequal application of criteria depending on the regulator. A bill proposing amendments to the LDC, currently before the Spanish parliament, offers the option of centralizing all competition issues in a competition tribunal.

A fundamental issue that must be resolved before creating such a centralized competition authority would be recruitment of persons sufficiently knowledgeable of the sector that they could effectively perform such regulatory functions. It is difficult to find such individuals, other than those coming from the former monopoly. Salaries offered must be comparable to those in the private sector. In recent years, the newly privatized enterprises have hired away nearly half the staff of the Electricity Commission, which has been seriously weakened as a result. The regulation governing recruitment of these personnel is ambiguous. Rules should prevent them from leaving their post and immediately accepting a post with private industry, as a gross breach of public functions. Such rules already exist in other areas.[22] The absence of such rules will facilitate institutional channels for corruption.

Whether members of independent regulatory commissions should have renewable posts is currently being debated. On the one hand, allowing renewal runs the risk that the regulator, in the latter years of the initial mandate, will become more docile towards governmental interests in the hope of being reappointed (governmental capture). On the other hand, eliminating that possibility increases the regulator's independence from government but places pressure on him/her to be more docile towards industry interests, in the hope of finding subsequent employment in industry (industry capture). Therefore, both options present problems.

In the electricity industry, the European directive creating a common market for electricity[23] was implemented in Spain.[24] This legislation opens the Spanish market to competition and creates a system of administrative supervision, partially based on the National Electricity Commission (*Comisión del Sistema Eléctrico Nacional*) (CSEN), the former sectoral regulator. The CSEN has existed since 1994, and has powers to initiate antitrust litigation and to conduct liberalization through the prohibition of anticompetitive practices. Despite those legal provisions, it has been reluctant to take action.

The first president of this body was Mr Fernández Ordóñez, an economist and former president of the TDC, who was nominated for a five-year term by the socialist government. However, resistance developed in both government and industry with respect to several characteristics of this body, including independence of the president, his activist policy and his firm resolution to introduce competition in the sector. The dispute over financing the cost of transition to a competitive market, which amounted to nearly one billion pesetas (six billion dollars), led Mr Ordóñez to resign in 1998.[25]

Thereafter, a new law was enacted which weakened the CSEN by substantially reducing its regulatory powers and its possibility of enforcing competition law in that sector, and replaced it with a more compliant National Energy Commission (*Comisión Nacional de la Energía*).[26] The powers that remain with the CSEN are only consultation and inspection: whenever it detects an anticompetitive measure, it can so notify the SDC.

## D.  INFRASTRUCTURES

Infrastructures are a hidden obstacle to competition in post-monopolist industries. The successful introduction of competition is dependent on the capacity of the infrastructure to absorb an increase in demand of its services. A government policy with respect to infrastructures is indicative of the genuineness of its commitment to a free market economy, and of its belief in the benefits of opening traditional public services to competition.

In Spain, the airline industry has been liberalized to some extent. For instance, flights connecting the major Spanish cities to other major cities are now offered by four companies instead of one. Prices have decreased by nearly 30 per cent as the result of competition, which has induced a significant increase in demand. However, the government's policy with respect to infrastructure may frustrate this process of liberalization. Problems with airport capacity, handling operations and air traffic congestion have caused chronic delays. A pilot strike worsened the situation. Normally, the delays caused by the strike would have been manageable. However, in a system already at the limit of its capacity, chaos ensued (considerable delays, cancellations, lost baggage and so on). The solution negotiated between companies and the Ministry of Transportation was a proportional reduction in flights operated by each company, which was a step backwards in the liberalization process. Thus, liberalization and suppression of legal obstacles to competition have not been accompanied by an effective policy providing that infrastructures can respond to a competitive environment.

Government inactivity with respect to infrastructure is not neutral. The slot allocation system is governed by the principle of grandfathering, which clearly favours large, post-monopoly incumbents. Where slots are scarce due to limitations of airport capacity, new entrants that can only offer non-competitive timetables will be disadvantaged, while former national monopolies will benefit.

The same is true in the telecommunications industry. Using Retevision, the second telephone operator in Spain, it is often impossible to make a connection because line capacity is saturated. Immediately after hanging up, and dialling the same number directly through Telefonica, the former national monopolist, the call is immediately processed. Again, the incumbent is favoured.

For liberalization to be successful, it is essential that capacity is sufficient to handle the increase in demand that lower prices and entry of new competitors produces. One solution might be to confer the European Commission with the powers to address infrastructure problems, when it is demonstrated that an inactive policy is deliberate, frustrates competition and favours former national monopolists.

## CONCLUSIONS

The process of economic liberalization in Spain is making progress. Although the TDC is understaffed and must cope with considerable institutional short-comings, it is nonetheless making admirable efforts to foster competition in the Spanish economy. Governmental resistance remains strong, however. Notwithstanding rhetoric in favour of competition and of creating economic opportunities in all sectors, in reality government and powerful interest groups make efforts to hinder the full potential of a competitive environment. This may be inevitable in the process of economic transition. Time is needed for the public and for government to understand the social and political potential of the competitive principle.

The TDC and the SDC were created when national monopolies dominated the economy and a transition to a competitive market economy was required by mandate of European competition law. These bodies suffer from both industry capture and government dependence. Industrial national champions directly influence government, which in the end establishes regulatory guidelines in an informal and secret way.

Transition from monopoly to competition without breaking up the former monopolies has proved to be inefficient, since the monopolist uses all its influence to retain its privileges. Therefore, it would be preferable to break up these former monopolies, and thereby limit the possibilities of influencing governmental regulation.

Competition authorities can be an effective tool for detecting and correcting the anticompetitive impact of regulation. However, these authorities must have several characteristics:

* total independence from government;
* possibility of effective antitrust enforcement; and
* jurisdiction over anticompetitive regulation.

In the abscence of these conditions, 'Mediterranean liberalization' (including Spain, France, Italy and Portugal), although formally impressive, has only slightly transformed dominant state-owned firms and economic interests, sometimes simply from public to private monopoly. Transformation of administrative and regulatory structures entrusted with creating a competitive market is needed. National competition law offers guidelines for this administrative transformation, but greater involvement of both European competition policy and the national judiciary is needed.

## NOTES

1. Manuel Ballbe and Carlos Padros, *Estado Competitivo y Armonización Europea* (The competitive state and European harmonization) (Barcelona, 1997).
2. Law 110/63, Ley de represión de las prácticas restrictivas de la competencia (Law against restrictive practices of competition), 175 *Boletín Oficial del Estado* 11144 (23 July 1963) (Aranzadi RCL 1963\1423).
3. One such external pressure was an agreement between the United States and Spain obliging the Spanish government to discourage monopolistic or protectionist arrangements and to promote competition, productivity and the conditions necessary for the development of international commerce. Luis Cases, 'Competition Law and Policy in Spain: Implementation in an Interventionist Tradition', in *Regulating Europe* 180 (Giandomenico Majone, ed., London, 1996).
4. Even some 'liberal' governments have been largely unconcerned about fostering competitive mechanisms and a free market economy.
5. Bruce Yandle, 'Sir Edward Coke and the Struggle for a New Constitutional Order', 4 *Constitutional Political Economy* (1993).
6. James Harrington, *The Commonwealth of Oceana* (London, 1924 ).
7. John Trenchard and Thomas Gordon, *Cato's Letters: or Essays on Liberty, Civil and Religious and Other Important Subjects* 213 (London, 1755).
8. George Stigler, 'Economic Competition and Political Competition', 1972 *Public Choice* 91.
9. Luis Cases, *Derecho Administrativo De Defensa De La Competencia* (Administrative law of defence of competition) 123 (Madrid, 1995) (quoting 123 *Congressional Record* 2, 457 (1890)).
10. Law 16/1989, Ley de defensa de la competencia (Law of defence of competition). *Boletín Oficial del Estado* 22747 (18 July 1989) (Aranzadi RCL 1989\1591).
11. Cases, *supra* note 3, at 190.
12. Tribunal Defensa De La Competencia, *La libre competencia en España* (1986–1988) (Free competition in Spain, 1986–1988) 27 (Madrid, 1989).
13. Michael Hutchings and John Levitt, 'Concurrent Jurisdiction', 3 *European Competition Law Review* 119, 123 (1994).
14. On one occasion, when a former Electricity Commission president attempted to obtain a government economic study, he was asked the reason for his interest.
15. *Industrial Enterprise and European Integration* (Jack Hayward, ed., London, 1995).
16. Alfred Steinherr and Pier-Luigi Gilibert, 'The Impact of Financial Market Integration on the European Banking Industry' 53 (Centre for European Policy Studies, CEPS Financial Markets Unit Research Report 1989).
17. Tobias Hoschka, *Cross-Border Entry In European Retail Financial Services* 137 (Florence, 1993).
18. John J. Flynn, 'Legal Reasoning, Antitrust Policy, and the Social "Science" of Economics', 33 *Antitrust Bulletin* 713 (1989).
19. Subsidiarity cannot be read as indicating that things should be done at the lowest possible level, without any reservation or any normative criterion. This clearly would constitute a recipe for anarchy. On the contrary, effectiveness must not be measured only in economic terms, but in a broader range of values described as effectiveness in implementing a social organization which protects markets, cities, families, consumers or less-favoured people.
20. Cornell W. Clayton, 'Law, Politics and the New Federalism: State Attorney General as National Policymakers', 56 *Review of Politics* 536 (1994).
21. *Id.* at 540.

22. Manuel Ballbe, 'Telefónica ficha al árbitro', *El Periódico de Cataluña*, 7 July 1999, at 7 (analysis of the Bangemann case and how Telefonica's president said that they had hired the telecommunications' Ronaldo, when Telefonica had instead hired the referee).

23. Council and Parliament Directive 96/92/EC of 19 December 1996. 1997 *Official Journal* (L 27) 20–29.

24. Law 54/97 of 27 November 1997, Reguladora del Sector Electrico (Regulation of the electricity sector) 285 *Boletín Oficial del Estado* 35097 (28 November 1997) (Aranzadi RCL 1997\2821).

25. The European Commission backed the former president of the CSEN's position by declaring that the public financing of the transition costs to competition was a state aid.

26. Energy Law 34/1998, 241 Boletín Oficial del Estado 33517 (8 October 1998) (Aranzadi RCL 1998\2472 vid; CSEN Internal Document n. 4. July 1997). These limitations are further reinforced with the passage of Royal Decree 1339/1999 of 31 July that regulates the Comision Nacional de la Energía. 202 Boletín Oficial del Estado 33425 (24 August 1999) (Aranzadi RCL 1999\2257).

# ANNEX   EXAMPLES OF ANTICOMPETITIVE REGULATIONS IN THE SPANISH ECONOMY

- *Air transport*   Although liberalized, the lack of infrastructure and the use of a grandfathering system for slot allocation favours the national-flag carrier, and thereby prevents the development of further competition.
- *Books*   Prices are fixed by administrative regulation; impossible to sell at discounts below the fixed price.
- *Bus (road transportation)*   Privatization of state-owned enterprise that controls 80 per cent of market now beginning.
- *Commercial activities*   Strict regional control of regulations of hours of operation and establishment of malls and large commercial areas; Sunday trading bans.
- *Electricity*   Dominated by state-owned enterprises; possibility of selecting the supplying firm only available to businesses (privileged consumers).
- *Pharmaceuticals*   State monopoly exercised through exclusive contracts, which are very restrictive.
- *Financial services*   Considerable competition, but second financial conglomerate is public and the savings banks provoke competitive distortions.
- *Gas*   State monopoly until 2013.
- *Highways*   State monopoly.
- *Maritime transportation*   Second operator recently introduced to connect mainland with Balearic Islands; timid competition.
- *Petrol distribution*   No effective competition among firms; de facto agreements not to compete in prices among different petrol stations.
- *Postal service*   Competition introduced in some parts, but ordinary urban postal distribution still in hands of state monopoly.
- *Professional services*   Several restrictions to entry in most professions, for example, lawyers and architects; fees normally fixed by professional associations.
- *Telecommunications*   Liberalization programme undertaken, but Telefonica enjoys dominant positions by law until 2025; problems of discrimination with new entrants, and of infrastructure, which prevent the full development of effective competition.
- *Railways*   Directives on separation of infrastructure and transportation services have been transposed, but state monopoly still totally dominant.
- *Undertakers' establishments*   Recently liberalized although still under local control.
- *Water supply*   Local monopolies under dominant holding; no competition.

# 19. Joining the electric industry policy debate at the state level

## John C. Hilke

*This chapter describes the main elements that are important in putting together a successful competition and consumer advocacy programme. It focuses on the efforts of the Federal Trade Commission (FTC) as advocate with respect to electricity deregulation in the US as an example. This is the last area of major reform in the US, since most of the other regulated industries have already been deregulated.*

*Both the federal and state governments have a role in electricity regulation. The federal regulator is responsible for wholesale electricity, while the state regulators are responsible for setting the rates that individual customers pay. The FTC's competition and consumer advocacy programme has worked primarily at the federal level, although it has recently changed its focus to try to have a greater impact at the state level.*

*Effective advocacy first requires the advocate to develop an understanding of the industry by reading the trade press, talking to executives and hiring experts. This process helps create an understanding of the concerns of the different interest groups, and how regulatory changes will affect them.*

*Second, the advocate must select the issues that it will address in its advocacy submission. The FTC focuses on issues related to competition policy and consumer protection, which are its mission areas.*

*Third, the FTC has increased its level of networking with decision makers. State and federal regulators tend to listen more if they know the FTC staff. This allows the FTC to be more effective in its comments.*

*Fourth, as a decision point for an agency or a court approaches, issues tend to shift suddenly. The FTC follows the issues closely enough to know when the argument is changing, in order to avoid appearing out of touch.*

*Finally, the FTC benefits from its combination of law enforcement and advocacy activities. Litigating a case in a given industry provides an opportunity for the FTC better to appreciate the pertinent history of the industry and its prospects. Research combined with internal documentation provides an excellent background for understanding the strategic issues of the managements of those companies. Thus, a more refined approach to suggesting regulatory reform can be developed. This background is also useful for understanding how the companies' incentives will cause them to react to regulatory changes.*

## INTRODUCTION

In many respects, the electric power industry is the last great arena for regulatory reform in the United States. Trucking, airlines, telephone, banking, natural gas and railroads have already undergone major restructuring and regulatory reforms.[1] By any measure, changes in the electric power industry are an important matter for the economic wellbeing of the US and for the living standards of its citizens. Annual revenues in the US electric power industry exceed $200 billion, and the industry accounts for as much as 10 per cent of the total capital stock of US industry. Electric power is nearly ubiquitous and arguably is interwoven into the fabric of everyday life to a greater degree than the products or services of any other industry. For this reason, reform of the electric industry is not undertaken lightly. At the same time, even modest improvements in the performance of the electric power industry would translate into substantial gains for consumers and businesses.

This chapter focuses on competition and consumer protection advocacy comments filed by the Federal Trade Commission (FTC) staff before state public utility commissions (PUCs), and complementary efforts before the Federal Energy Regulatory Commission (FERC). After providing necessary institutional background information, it sets forth the critical elements required to develop an effective advocacy effort by a national competition and consumer protection agency at the subnational (state) level of government. This discussion is based on the personal experience of the author in the FTC's competition and consumer protection advocacy programme over the past 15 years, with a focus on recent experience in advocating increased competition and consumer protection for electric power markets. The chapter aims to strike a balance between 'how-to' advice on competition and consumer protection advocacy, and observations on the potential anticompetitive and anti-consumer effects of some regulatory approaches taken in the electric power industry in the US. It will show that the critical elements in competition and consumer protection advocacy include: identifying major issues and organizing background infor-mation, developing positions on a subset of the major issues (those that are closest to existing areas of expertise in the agency), networking with partici-pants in the policy debate, ongoing monitoring of shifts in 'hot' topics, and integrating law enforcement efforts with competition and consumer protection advocacy. It expresses the general rationale for the significance of each of these elements and then illustrates how the FTC has sought to address some of these elements in its electric power industry competition and consumer protection advocacy efforts.

## A.   THE SETTING

Unlike many countries with nationalized power systems, the US elected to retain private, for-profit ownership for over 70 per cent of its electric power generation, transmission and distribution volume.[2] To control the natural monopoly aspects of these private enterprises, rate and service regulations covering final retail sales to customers were adopted in all of the states in the early part of the century. By the 1930s, the federal government started regulating rates and services for interstate wholesale transmission of electric power. This two-tier regulatory approach remains in effect to this day. Regulatory reform in the electric power industry consequently has proceeded on two tracks. The first is the federal track. FERC, as the primary congressionally authorized regulatory agency in the electricity sector at the federal level,[3] controls the pace and direction of regulatory reform in wholesale power sales. The second is the state track. The operating agencies at the state level are the 50 state PUCs.[4] State public utility commissions, with authority from state legislatures, control the pace and direction of reforms in retail electric power markets in each state. The National Association of Regulatory Utility Commissioners (NARUC) is organized to help the states coordinate their policies on restructuring at the retail level, and to coordinate state communication with FERC as well as with Congress and the administration.

The federal (and state) antitrust authorities have concurrent jurisdiction with FERC over mergers involving electric power industry members. The Antitrust Division of the Department of Justice (DOJ or Antitrust Division) has handled most mergers between electric utilities, while both the DOJ and the FTC have reviewed convergence mergers between electric power generators and fuel suppliers. In addition, the federal antitrust agencies have jurisdiction to prevent monopolistic or unfair acts and practices in the electric power industry. The FTC has additional jurisdiction regarding consumer protection issues such as advertising claims and other forms of consumer information.

The FTC has a competition advocacy programme that originated long before electric power restructuring became a significant public policy area. The competition advocacy concept within the FTC originated with the founding of the agency in 1914. President Woodrow Wilson envisaged the FTC as a vehicle for focusing public attention and debate on competition issues by conducting research and holding hearings on such topics. Subsequently, the agency developed primarily into a law enforcement agency, but it has always maintained its reporting and advocacy functions as well.

On the federal track, electric power industry reforms first arose in connection with the energy crisis of the late 1970s. At that time, legislation was passed to allow independent power suppliers to connect to the transmission grid. During this period and over the following decade, FERC advanced open-access reforms for the transmission grid on a utility-by-utility basis as part of its merger review process. FERC often conditioned its merger approval on an agreement by the merging firms to provide open access to their transmission system. The watershed events in electric power regulatory reform at the federal level have proved to be the Energy Policy Act of 1992 and the consequent FERC Order Nos 888 and 889.[5] The two FERC orders were presented for public comment in 1995 and issued in 1996. Order No. 888 requires transmission owners to offer open, non-discriminatory access to the transmission system for wholesale trades in electric power. Order No. 889 requires transmission grid owners electronically to disclose and update their available transmission capacity determinations.

On the state track, California was the first state to begin work on opening retail electric power markets to competition. Regulatory reforms in the UK's electric power industry were a touchstone for the California reform movement. California had some of the highest electric power rates in the country and was experiencing economic difficulties at the time. Its regulatory reform process began in the early 1990s and continues to this day.

## B.   DEVELOPMENT OF THE FTC'S COMPETITION AND CONSUMER PROTECTION ADVOCACY PROGRAMME REGARDING RETAIL ELECTRIC POWER COMPETITION

Like public awareness of electric industry competition issues generally, the FTC's involvement began slowly. The first comment concerning electric power regulatory reform came in a submission filed on 29 September 1987 with the Legislative Audit Council of the State of South Carolina. At that time, the FTC staff wrote:

> New technological developments in the production and transmission of electricity suggest that independent power producers may soon be able to compete effectively to serve distribution networks in both nearby and distant areas, thereby reducing or eliminating the natural monopoly aspects of electricity production and transmission that have been the rationale for regulation. Such a system would permit consumer access to the lowest cost available power and encourage utilities to locate generating plants at the most efficient sites. While electric utility deregulation may be premature at this time, the Council may wish to alert the legislature to the anticipated deregulation opportunities presented by technological advances.[6]

*Table 19.1   Guide to FTC staff comments on electric industry reform, October 1999\**

| Filings | Issues |
|---|---|
| *FERC filings* | |
| Docket No. RM99–2–000 (August 16, 1999) | Regional transmission organizations |
| Docket No. EL99–57–000 (May 27, 1999) | Entergy Services Transco proposal |
| Docket No. RM98–4–000 (September 11, 1998) | Revised merger filing requirements; problems with FERC's information sources |
| Docket No. PL98–5–000 (May 1, 1998) | Policy issues in formation of ISOs |
| Docket Nos ER97–237–000 and ER97–1079–000 (February 6, 1998) | Problems with ISOs remedying market power problems with behavioural rules |
| Docket No. RM96–6–000 (May 7, 1996) | Merger policy, adoption of the DOJ/FTC Horizontal Merger Guidelines |
| Docket Nos RM95–8–000 and RM94–7–001 (August 7, 1995) | Drawbacks to a behavioural Open Access approach; ISOs, transmission pricing; mitigation of stranded costs; public benefit programmes |
| *State filings* | |
| Arkansas Public Service Commission, Docket No. 00–048-R (April 13, 2000) | Analysis of existing retail market power |
| Commonwealth of Virginia, State Corporation Commission, Case No. PUE990349 (February 10, 2000) | Additional state rules for regional transmission entities |
| Public Utilities Commission of the State of California, Docket No. R98–12–015 (March 17, 1999) | Distributed generation |
| Alabama Public Service Commission, Docket No. 26427 (January 8, 1999) | Wide range of restructuring issues |
| Massachusetts Department of Telecommunications and Energy (October 8, 1998) | Affiliate rules |
| Nevada Public Utilities Commission, LCB File No. R087.98 (September 22, 1998) | Affiliate rules; use of parent firm logo by unregulated affiliates |
| Louisiana Public Service Commission, Docket No. U-21453 (September 11, 1998) | Consumer protection aspects of electric industry regulatory reform |

| | |
|---|---|
| Mississippi Public Service Commission, Docket No. 96-UP-3889 (August 28, 1998) | Transco proposal from Entergy raises horizontal and vertical competition concerns; efficiency advantages described for the proposed Transco may be addressed through an ISO |
| National Association of Attorneys General (August 10, 1998) | Advantages of maintaining flexibility in 'green guides' and of empirical research regarding consumer understanding of environmental claims |
| Michigan Public Service Commission, Case No. U-11290 (August 7, 1998) | Assessment and remedies for existing horizontal market power; computer simulation modelling |
| Louisiana Public Service Commission, Docket No. U-21453 (August 7, 1998) | Stranded cost recovery incentives to artificially deter entry; distortion effects; and mitigation incentives |
| West Virginia Public Service Commission, Case No. 98–0452-E-GI (July 15, 1998) | Market power issues in retail competition |
| Utah Public Service Commission (July 15, 1998) | Consumer protection issues |
| Commonwealth of Virginia, Joint Subcommittee Studying Electric Industry Restructuring, SJR-91 (July 9, 1998) | Market power issues in retail competition |
| Public Utility Commission of Texas, Project Number 17549 (June 19, 1998) | Affiliate transactions; use of the parent firm's logo by unregulated affiliates (potential for deception and cross-subsidization) |
| Louisiana Public Service Commission, Docket No. U-21453 (May 15, 1998) | Market power issues in retail competition |
| Maine Department of the Attorney General and Public Utilities Commission, 'Interim Report on Market Power in Electricity' (May 29, 1998) | Treatment of entry in market power analysis for retail competition |
| California Public Utilities Commission, Docket Nos R.94-04-031 and I.94-04-032 (August 23, 1995) | Retail competition elements |
| South Carolina Legislative Audit Council (February 28, 1994) | Institutions, rules, and effects of regulatory reforms abroad |
| South Carolina Legislative Audit Council (September 29, 1987) | Electric power industry regulatory reform may be appropriate in the near future |

*Note:*   *   FTC staff comments are available on the FTC's website at <www.ftc.gov/be/advofile.htm>

Two subsequent important milestones for the FTC competition and consumer protection advocacy effort have been (i) the Open Access Comment to FERC in 1995[7] and (ii) the recent increase in filings about electric power issues, including several comments filed at the state level. First, the Open Access Comment filed by the FTC staff before FERC took the position that behavioural rules, such as those proposed by FERC, are unlikely to function properly because they leave incentives in place to discriminate in providing transmission access to competing generators. The comment also identified independent system operators (ISOs) as a potentially lower-cost alternative to divestiture of generation assets. ISOs would also blunt incentives to discriminate in granting transmission access. The issues and positions taken in the Open Access Comment have formed the foundation for many subsequent comments. Second, by early 1997, it became apparent that electric power industry reforms would continue to grow in importance, but that much of the debate would shift to the state level as more and more states began to evaluate the merits of increasing competition and consumer protection in retail electric power markets. Since that time, the FTC's competition and consumer protection advocacy programme has filed a variety of comments in electric power industry proceedings, with increased emphasis on state-level comment opportunities (through more systematic identification of such opportunities) and increased visibility of the FTC's involvement in the industry (through greater participation by commissioners and staff in industry conferences and hearings). Table 19.1 is a listing of the FTC staff filings on electric industry regulatory reform issues.

## C.   IDENTIFICATION OF MAJOR ISSUES DURING THE EARLY PUBLIC POLICY DEBATES

An obvious early step in competition and consumer protection advocacy in an industry is developing a reasonable understanding of how the industry operates and the economic issues that have been raised in policy discussions about the industry domestically and abroad. A generalized understanding of an industry is essential in competition and consumer protection advocacy, as it is in litigation or industrial organization economics studies. With a general framework of the industry's economics, institutions and history in mind, it is much easier to understand how all the various details relate to one another and how the positions of various firms and other organizations relate to their respective interests. A framework of background information also allows a competition and consumer protection agency to develop more effective lines of inquiry in interacting with industry participants. Without such a general framework, it is easy to miss the significance of events and new developments, and not to be taken seriously in discussions with regulators and other policy makers.

There are a variety of common-sense methods for gaining an understanding of major issues in an industry such as electric power. A prudent initial step is to work with an economic expert in the industry in order to supplement the reading of the trade press and other research that the agency has done about the industry. Contacts with such an expert can have some strong advantages. First, economic experts with industry experience usually already have a 'cognitive map' of industry competition and consumer protection issues. Interacting with such an expert provides a very efficient way for the staff of the competition and consumer protection agency to acquire such a cognitive map of the industry. Second, the expert usually has a wide network of contacts and sources in the industry, both personal and evidentiary. This can make efforts to document industry facts, trends and peculiarities much more efficient. Third, the expert usually has developed a good understanding about which outside parties are the strongest advocates for different policy positions. This can allow a competition and consumer protection agency to ensure that it knows both sides of the main arguments and more effectively to evaluate conflicting claims of interested parties before developing its own position. Fourth, the expert can give the competition and consumer protection agency a sense of confidence that it understands the issues. This comes from repeatedly asking the expert if his/her understanding corresponds to the understanding that the agency has developed. Fifth, the expert can provide a yardstick for determining when the agency has developed a reasonable initial understanding of the industry. This test is satisfied when the staff of the agency can carry on an extended discussion of the industry with the expert without learning much that is new.

Another useful technique for obtaining background information may be to network with former employees of the competition and consumer protection agency who have become active in industry issues, both in government and in the private sector. Informal contacts with former staff members may help in the early stages of understanding the industry and its issues, because former staff members understand and appreciate the perspective that the agency brings to its competition and consumer protection advocacy efforts. Networking with individual interest groups may be another viable technique for gathering background information about an industry.

## D.   DEVELOPING POSITIONS ON A SUBSET OF ISSUES

Electric power industry restructuring, like previous regulatory reform movements, entails a vast number of potential issues ranging from those that are extremely technical to those that are primarily emotional. Since a competition and consumer protection advocacy programme is likely to have limited resources, the agency may need to pick and choose among possible comment opportunities. Perhaps the best general approach is to select issues that are closely related to the agency's mission(s). In the case of the FTC, its missions are to protect and enhance competition and to protect consumers. Plus factors in selecting issues to comment upon may include related experience in law enforcement efforts, research or prior advocacy work. Consequently, the FTC's advocacy comments have focused on competition and consumer protection aspects of proposed regulatory reforms. To conserve resources, energy and credibility, it may be important not to comment on every issue that arises.

The most substantive result of this type of review of potential issues at the FTC was a decision to take no position on several important issues that generally are outside the FTC's mission areas. For example, agency comments have taken no position on environmental portfolio standards, universal service requirements and the extent of stranded cost recovery.

The initial issue selection process culminated in the FTC staff's Open Access Comment to FERC in 1995.[8] The issues selected at the time were the following.

**Operational Unbundling**

Operational unbundling would likely be more effective than functional unbundling and less costly than industrywide divestiture. FERC's plan for functional unbundling of power generation from transmission services addresses a critical competitive issue by requiring vertically integrated utilities to grant open access and equal treatment to their competitors. This approach, however, would leave in place the incentive and opportunity for some utilities to exercise market power in the regulated system. Preventing them from doing so by enforcing regulations to control their behaviour may prove difficult. The problem would be most effectively prevented by completely separating ownership and control of generation from transmission. This separation would remove both the incentive and the opportunity to exercise market power, by eliminating the utilities' ability to discriminate in favour of their own generation operations. The additional benefits of full divestiture may be outweighed, however, by the costs and difficulties of implementing it industrywide. It may be sufficient to require operational unbundling, in which the dispatch of generating capacity and/or the operation of the transmission grid would be controlled by an independent entity. Operational unbundling could prevent discrimination and achieve the competitive benefits of open access more effectively and efficiently than would an attempt to mandate, regulate and monitor access. In addition, operational unbundling would not incur the costs of full divestiture.

## Open Access

Competition problems in concentrated generation markets must still be addressed under open access. Open access will affect, but not obviate, FERC's assessment of competitive conditions in electric power generation, including its analysis of 'generator dominance'. The DOJ/FTC Horizontal Merger Guidelines show how to evaluate likely competitive effects of concentration among suppliers and changes in market contours. Expanding the number of suppliers potentially available is likely to make the electric power system more efficient and more competitive, but there may be circumstances, even under open access conditions, in which dominant suppliers might be able to exercise market power. Competitive conditions among mid-cost plants could be particularly significant because they will determine price during most periods.[9]

## Efficient Transmission Pricing

Efficient transmission pricing must accompany open access. Procompetitive reforms will not achieve their objectives, and might even prove counterproductive, unless prices and terms for transmission services also become economically efficient signals about investment and output. Achieving the economic benefits of unbundling will, therefore, depend strongly upon FERC's concurrent reform of transmission pricing. An aspect of efficient transmission pricing is the regime for resale of transmission rights in secondary markets, which will be especially important if FERC opts for functional unbundling alone. For secondary markets to perform their procompetitive functions effectively, the cap on resale prices should be removed, so that resale prices can become economically accurate signals about expanding transmission capacity. Transmission pricing based on market factors should assist in discouraging local transmitting utilities from favouring their own potentially unmarketable generation capacity and reducing their incentives to delay expansion of wholesale transmission capacity. The utilities might well share these incentives for delay with the agencies that regulate them locally, because delay might favour the interests of local customers.

## Recovering Stranded Costs

Methods for recovering 'stranded costs' should avoid market distortions and reward efforts to mitigate. The FTC staff expresses no view about the net costs and benefits of recovering stranded costs from future, present or past customers. It offers some views about the methods that might be used if FERC commits to recovery of stranded costs. FERC's choice of method will take on additional importance if other jurisdictions use it as a model. First, structuring stranded cost recovery as excise charges is likely to distort price signals and may lead to inefficiencies. Instead, the method chosen should minimize market distortions. Second, shifting all costs to remaining customers could stimulate resistance and delay the transition to greater competition. To avoid that problem, FERC and state and local regulators should consider transitional rate caps or other methods to dampen the 'rate shock' to remaining customers. Third, requiring that all savings from mitigation be passed through is likely to undermine utilities' incentives to innovate with services, marketing and pricing. Alternatives that preserve those incentives to mitigate should be considered. Finally, recovery on a wider geographic basis may be appropriate for those investments that were undertaken to benefit a wider group of customers.

* * *

This selection of major issues during the initial public policy debate proved to be both appropriate at the time and of long-lasting significance for the FTC's competition and consumer protection advocacy programme. These issues have continued to be at the centre of debate, both at the federal and state levels.[10]

## E.    PERSONAL CONTACTS (NETWORKING)

In the US system, regulatory modifications generally require that the regulatory body publish its proposed changes, allow public comment, take the public comments into account, and then publish a final rule. The mechanics of this system do not require that filers interact with the decision makers or with other parties filing comments. It is just human nature, however, for regulators to give special heed to comments from a neutral competition and consumer protection agency whose staff and commissioners are personally known by the decision makers to be active participants in public policy discussions.

Another issue for the competition and consumer protection agency may be the timeliness of the notice that the agency receives concerning comment opportunities before individual states and FERC. It can be difficult to prepare and file a meaningful comment if there is only a short time period between when a comment opportunity becomes known to the agency and when the comment is due. If regulators know that a competition and consumer protection agency is likely to be interested in commenting, the regulators are more likely to inform the competition and consumer agency about upcoming invitations to comment on proposed regulatory changes. Thus, networking can be important in increasing both the effectiveness and timeliness of the competition and consumer protection agency's comments.

The goal of greater visibility can be pursued with several approaches. First, the competition and consumer protection agency may seek to affiliate itself formally with organizations of regulators. For example, the FTC accepted membership in NARUC, which allows the FTC's staff to participate on staff committees of NARUC (and to attend NARUC conventions at discounted rates). Often the NARUC staff committee members are the senior staff at the state commissions. Senior staff at the state commissions often organize and conduct evaluations of restructuring options in their respective states. Membership in NARUC also brings the agency into contact with the researchers at the National Regulatory Research Institute (NRRI) (supported by NARUC). NRRI researchers frequently consult with individual state PUCs. These types of contacts may create a natural source of invitations to comment on regulatory reform proposals and provide occasional invitations to testify before regulators or legislative committees.

Second, competition and consumer protection agency officials and staff may attend and make presentations at industry workshops, seminars and public hearings dealing with restructuring issues in the industry. Often, the audiences at these meetings include a wide variety of industry participants. The concerns and questions expressed in these meetings may help the competition and consumer protection agency to understand reactions to its comments and to update its understanding of technological and organizational developments in the industry. Industry workshops and hearings provide additional opportunities for contacts with regular participants, such that relationship building becomes self-sustaining. Attending such workshops and hearings also provides the potential benefit of 'showing the flag', in the sense that industry participants perceive that the competition and consumer protection agency is monitoring developments in the industry from a law enforcement perspective as well as from an advocacy perspective.

Third, the competition and consumer protection agency may find it useful to expand its contacts with other national-level agencies interested in regulatory reform. In the US electric power industry, these agencies are the DOJ, FERC and, to a lesser extent, the Department of Energy (DOE). To enhance its contacts with other federal level agencies, the FTC participated as a technical advisor in the development of the administration's proposals for electric power industry restructuring and initiated periodic meetings between FERC, FTC and DOJ staffs to share perspectives and concerns. Another aspect of contact between agencies at the federal level is to continue to file comments with national regulators. Often, similar issues are being considered both by subnational regulators and national regulators. In the electric power industry in the US, for example, wholesale competition (regulated by FERC) and retail competition (regulated by the states) are strongly related.

## F.   MONITORING CHANGES IN THE 'HOT' TOPICS

A common observation in public policy development is that the critical issues tend to change over time. These shifts may reflect crisis events or other changes in facts, changes in personnel, or tactical shifts by an interest group. Whatever the source, failing to keep pace with these changes can mean the difference between a credible competition or consumer protection comment and a largely irrelevant comment. Several shifts of this type have taken place over the past several months in the debate on electric power industry restructuring in the US. A prime example is stranded cost recovery. Although this issue continues to be controversial, the level of discord has diminished considerably, in large part because sales of stranded assets have generally occurred at prices far above book values. While this issue appears to have faded, new ones have arisen. These include: distributed generation connections to the transmission grid; for-profit Transcos; ancillary services price spikes; price spikes more generally during peak demand hours; and 'stranded benefits' in states with low generation costs. Other issues have waxed and waned and waxed again, such as locational marginal pricing, affiliate codes of conduct and remedies for existing market power.

Monitoring of shifts in issues can be facilitated by personal contacts, regularly reviewing the trade press, attending conferences and hearings, and making contacts with the interest groups working to develop such shifts in the policy debate. As the visibility of the competition and consumer protection agency's involvement in reform issues grows, more interest groups are likely to make an effort to brief the competition and consumer protection agency on new developments.

## G.   INTEGRATING COMPETITION AND CONSUMER PROTECTION ADVOCACY WITH LAW ENFORCEMENT

Ideally, competition and consumer protection advocacy and law enforcement efforts are complementary. Knowledge gained in competition and consumer protection advocacy work, for example, can provide much of the background necessary to identify and pursue competition issues in a law enforcement context. Moreover, general insights gained during law enforcement investigations can help to inform competition and consumer protection advocacy as well as add credibility to competition and consumer protection advocacy filings. Empirical research and policy reviews can play a similar supportive role in competition and consumer protection advocacy. Law enforcement investigations at the competition and consumer protection agency are likely to provide general insights beyond those available from normal competition and consumer protection advocacy work because law enforcement actions typically obtain corporate planning, marketing and operating documents that are confidential.[11] These documents often disclose methods of analysis and strategic considerations that are only alluded to in publicly available materials.[12] In addition, resources available in law enforcement investigations (and research) may allow use of quantitative methods that are not commonly available in competition and consumer protection advocacy work.

Important complementarities of this sort occurred in conjunction with the FTC's case against PacifiCorp in its proposed acquisition of Peabody Coal Company. The detailed work done for the case, particularly work using computer simulation modelling, gave greater impetus and credibility to FTC staff filings with the states, urging the states to consider using computer simulation modelling to assess existing market power in retail electric power markets. FTC Commissioner Thompson testified about the *PacifiCorp/Peabody* case before the House Judiciary Committee on 28 July 1999:

> The Commission's *PacifiCorp* case contained potential threats to competition both from raising rivals' costs and from abuse of proprietary information. ... A post-acquisition PacifiCorp would have had both the incentive and the ability to raise the price of coal to its competitors, Navajo and Mohave. Both the Navajo and the Mohave plants have substantial off-peak excess capacity which is used to supply other utility companies in the Southwestern states. Raising fuel costs to these plants would put upward price pressure on electricity over a wide regional area.
>
> The acquisition also would have given PacifiCorp access to proprietary information about its competitors. Through Peabody's coal supply relationships, PacifiCorp could have learned highly sensitive data about competitors' costs and generator operating conditions. Peabody provided coal to approximately 150 power plants in the Western states, many of them competitors of PacifiCorp. The order settling the complaint would have required PacifiCorp to divest the Kayenta and Black Mesa mines and to establish a firewall that would have forbidden Peabody from disclosing certain non-public information to PacifiCorp.[13]

## CONCLUSION

The FTC's competition and consumer protection advocacy programme in the electric power industry has its roots in the initial vision of the FTC as an agency to focus public attention on competition issues. By focusing the competition and consumer protection advocacy programme on the electric power industry, the FTC has created a procompetitive and pro-consumer presence in the electric power industry restructuring debate.[14] While this debate is ongoing, there is significant evidence that the FTC's competition and consumer protection advocacy comments have come to be an acknowledged, relevant resource in the policy-making process. Critical elements in developing this type of active competition and consumer protection advocacy programme may include: identifying major issues and organizing background information, developing positions on a subset of the major issues (those that are closest to existing areas of expertise in the advocacy agency), networking with participants in the policy debate, ongoing monitoring of shifts in 'hot' topics, and integrating law enforcement efforts with competition and consumer protection advocacy.

## NOTES

1. For a review of these reforms, see Clifford Winston, 'U.S. Industry Adjustment to Economic Deregulation', 12 *Journal of Economic Perspectives* 89 (1998).
2. Other suppliers include federal government electric power authorities, municipal power authorities, cooperatives and a few state power authorities.
3. FERC also has regulatory responsibilities in the natural gas industry. Competition reforms in that industry are continuing, but the process started approximately a decade earlier than in the electric power industry.
4. The state public utility commissions also have regulatory responsibilities in the telephone, transportation and water supply industries. The degree of authority and the level of staff support available to state public utility commissions vary from state to state. In most states, the public utility commission has the authority to determine allowable rates and conditions of service to final customers. These commissions also have authority to approve or disapprove of most generation, transmission and distribution investment decisions. Until recently, most state commissions encouraged public utilities to operate as largely self-sufficient entities with respect to generation capacity and siting. Transmission was viewed primarily as a reliability enhancement, not as a systematic source of power to meet anticipated demand levels. Due to this localized approach in siting of generation and transmission, as well as other factors, significant price disparities developed among different areas of the country, with high-cost states experiencing prices five times (or more) as high as those in low-cost states. For example, the least-expensive residential rate in the country in 1995 was 1.5 cents/kWh. The most expensive residential rate at that time was 16.1 cents/kWh. Ronald J. Binz, Thomas Feiler and Michael J. McFadden, 'Navigating a Course to Competition: A Consumer Perspective on Electric Restructuring', 9–11 (Unpublished paper on file with the Competition Policy Institute, 1997) <www.cpi.org/reports.htm>. These geographic price disparities helped spark interest in increased competition.
5. US Department of Energy, Federal Energy Regulatory Commission, Doc. Nos RM95–8–000 and RM94–7–001; Promoting Wholesale Competition Through Open Access Non-discriminatory Transmission Services by Public Utilities, Order No. 888; Recovery of Stranded Costs by Public Utilities and Transmitting Utilities, 61 Fed. Reg. 21 539 (1996).
6. Comments of the Federal Trade Commission Staff to the Legislative Audit Council of the State of South Carolina on Possible Restrictive or Anticompetitive Practices in South Carolina's Public Service Commission Statutes (29 September 1987) (available from the author).
7. Comment of the Staff of the Bureau of Economics of the Federal Trade Commission in the Matter of Promoting Wholesale Competition Through Open Access Non-discriminatory Transmission Services by Public Utilities, Recovery of Stranded Costs by Public Utilities and Transmitting Utilities, Proposed Rulemaking and Supplemental Notice of Proposed Rulemaking, FERC Docket Nos RM95–8–000; RM 94–7–001 (7 August 1995) <www.ftc.gov/be/advofile/htm>.
8. Comment of the Staff of the Bureau of Economics of the Federal Trade Commission, *supra* note 7.

9. In most electric power exchange markets, the price required to meet the last increment of demand at a particular period in time will be the price that is paid to all generators that are dispatched (utilized) during that time period.

10. For example, FERC's recent notice of public rulemaking on Regional Transmission Organizations concludes that 'continued discrimination in the provision of transmission services by vertically integrated utilities may ... be impeding fully competitive electricity markets'. US Federal Energy Regulatory Commission, Docket No. RM99–2–000, Regional Transmission Organizations, Notice of Proposed Rulemaking 6 (13 May 1999) (On file at the US Federal Energy Regulatory Commission, Office of the Secretary, 888 First Street, NE, Washington, DC 20426). This conclusion is consistent with the risks to competition that the FTC's staff cautioned about in its Open Access Comment in 1995.

11. No confidential information is disclosed in advocacy comments or presentations. However, general insights about business strategies, competitive concerns and consumer information from case work helps to enrich and validate competition and consumer protection advocacy work.

12. FTC, Comment to FERC on its revised merger filing requirements, FERC Docket No. RM98–4–000 (11 September 1998).

13. Prepared Statement of the Federal Trade Commission presented by Mozelle W. Thompson, Commissioner, Before the Committee on the Judiciary, United States House of Representatives (28 July 1999) (available from the author).

14. See, for example, Federal Energy Regulatory Commission's Regional Transmission Organization Notice of Public Rulemaking, FERC Docket No. RM99–2–000 at 65 (13 May 1999) ('The functional unbundling policy underlying Order No. 888 was an attempt to regulate the behaviour of transmission owners. There are growing indications, however, that the conflicting incentives that vertically integrated utilities have regarding transmission access may be too difficult to police ... The Federal Trade Commission advised the Commission that a functional unbundling approach ... would leave in place the incentives and opportunity for some utilities to exercise market power in the regulated system. Preventing them from doing so by enforcing regulations to control their behavior may prove difficult'.); Market Power in Electricity, final report to the Maine State Legislature by the Department of the Attorney General and the Public Utilities Commission at 57 (1 December 1998) ('Because of federal preemption, the State in most cases lacks jurisdiction to legislatively address market power within a load pocket on the New England grid. ... The Commission and the Department intend to monitor developments, using computerized simulation modeling where appropriate, to ensure as far as possible that anticompetitive activity with a wholesale price impact is detected. To the extent that such price effects are felt, it may be that (as the Federal Trade Commission has pointed out [Federal Trade Commission Staff Comment of 29 May 1998]) specific transmission enhancements or new generation projects can be proposed and encouraged as a practical remedy'); Consumer Energy Council of America, Research Foundation, quoting the FTC staff comment to California (17 March 1999) as a rationale for CECA/RF's decision to establish a Distributed Energy and Domestic Policy Forum ('Because DG [Distributed Generation] is likely to be at a critical state of development and particularly vulnerable to discriminatory behavior by incumbent utilities in connecting to the T&D grid, the California Public Utility Commission may wish to establish conditions for a fair market test of DG. ... After the CPUC has conducted a fair market test and evaluated DG's initial rate of market acceptance, it may then wish to address the longer-term questions of distribution competition that may arise if DG is adopted extensively').

# 20. Country experiences with targeted advocacy and enforcement programmes

## Michael O. Wise

*This chapter presents findings from Organization for Economic Cooperation and Development (OECD) studies of country experiences with targeted advocacy and enforcement programmes. Issues discussed include identifying 'success' and 'failure', requirements of consultation and their effectiveness, relevance of formal authorization to deal with policy issues and institutional independence, and sequencing and tactics. Some national experiences are described from the US, the Netherlands, Japan, Mexico, Denmark, Spain, Hungary and Korea (see Annex).*

*To be effective, the competition advocate must have a 'fist' in the process. Enforcement is the fist that most agencies have. An agency that is not actively enforcing the law may not be taken seriously in the debate. The relationship between advocacy and enforcement is delicate, but critical. Enforcement sets up advocacy. On several occasions when efforts to enforce have failed, the need to change the rule was clearly demonstrated.*

*Competition policy bodies can respond to the anticompetitive impact of regulation with measures other than law enforcement, such as public media debate, private advice and formal participation in court or agency proceedings. Tactics must be adapted to the political environment. For instance, the independent Mexican competition authority was empowered to deny participation in privatization auctions, and to make the ultimate decision as to whether there is market power justifying regulation. The Hungarian competition authority has the power to go to court to challenge anticompetitive action by other agencies, which has changed other agencies' behaviour towards it. Several other transition countries have created similar powers.*

*Advocacy is effective only to the extent that it is backed by political support and perhaps by some other legal powers. The details of how it is organized, of the structure and of the independence of the agency really are not as important as this political context and the existence of a strong constituency for the idea of competition. Establishing such a constituency is an especially worthwhile function of advocacy.*

## INTRODUCTION

Once it is established that regulation can be anticompetitive, the question of what to do about it arises. Most governments now have a body charged with promoting and defending competition. What can this body do about anticompetitive regulation? The usual answer, to enforce the law protecting competition, is not apt, for these restraints are put in place by other laws, against which the competition law is impotent. Most competition laws include an anti-gridlock protector, making the competition law inapplicable where other laws or official actions govern. Enforcement is not entirely out of the question in a setting dominated by anticompetitive regulation, but the target is usually conduct or rules that are *ultra vires* the regulatory authorization. Assuming enforcement alone will not solve the problem, what remains to be done are all the tactics typically lumped together under the awkward label, 'advocacy'.

## A.   ADVOCACY PROGRAMMES

Nearly every competition agency is involved in policy advice about regulation. In virtually every country where significant reform efforts have been undertaken, the competition agencies have been involved in some way in the reform process. For some agencies, however, the word 'advocacy' provokes discomfiture. The term implies direct confrontation, in public, with other agencies. That is one form that participation can take, and in some cultural and political contexts that is the role that is taken most seriously. The label was adopted quite deliberately in the US in the 1970s, because that was the function that the agencies wanted to emphasize. They wanted to step into the shoes of already recognized 'consumer advocates', but taking on other government agencies rather than corporations.

   Public confrontation is not the only tactic, and by itself, it may not even be a very effective one. The process can also include behind-the-scenes persuasion and publicity outside of formal proceedings. A few competition agencies have the power to initiate court proceedings challenging anticompetitive actions by other agencies or official or quasi-official bodies. More indirect, but still visible, is formal participation in another agency's public hearings and deliberations. Less visible, but often a critical complement, is continuous staff-level monitoring and collaboration, and strategic policy-level coordination with potential allies. What is appropriate and effective depends on the particular institutional setting.

Advocacy must be adapted to the political environment. It is, however, typically somewhat unusual in that environment. Effectiveness depends on taking advantage of that 'unusualness', balancing advocacy with enforcement and timing action for the occasion. Ultimately, advocacy is effective if and perhaps only if it is backed by legal or political power. Details of statutory authority, agency structure and management matter little; what really matters is whether the very idea of competition has a significant constituency. One of advocacy's functions is building and motivating that constituency.

In the 1997 OECD study of regulatory reform, some competition agencies attempted to quantify their participation in regulatory proceedings and reform issues. The efforts are not entirely comparable, because they cover different periods of time, and multiple presentations about the same issue are sometimes treated as one and sometimes as many. Nearly every sector commonly identified to be in need of reform, including telecommunications, electric power, professional services, agriculture and food, financial services, and product standards, has been the subject of substantial advocacy or enforcement attention. Of the approximately 20 OECD countries whose agencies have had the most active programmes, all have been involved in telecommunications issues, all but two in professional services, all but two in financial services, and well over half in the electric power and agriculture and food sectors. Most have also been involved in reform in airline and other transport sectors, and in issues about retail trade and distribution.

The programmes of longest standing are in North America. In Canada, the Competition Bureau listed 200 proceedings dating from 1976; the Office of Consumer Affairs reported an additional 110 since 1984. Most of these appear to have been formal, on-the-record public comments. The US Department of Justice (DOJ) Antitrust Division and Federal Trade Commission (FTC) have made about 2000 comments or other appearances about regulatory issues since 1975. The Mexican office was established only in 1993, but for reasons detailed below, it has been uniquely active.

Scandinavia is the hotbed of advocacy action in Europe. In Finland, the Office of Free Competition made regulatory reform a priority project since 1988, generating over 900 actions in dozens of sectors. The consumer agency also made over 800 appearances. In proportion to the size of the country and the agency, Finland's regulatory reform advocacy programme is the most active and ambitious anywhere. Sweden's agency was not far behind, producing an average of approximately 100 policy actions a year. Since 1990, the Danish Competition Council has initiated approximately 40 formal proceedings calling on other agencies to correct their actions, and has made more than 100 appearances at hearings and in other fora.

Transition situations invite a great deal of advocacy effort. The Office of Economic Competition in Hungary estimated its annual output on regulatory and policy issues to be 20 comments within the government, ten in parliament or the Cabinet, 30 in other formal settings, 30 informally, and five directly related to case enforcement. The Antimonopoly Office in Poland made approximately 200 presentations to other parts of government since 1990, and listed a total of over 1000 actions, some of them direct challenges to monopolization by public authorities. The Czech Office for the Protection of Economic Competition identified 34 proceedings since 1991, not including privatization actions; these were taken when the office was still a ministry within the government. In Spain, Mexico and Korea, three 'transition' settings outside of Central Europe, competition agency participation in reform has also been important in bringing about change.

In the rest of Western Europe, the most active programme appears to be Italy's. The Italian Competition Authority's formal actions included submission of 65 written reports to public authorities from 1990 to 1996, plus participation in hearings and production of fact-finding reports. About half of these actions involved telecommunications, professional services, maritime transport or electric power.

## B.  SUCCESS OF ADVOCACY EFFORTS

Assessing whether this extensive participation has made a difference requires judgements. The first difficulty is identifying what, in the relevant context, would count as success or effectiveness. If the outcome is less competitive than the agency would have liked, it still might be more competitive than it would have been without the agency's participation. The next difficulty is determining what action led to the success, and whose action it was. The process of changing major legislation and regulatory practice is complex and time consuming, so it is nearly impossible to assign responsibility for the results, particularly for the successes. Not only are there usually many issues at stake other than competitive and consumer effects, but there are also usually many other participants. Claims of credit and assignments of blame may have more to do with politics than persuasion. It may thus be practically impossible to isolate the effect of the agency's participation on the regulatory outcome. Given the extended period over which regulatory reform issues are typically debated and decided, it is even difficult to determine when the most important contributions were made. A presentation that seemed to make no difference in the short run may have contributed to a long-term paradigm change of thinking within the industry or regulatory body.

Hungary offers an illustration. The competition office failed to convince the transport ministry not to limit entry into taxi service. In a private suit, however, the constitutional court ruled that the limitation infringed the right to enter a business. The competition office attempted to prevent locally imposed rate regulation from being overly intrusive, but that effort was not persuasive. Although the resulting regulation was broader than the office would have liked, the price cap was ultimately set so high that it is not binding. Accordingly, after two advocacy 'failures', Hungary ultimately emerged with a reasonably competitive taxi system.

In Finland, the Office of Free Competition believes its most important accomplishments were in electric power, telecommunications, transportation, environment, and petroleum and alcohol products. In Sweden, action by the Competition Authority led to free market entry in the taxi industry, partial deregulation of long-distance bus services, and liberalization of the domestic airline market. Its studies and proposals, as well as some enforcement actions, have prepared the ground for change in banking and insurance, postal services and telecommunications. In Italy, the Competition Authority believed its intervention was instrumental in stimulating the adoption of European Union (EU) telecommunications directives and a new regulation for harbours. In the US, the most visible results of the agencies' programmes are probably in restructuring telecommunications and broadcasting, and in reducing barriers and collusion in professional services. Both of these successes involved a combination of highly visible enforcement action and sustained advocacy. The Australian and Canadian agencies also believe their most influential work has been in public utilities and professional services.

In transition settings, the visible successes are often in restructuring and privatizing state-owned enterprises; here 'success' may consist not of creating an optimal competitive market structure, but simply avoiding the creation of a private monopoly to succeed the public one.

Success may sometimes be an accident or an orphan. In one country with a strong record of neo-liberal reform, the competition office claims no responsibility; indeed, potential targets of reform effort had successfully terminated the agency's advocacy role. Another agency names transport sectors among its successes, but the transport ministry in that country denies that advocacy had any effect on its decisions, which are not particularly dramatic in any event. Sweden's competition agency thought its advocacy moved agriculture policy in the right direction, but that this policy took several steps backward when Sweden joined the EU.

Despite the ambiguities, a few agencies have attempted to assess their successes and failures. The Danish Competition Council believes that approximately 60 to 70 per cent of the time, the ultimate action is at least partially consistent with its recommendations. This implies that approximately 30 per cent of the time, its positions have been ignored or rejected. The Italian Competition Authority concludes that as many as two-thirds of its interventions have been unsuccessful. Outside support makes a difference; the Italian agency finds that its success rate improves to more than 70 per cent when a decision or directive of the European Commission or a ruling of the Court of Justice supports its position. Access and status may matter, too: the highest reported success rate, in some years over 75 per cent, is in Korea, where the head of the Korean FTC has ministerial rank and was, for a time, serving also as the head of the Deregulation Commission.

Difficulties are inevitable. Interests that benefit from the status quo actively oppose reform. And those who probably would benefit from reform do not realize it, or do not care very much. Thus, they passively support the status quo. A typical ground of resistance is consumer protection, where the claim is made that the regulation does what it should, which is to make consumers better off than they would be without it. For instance, professional associations say they must limit entry and retain power to expel members to ensure quality control. Even some consumer interests have resisted changes that would lead to lower prices, believing that the sacrifice in product quality would be unacceptable. That of course begs the question whether lower prices from greater competition would result in lower quality or just thinner profit margins. One way to overcome opposition is to show that procompetitive reform actually helps achieve other goals, such as increased innovation, productivity, competitiveness, growth and even environmental protection. Where a good story can be told, concretely and convincingly, it can sway the undecided or at least neutralize opposition.

## C.   CONSULTATION REQUIREMENTS

Competition laws usually require other bodies or ministries to consult with the competition agency about particular matters, or even about all actions that might affect competition. Where the laws are not so explicit, a similar right or power of consultation typically inheres in the agency's position in the government structure, as a matter of government decree, or as the usual or expected practice. Nearly all agencies offer advice and opinions on matters when requested by other parts of the government or the legislature. A few agencies have limited their regulatory and policy work to such responses, sometimes because their legal authority for other kinds of participation in regulatory issues is not clear. In New Zealand, for example, the Commerce Commission only responds to requests for advice, because its statutory authority limits its functions to law enforcement. In Germany, the *Bundeskartellamt* similarly limits its actions to responding to requests from the ministry and the *Bundestag*.

## D.  RELEVANCE OF FORMAL AUTHORIZATION TO DEAL WITH POLICY ISSUES AND INSTITUTIONAL INDEPENDENCE

The degree and nature of an agency's formal authority to participate in reform can be important, but is not necessarily critical to its effectiveness. Where competition is strongly established as the basic principle of economic policy, there may be less need for formal authority to promote that goal. But the lack of clear authority can prevent action even where procompetitive reform has support.

Basic laws in some countries explicitly authorize the competition agencies to participate directly in proceedings at other government agencies or with regulators, or to publicize recommendations about their decisions or about reforming their laws and regulations. Most of these agencies have had active regulatory reform programmes. In Canada, for instance, the Director of the Competition Bureau has specific, statutory power to appear before federal regulatory bodies, and may also appear before provincial boards and commissions with their consent. In Denmark, Finland, Norway and Sweden, the competition agencies are authorized by law to call attention to possibly anticompetitive rules or actions taken by public authorities (or subject to their control or approval), and to recommend measures to reform them.

Other agencies have general powers to study and report on competitive issues and problems. Where this power is interpreted to extend to the effect of government action as well, it has supported significant programmes of participation. A general power to study and report is the principal foundation for the advocacy work of the US FTC, for example. Sometimes this general power is supplemented by power to do such studies in response to particular requests. In Australia, for example, the agency may undertake research about areas affecting consumers that are within the legislative power, and make the findings available to the public. In addition, it may do research on matters referred to it by the National Competition Council (NCC), and review and report on laws when referred by the minister. The agencies in Japan, Italy, Mexico and Spain operate under similar conditions.

Another seemingly significant institutional factor is the degree of independence. This too, however, is ultimately ambiguous. A position of independence from government ministries can be both a strength and a weakness. Independence may be necessary for the agency's position as an impartial law enforcer. In their enforcement roles, competition agencies normally enjoy some degree of independence of action, regardless of their formal position in the government. The resulting image of impartiality might also strengthen their position in the reform process. On the other hand, a position outside the government may isolate the agency from the important reform decision process. Agency participation is hampered if regulators and other agencies are reluctant to make their own processes transparent. Moreover, an independent agency may have difficulty establishing a base of political or popular support for actions other than law enforcement. The degree of institutional independence, however, appears not to be determinative. Some of the most institutionally independent agencies, including the competition agencies in Italy, Mexico, Korea and the US FTC, have done substantial work on regulatory issues, while others in similar circumstances, such as Germany's *Bundeskartellamt*, have not.

## E.   RESOURCES, STRATEGIES, AND TACTICS

Participation in the reform process is costly, in terms of both resources and political capital. This must be weighed against the competition and consumer benefits of the reform outcome. A low likelihood of success in an advocacy effort must be balanced against the prospect that the benefits will be greater and more enduring. To participate effectively, agencies must have enough resources for the purpose, especially during transition periods. Competition agencies will be understandably reluctant to participate fully in regulatory reform efforts if that commitment would impair performance of their primary responsibilities in law enforcement. Fortunately, there are synergies, as regulatory issues become subjects of competition enforcement. Experience working on reform will make enforcement more effective, and vice versa.

A competition agency may initially lack expertise about a regulated industry and its regulatory regime. The agency's staff, although expert about principles, lacks direct knowledge of the industry, largely because exemptions have shielded the industry from the agency's jurisdiction. Agencies may retain staff specialists who have that expertise, or the agencies may establish new organizational units specializing in these issues. This poses some risks, for a separate staff responsible for regulatory issues may become a target for criticism that the agency is diverting resources from its primary mission. Moreover, as reducing regulation may correlate with increasing competition enforcement, offering advice directly may appear as empire building. As reform progresses, though, and the formerly regulated industries become increasingly subject to competition law enforcement, these potential liabilities become assets. Experts hired as specialists in regulated industry issues will later be analysts supporting law enforcement work in the same industries.

Many competition agencies rely on, and even sponsor, analysis and advice from outside experts and academic sources. Outside experts already know the subject, may appear to be more objective, and may be familiar with the relevant institutions, which can help the agency make useful contacts as the process proceeds.

At the agenda-setting stage, a major function is publicity, to construct a public and government consensus-supporting action. Despite its likely lack of particular industry expertise, the agency should not be bashful in the pre-reform period, as it may be the only voice in or near the government that is willing to put reform on the agenda. In Australia, the competition agency began discussion about reforming regulation of the taxi industry, which is an industry that other political decision makers are often loath to take on.

During the stage of formal consideration and decision, the competition bodies' chief role is to offer analysis and advice. The agencies may make formal or informal comments and proposed revisions to particular proposals. One important function is to advise about whether they will be compatible with law enforcement requirements. The agencies also contribute to the basic cost–benefit analysis, with insights about consumer effects and how businesses in a competitive market will respond to alternatives. Regulatory agencies typically understand cost–benefit effects in their own industry context, but may lack the broader consumer welfare perspective. The competition agencies, with their cross-industry perspective, bring concrete illustrations of how competitive institutions are likely to work to debates that sometimes stall, cautious in the face of counterfactual arguments. To be effective, the agency should be involved while proposals are being formulated, and active rather than merely reactive to other initiatives.

Enforcement authority can make advocacy more effective. Some agencies even recommend against undertaking an advocacy project unless they have reinforcement from enforcement power. Direct enforcement is not, however, always an option. Where an anticompetitive restraint follows directly from government action, advocacy may be the only way to help eliminate it. Enforcement can identify these regulatory problems. Enforcement action against anticompetitive conduct that falls outside the scope of formal exemptions can publicize the need to address conduct that remains exempt. The US offers many examples of enforcement related to regulatory issues, but other countries have undertaken similar actions. In Finland, debate about reform of the electricity industry in the late 1980s was accompanied by competition law enforcement actions, challenging restraints that were preventing the entry of competition.

## F.    IMPLEMENTATION OF DECISIONS

After decisions are made, they must be implemented. At this stage, the competition agencies' principal roles are enforcement and publicity, to apply the law and keep the process honest. The period of transition, before reform takes full effect, calls for special enforcement care. Even before the laws or rules actually change, the likelihood of new institutions can lead to anticipatory changes in firm behaviour. As firms adapt to the new, more competitive reality, enforcement should be sensitive to that process. Competition agencies and regulators must keep the reform goals in mind and adapt their actions accordingly. Where firms confront ambiguities and uncertainties about whether the regulatory or competitive regime applies, competition enforcement should offer guidance, more than discipline.

Enforcers must, however, strongly resist industry efforts to reverse or ignore the reform process and persist in familiar, non-competitive behaviour. Anticipating greater competition, industry players may take steps to reduce its impact on them, through alliances or mergers. Where these are likely to be anticompetitive in the post-reform environment, the competition agency must either take preventive action during the transition period (where permitted), or prepare for the possibility that enforcement and restructuring action will be needed after the parties no longer have regulatory immunity from competition law enforcement. Such enforcement actions complement and reinforce reform outcomes. For example, the French competition authorities played a role in ensuring that road freight deregulation functioned properly and the benefits materialized. Merger enforcement actions in the US have deliberately reinforced the restructuring decisions set out in the recent Telecommunications Act.

The competition agency can expect additional enforcement work in the post-reform period. In part, this increase corresponds to expansion of jurisdiction through removal of exemptions. In addition, some of it may represent backlash from the reform process, if firms attempt to revert to non-competitive pre-reform behaviour, or otherwise resist the implications of reform. Formerly monopolistic firms may have habits that are equivalent to abusing dominant positions, which must be curbed. Newly or prospectively competitive firms, uneasy about their prospects under the new conditions, may merge or collude to prevent competition. Those moves must be reversed or deterred. Exemplary enforcement actions will educate the industry about the new rules and inform the public that their interests are being protected in the new setting.

A strategic approach is recommended. The balance of costs and benefits must include a realistic assessment of how much influence the agency's participation is likely to have on the outcome. A strategic approach would take account of these considerations to concentrate resources on a few, well-chosen issues. By contrast, a comprehensive approach could join in any reform debate where the competition agency's views could be relevant. The comprehensive approach would strongly signal the agency's seriousness about participation. It may, however, spread the agency's efforts too thinly to be effective in any forum. Moreover, it may also incur much greater risks of generating distracting controversy, compared to the likelihood of achieving a commensurate benefit.

Demonstrable consumer benefit is a critical element in setting priorities. To emphasize the legitimate policy foundation of their actions and the link between regulatory issues and their usual enforcement work, agencies should concentrate their resources on settings where consumer benefits and effects are strongest and most clearly demonstrable.

Effective participation depends on access to the process. Regardless of its organizational position inside or outside the government structure, the agency must have enough access to the process to ensure that the important decisions are not already made before there is a real opportunity to participate. A good working relationship between the agency's staff and the staffs at the various regulatory bodies will broaden the perspectives of all parties, and enable the competition agency to keep abreast of technological and political developments that might affect the regulator's outlook on critical issues. Advocacy that takes a diplomatic approach, by respecting the complexity of the issues and the potential legitimacy of other policy goals, helps establish that relationship.

Effectiveness may depend on support from other participants. Because the cost in political capital can be great, agencies should carefully consider whether to participate in settings where no support from other parties can be expected. To increase effectiveness and help prevent damaging political counterattacks, the agencies should rely upon support from those with other policy interests – that is, they should be aware of, and capitalize on, linkages with other policies and institutions. Where possible, they should consider working with media, interest groups, and advocates in other fora to achieve regulatory reform goals.

This process entails a risk, because appearing to form alliances to achieve reform outcomes could compromise the independent stance necessary for law enforcement. Moreover, identifying allies is not always straightforward. Industry parties may change their positions, as those who oppose reform may have second thoughts later when it appears they may benefit from it. Allies on some issues may become adversaries on others. Sometimes a degree of leverage is useful. For instance, one competition agency announced it would support an industry in its effort to have price controls removed, if import restraints were removed as well. Consumer and labour groups can be uncertain allies to the extent they do not accept the benefits of promoting competition, or fear that market competition is equivalent to social disorder. Where reform is progressing one industry at a time, allies for further reform may be found in the previously reformed sectors. Ultimately, though, it is probably most important for the agency to find allies elsewhere in the government decision-making process.

An agency that includes both consumer protection and competition authorities has a unique advantage in promoting regulatory reform: it can be its own ally, because it can credibly contend that its advice to promote competition is consistent with its responsibility to protect consumers. A separate consumer protection agency faces special challenges. Distinctions between economic 'deregulation' and reform of other kinds are not always clearly drawn. Consumers, and consumer agencies, have expressed misgivings about whether advocacy of consumer interests and protections is consistent with advocacy of less, or different, regulation. Some consumer protection authorities report that one of their problems is resisting pressure for deregulation. Consumer interests in Denmark have resisted changes that would lead to lower prices, on the ground that product quality would also decline too much. Consumer groups are sometimes sympathetic to the arguments of professional associations that anti-competitive rules must be retained to provide consumer protection quality control.

Nonetheless, consumer agencies can play an important educational role. Increasing competition benefits consumers directly; thus, the ultimate goal of much economic regulatory reform is fundamentally a consumer protection goal. Where a single agency has both consumer protection and competition responsibilities, this point is often easier to make convincingly.

## CONCLUSION

The effectiveness of advocacy depends strongly on political context. Thus it is difficult to prescribe generally applicable rules or principles – except that principle itself. As the distinguished lawyer who heads the Dutch competition agency once put it, advocacy in policy making, just as in legal argumentation, is an art, not a science. Convincing a decision maker requires not just having a convincing argument, but also good timing and the other aspects of persuasion that make the argument compelling in context. Sometimes this will mean appeal to general principle, and sometimes evocation of analogy to a successful action, even law enforcement, in a particular sector. Credibility is typically based on successful law enforcement, and on the independent status that demonstrates its principled basis. Yet in settings where fundamental structural reform is a prominent policy goal, a competition agency's most important work can be advocacy. This applies not only to conventionally understood 'transition' countries, but also to the common policy relationship between central authorities and regional governments or elements of federal or quasi-federal structures.

## REFERENCE

Organization for Economic Cooperation and Development, *Report on Regulatory Reform, Thematic Studies* (Paris: OECD 1997).

# ANNEX    HIGHLIGHTS OF SOME NATIONAL ADVOCACY PROGRAMME EXPERIENCES

## United States[1]

In the late 1980s, the US competition agencies were unusually active, with over 100 advocacy appearances a year. By 1997, the annual total was fewer than 20. Activity revived to some extent in 1998, but then declined again in 1999. At present, neither the DOJ nor the FTC has a separate office for this function. The exact resource commitment is not clear, but is obviously very small. The overall decline in advocacy activity probably reflects that the easier and more obvious battles have been fought and won, at least at the federal level.

The US experience demonstrates the value of backing advocacy with enforcement. There, competition law enforcement has been used to break up the national telecommunications monopoly. Less dramatically, the need for reform can be demonstrated by law enforcement actions. Because regulation is often accompanied by exemption or exclusion from the competition law, this effect is indirect, and appears in two ways. First, as in the FTC's actions against 'ethical practice' agreements among professionals, enforcement usually succeeds because it is aimed at conduct that, for technical jurisdictional reasons, falls outside the regulatory exemption. This shows that the kind of conduct required by regulation has anticompetitive effects. Second, enforcement succeeds by failure. If an action brought against clearly anticompetitive behaviour must be dismissed because of a regulatory exclusion, the failure can support a call to eliminate the exclusion. Unsuccessful suits against trucking tariff bureaus, which were found to enjoy protection under the 'state action doctrine', helped set the stage for deregulation in that area.

Formal public advocacy is more effective when it is combined with informal cooperation with other regulators and policy makers. Airline deregulation was organized and promoted by a coalition of key staffers in Congress and the executive branch, enlisting support in some segments of the industry. Advocacy was at most a supplement, because the most important decision makers in the sectoral agency and the legislature were already nearly convinced. The success of deregulation in energy and communications might be traced to a long tradition of staff-level consultations and exchanges between the antitrust agencies, the Federal Energy Regulatory Commission (FERC), and the Federal Communications Commission (FCC), as well as shared ideas among political-level appointees.

## The Netherlands[2]

In the Netherlands, the Ministry of Economic Affairs has had major responsibility for the government's regulatory reform programme. The ministry houses the new competition agency, the NMa. In a sense, the competition agency's parent organization already is doing the advocacy role. However, the ministry must participate in the political balance of the government, and thus its advocacy is somewhat tempered by realpolitik. The NMa has taken on only a limited advocacy role, responding to requests from parliament or ministries for analysis and comment on particular legislation. The initial strategy of concentrating on enforcement tends to confirm the principle that the foundation of credible advocacy is a reputation as an enforcer. The new agency has not yet established its enforcement bona fides. Until it does so, it is reluctant to get involved in what could look like an unprincipled bureaucratic turf battle.

## Japan[3]

Japan's Fair Trade Commission (JFTC) has a statutory responsibility to advise about laws and regulations that could affect competition. When administrative bodies propose economic laws and ordinances, the JFTC may consult at the planning and drafting stage if there is concern that they will include exemptions from the Antimonopoly Act or provisions that may restrict competition. However, the process is nearly opaque to the outside, making it difficult to tell how well this consultation duty is carried out in practice. The JFTC does not make its disagreements public.

Because the JFTC is not in the cabinet, its views must be submitted through the prime minister's office, limiting its own direct involvement. Because government bodies cannot propose legislation outside their own jurisdiction, the JFTC has relied principally on outside experts to develop recommendations. Those recommendations are not usually presented as the JFTC's, although the relationship between it and its academic study groups is no secret: the research is done by the JFTC staff. The members of the study group may criticize and disagree with government policies, which the JFTC itself is unlikely to do.

Recommendations and reports by JFTC study groups are credited with helping accomplish several major goals. The single most significant project was probably the overhaul and repeal of many exemptions from the Antimonopoly Act. The group also played a role in changing the policy and the law about large-scale stores, as research about regional enforcement revealed problems due to local administrative guidance. In 1997, study group reports were published about the domestic airline industry, electric power, and natural gas.

## Mexico[4]

Mexico's experience demonstrates the importance of tenure, independence, good personal relationships, and above all, as one Mexican official stated, having 'a fist in the process'. The competition law gives the enforcement body, the independent *Comision Federal de la Competencia* (CFC), substantial authority to study and comment on competition-related policy matters. Comments on particular proposed laws must be offered in response to requests, but general issues are always appropriate for study and advice. The CFC participates directly in the deliberations of several important interministerial committees.

The CFC's most interesting regulatory and policy role has been in the processes of privatization and of awarding concessions and licences, both in the design of the law and regulations and in implementing them. The CFC has direct, final responsibility for competition aspects of sector-specific regulation. It can determine which firms may participate in auctions for public enterprises, concessions, licences and permits. In addition, in several sectoral schemes, the CFC has the power to determine whether effective competition exists, or whether a firm has substantial market power, as a condition for a sectoral regulator to impose regulation such as price caps.

The power to limit bidders is almost like enforcement. Rather than undo a monopoly or a merger after the fact, the CFC can prevent it from occurring in the first place. It has exercised the power sparingly. Conditions have often been imposed on particular bidders, typically limiting how much of a system they can obtain, but only a few have been barred outright. The power to identify the absence of effective competition has been more contentious.

### Denmark[5]

Denmark's competition office has made a substantial resource commitment to advocacy. In 1996, this amounted to approximately 15 person-years from a staff of approximately 70. The results, however, have been limited, largely because political and popular support for competition policy was weak until very recently. On the other hand, the political culture welcomes public debate, so advocacy is never out of place.

The Competition Council 'may approach the competent authority ... and make recommendations for promotion of competition'.[6] The only sanction is publicity, and perhaps embarrassment. The Council has estimated that approximately 60 to 70 per cent of its recommendations under this process resulted in some action or amendment consistent with them, and approximately 30 per cent of its recommendations have been neglected or rejected. It appears that many of the failures were in areas where there might be superficially plausible 'consumer protection' claims or tight, long-standing cartels defended their entry controls.

Council studies and statements about infrastructure deregulation may have had more impact than its efforts in health care, transport, professions and services. That may be because the recipients were more sympathetic, and were obliged to move toward the instructions of EU directives, in telecommunications and electric power.

## Spain[7]

Spain's experience illustrates the power of independent, authoritative advocacy to launch reform when the conditions are right. The two competition bodies, especially the Competition Tribunal (which is outside the government) have statutory roles in administrative and legislative processes. Given its independent position, the Tribunal can be more effective as a voice in public debate analysing and criticizing current policies.

Since 1992, the Tribunal has made more than 150 advocacy recommendations. The most important single action was probably its major, comprehensive report on structural reforms in response to a government request in 1992. The report not only recommended changes in legislation, but also set out a strategy to overcome special interest opposition.

The Tribunal has continued to issue reports and studies, but the pace and focus have changed to concentrate on particular sectoral problems and proposals. Recently, however, the number of these studies has sharply declined. The reduced rate of these reports, and their narrower focus, are explained by staff changes and by a management decision that workload constraints meant other matters should receive higher priority. Another reason may be that the early reports addressed the most important issues, and appeared when public acceptance of competitive, market approaches was still unclear. Now, persuading the public is less important, and many of the major subjects have been addressed. Moreover, there has been an election since the 1992 report and the period of strong advocacy activity. The opposition endorsed the Tribunal's 1992 programme. Now that the opposition has become the government, the need for analysis and criticism of government policy is not as obvious to it.

## Hungary[8]

Hungary has adopted an institutional design combining decisional independence with access to the policy process at several stages. It has also given its competition body a most powerful 'fist', the power to go to court to challenge other agencies' action.

The Hungarian Competition Office (HCO) occupies a position outside the government, which gives it flexibility to affect debate and encourages public expression of its views. There is a consultation requirement, enforced mostly by embarrassment. The views of the HCO must be sought with respect to all draft proposals or legislation that could restrict competition, grant exclusive rights, or regulate prices or terms of sale. If a ministry has failed to consult with the HCO about a proposal or draft, that omission can be corrected or at least identified either at the meeting of the Cabinet, which the HCO president attends, or at the state secretaries meeting, which the vice-president attends. The process does not, however, function perfectly. Despite the formal obligation to consult and the potential for embarrassment at a formal meeting if a ministry has failed to consult, the HCO still encounters proposals about which it should have been consulted, but was not. When the process functions correctly, it provides the HCO with the opportunity to have an impact.

The HCO's independent status implies that it is principally responsible to parliament. As a formal matter, it makes policy proposals to parliament, sometimes through its annual report, rather than through the government. The HCO has a long-standing, regular connection with the parliament's Economic Committee, and HCO ideas often appear first in public in the form of a committee report or even a legislator's proposed amendment to a government bill.

The HCO can challenge anticompetitive actions by other public bodies in court. This power in the current law has never formally been used; a similar procedure under the previous law was used once. Informal, non-public threats to use it have occasionally been effective. This power can only be used against particular decisions, though, and not against anticompetitive policy decisions or rules. To challenge those, the HCO (or a member of the public) can bring an action in the Constitutional Court, claiming that procedures were not properly followed or that constitutional standards of proportionality were not met. Filing or threatening Constitutional Court action has achieved results on several occasions involving taxis and auto imports.

### Korea[9]

Korea has a comprehensive requirement for interagency consultation, but as is often the case, it lacks means of enforcement and thus, is not always observed. The consultation process appears to have improved after the Korean Fair Trade Commission (KFTC) became independent, and again when its status was raised. The chairman and the vice-chairman now present the KFTC's views in person, in deliberations at the ministerial and vice-ministerial level. The KFTC chairman is also one of the four members of the Economic Ministries Council, which advises about regulations that are the responsibility of the Ministry of Finance and Economy.

The KFTC was the agency responsible for economic deregulation between 1988 and 1992, within the Economic Planning Board. When the KFTC became an independent agency in 1994, it began to take a more visible role. The KFTC chairman served as the president of the Inter-Ministerial Committee of Economic Regulatory Reform from April 1997 to December 1998.

# NOTES

1. Michael O. Wise, 'Review of United States Competition Law and Policy: The Role of Competition Policy in Regulatory Reform', 1 *OECD Journal of Competition Law and Policy* 9 (1999).
2. Michael O. Wise, 'Review of Competition Law and Policy in the Netherlands', 1 *OECD Journal of Competition Law and Policy* 73 (1999).
3. Michael O. Wise, 'Reviews of Competition Law and Policy in Japan, Mexico, Denmark, Spain, Hungary, Korea', *OECD Journal of Competition Law and Policy* (forthcoming 1999 and 2000).
4. *Id.*
5. Michael O. Wise, 'Review of Competition Law and Policy in Denmark', 2 *OECD Journal of Competition Law and Policy* 23 (2000).
6. Danish Competition Act, Statute No. 384 (10 June 1997).
7. Wise, *supra* note 3.
8. *Id.*
9. *Id.*

# 21. Competition advocacy within the European Commission: the role of DG competition

## Kirti Mehta[1]

*The European Commission is in a special situation with regard to competition advocacy: it is a competition authority with exclusive competencies under the Treaty of Rome in the domain of Competition Policy, and it is also an institution with an important role in the initiation, implementation and monitoring of Community-wide regulatory actions. Given that both the regulatory actions of the Commission and its role as competition authority are Treaty based, its regulatory actions must be coherent with the core principles of competition policy.*

*To date, the Directorate General for Competition (DG Competition) has not played a very major role as competition advocate to ensure this coherence. It could take on a much greater role in a number of respects, which are explored in this chapter and summarized here.*

*First, the Commission's regulatory responsibilities include product regulation – health and safety – through specification of standards. Product regulation can take the form of classification (a product meeting the standard can be put on the market). A reasonable standard should be adequate to protect health and safety, but other, more anticompetitive regulatory forms are also frequently used. These include setting standards at levels higher than necessary to achieve health and safety goals, controlling entry and establishing technological conditions. Incumbents favour drastic standards that cannot be met, which create high entry barriers for newcomers. National regulatory authorities also favour high standards, which conserve their enforcement resources. DG Competition could encourage adoption of procompetitive standards, which do not impose artificially high barriers, whenever a centralized standard-setting procedure is used. (Currently, centralized procedures are used infrequently, as they require a centralized agency which exists in few areas.)*

*Second, Article 81 is applicable with respect to regulation established by self-regulatory bodies. DG Competition could apply Article 81 more broadly in this regard.*

*Third, in the regulated industries, the Commission can rely upon Article 86 to launch liberalization, which it has done in the telecommunications sector. It can also rely on merger control to ensure that a competitive market structure results once restructuring occurs.*

*Fourth, with respect to anticompetitive national regulation, DG Competition could have a role in benchmarking the performance of national regulations, which currently is not done. With respect to internal market regulation, the Commission uses a 'scoreboard', through which it can ensure that improvements are made where needed. A similar system could be used to encourage member states to eliminate anticompetitive regulation.*

*Fifth, given the extent of regulation in the economy, it would be difficult for DG Competition to play a central role in all areas. Other power centres at different levels should also have the competition advocacy role. DG Competition could help design general guidelines that set forth competition principles applicable to all areas of regulation, or different sets of guidelines for product regulation based on safety and performance criteria, the regulated sectors, and still others where competition authorities would have a greater role. Guidelines should apply to a critical mass, and should not be designed on a sectoral basis.*

## INTRODUCTION

The European Commission is in a rather special situation with regard to competition advocacy: it is a competition authority in its own right with exclusive competences under the Treaty in the domain of competition policy (these tasks are primarily the responsibility of DG Competition), and it is also an institution with a very important role in the initiation, implementation and monitoring of Community-wide regulatory actions. The regulatory actions of the Commission are Treaty based, and competition rules are also an integral part of the Treaty, thus requiring that regulatory actions of the Commission are per force coherent with the core principles of competition policy. Can DG Competition have any specific role as a competition advocate within the Commission? To answer this question, this chapter outlines how competition advocacy works in practice within the European Commission.

## A. DESIGN OF REGULATORY POLICY

Competition advocacy is a mechanism to ensure that regulatory oversight is applied where necessary and that it satisfies certain rigorous criteria of optimality. An intuitive criterion for optimality could be that the regulation creates a level playing field, thus improving the functioning of markets. Prices of the regulated product/service should continue to be subject to competitive pressure, so that compliance costs do not reduce or alter the constraints on pricing. This could, for example, occur through the differential effects of compliance costs on certain incumbents and potential entrants. The problem for regulatory policy is how to internalize or 'endogenize' this mechanism in the design of regulation, its process and the institutional architecture. The issue for competition policy is how best to complement exogenously the regulatory policy currently in place. Competition advocacy would thus seem to have a role in both the design of regulatory oversight and in the application of competition policy.

The optimal regulation that would result under conditions of effective competition advocacy would be characterized by a number of properties that limit or mitigate inefficiencies:

- Regulatory scope should be strictly limited to what is necessary to achieve, for example, product safety, efficacy and performance standards or other social objectives.
- There should be objective, performance-based criteria for evaluation.
- Administrative procedures should be transparent, proportionate and non-discriminatory.
- Risk assessment procedures for products should be based on scientific criteria compatible with international standards and adaptable to technical progress.
- Legislation should either regulate market entry through mandatory qualifications on firms or should regulate product/service health and safety specification. Where both market entry and product/service specifications are regulated, the control of supply must be indispensable to meet some clear social objectives.

## B.   INCORPORATING COMPETITION ADVOCACY IN REGULATORY POLICY

Competition advocacy to attain these desirable properties is largely built into the process of regulation within the European Commission. Much attention has been devoted to the design of regulatory oversight, particularly with respect to product safety and efficacy legislation. From the origin of a regulatory proposal to its final adoption by the Commission, it passes through a number of filters, including interservice consultations, to ensure that it advances the desirable properties listed above. It is not only the process of preparing regulation that underlies the relative success in incorporating competition advocacy, but also the systematic phases of consultation of interested third parties (including national regulators), the obligation to undertake economic impact assessment of proposed regulation, and the institutional readiness to review oversight. The role of DG Competition in this process, while not negligible, is not especially significant.

## C.  THE COMPETITION AUTHORITY'S ROLE IN OPTIMIZING REGULATORY OVERSIGHT

There are two areas in which DG Competition's role is highly significant. First, it can use Treaty provisions directly or through secondary legislation to initiate a process of liberalization and deregulation in industries where the right of establishment is limited by national law. This instrument is relied upon only with respect to markets whose size considerably exceeds the exhaustion of internal scale economies, such as network industries. Second, where state authorities or state-delegated organizations carry out economic activities, DG Competition can ensure that they are linked directly or indirectly with a regulatory function, and that these authorities' actions are compatible with competition rules, including state aid provisions.

There are at least four other desirable properties of optimal regulation that competition advocacy, particularly by a competition authority, may reasonably seek to attain. First, the choice of regulation model should be influenced by competition considerations. For instance, in regulating product safety, a choice must be made between at least two models of regulation: harmonization with common and uniform standards at the Community level, or mutual recognition subject to minimum safety requirements, but with the possibility of imposing stricter national rules. The first model is likely to generate more rigorous competition than the second, unless the production factors are highly mobile and force competition between the different regulatory standards.

Second, competition advocacy can promote regulation that creates a 'one-stop shop' – that is, provides for regulatory approval of a product by all the agencies concerned simultaneously. For instance, where the product is subject to safety, environmental assessment and product performance or efficiency standards, a single notification should be relied upon to assess compliance with all three types of requirements. This policy of 'one door, one key' is especially helpful to small and medium-sized enterprises as it limits entry barriers. It also limits forum shopping and ensures a high degree of legal certainty for firms.

Third, competition advocacy can strive to ensure that sunk costs resulting from regulatory compliance are limited and proportionate to a regulation's social objectives. Regulation will normally increase the exogenously determined level of sunk costs. The sunk costs tend to generate a concentrated market structure, thereby impeding entry into and exit from the relevant market. A competition authority could also ensure that regulatory standards are not set in such a way that regulatory expenditures by firms are endogenous sunk costs – that is, that an individual firm's regulatory outlays stimulate demand for that firm's products. This type of sunk costs, associated with quality and ecological labels, would promote a high degree of market concentration without any major compensating gains in product safety. Its effect on product choice is uncertain.

Fourth, the competition authority should be concerned when regulation designed to promote product safety or energy efficiency, or to impose limit values on polluting raw materials, is implemented through explicit or implicit agreement among the incumbents. While some arguments can be made in favour of industry adoption of voluntary safety norms, these are likely to be vitiated if they are implemented through restrictive agreements between the incumbents. Such agreements are likely to facilitate concerted practices with respect to the important parameters of competition.

## D.  DG COMPETITION'S ROLE IN OPTIMIZING REGULATORY OVERSIGHT

With respect to the four areas of competition advocacy discussed above, DG Competition is most active with respect to the last, regulation through restrictive agreements. This is a limited (although growing) area of regulation, because the use of mandatory standards is the more common approach where regulation is required to ensure product or environmental safety. Voluntary agreements are used when the legislative process is blocked due to lack of convergence on the mandatory standards. Given its goal of promoting market integration, DG Competition has also favoured a one-stop shop for pre-market approval regulations. Community competition law, as currently applied and upheld by the Court of Justice, views market segmentation essentially as a *per se* violation. One-stop shop is viewed as a means of encouraging parallel trade between markets.

As regards the other desirable aims of competition advocacy, DG Competition's role is limited, for essentially two reasons. First, it devotes the bulk of its resources to the treatment of Article 81 notifications, which may themselves result from the externalities created by the regulatory framework for product approval. For example, given the high cost of clinical trials, product innovations by small firms can often only reach the market if developed through collaboration with competitors, principally the major players in the market. Second, in the formulation of product safety, health or environmental standards, competition advocacy can play only a secondary role. Much greater weight is given to the precautionary principle, which may tend to penalize innovation, as a guiding rule for regulatory oversight.

With respect to regulated sectors in which the right of establishment is in some way restricted or licensed by the state, competition advocacy can play a paramount role. In the case of public utilities, where the minimum efficient scale is larger than the relevant market, a statutory monopoly with guaranteed universal service is the necessary, appropriate and proportionate measure to achieve viable supply. This justification loses it validity, however, when technological innovations drive down the minimum efficient scale, or when single market measures in conjunction with globalization radically increase the size of the market. Competition advocacy should ensure that these efficiency-increasing forces are permitted to lead to deregulation. However, given the high costs of replicating the existing essential facilities, market entry must be stimulated by facilitating access to existing networks. It is unclear whether the competition authority or specialized industry regulators should be delegated the tasks of regulating access conditions and monitoring conduct and performance of former monopolists and new entrants. The Commission's experience with the telecommunications sector suggests that the role of a competition authority in initiating and advancing market liberalization is crucial. It is, however, less clear whether implementation of the comprehensive regulatory framework for access conditions, stranded costs, universal service and so on, which national regulators currently perform, could have been more effectively implemented by a competition agency.

There is much scope for competition advocacy with respect to entry regulation through licensing, professional standards and codes governing the activity of liberal professionals. This is an area in which competition agencies could be much more active in securing much greater competition, with no adverse impact on consumer protection.

## CONCLUSIONS

In conclusion, the following points are emphasized:

- The most significant area of Community legislation is product or technology related regulation – that is, mandatory health, safety or environmental standards. To be effective in this area, competition must be an integral part of the basic regulatory policy and philosophy. Thus, competition advocacy would promote common and uniform mandatory standards, centralized pre-market approval procedures based primarily on scientific criteria, and a single regulatory decision. If this first best is unattainable, then competition advocacy should strive to achieve the least-anticompetitive second best.

- Competition advocacy and enforcement should play a significant role with respect to regulation by voluntary or state-sponsored agreements among incumbents, and sectors subject to statutory monopoly, such as network industries (except information goods).
- The influence of a competition authority as advocate will differ where regulatory oversight relates to: (i) product safety approval subject to exogenous standards of efficiency, efficacy and performance; (ii) market entry conditions or tender procedures, subject to exogenous qualifying requirements on entrants; (iii) regulated sectors. Accordingly, it is vital for effective competition advocacy that different principles are in place. Where there is specific product/service regulation, competition advocacy is more effective when competition principles are internalized as essential elements of regulatory policy. In other situations, regulatory policy is the same as competition policy. The empowerment of the competition authority to apply competition rules to state or quasi-state bodies is a crucial element ensuring the effectiveness of competition advocacy.
- Where right of establishment or market entry is regulated, either explicitly or through standards and codes of professional bodies and self-regulators, it is increasingly evident that competition authorities could make greater use of liberalization and deregulation of entry conditions. This would be preferable to uncertain attempts to obtain improvements in performance and conduct through incremental changes in rules set by self-regulators.
- Finally, competition rules and the regulations applying them should not themselves escape competition advocacy. If non-transparent procedures, discretionary rules and high costs of notification are imposed on economic operators, particularly for cooperation agreements that amount to minor restrictions of competition, then the result is likely to be a heavy economic cost reducing entrepreneurial innovation and initiative, employment and growth. Similarly, the application of competition rules that do not reflect sound economic principles leads to increased social costs.

Competition advocacy is thus a major challenge that should not be underestimated by a competition authority. DG Competition is active in this regard.

## NOTE

1. The views expressed are those of the author and in no way reflect or represent the position of the European Commission. The author is indebted to Wouter Wils for helpful comments and suggestions.

# 22. Constitutional limits to anticompetitive regulation: the principle of proportionality

## Michael Kohl

*This chapter explores two main aspects of constitutional scrutiny of anticompetitive regulation. First, it addresses how constitutional principles legitimate scrutiny of anticompetitive regulation. Second, the chapter considers the proportionality principle as a framework for scrutiny of anticompetitive regulation.*

*The author concludes that convincing arguments can be made that scrutiny of anticompetitive regulation is constitutionally mandated. Such a constitutional mandate is best supported by the argument that freedom of competition is a direct constitutional interest. Somewhat weaker arguments are that competition is constitutionally protected because it is the indirect outcome of constitutionally protected basic individual economic freedoms, such as the right to property and the freedom to enter contracts; that it is the only tool available to safeguard the economic viability of the state; and that economic regulation is highly complex and therefore likely to escape normal democratic controls. Thus, it must be subject to court scrutiny to ensure constitutionally required democratic accountability. Taken together, all four arguments present a strong case for a constitutional requirement to scrutinize regulation to eliminate its anticompetitive effects.*

*The proportionality principle rationally structures the relationship between a regulatory aim and the means chosen to achieve such an aim by testing a regulation's appropriateness, necessity and proportionality. This principle has been formulated in German constitutional law, which has influenced European Union (EU) law, to scrutinize regulatory limitations of basic economic freedoms. It can be a useful tool for assessing and balancing the costs and benefits of anticompetitive regulation, and for deciding whether to repeal or amend such regulation.*

*Case law of the European Court of Justice (ECJ) and German Constitutional Court applies the proportionality principle. In the context of protecting basic economic freedoms, the courts have been reluctant to scrutinize measures that only indirectly restrict individual rights, but directly restrict the collective freedom of competition. This reluctance is related to the institutional nature of courts, and is not mandated by the proportionality principle. Courts are well suited to protect individual rights, and balance them against collective interests. In contrast, courts have difficulties substituting their discretion in balancing different collective interests for that of the legislature or executive, because they are committed to the principle of separation of powers. Thus, courts refrain from protecting collective freedoms and acknowledge extensive regulatory discretion. This implies a limitation of judicial oversight, which may be of little concern as long as political accountability is present (which is not the case with respect to anticompetitive regulation).*

*Moreover, courts are legal institutions, whose judges are trained to assess legal facts and clearly specified rights, but not to do economic analysis or advocacy. They are inherently passive, since they act only when called upon. Thus, perhaps they are not the best institutions to scrutinize anticompetitive regulation, although they could perform the function of a new oversight institution, invalidating regulations determined to be anticompetitive.*

*The author concludes that a new oversight institution, based on the model of the Court of Auditors, may be appropriate.*

## INTRODUCTION

Regulation[1] of economic activity is common in all industrialized countries and usually considered indispensable to the achievement of objectives of orderly planning and welfare in society. However, regulation often amounts to a restraint of competition, either as an intended or as a secondary effect. As the body of regulation expands each decade, and particularly with each slowdown of economic growth, much of it is viewed as out of date and in need of overhaul. This has led to considerable liberalization and re-regulation in the last decade. This chapter contends that competition policy, which aims to protect competitive and economic freedom by curtailing the abuse of private and public economic power, should be used as a general guiding principle in the process of regulatory reform.

Assessing the anticompetitive[2] effects of regulation raises many questions. Some are of a very technical nature, such as how to determine and quantify the anticompetitive effects of regulation. Others are of a more fundamental nature, such as the legitimacy of scrutinizing regulation for its anticompetitive effects, and then having to advise (or order) the regulator as to when regulation should be revised.

Constitutional courts[3] have employed constitutional arguments, such as protection of economic freedoms and the principle of proportionality, to scrutinize regulation. The proportionality principle has been particularly useful in structuring the correlation between means and ends, that is, between restrictions of freedom and benefits to social interests that often are the objective of regulation. This suggests that the legitimacy of scrutinizing regulation for its anticompetitive effects could perhaps be derived from constitutional law, and particularly the proportionality principle.

This chapter aims to explore this possibility. It will first clarify whether constitutional principles, in particular protection of economic freedoms and accountability of public power, require scrutiny of anticompetitive regulation, or whether this would be a policy choice. Constitutional protection of basic economic freedoms may give rise to a constitutional mandate to scrutinize regulation for its anticompetitive effects, if the freedom of competition is viewed as one aspect of the basic economic freedoms, or if competition is viewed as the only tool that can safeguard the economic viability of the state. Second, application of the proportionality principle by the European Court of Justice (ECJ) and the German Federal Constitutional Court (*Bundesverfassungsgericht*) to scrutinize regulation with anticompetitive effects when formally protecting basic economic freedoms will be explored. Finally, the institutional suitability of a court to safeguard the collective interest, which would be harmed by anticompetitive regulation, versus its suitability to safeguard individual interests, protected by economic freedoms, will be considered. The chapter concludes with remarks on possible guiding principles for scrutiny of anticompetitive regulation.

## A.   IS THERE A CONSTITUTIONAL MANDATE TO SCRUTINIZE ANTICOMPETITIVE REGULATION?

Constitutional principles provide constitutional courts with broad authority to scrutinize restrictive regulation. In liberal democracies, a constitution normally establishes that public power derived from the people is entrusted to the state and its institutions, and it defines their powers. All laws derive their legitimacy from the constitution and must therefore conform to its principles. If they do not, they must either be reinterpreted to avoid such conflict, or be declared null and void, often following a court procedure.[4]

Scrutiny of anticompetitive regulation may be seen as one aspect of the broader questions of accountability and control of public power, and preservation of individual liberties. Constitutional theory establishes accountability through separation of powers, periodic elections of representatives, the rule of law, the principle of proportionality[5] and a catalogue of civil and human rights. The protection of individual liberties must be balanced against the role of the state as a guarantor of 'social justice', order and social welfare. Does constitutional theory require that the legitimacy of regulation, promulgated to pursue social goals, be determined by balancing the need for it against individual freedoms or distortions of the competitive market process? Or is such accountability simply a policy option?

### Freedom of Competition as a Direct Constitutional Interest

A constitutional mandate to scrutinize anticompetitive regulation could be implied if the 'freedom of competition' were viewed as being directly constitutionally protected. This would follow if the freedom of competition were considered a consequence of the protection of basic economic freedoms, or if competition were considered the only tool that could safeguard the economic viability of the state.

Most national constitutions do not explicitly require that the state be managed under any particular type of economic system. For instance, the German *Grundgesetz* acknowledges neutrality towards choice of economic system.[6] In contrast, the EC Treaty contains positive acknowledgements of free competition as a basic treaty value, and thus a constitutional value.[7] As a consequence of the supremacy of Community law over national law,[8] the member states must accept the Treaty's constitutional requirement for free competition. The clear commitment of the member states to a free market economy and a system of undistorted competition implies that they are not free to adopt an economic system that does not permit free competition.[9] Moreover, the Treaty explicitly prohibits the member states from interfering with the competitive market process, through its rules on public and quasi-public undertakings and state aids.[10] Thus, free competition is a constitutional requirement in the EU and its member states.

### Basic Economic Freedoms Indirectly Protect the Freedom of Competition

In addition, constitutions normally establish basic individual civil and economic rights and freedoms, such as the freedom of contract and the right to property. These individual economic freedoms could legitimize scrutinizing regulation with anticompetitive effects if the freedom of competition is protected by those basic freedoms. The collective exercise of these individual economic freedoms results in markets driven by competition.[11] Thus, the competitive economic system is indirectly related to these freedoms, and therefore indirectly derives constitutional protection. The EC Treaty's reference to the freedom of competition requires interpretation of basic economic freedoms in this way. Thus, the Treaty must be seen as protecting the freedom of competition indirectly.

An important distinction must be made, however, between this indirect protection of the freedom of competition and the direct protection of individual economic rights and freedoms. As shown in Section B *infra*, courts are prepared to balance individual against collective interests when protecting individual basic economic freedoms. In contrast, courts seem less willing to balance the collective interest in free competition against other collective interests.

## Securing the Economic Viability of the State through Competition

Another approach to conceptualizing the freedom of competition as a constitutional interest is to view it as a means to the end of achieving economic soundness, sustainability and cost-consciousness of state administration. The economic viability of the state might be endangered when the state 'lives above its means', as when its budget is unbalanced. Economic viability could also be endangered through a state's interference with economic activity that goes beyond moderate taxation and public spending, such as through burdensome economic regulation. Thus, a collective interest in sound economic development that can be achieved through competition may be implied.

The absence of economic soundness and sustainability amounts to a factual or economic, rather than formally legal, restriction of freedom. Bankruptcy would excessively limit the state's freedom to pursue initiatives to advance social welfare, and could eventually lead to its self-destruction. Moreover, it would choke individual economic initiative that provides the economic basis for a state infrastructure. Thus, constitutions should require economic soundness and cost-consciousness from all state institutions. Only some states' constitutions in fact include such a requirement.[12]

The interest in economic soundness and cost-consciousness has its basis in economic theory of competition. The application of this theory in antitrust law leads to the scrutiny and prohibition of anticompetitive agreements between or among private actors. It is incomprehensible that the same economic theory is not applied to interactions between the state and private actors, such as to lead to scrutiny of regulation for anticompetitive effects. One explanation for this difference might be that at the time most liberal democratic constitutions were drafted, the regulatory state had not reached today's dimensions, and hence the danger of anticompetitive and economically unsound regulation was not a concern. At present, however, constitutional concerns about anticompetitive regulation have matured. Regulatory reform and re-regulation are difficult to achieve largely due to anticompetitive regulation. Society at large suffers because small groups that benefit from various types of anticompetitive regulation are capable of obstructing regulatory reform.

Therefore, the constitutional interest in economic self-preservation of the state is an indicator that economic soundness, cost-consciousness, the suppression of waste and lavishness should be viewed as constitutionally-based interests. The economic theory of competition has identified anticompetitive conduct that clarifies the notion of economic soundness, and provides a basis for scrutinizing anticompetitive regulation. Scrutiny of regulation to ensure that it interferes with economic activity only to the degree necessary would help safeguard the state's interest in its own economic sustainability.

## The Accountability of Public Power

A fourth approach to finding a constitutional basis for freedom of competition is to focus on the accountability of state institutions, particularly regulators or legislators. All liberal democratic states have recognized that accountability is a basic issue of public organization, and have developed mechanisms by which the populace can hold its representatives accountable. The classic tools are periodic elections, separation of powers, transparency, the rule of law and a catalogue of basic human and civil rights. These tools have been supplemented over time, responding to new challenges. For example, the growing complexity of the public budget has given rise to a lack of transparency. In response, courts of auditors have been instituted to monitor the legality and cost-effectiveness of public spending,[13] holding government accountable for wasting taxpayers' money.[14] The complexity of regulation has also grown considerably, but no comparable institutional response has been instituted. One explanation for this difference may be the difficulty in pinpointing any associated waste. However, wasting resources through anticompetitive regulation or through unjustified spending are equally improvident. Accordingly, as a matter of accountability, anticompetitive regulation warrants an institutionalized process of survey and scrutiny.

One could argue that courts, and especially constitutional courts, are already equipped with the tools necessary to safeguard constitutional interests, including the economic viability of the state. However, as shown in Section B, when courts are called upon to protect the individual from indirect effects of excessive regulatory intervention, they are often reluctant to assess the merits of regulation. Instead, they tend to scrutinize procedural questions, or acknowledge a wide area of legislative or administrative (that is, regulatory) discretion in economic policy matters.[15] In fact, the capacity of courts to deal effectively with the often highly complex nature of economic regulation may be seriously impaired by lack of knowledge and economic-regulatory expertise.

The complexity of economic policy choices often immunizes regulatory decisions from public understanding and electoral response. Therefore, it isolates the regulator or legislator from political accountability. Judicial self-restraint or the impotence of judges to assess the merits of economic policy matters isolates the regulator from legal accountability. A democratic constitution must not leave the exercise of public power unchecked; rather, it must require scrutiny under constitutional principles of any exercise of public power. Accordingly, the observation that economic regulation with anticompetitive effects escapes political as well as legal accountability is an argument for scrutiny under constitutional principles, since a democratic constitution cannot leave the exercise of public power unchecked.

### Scrutinizing Anticompetitive Regulation: Freedom of Competition and the Proportionality Principle

A constitutional mandate for scrutiny of anticompetitive regulation is best supported by the argument that freedom of competition is a directly protected constitutional interest. The arguments based on the guarantee of basic economic freedoms that indirectly protect the freedom of competition, the economic sustainability of the state and the accountability of public power, set forth in the second, third and fourth subsections above, are somewhat weaker. Together with the first argument, however, they show the constitutional necessity of scrutinizing anticompetitive regulation. Accordingly, scrutiny of anticompetitive regulation is constitutionally mandated and not merely a policy option.

Assuming, *arguendo*, that a constitutional mandate does not exist, the arguments set forth above present convincing evidence in favour of such scrutiny as a policy option.

## B. THE PROPORTIONALITY PRINCIPLE AND ITS APPLICATION BY THE COURTS

Neither the protection of the basic economic freedoms nor that of the freedom of competition is absolute. Rather, regulation can and does restrict these freedoms in the pursuit of other socially desirable goals. However, restriction of the basic freedoms must not be arbitrary, which means that the gravity of the restriction of freedom must be proportional to the importance of the socially desirable goal pursued. This concept is captured by the constitutional principle of proportionality, which requires the means used to be in proportion to the end sought. By looking at anticompetitive restrictions as costs and the socially desirable goals as benefits, the principle integrates the concept of an economic cost–benefit analysis into a constitutional democratic framework.[16]

Under German constitutional law, proportionality of a measure is established by satisfying a three-step test.[17]

- The measure must be appropriate for attaining the objective (element of appropriateness or suitability).

- The measure must be necessary, in the sense that no other measure is available which is less restrictive (element of necessity).
- The restrictions produced by the measure must not be disproportionate to the objective achievable (element of proportionality).

In the European context, the ECJ has recognized the proportionality principle under Community law, and has applied it, sometimes following a two-step test, sometimes a three-step test. The Maastricht Treaty added the proportionality principle to the text of the EC Treaty,[18] which was elaborated in the Protocol on the application of the principles of subsidiarity and proportionality.[19] The Protocol did not, however, specify any deviations from the Court's case law on proportionality, nor did it attempt to provide any clarifications. Accordingly, the ECJ decisions, which vary in their elaboration of the structure of the proportionality principle and in the rigidity of its application, remain the main source explaining the substance of the principle.

In *Fromancais*,[20] a two-step approach was used:

In order to establish whether a provision of Community law is consonant with the principle of proportionality it is necessary to establish, in the first place, whether the means it employs to achieve the aim correspond to the importance of the aim and, in the second place, whether they are necessary for its achievement.

In contrast, in *FEDESA*,[21] a three-step approach was used:

The principle of proportionality ... requires that the prohibitory measures are appropriate and necessary in order to attain the objectives legitimately pursued by the legislation in question; when there is a choice between several appropriate measures recourse must be had to the least onerous, and the disadvantages caused must not be disproportionate to the aims pursued.

This is very similar to the German three-step test, to which its origin is attributed.[22] Moreover, the EU approach is similar to the Australian approach and the US approach, discussed elsewhere in this volume.[23] The latter two approaches, however, are more specifically designed for scrutiny of regulation, while the former states a general constitutional principle.

**ECJ Case Law**

The ECJ case law offers rich material on judicial scrutiny of regulatory market intervention. In particular, relevant decisions include those in the area of the Common Agricultural Policy (CAP), pursuant to Articles 32 to 38 of the Treaty where traditional economic freedoms are at stake, and in the area of the fundamental freedoms, such as free movement of goods, services and persons, and freedom of establishment. In these cases, the Court follows a step-by-step analysis, which does not always follow the same formal structure and terminology. This produces some uncertainty as to the precise content and application of the principle. In particular, the Court does not always clearly distinguish the different elements of a proportionality test and does not always specify the factors used to identify relevant interests. The cases do, however, always identify a restriction on individual rights, and an objective in pursuit of which the restriction may be justified.

## Common Agricultural Policy cases

In *Bela-Mühle* (the skimmed-milk-powder cases),[24] the proportionality of certain preconditions imposed for receiving Community aids was considered. The cases related to a Council regulation[25] that was intended to reduce excessive stocks of skimmed milk powder held by intervention boards. It was to do so by subjecting recipients of aids for certain vegetable protein products to the condition that they purchase specified quantities of skimmed milk powder at a fixed price, which was approximately three times the value of the foodstuff that it replaced. The validity of the legislative measure was challenged on the ground that it violated the proportionality principle and the prohibition against discrimination. The Court ruled that the provision was invalid. Two elements played a decisive role in the Court's decision: that the objective pursued must be legitimate, and that the measure must be necessary. The Court stated the standard of scrutiny by reference to Articles 33 and 34:

> Although Article [33] thus enables the CAP to be defined in terms of a wide choice of measures involving guidance or intervention, the fact nevertheless remains that the second subparagraph of Article [34](3) provides that the common organisation of the agricultural markets shall be limited to the pursuit of objectives set out in Article [33]. Furthermore, the same subparagraph lays down that the common organisation of the markets 'shall exclude any discrimination between producers or consumers within the Community'. Thus the statement of the objectives contained in Article [33], taken together with the rules in the second subparagraph of Article [34](3), supplies both positive and negative criteria by which the legality of the measures adopted in this matter may be appraised.[26]

The Court looked at the redistributive effects of the measure that consisted of:

> the imposition, not only on producers of milk and milk products, but also, and especially, on producers in other agricultural sectors of a financial burden which took the form, first, of the compulsory purchase of certain quantities of an animal feed product and, secondly, of fixing of a purchase price for that product at a level three times higher than that of the substances which it replaced. The obligation to purchase at such a disproportionate price constituted a discriminatory distribution of the burden of costs between the various agricultural sectors.[27]

The Court concluded: 'Nor ... was such an obligation necessary in order to attain the objective in view, namely, the disposal of stocks of skimmed-milk powder. It could not therefore be justified for the purpose of attaining the objective of the CAP'.[28]

Thus, the Court held that the objective of non-discriminatory market regulation was not met, and that the measure used was not the least onerous and thus did not conform to the proportionality test's element of necessity. However, the decision does not make clear which factor was decisive.

The proportionality of the Commission's application of a legislative penalty was considered in several other CAP cases. In *Buitoni v. FORMA*,[29] a legislative provision required forfeiture of deposit if any condition attached to import, export and other licences was violated, without regard to whether the violation was substantive or formal. The purpose of the legislation was to control the volume of supply in the relevant product market. The Commission had imposed the penalties for formal, non-substantive violations. The provision was challenged on the ground that it was inflexible. The Court credited the argument of 'administrative efficiency', which the Commission made in defence of its practice. However, it held that forfeiture of the entire deposit as a consequence of violation of merely formal requirements (that is, not respecting time limits for the supply of documentation as to the accurate execution of an export licence), was disproportionate:

> That fixed penalty, which is applied to an infringement which is considerably less serious that that of failure to fulfil the obligation which the security itself is intended to guarantee, which is sanctioned by an essentially proportionate penalty, must therefore be held to be excessively severe in relation to the objectives of administrative efficiency in the context of the system of import and export licenses.[30]

The Court then referred to the necessity element of the proportionality test and a less onerous alternative. It instructed: '[The Commission] should have sanctioned failure to comply with that period only with a penalty considerably less onerous for those concerned than that prescribing the loss of the whole of the security and more closely allied to the practical effects of the omission'.[31] A similar conclusion was reached in *Atlanta BV v. Produktschap voor Vee en Vlees*:[32]

> [T]he absolute nature of Article 5 (2) of the above mentioned Regulation is contrary to the principle of proportionality in that it does not permit the penalty for which it provides to be made commensurate with the degree of failure to implement the contractual obligation or with the seriousness of the breach of those obligations.[33]

Accordingly, in the CAP cases, the Court established that the Commission holds wide legislative discretion, justified by its political responsibility.[34] The proportionality principle was narrowly interpreted to invalidate the Commission's practice of discriminating against licensees that violated only formal licensing obligations, while fulfilling the substantive obligations.

## Fundamental freedoms cases

A second group of cases in which the proportionality principle was considered involved the fundamental freedoms. Regarding free movement of goods, Articles 28 and 29 prohibit quantitative restrictions on the free circulation of goods between member states, unless they fall (i) within the derogation specified in Article 30, or (ii) under the *Cassis de Dijon*[35] exception to the broad definition of the concept of 'measures having equivalent effect' in the *Dassonville* formula.[36] In applying the proportionality principle to 'measures having equivalent effects' as quantitative import restrictions, the ECJ repeatedly invoked the necessity element, and probed measures as to the existence of less onerous means to achieve the envisaged objective.

In *Cassis de Dijon*, the German *Monopolverwaltung* (for alcohol) refused to grant permission for importation of Cassis de Dijon, a cordial liqueur, on the basis that its alcohol content was too low to comply with the German classification of cordial liqueurs (25 per cent alcohol content). The classification in France, the country of origin, had a lower requirement (15 to 20 per cent alcohol content). The Court followed the opinion of Advocate General Capotorti, who observed: 'The objective of the protection of the consumer against fraud may, in fact, be attained by other means which are *less harmful* to trade; in relation to that objective the obstacles placed in the way of the free movement of goods are excessive and, therefore, disproportionate'.[37]

*Groenveld v. Producktschap voor Vee en Vlees*[38] involved a dispute over the Dutch rule prohibiting all storage and processing of horsemeat. The Advocate General's opinion insinuated that less-restrictive means to protect consumers and fair competition existed: '[A] remedy such as that adopted by the Netherlands consisting in a complete prohibition on the production of horsemeat sausages is certainly out of proportion to that object'.[39]

Similarly, in the 'apple vinegar' cases,[40] an Italian rule excluding the marketing and importation of all non-wine vinegar was at issue. The Court concluded:

Whereas it is true, as confirmed by a consistent line of decisions of the Court, that in the absence of common rules relating to the marketing of a product it is for the Member States to regulate on their own territory all matters relating to the marketing of that product and that obstacles to movement within the Community resulting therefrom must be accepted, the fact remains that those requirements must still be acknowledged to be necessary in order to satisfy mandatory requirements such as the protection of public health, referred to in Article 36, consumer protection or fair trading, which does not appear to be the case here. As far as fair trading and consumer protection are concerned, those needs ... may be fulfilled by *means less restrictive* to free movement than a prohibition of the marketing of all kinds of natural vinegars other than wine vinegar.[41]

The necessity element played a similar role where the free movement of goods was restricted on the basis of an Article 36 derogation in *Commission v. United Kingdom*.[42] There, the British government imposed restrictions on the marketing in its territory of UHT-treated milk and cream for the purpose, *inter alia*, of preventing foot-and-mouth disease. The Court held:

> [W]hilst the protection of health of animals is one of the matters justifying the application of Article 36, it must none the less be ascertained whether the machinery employed in the present case by the United Kingdom constitutes a measure which is disproportionate in relation to the objective pursued, on the ground that *the same result may be achieved by means of less restrictive measures*, or whether, on the other hand, regard being had to the technical constraints already mentioned, such a system is necessary and hence justified under Article 36.[43]

Parallel reasoning of the Court can be found for the freedom to provide services, the freedom of movement and the freedom of establishment.[44]

\* \* \*

The above overview is intended to illustrate that scrutiny under the proportionality principle can be efficiently performed when the restriction is well defined (as in the cases involving forfeiture of a deposit and limitation of the free movement of goods), and the restrictive measure is not very complex or system embedded, and therefore does not obstruct the view of less-restrictive alternatives. Further analysis, including economic analysis, may be required when complex regulatory issues are at stake.

### Case Law of the German Federal Constitutional Court

In Germany, the principle of proportionality has been developed from the rule of law (*Rechtsstaatprinzip*), and plays an important role in combination with the guarantee of basic human rights. The decisions of the Federal Constitutional Court have given shape to the proportionality principle. Notwithstanding minor temporal changes in terminology, the Court has consistently applied a uniform set of criteria in analysing cases under the principle.

In *Apotheken Urteil*,[45] the landmark decision on pharmacy licensing, the legality of an entry restriction for pharmacies in certain regions of the country resulting from the Bavarian pharmacy licensing system was at issue. The Court established the fundamental relationship between the basic freedom to choose and exercise a profession or trade (*Berufs- und Gewerbefreiheit*) and the principle of proportionality. It identified different types of restrictions that typically limit those freedoms by different degrees, and elaborated the 'three-steps theory' (*Drei-Stufen-Theorie*).[46] A restriction on the choice of a certain profession or trade (entry/exit) was attributed a very high weight, and could only be justified by the pursuit of extremely important social objectives. A *subjective* restriction on the exercise of a trade or profession that lay outside a person's capacity to overcome (scope, behaviour) was attributed a lower weight, and an *objective* restriction on exercise that could be overcome was attributed the lowest weight. Thus, the intensity of the restriction of freedom decreased with each step, and the justification for the restriction was subject to decreasingly strict requirements as to the importance of the social objectives pursued.[47] The three steps were meant to be illustrative points on a scale of restrictions of decreasing intensity. There, the Court concluded that the licensing restriction at issue was null and void, because its social objective, the protection of public health,[48] could be achieved by less-restrictive means.[49]

Accordingly, the case law of the German Constitutional Court has been the driving force in the development of the proportionality principle. It has established that, to apply the proportionality principle, the starting-point is identification of the regulatory goal, followed by a precise and detailed description of the restriction of the basic freedom caused by the regulation. The importance of the goal, and the severity of the restriction, must both be ranked. This may be supported by a quantification of costs and benefits (although this will not be the only indicator for ranking). An objective comparison of competing means for the attainment of the goal must be made. An economic or competitive impact assessment can be a helpful tool.[50]

The principle has its most important role in limiting restrictions on basic human rights to what is necessary to achieve specified social interests. With respect to the freedom to choose and exercise a profession or trade, the principle has proved to be useful in assessing restrictions that could be considered anticompetitive. The case law shows also that the restriction of individual freedoms is readily assessable, while assessment of the restriction of collective freedom is more difficult.

## The Varying Rigidity of the Courts' Scrutiny

The ECJ has been more willing to engage in strict scrutiny of restrictions on traditional legal rights, such as civil or economic freedoms and individual rights, than of restrictions on collective or social interests.[51] The greater legal specificity of a traditional legal right permits the Court to engage in a more precise legal analysis, in which it relates the restriction to the objectives pursued. In contrast, the lack of legal specificity of many collective or social interests, and the broad dispersal of the harm, prevent the Court from a precise legal assessment of such interests. As a result, the Court attributes a wide area of discretion to the legislature or administrator with respect to such interests.

The varied strictness of scrutiny with which courts apply the proportionality principle is a result of institutional elements. Courts make up the judicial branch of government, and are committed to the separation of powers, which allows them to intervene with legislative or executive powers to only a limited extent. Accordingly, they do not decide conflicts between collective or legally unspecific interests. However, the borderline between legally specific and unspecific interests is not clear-cut. It may thus impose only a weak limitation on constitutional courts (or courts that decide questions of constitutional law such as the ECJ). Outside of civil rights, questions of constitutional law are often not purely legal, but also include political judgements. Therefore, constitutional courts more rigorously apply the proportionality principle, and are willing to make decisions with respect to legally less-specific interests, than other courts. Countries with constitutional courts are more accustomed to judicial scrutiny of the merits of legislative action.[52]

Even constitutional courts, however, seem to have difficulty in assessing the merits of anticompetitive regulation. For instance, in *Brandweinmonopol*,[53] the German Constitutional Court considered the compatibility of a public monopoly with the freedom to choose and exercise a trade. There, a fiscal monopoly with respect to alcohol created a fundamental conflict with the freedom to choose a trade. It survived constitutional challenge largely due to constitutional taxation provisions that specifically mentioned that type of monopoly. Similarly, in a case involving a public house insurance monopoly (*Gebäudever-sichungsmonopol*) of some of the *Länder*,[54] the Court relied on a constitutional norm on distribution of competencies to uphold the monopoly when it was challenged on the ground of infringement of basic freedoms. The decision in this case has been criticized as argumentative.[55]

Thereafter, the Court decided two cases involving the monopoly on employment agents (*Arbeitsvermittlungsmonopol*). The first decision upheld this public monopoly,[56] and its founding statute's total prohibition to work as a private employment agent, on the ground that it furthered the objective of a high level of employment, and protected the jobless and job-seeking from exploitation that could arise from private employment agents. The Court found that it would be impossible for the private sector to cope with the highly complex job market. It concluded that information on long-term workforce supply had to be concentrated in one place, because on the basis of job market statistics, students and workers could be advised as to viable career choices.[57] The second *Arbeitsvermittlungsmonopol* decision[58] concerned extension of the monopoly to cover 'body leasing' – the hiring out of employees on a temporary basis. An individual sought to engage in this activity, but the public monopoly claimed that it was a cover for acting as an employment agent, and fell within its legal monopoly. The Court distinguished employment contracts from temporary fixed working contracts with the body-leasing agency. It found that the hired-out worker was sufficiently protected by labour law, and therefore not in the same need of protection as the jobless, who are exposed to a higher danger of exploitation.[59] Accordingly, the Court held that extending the scope of the monopoly to cover this activity, and thereby impose a massive restriction on the freedom to choose a profession or trade, was not warranted.

Generally, the German Constitutional Court has performed a rigorous scrutiny when the case has presented straightforward facts, permitting clear separation of the interests at stake.[60] In contrast, in cases involving complex economic regulation designed to change industry structure, the Court has recognized wide legislative discretion.[61] This discretion, however, is not absolute. For instance, the Court has required the legislator to correct regulation that has been adopted based on erroneous forecasting assumptions.[62]

The reluctance of the German Constitutional Court to outlaw public monopolies based on constitutional challenges asserting basic economic and civil rights can be explained by the *Grundgesetz*' neutrality with respect to economic system.[63] Dismantling a public monopoly and requiring enactment of a regulation of the activity concerned, on the ground that the public monopoly interfered with the freedom to choose or exercise a profession or trade, could be viewed as at odds with the *Grundgesetz*' economic-system neutrality, which the Court is required to safeguard. It is, however, debatable whether the economic-system neutrality of the *Grundgesetz* is sufficient justification for the Court's hands-off approach, as it is not clear whether a tightly regulated industry is more or less capitalist or socialist than an uncontrolled public monopoly.[64] In light of competition as a constitutional interest in EU law,[65] it is questionable how the postulation of economic system neutrality can be upheld.

## C.   ACCOUNTABILITY: SEPARATION OF POWERS AND REGULATORY DISCRETION

Courts tend to invoke the constitutional principle of separation of powers in order to avoid a review on the merits that would require them to substitute their own discretion for that of the legislator or the regulator, both of whom are presumably politically accountable. However, it is debatable whether such judicial self-restraint is appropriate, given the role of the courts as guardians of the constitution. This role gives them an exceptional position within the matrix of separation of powers. It is especially important where political accountability of regulatory discretion is hampered by the complexity and lack of transparency of the regulation involved, thus leaving it subject to neither political nor judicial oversight.

The reluctance of courts to scrutinize regulation is often expressed through the acknowledgement of wide discretionary powers to the regulator when adopting economic regulation. This, however, is fundamentally at odds with the rule of law, which is an important limitation to the arbitrary use of public power. In particular, where basic economic freedoms are concerned, courts apply a legal standard of review to determine whether a restriction is justified. In contrast, where collective interests are concerned (such as the freedom of competition), they must be balanced with other social interests, and courts lack a concrete standard of review assessment. Even the proportionality principle, which provides a flexible framework for balancing the importance of a social aim against the severity of a restriction, does not encourage courts to review the merits of such cases. This may be because the proportionality principle does not provide an independent standard of review, but rather establishes a formal relationship between means and ends by reference to external values. This contrasts with the legal formalism that courts rely upon to assess restrictions of individual rights.

To overcome the problem created by this combination of judicial self-restraint and lack of political accountability with respect to complex economic regulations, several solutions are possible. First, a new institution could be created that is better suited for reviewing economic regulation, as the court of auditors was created to review public spending. Second, the wide discretion of the legislator or regulator could be narrowed by legally requiring them to make a structured assessment of the competing interests. This would also improve the transparency of their decision making, and may provide a standard for judicial review of anticompetitive regulation. A combination of these two options may be the most successful response.

The details of an institutional response will not be discussed in depth here.[66] However, scrutiny of anticompetitive regulation cannot occur in a court's predominantly adversarial and formalistic setting, driven by the defence of individual rights. A better institutional setting would be an auxiliary organ of the legislature designed to ensure greater self-control, which would not be limited in performing its oversight functions by concerns with separation of powers. Its sole function would be that of a controller, transparently supervising the regulator's use of discretion with respect to anticompetitive regulation.[67] It should have the capacity both to review the legislator's motivation for enacting anticompetitive regulation, and to balance various collective interests.

The proportionality principle could be the guideline for scrutiny, as it formalizes the relationship between a regulatory aim and the means employed to achieve it. Regulation would have to pass a proportionality test before implementation, and thereafter periodically, under which the regulator would have to show that the benefits of the regulation outweigh the costs from restrictions of competition. This would ensure transparency and accountability of the regulator in its exercise of public power.

## CONCLUSION

This chapter explores two main aspects of constitutional scrutiny of anticompetitive regulation. First, it addresses how constitutional principles (basic economic freedoms, economic viability of the state and accountability of public power) legitimate scrutiny of anticompetitive regulation. It concludes that a constitutional mandate for scrutiny is best supported by the argument that freedom of competition is a direct constitutional interest. Somewhat weaker arguments are those based on indirect protection of the freedom of competition through the guarantee of basic economic freedoms, the need of economic sustainability of the state, and accountability of public power. However, together with the first argument, they present a strong case for a constitutional requirement to scrutinize regulation to eliminate its anticompetitive effects.

Second, the chapter considers the proportionality principle as a framework for scrutiny of anticompetitive regulation. This principle has been formulated in German constitutional law, which has influenced EU law, to scrutinize regulatory limitations of basic economic freedoms. It can be a useful tool for assessing and balancing the costs and benefits of anticompetitive regulation, and for deciding whether to repeal or amend such regulation.

Case law of the ECJ and German Constitutional Court applies the proportionality principle. In the context of protecting basic economic freedoms, the courts have been reluctant to scrutinize measures that only indirectly restrict individual rights, but directly restrict the collective freedom of competition. This reluctance is related to the institutional nature of courts, and is not mandated by the proportionality principle. Courts are well suited to protect individual rights, and balance them against collective interests. In contrast, courts have difficulties substituting their discretion in balancing different collective interests for that of the legislature or executive, because they are committed to the principle of separation of powers. Thus, courts refrain from protecting collective freedoms and acknowledge extensive regulatory discretion. This implies a limitation of judicial oversight, which may be of little concern as long as political accountability is present.

It is doubtful whether political accountability is adequate with respect to complex economic regulatory policy decisions. The lack of transparency with respect to such decisions is similar to that with respect to the public budget, which is also highly complex. As a result, these matters are largely inaccessible to electoral response. The court of auditors was the institutional response chosen for lack of transparency with respect to the budget, but no institutional response has yet been made with respect to anticompetitive regulation. An institution similar to the court of auditors may be appropriate in this context as well. Like the court of auditors, the new institution should stand outside the classic separation of powers, and should be sufficiently endowed with legal and economic expertise.

One possible framework for scrutiny would be the following. Any regulation that produces anticompetitive effects must be proportional in order to be adopted or to remain in place. A regulatory measure with anticompetitive effects is proportionate when:

- it is suitable for attaining a legitimate legislative/regulatory objective (element of appropriateness or suitability); and
- it is necessary, in the sense that no less-restrictive measure is available to achieve the legitimate objective (element of necessity). This element may be the most burdensome with respect to complex economic questions, as determining the least anticompetitive solution may involve extensive economic analysis. The expertise in a specialized institution would allow it to apply economic analysis and compare even complex regulatory alternatives, which is a great advantage over judicial review. If a less-restrictive means to achieve the objective were revealed, the regulation would be deemed disproportionate.

The restriction is not disproportionate to the legitimate objective (element of proportionality), which may, to some extent, involve political choice. However, when the political choice has been reduced to this third step, the accountability of the decision maker, and thus the legitimacy of a regulatory decision, has been greatly improved.

## NOTES

1.  In the US, regulation refers to the 'sustained and focused control exercised by a public agency over activities that are generally regarded as desirable to society'. Giandomenico Majone, *Deregulation or Re-Regulation? Regulatory Reform in Europe and the United States* 1 (London, New York, 1990) (citing Philip Sleznick, 'Focusing Organisational Research on Regulation' 363–4, in *Regulatory Policy and the Social Sciences* (Roger Noll, ed., Berkeley and Los Angeles, CA, 1985). In Europe, regulation has a less clear meaning, mainly due to Europe's more recent embrace of the free market ideology and the traditionally stronger involvement of the state in the organization of economic production and distribution through ministerial bureaucracies, public monopolies, public enterprises and nationalized industries.
    Here, regulation is limited to the narrow meaning, relating to (i) sector-specific, market-specific or occupation-specific rules governing the entry/exit, scope, behaviour and form of ownership of an economic undertaking; (ii) procedural or institutional provisions serving the effective implementation of these rules in the pursuit of a socially beneficial objective.

Regulation can be a legislative measure as well as an administrative by-law or decision. In contrast, the broader meaning would also include general laws, criminal as well as civil, and thus any law that has impact on the running of a business.

Concentrating on the narrow understanding of regulation does not imply that the response of market actors to the general laws in devising their business strategies is ignored. However, the focus on regulation in the narrow sense is useful to explore the need for guidelines and institutions that limit the anticompetitive effects of such regulation. Awareness of the distinction between a narrow and a broad definition of regulation allows a holistic view of the behaviour of market actors, and for thinking about more sophisticated regulatory means that combine and substitute alternative elements between regulation in the narrow and in the broad sense, that is, combining and substituting dirigisme and control with/for decentralized incentives coordinated through the market. For a similarly broad reference to regulation, see Richard Posner, *Economic Analysis of Law* 367 (4th edn Boston, MA: Little, Brown, 1992).

Thus, regulation involves the level of intensity of state interference with economic activity and reality as hybrids located between two extremes: pure state control or monopoly, and pure private market control, governed by general laws. From such a perspective, all economic activity is regulated by hybrids, and deregulation and/or regulatory reform are essentially re-regulation. The awareness of regulation as a hybrid also has a significant impact on the search for potentially less restrictive but equally effective means of regulation for the achievement of a socially desirable objective.

2. The term 'anticompetitive' has a clear meaning in antitrust law, where it is the subject of highly technical legal and economic analysis geared towards the assessment of the most efficient combination of economic factors of production. However, opinions vary as to what constitutes economic efficiency. See Giuliano Amato, *Antitrust and the Bounds of Power* 109 (Oxford, 1997).

In general, anticompetitive agreements or behaviour are assessed in comparison to a hypothetical state of no restraint, and therefore an efficient combination of economic factors. The economically inefficient combination of productive factors, whether self-imposed or externally imposed, is considered undesirable and anticompetitive. Economic inefficiencies cause waste, which is a private concern as long as it takes place within the private sphere, but becomes a public concern when it takes place between private actors, or between the state and private actors.

Anticompetitive agreements or behaviour raise barriers to entry, and place limits on the scope of economic activity, on behaviour affecting the ability to inform (advertising) or freely determine price and quality, and on the form of ownership restricting a free choice as to financing or limitations of liability.

3. In this chapter, decisions of only the European Court of Justice and the German Federal Constitutional Court (*Bundesverfassungsgericht*) have been considered.

4. British lawyers may not agree with this and similar statements, as they attach a far greater importance to the sovereignty of parliament, which they see as unlimited. However, a common law constitution, like the UK's, even if not formally written, is nonetheless a constitution in a material sense.

5. British lawyers might doubt the existence of such a principle, at least with regard to British constitutional law. However, Lord Diplock has stated:

> My Lords, I see no reason why simply because a decision making power is derived from a common law rule and not a statutory source it should for that reason only be immune from judicial review. Judicial review has I think developed to a stage today when, without reiterating any analysis of the steps by which the development has come about, one can conveniently classify under three heads the grounds on which administrative action is subject to control by judicial review. The first ground I would call 'illegality', the second 'irrationality' and the third 'procedural impropriety'. That is not to say that further developments on a case by case basis may not in course of time add further grounds. I have in mind particularly the possible adoption in the future of the principle of 'proportionality', which is recognised in the administrative law of several fellow members of the European Economic Community ...

Jürgen Schwarze, *European Administrative Law* 865 London, 1992.

6.   4 *BVerfGE* 7, 17 (1954) (*Apotheken Urteil*).
7.   Treaty Establishing the European Economic Community, 25 March 1957, 298 *United Nations Treaty Series* 11, 1973 Great Britain Treaty Series No. 1 (Cmd. 5179-II) as amended by the Treaty of Amsterdam amending the treaty on European Union, the treaties establishing the European Communities and certain related acts, 2 October 1997, 1997 *Official Journal* (C 340) 1 (EC Treaty), preamble, Arts 3, 4, & 81–89.
     Reference to the principle of free competition in the EC Treaty: Preamble, para. 4 ('RECOGNISING that the removal of existing obstacles calls for concerted action in order to guarantee steady expansion, balanced trade and fair competition'); Art. 3(g) ('a system ensuring that competition in the internal market is not distorted'); Art. 4, para. 1 ('For the purposes set out in Article 2, the activities of the Member States and the Community shall include, as provided in this Treaty and in accordance with the timetable set out therein, the adoption of an economic policy which is based on the close coordination of Member States' economic policies, on the internal market and on the definition of common objectives, and conducted in accordance with the *principle of an open market economy with free competition*'); Art. 4, para. 2 ('Concurrently with the foregoing, and as provided in this Treaty and in accordance with the timetable and the procedures set out therein, these activities shall include the irrevocable fixing of exchange rates leading to the introduction of a single currency, the ECU, and the definition and conduct of a single monetary policy and exchange-rate policy the primary objective of both of which shall be to maintain price stability and, without prejudice to this objective, to support the general economic policies in the Community, in accordance with the *principle of an open market economy with free competition*.') (emphasis added).
     These principles are reflected and expanded in the more elaborate rules of Articles 81 to 89, which apply to undertakings, including public undertakings, and state aid.
8.   *Commission v. Italy*, 1972 *ECR* (Report of cases before the Court of Justice of the European Communities) 529, 534 paras 5–10 (holding that Community law must be 'fully applicable at the same time and with the same effects over the whole territory of the Community' without the member states being able to invoke any 'provisions whatsoever of national law' to override it).
9.   This means also that the economic system-neutrality of the German *Grundgesetz* has de facto been given up by joining the EC.
10.  EC Treaty, *supra* note 7, Arts 86–89.
11.  Professor Friedhelm Hufen stated: 'Der Plural von Berufsfreiheit heißt Wettbewerb' (The plural of the freedom to choose and exercise a profession or trade is competition.) Friedhelm Hufen, 'Berufsfreiheit – Erinnerung an ein Grundrecht' (The freedom of profession – in commemoration of a basic right), 1994 *Neue Juristische Wochenschrift* 2913, 2915.
12.  For example, the German Constitutional Court ruled that the constitutional limitation on the extent of the budgetary deficit was a principle in German constitutional law.
13.  See EC Treaty, *supra* note 7, Art. 248, which specifies the tasks of the Court of Auditors:

     1. The Court of Auditors shall examine the accounts of all revenue and expenditure of the Community. It shall also examine the accounts of all revenue and expenditure of all bodies set up by the Community insofar as the relevant constituent instrument does not preclude such examination. The Court of Auditors shall provide the European Parliament and the Council with a statement of assurance as to the reliability of the accounts and *the legality and regularity of the underlying transactions* which shall be published in the Official Journal of the European Communities.
     2. The Court of Auditors shall examine whether all revenue has been received and all expenditure incurred *in a lawful and regular manner and whether the financial management has been sound*. In doing so, it shall report in particular on any cases of irregularity. The audit of revenue shall be carried out on the basis both of the amounts established as due and the amounts actually paid to the Community. The audit of expenditure shall be carried out on the basis both of commitments undertaken and payments made. These audits may be carried out before the closure of accounts for the financial year in question.
14.  Professor Majone proposed a 'regulatory budget', which was a move towards more transparent accountability structures, as they exist for the public budget. See Giandomenico Majone,

'The Rise of the Regulatory State in Europe', in *A Reader on Regulation* 192, 210 (Robert Baldwin, Colin Scott and Christopher Hood, eds, Oxford, 1998).

15.  See Nicolas Emiliou, *The Principle of Proportionality in European Law* 61 et seq. (London, The Hague, Boston, MA, 1996); Peter Selmer, *Die Gewährleistung der unabdingbaren Grundrechtsstandards durch den EuGH* (Safeguarding the inalienable basic rights standard by the European Court of Justice) 134 et seq. (Baden-Baden 1998) (similar critique of the ECJ); Friedhelm Hufen, 'Ladenschluß: Zum verfassungsrechtlichen Kern eines politischen Dauerthemas' (Shop closing hours: comment on the constitutional essence of a never-ending policy debate), 1986 *Neue Juristische Wochenschrift* 1291 (critical remarks on the wide range of discretion accepted by the German courts with respect to limitations on the freedom to choose and exercise a profession or trade); Hufen, *supra* note 11, at 2913.

16.  However, the proportionality test is not a substitute for a quantitative cost–benefit analysis. Rather, it is a basic framework that derives its authority from the rule of law (*Rechtsstaatprinzip*).

   A similar reference to the democratic argument can be found in Cass R. Sunstein, 'The Cost–Benefit State', 39 *Chicago Working Paper in Law and Economics* 26 (1996).

17.  Schwarze, *supra* note 5, at 687.

18.  EC Treaty, *supra* note 7, Art. 5 states: 'The Community shall act within the limits of the powers conferred upon it by this Treaty and of the objectives assigned to it therein. In areas which do not fall within its exclusive competence, the Community shall take action, in accordance with the principle of subsidiarity, only if and insofar as the objectives of the proposed action cannot be sufficiently achieved by the Member States and can therefore, by reason of the scale or effects of the proposed action, be better achieved by the Community. *Any action by the Community shall not go beyond what is necessary to achieve the objectives of this Treaty*' (emphasis added).

19.  AT, *supra* note 7, Protocol No. 30.

20.  *Fromancais v. FORMA*,1983 *ECR* 395, para. 8.

21.  *R. v. Minister for Agriculture, Fisheries and Food et al.*, 1990 *ECR* I-4023, para. 13.

22.  Francis Jacobs, 'Recent Developments in the Principle of Proportionality in EC Law', in *The Principle of Proportionality in the Laws of Europe* 1–2 (E. Ellis, ed., Oxford, 1999).

23.  The Australian approach is discussed in the contributors to this volume and by Allan Fels in Chapter 16 and by Laraine Laudati in Chapter 17; the US approach is discussed by Laraine Laudati in Chapter 17.

24.  1977 *ECR* 1211; see also Granaria v. Hoofdproduktschap voor Akkerbouwprodukten, 1977 *ECR* 1247; *Oelmühle u. Becke v. HZA Hamburg u. HZA Bremen-Nord*, 1977 *ECR* 1269.

25.  Council Regulation 563/76 of 15 March 1976, 1976 *Official Journal* (L 67) 18.

26.  *Bela-Mühle*, *supra* note 25, 1977 *ECR* 1220–21.

27.  *Id.* at 1221.

28.  *Id.*

29.  1979 *ECR* 677.

30.  *Id.* at 685.

31.  *Id.*

32.  1979 *ECR* 2137.

33.  *Id.* at 2151.

34.  See Schwarze, *supra* note 5, 726 (1992) (providing references to that case law).

35.  *Rewe-Zentral AG v. Monopolverwaltung für Brandwein*, 1979 *ECR* 649. Under the exception, the Court accepted as compatible with Arts 28 and 29 provisions that were necessary 'in order to satisfy *mandatory requirements* relating in particular to the effectiveness of fiscal supervision, the protection of public health, the fairness of commercial transactions and the defence of the consumer'. *Id.* at 662 (emphasis added).

36.  1974 *ECR* 837. According to that formula, 'measures having equivalent effect' as quantitative import restrictions in Article 28 meant 'all trading rules enacted by Member States which are capable of hindering directly or indirectly, actually or potentially, intra-Community trade'. *Id.* at 852.

37.  1979 *ECR* 666, 674 (emphasis added).

38.  1979 *ECR* 3409.

39. *Id.* at 3421.
40. *Italy v. Gill*, 1980 *ECR* 2071; *Commission v. Italy*, 1981 *ECR* 3019.
41. Commission N Italy, *supra* note 40 at 3042 (emphasis added).
42. 1983 *ECR* 203.
43. *Id.* at 236 (emphasis added).
44. *See* Schwarze, *supra* note 5, at 814.
45. 7 *BVerfGE* 377 (1954).
46. This should not be confused with the three-step test of the proportionality principle.
47. The Court held:

> Das Grundrecht soll die Freiheit des Individuums schützen, der Regelungsvorbehalt aus-
> reichenden Schutz der Gemeinschaftsinteressen sicherstellen. Aus der Notwendigkeit,
> beiden Forderungen gerecht zu werden, ergibt sich für das Eingreifen des Gesetzgebers
> ein Gebot der Differenzierung etwa nach folgenden Grundsätzen: Die Freiheit der Beruf-
> sausübung kann beschränkt werden, soweit vernünftige Erwägungen des Gemeinwohls es
> zweckmäßig erscheinen lasser; ... Die Freiheit der Berufswahl darf nur eingeschränkt
> werden, soweit der Schutz besonders wichtiger Gemeinschaftsgüter es zwingent erfordert.
> Ist ein solcher Eingriff unumgänglich, so muß der Gesetzgeber stets diejenige Form des
> Eingriffs wählen, die das Grundrecht am wenigsten beschränkt. *Apotheken Urteil, supra*
> note 6, at 378.
>
> (The basic right protects the freedom of the individual, the reservation to regulate secures
> the adequate protection of social interests. From the necessity to conform to both demands
> the legislator is faced with the need to differentiate, roughly pursuant to the following
> principles: (a) The freedom to exercise a profession can be restricted when reasonable con-
> siderations of social interest indicate a usefulness; (b) The freedom to choose a profession
> can be restricted only as far as particularly important social interest compel to such a step.
> If such restriction is inevitable the legislator must always choose the least-restrictive means
> available.)

48. The Court has held that the protection of actual or potential competitors can never be a social
    interest justifying a restriction. *Id.* at 408; 11 *BVerfGE* 168, 183 (1960).
49. *Apotheken Urteil, supra* note 6, at 443.
50. A parallel can be drawn to the requirement of an environmental impact assessment as a
    condition for any building and operating permission of industrial or infrastructural installa-
    tions under Community law. Council Directive 85/337/EEC of 27 June 1985 on the assessment
    of environmental effects, 1986 *Official Journal* (C 175) 40 (1985).
51. See also Gráinne de Búrca, 'The Principle of Proportionality and its Application in EC Law',
    13 *Yearbook of European Law* 105, 110 (1993).
52. See Walter van Gerven, 'The Effect of Proportionality on the Actions of Member States of
    the European Community: National Viewpoints from Continental Europe', in *The Principle
    of Proportionality in the Laws of Europe* 37, 59 (Evelyn Ellis, ed., Oxford, 1999) (providing
    broader comparison and further reasons for varying degrees of rigor in scrutiny and its
    acceptance in different legal systems).
53. 14 *BVerfGE* 105, 111 (1962). See Hans-Jürgen Papier, 'Grundgesetz und Wirtschaftsord-
    nung' (The basic law and economic order), in *Handbuch des Verfassungsrechts* (Handbook
    for constitutional law) 799, 817 (Ernst Benda, Werner Meihofer and Hans-Jochen Vogel, eds,
    2nd edn Berlin, New York, 1994).
54. 41 *BVerfGE* 205 (1976).
55. The critique is that the decision had to employ an *argumentum e contrario* to the legislative
    competence norm, GG Art. 74 No. 11, to show that the *Länder* are allowed to establish such
    a commercial monopoly. Thus, it was outside the scope of application of basic freedoms.
56. 21 *BVerfGE* 245 (1967). This assessment could not be upheld once an ECJ decision found
    the monopoly to be commercial, and to violate Article 82. *Höfer-Elser v. Macrotron GmbH*,
    1991 *ECR* I-1979.
57. *Arbeitsvermittlungsmonopol, supra* note 56, at 252. However, important parts of the argument
    were deliberately omitted: 'Wie keiner näheren Ausführung bedarf, können diese schwieri-

gen, mannigfaltigen und weit gespannten Aufgaben nur von einer einheitlichen Arbeitsver-
waltung gemeistert werden'. *Id.* at 253. ('Without need of further elaboration [it is understood],
can these difficult, multi-faceted and far-reaching tasks only be mastered by a unified labour
administration.')

58. 21 *BVerfGE* 261 (1967).
59. *Id.* at 268.
60. For example, *Puffreis*, 53 *BVerfGE* 135, 145 (1980). (Prohibition to import a sweet on the basis
    that the content of cacao was too low was held to fail the necessity test, since less restrictive
    means, such as labelling, were available.)
61. For example, *Mühlenstrukturgesetz* 25 *BVerfGE* 1 (1968).
62. *Id.* at 13; 50 *BVerfGE* 335 (1979); 49 *BVerfGE* 89, 130 (1978).
63. See 4 *BVerfGE* 7, 17 (1954); 30 *BVerfGE* 292, 315 (1971); 50 *BVerfGE* 290, 337 (1979).
64. The constitution is not concerned with political classifications of 'left' or 'right', but with the
    control of power in whatever form it may appear. This may lead to the insight that the notion
    of economic-system neutrality has little meaning as a constitutional concept.
65. See notes 7–9 *supra.*
66. In any case, the institutional question will depend strongly on the procedural format of the
    regulatory process and its review. The court of auditors provides one model.
67. A good example may be the institutional balance between the German *Bundeskartellamt*
    (which is an independent authority, not politically accountable, and enjoys wide discretion,
    due to the wide formulation of the enabling statue, and therefore little legal accountability)
    and the *Monopolkommission* (which reviews and publishes a report every other year on the
    performance of the regulator).

# 23. Panel discussion

**Prof. Jenny**   This comment is in reference to the Ballbe/Padros study, on the concept of independence of competition authorities. They described a situation where, through lack of technical and financial means, and means of investigation, the Spanish Competition Authority could not fulfil its function in an independent way. Is it good to have heads of competition authorities as cabinet ministers? I am referring to the Korean case, for example. In Japan, there is an issue of the relationship between the Japanese Fair Trade Commission and the prime minister's office. When we talk about advocacy, it is obviously a great help. So what is the tradeoff between independence and being part of the government?

**Prof. Amato**   In transition economies, you can waive part of the independence for the sake of a higher influence on the political process. In Western Europe, we see authorities as part of the cabinets as something that is to be avoided for the sake of independence. In Central/Eastern European countries, competition authorities that are part of the cabinets have been far more effective than independent competition authorities would have been. Thus, it depends on the context.

**Prof. Fels**   I have always been struck by the European Commission position. It seems to me tremendously important that DG Competition has a seat at the cabinet table and therefore is in a key position to influence every law in every directorate, whether transport, energy, communications or whatever.

**Prof. Amato**   Many of us justify this astonishing concentration of power because we say that Europe is in a transition towards ever closer integration. Otherwise, it would be quite difficult to accept investigation, adjudication and regulation in the same hands. Some of us have already questioned whether we are still in a transition, and whether a change is needed. However, this is still a minority view.

**Prof. Fels**   We have also had a minor debate about whether we should have something like a competition minister. There is a view that a competition minister might end up having quite a junior position; it is preferable that the main economics minister, the treasurer or the finance minister or whatever, have this portfolio, notwithstanding conflicts which that minister might have on a couple of matters. But in some ways, it is so central to economic policy that the most important economic minister should be handling the job.

**Prof. Jenny**   Regarding the comment in Mr Wise's study that if you have to advocate, somehow you have already lost the battle, is there a difference between the countries that you have discussed, and countries like Poland, Hungary, Venezuela and Brazil? During the uncertain period of transition in these countries (which are also transitional in the sense that they are moving from autocratic government to democratic government) there was some scope for Jatar in Venezuela, Vissi in Hungary, and Gesner in Brazil to play a rather important advocacy role. They took over the matter, even with a political mandate, and convinced the political élite of their position. To a certain extent, it is a question of the personality who heads the competition authority.

**Mr Wise**   I am very impressed with what Vissi has done in Hungary. For 15 years now, he has managed to push the idea that competition policy should be at the centre. Their success is not the result of a particularly vigorous job with enforcement, but of a carefully calibrated job of picking their spots, and setting up an institution with a nice combination of contact and independence.

Professor Jenny's point about ministerial rank is nicely illustrated in Hungary, where the head of the agency has ministerial rank. He is present at the cabinet meeting, but does not vote. As a result, he is not involved in horse-trading. Meanwhile, case decisions are made within the organization by a separate entity that is independent from the head of the agency, so the latter cannot be accused of influence on the outcome of cases. They have excellent contacts with the parliament, and are therefore involved in the debate, in their own name. But I agree that the personality is very important.

**Prof. Amato**   Professor Fels, what is the source of the funds used for payments to the states that properly carry out their regulatory reviews?

**Prof. Fels**   This was mixed with the usual federal/state bargaining over money. Some additional funds were made available on the ground that the reforms would generate a large annual increase in GDP, that the revenue benefits went more to the centre in our tax system, and that the states would lose revenue, in particular as a result of the monopoly public utility bodies not being able to charge monopoly prices.

**Prof. Amato**   I have several comments. First, for continental lawyers, in the tradition of administrative law, powers of investigation and adjudication are held by a single authority. Continental lawyers view the separation of these powers as a shortcoming. In contrast, when the first common law lawyers entered the Community, they found it odd that the Commission could have both of these powers. Quite a significant controversy grew. Cases are still pending before the Court of Human Rights as to whether the joint exercise of these powers might be considered a violation of the Convention on Human Rights. However, the tradition continues, notwithstanding the convergence in European legal systems. This problem has not to do with the distinction between antitrust authorities and advocates for competition, which is our main issue, but with the issue of the concentration of power. People resent the fact that the same institution is doing everything. The minority view, represented by the German *Bundeskartellamt* and supported by me several years ago, advocates an independent cartel office. I am not completely sure whether this would be a solution, because the independent cartel office would also have shared the powers of investigation and adjudication.

Based on my experience, I have reached the conclusion that common law lawyers are correct. I headed an antitrust authority where my staff would investigate a case, and we ourselves, the board, would decide the case. Private lawyers expected us to be a third party *vis-à-vis* the investigative staff and the private undertaking. However, I was not a third party because I had authorized, step by step, what the investigative staff had been doing. Under the Convention of Human Rights and in the opinion of the European Court of Justice, the Commission is not accepted as an impartial judge, because it has investigated the case, and it will ultimately adjudicate that case. Currently, it is argued that the Commission is part of an administrative procedure, but the impartial judge comes later in the procedure, because the Court of First Instance, and ultimately the Court of Justice, can review the Commission's decision.

The real problem is advocacy and antitrust authorities. There are many reasons why antitrust authorities are well suited to be competition advocates, since they have the know-how. There is no significant difference between assessing the anticompetitive impact of private conduct and that of a regulation. The same kind of economic analysis, legal reasoning, the principal of proportionality and so on, apply with respect to both. Thus, the same know-how is useful for both. Yet people resent the same institution doing too many things. The Italian Competition Act empowers the competition authority both to adjudicate cases and to send recommendations to the cabinet and parliament in relation to pending or existing legislation that could distort competition. This recommendation is strictly limited to technical competition issues. Yet, whenever we sent a recommendation, the reaction was: 'Why are you interfering with the political process? This is our business'. I would explain that they were wrong, we were not interfering because we did not take part in making the decision. We were simply providing them with expert information, but it was up to them to decide. But of course, this is quite formalistic, in the sense that the competition authority's recommendation enters the political arena and becomes part of the game. Does it make sense for an independent competition authority, whose reputation as enforcer of antitrust law determines its legitimacy, to be perceived as part of the political process? When I was chairman of the Italian competition authority, I always gave the formalistic answer. I prefer the Australian solution. The National Competition Council was established precisely for the purpose of conducting an independent review. Political authorities accepted this, and now they cannot complain.

Finally, Mr Kohl correctly stated that all constitutional courts could use the principal of proportionality, which is recognized as a constitutional principle in many of our systems. In Italy, at least three books have been published on the principle of proportionality in our constitution within the last several years. The unanimous conclusion is that it is present, even though it is not spelled out. To use the principle of proportionality for judicial review of legislation with anticompetitive effects, with the possible outcome of voiding the statute in the end, would not differ from what is done to enforce the principle of equality. But *gleich ist gleich und gleich ist nicht gleich*. Why do courts not do this? Mr Kohl argued that the reasons were the separation of powers, the legal education of the judges and their lack of training in economic analysis. I agree with these arguments, but I wonder if there is not also a structural reason – that is, by the time a court is reached, a competition authority has already rendered a decision. The treaty allows national courts directly to decide cases involving violations of Articles 81 and 82. But in most of the cases, the court's involvement will be judicial review of a decision rendered by a national competition authority. Thus, the facts have already been assessed by the competition authority. Here, separation of powers plays a part, because national courts tend to say that their role is limited to correcting manifest errors made by the authority in assessing the facts. Moreover, the Court of Justice's jurisprudence makes clear that in complex economic matters, the only role that remains within the jurisdiction of the Commission is to correct manifest errors. Were the system more like the American system, the national courts would probably react differently. Were our competition authorities simply empowered to investigate and litigate, but not to decide, I am confident that the courts would automatically assess the facts by using economic analysis. Accordingly, the reluctance of the courts to assess the facts is the result of the enduring prevalence of administrative law institution building in continental Europe.

**Prof. Joerges** My comment refers to the interdependence between the idea of competition and efficiency, on the one hand, and regulation, on the other. Competition advocates are defending efficiency against other public interests, such as environmental protection or concerns for safety. However, such objectives should not always be viewed as alternatives to efficiency; their introduction can often be understood as an effort to seek solutions which make the delegation of economic activities to competitive processes compatible with society's concerns for certain regulatory goals. A part of the American literature, such as that of the constitutionalist Cass Sunstein from Chicago, views the problem in this way. Mr Kohl has reviewed our constitutional debate, which is too narrow. The German ordo-liberals have, in the formative era of European integration, invented the notion of a European supranational 'economic constitution', which would 'trump' certain regulatory objectives of the member states. This type of argument, however, seems hopelessly outdated.

The Treaty, which is to be interpreted much more prudently, does not build up a pre-established hierarchy of 'economic' and 'non-economic' objectives. Rather, it acknowledges both of them – and the jurisprudence of the European Court of Justice documents how these can be made compatible. The principle of proportionality as understood and applied by the Court provides a mechanism of supervising rather than of striking down national legislation. Professor Amato noted the reluctance of the courts to interfere with the assessment of complicated so-called technical matters that have been assessed by DG Competition. This self-restraint is in striking contrast with any comprehensive control of regulatory objectives; the Court cannot do more than to require member states to pursue a given regulatory goal in such a way that it is less intrusive of the goals pursued under article 28. In principle, they can be said to provide civil society or the market a greater reach or a broader domain – but not the power to 'overrule' legitimate regulatory concerns.

Thus, in framing the debate on how to control anticompetitive regulation, it would be overly defensive to assert that a higher law is needed. The bridging principle is not a higher law, but principles such as proportionality and other procedural standards. The jurisprudence on the compatibility of national regulatory legislation with Article 81 and Article 5 points in the same direction. Here again, the Court has, without directly interfering, found ways to establish certain criteria under which national regulation is compatible with Article 81 and Article 5 of the Treaty. It is not the search for hierarchy, but for compatibility, which is the long-run goal of this kind of exercise. We must learn to mitigate among a plurality of objectives if we want Europeans to accept the Treaty as the overall constitutional framework for the regulation of the European economy.

**Prof. Jenny**    Professor Amato has argued that structure creates the bias in the relation, that administrative decisions are reviewed by courts, which tend only to look at the manifest error of appreciation as opposed to assessing the facts. But is this really a question of structure, or is it a question of the preference of courts to limit their role, even if they are not legally obliged to do so? The Court of First Instance, which has gone much further in reviewing the facts than the Court of Justice, proved that there is no structural necessity. A court can make a factual appreciation of the case. At the beginning of the nineteenth century in France, judges had no freedom to interpret the law; they were required to ask parliament for authorization to interpret it. Ever since then, the *Court de Cassation* has taken an extremely narrow view of its role, in strong contrast to the role of the US Supreme Court, which gives direction. Thus, I question whether there are phenomena beyond the structure, which may have an impact, and whether, even with that structure, the system could evolve to improve the judicial oversight of administrative decisions by competition authorities.

**Prof. Amato**   This evolution is already visible. The Court of First Instance is reviewing the facts now much more than had previously been the case. The manifest error screen is getting increasingly narrow. The legal tradition that we have inherited partially explains the limited role of the courts, but there is no reason for a court to consider the assessment of facts to be out of its scope on the ground that such an assessment is part of administrative discretion. Administrative discretion was invented centuries ago in order to balance various public interests against each other. However, whether a fact is blue or black is not covered by administrative discretion. The boundary is much less neat than would appear. But the courts have repeatedly said that the assessment of complex economic facts is covered by the Commission's discretion.

Can the principle of proportionality be used as a justification for applying economic analysis? In other words, can a court determine whether a measure is proportionate by applying economic analysis? This is what it must do to determine whether a regulatory goal could be achieved in a less anticompetitive fashion than it is with the regulation under review. Economists should also be thinking in terms of the principle of proportionality, in order for their tools to be more useful in the legal process.

I had raised the point of hierarchy not because it is essential, but because at the European level, no general instrument exists empowering a court to declare that an anticompetitive measure is null and void. There are several specific instruments which apply only in limited areas: Article 81, when powers are delegated to private undertakings; Article 86, when there is an exemption of services of general economic interest; ex Article 87, when there is a state aid that does not comply with certain criteria. Beyond these areas, the state action doctrine applies, leaving the Commission powerless. Hierarchy might be relevant in determining whether a constitutional court could take action. Assuming that the principle of proportionality is a constitutional principle, in cases that cannot be reached by the Commission, a constitutional court could consider whether a measure is anticompetitive because it violates the principle of proportionality. This is the only reason that I was connecting proportionality with hierarchy of laws.

**Prof. Joerges**    The term in German constitutional doctrine coined by Konrad Hesse was *praktische Konkordanz* – that is, a twofold commitment to a competitive market, and simultaneously, to legitimate regulatory concerns. This notion implies that there be no pre-conceived hierarchy between the two.

**Prof. Siniscalco**    I have been disturbed by our continuous switching between optimality, or normative, analysis (what should be done), and political economy (why things do not change, why anticompetitive institutions are there and so on). In our field, these are almost two different disciplines, which follow different methodologies. The people who do optimality analysis hardly talk to those who do political economy, because they are two different trades. They should talk to each other.

Second, the principle of proportionality can indeed be the fundamental instrument for the evolution of norms. It is a powerful means for selection of institutional and other norms that allows the survival, not of the fittest, but of the most competitive. Thus, I see it as a functional tool exerting leverage to have the fittest, or the most competitive, prevail.

**Dr Mehta**    As an economist, I am also a bit worried about using economic analysis to make an assessment of proportionality. An economist needs the framework in which to make an economic analysis. Article 30 allows countries to go beyond the measures that are adopted at Community level. The Court has done an economic analysis in many cases applying Article 30. The Commission must be careful not to try to harmonize at a low level, because then the measures that go beyond will tend to be upheld. Article 95 of the Amsterdam Treaty gives a short period for the Commission to challenge that view with a very sophisticated analysis. It remains to be seen what the Court will decide. It may decide not to review the facts, and to leave the economic evaluation to the Commission. In concrete cases, however, the court has reviewed the facts and decided not to follow the Commission's suggestion. In cases involving competition law, the Court of First Instance has asked the Commission to apply Article 81 in the appropriate legal and economic context. Economists tend to suggest solutions that are within the framework of the policy objective, but if diverse other interests are recognized in the policy objective, then it is difficult to show that a particular policy option was proportionate and optimal in that context.

**Mr Kohl**    Proportionality is a formal principle relating means to ends in a structural way. Under German law, a three-step analysis is used; European law is somewhat more ambiguous, sometimes using a three-step test, sometimes a two-step test. The principle is devoid of inherent value apart from relating means to ends. The courts consider civil rights that are being restricted by certain measures, and then relate them to ends for which these restrictions are imposed, which are usually public interest ends.

I agree that courts could scrutinize anticompetitive regulation, but the European Court of Justice and the German Constitutional Court do not. There are two explanations for why they do not. First, the restriction at issue must be very concrete, usually an individual right. Competition is a more general interest, such as health, safety, consumer protection and environmental protection. Courts are not comfortable relating restrictions to a general public interest, such as competition.

Second, courts are trying to respect the separation of powers. Thus, they do not want to substitute their balancing of different general interests for the balancing of general interests by the legislature or the administration.

Finally, much regulation is promulgated on a national level, purely within the national boundaries, where European competition law does not apply. There is no general principle at national level that every regulation must be procompetitive.

**Mr Heimler**   Regarding the question of who should be responsible in Europe for a regulatory review, I believe reputation with the public, the parliament and the government is the key concern. The European Commission has the best reputation in the EU, and is the best advocate for competition because it is far away from national governments and lobbies. It can take a broader view, which will be widely accepted. For instance, Italy was required by the Treaty to reduce its budget deficit. It was in Italy's own interest to do so, and not that of other member states. Italy succeeded in doing this because it was a constraint imposed by the Treaty. Thus, Europe is very important.

I believe that guidelines both for product market regulation and public utilities are also very important. The Commission recently produced a White Paper on Retail Trade, in which competition issues are very vague. It is a white paper that makes no progress. It is of no help to a national government that wants to reform regulation affecting retail trade, because it fails to specify whether member states should have structural regulation, or what they should do about sales below cost. It says that competition is important, but does not specify the optimal structure of regulation necessary for the sector to flourish to the benefit of society or the dimension of competition that the member states should use. Directorates other than DG Competition, or perhaps the European Parliament, prepared this White Paper. However, competition experts did not review it. It is a lost opportunity, because it could have been a great help in the political debate in every country if the Commission had issued a real guideline for competition-orientated reform.

However, I share the views of Professors Amato and Fels, that a body other than DG Competition should be responsible for these guidelines. DG Competition is too much involved in decision making within the Commission. It cannot also be the judge of member state regulations. The idea of having an outside, independent agency for issuing guidelines is very important, and could greatly enhance the possibilities for the guidelines to be effective.

Regarding interference with the political process through competition advocacy, I believe that timing is important. If a report arrives at the end of the political process, it will be considered interference, but if it arrives sufficiently early, then it will not. Guidelines should be presented with sufficient leadtime so that they can be placed on the agenda of national parliaments or governments. The Italian Competition Authority produced a report in 1993 on retail trade reform, well before the reform of retail trade was put on the Parliament's agenda. This document was reflected in the subsequent legislation. Early publication of the guidelines is also important.

Finally, specificity is important. For instance, the Commission communications on public utility regulation are not very clear. They speak about how prices should be proportional to costs, but they never define the costs. This creates difficulties for national regulators, who do not understand what is meant by the communications, and do not know how to apply them. Thus, specific guidelines would be extremely important to help national governments and the Commission.

**Prof. Schwartz**    I am asking for a clarification of the European legal system as compared to the US system with respect to administrative procedure law. US courts are indeed reluctant to substitute their own judgments for those of either the legislature or a government agency. However, it is quite common for a US court to invalidate an administrative agency's decision on the ground that it is 'arbitrary and capricious', meaning that the agency has not explained the basis for what it has done. Recently, when the FCC implemented the Telecommunications Act, it singled out seven elements of the local network that must be supplied on an unbundled basis. The reviewing Court rejected this action because the Federal Communications Commission had not adequately explained why competitors would need all of these elements. My question is whether there is more deference to a government agency in Europe.

**Prof. Amato**    In your example, it would be precisely the same. Courts may use this shield between themselves and the facts to accept a principle, but reject the use of the principle in the case before it, which is typically American as well. A case was before the Court several months ago where the issue was whether the Merger Regulation covers collective dominance. The advocate general had flatly said that it did not, but the Commission had always said that it did. The Court decided that in principle, the notion of collective dominance must be included in the Merger Regulation. The Commission lost, however, because the Court held that it had not proved the facts.

**Prof. Schwartz** On the question of whether competition conflicts with other public policy goals, in the area of disciplining market power, traditionally it has been dealt with through natural monopoly regulation or public ownership. The alternative is to have competition and enforce it through antitrust rules, if what used to be a monopoly can now become competitive. But in the areas like safety and pollution, economists generally accept the goals as given, and advise on the most cost-effective way to achieve them. Probably the most important advance in industrial organization economics in the last 20 years is looking for more market friendly mechanisms to achieve goals. For instance, with pollution problems, we have attempted to harness competition and market forces to meet given goals by specifying permit limits, but leaving the permitee to determine how to meet the limits. They can even buy and sell pollution permits. Another example is universal service. To ensure that poor people have a telephone, one solution is to create cross-subsidies, but this distorts the price structure. An alternative would be to use targeted subsidies: give the poor people vouchers. Economists are undoubtedly better at criticizing and asking questions than at providing solutions, but it is unfair to characterize them as never providing any answers. Some of the best work has been at trying to find market-friendly mechanisms.

Finally, we at the Justice Department always try to find less-restrictive alternatives. When a merger is notified, and the companies argue that it will achieve certain efficiencies, the first question we ask is whether the same efficiencies could be achieved without the merger, in a way that is less restrictive of competition. It is part of our culture naturally to ask these questions.

**Prof. Joerges** Under Article 28 and according to the jurisprudence of the Court, our national legislatures are under a duty to consider whether their regulatory means are the least restrictive conceivable.

Directive 83/189 is one of the means which can be used to ensure compliance with that duty. This directive requires that all regulatory measures affecting the functioning of the internal market must be presented to a European committee; a standstill can be imposed where a common European response to a regulatory concern seems preferable. Before such a decision is handed down, DG Enterprise will search for and suggest less-restrictive means which seem more compatible with the free market objective. These review procedures are designed to initiate a search for solutions which respect the legitimacy of regulatory concerns, but are nevertheless compatible with the functioning of the free market and competition.

**Dr Mehta**    Regulation 83/189 requires that all standards must be presented to a committee, and a standard procedure must be followed. Before a decision is handed down following this review procedure, DG Enterprise asks whether it could not be done in a less-restrictive way or in a way that is more compatible with the free market objective. These review procedures are designed to control the legitimacy of the standards in terms of free market and competition. Regulation 83/189 may incite more regulation, because those member states that want to regulate can only be dissuaded from doing so if the Commission decides to take action at Community level. Sometimes the question whether regulation is needed is not asked. In this sense, less anticompetitive solutions are not evaluated. For instance, in some cases, a material would simply be banned rather than limited by imposing higher charges if it was more polluting, which may well be a preferable response. Such action is very difficult to counteract in the absence of comprehensive cost–benefit analysis. I agree that the mechanisms are there, but I question how they are used in practice.

**Dr Laudati**    I would like to return to the Australian experience and the review. Professor Fels has given us an indication that maybe it is not working out the way he had hoped, or at least that all the evidence is not yet in. It is the unique experience in the world of doing a comprehensive review and doing it in a federal context. It would be helpful if Professor Fels could expand on what, institutionally, could have been changed or could be changed to help the review to work better. Is there an institutional problem, and if not, what is the nature of the problem?

**Mrs Bruzzone**    I would like to comment on the main weaknesses of competition advocacy by national competition authorities, taking into account the Italian experience. Interventions are often too late and not systematic. Moreover, competition authorities sometimes have quite a hostile audience, especially in other public administrations. To overcome such obstacles, the establishment of another central commission or agency in the government, with the task of carrying out a systematic review of regulation and issuing guidelines for pro-competitive reform, might be useful. But it should be a complement, not a substitute, of the competition authority role in promoting liberalization. If we have to start with a new system, it seems better to keep a competition advocacy role for a plurality of institutions, basically because we do not know whether the new commission will be effective.

The same arguments can be made with respect to the courts. Maybe the courts can play a role by applying the proportionality principle to these matters. But it is quite a technical job, requiring a good economic knowledge, to balance various goals and to establish the least-restrictive instrument that will ensure that the market failures resulting from the provision of a credence good are corrected. Are our courts prepared to do this?

In summary, the creation of several bodies with different roles working all together in the same direction will be better than choosing just one way to attain these objectives. The courts may need some technical advice, which may come either from the competition authority, or from another commission.

**Prof. Amato**   I was not considering the national level, I was simply considering the European level.

**Prof. Siniscalco**   At any level, it might depend on the weakness or strength of the head of this authority. To have multiplicity in an uncertain world is always better.

**Prof. Fels**   Returning to the question of mixing the investigative and adjudicative roles, and to a degree the discussion on proportionality, I would like to present a hard-line economics view. Competition policy is simply an instrument of economic policy, which has certain economic aims. We want certain results in our economy, and it is pragmatic to use legal instruments to achieve those results because they are the most accepted in the community. It is not just beautiful legal processes that we are setting up for their own sake. Moreover, the pursuit of an economic goal that is mainly affecting corporations and business is not the same as the processes that are involved where individual rights and so on are concerned, or where there is a criminal issue to be decided. Against that background, the questions are more pragmatic apropos of mixing the investigative and adjudicative role. Does it work well? On the whole, it does, because it is efficient to have the two functions together, and it is often inefficient to separate them. In any event, some safeguards are in place: the appeal rights to courts and tribunals and so on.

Assuming it is acceptable to link up the investigative and the adjudicative roles, and then advocacy is added, or even the powers to override laws on competition grounds, that is quite a significant accumulation of power. In certain economies, such as East Europe, that is the appropriate thing to do. But it is quite a major concern.

On the question of the institutions, in Australia we currently have the Productivity Commission, which was until recently called the Industry Commission, and before that the Tariff Board. It started when, years ago, an independent body was needed to decide what the level of tariff protection should be. Initially, it decided on generous tariff protection. Along the way, it was converted, and decided that what it was doing was bad. Thereafter, it turned out reports denouncing high tariffs, and seeking to educate the public. It had slightly mixed effects. Governments were able to avoid taking decisions on issues by asking the Productivity Commission to prepare a report. It could then delay for a couple of years. Nevertheless, in the long run, it had quite an effect on public opinion regarding trade liberalization. When it had completed that work, it turned its attention to internal microeconomic reform. 'Micro' comes from Greek and means a little bit, and 'microeconomic' means a little bit of economic reform. The Commission has prepared many reports. About ten years ago, it did a fundamental analysis and devised quite a good framework for reform of energy. Similarly, we had an independent inquiry by someone else into the financial sector, which set the pattern for reforms that took about ten years to deliver.

When Mr Hilmer did his review, it was decided not to use this commission for policy advocacy, because it was very unpopular with the states, who viewed it as a national body that was unsympathetic to them, and as taking a very hard line on economics, which they did not like. I would like to think that we come up with value-free work in economics, but it was by no means value free.

On the question of what would be the appropriate institutions in Europe to do a regulatory review, I have several reactions to Mr Heimler's comments. First, I agree that reputation is extremely important in this. At the European level, DG Competition would seem to be the body with the reputation. Moreover, knowledge of the market is important in a regulatory review, especially on microeconomic issues. In Australia, for example, we had a national agreement to introduce reform into the gas market. Bureaucrats devised principles for free and fair trade in gas and removal of interstate barriers to competition. The industry said it would go along with this, but it needed a one-year transition period, and succeeded in getting a clause added to the legislation specifying that pre-existing contracts should not be disturbed. They spent the year entering into 30-year contracts to ensure that nothing happened for 30 years. Our commission watched this process with horror, because we knew the market, and we knew that this was what would happen. Thus, the reformer must have knowledge of the industry. Often the competition agency has precisely the knowledge of how the market is working that is vital in these reform questions. I am not concluding that this job should be done by DG Competition. Perhaps the process should be initiated by having an independent inquiry separate from DG Competition to get the whole agenda moving. As to who does the work after that, I am not quite so sure.

On Dr Laudati's question about Australia, it is still a little early to say. There have been some reforms we would not otherwise have had, but the hard issues are going to come up in the next two years. What have been the problems? I do not know that there have been many institutional problems. But what is needed for this to work is ongoing leadership at the top level, which does not seem to be very easy. Unless the national leader is a fanatic about competition policy, and only that, then the pressure will not be sufficient. About one year after our review started, I told our prime minister that we appreciate that every 6–12 months he would give it a push, a little speech, but more is needed. He replied that it was difficult for him, because he had 50 other major issues: foreign policy, aborigines and so on, and every one of them requires a huge effort in learning and negotiating, and that he could not give that much time to the review. Thus, there is the problem of getting ongoing commitment from the top.

Second, when we were pushing for this reform, we presented it to all the political leaders, they agreed to it, but they did not understand what they were in for. It went through because they were happy to have a general competition policy, which is a worthy and wonderful goal that everyone agrees on. After that, the interest groups – the farm groups, the state governments – get organized in all sorts of ways, and they organize well, both in terms of putting pressure on, and in terms of their ability to advocate their own cause, to present the issues as a threat to rural culture, or as a threat to the autonomy of state governments.

On the other hand, we have this big ugly National Competition Council that is going to withdraw the money from them, which is quite an important pressure. It can be used to push for reforms that the governments secretly want.

PART IV


*Tour de Table*

# 24. Practical economic guidelines for reforming regulation to eliminate its anticompetitive effects

**Prof. Amato**  I have in mind that we propose that the European Commission do something in terms of screening national regulations, availing ourselves of the Australian precedent. To be impressive, as we must, because at some point I see some or all of us going to Brussels, meeting the President of the Commission and the Commissioner for Competition, and offering them the product of our work, prepared by Dr Laudati. In order to be effective, our volume should have a final part, which is a clear indication on how the screening could be done. It should provide guidelines both for regulators and reviewers of regulation, and suggest which institution at the European level should be given the job. We have already discussed all of these things. Now we shall have a *tour de table* to make it more specific, and focus upon it more.

Let us begin with my suggestions for an outline of possible economic guidelines. First, the regulator should be required to indicate the objective of the regulation, and whether it is aware of restrictions of competition that might result from the regulation, even if not apparent, indirect and affecting other markets. This is typical of tax and health regulations in many cases. For example, under the regulation of the health system in Italy, each local unit makes its own equipment procurements. For several reasons, including the delay in payments, this produces enormous anticompetitive effects in the markets of the suppliers. By a different organization of procurements, these markets could be made far more competitive. This is the typical case where the restriction is not the direct objective of the regulation.

Second, the items in relation to which the restriction must be assessed should be specified. We should certainly include the standard types of restrictions, such as limiting entry, fixing prices and sharing markets. We should also include anticompetitive effects on other aspects, such as innovation, the range of products available to consumers and the distribution system. These must be analytically indicated, because people are not necessarily aware of such inefficient and anticompetitive side-effects.

Until now, no one has screened the effects on production of collective agreements and the labour markets. In the *Albani* case, which is currently pending, the Advocate General is accepting the view that collective agreements are not in principle outside the coverage of the antitrust rules. We do not yet know what the decision of the Court will be, but it is very difficult to imagine Europe as an arena in which courts revise collective agreements because of their anticompetitive effects. However, it is very different, and much less disruptive, if a screening institution indicates, without any legal consequence, the effects of a given collective agreement. This is not *regulation*, it is *self-regulation*. Is there room in this sort of screening for self-regulations that are publicly authorized or approved, and therefore a hybrid mix of self-regulation and public measures? This is a typical area in which there is no restrictive intent, but there are restrictive effects. Therefore, these items must be indicated in our guidelines, otherwise the anticompetitive effects will not be reached.

Third, a crucial aspect of the guidelines will be to specify how to assess the impact or intensity of the effect. Should we indicate the principle of proportionality? This is crucial. We should indicate that economic analysis applies, how it applies, what kind of intellectual path it opens and what kind of economic arguments should be used. This is something that we do in antitrust.

Fourth, an essential aspect of the guidelines will address how to identify less-restrictive alternatives. Here there are both legal and economic arguments. In legal terms, it should be clarified in advance that to regulate does not mean to prohibit. There is a heritage that comes from Kelsen and others of his legal culture, which holds that a regulation scheme specifies obligations and entitlements. However, a legal rule might be framed differently. For example, to control pollution, the regulator can oblige companies to use specified machinery, with the only impact that more of this machinery will be sold, but not necessarily that the rate of pollution will be reduced. It might make more sense to specify a level of pollution, and allow the sale of pollution rights in secondary markets. This is something that Kelsen had not thought about because it is beyond the scheme of specifying obligations and entitlements.

In many cases of information asymmetry, the spreading of information is the concern. This is an area where by instinct, and not by the pressure of vested interests, regulators tend to use a compulsory system of prohibition: consumers are not informed, therefore a mandatory tariff is imposed. What may be a less-restrictive alternative?

Fifth, and another essential point, is the relation between general and specific, how different contexts might change the assessment of a single measure. We discussed an example where Section 271 of the US Telecommunications Act creates a limitation to entry that is intended to help open up a related market. But this is not necessarily so. Generally, limiting entry implies that fewer firms will be present in the market, so it is a restriction. In context, however, it might produce the opposite effect, even though in connected markets. This is the typical example of how contexts may determine the result. This indicates how essential it will be in our guidelines to have footnotes under each of the headings providing examples. We cannot make the guidelines specific, sector by sector, country by country. We must leave the impression on the reader that the guidelines are general, but none of them can be used in general terms. The guidelines remain general, but the footnotes give examples that open up the range of possible solutions, sometimes opposites. This gives our regulators the flexibility they will need in implementing the guidelines.

The final point should be to suggest an institutional architecture. This should be designed for a European screening of national measures. What would be the most appropriate institutional architecture in Europe? It might be more appropriate to recommend an independent European competition council, with prestigious members. It should be supported by DG Competition, which already has great expertise, so that it would be inefficient to reinvent the wheel. National competition authorities could also support the European competition council. Something can be invented.

We should also suggest a procedure. No one can specify the article in the Treaty whereby something like this can be established. No treaty article is needed, however, to empower someone to do something that is powerless in the sense that it is simply performing a screening analysis that has no legal consequences. It is providing national regulators as well as European institutions information as to the quality of their existing regulations. There may, of course, be political reactions, but no legal objection can be raised. Since there might be political reactions, perhaps we should suggest a procedure which begins with hearings in the European Parliament. Perhaps one of the standing committees of Parliament could vote to request the Commission to organize this review.

I would like to get your reactions to this preliminary architecture, your suggestions for how it can be strengthened, or how it should be modified.

**Dr Hilke**    What worries me about the first part of your suggested structure is that it seems to give a lot of credence right up front to the need for regulation in an area. An alternative approach is one that I would label 'zero-based regulation', going back to the Jimmy Carter era with a zero-based budget. It would suggest that we should not presume that a regulation is needed. Instead, policy makers should do a more extensive evaluation of whether other countries or sections of the country in question make do without this type of regulation. Do market failures arise in these other jurisdictions, and if so, how big are they?

My second point is that we must distinguish between new regulations and existing regulations. As to new regulations, in the United States we have requirements imposed by Congress for a Small Business Impact Statement and an Environmental Impact Statement. Why not add to these a Competition Impact Statement, requiring every proposed regulation to be accompanied by an analysis of the impact on competition in that industry and all upstream and downstream industries? This would create much more transparency as to the likely effects, and ensure that problems are not buried in the fine print.

In the European context, it seems that DG Competition is already potentially in that review capacity, and it might not be all that much of an extension of its power to take on a screening function. However, with respect to existing regulations, a separate commission might be appropriate, even if it has DG Competition support.

Finally, the notion of 'sunset provisions' is extremely powerful. It means that on a regular cycle, regulators would have to re-justify what they are doing. It is a convenient mechanism, because rather than having to review all existing regulations at once, only one-fifth of the existing body of regulations would be up for review in a given year, and those coming up next are clearly indicated. It enables the staff to be well prepared. In the United States, many states have used this type of sunset review, and have eliminated innumerable regulations on the books that have no effect. For instance, the US Federal Trade Commission reviewed the South Carolina public utility statutes, and found that provisions were still on the books for separate washrooms for Negro Americans as opposed to Whites. They were still regulating streetcars, although there have not been streetcars in South Carolina for 70 years. Therefore, it is possible to get rid of a lot of dead wood right from the start, which enables policy makers to focus on what they still want to do. An important example from the electricity experience is that technology drives what market failures come into being, and can change them. Unless the appropriateness of the regulation is reviewed, there is a high probability of being substantially behind the times. Often, some of the most anticompetitive provisions are there simply because they were there historically, and have never been reconsidered. Once a legislature says, 'Every five years, we have to look at this again', it creates a very strong mechanism to ensure that everything comes to the public agenda on a regular basis.

**Prof. Motta**   Our project is highly ambitious, but also very interesting and potentially with a strong impact. The guidelines seem similar in spirit to what the US Supreme Court has ruled with respect to commercial speech. Dr Fumagalli and I had written our study about the impact of advertising before reading Dr Laudati's study, but we were surprised to arrive at basically the same conclusions. It was comforting to see that the economic analysis and the US Supreme Court arrived at similar conclusions.

The guidelines can employ a regulatory tool that directly affects and directly addresses the externality that has been identified in the market. Our study had an example of information asymmetries in the professions. Advertising restrictions go in the direction opposite from that needed to solve the problem, because they tend to widen the information gap between consumers and professionals, when we should be attempting to narrow it. Consumer protection legislation, such as quality certification by the state, could help narrow the gap.

Our guidelines should be applied not only to regulation, but also to the way in which competition policy is enforced. For example, when DG Competition is dealing with vertical restraints, it must take into account two different objectives: promoting efficiency and market integration. Therefore, enforcement of competition policy in the realm of vertical restraints has often focused on the market integration objective rather than the efficiency objective. One example is the *per se* rule against the prohibition of parallel imports, which has a strong impact on innovation. Thus, these guidelines should extend to the way in which competition policy is enforced.

Finally, on the institutional issue, there are good reasons why DG Competition should be in charge of this reform effort, others why it should not. But it is clear that whatever institution is designated, it should not be operating behind closed doors. Rather, it is fundamental that this institution should have an impact on the public, and thereby build up the constituency that is necessary to create a consensus. For example, it would be difficult to remove protectionist regulation in a sector such as trucking, where the operators in the industry are very powerful, and the public does not see any direct impact on themselves from intervention. A good study should show the public that trucks have a strong negative environmental impact and that the number of accidents on the road is related to trucking legislation. Such a study might make the public sympathetic to reform, because it would dispel the notion that these poor truckers are generally people with just a small truck who would not be able to survive without the government's help. In fact, those who benefit most from protectionist legislation are large firms. The same is true with respect to agricultural policy. People have the idea that the small farmer will benefit most from protection. In truth, those who benefit most from protection are large and efficient farmers who do not need this to survive.

**Prof. Siniscalco**   First, when a regulation is designed, its enforcement provisions should be carefully crafted. The regulation may be self-enforcing, like price regulation, or it may need an enforcement body. We should be cognizant of the incentives to corruption, fraud, free-riding and so on. I believe that is the most important chapter to add to the guidelines.

Second, a mechanism should be created, whether based on proportionality or something else, for systematically reviewing and updating a regulation over time. Given the evolution of technology, optimal regulation today will be suboptimal tomorrow. Each regulation should embody its own self-revision, roughly every five years. I believe that international benchmarking is the most powerful instrument for accomplishing this – not so much at the research level, but as multilateral benchmarking as is currently done in Europe. Each government would explain what it does, and all would discuss whether it is right or wrong. This would eliminate the risk of technocracy, which is always present when something is delegated to the Commission, and which many member states simply do not trust. Last week, I was with Premier Asner, who gets extremely annoyed whenever Mario Monti talks about anything concerning harmonization. Countries do not like this kind of delegation; they prefer to sit around the table and discuss their own practices and to benchmark. Perhaps this is not efficient, but from a political perspective, it makes things easier.

Finally, a research network should be a part of this process. Brussels should be a clearing room for ideas, rather than the producer of ideas.

**Mr Heimler**　I should like to make a comment regarding equity versus efficiency, and interests other than competition. The competence we competition authorities have is not to discuss whether the environmental or safety goals that are given to us are correct.

**Prof. Amato**　We should take those goals for granted. I am not proposing a system under which we argue about the goals. We ask the regulators to indicate the goals, because the goals have to be clear. This is the first item of the analysis.

**Mr Heimler**　We can find the least-restrictive way of achieving those goals. This is where we have our strength and our abilities.

Second, I do not think we should have one guideline, but a number of guidelines, according to the sector to which the guidelines must be applied. A single guideline could not adequately address the health sector, or education, or the retail trade, or agriculture. Sectoral guidelines are preferable, not necessarily addressing specific-country legislation, but addressing the goals of the regulation, and how these goals can be achieved in the least-restrictive way, giving examples. For instance, regarding education, we should not care whether it is private or public. Rather, we should focus on how competition, also in a public or subsidized system, can function. We should also address efficiency considerations, even if everything remains in the public domain. I believe this is a good exercise and it can be done.

These guidelines should be addressed to regulators, and the goals must be clear. They cannot have various goals. Perhaps we need other means to accomplish this task, not simply guidelines or studies. It would be better to have this work done by an independent institution. Within the Commission, it would be more difficult to do the type of work that is needed and to ignore specific interests that some commissioners or some directors general pursue.

**Dr Biggar**　I favour having some sort of screening of regulatory proposals and a regulatory review process. However, these guidelines should include a provision to address the separation/integration issue that I discussed in my study. Regulations alone do not determine the level of competition in the marketplace; competition also depends on the structure of the market. A regulation could be in total compliance with these guidelines, but competition could still be absent or insufficient. For example, if the legal monopoly of the Italian postal service were abolished, competition in the delivery of mail may still not develop to an adequate level, even over a five-year period. This would pose no problem if some other body, such as the competition authority, had the power to introduce competition by separating down the track. As long as the separation decision remains with the central government rather than being delegated, then the guidelines should question whether all separation options have been considered.

**Dr Dutz**   First, a rejoinder to what Dr Biggar just suggested, we should consider a more expansive definition of competition advocacy. Traditionally, competition advocacy focuses on recommendations of either new or existing rules. One extension could be also to focus on whether anything is missing. Sometimes, a new rule is needed, or something should be enforced that is not currently being enforced. The failure to take a separation action could be part of that. The idea is to have this regulatory reform make markets more effective in meeting society's goals. Another way of expanding the competition advocacy role that a number of transition economies have adopted is for the competition authority to recommend new laws. This could include ordering new rules. Some competition authorities have the power to order procompetition changes to existing laws, or the power to introduce new laws where necessary, subject to review. It is not clear that this is necessary in the European context, but it is one way to expand competition advocacy.

Second, it is generally desirable, where possible, to mobilize key support constituencies. The Mexican example, however, may be one where too much education up front would have been counterproductive because it would have allowed groups strongly affected by reform to mobilize against it. For instance, when they pushed through the regulatory reform in trucking, the agreement emphasized the advantages of modernizing industry, but said nothing about enhancing competition.

I agree with the suggestions of regulatory reform through international benchmarking, and putting forward criteria that could be transparently reported is another powerful way to achieve education.

**Prof. Jenny**   First, I would like to state a word of caution. We assume that the objectives of regulations are easily described. For six years, I have been a member of a commission designated to evaluate legislation. I have seen that it is extremely difficult to specify the objectives of a regulation. There are several layers of both explicit and implicit objectives. For instance, the written objective of the French telecommunications law, 'free and fair competition', provides little guidance. Whoever is in charge of finding less-restrictive ways to meet the objectives is going to have a very difficult time. I question whether a review of whether there are less-restrictive ways of achieving the theoretical goals is worthwhile, without considering first whether a law has achieved its explicit or implicit goals. This would be a much wider regulatory review. Some will be critical if the question of whether the regulation has worked well is not asked.

**Prof. Amato**   We should write: 'Be sincere in stating your objectives'.

**Prof. Jenny**   Second, are the guidelines a checklist of questions that should be asked, or are they a methodology of how to solve some of the problems?

**Prof. Amato**   They are a methodology of how to solve the problems.

**Prof. Jenny**   A problem is that economists are not so good at telling you how to do it. They know what should be done, but in terms of specifying the methodology, there is a failure. In Panel 2, we had a discussion of vertical integration, and of economies of scope versus competition in downstream markets. Will the guidelines say that the question should be asked whether economies of scope are present, or will they say this is how we could assess economies of scope, which is the real problem? If the latter, then they will be rather extensive. Economies of scope are very difficult to assess empirically, and it would be difficult to specify the methodology. This would require us to do more work, since we have not addressed the issue of how to assess economies of scope. We must be clear on where we want to go.

I disagree with Mr Heimler, with respect to sectoral guidelines. I understand why he says that, and I have a certain sympathy. However, I refer back to Dr Hilmer's statement that he never would have got anywhere if he had done sectoral studies because the lobbies would have immediately taken him on. There must be a level of generality in identifying the problems.

Finally, on the institutional issue, presumably this applies to regulatory review of domestic regulations in Europe, even regulations that have no impact on trade between member states. We agree that it cannot easily be done at domestic level. Then the question is whether it is politically conceivable that the European Parliament or the European Commission or some other European body would decide that it has jurisdiction or the duty or power to review purely national regulations that have no impact at European level. I favour international benchmarking, and therefore I assume that it is only feasible at the European level.

**Prof. Amato**   The delicate issue of the preliminary procedure of how to set up this review process should involve the intervention of a wide consensus. Part of it could be that member states would submit their domestic legislation to this kind of screening.

**Dr Laudati**   To pick up on this issue of objectives, I think that the US Supreme Court's idea of 'substantial state interest' and examining whether the legislation involved directly advances the substantial state interest is a very good way of looking at it. In the process of doing that, some of the anticompetitive problems can be revealed. Taking the example of one case where lowering the level of gambling was the objective of having an advertising ban on gambling, the Court held that there are more direct ways to achieve this objective, such as a ban on gambling, or limiting the number of hours in which gambling casinos could be open. But having the advertising ban is not a direct way of achieving this goal, and is anticompetitive.

Second, when analysis reveals that a piece of legislation is anticompetitive, but that it is still a desirable piece of legislation because it achieves other objectives that are socially desirable, then what should be done? What kind of a balancing process should there be for determining that the legislation should remain in effect even though it is anticompetitive and there are no alternatives?

**Prof. Amato**   It is not the function of the guidelines to determine whether the law will survive or not.

**Mrs Bruzzone**   Perhaps we should take a broader approach to assessment of competitive effect, and call it assessment of economic impact on the market. That is, we may want to consider more factors than we would if limited only to whether a restriction of competition is present. Therefore, I would call the second step, 'analysis of economic impact on the market'. The guidelines should specify the relevant variables to be considered.

Regarding the relation of general and specific, an important point came out of an earlier discussion: a regulatory constraint cannot be evaluated independently of other regulations. In some cases, partial deregulation is fine, in some cases not. The guidelines should address this.

Finally, considering the level of generality of the guidelines, I understand that they must be general enough. However, to make practical suggestions, we need sectoral detail. Here, we meet a serious tradeoff. A compromise solution might be to keep at least a distinction in the guidelines between structurally competitive services and public utilities. The relevant questions are different for the two. Guidelines may be too general if they do not separate public utilities from structurally competitive services.

**Prof. Scarpa**   This task is already ambitious enough as has been outlined. Trying to go into sectoral guidelines would require three or four more days of work around this table, and competence that many of us probably have, but others do not. Perhaps this could be dealt with at the next set of meetings.

I liked Dr Hilke's recommendation on zero-based regulation. I think we could apply that to several cases. For instance, as to information asymmetries and providing more information to consumers, the guidelines could specify that licences are presumed as negative, and should, in principle, be replaced by certification. Following a case-by-case analysis, a given licensing requirement may be proved necessary, because the consequences of wrong choices by consumers could be devastating.

I appreciate what Professor Jenny was saying about national markets. However, I wonder whether national markets still exist in Europe. There are markets where the consequences for consumers refer to local consumers, but markets are not local for firms. Whatever a firm does in a market affects what that firm is able to do somewhere else. Restrictions that a firm must face in one place entail costs that do not allow it to compete in other markets. Therefore, I wonder where the boundary really is. I think that challenging the definition of national markets would be very important. Many recommendations about how to free national markets come from the centre. In Italy, national legislation on local public services met resistance at local level. General decisions by the EU often meet resistance at national level. Whenever the discussion takes place at a higher level, we have an easier time affirming and finding support for general principles, which is what we are interested in at the moment. I believe that raising the level of discussion on these factors might generally be helpful.

**Dr Mehta**   We should consider for whom we are writing these guidelines. The concern is primarily with national regulation. We should consider how these guidelines would be implemented. The scoreboard was a very good idea of Professor Amato, because it increases transparency.

Compliance cost should be included when measuring intensity of effect. This is where most of the cost–benefit analysis is focused.

We have seen in other work that performance-based regulations are often better than prescriptive regulations. The latter focus on issues such as who sets the standard, is the procedure for setting standards open and is there an appeal process? This is a general issue.

On the question of whether general or sectoral guidelines are more appropriate, there are many general elements common to both. However, as regards certain sectors, such as telecomunications, media and other regulated sectors, we now have much experience. If the guidelines are not specific, they will be criticized for reinventing the wheel. Many of the studies presented here went beyond generalities, and contain much specific content, which should be organized. I would be keen for the guidelines to specify methodology rather than simple checklists, because checklists have little impact.

On procedure, the Commission has had the Competitiveness Council of Alexis Jacquemin, which was supposed to consider national as well as European rules, because it was dealing with the problem of too much regulation. The original task was to look at whether regulatory reform was needed. I do not know what its final conclusion was, but it does prepare reports from time to time.

On the institutional question, these guidelines would have to be quite substantial to cover the issues and be of interest to a critical mass. On the other hand, perhaps it should be taken further before the screening and benchmarking of national measures. Expertise may be needed to do the screening. DG Competition and other services will certainly be supportive. Also, prominent people should be involved for this effort to have any effect. Experts are needed to expand these guidelines into something that starts and creates a momentum to the process. If the process begins by screening certain regulations in certain areas, and a scoreboard is established by benchmarking and determining the one that has achieved the best results, and this is done with a high degree of credibility, it would have a very important effect. It would help build the necessary constituency, as people would see that this would mean much better regulation. There, the national antitrust authorities have an important role to play.

**Prof. Ballbe**   The role of information is crucial in this process. At the national level, the regulator should be obliged to provide information on the motivation for adopting a given type of regulation. Also, as noted by Professor Siniscalco, information should be used as a regulatory tool. An independent agency that can put together all the information on regulation in Europe would be very useful. For instance, the European Agency for the Environment publishes reports on who is polluting, where, and at what level. No state wants to be at the top of their list of polluters.

Regarding independence, the prosecution power of the competition authority should be taken out of the hands of government. National competition authorities should be independent from government, at least in an economy like Spain's, which is in the process of liberalizing.

Regarding infrastructures, we should look not only at what the government does, but also at what it does not do. Inaction in some areas is not neutral, such as for network services, transportation and so on.

Finally, we should consider involvement of the judiciary. We should employ human capital to make these guidelines effective. On the curriculum of Spanish legal studies, there is no competition law. Judges are not trained, and have no idea of competition law. Thus, we must create human capital capable of applying these guidelines. We should also consider the involvement of supra-national powers.

**Mr Kohl**    The search for less-restrictive alternatives can perhaps be supplemented by the zero-based regulation approach. In looking for alternatives, non-public regulation would be private law. For example, reducing search costs can be accomplished by public regulation, by minimum quality standards. However, it can also be done by labelling or trademarks/service marks, which would cause firms to discipline themselves towards achieving a certain quality. Another example of this is what Marius Schwartz told us with respect to the telecommunications sector: attempting to open the local monopoly by inducing the incumbent to establish technological mechanisms that serve as intermediaries and overcome transaction costs which are there for new entrants. The search for alternatives is thus geared towards private law regulation as opposed to public regulation.

Second, I am very much in favour of the sunset provision. It should be supplemented with provisions to measure a regulation's efficacy in reaching the proposed aims, assessing data on the market situation.

**Dr Nicoletti**    First, I think we should avoid reinventing the wheel. Much has been written on guidelines for governments. The OECD has recently done a lot of work in this area, coming up with a set of recommendations (including for instance the use of Regulatory Impact Analysis).

Second, in the context of this work, peer pressure is very important, which is why benchmarking is so important. We should suggest that it be pursued. It is particularly important with respect to the zero-based regulation proposal. It is useful for a country to see that another country has no regulation in a sector and yet everything works very well.

Third, the guidelines should include a provision on how to ensure that the regulatory review is successful from a political standpoint. The bodies that review regulations should publish their opinions. To avoid that the lobbies be too powerful in opposing change, the proposal should also be packaged correctly to show that it can produce benefits which are clearly understandable to politicians and consumers.

Fourth, we must distinguish between economywide and sector-specific regulations. For instance, the guidelines should say something about administrative burdens. This has a very strong impact on economic performance and on entry at the national level. We should say something about this, but then we are enlarging, as Dr Bruzzone suggested, from impact on competition to impact on economic performance in general.

Fifth, it is important to highlight the interaction between regulations in the product and labour markets and their combined effects on labour market performance. Different regulatory arrangements in the two markets can make regulatory reforms easier or more difficult, and their repercussions on employment can be important. Stressing the potential impact of procompetitive reforms on employment is crucial because politicians always have employment in mind.

Finally, we should insist on the concept of sunsetting. Regulations can be sunsetted, notably when they address technology-specific market failures that have disappeared due to technical progress. For this reason, it is generally preferable that regulations be as little technology specific as possible. But we should extend the concept of sunsetting regulations to regulatory institutions themselves. Institutions should disappear when markets have become sufficiently competitive.

Given the huge amount of regulation at the domestic level, it is impossible to avoid the subsidiarity principle in reviewing regulations. It would be best to have national authorities reviewing the national regulations and submit these reviews to a European-wide commission, and to link this process to the ongoing Cardiff process. The review at national level should be done by independent entities, because the Cardiff process implies self-assessment by the countries of what they have done, which is made by finance ministers who are not always self-critical enough.

**Prof. Fels** The main point that everyone has recognized is the need to create a political momentum for these changes to happen, then to maintain the political momentum and drive for them to be implemented successfully. That seems like the greatest challenge, because in many countries, regulatory review processes and requiring regulatory impact statements have been attempted, but after a year or two have faded away to insignificance. It is up to the political leaders to create the conditions that would lend support for this.

**Prof. Amato** We shall try to summarize a scheme of guidelines. You will receive them soon, so you will have time to comment, then something hopefully will happen. Thank you all for what was a very good seminar. It was the first time for many of us for a joint meeting, and it has worked. This is a sign of a successful group of people in discussing their respective ideas, and if the process moves ahead at least at European level initially, there might be reasons for us to meet again as a group in this format to supervise what is going on.

PART V

Recommendations for the Reform of Regulation
to Promote Competition

# 25. Draft guidelines

## Giuliano Amato and Laraine L. Laudati

## A. STATEMENT OF PURPOSE

The participants in the Round Table on Anticompetitive Regulation recommend that a means be established in the EU to promote the elimination and/or revision of anticompetitive regulation in the Community and its member states. Laws and regulations extending across all sectors, including agriculture, construction, manufacturing; and various services, such as financial, health, retailing, road and air transport, personal, professional, education, post, communications, electricity, gas, and water, can have anticompetitive effects.[1] Accordingly, the participants recommend that all existing laws and regulations, both Community level and national level, be reviewed pursuant to a Regulatory Review Action Plan to determine whether they unjustifiably restrict competition. The results of such review for the Community and each member state should be benchmarked against the results for the other member states, and an 'anticompetitive effects' rating should thereafter be attributed to each law or regulation of the EU and each member state.

A Procompetitive Regulation Scoreboard should then be prepared (which will function in a manner similar to the EU's Single Market Scoreboard[2]), comparing the 'procompetitive regulation' score for the EU and each of the member states for each law and regulation. The Procompetitive Regulation Scoreboard should be published on a regular basis, and should spell out, in a manner easily understood by consumers, the costs of anticompetitive regulation. Thus, the end result should be to increase the level of transparency as to the existence and effects of anticompetitive regulation throughout the EU. This should, in turn, create a constituency that will demand revision of anticompetitive regulation, and place pressure on the Community institutions and the member states to make such revisions.

With respect to proposals for new legislation, a Competition Impact Statement should be prepared, addressing each of the questions listed in Section C below. For Community legislation, the Competitive Impact Statement should be prepared by one of the European institutions; for national legislation, by a national institution.

It should thereafter be provided to legislators deciding whether to pass the law or regulation. It should also be published.

## B.    ESTABLISHMENT OF A PROCOMPETITIVE REGULATION TASK FORCE

A new, independent European Procompetitive Regulation Task Force[3] should be established,[4] which should be composed of competition experts from all of the member states (and perhaps some third countries, such as Australia and the US, as well as some Central and Eastern European countries). Its functions would be:

1. To conduct the further research necessary to eliminate anticompetitive regulation in the EU, including: research on the anticompetitive effects of EU or national regulation; and analysis of the means by which public policy objectives in different sectors can be achieved with less harm to competition.

   a. With respect to better use of tools that already exist at European level:
      • legal research of what further use could be made by the European institutions, national courts, and national competition authorities, of Treaty provisions, especially Articles 81 (in combination with Articles 3 and 10), 86, and 99[5] to eliminate anticompetitive regulation in the member states;[6]
      • legal research as to how the proportionality principle could be further exploited as a mechanism of supervising anticompetitive national legislation, bearing in mind that the Treaty is the overall framework for regulation in Europe;[7]
      • research as to how the Commission might include a screening device for anticompetitive regulation in its normal interagency consultation procedures, which are followed with respect to all proposed regulations, directives, and decisions, such as by incorporating a requirement that a Competitive Impact Statement accompany each Commission legislative proposal.
   b. With respect to conducting a regulatory review:
      • research to specify methodology for analysing the economic impact of anticompetitive restriction (item C4 below);
      • research as to what means might be used to create incentives (or disincentives) for member states to satisfy (against failure to satisfy) review and reform efforts.[8]

2. To work with DG Competition and the national competition authorities to:

    a. develop, revise and refine these proposed guidelines;

    b. develop a Regulatory Review Action Plan, which would include a schedule for review of all regulation in the EU under the guidelines, and rules for subsequent review of each regulation on a regular basis, such as every five years, under a 'sunset provision'.[9]

    c. determine what further role DG Competition should play in the process;[10]

    d. determine which institutions within the member states should be responsible for the regulatory review, how they should be structured, and what should be their responsibilities in the review process;

    e. determine which institutions at Community level and at national level should be responsible for preparing Competitive Impact Statements on new legislation;

    f. determine how to raise public (and business) awareness of the importance of this project, and thereby build a constituency in support of it, and how else to create and maintain highest level political support for the review process in the member states;[11] and

    g. conduct international benchmarking among the member states with respect to each category of regulation.[12]

3. To maintain and publish, on a regular basis, the Procompetitive Regulation Scoreboard.[13]

[Note: Perhaps some of these tasks should be performed by a special temporary study group, and some should be performed at a later time by a permanent Task Force.]

## C. THE GUIDELINES

Based on the chapters and discussion at the Round Table on Anticompetitive Regulation, the following preliminary outline of questions has been developed for purposes of the regulatory review. It is meant to be a starting-point; additional work is needed to specify in further detail the exact information that should be gathered, and how it should be analysed.

1. What is the objective of the regulation?[14]   The objective of the regulation must be established, as the task at hand is to determine whether the existing or proposed regulation is the least-restrictive way to achieve that objective. The national regulator should provide detailed and substantial information on the motivation for adopting a regulation. General statements of objective,

such as 'the promotion of free and fair competition', are not sufficient for this purpose. Rather, the regulator should specify the market failure or other public interest goal that the regulation is designed to address. Market failures can take various forms, including:

a. natural monopolies;
b. asymmetric information problems;[15]
c. negative or positive externalities (including environmental considerations); and
d. public goods (market equilibrium level of good or service different from that socially desirable).

When the market failure concerns the provision of a very general and not easily quantifiable good, such as the protection of health or safety of citizens, one may simply speak of public interest objectives, since from a practical policy-making viewpoint the adoption of the market failure notion does not add significant information. Moreover, some objectives involve public interests other than the correction of market failures; an example is provided by distributional considerations. Therefore, public interest objectives other than correction of market failures might include:

a. protection of health, safety, welfare of citizens;[16]
b. energy conservation;
c. distributional considerations (especially those concerned with universal service obligations with respect to public utilities);
d. issues involving national security; and
e. obligations under international treaties.[17]

2. Is there a nexus between the regulatory objective and the regulation?

a. Is regulation necessary to achieve the objective?[18]   (Principle of zero-based regulation.) The regulator should be asked to show that the regulation prevents the occurrence of real harms. The regulation must be suitable to achieve the envisaged objective, that is, it must be capable of remedying the identified market failure in an objectively observable way.
   International benchmarking associated with an analysis of 'optimal' regulation may reveal that some member states have regulation which other member states do not have. This provides the opportunity to determine whether market failures occur in the absence of regulation, and if so, how substantial they are. Such benchmarking may indicate that regulation is not really necessary.

b. Does the regulation directly advance the objective? An anticompetitive regulation may, at times, not even advance the regulatory objective, and should therefore be eliminated.[19] The regulator should be asked to show that the restriction will, in fact, alleviate real harms to a material degree.

3. What restrictions on competition might result, directly or indirectly, from the regulation (or from what the regulation fails to do)?[20] All restrictions should be listed, including both direct or intended restrictions as well as indirect or unintended ones.

   a. With respect to structurally competitive industries, restrictions on competition can take various forms, including:
      i. Restrictions on entry:[21]
         • direct: For example, licensing, certification, training requirements, registration, accreditation; ceilings on the number of competitors in a market; requiring minimum distances between retail outlets; and
         • indirect: For example, licence fees or otherwise increasing costs, modifying equilibrium conditions for entry.
      ii. Restrictions affecting business conduct:
         • fixing or otherwise impacting prices;
         • limiting the scope of activities;
         • limiting possible innovations;
         • limiting truthful advertising;
         • limiting hours of operation;
         • establishing minimum standards; and
         • establishing information requirements.
      iii. Restrictions on organizational form and ownership relations.
   b. With respect to structurally non-competitive industries, restrictions on competition can take various forms, including:
      i. Restrictions on entry:
         • government monopoly[22] or monopoly franchise;[23] and
         • assisting entry by placing limits on further entry.[24]
      ii. Failing to regulate access charges or other access elements.[25]
      iii. Failing to require vertical separation (where firm has vertically integrated non-competitive component and competitive component).[26]
      iv. Absence of a level playing field, for example, granting subsidies to incumbents,[27] or restricting incumbents, but not entrants, to encourage entry.[28]
      v. Imposing retail tariffs on incumbents that are not cost reflective (universal service obligations; cross-subsidization).[29]

    vi.  Some forms of average price regulation.[30]

   vii.  Imposing market share targets to reduce the incumbent's market share.[31]

  viii.  Prematurely deregulating the market.[32]

    ix.  Prohibiting incumbents from practising some forms of price discrimination.[33]

4.  What is the impact of the restriction on competition?[34] (The guidelines should specify the methodology to be used to assess impact, and to measure it quantitatively.)[35]    The impact of a restriction on competition can only be determined by viewing it in the context of the market in which it applies.[36] To avoid distributional problems, restrictions should also be analysed from an economywide perspective (as opposed to the perspective of only the regulated group).[37] The interaction with other government regulations should be taken into account when analysing a regulation's economic impact.[38] The factors that should be considered relate both to the direct impact of a regulation on market conditions and its indirect impact, through the influence on the strategic conduct of undertakings. These factors may include:

- demand conditions;
- technology (capital intensity, economies of scale and economies of scope);
- entry conditions, such as entry restrictions imposed by government regulation;
- nature of import competition;
- number and size distribution of market participants;
- existence of substitute products and product differentiation;
- provision of information to the market by firms, such as through advertising;
- degree of vertical integration;
- arrangements among firms, such as cartels;
- level of prices, quantity and quality;
- level of profit margins;
- efficiency;
- innovation and technological progress;
- effect on labour markets; and
- effect on entry into and performance in downstream markets (with respect to infrastructure services).

5. Are less-restrictive alternatives available to achieve the objective of the regulation? If so, what are they? [39]

   a. Is the regulation as narrowly drawn as possible to achieve the regulatory objective, or could a more limited restriction achieve it? This is essentially the same as asking whether the regulatory restriction is proportional to the regulatory objective. [40]

   b. A presumption might be created that certain types of regulations have an unacceptable negative impact on the market, and that they should be eliminated or reformed, unless it can be demonstrated that this effect is not present, or that it is necessary to achieve other social objectives. For instance, a licensing requirement could be necessary in a profession to protect the public from grave consequences. Categories of 'presumably more-restrictive' and 'presumably less-restrictive' regulations could be established. For instance:

|  | Presumably more restrictive | Presumably less restrictive |
| --- | --- | --- |
| Environmental, safety standards | Prescriptive standards (e.g., requiring use of specific pollution control technology) | Performance-based standards (e.g., emission standards)[41] Economic instruments (tradable emission or noise rights, taxes proportional to emissions) |
| Regulation of professions | Quantitative entry restrictions Licensing Bans on truthful advertising[44] Bans on in-person solicitation of clients[45] | Minimum quality standards[42] Self-regulation of quality[43] Certification Time, place, manner restrictions on advertising[46] Information requirements Minimum quality standards Licensing requirements |

   c. How effective are the less-restrictive alternatives at achieving the regulatory objective? If they are less effective than the regulation currently in effect, is the lower effectiveness tolerable, given the social benefits from a less-restrictive regulation?

6. What institutional obstacles to eliminating anticompetitive regulation exist in the member state? What reforms are needed?

a. Should there be self-regulation? Self-regulation has the advantages of passing the role of regulator to firms that have more information about their industry than the regulator has; providing greater flexibility than public procedures; and internalizing the cost of regulation.[47] However, self-regulation should be accompanied by certain controls, such as:

- General principles of self-regulation [by professionals] should be established.
- Self-regulation should be subject to competition law (and not exempted from its coverage).[48] The competition authority should scrutinize the rules and practices of business and professional associations to permit them to maintain and enforce rules that protect the public on matters such as safety, but to prevent them from using the association to promote anticompetitive goals.
- Members of the regulated group should not dominate the professional governing body.

b. Does the regulation include mechanisms for its adjustment, updating, review or eventual sunsetting, in response to changes in the markets over time?

c. Is the institutional structure in place capable of consistently generating high-quality regulation?

- What regulatory institutions are in place? Are these institutions necessary?
- Are the regulatory institutions sufficiently independent to efficiently perform their job effectively?
- Does the regulatory institution perform its tasks in a manner that is clear, transparent and involves adequate opportunity for consultation?
- Is the interaction between the various responsible regulators an obstacle to the development of competition?

d. Should the regulatory authority responsible for administering the regulation be at a different level?   Some participants suggested that closeness of the regulatory authority to the regulated firm could result in regulatory capture, and protectionist implementation of a regulation that might not otherwise be anticompetitive.[49] A solution might be to shift responsibility for implementation of the regulation to a more centralized authority. For instance, problems of ineffective liberalization by sectoral regulators might be solved by centralizing the regulatory authority in charge of liberalization.[50] Reform of regulation of professionals should be the responsibility of central government agencies rather than professional groups.[51] Another solution to protectionist implementation is structurally to increase the incentives of local regulators to take competition arguments into account.

e. How should regulation be organized? Should there be sectoral regulators or economywide regulators? How should sectors be defined? Should regulators be concerned also with enforcement of the antitrust law? What is the 'optimal' institutional setting?

f. Should the national competition authority and/or DG Competition change the way they perform their role as competition advocate? The present role of DG Competition, and of the national competition authorities, as competition advocate may not be effective in convincing other government agencies to consider competition policy in their regulatory efforts.[52] The competition authority may need to take steps to improve its effectiveness as a competition advocate.[53] Weaknesses in competition advocacy may be due to intervening too late; intervening randomly, rather than systematically; poorly marketing advocacy opinions; and having a hostile audience.[54] Changes may be needed, such as institutional modifications with respect to national competition authorities,[55] modifications to government decision-making procedures,[56] or modifications of the competition agency's legal authority to participate in proceedings of other government agencies.[57] National competition authorities could be especially useful in identifying competition problems that regulation fails to address, or resulting from a failure to enforce regulation that already exists, and they could recommend new laws or regulations to address such problems.

g. Should steps be taken to encourage national judges to apply the principle of proportionality to anticompetitive regulation, and if so, what should these steps be? If not, should a specialized body be created for 'judicial oversight' of anticompetitive regulation?[58] European judges have been reluctant to apply the principle of proportionality to invalidate anticompetitive regulation. A number of reasons have been suggested for this, including that competition authorities have power both to investigate and adjudicate. In reviewing the authority's decisions, constitutional courts limit their role to assessing manifest error by the competition authority, in deference to the principle of separation of powers. Thus, if competition authorities did not have the power to decide, courts would be likely to assess the facts automatically by using economic analysis. Another reason cited was lack of training in economic analysis. Perhaps if they had more training, or if they could obtain expert advice from an independent body, they would apply the proportionality principle more aggressively in these matters.

h. Once anticompetitive regulation is reformed, should other mechanisms be instituted to deal with the side-effects of the reforms? Eliminating anticompetitive regulation may not be sufficient in itself to make markets more competitive, due to problems of information asymmetries, and consumers' lack of understanding of the quality of the goods or services that they purchase. Consumers may need help to understand a more competitive market.[59] Some possible solutions would be:

i.  With respect to professional services:
    *   independent auditing, through private or government bodies (the latter may be more trustworthy because they do not operate on the profit motive),[60] or a privately produced catalogue of professionals, including quality ratings;[61]
    *   elimination of any regulations that might hamper the consumer's ability to get a second opinion (especially with respect to medical services).
ii. With respect to products:
    *   a regulation requiring manufacturers of products to reveal the quality of the product according to a rating system established by the regulation.[62]
    *   privately produced information about the quality of products.[63]

## NOTES

1.  A general approach, requiring that all regulation be subject to review, is preferable to a sectoral approach, because the latter would be more likely to encounter resistance from lobbies within each sector.
2.  The Single Market Scoreboard documents the progress made by each of the member states towards complying with the undertakings announced in the Single Market Action Plan, endorsed by the Amsterdam European Council in June 1997.
3.  Several participants emphasized the importance of having a centralized authority to conduct the review, in order to avoid problems of regulatory capture.
4.  Professor Amato suggested that the process might begin with hearings in the European Parliament, where a standing committee could vote to organize the review.
5.  Under Article 99, the Council, on the basis of a proposal by the Commission, may adopt recommendations containing general guidelines on the economic policy of member states. The Commission should then submit reports to the Council on the relevant developments in each member state. On this basis, the Council may adopt and publish a specific recommendation directed at a member state, whenever its economic policy is significantly inconsistent with the guidelines. This multilateral monitoring system, operating on the basis of a qualified majority rule, is currently used only for macroeconomic issues. Article 99, however, refers more generally to the economic policy of member states. Therefore, in principle, Article 99, if read together with Articles 4 and 98 of the Treaty (establishing that the economic policy of member states must be consistent with the principles of a free market and competitive economy, aimed at fostering an efficient allocation of resources) may be used also with respect to microeconomic policies and therefore regulatory issues.
6.  For instance, Dr Laudati reported that the Commission has relied on Article 81 to eliminate advertising restrictions from professional codes of conduct. A comprehensive analysis of other instances where Article 81 could be applied to eliminate anticompetitive self-regulation should be made.
7.  Professor Joerges observed that in other contexts, the Court of Justice has been very willing to assess the legitimacy of regulatory objectives and to require member states to pursue a

regulatory goal in a manner less intrusive to other regulatory goals, generally those pursued under Article 28.

Mr. Kohl argued that scrutiny of anticompetitive regulation is constitutionally mandated because 'freedom of competition' is a direct constitutional interest; because it is the indirect outcome of constitutionally protected basic individual economic freedoms; and because it is the only tool to protect the economic viability of the state. Further, he argued that the proportionality principle could be a useful tool for assessing and balancing the costs and benefits of anticompetitive regulation, as it rationally structures the relationship between a regulatory aim and the means chosen to achieve it by testing a regulation's appropriateness, necessity and proportionality.

8. Professor Schwartz observed that in the US, a common tool used is the withholding of federal funding from the states, such as when a state fails to meet a federal pollution standard.

9. Dr Hilke noted that a sunset provision would require regulators to re-justify what they are doing on a regular basis, and would enable policy makers to focus on what they still want to do. Especially in high-technology industries, if the appropriateness of the regulation is not reviewed regularly, there is a high probability of its being substantially out of date. Often, some of the most anticompetitive provisions are there simply because they were there historically, and have never been reconsidered.

Professor Schwartz indicated that this task can be very time consuming. For instance, the US DOJ's Antitrust Division at one time tried to repeal many of its outdated consent decrees (court orders entered to settle antitrust cases), and found the task difficult – both because of the sheer volume, and because an interested party will often oppose repeal, resulting in a court hearing.

Further, Professor Schwartz provided several examples of how a sunset provision could work. In the US, the abolition of the Civil Aeronautics Board (CAB) corresponded to the deregulation of the airlines and helped to prevent a return to regulation. (By contrast, the Interstate Commerce Commission (ICC) was targeted for abolition, but some of its functions have simply been taken over by the Surface Transportation Board.) Sunsetting an agency may be a dramatic but effective course, where the industry truly does not merit regulation.

Regarding individual rules or regulations, the Antitrust Division used to enter consent decrees to settle antitrust cases of unlimited duration. The Division found that decrees became outdated, and often anticompetitive. Accordingly, it changed this policy around 1980 to limit new decrees to a ten-year duration. This term can be longer in very special circumstances, but it is sometimes even shorter.

Finally, Professor Schwartz observed that in the US, the Stevens Act, which took effect in the mid-1990s, requires regulatory agencies to track the costs and benefits of their regulations and transmit annual reports to Congress. While the reports themselves are sometimes uninformative or biased, the process creates a forum for other concerned and informed parties to express their views.

10. Professor Amato raised the concern that people resent the same institution doing too many things, noting that the Italian Competition Authority is empowered both to adjudicate cases and to send recommendations to the cabinet and parliament in relation to pending or existing legislation that could distort competition. When it sends a recommendation, the reaction of government officials is often that this constitutes interference with the political process. Although it is expert information, the competition authority's recommendation would become part of the game, injecting the competition authority into politics. Professor Amato concludes that in Europe, a solution similar to that adopted in Australia, that is, creation of an independent National Competition Council to conduct the review, would be preferable to having it done by the existing competition authority.

Mr Heimler commented that DG Competition has the best reputation of any competition authority in the EU because it is far from national governments and lobbies, and because it can take a broader view that will be widely accepted by the member states. However, he concluded that an outside, independent body should be responsible for these guidelines and the regulatory review, as DG Competition is too much involved in decision making.

Professor Fels agreed that reputation is important, and that DG Competition is the body with the best reputation. He added that knowledge of the market is also important, especially on microeconomic issues. He suggested that the review process in Europe might begin with an independent inquiry separate from DG Competition, but he was uncertain of who should do the work after the initial phase.

11. Participants in the Round Table persistently emphasized the importance of creating and maintaining political momentum for change, including continued support at the highest political level. Professor Fels cited difficulties in maintaining sufficient high-level political support as one of the main problems with carrying out the Australian review in an effective manner. This support is crucial at the point when interest groups have organized and begin lobbying to oppose reform. He believes that the monetary incentive payments to states and territories for satisfying review requirements have been an important countervailing force.

12. Mr Nicoletti stressed that peer pressure is very important to further regulatory reform, which is why benchmarking is so useful. It is particularly relevant with respect to the zero-based regulation proposals: it is instructive for policy makers and the wider public to see that another country has no regulation in a specific area, and yet economic performance and/or consumer protection are no worse and possibly better than in the home country.

13. Participants emphasized the important role that could be played by the Procompetitive Regulation Scoreboard to build a constituency in support of reform. For instance, revealing the costs to society of anticompetitive regulation in a given industry, and that those who benefit most are large firms, could be forceful evidence to help build a constituency.

14. The Guidelines and the Scoreboard do not have the purpose of judging the social value of regulatory objectives. Thus, these objectives are accepted as given, and not questioned in this process. However, international benchmarking of objectives may provide useful information to national regulators to help them reflect on regulatory objectives, and whether they remain relevant concerns.

15. Professor Fels stated that the consequences of making incorrect judgements of quality for relatively simple goods with few characteristics is likely to be small, as consumers are likely to be able to form a reasonably accurate estimate of the value of the good. When consumers face difficulties in evaluating the quality of goods *ex ante*, their ability to estimate accurately is most likely when they can assess the quality of the goods after consumption, and they undertake repeat purchases.

    Professional services are significantly more difficult for consumers to assess, because services are generally not observable before they are purchased in the same way as goods; they are, by nature complex, and it is thus difficult to assess quality before, and sometimes after, they are purchased; consumers are infrequent purchasers of professional services; and the consequences of poor professional services can be significant. These characteristics can justify regulation aimed at quality assurance, which are intended to provide a guaranteed level of service quality to consumers.

    Professor Jenny observed that consumers face difficulties in evaluating quality of professional services, either *ex ante*, or sometimes even *ex post*. In addition, they do not even know where their demand curve lies because they do not know what services they need.

    The US Supreme Court has ruled that the state has a 'substantial interest' in the maintenance of professionalism, and in controlling various aspects of professionalism (preserving professionals' independence, preventing them from fraud or overreaching, ensuring against conflicts of interest) in order to protect consumers, given the information gap between professionals and consumers.

16. The US Supreme Court has recognized a 'substantial state interest' in reducing the demand for gambling, reducing the consumption of alcoholic beverages, preventing brewers from competing on the basis of alcohol strength (which could lead to more alcoholism), and aiding parents' efforts to discuss birth control with children.

17. It may go beyond the powers of one country to correct a market failure in another. Thus, international treaties may be needed.

18. This standard is similar to that included in the legislative proposal of the National Committee to Review the Antitrust Laws (NCRAL): that a regulation be 'necessary to accomplish an

overriding statutory purpose of the agency'. It is also similar to the US Supreme Court's requirement that the state has a 'substantial interest'.

19. For example, restrictions on truthful advertising, particularly advertising bans, imposed to address the problem of asymmetric information with respect to professional services not only fail to address this problem, but widen the information gap between professional and consumer. Moreover, as argued by Professor Motta and Dr Fumagalli, advertising professional services increases welfare by decreasing prices and promoting entry.

    Professor Jenny suggested that eliminating anticompetitive regulations may not be enough and that governments should seek ways to allow consumers to make better-informed choices.

20. The failure of regulation to address an aspect of a problem can give rise to anticompetitive effects. For example, Professor Ballbe's chapter discusses how the failure to deal with infrastructure limitations in Spanish airports has undermined efforts to liberalize the airline industry. Mr Nicoletti's chapter shows that the failure to address congestion and airport dominance problems has limited the benefits of airline liberalization in OECD countries.

    Professor Schwartz observed that failure to expand airport capacity has been a problem in the US as well. This has created a negative public impression of competition and deregulation, because people mis-attribute their problems (congestion, delays) to competition, rather than to the failure to expand the needed complementary infrastructure.

21. Dr Bruzzone stated that restrictions on entry to a profession can be expected to limit supply and raise prices and incomes of those providing the service. The unintended effect may be to redistribute wealth from consumers to the regulated profession.

22. Professor Siniscalco reported that his empirical evidence supports the notion that a government monopoly market should be liberalized first, then privatized, rather than the reverse. This conclusion is based on the findings that: a negative relationship exists between privatization and vertical integration; a positive relationship exists between privatization and regulation (that is, if a market is not fully regulated at the time of privatisation, investors are willing to pay less for it, because they assume that at some point it will be regulated); and the percentage of stock sold in a privatization is related to both vertical integration and regulation (i.e., less stock is sold if the government has not yet completely regulated the industry, or if the monopoly has not yet been separated).

23. Mr Heimler argued that local governments should intervene in the market whenever the competitive system does not satisfy general interest requirements. For goods that local governments must supply, it must decide whether to provide these services directly, or contract them out. Local government must supply public goods (for example, street lighting, street cleaning, traffic control) because the amount otherwise supplied by the market would be less than socially optimal. Non-public goods with a natural monopoly component (for example, water, gas and electricity) allow for only a partial opening of competition. Non-public goods with no natural monopoly component (for example, local transport, waste disposal, recreational services) should be supplied by the market, but intervention may be justified when local governments are pursuing goals that the market would be unable to attain on its own.

    Since local taxes are administered centrally in Italy, the effects of tax savings are felt nationally rather than locally, which means that local governments have little incentive to achieve efficiency in the provision of services. To address this problem, the Italian government has submitted a legislative proposal to parliament that the right to provide local services for a specified period of time should be auctioned. This proposal is designed to enhance efficiency in the provision of local services, by creating competition *for* the market as a substitute for competition *in* the market. This may be viewed as the most efficient solution for services with low sunk costs, while privatization may be preferable for services with high sunk investments.

24. For instance, Professor Armstrong describes the 'duopoly policy' in fixed-link telecommunications in the UK from 1984 to 1991, which was designed to assist potentially more efficient entrants by allowing only one firm to offer a nationwide service in competition with BT.

25. For instance, Professor Armstrong described the failure to regulate the access charges of British Gas to its gas pipeline. The result was that more-efficient entrants were unable effectively to compete.

Professor Schwartz described the innovative effort of the US Telecommunications Act of 1996 to create competition in local telecommunications markets. It envisages entry not only by facilities-based competitors building their own networks (which requires relatively modest cooperation from the incumbent), but also by competitors who use some or all of the incumbent's unbundled network elements, or who resell the incumbent's existing retail services. It mandates incumbents to cooperate with entrants with respect to: interconnection; access to unbundled elements of the local networks, at rates based on these facilities' cost; and offering competitors, at discounted wholesale rates, any existing retail service for resale.

26.    Professor Biggar observed that many industries have a non-competitive component vertically integrated with a competitive component (for example, railways, postal services, telecommunications, electricity, gas, air services, waste management, water, maritime transport). He argued that there should be a presumption in favour of vertical separation, because (i) when a firm is vertically integrated, it has an incentive to keep competition out of downstream markets; (ii) the firm will always attempt to shift costs away from the regulated component to the non-regulated component, and may be able to engage in predatory pricing in the competitive component; and (iii) it is easier to reintegrate a separated firm, than to separate a firm.

27.    Professor Armstrong described the subsidies paid to the BBC, funded by taxing viewers, which places other broadcasters at a significant competitive disadvantage.

28.    Professor Armstrong gave various examples of this practice, such as placing universal service requirements on the incumbent, but not on entrants; and prohibiting an incumbent from serving related markets or participating in an important aspect of the market.

Professor Schwartz stated that the local Bell operating companies had been barred from providing long-distance services by a 1982 court decree. The US Telecommunications Act of 1996 provides that the local Bell operating companies are prohibited from entering the long-distance market until they have implemented a 'competitive checklist' designed to assist entry into their local markets. He explained that this provision has been criticized as anticompetitive, but that he believes that relying on 'sticks' alone to try to force monopolists to do what they do not want to do is very difficult. Providing an incentive device, if not too costly, can help.

29.    Professor Armstrong noted that tariffs that do not reflect costs are one of the most potent sources of regulation-induced problems with competition, as this will attract an undesirable pattern of entry, including cream skimming and lack of efficient entry in loss-making markets. This will also give rise to problems for the incumbent in funding its loss-making service.

30.    Professor Armstrong described the situation where price cap regulation takes the form whereby a measure of the average price of a basket of the incumbent's prices is controlled, but the firm has leeway in choosing the pattern of relative prices in the basket. This can give rise to incentives to react overly aggressively to entry.

31.    Professor Armstrong noted that this policy requires the incumbent to compete *less* effectively, with the likely result that inefficient entrants will prosper.

32.    Professor Armstrong suggested that if the market is deregulated when substantial market power is still present, prices will be high, which may induce a high level of entry that may not be efficient entry. Dr Hilke noted that problems of predation may then arise.

Professor Schwartz observed that another risk is that there will be a consumer backlash if prices rise when regulation is eliminated, and this can make it harder to retain the deregulation or to attain future deregulation. For instance, in the US, policy has oscillated back and forth several times between deregulation and regulating cable rates.

33.    Professor Armstrong suggested that such policies blunt the incumbent's incentive to compete in markets where entry occurs. As a result, less-efficient rivals may succeed in their chosen markets because the incumbent cannot afford to compete with them.

34.    The analogous Australian Regulatory Review standard is that 'the benefits of the restriction to the community as a whole outweigh the costs'. Similarly, the NCRAL legislative proposal contained an analogous provision: that 'the anticompetitive effects of such action are clearly outweighed by significant and demonstrable benefits to the general public'. These standards imply a broader inquiry into the costs and benefits of the existing or proposed regulation. In contrast, the present guidelines are designed to focus specifically on the problem of anti-

competitive effects of regulation for purposes of preparing a Competitive Impact Statement (for proposed legislation) or the Scoreboard (for existing regulation). However, the Australian standard and the NCRAL standard would seem appropriate for a legislature considering whether an existing anticompetitive regulation should be repealed, or a new anticompetitive regulation should be enacted, when there is no less-restrictive alternative.

35. Professor Amato observed that there is no significant difference between assessing the anti-competitive impact of private conduct and that of a regulation – the same kind of economic analysis, legal reasoning and so on apply with respect to both.

Mr Heimler underscored the importance of specificity as to methodology, which will be very helpful to national governments and the Commission in implementing the guidelines for regulatory review. For instance, the Commission's communications on public utility regulation are not clear: they state that prices should be proportional to costs, but they do not define costs. This creates difficulties for national regulators, who do not understand what is meant by the communications, and do not know how to apply them.

36. For example, Professor Schwartz's chapter shows that Section 271 of the Telecommunications Act of 1996 creates a limitation on entry by the Bell companies into the long-distance market. The intention of this restriction is to help open the local markets, which the Bells now dominate. Limiting entry generally implies that fewer firms will be in the market, and it is therefore a restriction on competition. In this context, however, the entry limitation might produce the opposite effect.

37. Restrictions in other markets may also be important since technical progress or changes in consumer demand often lead to an enlargement of the product characteristics on which firms compete. This is why, to be efficient, liberalization should occur simultaneously, to the extent this is possible.

38. Regulations cannot be evaluated independently of other regulations, as they may affect each other. Dr Laudati's chapter refers to a decision of the US Supreme Court, which held that a blanket ban on advertisement which was part of an irrational and inconsistent regulatory scheme failed to meet the requirement of a 'direct and material link' between a regulatory objective and the means chosen to achieve the objective. It concluded that the overall irrationality of the regulatory scheme meant that the regulation in question could not directly and materially advance the state's interest.

39. The NCRAL legislative proposal required only that 'the objectives of the action and the overriding statutory purpose cannot be accomplished in substantial part by alternative means having less-anticompetitive effects'. This suggests that if it is possible to achieve only a substantial part of the government's overriding statutory purpose by less-anticompetitive means, then the regulation is overbroad. Similarly, the Australian standard requires only that a review 'consider alternative means for achieving the same result including non-legislative approaches'. Thus, it does not require any showing that the objectives of the legislation cannot be achieved by means having a less-anticompetitive effect.

Dr Hilke and Professor Schwartz noted that identification of less-restrictive alternatives is at the heart of treatment of efficiency claims in merger evaluations under the DOJ/FTC Horizontal Merger Guidelines. Accordingly, when the parties to a merger argue that it will generate certain efficiencies, the DOJ/FTC view this as a defence to an otherwise anticompetitive merger only if the efficiencies are 'merger specific' – that is, only if they cannot be secured through a less-restrictive means than a complete merger.

40. The US Supreme Court has imposed such a requirement in its commercial speech cases.

41. Professor Fels suggested that performance-based regulation is preferable to prescriptive regulation because the latter tends to impose greater restrictions on innovation and competition.

42. It is debatable whether minimum quality standards actually provide a less-restrictive alternative. Professor Scarpa argued that minimum quality standards can result in entry barriers, predatory behaviour, and welfare-reducing effects, because they restrict the pace at which a firm can move, and thus restrict its options. Moreover, rivals have an easier time ousting the firm from the market, because it cannot sufficiently differentiate its product from those of the rivals.

43. Professor Scarpa argued that self-regulation of quality may be a less-restrictive alternative to minimum quality standards when the number of agents is limited, the mobility of customers is high, and the regulator's uncertainty of the firm's costs is substantial.

44. Dr Laudati reported that the US Supreme Court has appropriately made a distinction between advertising bans and 'time, place, and manner restrictions'. The latter regulations help ensure that consumers receive truthful, non-misleading information in advertisements; the former prohibit the dissemination of truthful information. Accordingly, the former are a far more restrictive form of regulation than the latter.

    With respect to legal services, the Court has ruled that 'routine legal services', such as uncontested divorces, simple adoptions, uncontested personal bankruptcies, and name changes, are the only ones that lend themselves to non-misleading advertising. Thus, by implication, non-routine legal services could lawfully be the subject of an advertising ban because they are inherently misleading.

45. The US Supreme Court allowed a ban on in-person solicitation of clients by lawyers due to the inherent dangers of overreaching and undue influence. However, it did not allow a ban on in-person solicitation of clients by accountants, because the danger of overreaching and undue influence was not present. Thus, the danger of overreaching depends on the type of professional making the solicitation, the type of client likely to be solicited, and the circumstances underlying the solicitation.

46. For instance, the US Supreme Court has indicated that a state bar association could specify the exact services that must be included in advertised 'routine legal services'.

47. Professor Fels suggested that government action will not be the most effective solution when the government lacks information and capacity to enforce regulations; dispersed information, held by groups and individuals closer to the industry, may be more reliable and a better basis for action. In such situations, self-regulation may be preferable.

48. Professor Fels noted that Australian law condemns any self-regulation that is the result of private agreement in a profession and is anticompetitive, or is otherwise likely to violate the antitrust laws, unless the profession comes forward to the Australian Competition and Consumer Commission and seeks authorization on the ground that a sufficient public benefit is present.

49. For instance, standards for entry in a profession, which are positive to the extent that they protect consumers from incompetent professional services, may be set above the level needed to maintain quality, and instead be designed to maintain the incomes of existing practitioners.

50. Professor Ballbe provided a vivid example of how liberalization of the Spanish airline industry would be better handled at a more centralized level. The industry has been liberalized to some extent, resulting in price decreases of nearly 30 per cent and a significant increase in demand. However, the government's policy with respect to infrastructure may frustrate the process of liberalization. Problems with airport capacity, handling operations, air traffic congestion and pilot strikes have caused chronic delays. As a result, the companies and the Ministry of Transport negotiated the solution of a proportional reduction in flights operated by each company, which was a step backwards in the liberalization process. Thus, for liberalization to be successful, infrastructure capacity must be sufficient to handle the increase in demand that lower prices and entry of new competitors produces.

51. Professor Fels observed that in Australia, efforts to reform professional regulation have made little progress because the professional associations themselves have been delegated the task of analysing the need for reform.

52. Dr Mehta acknowledged that DG Competition has not played a very major role as competition advocate to ensure coherence of its regulatory actions with the Treaty's core principles of competition policy.

    Mr Heimler provided a vivid example of the failure to take account of competition considerations in the European Commission's recently published White Paper on Retail Trade. He observed that this White Paper says that competition is important, but does not specify the dimension of competition that the member states should use. Thus, it is of no help to national governments that want to reform retail trade, because it fails to specify whether they should have structural regulation, or what they should do about sales below cost.

53. Dr Hilke suggested that in order to be an effective advocate, a competition authority must develop an understanding of the industry in question, be selective as to the issues that it will address in its advocacy submissions, 'network' with decision makers, follow shifts in issues, and take advantage of learning opportunities from its dual role as competition advocate and competition enforcer.

    Dr Dutz suggested that the competition authority has a critical role to play in any regulatory reform initiative, both in terms of *ex ante* advocacy and *ex post* enforcement. *Ex ante*, it should help establish the groundwork for the reform through media relations and systematic relationships with representatives of consumer and producer interests. Following reform, it should strictly enforce competition laws, ensuring that anticompetitive regulation is not replaced by anticompetitive interfirm agreements.

54. Mrs Bruzzone argued that the advocacy experience of national competition authorities shows these weaknesses.

55. For instance, Professor Jenny observed that there is a tradeoff between independence and being part of the government – whether it is good to have heads of competition authorities as cabinet ministers, which would be helpful for purposes of competition advocacy; or whether it is more important to have an independent competition authority.

    Professor Schwartz commented that in advocating 'independence' above all, the fact that independence can mean irrelevance is sometimes overlooked. In the US, the Department of Justice's Antitrust Division is powerful, and relatively politically insulated (even as compared to some administrative agencies that nominally are more independent) partly because it is located in the Department of Justice, a strong ministry with a mandate for law enforcement.

    Professor Amato suggested that in transition economies, it is worthwhile to sacrifice some degree of independence in order to have a higher influence in the political process.

    Professor Fels observed that DG Competition has a seat at the cabinet table, and is therefore in a key position to influence every law in every directorate. Further, he suggested that competition policy should be injected into the central areas of government decision making, through the most powerful agencies and ministers of government. A competition minister might have quite a junior post, so that it is preferable that the main economics minister, the treasury or finance minister, have this portfolio.

    Mr Wise argued that to be effective, a competition advocate must have a 'fist' in the process, and that enforcement is the fist that most competition authorities have. He suggested that an agency that is not actively enforcing the law is not likely to be taken seriously in the debate. Moreover, he observed that the advocacy tools used (for example, public media debate, private advice and formal participation in court or agency proceedings) must be adapted to the political environment. Finally, advocacy is effective only to the extent that it is backed by political support and perhaps some other legal powers.

56. For instance, Mr Wise explained that some competition laws require other government agencies to consult with the competition authority about particular matters, such as new legislation for which they are responsible. Perhaps competition laws that do not contain such a consultation requirement should be modified to include one.

57. Mr Wise reported that in some countries, laws explicitly authorize such participation; in others, competition agencies have general powers to study and report on competition issues and problems, or to prepare such studies in response to particular requests. Effective participation depends on the competition agency having access to the process before important decisions are made.

58. Mr Kohl argued that a new oversight institution, based on the model of the Court of Auditors, may be appropriate to provide review of anticompetitive regulation.

59. Professor Fels suggested that addressing side-effects of reforms might appropriately be delayed to a second step in the process. The priority should be first to eliminate the anticompetitive aspects of regulation.

60. Professor Jenny noted that in France, independent service auditors have been emerging to address this problem. Professor Schwartz noted that in the US, private firms have been started to benchmark the performance of lawyers.
61. Professor Siniscalco suggested that such a guide could help solve the problems of incentives of professionals to provide high-quality services.
62. Dr Hilke described Federal Trade Commission trade rules that require the publication of easily understood technical information that consumers can use to compare products.
63. Dr Hilke noted that in the US, *Consumer Report* (a monthly magazine) provides quality information about a broad variety of consumer products. Similar magazines are now also being published in the US in areas such as quality of hospital services and educational services.

# Index

Abdala, Manuel A. 244n
access to facilities 373–4
  introduction of competition into
    regulated industries 154–5,
    158–9, 165, 168–70
accountability 267, 274–5, 424–5, 433–6
accounting separation 190
accreditation 109
Adenauer, Konrad 221
administrative law xvii, 443–4, 445, 450
adverse selection 8
advertising 136
  auditing 125–6
  effects of
    economic analysis 56–61
    empirical evidence 61–4
  prices 54–5, 56, 57–8, 61–3
  quality and 49, 60, 63–4
  restrictions on 3, 5, 13, 35, 49–67,
    128–30, 133–4, 136–7, 141–2,
    462–3, 467
    blanket bans 77–80
    product markets 50, 64–6
    professional services 49–64, 66–7,
      81–5, 86–7, 88–91, 128,
      129–30, 133–4, 136–7, 142
    rationale for 52–6, 129
  vulnerable people 137–8
advocacy
  competition xxii–xxiii, 5–6, 20–5,
    131–2, 442–55
  consultation requirements 399
  country experiences with targeted
    advocacy and enforcement
    programmes 394–410
  development of 381–4
  development of position on subset
    of issues 385–8
  electricity industry competition and
    consumer advocacy
    programme 378–92

European Union and 358, 360,
    412–18, 442, 444, 449–52
  formal authority 400–1
  guidelines for reform 465
  identification of major issues
    384–5
  implementation of decisions 402–5
  institutional setting 380–1
  law enforcement and 390–1
  monitoring changes 390
  networking/personal contacts
    388–9
  programmes 5–6, 20–5, 131–2,
    343, 356–8, 360, 378–92,
    395–7, 442–55
  resources, strategy and tactics
    401–2
  success of 397–9
Aghion, Philippe 259n
air transport 373
  cross-country regulation patterns
    296–7, 304–9
Akerlof, George 34, 46n, 68n, 311n
Alchian, Armen A. 243n
alcohol advertising restrictions 64–6, 79
Amato, Giuliano 437n
Argentina
  privatization in 222
    electricity industry 233, 235
Armstrong, Mark 167n, 196n
assets, ownership of 266–7
asymmetric information problems 8,
    106, 109, 134, 137, 141–2, 460
  advertising restrictions and 49, 53–4
  minimum quality standards and 29,
    34–8
AT&T 184,200,205–7
auctions, local public services in Italy
    and 263, 270–2

market failures 8–9, 11, 111,
119–20, 143
public choice theories 21
scope of 7–8
economic guidelines for reforming
regulation xxiv, 459–71, 475–84
establishment of procompetitive
regulation task force 476–7
guidelines 477–84
panel discussion on 459–71
statement of purpose 475–6
electricity industry 147, 148
competition authorities and 372–3
competition and consumer advocacy
programme 378–92
development of 381–4
development of position on subset
of issues 385–8
identification of major issues
384–5
institutional setting 380–1
law enforcement and 390–1
monitoring changes 390
networking/personal contacts
388–9
cross-country regulation patterns
296–7, 299–304
privatization 220–43
data and variables of study 228–37
empirical results of study 237–42
quantity and quality of 229
reasons for 220
regulatory framework and 234–6
vertical integration and 221, 229,
233–4, 237
vertical separation in 191
Elmeskov, Jorgen 312n
Emiliou, Nicolas 439n
employment
employment protection legislation
(EPL) 283, 287–9, 290
regulation and
composition of employment 293
lower rates of employment 290–2
road freight transport 254
self-employment 293
energy sector *see* electricity industry; gas
industry
enforcement
competition law 369–71, 390–1

country experiences with targeted
advocacy and enforcement
programmes 394–410
entry to markets
advertising and 64
introduction of competition into
regulated industries 151–66,
171, 172
consumer protection 159–66
incumbent protection 153–5
new entrant protection 155–9
pricing of network elements 168–70
restrictions 5, 9–11, 14, 53, 122–3,
316, 460
accreditation 109
Bell companies in US 198–215
certification 37, 38, 109
licensing 10, 37, 109, 249
limitations on further entry 155–6
minimum quality standards and 33
registration schemes 108–9
self-regulation and 40–1
vertical integration and 182–3
environmental issues 110, 464, 469
ethics, advertising and 54
European Union 366
advertising restrictions and 52, 128–9
banking sector and 15, 16, 22
competition and 422
advocacy programmes 358, 360,
412–18, 442, 444, 449–52
design of regulatory policy 413–14
dual enforcement of competition
law 369–71
optimizing regulatory oversight
415–17
courts 419–20
electricity market and 234–5
guidelines for reform and xxiv,
459–61, 462, 463, 466, 475–84
laws and regulations xvi
private services and 20
professional services and 19
proportionality principle and xvii,
xxiii, 419, 426–30, 431–2, 435,
446, 447–8, 449
public services and 147–8
retail sector and 18
experience goods 5, 8, 14, 35, 60
externalities 8, 173–4